Handbook of
Social and
Evaluation Anxiety

Handbook of Social and Evaluation Anxiety

EDITED BY

HAROLD LEITENBERG

University of Vermont
Burlington, Vermont

Plenum Press • New York and London

Library of Congress Cataloging-in-Publication Data

Handbook of social and evaluation anxiety / edited by Harold
  Leitenberg.
      p.   cm.
  Includes bibliographical references.
  ISBN 0-306-43438-5
  1. Anxiety--Social aspects. 2. Self-consciousness. 3. Social
role. 4. Bashfulness.   I. Leitenberg, Harold.
HM251.H2236 1990
152.4'6--dc20   90-6853
                                                              CIP

© 1990 Plenum Press, New York
A Division of Plenum Publishing Corporation
233 Spring Street, New York, N.Y. 10013

Printed in the United States of America

To my wife, Barbara,
and children, David, Elliot, and Joe

Contributors

DAVID H. BARLOW, Department of Psychology, State University of New York at Albany, Albany, New York 12203

JOSEPH L. BREITENSTEIN, Department of Psychology, West Virginia University, Morgantown, West Virginia 26506-6040

TIMOTHY J. BRUCE, Department of Psychology, State University of New York at Albany, Albany, New York 12203

JONATHAN M. CHEEK, Department of Psychology, Wellesley College, Wellesley, Massachusetts 02181

PAUL M. G. EMMELKAMP, Department of Clinical Psychology, University of Groningen, Academic Hospital, 9713 EZ, Groningen, The Netherlands

WILLIAM J. FREMOUW, Department of Psychology, West Virginia University, Morgantown, West Virginia 26506-6040

PAUL GILBERT, South Derbyshire Health Authority, South Derbyshire DE3 5DQ, England

CAROL R. GLASS, Department of Psychology, Catholic University of America, Washington, DC 20064

RICHARD G. HEIMBERG, Department of Psychology, State University of New York at Albany, Albany, New York 12203

ROBERT K. HEINSSEN, JR., Chestnut Lodge Research Institute, 500 West Montgomery Avenue, Rockville, Maryland 20850

DEBRA A. HOPE, Department of Psychology, State University of New York at Albany, Albany, New York 12203

WARREN H. JONES, Department of Psychology, University of Tulsa, Tulsa, Oklahoma 74104

NEVILLE J. KING, Faculty of Education, Monash University, Clayton, Victoria 3168, Australia

ELLEN TOBEY KLASS, Department of Psychology, Hunter College, City University of New York, New York, New York 10021

HAROLD LEITENBERG, Department of Psychology, University of Vermont, Burlington, Vermont 05405

SUSAN P. LIMBER, Department of Psychology, University of Nebraska, Lincoln, Nebraska 68588-0308

JENNIFER ALANSKY MAURO, Department of Psychology, University of Oregon, Eugene, Oregon 97403

LISA A. MELCHIOR, The Measurement Group, 6245 Bristol Parkway, Suite 242, Culver City, California 90230

THOMAS H. OLLENDICK, Department of Psychology, Virginia Polytechnic Institute and State University, Blacksburg, Virginia 24061

RONALD J. PRINZ, Department of Psychology, University of South Carolina, Columbia, South Carolina 29208

JAYNE ROSE, Department of Psychology, Augustana College, Rock Island, Illinois 61204

MARY K. ROTHBART, Department of Psychology, University of Oregon, Eugene, Oregon 97403

ESTHER D. ROTHBLUM, Department of Psychology, University of Vermont, Burlington, Vermont 05405

DANIEL RUSSELL, Graduate Program in Hospital and Health Administration, College of Medicine, University of Iowa, Iowa City, Iowa 52242

BARBARA R. SARASON, Department of Psychology, University of Washington, Seattle, Washington 98195

IRWIN G. SARASON, Department of Psychology, University of Washington, Seattle, Washington 98195

AGNES SCHOLING, Department of Clinical Psychology, University of Groningen, Academic Hospital, 9713 EZ, Groningen, The Netherlands

GEORGINA SHERLING, Northwick Park Hospital, Harrow, Middlesex HA1 3UJ England

RONALD E. SMITH, Department of Psychology, University of Washington, Seattle, Washington 98195

FRANK L. SMOLL, Department of Psychology, University of Washington, Seattle, Washington 98195

ROSS A. THOMPSON, Department of Psychology, University of Nebraska, Lincoln, Nebraska 68588-0308

PETER TROWER, Solihull Health Authority, Solihull, West Midlands B93 OPX, England.

Preface

For a long time I have wanted to put together a book about social and evaluation anxiety. Social-evaluation anxiety seemed to be a stressful part of so many people's everyday experience. It also seemed to be a part of so many of the clinical problems that I worked with. Common terms that fit under this rubric include fears of rejection, humiliation, criticism, embarrassment, ridicule, failure, and abandonment. Examples of social and evaluation anxiety include shyness; social inhibition; social timidity; public speaking anxiety; feelings of self-consciousness and awkwardness in social situations; test anxiety; performance anxiety in sports, theater, dance, or music; shame; guilt; separation anxiety; social withdrawal; procrastination; and fear of job interviews or job evaluations, of asking someone out, of not making a good impression, or of appearing stupid, foolish, or physically unattractive.

In its extreme form, social anxiety is a behavior disorder in its own right—social phobia. This involves not only feelings of anxiety but also avoidance and withdrawal from social situations in which scrutiny and negative evaluation are anticipated. Social-evaluation anxiety also plays a role in other clinical disorders. For example, people with agoraphobia are afraid of having a panic attack in public in part because they fear making a spectacle of themselves. Moreover, even their dominant terrors of going crazy or having a heart attack seem to reflect a central concern with social abandonment and isolation. People suffering from obsessive–compulsive disorders are often overwhelmed by guilt-provoking sexual and aggressive thoughts and dread that these will be acted upon and discovered. Women with bulimia nervosa believe they have flawed characters as well as flawed bodies and they try to achieve a perfect shape because they fear rejection otherwise. Men with sexual dysfunctions are often said to suffer from performance anxiety. School phobia, social isolation in children, severe anxiety in anticipation of loss of employment or loss of a loved one, homophobia, social deficits linked to social anxiety in schizophrenia, avoidant personality disorder—the list can go on and on.

Social-evaluation anxiety is obviously an important issue affecting people of both genders, all ages, and all walks of life. It has been relatively neglected for many years and research has been scattered across different subdisciplines. Of late, however, interest in this topic appears to be on an upswing. Clinical researchers, personality theorists, developmental psychologists, and social psychologists have all made important contributions to this area. My goal in this book was to combine the clinical perspective on social and evaluation anxiety with that of basic research in development psychology. I wanted the book to provide a relatively comprehensive review of the varied topics in this area. Aside from the convenience of gathering this disparate research into one source, I hope that this book will serve a useful integrative function and stimulate further study.

Many people have worked hard to bring this book to completion. Most obviously I am grateful to the authors of the chapters in this book. An edited book is only as good as its contributors make it. Writing review chapters involves time, effort, and sacrifice from people with very busy schedules and competing demands. I would also like to thank our editor at Plenum, Eliot Werner, for his patience, flexibility, and support.

HAROLD LEITENBERG

Burlington, Vermont

Contents

Introduction... 1

Harold Leitenberg

Definition 1
Types of Social Anxiety 1
Phenomenology 3
Consequences of Social Anxiety 4
Organization of This Book 5
References.. 8

PART I. OVERVIEW

1. Social Anxiety, Evolution, and Self-Presentation 11

   Peter Trower, Paul Gilbert, and Georgina Sherling

   Description and Definition of Social Anxiety 12
   A Psychobiological Account of Social Anxiety 13
   An Appraisal-Coping Model of Social Anxiety 22
   Evaluation and Application 36
   Concluding Summary 41
   References 42

2. Shyness, Self-Esteem, and Self-Consciousness 47

   Jonathan M. Cheek and Lisa A. Melchior

   Defining Shyness as a Three-Component Syndrome 48
   Shyness as a Dimension of Self-Esteem 58
   Shyness and Self-Concept Processes 67
   Conclusion 71
   References 73

PART II. SOCIAL ANXIETY IN CHILDHOOD:
DEVELOPMENTAL AND CLINICAL PERSPECTIVES

3. Social Anxiety in Infancy: Stranger and Separation
   Reactions 85

   Ross A. Thompson and Susan P. Limber

   Theoretical Perspectives 86
   Stranger Reactions in Infancy 95
   Separation Reactions in Infancy 118
   Concluding Comments: Directions for Future Inquiry 127
   References 130

4. Temperament, Behavioral Inhibition, and Shyness in
   Childhood 139

   Mary K. Rothbart and Jennifer Alansky Mauro

   Behavioral Inhibition 142
   Issues in the Assessment of Behavioral Inhibition 145
   Shyness and Social Anxiety 147
   Biological Models for Behavioral Inhibition 150
   Behavioral Genetics Approaches 151
   Jeffrey Gray's Model for Behavioral Inhibition 153
   Behavioral Inhibition, Shyness, and Psychopathology in Children 155
   Summary 156
   References 157

5. Socially Withdrawn and Isolated Children 161

   Ronald J. Prinz

   Overview 161
   Conceptualization of Social Withdrawal and Isolation 161
   Assessment Methods 163
   Intervention Strategies 170
   Significant Issues 173
   References 176

6. School Phobia and Separation Anxiety 179

   Thomas H. Ollendick and Neville J. King

   Introduction 179
   Description 180

Diagnostic Issues 182
Etiology 186
Assessment 189
Intervention 195
Summary 208
References 209

PART III. SOCIAL ANXIETY IN ADULTHOOD: ESTABLISHING RELATIONSHIPS

7. Dating Anxiety 217

Debra A. Hope and Richard G. Heimberg

The Disruptive Effects of Dating Anxiety 217
Issues in the Research Literature 218
The Nature of Dating Anxiety 220
Assessment of Dating Anxiety 227
Modification of Dating Anxiety 228
Case Example 234
Summary and Conclusions 240
References 242

8. Loneliness and Social Anxiety 247

Warren H. Jones, Jayne Rose, and Daniel Russell

Review of the Loneliness Literature 248
Linkages between Loneliness and Social Anxiety 259
References 263

PART IV. SOCIAL ANXIETY IN ADULTHOOD: CLINICAL PERSPECTIVE

9. Social Phobia: Nature and Treatment 269

Agnes Scholing and Paul M. G. Emmelkamp

Introduction 269
Definition of Social Phobia 270
Epidemiology 278
Characteristics of Social Phobia 278

Etiology 284
Assessment 287
Treatment of Social Phobia 298
Concluding Remarks and Future Directions 314
References 316

10. Social Skills, Social Anxiety, and Cognitive Factors in
    Schizophrenia 325

    Robert K. Heinssen, Jr. and Carol R. Glass

    Introduction 325
    Social Functioning in Nonschizophrenic Populations 326
    Models of Social Disability in Schizophrenia 327
    Social Anxiety and Dysfunctional Cognitions in Schizophrenia 341
    Future Directions 348
    References 350

11. The Nature and Role of Performance Anxiety in Sexual
    Dysfunction 357

    Timothy J. Bruce and David H. Barlow

    Introduction 357
    Conceptual Groundwork 359
    The Role of Anxiety in Sexual Responsivity 361
    The Role of Cognition in Sexual Responsivity 366
    The Interaction of Autonomic and Attentional Factors 375
    Working Model and Summary 377
    Related Areas of Performance Anxiety 379
    Future Directions 380
    References 381

12. Guilt, Shame, and Embarrassment: Cognitive-Behavioral
    Approaches 385

    Ellen Tobey Klass

    Introduction 385
    Defining Guilt, Shame, and Embarrassment 386
    Assessment Considerations 388
    Guilt 390
    Shame 403
    Embarrassment 405
    Conclusions and Open Issues 408
    References 412

PART V. EVALUATION ANXIETY

13. Sport Performance Anxiety 417

    Ronald E. Smith and Frank L. Smoll

    Arousal, Stress, and Anxiety 418
    The Nature of Sport Performance Anxiety 421
    The Measurement of Anxiety in Sports 424
    Determinants of Sport Performance Anxiety 428
    Consequences of Performance Anxiety 435
    Future Directions in Sport Performance Anxiety Research 448
    References 449

14. Speech Anxiety 455

    William J. Fremouw and Joseph L. Breitenstein

    Introduction 455
    Assessment of Speech Anxiety 456
    Treatments for Speech Anxiety 460
    Defining Effectiveness of Treatments 463
    Prediction of Treatment Outcome 466
    Future Directions 470
    References 471

15. Test Anxiety 475

    Irwin G. Sarason and Barbara R. Sarason

    Test Anxiety and Performance 477
    Cognitive Interference, Worry, and Self-Preoccupation 482
    Components of Test Anxiety 485
    Intervention Strategies 486
    Test Anxiety and Social Anxiety 490
    References 493

16. Fear of Failure: The Psychodynamic, Need Achievement,
    Fear of Success, and Procrastination Models 497

    Esther D. Rothblum

    Psychodynamic Views of Fear of Failure 497
    Fear of Failure versus Need Achievement 501

Fear of Success 512
Fear of Failure as an Antecedent of Procrastination 524
Conclusion and Future Directions 530
References 531

Index 539

Introduction

HAROLD LEITENBERG

DEFINITION

Social anxiety involves feelings of apprehension, self-consciousness, and emotional distress in anticipated or actual social-evaluative situations. Such anxiety occurs when people want to make a favorable impression but doubt that they will succeed (Schlenker & Leary, 1982). There has to be a belief that the situation involves scrutiny or evaluation by others regardless of whether this is actually true or not, that negative evaluation is a possible or even a likely outcome, and that the consequences of such negative evaluation would be harmful. The essence of social anxiety is that the person fears that he or she will be found to be deficient or inadequate by others and therefore will be rejected.

TYPES OF SOCIAL ANXIETY

Social anxiety is a ubiquitous phenomenon. At some time or another most everyone has experienced some degree of anxiety related to a social situation. It may have occurred just before giving a speech; after having done or said something you considered shameful, humiliating, or embarrassing; when trying to arrange a date with an attractive person of the opposite sex for the first time; when going to a party where you hardly know anyone; when going on a job interview; when being criticized or when expressing disagreement with someone in authority; or when you felt weak, stupid, foolish, or inadequate in some way. These are common everyday situations, and they demonstrate that fear of the prospect of negative evaluation and social rejection is probably inherent in being human. Ridicule, humiliation, contempt, embarrassment, loss of affection, loss of acceptance, loss of respect, negative evaluation, and rejection are distinctly unpleasant experiences to almost all of us. The ultimate imaginable consequence of negative evaluation and social rejection is to be shunned and abandoned, something we may learn to dread from the dependency of infancy.

HAROLD LEITENBERG • Department of Psychology, University of Vermont, Burlington, Vermont 05405.

(For an evolutionary account of the origins of social anxiety see Trower, Gilbert, and Sherling, Chapter 1 this volume.)

Social anxiety has been studied in various guises. Shyness, performance anxiety, social phobia, avoidant personality disorder, social withdrawal, social isolation, public speaking anxiety, speech anxiety, communication apprehension, fear of interpersonal rejection, dating anxiety, separation anxiety, stage fright, fear of strangers, shame, embarrassment, social inhibition, social timidity—all of these and more fall under the umbrella of social anxiety.

One can also make an argument for including test anxiety, and essentially any form of evaluation anxiety, under this umbrella. Even if there is no immediately visible interpersonal context or audience present, what one fears about failure often implicitly involves some expectation of a negative interpersonal consequence. This could be short-term expectations (e.g., disapproval or rejection by family, superiors, or peers), or it could be a more long-term and extended chain of expected negative consequences (e.g., poor performance will lead to loss of status (or job) which will lead to loss of respect to loss of love and eventually to being abandoned). Note that these do not have to be realistic expectations. In fact, the catastrophic interpersonal consequences imagined by a person suffering from high evaluation anxiety of any kind are seldom accurate predictions of what will truly take place. It could also be argued that social anxiety is a subset of evaluation anxiety rather than vice versa. In any case, there is substantial overlap between the two constructs, and this book includes chapters on both social and evaluation anxiety.

Social-evaluation anxiety in its various forms is extraordinarily common and upsetting. For example, fear of speaking before large groups is the most frequently reported fear of adults. And approximately 40% of people in this country consider themselves to be generally shy. Most of these individuals don't like being this way, and they report that it has caused problems for them in their daily lives.

This array of different types of social-evaluative anxieties could be distinguished in various ways. One distinguishing characteristic is intensity, which can also be used to differentiate clinical versus nonclinical levels of social anxiety. How much functioning is being disrupted by the social anxiety? How incapacitated is the individual? How much autonomic arousal or emotional distress is being experienced? How much avoidance behavior is being exhibited? The greater the disruption, distress, and avoidance, the more likely one would seek clinical assistance and the more likely the individual would be considered to have a clinical disorder. It is bemusing to note in this regard that social phobia did not make it into the standard psychiatric diagnostic manual as a distinct disorder until 1980. This, of course, did not mean it was not in existence until then.

Another distinguishing characteristic is the extent to which the anxiety is generalized across different social situations. Some social anxieties involve only one limited type of social event (e.g., eating in public), whereas others involve a variety of social situations. It should be noted that this characteristic of generalization is often independent of intensity or the clinical versus nonclinical distinction. For example, the shy person who feels awkward and uncomfortable in many social encounters but whose life is not significantly impaired would not be considered to have a clinical disorder, whereas the person who is afraid of only one situation, eating in public, but to such an extent that he or she cannot go on trips, to work, or to school because he or she is unable to eat around others would be considered to have a disorder.

The types of situations provoking social anxiety can also be differentiated. For example, one distinguishing characteristic entails the degree to which contingent interaction is involved (Leary, 1983). In a conversation, one has to respond to what another person says or does not say. A public performance, on the other hand, such as giving a prepared speech or music recital has less of this interactive quality, although it is not completely absent. Actors and other performers, after all, do respond somewhat differently depending on audience reaction. But clearly there is a script to follow and there is less of a reciprocal exchange. Some people may feel quite secure in a party situation but be terrified of giving a prepared talk to a large audience. Others may feel fine giving public presentations but experience considerable anxiety at the prospect of going to a party. Note that contingent interaction is often inversely correlated with size of audience. Interactive situations tend to be more one-on-one, whereas noninteractive situations tend to consist of performances before a group. Evaluative situations involving no immediate audience at all (e.g., handing in test or job assignments) are also obviously noninteractive.

PHENOMENOLOGY

Aside from self-reported uncomfortable feelings, social anxiety can be expressed in various ways: physiologically, behaviorally, and cognitively. Though one can feel tense and anxious without any measurable sign of bodily symptoms, it is not uncommon for people who are experiencing social anxiety to exhibit some physiological reaction such as excessive sweating, racing heart, blushing, trembling, stomach distress, numbness, dizziness, and so on. Socially anxious people may experience all, some, or none of these somatic symptoms of autonomic arousal.

Behavioral signs of social anxiety are also variable. When social anxiety is intense, people avoid or escape from social situations. This may apply only to specific social situations, for example, avoiding talking in front of groups or avoiding use of public bathroom facilities. Avoidance can also be quite extensive. People suffering from social anxiety may avoid parties, avoid engaging in conversations with people they do not know well, avoid meetings at work, avoid eating in public, avoid asking for directions, avoid jobs or tasks involving any evaluation—in other words, they may isolate themselves from most social encounters.

Less extreme behavioral signs of social anxiety include procrastinating, averting one's eyes during conversation, stammering, fidgeting nervously, being reticent about instigating conversation, and being inhibited about expressing opinions. Some of these behavioral signs of social anxiety may suggest that the socially anxious individual lacks social skill. It should be emphasized, however, that one can be socially inept without experiencing any social anxiety; and one can be socially anxious without showing any visible sign of social awkwardness or deficiency. When both social anxiety and social deficiency are present in the same individual, however, then one is confronted with a classic cause-and-effect question. Which came first? Did preexisting social anxiety interfere with social performance? Or did a lack of social skill cause the individual to develop social anxiety? In most instances, albeit certainly not all, the former seems to be the case.

Unlike physiological and behavioral signs of social anxiety, which need not always be present, it is difficult to conceive of social anxiety without certain characteristic cognitions. The most salient is a painful self-consciousness, what Buss (1980) has referred to as public self-consciousness. People who chronically experience social anxiety are preoccupied with thoughts about being the object of scrutiny and evaluation, and they fear the worst. They have a low opinion of themselves and underestimate what they are capable of and how they appear in a social situation. They also overestimate what is expected or required. It often appears that socially anxious individuals are concerned that their worst fears about themselves will be confirmed by the negative judgment of others. This overconcern with negative evaluation leads the socially anxious person to become self-focused and preoccupied with how he or she may appear in others' eyes. This hypervigilance against appearing foolish, stupid, awkward, or inadequate can indeed produce anxiety.

There are a host of self-deprecating thinking patterns associated with social anxiety. Socially anxious individuals tend to perceive their performance as deficient even when it is not; they think they are being observed by others when they are not; their standards and judgments are perfectionistic—if one does not do an excellent job one is a failure, with nothing in between; they recall past negative social encounters but ignore or forget the positive ones; they accept negative but reject positive feedback; they blame themselves for negative social outcomes but do not take credit for positive ones; they believe that certain behaviors that others would take in stride are shameful and humiliating; they catastrophize the consequences of any social misstep or sign of anxiety in social situations.

People who often experience social anxiety dread that other people will notice. They believe that signs of anxiety are visible, even if they are not. They also believe that showing signs of anxiety means they are making a pathetic spectacle of themselves. Being anxious is interpreted as being weak and inferior and incompetent. They believe that the appearance of any anxiety will be further cause for people to reject and abandon them. And, of course, the more they fear being seen as anxious the more anxious they become.

CONSEQUENCES OF SOCIAL ANXIETY

Social-evaluation anxiety can adversely affect children as well as adults. It seems to affect both men and women nearly equally, with some variation depending on the type of social encounter or behavior a person believes is being evaluated. It can inhibit and disrupt performance in a variety of settings. It can hinder the development of close friendships and sexual relationships. It can prevent reaching goals at school, at work, and in the community. At the extreme end it can develop into a serious personality disorder (avoidant personality) or into an anxiety disorder (social phobia). It also has been associated with a wide range of other clinical problems including alcohol abuse, loneliness, guilt reactions, depression, school phobia, social withdrawal in childhood, severe eating disorders such as anorexia and bulimia, schizophrenia, sexual dysfunctions, and sexual offenses. It also is an important component of other anxiety disorders including agoraphobia, panic disorder, generalized anxiety disorder, and obsessive–compulsive disorder.

Although we normally think about and study these negative aspects of social anxiety, it should be observed that sometimes social anxiety can be adaptive. A concern about others' opinions can inhibit behavior that is socially unacceptable. Fear of negative evaluation can therefore be a powerful force in society, motivating people to obey existing rules and conventions. At moderate levels, such anxiety may also motivate people to prepare better and therefore perform better on a variety of social tasks.

ORGANIZATION OF THIS BOOK

As can be gathered from what has been said so far, social anxiety is a generic term for many related topics. The purpose of this book was to bring these all together in one place. It is only in the last decade that the topic of social anxiety has begun to receive the detailed attention it deserves considering its prevalence and distressing personal impact. Personality theorists and researchers, social psychologists, developmental psychologists, and clinical investigators have studied different facets of social anxiety. Bringing this body of work together in one sourcebook can lead to an integration of this research and be a stimulus for further investigation.

The book is organized into five sections. The first section provides an overview of social anxiety. Trower, Gilbert, and Sherling describe a psychobiological model of social anxiety, with a consideration of its evolutionary origins. Cheek and Melchior review the literature on social anxiety as a personality characteristic (shyness), describing in detail how self-esteem and other self-focused cognitions play a central role in understanding social anxiety.

The second section focuses on social anxiety in childhood, with two chapters written from a developmental perspective and two written from a clinical perspective. Thompson and Limber review the literature on stranger wariness and separation distress in infancy. In both cases a complex set of interacting factors—some transient, some enduring, some having to do with the child, and some having to do with the situation—influence the degree of "anxiety" exhibited in response to a stranger's presence or separation from a caretaker. Rothbart and Mauro review the research on temperament and genetic factors that may influence social timidity, inhibition, and shyness in the young child. Considerable evidence suggests that individual differences in these characteristics in young children are in part related to different temperamental dispositions. From a clinical perspective, Prinz describes what is known about socially withdrawn, isolated, and avoidant children, reviewing issues involved in the assessment and treatment of these children. He raises a point here that appears in later chapters concerned with treatment issues: because not all withdrawn children have the same problems, just as not all social phobics are the same, more flexible matching of different treatment strategies to different subgroups may be needed to achieve greater treatment success. Also with a clinical emphasis, Ollendick and King review the literature on assessment and treatment of school phobia and separation anxiety in children.

The third section is devoted to the role of social anxiety in establishing relationships. Hope and Heimberg review the research literature on dating anxiety, including etiology, assessment, and treatment alternatives. Such anxiety about rejection from potential romantic or sexual partners can sometimes be paralyzing, preventing many men and women from developing any close relationships. Extreme dating anxiety is an excellent illustration of how not only the individual but all of society can suffer from the negative consequences of social anxiety. As just one example, fear of sexual rejection in men is sometimes a major contributing factor in the commission of certain sexual crimes, particularly child molestation and exhibitionism. In the next chapter in this section, another potentially serious negative consequence of social anxiety is considered. Jones, Rose, and Russell summarize the literature on emotional and social loneliness, reviewing assessment of loneliness and factors that contribute to loneliness, including social anxiety.

The fourth section of the book is devoted to some of the clinical disorders associated with social anxiety during adulthood. Scholing and Emmelkamp describe the nature of social phobia, its prevalence, etiology, assessment and treatment, and similarities and differences between social phobia and avoidant personality disorder. Because the diagnostic distinction between generalized social phobia and avoidant personality is not always easy to make, and because there is so little research literature devoted to this topic, a separate chapter on avoidant personality disorder was not included in this book. Heinssen and Glass examine the role of social anxiety in schizophrenia. Social withdrawal and avoidance are significant problems in this population, and although schizophrenia is multideterminded, it appears that social anxiety is one important contributing influence. Bruce and Barlow examine how fear of failure, or performance anxiety, contributes to sexual dysfunction, especially erection difficulties of men. The way in which such performance fears and concerns about being perceived as inadequate inhibits sexual arousal may not be as simple as it sometimes appears. The authors show how basic research conducted in the past decade can explain this phenomenon. In the last chapter in this section, Klass addresses the topic of assessment and treatment of dysfunctional guilt, shame, and embarrassment. One might question why the topic of guilt should even be included in a book on social and evaluation anxiety. But as pointed out by Klass, guilt, shame, and embarrassment have considerable overlap and differ in degree but not in kind on two dimensions: (1) the extent to which one is concerned about moral transgression; and (2) the extent to which one is concerned about negative evaluation. Guilt involves the greatest concern with morality and is least explicit about a concern with others' reactions. Nevertheless, fear of other peoples' negative evaluation "if they knew how bad I am" and fear of rejection is often implied in guilt, even if not as obvious as with shame or embarrassment.

The final section of the book is concerned with performance and evaluation anxiety where the audience or interpersonal context is less interactive or less immediate. Smith and Smoll review the research literature and provide a theoretical model for understanding performance anxiety in sports. Their exposition of the factors involved in sport performance anxiety often appears to be applicable to anxiety experienced in other public performance situations as well, whether it be music, dance, or theatre. Fremouw and Breitenstein summarize the research on assessment and treatment of speech anxiety (anxiety about speaking before an audience). The extent to which people fear appearing foolish or ignorant or anxious, or all three, in public speaking situations is truly remarkable. Because it is so common an occurrence and, in some jobs and in school, so unavoidable, this topic has received more attention than many of the others in this book. A higher level of attention has also been paid to the topic of the next chapter, test anxiety. Sarason and Sarason describe some of the first research in the area of social-evaluation anxiety to elucidate how task-irrelevant self-deprecating thoughts underlie evaluation anxiety and impair performance. They also summarize issues in assessment and treatment of disruptive test anxiety. In the final chapter of the book, Rothblum provides an extensive review of fear of failure research, including achievement motivation, gender differences, so-called fear of success, procrastination, and various self-handicapping strategies used as excuses to protect against the threat to self-esteem and the "shame" of failure.

The most obvious conclusion from reading these various chapters is that social and evaluation anxiety is a diverse and pervasive problem, affecting millions of men, women, and children. In some instances, it is just a vexing problem, something that one can adjust to and live with despite considerable discomfort. In other instances, however, it can be disabling, causing untold personal misery and social harm. As the chapters in this book testify, research in this area has begun to gain some momentum. We now know much more about the biological and developmental factors associated with the origins of social and evaluation anxiety. We also know much more about the role that distorted and dysfunctional thinking patterns play in every kind of social and evaluation anxiety so far studied. These chapters also indicate that we have made considerable progress in refining assessment tools and in developing effective treatment approaches for social and evaluation anxiety. However, the broad cultural forces that contribute to social anxiety are not easily changed, and if one is seriously concerned about totally preventing or eradicating the negative aspects of social and evaluation anxiety, these will need to be addressed. The utopia where people need not be afraid of being hurt by negative evaluation and rejection is still far in the future. Social and evaluation anxiety, after all, is not always irrational.

REFERENCES

Buss, A. H. (1980). *Self-consciousness and social anxiety.* San Francisco: W. H. Freeman.
Leary, M. R. (1983). Social anxiousness: the construct and its measurement. *Journal of Personality Assessment, 47,* 66–75.
Schlenker, B. R., & Leary, M. R. (1982). Social anxiety and self-presentation: A conceptualization and model. *Psychological Bulletin, 92,* 641–669.

I

Overview

1

Social Anxiety, Evolution, and Self-Presentation
An Interdisciplinary Perspective

PETER TROWER, PAUL GILBERT, AND GEORGINA SHERLING

An old but radical idea in social psychology is that the "person" is not a passive product—of environmental conditioning or genetic abnormality or biochemical factors or unconscious psychic phenomena—but is an active creation of the individual him- or herself (Gergen, 1984). Any approach to understanding and studying social anxiety has to take a position on this issue, since it has a major influence on subsequent model building, research, and therapeutic developments. Clinical psychology and psychiatry have traditionally favored one or other versions of the former paradigm, that people are products of various forces, be it internal or external. However, variants of the latter idea (that people are agents of their own creation [Trower, 1984, 1987]) is now well established in social psychology and becoming an emergent paradigm in the clinical field. For example Heimberg, Dodge, & Becker (1987) list five models of social phobia, all of which are arguably of the latter rather than the former school. Following Goffman's seminal dramaturgical model (Goffman, 1959), the explicit or implicit theme in these types of models is that individuals are the architects of their own self-presentations, are motivated to present themselves favorably, and social anxiety is a fear of negative evaluation of the self that is likely to follow from predicted failures in self-presentation performances.

However, there has recently been an equally radical idea that seems to run counter to the model of self as agent and indeed seems to fall within the "passive product" school. This is that social anxiety is a part of our genetic endowment and, in fact, played a critical role in the evolution from individual to social living (Chance, 1988; Gilbert, 1989). Perhaps surprisingly, the two paradigms are not in conflict but form integral parts of a whole which, we believe, provides a potentially comprehensive picture of social anxiety.

PETER TROWER • Solihull Health Authority, Solihull, West Midlands B93 OPX, England. PAUL GILBERT • South Derbyshire Health Authority, South Derbyshire DE3 5DQ, England. GEORGINA SHERLING • Northwick Park Hospital, Harrow, Middlesex HA1 3UJ, England.

Following these leads, the plan for the chapter is, first, a description and definition of social anxiety; second, an evolutionary account of social anxiety; third, within the framework of the evolutionary account, an account of the particular evolved psychological mechanisms characterized by social anxiety; fourth, a description of pilot evaluative research by the authors on the models; and finally, some suggestions about potential clinical applications.

DESCRIPTION AND DEFINITION OF SOCIAL ANXIETY

Clinical researchers have expressed dissatisfaction with or offered divergences from current medical nosologies such as the DSM-III (American Psychiatric Association [APA], 1980) diagnosis of social phobia (Liebowitz, Gorman, Fyer, & Klein, 1985; Turner, Beidel, Dancu, & Keys 1986; Tyrer, 1986). Some have tried to identify different types of social anxiety under different diagnostic categories, for example, social phobia versus avoidant personality disorder (Turner et al., 1986), social phobia versus generalized anxiety disorder (Beck, Emery, & Greenberg, 1985), and most recently, the new DSM-III-R (APA, 1987) makes a distinction between generalized and specific social phobia. Forms of social anxiety also form part of the picture of other disorders and problems, including schizophrenia and substance abuse.

Social psychologists have sought to classify characteristics of social anxiety in other ways, and they have produced different descriptions (Jones, Cheek, & Briggs, 1986).

We use the term *social anxiety* as a generic term to include a varied cluster of characteristics that have been identified in the literature. Some of these reflect differences along a severity dimension—social phobia may represent the more specific and severe clinical end of the spectrum, whereas shyness and communication apprehension appears more diffuse, and it tapers into experiences that would not warrant a classification of disorder. Other characteristics may reflect differences of kind, with different subtypes (Buss, 1986). We believe there are several subtypes of social anxiety and make some suggestions about these. However, we will narrow the main focus of this chapter to one major subtype often called *evaluation anxiety* (Beck, Emery, & Greenberg, 1985).

Definition of Evaluation Anxiety

We suggest the following definition of evaluation anxiety: An anticipatory anxiety cycle beginning with primary fear of negative evaluation of the social self by others—the social self here being defined in terms of self-presentation performances—and secondary fear of the consequences of fear symptoms interfering with self-presentation performances.

We include components in the subjective domain: feelings of anxiety, cognitions related to evaluative concerns, physiological arousal and behavior (although some desynchrony in anxiety states is well known [Rachman & Hodgson, 1974; Weiner, 1985]). Our main concern from a theoretical perspective is the psychological meaning of social anxiety and the difference between this and the meaning of other forms of anxiety. The term *social anxiety* can be taken to refer to an aversive awareness of the self (me) as object to another. Specifically—and unlike other forms of anxiety—the focus of social anxiety is "me as I appear to the other" (as object), and the content of anxiety is the fear of the other holding a negative impression of me, or holding me in low esteem.

The apprehension of oneself as a negative object for the other is experienced as shame, and social anxiety is the anticipation of this. Sartre (1943/1957), cited aptly by Mollon (1984), portrays this experience vividly in his discussion of being-as-object for the other:

> To "feel oneself blushing", to "feel oneself sweating" etc., are inaccurate expressions which the shy person uses to describe his state; what he really means is that he is vividly and constantly conscious of his body not as it is for him but as it is *for the Other*. This constant uneasiness, which is the apprehension of my body's alienation as irremediable, can determine . . . a pathological fear of blushing; these are nothing but the horrified metaphysical apprehension of the existence of my body for the Others. We often say that the shy man is "embarrassed by his own body". Actually this expression is incorrect; I cannot be embarrassed by my own body as I exist it. It is my body as it is for the Other which may embarrass me. (p. 353).

We can take this a stage further and say that it is out of his predictions of what the other may do once he has a negative impression of him, that social anxiety truly arises. "What happens if I make a bad impression? Will the other humiliate me, lose interest, turn others against me, or generally hold me in low esteem?"

A PSYCHOBIOLOGICAL ACCOUNT OF SOCIAL ANXIETY

Whichever way we may look at it, social anxiety seems to pervade human nature. As shyness, it is experienced by the majority of people (Zimbardo, 1977). It affects every corner of our lives, as the following passage from *Time* magazine (cited by Spielberger, 1979) so vividly described:

> Anxiety seems to be the dominant fact . . . and is threatening to become the dominant cliche . . . of modern life. It shouts in the headlines, laughs nervously at cocktail parties, nags from advertisements, speaks suavely from the boardroom, whines from the stage, clatters from the Wall Street ticker, jokes with fake youthfulness on the golf course, and whispers in privacy each day before the shaving mirror and the dressing table. Not merely the black statistics of murder, alcoholism and divorce betray anxiety (or that special form of anxiety which is guilt) but almost any innocent every day act: the limp handshake, the second pack of cigarettes or the third Martini, the forgotten appointment, the stammer in mid-sentence, the wasted hour before the TV set, the spanked child, the new car unpaid for. (*Time* magazine, March 31, 1961, p. 44)

Social anxiety is a central feature not only of ordinary experience and social life, but as we have seen, it also pervades abnormal psychological conditions. We are witnessing a major growth of interest at both ends of this continuum, with social psychologists developing and researching the emergent concept of shyness (e.g., Jones, Cheek, & Briggs, 1986; Crozier, in press), while clinical psychologists and psychiatrists are promoting the study of the neglected topic of social phobia (Heimberg, 1989; Scholing & Emmelkamp, Chapter 9, this volume) as part of a major thrust into the study of the anxiety disorders (e.g., Tuma & Maser, 1985). This marks a late but welcome recognition of the importance of this phenomenon in human life. Social phobia was not even recognized as a diagnostic group until 1980 (APA, 1980). Now it is accepted, not only in its own right, but as a component in many other disorders—in other forms of anxiety such as agoraphobia and generalized anxiety disorder, in the personality disorders (especially avoidant personality disorder), in schizophrenic disorders, in depressive disorders, as a predisposing factor to addictions, and as a consequent factor in brain damage.

Needless to say, this remarkable pervasiveness of social anxiety exists not just throughout Western society but throughout the human race, and not just in humans but in other primates and some other mammalian species as well. Perhaps most significant of all is that social anxiety is not a recent development but has a long phylogenetic history (Gray, 1985), from which its "modern" (relatively speaking) form is derived.

Given that social anxiety is one of the universal components in humans and other species, it is interesting to note that the social and clinical science research communities (with some notable exceptions) have not taken a greater interest in its evolution. (This is, of course, a quite different perspective to that of the school that attributes psychological disorders [like social phobia] to hereditary factors, i.e., genetic anomalies that run in families.) Many researchers and clinicians are probably sceptical of the relevance of the evolutionary approach, or they may assume that man is a tabula rasa whose repertoire is entirely learned, or they may even have failed to wonder how or why human potentialities like social anxiety exist and take the form they do.

Research has not yet provided clear evidence on the role of evolutionary factors in anxiety. For example, in a review of the literature, McNally (1987) found little support for the specific predictions of the preparedness theory of phobia (Seligman, 1971), which holds that humans are biologically prepared to learn to fear objects and situations that threatened the survival of the species throughout its evolutionary history. In contrast, Ohman (1986) has reviewed considerable evidence that classically conditioned stimuli within the prepared modality are much more likely to elicit defensive reactions which remain resistant to extinction than are conditioned stimuli which are not within the prepared modality. In other words, prepared stimuli act as preparatory signals priming the attentional and action systems.

Though McNally asserts there is little evidence specifically for Seligman's theory, he nonetheless cites evidence that most phobias are associated with threats of evolutionary significance, and there is good evidence that people are "prepared" for threat cues of evolutionary significance and that they process these cues at an unconscious level—a point we return to. McNally urges an increase in research and suggests strategies for making future research more relevant than that so far conducted.

Apart from the need for further research, there is a need for a wider conceptual understanding of the evolutionary perspective. The classic nature–nurture argument reemerges here, in which we are invited to make a choice between learning and heredity. However, as Ohman (1986) clearly shows, learning cannot be regarded as independent of evolutionary history but is constrained and shaped by evolution.

Whatever attitude is adopted, the evolutionary perspective is not one that can be ignored, for if it is correct, it has quite radical implications for the study and treatment of social and other forms of anxiety (and other problems, such as depression). It can potentially throw light not just (or even mainly) on the history of human development, but on the fundamental psychobiological structure of human nature, particularly the evolved patterns of physical, emotional, cognitive, and behavioral potentialities with which the modern person is endowed as a result of that phylogenetic development. However, clinical and social psychology researchers and others usually take these potentialities as givens—social anxiety being one such—and models are developed and research is undertaken from that point. This is not really satisfactory, since to understand social anxiety and similar human phenomena, we need a theoretical structure of the meaning and evolved purpose and function of social anxiety within which to build our models.

Such a structural theory can, we hope to show, answer such vital questions as: Is there such a phenomenon as social anxiety, distinguishable meaningfully from other forms of anxiety? And if so what is it? Why and how is it different from other forms of anxiety? Why do humans *have* social anxiety? What purpose does it serve—given its apparent pervasiveness—in the organization of human (and primate) social life? Why is it that people are *socially* afraid (i.e., afraid of disapproval by others) rather than just physically afraid (i.e., afraid of being physically hurt by others)?

Tentative answers to these types of questions have recently begun to take shape. For example, from the painstaking observational research of ethologists, anthropologists, comparative psychologists, psychophysiologists, psychiatrists, and others over the past three decades or so, a conceptual picture of the likely evolution of social, as opposed to individual, forms of living in the ancestors of humans and other mammals has recently emerged (Bailey, 1987; Beck, *et al.*, 1985; Chance, 1980, 1988; Gilbert, 1984, 1989; Ohman, 1986; Price, 1988; Price & Sloman, 1987). One aspect of this picture shows that social anxiety played a major role in the transition, in that (ironically) it made it possible for individuals to live together in groups—an important survival advantage. Social anxiety in modern humankind probably still conforms to the same form and function. However, to explain the significance of this idea and develop some of its ramifications, we will first briefly describe the theory, developed principally by Gilbert (1989) and Chance (1988).

The Defense System

Anxiety and fear are important biological attributes that form part of a defense system in animals and humans to aid the survival of the individual.

These emotions are responses to real or imagined threat, and they mobilize psychobiological resources to defend, escape, or avoid the danger. Emotions are in this sense energizers (Tomkins, 1981; Zajonc, 1980, 1984). In the anxiety disorders these psychobiological mechanisms have a low threshold for activation in that minimum or improbable dangers are amplified by the appraisal and coping systems (described later). In this section we outline the defense system and the role that social anxiety plays within it. We also briefly describe the safety system (Gilbert, 1989), which has been overlooked in many theories but which throws significant light on the maladaptive nature of social anxiety. We then turn, in the next section, to a psychological model of the individual, in which the influence of these evolved systems can be seen to operate.

Antipredator System

Gilbert (1989) has suggested that the defense system is made up of three subsystems which serve different purposes and were laid down at different points in phylogenetic time. These are an antipredator system, a territorial breeding system, and a group living system.

The antipredator system is phylogenetically the oldest system and is probably universal across all species. It means that animals are biologically prepared to automatically detect threat signals, activate arousal, and take defensive action. These actions involve fight, flight, freeze, faint (feigning incapacitation), and camouflage or complex interactions of these. The focus here is primarily physical danger to the self, and it probably underlies animal phobias (Ohman, 1986) and panic disorder (Gilbert, 1989).

Territorial Breeding System

It is clearly the case that predators and nonsocial aversive events are not the source of social anxiety in humans. Hence we must look at later phylogenetic developments of the defensive system. Chance (1980, 1984, 1988) has reviewed much of the evidence suggesting that these latter adaptations fall into two domains which relate to breeding behavior.

The first is concerned with the development of territorial acquisitions. Here we begin to see the arrival of a social (pertaining to members of the same species) communication system designed to signal, analyze, and respond to conspecific threat. Territorial contests involve what Price (1988) called ritual agonistic behavior (RAB). This behavior is designed to aid the communication between contestants by means of ritualized threat displays, conveying information about what is called resource holding potential (RHP), allowing each to weigh up the strengths and weaknesses of the other and to decide the outcome with minimal or no actual fighting. The loser loses access to the territory contested and to breeding opportunities and other resources within that territory, and disperses to other territories. So long as there are other territories this dispersion need not be a problem. However, in limited territories a new system evolved. In order not to continually activate RAB, the loser not only gives up claim to breeding resources within the winner's territory, but also signals nonthreat to the winner. Price (1988) calls this defensive routine the yielding subroutine of RAB (YS/RAB). As Price makes clear, this routine is designed to signal to the winner that the loser is no longer a threat. Furthermore, it is also designed to reduce the loser's capability to continue fighting by producing in the loser a state of incapacity which has many of the characteristics of, and may be a precursor of, clinical depression (Price & Sloman, 1987). It is probable that the rudiments of a nondispersant, group living system evolved from this period through the YS/RAB routine, with the more dominant and powerful individuals occupying the largest and more central territories.

The antipredator system puts an emphasis on distance from the predator—the minimum safe distance that would prevent a surprise attack. The YS/RAB of the territorial period allows for a much greater degree of neighborhood closeness, but the defensive response options still emphasize a respectable degree of separation between conspecifics. Just how strong these forces for separation are in the territorial period can be gauged by (1) the fact that proximity is one of the major triggers for RAB and (2) the fact that courtship—despite being such a central activity to species survival—is a long and dangerous process (which researchers recognize as a major type of social anxiety in male and female humans). In many species, in order to breed, the male and the female need to go through a ritualized courtship procedure to overcome the innate predisposition to attack or flee from each other, which would prevent copulation.

Group Living System (Agonic)

The attentional focus in the territorial system is clearly on conspecific threat with (ritualized) fighting and withdrawal behavior. Nonetheless, the territorial defense system provides the rudiments for the next development—the group living system. One consequence of this is the emergence of the social conditions out of which the phenomenon we call social anxiety arose (though a form of social anxiety — stranger anxiety — may emanate from the territorial system).

This next evolutionary step brought truly social forms of living. To enable conspecifics to live together in groups, the "agonic" system evolved (Chance, 1980, 1988; Price, 1988). The agonic system took over from the territorial system the structure of hierarchical relationships, in which individuals occupied positions of dominance or subordination to each other. The same concern with access to resources is at stake too, except that animals living in groups are not territorially dispersant. In order to overcome the tendency to separate, the various defense responses of the territorial stage had to be inhibited so that individuals could stay together in groups. If the losing animal was not to withdraw, it must be able to send signals which appeased the dominant animal in such a way that it made it relatively safe to remain in close proximity. This has enabled the phenomenon of "reverted escape" (Chance, 1986) to develop—the fact that the threatened animal may move away temporarily only to return to the source of threat. It can only do this if it signals a submissive, no-threat response. This acts as an automatic signal which inhibits the dominant animal from inflicting injury, and thereby enables survival without fleeing the confines of the group. Submission is also common in primates. Many species that have developed the agonic mode share a common repertoire of nonverbal submissive behavior, such as gaze avoidance, crouching, the fear face, and various forms of behavior which originate from the infant (care eliciting) and from the courtship repertoires. In addition, humans have developed complex behaviors relating to verbal skills which are concerned with the problem of being in close proximity but inhibiting various kinds of status attack.

Agonic behavior in a subordinate (such as submission) probably evolved out of the yielding subroutine (YS) but is quite different from the latter, in that its function is to enable dominant and subordinate to live together. The subordinate is not in a defeated, depressed state but rather in a state of high but inhibited tension or "braked readiness" to take self-defensive action with regard to the dominant, to whom the subordinate is highly attentive. Nevertheless, the subordinate's access to resources is seriously curtailed, as is access to and control over social reinforcing opportunities.

It is our contention that social anxiety evolved primarily as part of this agonic mode. In new situations it would operate as an early warning system for discriminating the likelihood and degree of threat from another animal, trigger a self–other comparison of strengths and weakness, and, depending on the decision, prepare the animal for an appropriate response option, such as submission. Once established in a hierarchy, it would enable a subordinate to read potential threat from a dominant and prepare the animal to signal further submission if necessary.

It is clear that social anxiety in many species that live in close proximity is not abnormal. Indeed, a failure of anxiety in a subordinate in close proximity to a dominant, or where the dominant is closely observing the subordinate, would be disadvantageous. Under such conditions the subordinate needs to signal "no threat" and, via anxiety, be alerted to danger as quickly as possible. Social anxiety becomes "abnormal" in the context of hedonic modes of social behavior, as we shall later explore.

The Safety System

We have so far looked at defense systems—systems which evolved to enable animals to live socially but defensively in an environment of intraspecies threat. We have explored how social anxiety developed in this context. However, this is only half the story, since the degree of threat in well-functioning ecological environments is counterbalanced by the degree of safety. We must therefore look at the evolution of systems which enable animals to develop in safety as well as under threat.

This brings us to the safety system (Gilbert, 1989). As in the case of defense, Gilbert postulates three subsystems in the safety system, classified as individual, attachment, and hedonic.

The Individual Safety System

This system is concerned with the recognition and detection of nonsocial safety cues. For example, animals emerging out of their burrows will sample the local environment for the presence of threat, and if no threat is detected then exploration and various species-specific activities are facilitated (e.g., nest building, food seeking, etc.). The safety system works through positive reinforcement and is responsible for the seeking out and attending to various cues and stimuli that signal such reinforcement (Gray, 1971). As Rachman (1984) points out, anxiety can be regarded as resulting from the presence of danger or the absence of safety.

The Attachment System

In primitive species there is no recognition of genetically related offspring. A major phylogenetic jump occurs, however, when parents do recognize their own offspring and do not cannibalize them (MacLean, 1985). Successive adaptations increased the care-giving and nurturing interactions between parent and infant. By the time the primates arrived on the evolutionary stage, the parental attachment system had taken on profound importance for the development of the infant.

The mother (or primary care giver) is responsible for supplying many inputs essential to survival of the young. One of these is safety under threat. The infant returns to the mother for protection. The interaction has evolved such that the provision of tactile stimuli has a profound effect on reducing the infant's defensive arousal and, after calming, enables the infant to recommence exploring. Evolution has therefore made it possible for significant others (at least during early life) to have significant safety-bestowing properties. A good deal of work has now gone into understanding the attachment system and the deleterious effects that disruption to these interactions can bring (Bowlby, 1969, 1973, 1980; Hollow & Mears, 1979; Reite & Field, 1985). At the time the human child is becoming mobile (at around 9 months), we see the emergence of the first possible precursors of one form of social anxiety—fear of strangers (Bee, 1985)—and how this is handled within the attachment system has clear implications for the development of social anxiety.

The Hedonic System

Many researchers have noted the importance of attachment behavior in adult life (Heard & Lake, 1986). However, Gilbert (1989) has argued for the evolution of a more general form of cooperative behavior which has made it possible for adult conspecifics to operate in close proximity to each other without activating antagonistic behaviour. Chance (1988) has identified a mode of cohesion in the great apes which he calls the *hedonic mode*. In this mode primates act together in joint exploratory and defense actions (e.g., hunting and defending against predators). More importantly, their social activity is not centered on the sending and receiving of threat signals as part of a ranked group, but of reassurance signals between mutually dependent individuals. These are shown in various greetings, kissing, hugging, lip smacking, and other forms of reciprocated social behavior. In humans it is exemplified by the vast network of etiquette and politeness routines, such as greetings, partings, indirect requests, turn taking, apologies, and so on, as well as displays of more intimate affection, which are deeply embedded in social behavior of everyday life, and which have been so well clarified and identified by Goffman (1972) and by socio- and psycholinguists (e.g., Brown & Levinson, 1978).

Activity in this mode renders the social environment as one of safety (rather than threat) and one of positive reinforcers (rather than negative) during interpersonal interaction—something rarely seen in more agonic species. Consequently, attention is liberated away from defensive social monitoring. From an evolutionary point of view, the agonic mode, with its vertical form of ranks, does not facilitate cooperative enterprise, yet cooperative enterprise was to provide a major advance in that individuals working and problem solving together could achieve more than individuals working alone or in a threatening environment. The cooperative, horizontal form of organization, marked by equality among peers, was much better fitted for the purpose. This cooperation has been at the heart of human social life and also the route to our intelligence development (Chance, 1986, 1988) and capability for culture.

To summarize, whereas appeasement functioned in agonic structures to reduce conspecific threats, reassurance worked in cooperative (hedonic) social structures as a communication system for reducing status conflict in the social discourse of both parties.

When individuals do not feel valued or respected, there is an automatic tendency to regress to more hostile (primitive) forms of attempting to regulate their status. When parents and peers send signals of valuing to the child or other, there is a greater probability that status and self-esteem become regulated in prosocial and safety-enhancing modes rather than regressing to more primitive agonic or even earlier forms.

Interaction of the Defense and Safety Systems

It seems probable that most people experience both the defense and safety systems, but they are able to interact within the safety system most of the time so long as individuals who make up that system continue to send the appropriate reassurance gestures and receive and interpret them accurately. The motive for these transactions is to communicate mutual respect and valuing. Status is bestowed on the other by means of the complex rules of social interaction referred to earlier, and generally by the communication of appreciation of the other. A failure to do these things may invoke in the other a more primitive dominance set of actions and a return to a more hostile competitive form of social interaction, and cooperation breaks down. Social anxiety may then serve as a mechanism to alert people to threat signals, to say that the situation is no longer safe (e.g., that they are not valued and respected but seen as a subordinate) and that they may have to prepare themselves for defense in a hierarchical struggle of assertion or submission (or flight).

We postulate that socially anxious individuals are predisposed to use evaluative mentalities from the defense system, so that, unlike the majority who operate mostly within the safety system, they perceive the social world as a unitary, not a dual, system and have few or no constructs for the recognition and construction of hedonic forms of social interaction. They are unable to rely on the other to bestow status (indeed, they may not see it as in the nature of the other to do so), but see the world of others as dominant, able, hostile (to them), and worthy, and see themselves as submissive, low ranking, weak and vulnerable, and unworthy. They may misinterpret social signals as indicating threat, and underrate their ability to skillfully deal with the threat. They may characteristically exhibit intentional or automatic attempts to escape, freeze (automatic inhibition), behave submissively, and avoid future encounters. There is forensic evidence, too, that on rare occasions they may show an extreme fight reaction (Howells, 1986). Socially anxious individuals may also invoke in others the very defensive responses that they predict. Having a sense of inferiority, they may exhibit behaviors which actually provoke dominance behavior in the other (Leary, 1957)—a phenomenon well recognized in psychoanalysis as negative fit (Singer & Luborsky, 1977).

Chance (1988) has argued that what the above represents is two fundamental forms of "mentality," which he names after the agonic (or defensive) and hedonic (safety) modes. They are marked by very different classes of attention and information processing. The agonic-defensive focuses attention on the self, which in the social domain is a self–other comparison. In the hedonic mode attention has no need to be focused on the self since the friendship signals (if believed, and this may be crucial) render the system unnecessary.

Potential Developments of the Theory

There are a number of potential developments of the theory both within and outside the area of social anxiety. One is a potential contribution to understanding the relationship between psychological disorders, particularly depression, anger and aggression, and anxiety. Another—germane to our present discussion—is for distinguishing and understanding different kinds of social anxiety. It may be possible, for example, to map different kinds of social anxiety onto the phylogenetic stages, with more severe kinds linked to the more primitive stages. We make tentative proposals in this direction in the next section. The proportion of paranoia (perceived hostile threat) may be diagnostic in this regard, with increasing paranoia present in more serious disorders corresponding to the more primitive stages.

For example, a recent study shows a clear distinction between stranger anxiety and evaluation anxiety (J. Asendorpf, personal communication, October 1987), though both may be present in the same person (and certainly the potential is present in everyone). The theory suggests that stranger anxiety has less focus on performance than on hostile forms of being observed, and a preoccupation with threat not to the psychological but the physical self. Stranger anxiety probably relates to the earlier territorial system rather than the agonic system, and it starts much earlier in life, probably around 9 months, than evaluation anxiety, which starts at around puberty and the onset of self-consciousness. The theory also suggests high arousal and an experience of panic more typical of animal phobias than social phobias (Ohman, 1986). It is almost certain that fear of strangers may combine with evaluation anxiety, such as in agoraphobia, where there is, for example, a fear of doing something "shameful" in a crowded supermarket.

Another area of potential interest is avoidant personality disorder and schizoid personality disorder, both of which have social anxiety as a major component (Pilkonis, 1984). There is some recent empirical evidence for a distinction between avoidant personality disorder and social phobia, with the former showing greater avoidance and less social skill and a greater degree of general psychopathology (Turner *et al.*, 1986). It seems worth investigating whether avoidant personality disorder includes stranger anxiety, with a degree of damage to any relationship-forming potential. This picture could be progressively worse in schizoid personality disorders and other schizo-form disorders, where access to hedonic modes of relating may be completely or partially absent.

Summary

The pattern of social behavior of individuals—anxious and nonanxious alike—does not develop by learning alone but unfolds according to innate programs through which learning takes place. Social anxiety forms an integral and normal part of the innate defensive system, and it operates as an alerting mechanism to trigger defensive behavior and the learning of many subtle forms of such behavior. Our thesis is that social anxiety becomes abnormal when there is a low threshold for defensive activation, continues to alert individuals to status threats even when they do not exist, and switches off their ability to perceive safety (no-threat) and status-bestowing signals in cooperative situations. We also suggest that when individuals have inferiority beliefs about themselves they automatically start encounters from an agonic situation. This immediately sets up the recruitment of mental mechanisms evolved to help the subordinate to coordinate defensive behavior, such as submissiveness, to avoid dominant threat. This in turn tends to elicit more dominant behavior from others, including hostility, control, or lack of interest or valuing, which increases the probability that the subordinate will continue to believe that all social interactions are competitive.

We now turn to a psychological model that builds on this structure and attempts to explain the part these processes play in the maladaptive functioning of socially anxious individuals in everyday social interaction.

AN APPRAISAL-COPING MODEL OF SOCIAL ANXIETY

According to the theory outlined above, people are endowed with a set of innate repertoires, or "mentalities," which have evolved in phylogenetic time to aid survival and development. Once triggered, any one of these mentalities will recruit the psychological processes of attention, perception, cognition, emotion, and behavior to serve the goal of that particular mentality and will facilitate a particular type of learning congruent with that mentality. There is now considerable indirect evidence for this type of approach in general terms. For example, the literature on mood–state-dependent phenomena shows that perception, learning, and retrieval are all strongly channelled by the mood state of the individual, such that a person will, for example, perceive or recall events congruent with the mood, but not events that are mood incongruent.

We argue that social anxiety is closely linked with one of these biologically prepared states, namely, the agonic mentality, and is characterized by a particular recruitment of psychological processes geared to the goal of social defense explored earlier. We believe it is important to evaluate existing models of social anxiety from this perspective, and that to do so will give us new insights. We can best illustrate this by such a reevaluation and redevelopment of a model of social anxiety, first put forward by Trower and Turland (1984). We assume that a socially anxious person, being in the agonic state, is biologically prepared to (1) perceive social groups as structured in terms of dominance–submissive hierarchies, (2) selectively perceive and interpret threat cues within such a structure, (3) focus on the self under threat (perceived as if through the eyes of others), and (4) take action to defend the self in the struggle to avoid a potentially catastrophic loss of status in the hierarchy. We shall also emphasize the significant failure of the socially anxious to recruit a prepared hedonic mentality to recognize social groups being differently organized—along cooperative lines—and the problems that this failure creates.

Description of the Model

Following Trower and Turland (1984), we postulate that there are two major, interconnected processes in human social functioning in general—an appraisal system for perceiving, inferring, and evaluating the desirability or otherwise of various states of affairs (both internal and external) and a coping system for responding to those states of affairs if necessary in order to bring about a change to a desired state. The desired state is represented by cognitive schemata which contain standards against which comparisons are made. The overall process operates as a continuous, sequential feedback loop in a manner first described by Miller, Galanter, and Pribram (1960) in the TOTE (test-operate-test-exit) and later developed by Carver (1979) and others.

We can now develop the model in the following way. We can postulate that there are many potential forms that appraisal-coping systems can take, each characterized by a particular emotion and an associated network of cognitive schemata which prime an individual to make a particular type of interpretation of the social environment and a particular pattern of responding.

Social anxiety is typified by one type of schema, which as we have seen derives from the competitive, or agonic, mode, which primes the individual to appraise social "reality" as structured in terms of dominance hierarchies. We refer to this schema as the superordinate dominance schema—superordinate because it dictates the nature of the perceptual–conceptual background (social reality) within which all other perceptions and activities take their meaning. The most important subsets of schemata within the dominance schema are the self-schemata, since the self plays a central role in social anxiety. Indeed, in social anxiety the appraisal-coping process is recruited by the self, both to appraise threats to the self and to cope with those threats.

Structure of the Model

Within the general system, individuals as agents are deemed to actively anticipate and act rather than passively register and respond to environmental events as they occur. In other words, individuals make predictions (conscious and unconscious) or probable desirable or undesirable outcomes on the basis of certain specific behavioral or other cues and then choose their actions (or nonactions) on the basis of those predictions. Mischel (1973) has developed the concept of expectancy–outcome relationships to exemplify this predictive function. We postulate three kinds of *expectancies* (Figure 1). Within the appraisal system we have *stimulus–outcome* expectancies (e.g., predictions from social cues of various consequences), and within the coping system we have *behavior–outcome* expectancies (predictions that certain actions will produce certain consequences) and *efficacy–outcome* expectancies (Bandura, 1977; predictions about whether one can successfully execute certain actions). We describe the kinds of appraisal and coping which flow from the anxious person's dominance schema in the relevant sections below.

As a result of such expectancies, four kinds of *effects* are produced in the individual. First, within the appraisal system of a socially anxious individual, negative stimulus expectancies elicit anxiety experiences (effects), defined in terms of *physiological arousal, emotional experience*, and *cognitive self-schemata*. For example, an anxious individual may have a negative stimulus–outcome expectancy ("X is dangerous and about to happen") which provokes anxiety experi-

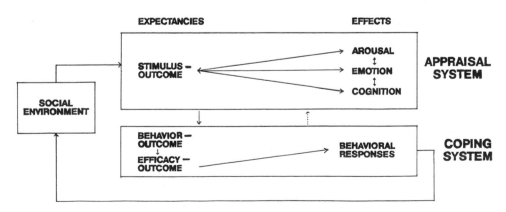

FIGURE 1. Based on the model of social anxiety first put forward by Trower and Turland (1984), the figure shows the structure and function of the appraisal and coping systems and their components (see text for details).

ences ("I am under threat!"). Second, on the basis of the appraisal, the individual selects *behavioral responses* as a consequence of his or her behavior–outcome and efficacy–outcome expectancies referred to earlier. For example, the individual settles on a coping response by deciding what he or she should and could do ("action Y should reduce the danger and I can implement Y") and then implements the response (or nonresponse) chosen.

Function of the Model

The appraisal and coping systems operate integrally as parts of an overall self-regulating, or cybernetic, system (Carver, 1979; Carver & Scheier, 1984). At a general level, they form a discrepancy-reducing loop, the main function of which is to negate or minimize any sensed difference between two given values. A given state of affairs is perceived and compared with a reference value or standard, to see if there is a discrepancy between them. In our terms this is the function of the appraisal system. If there is no discrepancy, no further action is taken. If there is a discrepancy, action is taken to try to reduce it—the function of the coping system. This self-regulating process does not continue indefinitely but can be interrupted by a variety of conditions. Once interrupted, an assessment is made of how likely it is that discrepancy reduction can be brought about, based on the present situation and the person's resources. If the outcome of this assessment is favorable, discrepancy reduction continues, but if it is unfavorable, the person disengages from further discrepancy reduction attempts.

One influential account of social anxiety which draws upon this model is that of Schlenker and Leary (1982). They argue that in social anxiety the focus of discrepancy is between a desired self-identity—the standard—and a low expectation that the desired self-identity will be constructed and/or maintained. The greater the expected discrepancy, the greater the level of social anxiety, and presumably the more likely it is that the individual will disengage from further discrepancy reduction.

This account, as stated, is rather too general for the theory we have developed (though it is much more fine-tuned in Schlenker, 1987), but we adapt the account in the following section.

Integration of the Theories

It may at this point be useful to integrate the biological and psychological theories in terms of a framework of levels of defense system goals or standards. Each level has an associated interpersonal strategy or set of rules to achieve the goal, which is discussed later. We stress that these levels only apply to the defense system, and that part of the problem with the socially anxious is that they do not utilize components of the hedonic system. In the description of the levels, we use the terms *goal* and *standard* interchangeably.

First-level goal. (1) This goal is to achieve the dominant position or increase relative resource holding potential (RHP) in a new or existing relationship (i.e., to be identified as the dominant individual in a relationship). The strategy used is some form of ritual agonistic behavior (RAB). (2) This goal also is to be dominant, but in this case the goal is to maintain an existing relationship position. The strategy used is RAB whenever the other is perceived to be behaving in an insufficiently subordinate manner.

Second-level goal. This goal is both to avoid harm and rejection or expulsion by a dominant and to maintain a position next to the dominant (e.g., to be dutifully subordinate). The strategy used is reverted escape (i.e., submissive appeasement and the adoption of a subordinate position).

Third-level goal. This goal is to avoid a perceived threat from a dominant or dominants when the strategy of submission is not working. The strategy used in this case is escape, fight, freeze, faint, camouflage, or a combination of these, or avoidance of the other(s).

There is a fourth stage which is not a goal but a state of resignation or "despair," in which depression is the predominant mood and helplessness the "strategy."

We would speculate that the primary desired self-identity for socially anxious people (given the influence of their dominance schemata from the agonic mode) is to be more dominant and have higher status (more RHP) than the other or others (the first-level goal), but they have low expectations of being able to construct and/or maintain this identity and therefore would have high anxiety about attempting a dominance strategy. The greater the discrepancy between the desired outcome and the expected outcome, the greater the anxiety, and the greater the likelihood of disengagement from this goal. In other words, if they attempt a dominance strategy (first-level goal) they expect to come off worst, so in order to limit their potential loss of status, they disengage from the dominance goal, settle for the subordinate position (second-level goal), and appease the other as dominant. If that fails (e.g., they fail to appease the dominant) they may opt for defensive alternatives which serve a more primitive and basic survival need (third-level goal), such as escape (by fight, flight, freeze, faint or camouflage) or avoidance, or given up altogether in a state of defeat and depression, and thereby give up the survival struggle. Expanding this in terms of Schlenker and Leary's theory, we might further speculate that a socially anxious person may opt to progress through some or all of the levels in the following way:

> *First-level goal.* (1) Am I able to construct my desired self-identity goal (i.e., one higher in dominance to the other) by successfully challenging the other (where the other is a new individual or existing dominant)? I doubt it. My ability level is too low and/or the risks too high. Disengage from this goal and go to Level 2. (2) Am I able to maintain an existing desired standard (dominant position to another) by limiting the challenge of the other (where the other is a potentially rising subordinate)? I doubt it. Disengage and go to Level 2.
>
> *Second-level goal.* Acquiesce by adopting a subordinate self-identity to the other, but limit the loss of status by appeasing the other—do as the other wants. If expectations for achieving this are also too low, disengage and go to Level 3.

Third-level goal: Avoid the other; escape, freeze, faint (feign incapacitation) or use some means of camouflage to reduce likelihood of attack; fight and show aggression if cornered. Use these tactics if physical or psychological survival seems at stake. If these strategies fail, admit defeat and give up.

The three levels can also be used to characterize different agonic (or earlier) dispositional tendencies, or types, following Gardner (1988). For example, the dominant type (e.g., Type A personality or narcissistic personality) would characteristically have first-level goals and be highly socially skilled in first-level dominance strategies. The subordinate follower type, or medium to low ranker (which might include a broad range from Type B personality to the socially anxious or shy and dependent personality), would characteristically pursue second-level goals and be highly socially skilled in second-level (submissive) interpersonal strategies. The lonely introvert type (social isolates, avoidant and schizoid personality disorders) would characteristically pursue third-level survival goals and would use high-arousal antipredator routines like escape and avoidance. Since these are not *social* skills, this type would probably be lacking in most social skills.

The three-level framework can be used to generate a variety of further hypotheses and may throw light, for example, on the issue of generalized versus specific social phobia distinguished in DSM-III-R. For example, dominant ("confident") types might be vulnerable to specific social phobias, where specific weaknesses in their dominance repertoires may be exposed or anticipated in specific situations. However, they may lack second-level appeasement skills and therefore tend to respond with third-level high-arousal reactions, which will further disrupt their dominance repertoires. Subordinate, follower types might be vulnerable to more generalized social anxiety as a function of their role, since subordinates are exposed to status attack, but being skilled in appeasement skills, they would generally cope within the group. However, we might expect subordinates to also experience specific, high-arousal social phobias under at least two conditions: (1) when they undertake first-level dominance goals (like public speaking), since they will be undertaking tasks with low expectancies of success and high expectancies of risk (threat response), and (2) when their appeasement strategies appear to be failing and they come under attack from a dominant. Under such circumstances, they would be strongly inclined to recruit third-level defense tactics.

We now turn to the various components of the model, dealing first with the social environment, second with the appraisal system, and third with the coping system. The order of the appraisal and coping systems is arbitrary, since they do not function linearly but in a continuous feedback cycle, and discussion of the one has to assume a particular state in the other.

The Social Environment

Social anxiety is uniquely a product of the social, as opposed to the physical, environment. While the physical environment is determined by impersonal laws of nature, the social environment is *constructed* by and for human beings, by means of rules and conventions which influence and shape, through reward and punishment, the behavior of individuals (Berger & Luckmann, 1966; Trower, 1984). Goffman (1972) refers to these as the ground rules by which the "social order" is maintained, and he distinguishes those that affirm and support actions from those that penalize and impose sanctions. There are various possible "constructions" of the social environment, and we have shown that the socially anxious tend to construct their social world in more primitive (hostile) hierarchical and agonic terms.

By means of the process of socialization, individuals internalize the social environment—they employ the complex web of rules and conventions as standards by which they evaluate and generate their own social behavior. It is in this context that we can understand the idea of self-presentation—the construction of the social self by means of self-presentation behavior, according to social rules and standards (Baumeister, 1982). The purpose of self-presentation, in the eyes of the socially anxious, is to avoid negative self-evaluation and the loss of status that this entails.

Fear of negative evaluation is a powerful stabilizing force in hierarchical social organization, in that people will go to extraordinary lengths to obey social rules, especially when directed to by dominant others, as the literature on conformity shows (e.g., Milgram 1965). We suggest that these social rules, particularly status-defining rules (i.e., who is dominant and who is subordinate), have an extreme influence on the behavior of the socially anxious.

However, we have also argued that there is another form of social organization which evolved out of the cooperative "safety" system, based on mutual reassurance giving. Here social rules form the backdrop and not the focus of social interaction (i.e., the interaction is not concerned with the enactment of dominance–submissive roles). As we shall argue, however, socially anxious individuals seem unable to make this switch.

The Appraisal System

The appraisal system is concerned with the interpretation and evaluation of events which may have significance for the individual, given his or her goals and needs at the time. In the socially anxious this appraisal is mainly concerned with the status of the self in a hierarchically organized social group. In this section we look at the components of the appraisal system in more detail.

Expectancies

People in general make interpretations and draw inferences from external and internal stimuli, and anxious people are particularly concerned with inferences about the future. These inferences have been termed *stimulus–outcome expectancies*, by means of which they come to forecast what will happen, given certain stimuli (Mischel, 1973).

One set of expectancies any individual will have is an estimate of other people's evaluations of his or her appearance, behavior, and other self-identifying characteristics. For most people, such expectancies only come into prominence periodically, such as when dominance schemata are triggered—when attention is drawn to the self, for example in self-enhancing or self-threatening situations—but in normal, routine, everyday situations they will remain latent. However, for the socially anxious, such dominance schemata and the consequent expectancies may be ever present. Given this salience of dominance schemata, combined with low-efficacy expectations (Bandura, 1977), the main concern of the socially anxious is the construction and maintenance of a social self-identity which is perceived as highly vulnerable. This leads to the hypervigilant monitoring of situations, potential audiences, and the individual's own self-presentation behavior for extensive periods of time. The socially anxious person is locked into a constant search for social cues, such as certain facial expressions (Ohman & Dimberg, 1984), which indicate hostile appraisal of his or her self-presentation behavior. Research shows such individuals are prone to monitor such cues more than average, and they are more likely to predict, perceive, and recall negative appraisal from others (e.g., Carver & Scheier, 1981; Fenigstein, 1979; Halford & Foddy, 1982; Lucock & Salkovskis, in press; Mathews & MacLeod, 1987; Smith, Ingram, & Brehm, 1983). This is exactly what would be expected from subordinate concerns. For example, Smith *et al.* (1983) had high and low socially anxious subjects participate in either a high-stress socially evaluative interaction or one that was low in stress and socially innocuous. High socially anxious subjects in the evaluative situation differed from the other three groups in demonstrating enhanced processing of information concerning potential evaluations of them by others also present in the stressful situation. Recently, Asendorpf (in press) showed specifically that dispositionally shy subjects were significantly more fearful of being socially evaluated than were non-shy subjects.

We suggested above that one of the main targets of other people's perceived negative evaluations is the anxious person's self-presentation behavior. The person would not be anxious, however, were he or she not also appraising his or her behavior as flawed in some way. Indeed, Schlenker and Leary (1982) propose that "social anxiety arises when people are motivated to make a preferred impression on others but doubt that they will do so, and thus perceive or imagine unsatisfactory evaluative reactions from subjectively important audiences" (p. 641). We would construe this as meaning that anxious people doubt their ability to perform status-enhancing or -maintaining behavior, and that they believe flawed attempts would lead to loss of status (resource holding potential, or RHP) in the eyes of others. This set of expectancies leads to social anxiety. While we have no direct evidence for our interpretation, there is abundant evidence that socially anxious people perceive themselves as lacking in social competence, particularly assertion skills, which we interpret as status enhancing or maintaining.

To recapitulate, we are suggesting that the socially anxious individual is characteristically locked into the dominance schema, which governs information processing, and, in particular, the type of expectancies and inferences the individual makes.

Typically, such inferences link some aspect of the person's behavior, appearance, or other self-identifying aspect to a negative evaluation of his or her self-presentation behavior by others. Often these inferences form a chain wherein the conclusion of one inference forms the premise for the next, as follows:

If I lift a cup, I'll shake.
If I shake, people will look at me.
If they look, they will know I'm anxious.
If they know I'm anxious, they will think I'm inferior and incompetent.

Behind these inferences are more central assumptions inherent in the dominance schema which give them their meaning. These assumptions include the innate fear of rejection, abandonment, and loss of access to resources, which is the worst outcome for the biological survival of the individual in a hierarchically organized society. For example, fear of inferiority is only understandable if the individual is making the connection that inferiority will lead to rejection and loss of social control, and that rejection will lead to abandonment and constitutes a threat to survival. Though these connections are predisposed in the dominance schema, an individual will have learned specific forms of such connections through parental or other significant figures. He or she may have assimilated social rules and standards about proper conduct into his or her cognitive schemata (discussed above) which, if breached, may lead to inferiority judgments by others and rejection. For example, a client may have the following beliefs: "A man is inferior if he is anxious; I will be abandoned if I am seen as inferior." From these he will derive an imperative: "I must not show I'm anxious."

Once formed, these beliefs operate as recognitory schemata against which performances can be judged (Carver, 1979). The individual will process new behavioral information by comparing it with such preexisting schemata and thereby recognizing and judging it as conforming to his or her desired self-schema or not. Schemata can affect what the observer attends to and can cause selective filtering, interpretation, recognition, and recall of information to fit the schema (Kihlstrom & Nasby, 1981; Nasby & Kihlstrom, 1986). There are intra- and interindividual differences in the extent to which a person is schema driven—makes judgments by means of his or her schemata—or stimulus driven—makes judgments by means of situation cues. As we have seen, socially anxious people are generally strongly schema driven as regards judging others' reaction.

Effects and Expectancy–Effect Cycles

We turn now to the way the individual subjectively experiences the world as perceived, and the interaction between expectancies and effects.

Following Trower and Turland (1984), we define subjective experience in the present context as consisting of (1) characteristic physical sensations which arise from physiological arousal and which contribute to (2) an emotional state expressible in ordinary language linked to (3) a perceived threat to the desired self-schema (Schlenker, 1986).

Ohman and others (e.g., Ohman, Dimberg, & Ost, 1985) demonstrate that social-evaluative anxiety is marked by continuous rather than episodic physiological arousal, and heightened but markedly lower levels of physiological arousal than that found in animal phobias, and this would seem to tally with the feelings of wariness and uncomfortable tension (as opposed to panic) that accompanies shyness-related emotions and exemplifies the state of braced readiness in the agonic mode. It also demonstrates that antipredator-type anxiety operates via a different system. The aim in the latter case is rapid avoidance, not submission. Like Ohman *et al.*, we would therefore expect these particular physiological and emotional effects to facilitate submissive, concealment, and conformity behavior, as opposed to panic, which would disrupt them.

The pursuit of a second-level defensive goal by means of a submissive self-presentation strategy is the only way that the socially anxious person believes he or she has of protecting against the threat to self in a competitive, dominance-seeking environment. Moderated arousal levels are what we would expect so long as the individual believes these coping behaviors will be successful. But the socially anxious person becomes periodically anxious about *failing* to behave submissively, revealing his or her fear (fear of sending signals revealing fear), or failing to conform to social rules and thus increasing the probability of some negative response from the other. As the perceived probability of failure of defensive behavior increases, we might expect the anxious individual's arousal to rise to panic-like proportions, and thereby to recruit (automatically and unconsciously) the phylogenetically older (third-level) defense responses, including fight, flight, freeze, and faint. Or the same thing may happen if the anxious person pursues a first-level goal (like public speaking). Indeed, Heimberg, Hope, Dodge, and Becker (1988) have found that "generalized" social phobics had heart rate reactivity which confirmed the pattern reported above, but public speaking phobics had extreme cardiovascular arousal, perhaps more akin to a panic state.

In both cases, increased physiological arousal and automatic behavioral responses such as stuttering, muscle twitching, and other responses derived from the fight–flight–freeze–faint system will severely disrupt self-presentation. These subjective effects of prior expectancies may in turn become anticipatory cues for serious, even catastrophic, failure in any kind of self-presentation behavior. In other words, fear-produced autonomic and behavioral reactions become fear-producing cues in a fear-of-fear cycle (Beck *et al.*, 1985).

Candidates for this fear-of-fear cycle include those reactions that are publicly obvious: shaking and other muscular reactions provoke fear of situations that involve writing, lifting cups, speaking in public, and other tasks for which dexterity is required; gastrointestinal reactions produce fear of vomiting, eating difficulties, urinating, and defecating; cardiovascular reactions produce fear of blushing and fainting.

It is predictable from our psychobiological theory that the degree to which a person tries to conceal his or her anxiety reflects the extent the situation is perceived as a dominance situation. Not all individuals feel it necessary to conceal. Equally, inadvertent social rule breaking also reveals vulnerability with a similar consequence. Arousal-disrupted self-presentation behavior of the kinds we have described causes both problems—revealing anxiety and causing inadvertent rule breaking—while at the same time increasing conspicuousness at the moment the individual wishes for concealment. It is this kind of spiralling effect that is likely to lead to what is properly defined as social *phobia* with an element of panic.

It is also an interesting question whether people with avoidant personality disorder are more avoidant and more interpersonally sensitive because they do not have the skills for defensive self-presentation and are thus more exposed to the kind of scenario we have just described.

We have so far talked about the psychological and physiological effects arising from the *expectation* of failed (or unavailable) defensive self-presentation and subsequent probable threats to the self and loss of status. A different set of effects arises, however, from the perceived *realization* of failed self-presentation in the presence of potential status-threatening others. The two main emotional effects of this kind are shame and embarrassment. The kinds of behaviours most studied are social rule-breaking behaviors, like gaffes, faux pas, and social accidents (Edelmann, 1987), which may so easily arise from the primitive fear responses explored above. Here the emotional effect is embarrassment, with probable *lowered* levels of arousal, an urge to escape from the presence of others, and a set of behaviors such as gaze aversion and, most importantly, blushing (Amies, Gelder, & Shaw, 1983), which may signal to both the victim and the observers that a performance failure has occurred and the client has lost status.

Schlenker & Leary (1985) are among a number of authors who have pointed out that the socially anxious have unrealistically high self-standards, which inevitably increases the doubts that the individual will be able to perform successful self-presentations. But it is the existence of the dominance schema which turns such doubts into social anxiety. For example, it contains a representation of a critical and competitive social world. The perception of a world implies that only the most powerful dominance displays will succeed, and the consequences of failing are potentially (in the perceiver's eyes) catastrophic.

Another factor that exacerbates anxiety is that discrepancies between self-presentation performances and self-standards causes the individual's focus of attention to be turned on the self (Carver & Scheier, 1984). Indeed, all subordinates need to be particularly attentive to their outputs. High self-consciousness is a central characteristic of the socially anxious (Buss, 1986). Such self-focus is classically triggered by an audience, and it amounts to an awareness that the self is the object of evaluative scrutiny. Self-focus makes the individual aware of the discrepancy and leads him or her to believe the discrepancy is transparent to the audience (Trower & Kiely, 1983). Buss (1986) and others have pointed out that the socially anxious are in a chronic state of self-awareness—known as dispositional self-consciousness—leading to excessive self-monitoring and constant awareness of discrepancies between appearances and standard. The perceived discrepancy is characteristically large in the socially anxious, since standards tend to be perfectionistic or idealized, while perceived performance attainment is low (Trower & Turland, 1984). Another effect of this self-focus is the tendency to self-attribute more responsibility for failure than for success, which is a reversal of the normal self-serving attributional bias (Arkin, Appelman, & Burger, 1980).

The Coping System

We have argued that in a socially anxious state, a person's appraisal system is fine tuned to selectively perceive, monitor, and evaluate threats to self, while the coping system is set to generate responses designed to defend the self, and it is in this area that we would expect to find appeasement or submissive behavior and various adaptations of behavior which may serve the function of reverted escape. In this section we try to show theoretically how the anxious individuals come to select such defensive behaviors, and we review some of the forms that such defensive behavior may take.

Anxious individuals make a comparison between their actual and desired self-presentations—an appraisal—and, in the case of a discrepancy, either make a further attempt or disengage a coping response. We earlier suggested that the desired self-presentation for the evaluatively anxious is "perfectionistic" in that (1) they aspire to be dominant and high status (first-level goal) but believe this requires flawless performances to be successful in the fiercely competitive world they perceive. However, the evaluatively anxious have (2) low expectations of their own efficacy and believe their flawed performances will expose them to criticism, humiliation, and further, possibly catastrophic, loss of status. In other words, there is perceived to be a vast and unbridgeable gap between what Bandura (1977) terms outcome expectancies (what they think is required) and efficacy expectancies (what they think they are capable of), such that any status-enhancing behavior is far too risky, resulting in (3) disengagement from the matching-to-standard (in this case, first-level standard) process.

Translating point (3) into the terms of our psychobiological theory, we argued that disengagement from a first-level goal would probably lead to engagement of a second-level goal, which in the agonic mode would be some form of reverted escape. Reverted escape behavior provides a form of self-defense from threats from above in the hierarchy, without having to flee from or avoid dominant others—which in extreme cases can lead to complete isolation. It provides a defense from threats from above in that it reassures higher-status others that no threat to their status is intended. Here the emphasis will be strongly on submissive self-presentations. Reverted escape represents disengagement from a first-level (dominant) goal in that the individual is giving up his or her preferred, status-enhancing presentation for one that indicates an acceptance of a lower position in the hierarchy.

However, socially anxious people experience threat not only from dominant others but also from subordinates and peers, especially those that may be upwardly mobile and perceived as potential challengers for dominance and who have a high probability of success. Indeed, a highly anxious individual may catastrophize about descending to the lowest position in the hierarchy. The state of braced readiness in the agonic mode allows maximum defense against these threats, because it can be used to reduce to a minimum the danger of faulty self-presentations which leave the individual exposed to status challenges. Here we suggest the emphasis will be more on neutral self-presentations and "correct" and rule-conforming social behavior, camouflage or concealment of felt anxiety, or any other strategies that will prevent the exposure of weakness or vulnerability which will give a peer or subordinate the opportunity to make a successful challenge.

There is no direct evidence for our thesis that the evaluatively anxious behave in ways that exemplify the agonic mode in the way we are claiming, since no research has yet addressed the issue. However, there is considerable indirect evidence, including the following lines of enquiry.

Strategies of Defensive Coping

There is evidence from many studies that socially anxious people behave more submissively than other groups, even though they know how to be assertive (e.g., Alden & Cappe, 1981; Alden & Safran, 1978; Arkowitz, Lichtenstein, McGovern, & Hines, 1975; Glasgow & Arkowitz, 1975; Goldfried & Sobocinski, 1975; Schwartz & Gottman, 1976; Sutton-Simon & Goldfried, 1979). This suggests that submissive behavior is not the manifestation of a skills deficit but is an intentional (second-level) strategy which may exemplify the agonic mode. Indeed, we shall show later that submissive or appeasement behavior requires good social skills. The evaluatively anxious rather *choose* to behave submissively for fear of the negative consequences that they believe would follow from behaving assertively (Fiedler & Beach, 1978). For example, Schwartz and Gottman (1976) found that in less stressful conditions, "nonassertive" subjects were just as competent as assertive subjects in providing refusal responses, but in a stressful situation they provided significantly fewer such responses. More recently Vitkus and Horowitz (1987) showed that "lonely" people, who are shown to be generally characterized by passive social behavior, were just as able as "nonlonely" people to behave more dominantly when they were *assigned* such a role. Vitkus and Horowitz construe their results as showing that lonely people adopt a passive role (which leads to poor social performance) and do so because they have low self-esteem. In our terms, the passive role exemplifies the agonic mode.

A number of other authors have put forward theories with experimental evidence that we would construe exemplifies the agonic mode. Arkin (1981) coined the term *protective self-presentation* to describe a "safe" style where the individual is motivated to avoid social disapproval but remain engaged in (rather than avoid) social interaction, in contrast to *acquisitive self-presentation*, where the individual is motivated to achieve social approval (and, we would add, improved status). Schlenker and Leary (1985) reviewed a number of studies that showed the protective self-presentational style. In two cited studies, highly anxious subjects responded in ways that allowed them to remain engaged in the conversation while contributing as little substantive information as possible. For example, they asked more questions and used more listener responses than nonanxious subjects. In other studies anxious females smiled more in conversations with the opposite sex and during speeches. These sorts of interactions permit the anxious individual to interact in a "passive yet pleasant fashion" (Schlenker & Leary, 1985, p. 183). Schlenker and Leary also reported that subjects had behaved in a way designed not so much to create a good impression but rather prevent a bad one. They avoided discussions of factual topics, which might portray them as unknowledgeable or might start an argument, but agreed more with the other person, were more likely to give helpful and friendly advice, and used more "reflective" listener responses. These subjects also disclosed less information about themselves, especially of an intimate nature.

When expectations by others are high, the anxious individual will not necessarily be helped by a protective style, since such a modest presentation may in such circumstances be judged negatively. This may be because when others are in the hedonic mode they are looking for a more positive contribution. However, there is evidence that shy people may strategically *use* their shyness as a handicap in order to reduce people's expectations of them and provide an explanation for failure which will protect them from negative self-evaluation (Snyder & Smith, 1986). This idea, which originated with Adler some 70 years ago, was developed and demonstrated by Jones and Berglas (1978), who termed it *self-handicapping*, the handicap being a self-confessed weakness to which a person can attribute failure rather than attribute the weakness of his or her self. Support for this is shown in a number of recent studies. For example, Baumgardner and Brownlee (1987) showed that individuals who were doubtful about their ability to perform well were inclined to fail strategically at the outset of social interaction as a means to create lower and safer standards. Strategies of this kind are interesting in that they appear to achieve the function of agonic behavior in signalling no threat, but at the same time limit the loss of status that such behavior entails. They also protect the individual from status attacks, or limit such attacks.

Another area for potential research is for a new look at the specific behavior elements in socially anxious self-presentations. Edelmann (1987) reports grinning and smiling was one of the most common reported reactions to embarrassing events, and he gives a useful discussion of the distinction between embarrassed and nonembarrassed smiles. For example, he cites a 1985 study by Asendorpf in which 85% of embarrassed smiles were accompanied by gaze avoidance. This seems to be the reason why embarrassed smiles carry a flavor of ambivalence: approach (smiling) and avoidance (gaze aversion) at the same time. Our theory would account for this behavior as a manifestation of appeasement and, more specifically, of reverted escape, where gaze aversion marks the impulse to escape (and serves to cut the threat stimulus), and smiling serves to appease the dominant other. Ethologists make a distinction between the smile and the appeasement grin or fear face with mouth corners pulled back, though this kind of distinction is not made in the above research.

Despite the cautiousness with which evaluatively anxious people may present themselves to minimize negative evaluation, they nonetheless anticipate, and in some ways bring about, faulty performances—social transgressions, faux pas, or accidents. Such events may be caused, as we have seen, by the physiological, behavioral, and cognitive states of readiness with which a person is biologically prepared to "cope" with a perceived danger, particularly those which come from the more primitive levels of the defense system. Stammering, freezing, and other manifestations of Level-3 responses are precisely what the anxious individual is endeavoring to conceal but is unable to control. When the faux pas has occurred, anticipatory anxiety gives way to shame and embarrassment, with their own give-away signals of blushing, gaze avoidance, and embarrassed smiling and laughing (Edelmann, 1987). We have already seen how the fear of (observable) fear may constitute a vicious cycle, in which rising anxiety about faulty performances triggers primitive escape routines, which give rise to yet further anxiety, and so on. We might speculate that the more intense the anxiety, the more likely it is that phylogenetically earlier response systems will be triggered (Bailey, 1987).

Evaluatively anxious people vary in their social skills, and because of this, they vary with regard to the point at which they become unable to sustain their place in the group by means of forms of reverted escape. Skilled individuals have further resources to tap, even when status-lowering overt social failure has been recognized and made cruelly visible by blushing and allied embarrassment behavior. These further skills involve face-saving explanations for conduct, described and researched by a number of authors, including various types of justifications to "reframe" spoilt identities, such as accounts, apologies, and excuses (Edelmann, 1987; Harré, 1979; Schlenker, 1987; Snyder, 1985; Snyder, Higgins, & Stucky, 1983; Tedeschi & Norman, 1985).

EVALUATION AND APPLICATION

In this chapter we have described and developed two theories of human social functioning which we have attempted to combine and integrate in an overall psychobiological account as applied to social anxiety. In this last section we briefly outline the work that has been and needs to be done to (1) evaluate the theoretical integration and (2) explore its clinical applications.

Evaluation of the Theories

Any theory requires two forms of evaluation: first, at the level of conceptual analysis, and second, at the level of empirical testing. With regard to the second of these, there is little in the way of research that has looked at the theories as an integrated system—hardly surprising, given their newness. Certainly there is much research on components and variables within the overall theories, and some of this research had been cited. We report below some preliminary results from two studies from our own research, which has at this stage tried to look in a broad and exploratory way at the interrelationship and interaction of the variables we have been discussing.

Survey of Standards and Styles

A survey study (Trower, in preparation) was undertaken with the first-year intake of psychology undergraduates at the Department of Psychology, Leicester University, who participated in order to obtain credits toward course work. The 115 participants (out of a total intake of 125) filled in a number of questionnaires and scales selected or tailor-made to measure the main variables we have discussed. We report a few of the findings relevant to the present discussion.

The most popular standards for desired self-presentations for the group as a whole were to be likeable, happy, interesting, humorous, confident, and attractive. Significantly more people put likeable or happy as their first choice. The bottom standards were being assertive and being the leader. In other words, the students universally strongly preferred hedonic over agonic goals, whether they were socially anxious or not. This may represent a universal ideal, or it may represent an ideal for this particular sociocultural group.

It also emerged that the students on the whole were fairly relaxed about achieving their standards, were not perfectionistic, did not make unreasonable demands on reaching them or catastrophize over failing to reach them.

The students who had the largest discrepancies between their minimum acceptable levels of performance on desired standards and the actual performance achieved tended also to be shy and socially anxious, supporting the theoretical link between such discrepancies and social anxiety. We also found that highly anxious groups scored high on Concern for Appropriateness Scale (Lennox & Wolfe, 1984; Wolfe, Lennox, & Cutler, 1986), described by the authors as a measure of the protective self-presentation style. This is an indirect indication that the socially anxious adopt the role of the agonic subordinate in social interaction (i.e., submission or appeasement, conformity, etc).

A Conversation Test

It was felt that we needed a more direct approach, based upon face-to-face interaction, in order to investigate the way socially anxious versus nonanxious people related interpersonally. The following study was designed for this purpose (Sherling, Trower, & Beech, in preparation).

Two groups of 12 first-year undergraduate students were selected on the basis of their scores on the Fear of Negative Evaluation (FNE) Scale (Watson & Friend, 1969). (These subjects were from another intake year and quite different from those in the survey just reported). The high-FNE group had scores similar to subjects in other studies who were clinically socially anxious. All subjects had a 3-minute videotaped conversation with a male member of the academic staff— an authority figure—who broke conversation rules in a systematic way. A variety of pre- and postconversation measures were taken. Immediately after the conversation, the subjects were shown the video and asked to stop it at points where they had felt discomfort, to report the associated emotion, the conversation rules being followed or broken, the strategy for coping, and to evaluate the success of the strategy and the emotion consequent to that. Independent judges also made ratings of the tapes. Results of interest to our present discussion include the following:

All subjects reported points of discomfort. The most common emotions reported during these points were embarrassment, nervousness, discomfort, and uneasiness. These are comparatively mild reactions which allow the individual to stay in the situation, rather than panic, which might cause a person to flee the situation. This might support our theory that reverted escape behavior is operating as the mechanism to enable people to stay together.

The most common emotion reported by the anxious group was embarrassment, whereas the nonanxious group reported discomfort. Most situations leading to reports of embarrassment involved negative self-evaluations, whereas most situations leading to reports of discomfort were to do with concern about the inequality of the interaction. Nearly all low-anxious subjects said they believed the conversation should be reciprocal, whereas only a minority of high-anxious subjects thought this. This can be construed as showing that high-anxious subjects were more accepting of a subordinate position.

Most high-anxious subjects thought the stooge (the staff member) should start the conversation—a subordinate's rule—whereas most low-anxious subjects did not. High-anxious subjects were also more inclined than low-anxious subjects to use submissive strategies for coping (such as admitting they felt nervous) and less inclined to use dominant ones (such as asking questions).

The most popular desired standards for self-presentation style were very similar to the hedonic standards for the survey sample described above. The only difference between the groups was a greater tendency for the low-anxious group to choose "be equal" as an important standard.

As might be expected, high-anxious subjects reported more discomfort at difficult points in the interaction than did low-anxious subjects. They also rated themselves as more submissive, and the stooge as more dominant, whereas the low-anxious subjects showed the *reverse* evaluations.

The high-anxious subjects had greater discrepancies than the low-anxious subjects between their minimum acceptable standards and those standards actually achieved—a result similar to that found in the survey.

Finally, a factor analysis was carried out to look for commonalities among the variables. We will report just the first factor here. This accounted for 32% of the variance, and the highest loading was self-rated discomfort at points when the tape was stopped. Discomfort was positively related to high scores on the FNE, high-discrepancy scores between desired and actual achievement of standards, number of anxiety symptoms reported during the interaction and independent ratings of anxiety, and it was negatively related to perceived level of attainment of standards and self-rated dominance and social skill in the interaction. Thus the discomfort factor seems to be a combination of high FNE, judging oneself to be submissive, and unfavorable self-assessment of performance both prior to and during the interaction. This therefore seems to reflect the combined psychobiological and self-presentation theories of social anxiety.

These are pilot studies and the results need to be treated with caution. Nonetheless, they support the integrated theories at a general level and give a lead as to where and in what way more research might be specifically directed.

Application of the Theories

The main argument in our theoretical integration is that socially anxious people are locked into an "agonic mentality" which precludes them from processing information or recruiting response repertoires in any other than a defensive way. This leads them to perceive themselves as subordinates in hostile hierarchies and to utilize submissiveness and other "reverted escape" behaviors to minimize loss of status and rejection. This has one particular clear implication for therapy, namely, that where possible (and it may not always be possible) the client's goal in therapy will be to learn to recruit his or her "hedonic mentality" and thus release a different set of appraisal and coping strategies, in which the client sees him- or herself in a situation of safety as one of a number of cooperating equals.

Setting aside the important question of assessment (important because some clients may be too harmed by early environmental learning to be able to recruit their hedonic mentalities), what directions might we pursue in terms of treatment?

One obvious area of development is in cognitive psychotherapy. We would certainly argue that the philosophy of rational-emotive therapy, for example, is consistent with (though by no means identical with) the hedonic mentality. Irrational beliefs, like "I must succeed to be worthy," are truly agonic, while the notion of self-acceptance and intrinsic worth which Ellis (1962) consistently emphasizes is a component of the hedonic mentality. Recent, well-controlled outcome studies support the view that cognitive restructuring along these lines is the treatment of choice. Mattick and Peters (1988) showed that a combined treatment including rational restructuring was significantly more effective than guided exposure alone on the principal outcome variables for socially phobic subjects. Similarly, Heimberg, Dodge, and Hope (1988) found that 75% of socially phobic patients were clinically improved at the conclusion of a cognitive-behavioral program, compared to 45% of patients who had been through an equally "credible" program based on education and group support. This outcome was maintained at 6-month follow-up.

Another area of development is in social skills training. Our theoretical integration suggests that the apparently "obvious" goal of giving socially anxious clients assertion training is an agonic goal, where the perhaps unstated aim is to help the client become dominant rather than submissive. Our approach suggests on the contrary that the obvious goal is to help the client perform more "hedonically." Training in friendship skills—conspicuously underdeveloped compared with assertion training—is clearly indicated. Ideas in this direction have been offered (Argyle, 1987; Argyle & Henderson, 1984; Trower, Bryant, &

Argyle, 1978) but need development. One area where they have been developed is in heterosocial skills training. For example, Muehlenhard and her colleagues (Muehlenhard, Koralewski, Andrews, & Burdick, 1986) have identified no less than 36 verbal and nonverbal behaviors which women can use to convey their interest in dating a man. Interestingly, the function of some of these cues was to reduce a man's possible fear of rejection. This is an important use of a hedonic strategy designed to turn off an agonic (anxious-submissive) response. The work of Muehlenhard and her colleagues has an obvious extension to friendship initiation in general—for signalling to another that one is initiating a cooperative rather than a competitive encounter and, therefore, for making the other feel safe rather than threatened.

Clearly, however, a cognitive therapy and social skills training approach need to be combined. The client has to function cognitively (and emotionally) *and* behaviorally in the hedonic mode. A client who still thinks in terms of dominance hierarchies will continue to misinterpret the other's cooperative intentions as challenges and would perceive his own "friendly" behavior as a challenge to the other and liable to a further put-down. These treatment suggestions and complications can best be illustrated with a case example.

Alf

"I feel completely inferior to everyone else. Whenever I am in the company of others, I feel their critical gaze, their derision and scorn, and my humiliation and shame at almost every move I make. The most ordinary daily activities are like torture, whether it be eating, talking, playing a game of snooker. I am trying all the time to behave in a way that I think other people would approve of, but I become so tense that I do the very things I try so hard to avoid—shaking, blushing, perspiring, drying up in conversation, not being able to swallow my food, not even being able to urinate in public lavatories. I am terrified of becoming a figure of ridicule, of contempt. I so want to be able to assert myself and be able to hold my head up, but I dare not, for fear of losing what little sense of self-esteem I still have. It sounds crazy, but I fear that my very survival is at risk."

This is a written account of distressing experiences by a client, Alf, a 27-year-old single man who has suffered from severe social anxiety since the age of 11. Despite his anxiety, he is by no means a social recluse, and he prefers to struggle with the torment of anxiety in the company of others rather than the depression of loneliness. No matter what he is doing—eating, playing snooker, or just standing—he feels people are strongly disapproving of him—his gestures, his speech, his appearance. He is in a constant state of high arousal and muscular tension, ready to change his behavior in a second. His main strategy for coping is to studiously do whatever he believes the other person wants him to do—to comply. This, of course, is rather difficult, since he rarely knows what people want him to do. Alf always has an overpowering sense of inferiority—or more accurately perhaps, a sense of the other's superiority. He hates feeling inferior and would dearly like to be the dominant one. One thing is clear: Alf has no sense of there realistically being any other kind of relationship with another person other than one up or one down. And yet paradoxically, what he most yearns for in life is to love and to be loved.

There are major childhood experiences which explain much of Alf's problem but which we shall not describe here. Instead we will describe a therapeutic approach which was based on the notion of Alf learning to send and receive cooperative interactions with others, rather than competitive ones, and the problems this created.

One week Alf had to apply the cooperative skill rule of reciprocation—if he is asked a personal question, answer it and ask a personal question back. Alf was unable to do this. The block was fundamental. After some discussion, the following emerged: To be actively friendly and reciprocal, you have to assume equality ("we're of equal value"). But if you don't think you're equal, then it won't seem right to treat the other that way (e.g., ask a question back). It would seem presumptuous, arrogant even. And if *they* don't think you're equal, they won't see you as sending out friendship signals, but rather, dominance signals. You're challenging their status!

This shows how Alf is locked into the agonic mentality. And whilst in that mode, he cannot see that friendly behavior will pull friendly behavior, but only that arrogant behavior will pull hostile dominance. So he inevitably returns to his defensive strategy of appeasing conformity, because that will be perceived as no threat, and maybe the other will *then* come to like him. But this hope is never fulfilled, because friendship is based upon reciprocation between equals.

It is only when Alf can *conceive* of a cooperative interaction that he can begin to utilize a social skills training approach, and this is what the next stage of therapy entails—to help him develop this conception, to get him in touch with his hedonic mentality. This can probably be best achieved in Alf's case through rational-emotive therapy and personal-construct therapy, but in other cases through other approaches, depending upon which approach may gain best access to the particular client (Dryden, 1984).

Concluding Summary

In this chapter we have argued that social anxiety in humans has an ancient ancestry, in that it developed as a vital part of a mechanism that enabled the evolution of group (social) living and that it allowed individuals to stay together rather than disperse under threat. An understanding of the nature of this innate potentiality must, we suggested, provide the framework for understanding the psychology of social anxiety. First, we outlined a psychobiological theory that attempted to explain the systems within which social anxiety developed and operated. Second, we developed a psychological information processing model to show how these innate potentialities, when triggered, influence appraisal and responding at the individual level. Third, we reported some evaluative research that gives tentative support for our theories (and referred to a variety of research papers that we interpreted as giving support), and finally, we developed some clinical implications of the theories, illustrated by an actual case study.

REFERENCES

Alden, L., & Cappe, R. (1981). Nonassertiveness: Skill deficit or selective self-evaluation? *Behavior Therapy, 12*, 107–114.

Alden, L., & Safran, J. (1978). Irrational beliefs and nonassertive behavior. *Cognitive Therapy and Research, 2*, 357–364.

American Psychiatric Association. (1980). *Diagnostic and statistical manual of mental disorders* (3rd ed.). Washington, DC: Author.

American Psychiatric Association. (1987). *Diagnostic and statistical manual of mental disorders* (3rd ed., rev.). Washington, DC: Author.

Amies, P. L., Gelder, M. G., & Shaw, P. M. (1983). Social phobia: A comparative clinical study. *British Journal of Psychiatry, 142*, 174–179.

Argyle, M. (1987). *The psychology of happiness*. London: Methuen.

Argyle, M., & Henderson, M. (1984). The rules of friendship. *Journal of Social and Personal Relationships, 1*, 211–37.

Arkin, R. M. (1981). Self-presentation styles. In J. T. Tedeschi (Ed.), *Impression management theory and social psychological* (pp. 311–333). New York: Academic Press.

Arkin, R. M., Appelman, A. J., & Burger, J. M. (1980). Social anxiety, self-presentation, and the self-serving bias in causal attribution. *Journal of Personality and Social Psychology, 38*, 23–25.

Arkowitz, H., Lichtenstein, E., McGovern, K., & Hines, P. (1975). The behavioral assessment of social competence in males. *Behavioral Therapy, 6*, 3–13.

Asendorpf, J. (in press). The nonverbal expression of shyness and embarrassment. In R. Crozier (Ed.), *Shyness and embarrassment*. Cambridge: Cambridge University Press.

Bailey, K. (1987). *Human paleopsychology: Applications to aggression and pathological processes*. Hillsdale, NJ: Lawrence Erlbaum.

Bandura, A. (1977). *Social learning theory*. Englewood Cliffs, NJ: Prentice-Hall.

Baumeister, R. F. (1982). A self-presentational view of social phenomena. *Psychological Bulletin, 91*, 3–26.

Baumgardner, A. H., & Brownlee, E. A. (1987). Strategic failure in social interaction: Evidence for expectancy and disconfirmation processes. *Journal of Personality and Social Psychology, 52*, 525–535.

Beck, A. T., Emery, G., & Greenberg, R. (1985). *Anxiety disorders and phobias: A cognitive perspective*. New York: Basic Books.

Bee, H. (1985). *The developing child* (4th ed.). New York: Harper & Row.

Berger, P. L., & Luckmann, T. (1966). *The social construction of reality: A treatise in the sociology of knowledge*. Garden City, NY: Doubleday.

Bowlby, J. (1969). *Attachment and loss: Vol. 1. Attachment*. London: Hogarth Press.

Bowlby, J. (1973). *Attachment and loss: Vol. 2. Separation, anxiety and anger*. London: Hogarth Press.

Bowlby, J. (1980). *Attachment and loss: Vol. 3. Loss: Sadness and depression*. London: Hogarth Press.

Brown, P., & Levinson, S. C. (1978). Universals in language use: Politeness phenomena. In E. Goody (Ed.), *Questions and politeness* (pp. 132–184). Cambridge: Cambridge University Press.

Buss, A. (1986). *Social behavior and personality*. Hillsdale, NJ: Lawrence Erlbaum.

Carver, C. S. (1979). A cybernetic model of self-attention processes. *Journal of Personality and Social Psychology, 37*, 1251–1281.

Carver, C. S., & Scheier, M. F. (1981). Self-consciousness and reactance. *Journal of Research in Personality, 15*, 16–29.

Carver, C. S., & Scheier, M. F. (1984). A control theory approach to behavior and some implications for social skills training. In P. Trower (Ed.), *Radical approaches to social skills training* (pp. 144–179). London: Croom Helm.

Chance, M. R. A. (1980). An ethological assessment of emotion. In R. Plutchik & H. Kellerman (Eds.), *Emotion: Theory, research and experience* (Vol. 1, pp. 81–111). New York: Academic Press.

Chance, M. R. A. (1984). Biological systems synthesis of mentality and the nature of the two modes of mental operation: Hedonic and agonic. *Man–Environment Systems, 14*, 143–157.

Chance, M. R. A. (1986). The social formation of personality systems: The two mental modes and the identity of recursive mental processes. *American Journal of Social Psychiatry, 6*, 199–203.

Chance, M. R. A. (Ed.). (1988). *Social fabrics of the mind.* Hove and New York: Lawrence Erlbaum.
Crozier, R. (in press). *Shyness and embarrassment.* Cambridge: Cambridge University Press.
Dryden, W. (1984). *Individual therapy in Britain.* London: Harper & Row.
Edelmann, R. J. (1987). *The psychology of embarrassment.* Chichester: Wiley.
Ellis, A. (1962). *Reason and emotion in psychotherapy.* New York: Lyle Stuart.
Fenigstein, A. (1979). Self consciousness, self-attention, and social interaction. *Journal of Personality and Social Psychology, 37,* 75–86.
Fiedler, E., & Beach, L. R. (1978). On the decision to be assertive. *Journal of Consulting and Clinical Psychology, 46,* 537–546.
Gardner, R. (1988). Psychiatric syndromes as infrastructure for intraspecific communication. In M. R. A. Chance (Ed.), *Social fabrics of the mind* (pp. 197–209). Brighton: Lawrence Erlbaum.
Gergen, K. J. (1984). Theory of the self: Impasse and evolution. In L. Berkowitz (Ed.), *Advances in experimental social psychology* (pp. 49–117). Orlando: Academic Press.
Gilbert, P. (1984). *Depression: From psychology to brain state.* London: Lawrence Erlbaum.
Gilbert, P. (1989). *Human nature and suffering.* Brighton: Lawrence Erlbaum.
Glasgow, R., & Arkowitz, H. (1975). The behavioral assessment of male and female social competence in dyadic heterosexual interactions. *Behavior Therapy, 6,* 488–498.
Goffman, E. (1959). *The presentation of self in everyday life.* Garden City, NY: Doubleday.
Goffman, E. (1972). *Relations in public: Micro-studies of the public order.* Harmondsworth, Middlesex: Penguin.
Goldfried, M. R., & Sobocinski, D. (1975). Effect of irrational beliefs on emotional arousal. *Journal of Consulting and Clinical Psychology, 43,* 504–510.
Gray, J. A. (1971). *The psychology of fear and stress.* London: Weidenfeld & Nicolson.
Gray, J. A. (1985). Issues in the neuropsychology of anxiety. In A. H. Tuma & J. D. Maser (Eds.), *Anxiety and the anxiety disorders* (pp. 5–26). Hillsdale, NJ: Lawrence Erlbaum.
Halford, K., & Foddy, M. (1982). Cognitive and social skills correlates of social anxiety. *British Journal of Clinical Psychology, 21,* 17–28.
Harré, R. (1979). *Social being: A theory for social psychology.* Oxford: Blackwell.
Heard, D. H., & Lake, B. (1986). The attachment dynamic in adult life. *British Journal of Psychiatry, 149,* 430–438.
Heimberg, R. G. (1989). Social phobia: No longer neglected. *Clinical Psychology Review, 9,* 1–2.
Heimberg, R. G., Dodge, C. S., & Becker, R. E. (1987). Social phobia. In L. Michelson & M. Ascher (Eds.), *Anxiety and stress disorders: Cognitive-behavioral assessment and treatment* (pp. 280–309). New York: Guilford Press.
Heimberg, R. G., Dodge, C. S., Hope, D. A., Kennedy, C. R., Zollo, L., & Becker, R. E. (1988). *Cognitive-behavioral treatment of social phobia in a group setting: Comparison to a credible placebo control.* Manuscript submitted for publication.
Heimberg, R. G., Hope, D. A., Dodge, C. S., & Becker, R. E. (1988). *DSM-III-R subtypes of social phobia: Comparison of generalized social phobics and public speaking phobics.* Unpublished report, Center for Stress and Anxiety Disorders, University at Albany, State University of New York.
Hollow, H. F., & Mears, C. (1979). *The human model: Primate perspectives.* New York: Winston & Sons.
Howells, K. (1986). Social skills training and criminal and antisocial behaviour in adults. In C. R. Hollin & P. Trower (Eds.), *Handbook of social skills training* (Vol. 1). Oxford: Pergamon Press.
Jones, E. E., & Berglas, S. (1978). Control of attributions about the self through self-handicapping strategies: The appeal of alcohol and the role of underachievement. *Personality and Social Psychology Bulletin, 4,* 200–206.
Jones, W. H., Cheek, J. M., & Briggs, S. R. (1986). *Shyness: Perspectives on research and treatment.* New York: Plenum.
Kihlstrom, J. F., & Nasby, W. (1981). Cognitive tasks in clinical assessment: An exercise in applied psychology. In P. C. Kendall & S. D. Hollon (Eds.), *Assessment strategies for cognitive-behavioral interventions* (pp. 287–318). New York: Academic Press.
Leary, T. (1957). *Interpersonal diagnosis of personality.* New York: Ronald.
Lennox, R. D., & Wolfe, R. N. (1984). Revision of the self-monitoring scale. *Journal of Personality and Social Psychology, 46,* 1349–1364.

Liebowitz, M. R., Gorman, J. M., Fyer, A. J., & Klein, D. F. (1985). Social phobia: Review of a neglected anxiety disorder. *Archives of General Psychiatry, 42*, 729–736.

Lucock, M. P., & Salkovskis, P. M. (in press). Cognitive factors in social anxiety and its treatment. *Behaviour Research and Therapy.*

Mathews, A., & MacLeod, C. (1987). An information-processing approach to anxiety. *Journal of Cognitive Psychotherapy, 1,* 105–115.

Mattick, R. P., & Peters, L. (1988). Treatment of severe social phobia: Effects of guided exposure with and without cognitive restructuring. *Journal of Consulting and Clinical Psychology, 56,* 251–260.

MacLean, P. D. (1985). Brain evolution relating to family, play and the separation call. *Archives of General Psychiatry, 42,* 405–417.

McNally, R. J. (1987). Preparedness and phobias: A review. *Psychological Bulletin, 101,* 283–303.

Milgram, S. (1965). Some conditions of obedience and disobedience to authority. *Human Relations,* 57–76.

Miller, G. A., Galanter, E., & Pribram, K. (1960). *Plans and the structure of behavior.* New York: Holt.

Mischel, W. (1973). Toward a cognitive social learning reconceptualization of personality. *Psychological Review, 80,* 252–283.

Mollon, P. (1984). Shame in relation to narcissistic disturbance. *British Journal of Medical Psychology, 57,* 207–214.

Muehlenhard, C. L., Koralewski, M. A., Andrews, S. L., & Burdick, C. A. (1986). Verbal and nonverbal cues that convey interest in dating: Two studies. *Behavior Therapy, 17,* 404–419.

Nasby, W., & Kihlstrom, J. F. (1986). Cognitive assessment of personality and psychopathology. In R. E. Ingram (Ed.), *Information processing approaches to clinical psychology* (pp. 217–239). Orlando: Academic Press.

Ohman, A. (1986). Face the beast and fear the face: Animal and social fears as prototypes for evolutionary analyses of emotion. *Psychophysiology, 23,* 123–145.

Ohman, A., & Dimberg, U. (1984). An evolutionary perspective on human social behavior. In W. M. Waid (Ed.), *Sociophysiology* (pp. 47–86). New York: Springer-Verlag.

Ohman, A., Dimberg, U., & Ost, L.-G. (1985). Animal and social phobias: Biological constraints on learned fear responses. In S. Reiss & R. R. Boutzin (Eds.), *Theoretical issues in behavior therapy* (pp. 123–175). Orlando: Academic Press.

Pilkonis, P. A. (1984). Avoidant and schizoid personality disorders. In H. E. Adams & P. B. Sutker (Eds.), *Comprehensive handbook of psychopathology* (pp. 479–494). New York: Plenum.

Price, J. (1988). Alternative channels for negotiating assymetry in social relationships. In M. R. A. Chance (Ed.), *Social fabrics of the mind* (pp. 157–196). Hove and New York: Lawrence Erlbaum.

Price, J., & Sloman, L. (1987). Depression as yielding behaviour: An animal model based on Schjelderup-Ebbe's pecking order. *Ethology and Sociobiology, 8,* 85–98.

Rachman, S. (1984). A reassessment of the "primary of affect." *Cognitive Therapy and Research, 8,* 579–584.

Rachman, S., & Hodgson, R. (1974). 1. Synchrony and desynchrony in fear and avoidance. *Behaviour Research and Therapy, 12,* 311–318.

Reite, M., & Field, T. (Eds.) (1985). *The psychology of attachment and separation.* New York: Academic Press.

Sartre, J.-P. (1957). *Being and nothingness.* London: Methuen. (First published by Gallimard, 1943.)

Schlenker, B. R. (1986). Self-identification: Toward an integration of the private and public self. In R. Baumeister (Ed.), *Public self and private self* (pp. 21–61). New York: Springer-Verlag.

Schlenker, B. R. (1987). Threats to identity: Self-identification and social stress. In C. R. Snyder & C. Ford (Eds.), *Coping with negative life events: Clinical and social psychology perspectives* (pp. 273–321). New York: Plenum Press.

Schlenker, B. R., & Leary, M. R. (1982). Social anxiety and self-presentation: A conceptualization and model. *Psychological Bulletin, 92,* 641–669.

Schlenker, B. R., & Leary, M. R. (1985). Social anxiety and communication about the self. *Journal of Language and Social Psychology, 4,* 171–192.

Schwartz, R. M., & Gottman, J. M. (1976). Toward a task analysis of assertive behavior. *Journal of Consulting and Clinical Psychology, 44,* 1276–1283.

Seligman, M. E. P. (1971). Phobias and preparedness. *Behavior Therapy, 2,* 307–320.

Singer, B. A., & Luborsky, L. (1977). Countertransference: The status of clinical versus quantitative research. In A. S. Gurman & A. M. Razin (Eds.), *Effective psychotherapy: A handbook of research.* Oxford: Pergamon.

Sherling, G., Trower, P., & Beech, J. (in preparation). Standards styles and rules of self-presentation: A comparison of socially anxious and non-anxious students. Department of psychology, Leicester University.

Smith, T. W., Ingram, R. E., & Brehm, S. S. (1983). Social anxiety, anxious preoccupation and recall of self relevant information. *Journal of Personality and Social Psychology, 44,* 1276–1283.

Snyder, C. R. (1985). The excuse: An amazing grace. In B. R. Schlenker (Ed.), *Self and identity: Presentations of self in social life* (pp. 235–260). New York: McGraw-Hill.

Snyder, C. R., Higgins, R. L., & Stucky, R. J. (1983). *Excuses: Masquerades in search of grace.* New York: Wiley.

Snyder, C. R., & Smith, T. W. (1986). On being "shy like a fox." In W. H. Jones, J. M. Cheek, & S. R. Briggs (Eds.), *Shyness: Perspectives on research and treatment* (pp. 161–172). New York: Plenum.

Spielberger, C. (1979). *Understanding stress and anxiety.* London: Harper & Row.

Sutton-Simon, K., & Goldfried, M. R. (1979). Faulty thinking patterns in two types of anxiety. *Cognitive Therapy and Research, 3,* 193–203.

Tedeschi, J. T., & Norman, N. (1985). Social power, self-presentation, and the self. In B. R. Schlenker (Ed.), *The self and social life* (pp. 293–322). New York: McGraw Hill.

Tomkins, S. S. (1981). The quest for primary motives: Biography and autobiography. *Journal of Personality and Social Psychology, 41,* 306–329.

Trower, P. (1984). A radical critique and reformulation: From organism to agent. In P. Trower (Ed.), *Radical approaches to social skills training* (pp. 48–88). London: Croom Helm.

Trower, P. (1987). On the ethical basis of "scientific" behaviour therapy. In S. Fairbairn & G. Fairbairn (Eds.), *Psychology, ethics and change* (pp. 74–90). London: Routledge & Kegan Paul.

Trower, P. (in preparation). A survey of standards and styles in self-presentation. Department of Psychology, Solihull Health Authority.

Trower, P., Bryant, B. M., & Argyle, M. (1978). *Social skills and mental health.* London: Methuen.

Trower, P., & Kiely, B. (1983). Video feedback: Help or hindrance? A review and analysis. In P. W. Dowrick & S. J. Biggs (Eds.), *Using video: Psychological and social applications* (pp. 181–197). Chichester: Wiley.

Trower, P., & Turland, D. (1984). Social phobia. In S. M. Turner (Ed.), *Behavioral theories and treatment of anxiety* (pp. 321–365). New York: Plenum.

Tuma, A. H., & Maser, J. D. (1985). Anxiety and the anxiety disorders. Hillsdale, NJ: Lawrence Erlbaum.

Turner, S. M., Beidel, D. C., Dancu, C. V., & Keys, D. J. (1986). Psychopathology of social phobia and comparison to avoidant personality disorder. *Journal of Abnormal Psychology, 95,* 389–394.

Tyrer, P. (1986). The classification of anxiety disorder: A critique of DSMIII. *Journal of Affective Disorders, 11,* 99–104.

Vitkus, J., & Horowitz, L. M. (1987). Poor social performance of lonely people: Lacking a skill or adopting a role? *Journal of Personality and Social Psychology, 52,* 1266–1273.

Watson, D., & Friend, R. (1969). Measurement of social-evaluative anxiety. *Journal of Consulting and Clinical Psychology, 33,* 448–457.

Weiner, H. (1985). The psychology and pathophysiology of anxiety and fear. In H. A. Tuma & J. D. Maser (Eds.), *Anxiety and anxiety disorders* (pp. 333–354). Hillsdale, NJ: Lawrence Erlbaum.

Wolfe, R. N., Lennox, R. D., & Cutler, B. L. (1986). Getting along and getting ahead: Empirical support for a theory of protective and acquisitive self-presentation. *Journal of Personality and Social Psychology, 50,* 356–361.

Zajonc, R. B. (1980). Feeling and thinking: Preferences need no inferences. *American Psychologist, 35,* 151–175.

Zajonc, R. B. (1984). On the primacy of affect. *American Psychologist, 39,* 117–123.

Zimbardo, P. G. (1977). *Shyness: What it is and what to do about it.* New York: Addison-Wesley.

2

Shyness, Self-Esteem, and Self-Consciousness

Jonathan M. Cheek and Lisa A. Melchior

Shyness is the ordinary language term most often used to label feelings of anxiety and inhibition in social situations. It is a remarkably common experience. Less than 10% of respondents to a cross-cultural survey reported that they had never felt shy (Zimbardo, 1977). Ratings of shyness-eliciting events reveal that interactions with strangers, especially those of the opposite sex or in positions of authority, situations requiring assertive behavior, and explicitly evaluative settings such as job interviews, provoke the strongest feelings of social anxiety (Russell, Cutrona, & Jones, 1986; Watson & Cheek, 1986).

From an evolutionary perspective on emotional development, a moderate amount of wariness regarding strangers and unfamiliar or unpredictable situations has considerable adaptive value (Izard & Hyson, 1986). Social anxiety is functional when it motivates preparation and rehearsal for important interpersonal events, such as planning ahead for the first day of teaching at a new school (Thyer, 1987). As a social emotion, shyness also helps to facilitate cooperative group living by inhibiting individual behavior that is socially unacceptable (Ford, 1987). The complete absence of susceptibility to feeling shy has been recognized as an antisocial characteristic since at least the time of the ancient Greeks (Plutarch, 1906). Situational shyness as a transitory emotional state thus appears to be a normal aspect of human development and everyday adult life.

For some people, however, shyness is more than a temporary situational response. About 30 to 40% of Americans label themselves as dispositionally shy persons (Gough & Heilbrun, 1983; Lazarus, 1982a; Pilkonis, Heape, & Klein, 1980; Zimbardo, Pilkonis, & Norwood, 1975). Three-quarters of the shy respondents said that they did not like being so shy, and two-thirds of them considered their shyness to be a personal problem. Although some psychologists have argued that the positive connotations of shyness, such as modesty or gen-

Jonathan M. Cheek • Department of Psychology, Wellesley College, Wellesley, Massachusetts 02181. Lisa A. Melchior • The Measurement Group, 6245 Bristol Parkway, Suite 242, Culver City, California 90230.

tleness, should not be neglected (Gough & Thorne, 1986; Keen, 1978), it is generally viewed as an undesirable personality trait, especially for men (Bem, 1981; Hampson, Goldberg, & John, 1987). Shy adolescents regard their shyness as an unacceptable and even shameful characteristic, and shy adults complain that their problem is not taken seriously enough by other people (Harris, 1984a; Ishiyama, 1984).

A growing body of contemporary research supports this negative image of shyness as a personality trait. Rather than simply promoting cooperative social life, an enduring tendency to experience shyness frequently, intensely, and in a wide range of situations creates self-defeating behavior patterns (Cheek, Melchior, & Carpentieri, 1986). As a result, dispositional shyness becomes a barrier to personal well-being, social adjustment, and occupational fulfillment (Jones, Cheek, & Briggs, 1986).

In this chapter we review research on shyness within a framework that is organized in terms of the shy person's self-concept. We begin by considering a three-component definition of shyness and the role of dysfunctional metacognition as the unifying theme in the experiences of shy people. Next, we examine the place of shyness in a multidimensional model of the structure, dynamics, and development of self-esteem. Then we discuss the private experience of shyness as revealed in self-concept processes such as expectancies, attributions, memories, self-consciousness, and self-presentational strategies. Finally, we conclude with the implications of our review for future directions in theory, research, and treatment.

DEFINING SHYNESS AS A THREE-COMPONENT SYNDROME

The word *shyness*, like other trait names, is a socially devised symbol for describing and explaining a salient aspect of human experience (Briggs, 1985). Its origin in ordinary language has, however, created a debate about the precise definition of shyness as a psychological construct (Cheek & Watson, 1989; Harris, 1984b; Leary, 1986). Nevertheless, there is considerable agreement among clinical, psychometric, experimental, and observational studies concerning the typical reactions of shy people during social interactions: global feelings of tension, specific physiological symptoms, painful self-consciousness, worry about being evaluated negatively by others, awkwardness, inhibition, and reticence (Briggs, Cheek, & Jones, 1986).

We believe that the best way to organize this list of typical shyness symptoms is to employ the standard tripartite division of experience into the three components of affect, cognition, and observable behavior. This trichotomy of feeling, thinking, and acting has a long history in psychology (Breckler, 1984). Recently, Buss (1984) has advocated the formal elaboration of a three-component model of shyness. Jones, Briggs, and Smith (1986), however, conducted a factor analysis of 88 shyness items from five personality scales and concluded that "there are persuasive reasons to suspect that a single dimension underlies the construct of shyness" (p. 638). We do not question their factor analysis; it is quite consistent with our own factor analytic work indicating only one major factor in shyness items (Cheek & Buss, 1981, p. 332; Cheek & Melchior, 1985). Rather, it is the research described below, employing a variety of methods other than factor analysis, that has persuaded us to continue to hold our previously stated preference for the three-component, rather than the unidimensional, conceptualization of shyness (Cheek, Carpentieri, Smith, Rierdan, & Koff, 1986; Cheek, Melchior, & Carpentieri, 1986).

The first category of shyness symptoms includes global feelings of emotional arousal and specific physiological complaints, such as upset stomach, pounding heart, sweating, or blushing. These reactions define the somatic anxiety component of shyness. Several surveys of high school and college students indicate that from 40 to 60% of shy students experience difficulties with multiple symptoms in this category (Cheek & Melchior, 1985; Fatis, 1983; Ishiyama, 1984). In a study that employed content codings of free descriptions by shy women, 38% of them volunteered at least one somatic anxiety symptom when describing why they consider themselves shy (Cheek & Watson, 1989). The somatic component is clearly an important aspect of shyness, but these results also help to clarify why it has been relatively easy for researchers to identify a subtype of socially anxious individuals who are not troubled by somatic arousal symptoms (e.g., McEwan & Devins, 1983; Turner & Beidel, 1985).

Acute public self-consciousness, self-deprecating thoughts, and worries about being evaluated negatively by others constitute the second, cognitive component of shyness. The argument for distinguishing the somatic and cognitive components of shyness is based on the general distinction between somatic anxiety and psychic anxiety (Buss, 1962; Schalling, 1975), which recently has received additional empirical support (Deffenbacher & Hazaleus, 1985; Fox & Houston, 1983). Between 60 and 90% of shy students identified various cognitive symptoms as part of their shyness (Cheek & Melchior, 1985; Fatis, 1983; Ishiyama, 1984). However, only 44% of the shy adults in the Cheek and Watson (1989) study described specific cognitive symptoms. Although this figure is unusually low (cf. Turner & Beidel, 1985), even among men and women clinically diagnosed as socially phobic, there is a meaningful amount of variability in public self-consciousness and other cognitive symptoms of anxiety (Hope & Heimberg, 1988).

The third component concerns the social competence of shy people. The relative absence of normally expected social responsiveness defines the quietness and withdrawal typical of shy people (Buss, 1984). Nonverbal aspects of the behavioral component of shyness include awkward body language and gaze aversion. About two-thirds of the shy respondents in the studies described above reported behavioral symptoms of shyness. Similarly, the results of several laboratory experiments indicate that most, but not all, shy people show observable deficits in social skills (e.g., Cheek & Buss, 1981; Curran, Wallander, & Fischetti, 1980; Halford & Foddy, 1982).

All three components of shyness are important, but none of them is a universal aspect of the experience of shy people. In order to investigate the degree of relationship among the three components, we wrote a short paragraph describing each component and asked two groups of college students to rate on a 5-point scale how frequently they experienced each aspect of shyness (Cheek & Melchior, 1985; Melchior & Cheek, 1987). The intercorrelations among the somatic, cognitive, and behavioral components ranged from .23 to .48, with an average of .30 for men ($n = 266$) and .39 for women ($n = 313$). The results from this rating method suggest more meaningful discrimination among the components of shyness than do the factor analyses of inventory items described earlier (e.g., Jones, Briggs, & Smith, 1986; see also Leary, Atherton, Hill, & Hur, 1986). Moreover, in the codings of self-descriptions by shy women, 43% gave responses from only one shyness component category, 37% reported symptoms from two categories, and only 12% mentioned symptoms of all three components; the remaining 8% defined their shyness exclusively in terms of its consequences (e.g., being alone, not getting a job, etc.; Cheek & Watson, 1989).

Evidence supporting the three-component model suggests that shyness as a global or nomothetic trait should be conceptualized as a personality syndrome that involves varying degrees of these three types of reactions (Cheek, Melchior, & Carpentieri, 1986). But do the three components converge toward defining such a global psychological construct? To find out, we correlated the self-ratings on each component with scores on a recently revised and expanded version of the Cheek and Buss (1981) scale for assessing global shyness. This 20-item scale has an alpha coefficient of .91, a 45-day test–retest reliability of .91, a .69 correlation with aggregated ratings of shyness made by family members and close friends, and a correlation of .96 with the original scale (Cheek & Melchior, 1985). The self-ratings of the somatic, cognitive, and behavioral components all correlated between .40 and .68 with the global shyness scale for each gender in both of our samples (average $r = .50$, $N = 579$; Melchior & Cheek, 1987).

The research reviewed in this section validates Buss's (1984) theoretical argument that it is reasonable to infer shyness when symptoms of at least one of the three components are experienced as a problem in a social context, as well as his contention that "it makes little sense to suggest that any one of the components represents shyness to the exclusion of the other two" (p. 40). From the perspective of the three-component syndrome model, dispositional shyness is defined as the tendency to feel tense, worried, or awkward during social interactions, especially with unfamiliar people (Cheek, Melchior, & Carpentieri, 1986; Cheek & Watson, 1989). Although the focus of this definition is on reactions that occur during face-to-face encounters, it should be noted that feelings of shyness often are experienced when anticipating or imagining social interactions (Buss, 1980; Leary, 1986). It also should be clear that discomfort or inhibition of social behavior due to fatigue, illness, moodiness, or unusual circumstances, such as the threat of physical harm, are excluded from the definition of shyness (Buss, 1980; Jones, Briggs, & Smith, 1986).

Metacognition as the Unifying Theme in Shyness

Regardless of their relative positions in experiencing the somatic, cognitive, and behavioral components of shyness, shy people have one obvious thing in common: they think of themselves as being shy. Rather than being a trivial observations, this may be a crucial insight for understanding the psychology of shyness. Hartman (1983, 1986) has argued that we need to move beyond the tripartite division of symptoms into three components to a higher level of abstraction for conceptualizing shyness. The unifying theme here is his suggestion that all shy people are alike at the metacognitive level of psychological functioning.

Metacognition is defined as a person's awareness, knowledge, and active monitoring of her or his cognitive processes and strategies. Metacognitive phenomena include "any conscious cognitive or affective experiences that accompany and pertain to any intellectual enterprise" (Flavell, 1979, p. 906). In the psychology of shyness, we are interested in metacognitive processes pertaining to social cognition and the self-concept. Flavell has pointed out that metacognition is especially likely to occur in novel roles and unfamiliar situations, but also that affective arousal interferes with its effectiveness. For the shy person, this means that anticipating or entering a shyness-eliciting situation will activate metacognitive processing, yet, at the same time, the shyness symptoms of tension and worry will impair the effectiveness of such processing.

Control processes involve the executive functions of directing and regulating one's social performance (Ford, 1987). Impairment of metacognitive functioning leads to disorganization of the control processes for perception, cognition, and motor performance. As Hartman (1986) put it, shy people become "preoccupied with metacognition: thoughts about their physiological arousal, ongoing performance, and other's perceptions of them as socially incompetent, inappropriately nervous, or psychologically inadequate" (p. 269). Such excessive self-focused metacognition not only disrupts smooth social discourse, but it also contributes to shy people's overestimation of the visibility of their somatic arousal to others, underestimation of their level of social skills, and inability to judge accurately how others evaluate them (Jones & Briggs, 1984; McEwan & Devins, 1983; Melchior & Cheek, in press).

Viewed at this higher level of metacognitive functioning, shyness may be conceptualized as the tendency to become anxiously self-preoccupied about social interactions (Crozier, 1979, 1982). Because this tendency represents only one specific aspect of metacognition, we will refer to the shy person's metacognitive processing of self-relevant social cognitions as *meta-self-consciousness* (cf. Dissanayake, 1988). As may be seen in Figure 1, this model allows us both to consider shyness as a global psychological construct and, at the same time, to acknowledge the empirically demonstrated variability among shy people in their experience of the three components of shyness symptoms.

Although the model of shyness as meta-self-consciousness provides a heuristic organization for reviewing the available research, we should mention that psychologists disagree about the details of precisely how and when metacognitive control processes become maladaptive for shy people during social interactions (Arkin, Lake, & Baumgardner, 1986; Carver & Scheier, 1986; Schlenker & Leary, 1982, 1985). It also should be clear that this model applies to *adult* humans, and not to shyness in children or other animals, with the possible

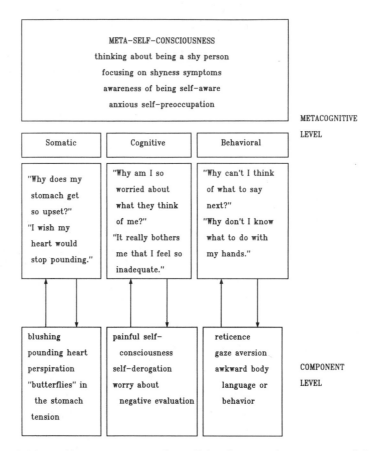

FIGURE 1. Meta-self-consciousness as the unifying theme in the experience of shyness.

exception of chimpanzees. The cognitive component of shyness first appears in human development around age 5 or 6, and the transition from social cognitions involving comparisons with others to metacognitions about oneself occurs in late adolescence (Buss, 1980; Damon & Hart, 1982; Guidano, 1986).

Moreover, we believe that the meta-self-consciousness of shy people should be viewed as unusual; it is experienced mainly when they are engaged in shyness-eliciting interactions. For those who are not shy, social behavior tends to be guided by strategies that are predominantly habitual and not subject to continuous conscious monitoring, except when they are involved in a dramatic social encounter such as a job interview, a first date, or a social psychology experiment (Berger, 1980; Cheek & Hogan, 1983; Cheek, Melchior, & Carpentieri, 1986; Langer, 1978). Even the behavioral inhibition of a very shy person often may be a habitual social strategy, with meta-self-consciousness only becoming salient when problematic interpersonal communication is unavoidable or strongly desired. Shy people also may vary in the extent of their maladaptive metacognitive functioning depending on the centrality of the imago "I am a shy person" in the structure of their identity (Cheek, 1989a; McAdams, 1985; Wurf & Markus, 1983).

In spite of these limitations, the metacognitive model of shyness may help to illuminate the decisive differences between dispositionally shy and not shy people. As Crozier (1982) has pointed out, a successful explanation of dispositional shyness must account for the findings that shy and not-shy people agree on the rank ordering of shyness-eliciting situations, and that almost all people who do not consider themselves shy still do report experiencing some shyness symptoms in those situations. Ishiyama (1984) suggested a distinction between two phases in the experience of shyness: the primary phase is the normal social anxiety experienced by most people in difficult interpersonal encounters; the secondary phase involves dysfunctional cognitive processing that occurs only in shy people, which is similar to what we are calling meta-self-consciousness. The differences between shy and not-shy people are not only quantitative, in terms of the frequency and intensity of shyness symptoms, but also qualitative, in terms of how those symptoms are interpreted metacognitively. The details of these differences in self-concept processes will become clear in the final section of this chapter as we review research on self-perceptions, expectancies, attributions, memories, goals, and strategies.

Conflict Models of Shyness

As we have seen in the preceding sections, the shy are far from indifferent to other people. Therefore, it is important to distinguish shyness from introversion–extraversion and the personality dimension variously labeled gregariousness, need for affiliation, or sociability. Unfortunately, these constructs frequently are confounded in both everyday discourse and the psychological literature (cf. Crozier, 1986; Semin, Rosch, & Chassein, 1981). For example, the Social Introversion Scale of the MMPI correlates .74 with a shyness scale (Wink & Cheek, 1989). Conceptually, however, it is both possible and desirable to define introversion independently of shyness:

> The typical introvert does not value social participation very much but he can engage in social activity perfectly adequately and without any anxiety or fear. Neurotic social shyness, however, is quite different; here we have a tendency to wish to indulge in social activity but an active fear which prevents the person from doing so in case he might be snubbed, hurt, offended, etc. (Eysenck & Eysenck, 1969, p. 27)

As Lewinsky (1941) observed concerning the shy person's approach–avoidance conflict in social situations, "this ambivalent attitude seems of great importance in the understanding of shyness" (p. 106; see also, Campbell, 1896, and Hampton, 1927). We agree with Lewinsky that shy people experience their own social inhibition not as a voluntary choice but as a barrier that prevents them from participating in social life when they want or need to (Cheek, 1987; Murphy, 1947, p. 606).

In spite of their advocacy of the conceptual distinction between shyness and introversion, the Eysencks did not include a separate shyness scale in their personality measurement model. Shyness scales tend to correlate around −.40

with their extraversion dimension and +.40 with their neuroticism dimension (Jones, Briggs, & Smith, 1986; for an item analysis, see Briggs, 1988). Other research indicates that the average correlation between shyness and various measures of sociability and affiliation motivation is about −.30 (Cheek & Zonderman, 1983; Cutler & Cheek, 1986; Hill, 1987). Whereas shyness tends to correlate around .50 with measures of psychological insecurity, such as fearfulness and low self-esteem, sociability is usually uncorrelated with such measures (Cheek, 1982; Cheek & Buss, 1981). Moreover, shyness is only weakly related to private self-consciousness, which is a measure of thinking introversion rather than social introversion (e.g., $r = .10$ in Cheek & Buss, 1981). Most importantly for a conflict model, people high in *both* shyness and sociability sometimes experience the greatest difficulties during social interactions and report the most severe adjustment problems (Briggs, 1988; Cheek & Buss, 1981; Cutler & Cheek, 1986).

The ambivalence of shy people can be conceptualized as a conflict experienced at the metacognitive level of processing self-relevant social cognitions. Such conflicts have been characterized from a wide variety of theoretical perspectives on shyness and closely related constructs: oscillation between interest and fear as social emotions (Izard & Hyson, 1986); tension between the social motives of seeking approval and avoiding disapproval (Arkin *et al.*, 1986); wanting to make a good impression but doubting one's ability to do so (Schlenker & Leary, 1982, 1985); perceiving that what one can gain through social participation may be outweighed by one's projected losses (Phillips & Metzger, 1973); having both positive and negative expectations for social reinforcement (Mehrabian, 1976); contradictory impulses of curiosity and timidity (James, 1890); a self-conscious struggle between the instincts of self-display and self-abasement (McDougall, 1963); and conflict between the social goals of getting along and getting ahead (Hogan, Jones, & Cheek, 1985; Wolfe, Lennox, & Cutler, 1986).

Our focus here is on the metacognitive conflicts experienced by shy adults, but similar tensions can be traced back to the earliest stages of cognitive and emotional development. Four relevant examples are: anxious attachment patterns (Bowlby, 1988; Pilkonis *et al.*, 1980); the mixture of wary and sociable behaviors displayed by most infants and preschool children when meeting a friendly stranger (Greenberg & Marvin, 1982); the combination of high levels of two temperaments, emotionality and sociability (Buss & Plomin, 1975); and an approach–avoidance conflict among elementary school children who scored high on measures of both exhibitionism and self-consciousness (Levin, Baldwin, Gallwey, & Paivio, 1960). At any level of analysis, it is clear that shyness involves a fundamental ambivalence toward social interactions. It simply cannot be equated with introversion or low sociability. The opposite of shyness is social self-confidence, not extraversion.

Shyness and Related Constructs

Shyness is related to a number of variables that together form a higher-order construct of adjustment which Maslow (1942) called "psychological insecurity" (cf. Watson & Clark, 1984). Conceptually, shyness is most closely related to three other varieties of social anxiety: embarrassment, shame, and audience anxiety (Buss, 1980). All four involve discomfort in the presence of other people. Embarrassment and shame are viewed as transitory affective reactions to specific social situations; audience anxiety and shyness, on the other hand, are considered to be personality traits as well as states. Embarrassment involves acute awareness of oneself as a social object and a brief parasympathetic response (blushing) in response to a minor interpersonal blunder or the accidental violation of a social norm (Edelmann, 1985). Shame, though related to embarrassment, is a much more serious reaction because the ashamed person suffers a threat to his or her enduring social reputation and self-esteem (Buss, 1980; see also Mosher & White, 1981).

Audience anxiety refers to social anxiety that is experienced while speaking or performing in front of a passive group of spectators (Buss, 1980). Shyness pertains specifically to contingent social interactions in which the individual must continually monitor and respond to input and feedback from other people (Cheek & Buss, 1981; Leary, 1983). Although shyness and audience anxiety scales typically correlate about .45, Cheek, Tsang, & Yee (1984) found that audience anxiety scores significantly predicted performance on a public speaking task, whereas shyness scores did not. Thus the conceptual distinction between these two varieties of social anxiety has received some empirical support. Buss (1986) also suggested that test anxiety usually should be classified as a nonsocial evaluation anxiety; in a recent empirical study, Sarason's Reactions to Tests Scale correlated .25 with social anxiety (Flett, Blankstein, & Boase, 1987).

Fenigstein, Scheier, and Buss (1975) constructed a personality scale to assess global social anxiety. It contains six items: two for audience anxiety, two for shyness, one for embarrassability, and one for general social anxiety. The shyness items were used in the development of the original nine-item version of the Cheek and Buss (1981) Shyness Scale, which correlates .75 with the partially overlapping Social Anxiety Scale (Cheek, 1982). Although the three-component model of shyness had not yet been developed, the initial set of items contained at least one for each of the somatic anxiety, cognitive, and behavioral categories of shyness symptoms. Subsequent work on scale development to improve reliability, content validity, and item wording resulted in 11-item and 13-item versions of the Cheek and Buss Shyness Scale (Cheek, 1982, 1983). All 14 items employed in the development and revision of the Shyness Scale are presented in Table 1.

Inspection of the questionnaire items in Table 1 will enable the reader to understand the type of operational definition used to identify participants as being "shy" or "socially anxious" in the research we are reviewing in this chapter. The Shyness Scale correlates between .75 and .87 with all of the other major scales commonly employed in this domain of research: Social Avoidance and Distress (Watson & Friend, 1969); Social Reticence (Jones & Briggs, 1986); Interaction Anxiousness (Leary, 1983); and the Fenigstein et al. (1975) Social Anxiety Scale described above (Jones, Briggs, & Smith, 1986). Labeling oneself as a shy person in response to a single question or Zimbardo's (1977) Stanford Shyness Survey correlates between .66 and .81 with the Shyness Scale (Cheek & Buss,

TABLE 1. Items from the Revised Cheek and Buss Shyness Scale

---

1. I feel tense when I'm with people I don't know well.
2. I am socially somewhat awkward.
3. I do *not* find it difficult to ask other people for information.
4. I am often uncomfortable at parties and other social functions.
5. When in a group of people, I have trouble thinking of the right things to talk about.
6. It does *not* take me long to overcome my shyness in new situations.
7. It is hard for me to act natural when I am meeting new people.
8. I feel nervous when speaking to someone in authority.
9. I have *no* doubts about my social competence.
10. I have trouble looking someone right in the eye.
11. I feel inhibited in social situations.
12. I do *not* find it hard to talk to strangers.
13. I am more shy with members of the opposite sex.
14. During conversations with new acquaintances I worry about saying something dumb.

Note. The response format ranges from 1 = very uncharacteristic or untrue to 5 = very characteristic or true. Items 3, 6, 9, and 12 are reverse scored. Item 14 is a revised wording of one of the original 9 items that was not included in the 13-item version. The average item mean is 2.55.

1981), and in the .60 to .69 range with popular measures in the closely related area of communication apprehension research (Daly & McCroskey, 1984; Kelly, Phillips, & McKinney, 1982; McCroskey & Beatty, 1986). The crucial point here is that, in spite of continuing debates among the test constructors about potentially important conceptual distinctions, these measures generally intercorrelate to an extent which permits us to consider them in our literature review as alternative operational definitions of the same global psychological construct (Nunnally, 1978).

We do distinguish the normal range of individual differences in shyness from the clinical extreme of phobic social avoidance. Harris (1984b) criticized Pilkonis and Zimbardo (1979) for continuing to include social avoidance in their definition of shyness even though research by Pilkonis (1977a) had found that shy students rated avoidance of social situations as by far the least important of five aspects of their experience of shyness. In the coding study of adult women's descriptions of their shyness that we discussed earlier (Cheek & Watson, 1989), only 6% of the respondents mentioned avoiding interactions, whereas about 66% listed other behavioral symptoms of shyness such as quietness and awkward nonverbal behavior. Moreover, shyness questionnaire items show at least a moderate degree of distinction from social avoidance items in psychometric analyses (Leary *et al.*, 1986; Patterson & Strauss, 1972).

Shyness and the clinical anxiety disorders differ substantially in their prevalence. Viewed as an adjustment problem in the psychopathology of everyday life, distressing shyness affects 25 to 33% of Americans, but the prevalence of meeting clinical diagnostic criteria for anxiety is probably around 8% (Pilkonis *et al.*, 1980; Thyer, 1987). Therefore, we believe that active efforts to avoid social contacts should not be included in the definition of shyness but should be reserved as a criterion for the clinical diagnosis of social phobia or the avoidant personality disorder (Meyer, 1983). Deciding whether or not shyness and social phobia belong on a single psychological continuum, with the extremely shy classified as "borderline" social phobics, appears to require further research, especially on possible similarities in etiology, biological mediators (e.g., phenelzine), and cognitive symptoms of social phobia and shyness (Bruch, 1989; Hugdahl & Ost, 1985; Liebowitz, Gorman, Fyer, & Klein, 1985; Liebowitz *et al.*, 1988). It is also worth noting that the presence of an approach–avoidance conflict toward social contacts appears to be a useful criterion for distinguishing social phobia from schizoid or avoidant personality disorders (Bruch, 1989; Liebowitz *et al.*, 1985). We share with R. G. Heimberg (personal communication, February 13, 1989) the hope that the revisions currently being developed for DSM-IV will clarify the relationships among shyness and the relevant clinical diagnostic categories.

Significant symptoms of clinical depression are quite common among social phobics (Liebowitz *et al.*, 1985). The relationship between shyness and depression seems to be weaker; measures of shyness and social anxiety usually correlate only in the .15 to .30 range with the Beck Depression Inventory (Anderson & Arnoult, 1985a; Cheek, Carpentieri *et al.*, 1986; Flett *et al.*, 1987; Traub, 1983). There are both similarities and differences in the cognitive symptoms of shyness and depression (Anderson & Arnoult, 1985b; Beck & Clark, 1988). Depression and the cognitive component of shyness symptoms may share a common pathway of genetic influence on psychological vulnerability, but they differentiate into distinct symptom clusters as a result of environmental factors (Kendler, Heath, Martin, & Eaves, 1987). The extension of recent developmental research (e.g., Blumberg & Izard, 1986) into longitudinal studies is needed to clarify the relationship between shyness and depression.

Both shyness and depression correlate around .40 with self-reports of loneliness (Anderson & Arnoult, 1985a). Short-term longitudinal research indicates that shyness is a significant characterological cause of loneliness, although situational factors are also important (Cheek & Busch, 1981). Concerning another aspect of psychological insecurity, the Shyness Scale correlates .50 with Buss and Plomin's (1975) global measure of temperamental fearfulness (Cheek & Buss, 1981). Jones, Briggs, and Smith (1986) replicated this finding, but they also included two subscales composed of items from the Fear Survey Schedule that distinguish social fears (e.g., meeting someone in authority and blind dates) and nonsocial fears (e.g., high places, sharp objects, and germs). They reported an important discriminant validity finding: the Shyness Scale correlated .50 with social fears but only .12 with nonsocial fears (see also Crozier, 1981; Efran & Korn, 1969; Foley, Heath, & Chabot, 1986).

Overall, the research reviewed thus far has provided strong support for three conclusions suggested by Cheek and Buss (1981): (1) shyness is a distinctive and important psychological construct in the normal range of individual differences in personality and social behavior; (2) shyness is not simply low sociability or lack of affiliation motivation; and (3) shyness is related to, but not identical with, other dimensions such as low self-esteem, audience anxiety, depression, fearfulness, and loneliness that together form Maslow's (1942) higher-order construct psychological insecurity. Cheek and Buss made only passing reference, however, to the important implications of the cognitive component of shyness, which became a major focus of attention in the 1980s as researchers explored the structure and dynamics of self-concept processes among shy people. We review this research in the remaining sections of the chapter.

Shyness as a Dimension of Self-Esteem

Personality may be regarded as an open, interacting system of feelings, thoughts, and behaviors that is involved, both developmentally and concurrently, in complex transactions with the individual's physical and social environment (e.g., Murphy, 1947). The crucial question raised by such an approach is, as Allport (1960) aptly put it, "what makes the system cohere in any one person?" (p. 308). McDougall (1963) grounded his theory of personality on the argument that unity is maintained by purposive, goal-seeking activity. He explained individual differences in the organization and regulation of volitional conduct as a consequence of the strength of the self-regarding sentiment, "the system of emotional and conative [i.e., striving] dispositions that is organized about the idea of the self and is always brought into play to some extent when the idea of the self rises to the focus of consciousness" (McDougall, 1963, p. 213).

From this perspective, the self-concept is not just our subjective picture of who we are; it is also a dynamic motivational system that influences the organization and direction of behavior. McDougall's personality theory has been neglected unreasonably for several decades (Hogan, 1976), but the cognitive and conative parts of it appear to be enjoying a recent revival (e.g., Pervin, 1989). We hope that renewed attention to the evolutionary, developmental, and affective aspects of McDougall's theory will not be far behind (Cheek, 1985). In any case, we accept his position that understanding any character trait such as shyness requires consideration of its function in the structure and dynamics of the self-concept.

The most consistent finding from research on the self-concepts of shy people is the inverse relationship between measures of shyness and global self-esteem. The typical correlation hovers around the $-.50$ level (Cheek & Buss, 1981; Fehr & Stamps, 1979; Jones, Briggs, & Smith, 1986), although some results closer to the $-.30$ level also have been reported (Cheek, 1982; Crozier, 1981). Items on global self-esteem scales, such as "I have a low opinion of myself" (reverse scored) and "I feel that I have a number of good qualities" (e.g., Rosenberg, 1979), do not refer specifically to shyness, so the correlation is not an artifact of overlapping item content (compare to Table 1). Rather, shyness versus social self-confidence is one of several self-relevant dimensions about which one has an opinion, a particular quality that one may feel good, bad, or indifferent about (Fleming & Courtney, 1984; Mamrus, O'Connor, & Cheek, 1983). Global self-esteem is a complex higher-order construct, and recent research indicates that self-esteem should be conceptualized and assessed by employing a multidimensional model (for a review, see Briggs & Cheek, 1986).

Shyness and Self-Regard

Shyness and personal self-esteem or self-regard have been conceptualized as two related dimensions of self-evaluation: at the metacognitive level, shyness pertains to evaluation of one's social competence and interpersonal value, whereas self-regard involves evaluation of one's private feelings about being a worthwhile individual (e.g., "I am basically worthwhile"; Cheek, 1982). Other major dimensions of self-evaluation include self-confidence about one's academic ability, physical appearance, physical ability, and vocational certainty (Fleming & Courtney, 1984; Mamrus et al., 1983). In this multidimensional model, total or general self-esteem refers to the sum of these six dimensions (after reverse scoring shyness as social self-confidence), preferably with the importance of each facet weighted to reflect its centrality in the organization of each individual's self-concept system (Cheek, 1989a; Harter, 1986; James, 1890; Rosenberg, 1979).

In order to examine the relationships among these dimensions of self-evaluation, we administered the Shyness Scale and the self-esteem measures used by Mamrus et al. (1983) to a sample of 106 college students (Cheek, Melchior, & Carpentieri, 1986). As may be seen in Table 2, shyness correlated negatively with all five of the other dimensions of self-esteem (average $r = -.40$). These correlations are not high enough, however, to demonstrate that shyness is identical to any of the other dimensions of self-evaluation; for this to be true, the scales would have to intercorrelate within the .70 to .90 range of their reliability coefficients (Nunnally, 1978). Yet it is also clear that shy people tend to have fairly extensive problems with low self-esteem.

The distinction between personal self-regard and shyness, defined as low social self-confidence, appears to be one of many examples of a pervasive differ-

TABLE 2. Correlations among Dimensions of Self-Esteem

	Shyness	Self-regard	Academic ability	Physical appearance	Physical ability	Vocational certainty
Shyness		-.57***	-.39**	-.55***	-.30*	-.40**
Self-regard	-.49**		.53***	.56***	.19	.52***
Academic ability	-.16	.50***		.44**	.14	.37**
Physical appearance	-.44**	.55***	.19		.27*	.43**
Physical ability	-.27	.23	.17	.33*		.19
Vocational certainty	-.43**	.51***	.37*	.35*	.02	

Note. The correlations for 59 women are presented above the diagonal, and those for 47 men appear below the diagonal.
* $p < .05$. ** $p < .01$. *** $p < .001$.

entiation between private and public aspects of the self (Hogan & Cheek, 1983). To investigate the impact of the centrality of shyness in one's self-concept, Cheek (1982) divided high scorers on the Shyness Scale into upper and lower thirds on their responses to the question, "How important to your own self-concept is the characteristic shyness?" (on a 1 to 5 scale). The shy people who rated shyness as important scored significantly higher on a scale assessing the value placed on social aspects of identity, but they were not different on a scale assessing the value placed on personal aspects of identity. Thus it appears that the self-evaluation measured by the Shyness Scale is most relevant to the domain of the social self, even though, not surprisingly in an inherently social species, it also relates to the more personal realm of self-regard. The differentiation of private and public aspects of the self is a developmental outcome, not an innate category (Buss, 1980; McDougall, 1963); we should also note that contemporary American culture appears to represent an extreme of comparative preoccupation with private aspects of the self (Cheek, 1989a).

Gender Differences

The pattern of correlations between shyness and the other dimensions of self-evaluation reported in Table 2 is slightly stronger for women (average $r = -.44$) than for men ($r = -.36$). In a much larger sample of college students ($n = 912$), Cheek (1979) obtained correlations between shyness and self-regard of $-.55$ for women and $-.43$ for men. Viewed in conjunction with research on adolescent shyness (Cheek, Carpentieri et al., 1986), these findings suggest the interpretation that the burden of shyness as a problem of self-concept disturbance may be greater for females in our culture, whereas behavioral problems related to taking the initiative in social encounters may be more salient for shy males (see also, Bruch, Giordano, & Pearl, 1986).

In the United States, the prevalence of labeling oneself as a shy person is higher for females than males in age groups that do show gender differences: 49% of girls versus 26% of boys in the 5th grade (Lazarus, 1982a; but Zimbardo [1977, p. 15] reported 42% for both boys and girls in a combined sample of 4th–6th graders); 60% of girls versus 48% of boys in the 7th and 8th grades (Zimbardo, 1977; consistent with other research on early adolescence reviewed by Cheek, Carpentieri et al., 1986); and 37% of women versus 28% of men in a normative sample of 10,000 adults (Gough & Heilbrun, 1983). College men, however, tend to score slightly, but not significantly, *higher* than women on the Shyness Scale (Cheek & Buss, 1981; Cheek & Melchior, 1985); college women score slightly yet significantly higher on sociability and meaningfully higher on global fearfulness (Cheek, 1979). In a clinic sample of phobic adults, women reported more simple phobias, but there were no gender differences for social phobia (Thyer, 1987).

College men rate shyness as being a more undesirable personality characteristic than do women (Gough & Heilbrun, 1983), and both genders agree that shyness is less socially desirable for a man than for a woman (Bem, 1981). Indeed, raters of both actual and hypothetical individuals regard a shy male as less likeable than a shy female (Gough & Thorne, 1986; Sigelman, Carr, & Begley, 1986). Although such sex–role-related effects for shyness are undoubtedly real and important, Gilmartin (1987) has exaggerated their consequences rather dramatically (Cheek, 1989b).

Gilmartin's fundamental assumption that "shyness does not force women to remain against their wills in the 'single, never married' category, as it often does with men" (1987, p. 5) is flatly contradicted by the data in Wilson's (1958) summary of the records of 500 women who sought counseling because they wanted to marry but were still single. Part of the problem in Gilmartin's orientation stems from his reliance on two studies by Pilkonis (1977a, 1977b) which indicated that shyness is much less of a personal and social adjustment problem for women than men; however, Pilkonis himself speculated that his sample of women might be unrepresentative (1977a, p. 589), and his speculation was confirmed in subsequent research (Cheek, 1979; Cheek & Buss, 1981; Cheek, Carpentieri *et al.*, 1986). Because shyness researchers often have either studied only one gender at a time or have not analyzed their data separately by gender, more systematic work on gender differences in shyness and their connection to cultural roles needs to be done (e.g., DePaulo, Dull, Greenberg, & Swaim, 1989; Snell, 1989).

The Developmental Relationship between Shyness and Self-Regard

Cross-sectional survey research reveals that the significant negative correlation between the trait shyness and dispositional measures of self-regard or global self-esteem (e.g., Rosenberg's [1979] scale) obtains across a wide age span: elementary school (Lazarus, 1982b), junior high school (Cheek, Carpentieri *et al.*, 1986), high school and college (Cheek & Buss, 1981; Jones, Briggs, & Smith, 1986), and among older adults and the elderly (Hansson, 1986). This consistent negative correlation does not, however, make it clear whether shyness is a cause or a consequence of low self-regard. Perhaps they are simply two concurrent feelings of self-evaluation within the structure and interacting dynamics of a person's self-concept, which may viewed as "a conceptual trait system" (Murphy, 1947, p. 506). Therefore, we need to ask a question about personality development: which comes first, shyness or low self-esteem?

The answer to this question may depend on the type of shyness that characterizes a particular individual. Baldwin (1894) described a developmental distinction between "primary" or "organic" bashfulness—the shyness seen in infants, young children, and animals—and "true" bashfulness, the kind of shyness seen in humans only after age 3, "which shows reflection in its simpler form, upon self and the actions of self [and] represents the child's direct application of what he knows of persons to his own inner life" (p. 439). McDougall (1963) extended Baldwin's analysis to explain the development of individual differences in the trait shyness, and he suggested a third stage of development in which the intensification of self-consciousness at the onset of puberty interacts with the development of the self-regarding sentiment to shape shyness and modesty as qualities of adult character and conduct. McDougall's third stage corresponds to what we are calling meta-self-consciousness, which is not fully developed until late adolescence (Damon & Hart, 1982).

More recently, Buss (1980, 1986) has proposed a distinction between early-developing, fearful shyness and later-developing, self-conscious shyness that is framed in the language of contemporary research on temperament and personality development. The fearful type of shyness typically emerges during the first year of life and is influenced by temperamental qualities of wariness and emotionality that include a substantial genetic component (Kagan & Reznick, 1986; Plomin & Rowe, 1979). Because the effects of these temperamental factors precede the development of a cognitive self-concept, Buss specifically excluded low self-esteem as a potential cause of early-developing shyness. In light of attachment theory (Bowlby, 1988), however, it might be better to conceptualize a concurrent transactional development of temperament and the "working model" of emotional self-esteem during early childhood, even though such a theoretical integration is controversial (e.g., Sroufe, 1985; cf. Lamb, 1982). Further prospective longitudinal research is needed to adequately test the interactionist model of temperament; it will be important to distinguish shyness from need for affiliation or social responsiveness to familiar people in such research (Goldsmith & Gottesman, 1981).

Buss's self-conscious type of shyness first appears around age 4 or 5, when the cognitive self has already begun to develop, and peaks between 14 and 17 as adolescents cope with cognitive egocentrism (the "imaginary audience" phenomenon) and identity issues (Adams, Abraham, & Markstrom, 1987; Cheek, Carpentieri et al., 1986; Hauck, Martens, & Wetzel, 1986). In contrast to the fearfulness and somatic anxiety that characterizes early-developing shyness, later-developing shyness involves cognitive symptoms of psychic anxiety such as painful self-consciousness and self-preoccupation (i.e., the level of meta-self-consciousness depicted in Figure 1).

Surveys employing retrospective reports of college students reveal four findings relevant to Buss's conceptualization: (1) about 36% of currently shy respondents indicated that they had been shy since early childhood; (2) early-developing shyness is more enduring, with about 75% of those who said they were shy in early childhood reporting still being shy currently, but only about 50% of those who were first shy during late childhood or early adolescence saying that they are currently shy; (3) the early-developing shy respondents also had developed cognitive symptoms of shyness upon entering adolescence, so that they differed from those with later-developing shyness by having more somatic anxiety symptoms but did not have fewer cognitive symptoms; and (4) early-developing shyness appears to be more of an adjustment problem, with males in that group reporting the most behavioral symptoms of shyness (Bruch et al., 1986; Cheek, Carpentieri et al., 1986; Shedlack, 1987).

From his perspective on development, Buss theorized that low self-esteem in middle childhood would be one factor causing susceptibility to self-conscious shyness in later childhood and adolescence. Three studies of adolescents, of which one was a short-term longitudinal design and the other two employed structural equation models, support Buss's conceptualization by showing that

low self-esteem predicts the presence of shyness and related interpersonal problems (Bohrnstedt & Felson, 1983; Elliott, 1984; Kahle, Kulka, & Klingel, 1980).
These preliminary findings suggest that longitudinal studies involving complete
assessment of multiple self-concept dimensions should prove worthwhile (e.g.,
Harter, 1986).

The ongoing longitudinal study of childhood "behavioral inhibition to the
unfamiliar" being conducted by Kagan and his colleagues is relevant to both
types of shyness described by Buss. Kagan's construct is essentially equivalent
to Buss's early-developing shyness (e.g., Kagan & Reznick, 1986), and the results
from 21 months to age 5 years support Buss's ideas about the physiological
correlates and enduring quality of early-developing shyness. The most recent
assessment occurred at age 7, which is after the time when later-developing
shyness theoretically begins to emerge. At this point, about three-quarters of the
children who were extremely shy when they were 21 months old were still shy,
and about three-quarters of those not shy previously continued to be uninhibited (Kagan, Reznick, Snidman, Gibbons, & Johnson, 1988). The first finding
suggests that beneficial socialization experiences can ameliorate the impact of a
problematic temperament, for as James (1890) argued, in humans an instinct is
only expressed in its pure form once and is thereafter subject to modification
through interaction with the environment (see also Buss & Plomin, 1975, 1984).

Although Kagan et al. (1988) do not invoke it, Buss's theory may also help to
explain the finding that one-quarter of the previously uninhibited children had
become shy. This outcome is, in fact, absolutely necessary if his construct of
later-developing shyness is valid! If no one becomes shy for the first time after
age 5, then Buss's theory of a distinct type of shyness that primarily involves
self-concept disturbances, rather than infant temperament, is superfluous. The
early–late distinction implies that the ordering consistency assessed by test–
retest stability should be high from infancy to age 5, more variable for assessments during middle childhood, depending on the exact age of each measurement, and then increasingly stable once again within adolescence and adulthood.

The results from Kagan's project so far and from several other longitudinal
studies generally support these expectations, although no one has yet analyzed
longitudinal data specifically to test Buss's theory (for reviews see Cheek, Carpentieri et al., 1986, and Moskowitz, Ledingham, & Schwartzman, 1985). Damon and
Hart's (1982) comments about qualitative changes in the trait self-esteem across
three stages of maturation also may apply to developmental discontinuities in
shyness, as we suggested earlier when we introduced the term meta-self-consciousness. Moreover, McDougall's (1963) theoretical position that cognitive-
affective sentiments will replace biological propensities as the prime organizers of
behavior during development may help to explain why Kagan et al. (1988) found
that physiological measures were less strongly related to shyness at age 7 than
they had been at age 5 (see also White, 1965; and see Murphy, 1947, on the
transition from "organic" to "symbolic" traits for a more fully explicated systems
theory of personality development).

Two prospective studies that traced the consequences of shyness from middle or late childhood into adulthood (average age about 35) found meaningful continuities in the trait and a coherent influence on the shy person's style of life but uncovered little psychopathology (Caspi, Elder, & Bem, 1988; Morris, Soroker, & Burruss, 1954). Gilmartin's (1987) retrospective study of extremely shy adult men, however, demonstrates that early-developing shyness sometimes can have devastating consequences. These maladjusted men reported that their childhood relationships with *both* their peers *and* their parents, especially their mothers, were simply terrible. In contrast, the typical pattern for shy children is poor relationships with peers but positive interactions at home, especially with their mothers (Stevenson-Hinde & Hinde, 1986).

Thus the home environment appears to be a decisive factor for developmental outcomes of shyness. This conclusion is supported by a growing body of literature demonstrating a relationship between increased shyness and measures of inhibition of emotional expressiveness in the family environment and a perceived lack of parental support, which has been found in studies from infancy through college age (Bell, Avery, Jenkins, Feld, & Schoenrock, 1985; Halberstadt, 1986; Ishiyama, 1985; Langston & Cantor, 1989; Plomin & Daniels, 1986; Riley, Adams, & Nielsen, 1984). Of course, positive experiences with peers at an early age help to develop social skills (Roopnarine, 1985), but such experiences are not easily available for the shy child (Richmond, Beatty, & Dyba, 1985). And elementary school teachers are not likely to help the shy child much because they tend to appreciate the passive compliance of such children, while their energy is focused on problem children who act out aggressively (Friedman, 1980). So the home environment appears to be the shy child's best hope, which is why we regard attachment, parental support, and sibling relationships as promising targets for future research on the development of shyness.

We also should point out that broader cultural values influence both the prevalence of shyness and the extent to which it is perceived as a problem (Klopf, 1984; Zimbardo, 1977; see Murphy, 1947, Chapter 40, for a theoretical discussion of the degree of fit between a culture and the biological individuality of its members). In particular, the cross-cultural findings that the Japanese tend to be substantially *more* shy than white Americans, whereas Filipinos, and perhaps also Koreans, tend to be significantly *less* shy than Americans, appear to undermine a recent claim of systematic between-group race differences for "Mongoloids" versus "Caucasoids" on the personality dimension of behavioral restraint (Rushton, 1988).

As Plomin and Daniels (1986) have pointed out, however, findings of family environmental influences on shyness do not necessarily undermine interpretations of the substantial genetic component found in early-developing shyness (within a studied population or group). In their study, the emotional expressiveness factor of the family environment measure had a much stronger negative correlation with infant shyness in nonadoptive families (i.e., biological parents were present) than in adoptive families. This is an important example of how genotype–environment correlations may influence the course of personality development (Scarr, 1987).

Although subsequent research continues to support Buss's (1980) theory of a strong genetic contribution to early-developing fearful shyness, there appear to be problems with his theoretical position that the later-developing, "self-conscious kind of shyness has no genetic component" (Buss & Plomin, 1984, p. 79). When we recall the findings that only about 36% of currently shy college students report having been shy since early childhood, we might expect that twin studies of late adolescents, which would presumably include more self-conscious than fearful shy children, should yield meaningfully lower heritability estimates for the trait shyness compared to twin studies of infants and young children. But they do not (e.g., Cheek & Zonderman, 1983). In their comprehensive review, Plomin and Daniels (1986) concluded that "heredity plays a larger role in shyness than in other personality traits in infancy . . . early childhood . . . middle childhood . . . adolescence . . . and adulthood" (p. 63; their reference citations are omitted here).

One solution to these paradoxical data is to suggest that the genetic predisposition for fearfulness and somatic anxiety shows up phenotypically in a gradual manner depending on exposure to environmental stressors. This is probably a factor in the development of shyness, but it does not explain either the significantly lower scores on somatic anxiety symptoms of shyness obtained for self-conscious compared to fearful shys (Bruch et al., 1986) or the identification of a substantial group of shy college students who experience little somatic distress (McEwan & Devins, 1983; Turner & Beidel, 1985). Our solution is to invoke the behavior genetics study by Kendler et al. (1987) that identified separate genetic factors contributing to somatic and psychic anxiety symptoms, and to suggest that it could apply to the early- versus later-developing shyness distinction.

Our speculation about a separate genetic effect on later-developing, self-conscious shyness might connect with Scarr's (1987) discussion of changes in the genetic program that are "turned on" just before puberty and involve becoming sensitive to the attractiveness of the opposite sex. McDougall (1963) also commented on this development around the age of 8, and he explicitly linked it to a new phase in the development of shyness and modesty (see also Harter, 1986). Moreover, Gilmartin (1987) observed that precocious development of this heterosexual sensitivity was strikingly characteristic of his sample of extremely shy men. In any case, our speculation suggests the need for further behavior genetics research on the development of shyness. We are not, of course, suggesting that low self-esteem, adolescent public self-consciousness, and relationship problems with parents and peers are not also important factors contributing to later-developing shyness.

Shyness and Other Dimensions of Self-Esteem

In spite of residual ambiguities about the developmental relationship of self-regard and shyness, it remains clear that shy people generally tend to have a low opinion of themselves. The other, more specific dimensions of self-esteem reported in Table 2 are: self-evaluation of physical appearance and physical ability, self-confidence in academic ability, and vocational certainty. To varying degrees, shyness correlates negatively with all of them among both men and women. We will mention a few key shyness findings in each domain as we review these correlations.

The substantial negative relationship between self-evaluations of physical attractiveness and shyness is generally consistent with other research (e.g., Bruch *et al.*, 1986); observer ratings of attractiveness, however, usually do not correlate negatively to a significant degree with self-reports of shyness (Jones & Briggs, 1984; Jones, Briggs, & Smith, 1986). Liebman and Cheek (1983) found that shy college women underestimated their level of attractiveness compared to observer ratings, whereas those who were not shy tended to overestimate their attractiveness. Concerning the psychological centrality of aspects of self-concept, they also found that the negative correlation between shyness and self-reports of attractiveness was significant only for those who rated physical attractiveness as being very or extremely important to their overall self-concept.

The underlying issue in perceptions of attractiveness is often sexuality; other research has shown that shyness correlates positively with sex anxiety and sex guilt, and negatively with the frequency of engaging in sexual activities (Carpentieri & Cheek, 1985; Fehr & Stamps, 1979). A discrepancy effect between self-perceptions and objective standards also has been obtained in the realm of sexuality: socially anxious subjects rated their level of knowledge about sexual matters significantly lower compared to nonanxious subjects, but the two groups did not differ on an objective test of sexual knowledge (Leary & Dobbins, 1983). Viewed in conjunction with the attractiveness research, the previously described tendencies of shy people to overestimate the visibility of their somatic anxiety and to underestimate their level of social skills (e.g., Clark & Arkowitz, 1975; Curran *et al.*, 1980; McEwan & Devins, 1983), and other research on self-concept processes such as attributions and memories mentioned in the next section, the discrepancy effect comes into focus as a crucial dynamic in the psychology of shyness.

Put succinctly, shy people are their own worst critics (Cheek, 1987). The weight of the empirical evidence from the past 15 years of research on shyness, self-esteem, and other aspects of psychological insecurity requires reevaluation of Greenwald's widely cited formulation of a general social psychological law called "beneffectance," which is based on the assumption that "the pervasiveness of cognitive biases that build and maintain an inflated sense of self-worth was demonstrated in a review by Greenwald (1980)" (Greenwald, 1988, p. 38). Empirically, this cognitive bias operates clearly only among those who score in the top third of the distribution on measures of psychological security, but it is either absent or significantly *reversed* among those who score in the bottom third of the normal range of individual differences in self-regard and social self-confidence (e.g., Harter, 1986). Although it may appear credible to explain the results from shy people that contradict beneffectance in a particular study as an effect of cautious public self-presentation (Greenwald, Belleza, & Banaji, 1988), the consistency of recent research findings has strengthened our earlier conclusion that beneffectance is really a dimension of individual differences in intrapsychic personality rather than a general law of social psychology (Cheek & Hogan, 1983; Cheek, Melchior, & Carpentieri, 1986).

Less research has been conducted on the dynamics of the moderately negative relationship between shyness and self-confidence in physical abilities (see Table 2). Concurrent, prospective, and retrospective studies all agree, however, that boys who dislike and avoid culturally masculine athletic activities are particularly vulnerable to problematic shyness (Gilmartin, 1987; Kagan & Moss, 1962; Zimbardo & Radl, 1981). In fact, Gilmartin quite persuasively attributes the maladjustment of his sample of extremely shy men to their lifelong experience of being "psychologically feminine" in a macho culture. The possibility of a biological basis for these findings is suggested by research indicating that neonatal levels of sex-steroid hormones (e.g., testosterone or progestin) influence subsequent individual differences in timidity, especially among boys (e.g., Jacklin, Maccoby, & Doering, 1983).

In our sample, the correlation between shyness and self-confidence in academic abilities is more strongly negative for females than males; this finding is consistent with earlier work by Fleming and Courtney (1984), although the correlation for males also was statistically significant in their sample. In contrast to these negative self-perceptions, shyness usually correlates near zero with aptitude test scores and grade point averages (Arnold & Cheek, 1986; Maroldo, 1986a; Traub, 1983). Shy students, however, do seem to take a passive approach to their own educational development by remaining silent in the classroom and failing to use available resources such as academic advising (Friedman, 1980).

Passivity and caution also characterize the vocational development of shy people. Not only are shy college students uncertain about their vocational choice (see Table 2), they also do not engage in appropriate information-seeking activities to explore the careers that they might decide to pursue (Bruch et al., 1986; Phillips & Bruch, 1988). Shy adults tend to be unambitious, underemployed, and relatively unsuccessful once they have made a choice from the restricted range of careers that they are willing to consider (Caspi et al., 1988; Gilmartin, 1987; Morris et al., 1954). Next to loneliness and other relationship difficulties (e.g., Jones & Carpenter, 1986), dysfunctional career development appears to be the most severe long-term consequence of chronic shyness. In fact, shyness and the availability of social support affect one's ability both to cope with involuntary unemployment in later life and to adjust to retirement (Hansson, 1986). Even though the roots of shyness go back to biologically based individual characteristics and childhood experiences, the behavioral consequences of shyness are maintained and mediated by maladaptive cognitive processes, which we consider in the closing section of this chapter.

SHYNESS AND SELF-CONCEPT PROCESSES

We reviewed the available research on shyness and self-concept processes in mid-1985 (Cheek, Melchior, & Carpentieri, 1986). We present a summary of

Table 3. Summary of Shy People's Cognitive and Metacognitive Tendencies before, during, and after Confronting Shyness-Eliciting Situations

Unlike those who are not shy, dispositionally shy people tend to:

1. Perceive that a social interaction will be explicitly evaluative.
2. Expect that their behavior will be inadequate and that they will be evaluated negatively.
3. Hold "irrational beliefs" about how good their social performance *should* be and how much approval they *should* get from others.
4. Become anxiously self-preoccupied and not pay enough attention to other people.
5. Think about "who does this situation want me to be?" rather than "how can I be me in this situation?"
6. Adopt a cautious self-presentational strategy of trying to get along, rather than an acquisitive style of trying to get ahead.
7. Blame themselves for social failures and attribute successes to external factors.
8. Selectively remember negative self-relevant information and experiences.
9. Judge themselves more negatively than others judge them.
10. Accept negative feedback and resist or reject positive feedback.

that review in Table 3. We will comment briefly on each set of findings as we describe some relevant work that has been completed since that time. As an overview, a glance at Table 3 makes it clear that shy people suffer from a pervasive lack of beneffectance in their processing of self-relevant information.

Perceptions, Expectancies, and Beliefs

The idea that personality dispositions profoundly influence the way different individuals perceive the same "objective" social situation is a fundamental assumption of many personality theorists (e.g., Hogan, 1976; Jung, 1933; Murphy, 1947). This assumption is certainly true for the personality trait shyness. For example, shy people perceive various social situations as being inherently less intimate and more evaluative, and they perceive identical interpersonal feedback as being more evaluatively negative, compared to those who are not shy (e.g., Goldfried, Padawar, & Robbins, 1984; Smith & Sarason, 1975).

When the prospect of interpersonal evaluation is made explicit, the disruptive effects of shyness are exacerbated. Cheek and Stahl (1986) asked college women who had previously completed a shyness scale to write a poem. Before writing their poems, half of the subjects had been told that their work would be judged for creativity by a committee of poets and that they would receive a copy of this evaluation, whereas no mention of evaluation had been made to the other subjects. In the evaluation condition, shyness correlated $-.57$ with the creativity ratings of the poems, but in the control condition the correlation was only $-.13$. These findings illustrate Allport's (1937) general point that the extent to which a trait influences behavior may vary depending on specific circumstances.

Recent research continues to demonstrate that shy individuals expect that their social behavior will be inadequate and that they will be evaluated negatively by others (DePaulo, Kenny, Hoover, Webb, & Oliver, 1987; Leary, Kowalski, & Campbell, 1988). The consistency of such findings has encouraged attempts to apply Bandura's (1982) self-efficacy theory to social anxiety (e.g., Leary & Atherton, 1986). In the terminology of that approach, shy people tend to have both low self-efficacy expectancies and low outcome expectancies (Maddux, Norton, & Leary, 1988). This line of work appears to be a useful contribution to our understanding of the cognitive component of shyness, even though certain aspects of self-efficacy theory continue to be controversial (e.g., Kirsch, 1986). Moreover, research on the perceptions and expectancies of shy people may help to explain why the shy often seem pessimistic, jealous, suspicious, unsympathetic, or even resentful toward others (Gilmartin, 1987; John, 1983; Jones, Briggs, & Smith, 1986; Maddux *et al.*, 1988; Zimbardo & Radl, 1981).

Cognitive therapies for shyness typically assume that irrational beliefs also play an important role in social adjustment problems (e.g., Glass & Shea, 1986). Additional support for this assumption has been provided recently by a comprehensive study of anxiety and irrational beliefs (Deffenbacher, Zwemer, Whisman, Hill, & Sloan, 1986). Measures of shyness, especially of the cognitive component, were related significantly to four scales of the Irrational Beliefs Test: demand for approval ("it is essential to be loved and approved by all significant others"); personal perfection ("one must be perfect to be worthwhile"); anxious overconcern ("threatening events are cause for great concern, and their possibility must be continuously dwelt upon"); and helplessness ("past experiences determine present feelings and behaviors, and the influence of the past cannot be changed"; Deffenbacher *et al.*, 1986, pp. 283–287). These results suggest that further work toward applying Ellis's rational-emotive therapy to shyness should be worthwhile (Watson & Dodd, in press).

Anxious Self-Preoccupation and Self-Presentation

The perceptions, expectancies, and beliefs typical of shy people illuminate how they tend to approach social situations with maladaptive and conflicted metacognitive processing of self-relevant social information (refer to Figure 1). Metacognitive explanations of what shy individuals actually do during social interactions are based on a distribution-of-attention model; because the cognitive load of meta-self-consciousness interferes with the attention that should be paid to other people, shy people are believed to suffer from a "selective attention deficit" that impairs their ability to participate effectively in social transactions (Crozier, 1979; Hartman, 1983).

In support of this conceptualization, Melchior and Cheek (in press) found that shy college women reported spending 33% of a 5-minute social interaction engaged in self-focus compared to about 20% of the time for those who were not shy. Moreover, the content of their self-focusing was dominated by negative thoughts about being tense and making a poor impression, as would be expected by Crozier's (1979, 1982) model of shyness as a propensity for engaging in *anxious* self-preoccupation. Other laboratory research adds support for the idea that shyness involves excessive and dysfunctional metacognitive processing (Arnold & Cheek, 1986; Cappella, 1985; Greene & Sparks, 1983; Smith, Ingram, & Brehm, 1983). Not surprisingly, shyness is related to poor performance on a measure of sensitivity to the verbal and nonverbal communications of other people (Schroeder, 1989).

Therapeutic interventions aimed at getting the shy client to "decenter" by paying more attention to other people appear to be quite effective in treating this aspect of shyness (Alden & Cappe, 1986). For example, when Leary, Kowalski, and Bergen (1988) gave instructions "to find out as much as you can about the other person," participants in a social interaction reported reduced levels of apprehension, insecurity, and awkwardness, and so did their conversational partners. Such training in cognitive social skills is a promising substitute for the use of alcohol as a self-help treatment for reducing shyness symptoms (Hartman, 1986; Maroldo, 1986b).

The tendency to be anxiously self-preoccupied has a pervasive influence on social behavior. Rather than viewing the attentional model as a competitor with a self-presentational approach (cf. Asendorpf, 1987), we suggest that the social strategies of shy people make sense for individuals who are preoccupied with worry and self-doubt. Shy people typically choose to adopt a cautiously conservative or "protective" style of self-presentation, seeking to get along with others rather than to get ahead (Arkin et al., 1986; Briggs & Cheek, 1988; Langston & Cantor, 1989; Wolfe et al., 1986). For example, they tend to conform to majority opinion, to change their personal attitude toward the position advocated by an authority figure, and to avoid disclosing much information about themselves (e.g., Santee & Maslach, 1982; Turner, 1977; for a review see Schlenker & Leary, 1985). When faced with a situation in which others hold high expectations of them, shy individuals may even fail strategically as a means of creating lower and safer standards of evaluation (Baumgardner & Brownlee, 1987). Those who are not shy are more likely to pursue an acquisitive self-presentation style by actively seeking to obtain social rewards (Arkin et al., 1986).

Attributions, Memories, and Judgments

Our previous review made it clear that shy people typically reverse the general social psychological process known as "the self-serving bias in causal attribution" by accepting more personal responsibility for social failures than for successes (e.g., Arkin, Appelman, & Burger, 1980). They tend to attribute successes to external, unstable causes (e.g., Teglasi & Hoffman, 1982). More recent work continues to indicate that maladaptive attributional styles are an important part of the psychology of shyness (Alden, 1987; Anderson & Arnoult, 1985a; Leary et al., 1986). This line of research confirms Zimbardo's (1977) suggestion that, when they encounter social difficulties, "shy people blame themselves; the not-shy blame the situation" (p. 54).

Shyness is also related to high scores on the Turning Against Self scale of the Defense Mechanisms Inventory, which indicates relatively pervasive self-punitive tendencies (Foley et al., 1986). It is worth noting that women score higher than men on Turning Against Self, and the only failure to obtain the typical attributional pattern for shy people employed only male subjects (Miller & Arkowitz, 1977; cf. Girodo, Dotzenroth, & Stein, 1981). As we mentioned in our discussion of the self-esteem correlations reported in Table 2, the cognitive processes involved in shyness appear to be somewhat more salient among women than men, which would be consistent with research on self-focused attention and depression (Ingram, Cruet, Johnson, & Wisnicki, 1988).

Selective memory is another cognitive mechanism by which shy people maintain their negative self-images. Two laboratory studies have found that shy college women remember negative self-relevant information better than do those who are not shy (Breck & Smith, 1983; O'Banion & Arkowitz, 1977). In the study by Breck and Smith, the shy women also recalled a higher proportion of negative than positive self-descriptive traits. In order to examine possible gender differences in these selective memories, Akert, Cheek, and Young (1989) asked college students to recall a time when they felt embarrassed. The tendency of shy people to write longer accounts of embarrassment than did those who were not shy was more pronounced among women than men. Here again, the need for more attention to gender differences in future research on shyness is evident.

In light of the various cognitive tendencies typical of shy people, it is not surprising that they judge themselves even more harshly than others judge them (Cheek, Melchior, & Carpentieri, 1986). Given that shy people expect to be evaluated negatively, we might anticipate that they would welcome some positive feedback. Unlike those who are not shy, however, shy individuals more readily accept negative feedback than positive feedback, and they tend to ignore, resist, or doubt the accuracy of positive evaluations (Alden, 1987; Asendorpf, 1987; Franzoi, 1983; Greenberg, Pyszczynski, & Stine, 1985; Lake & Arkin, 1983; Wurf & Markus, 1983). This striking pattern of consistent results validates Teglasi and Hoffman's (1982) speculation that the shy have a psychological "immunity" to positive feedback. Looking back at Table 3, we see that the cognitive tendencies involved in shyness are persistently maladaptive before, during, and after social interactions.

CONCLUSION

The present review reinforces our earlier portrait of the shy person's self-concept: low self-esteem, low expectancies for social success, worry about receiving negative evaluations from others, irrational beliefs, anxious self-preoccupation, preference for adopting a protective self-presentation style, self-blaming causal attributions, selective memory for negative self-relevant information, and unrealistically harsh self-perceptions (Cheek, Melchior, & Carpentieri, 1986). Our interpretation of dysfunctional meta-self-consciousness as the unifying theme in the experience of shyness suggests a strongly affirmative answer to Allport's (1955) challenging question: "Does psychological science need the concept of *self*?" (p. 36).

Moreover, we have seen that shy people actively resist information that would disconfirm their negative self-images by attributing success to external factors, selectively focusing on negative feedback, and doubting the accuracy of positive feedback. This "vicious cycle" of self-defeating cognitions is exacerbated by the cautious self-presentation style of shy individuals because playing it safe in social situations deprives them of opportunities for receiving approval from others and developing close relationships (Arkin *et al.*, 1986; Baumeister & Scher, 1988). Some shy people may even cling to their shyness as an excuse for their unwillingness or inability to cope with social pressures (Snyder & Smith, 1986), but for most it is probably a reflection of the general human tendency to maintain and defend one's self-concept even if it is unrealistic or negative (Epstein, 1980; Swann, 1987).

The pervasiveness of these self-concept processes suggests that the cognitive component is the predominant aspect of the shyness syndrome. That is, shy people's cognitions regarding their somatic anxiety symptoms and degree of social skill may be more consequential than their objectively assessed levels of tension or awkwardness. Such an interpretation would be consistent with recent anxiety research that emphasizes worry as the strongest predictor of performance outcomes (Borkovec, Metzger, & Pruzinsky, 1986; Deffenbacher & Hazaleus, 1985). We believe, however, that it is essential to keep in mind a rather fundamental point about human nature: "In both evolutionary and ontogenetic terms, affective experiences precede the development of evaluative thought as regulatory processes" (Ford, 1987, p. 638; see also McDougall, 1963, pp. 481–492). Recall that many shy people do have disruptive somatic anxiety symptoms, and that shyness is the personality trait with the strongest genetic component. Therefore, we agree with Sarason (1988) that anxiety researchers need to focus more attention on the interactions among cognitive, emotional, physiological, and behavioral symptoms.

Because humans are complex, self-constructing living systems, no narrow approach to the psychology of shyness, whether based on genetics, physiology, learning, emotion, self-esteem, psychodynamics, self-attention, self-efficacy, or self-presentation, can succeed by itself (Cheek & Briggs, in press). Our understanding of shyness will advance to the extent that psychologists are able to develop a biocultural systems theory of personality, social behavior, and psychopathology. Future research also should continue to investigate individual differences among shy people (e.g., Cheek & Watson, 1989), the impact of shyness on individual lives (e.g., Wright, 1930), the interpersonal dynamics of shy people in relationships (e.g., Read & Miller, 1989), and the psychodynamic patterns that maintain shyness across the life span (e.g., Thorne, 1989).

At present, the self-concept processes typical of shy people provide an interesting challenge to psychologists who are developing new cognitive therapies for shyness, especially because the shy can be surprisingly difficult clients (e.g., Nocita & Stiles, 1986). Nevertheless, research on combining cognitive restructuring, social skills training, and systematic desensitization, and investigations of potential interactions between client characteristics and treatment strategies, indicate that progress is being made in the development of effective techniques for overcoming shyness (Cappe & Alden, 1986; Cheek & Cheek, 1989; Elder, Edelstein, & Fremouw, 1981; Hollin & Trower, 1988). From our theoretical perspective, we view the "constructivistic" approach to cognitive therapy, which focuses on the developmental deep structures of self-organization and attachment, as being particularly promising (Guidano, 1986; for a case illustration see Leahy, 1985). We conclude that the personal revolution necessary for reorganizing the shy person's self-concept and social behavior is a difficult but achievable goal.

ACKNOWLEDGMENTS. Preparation of this chapter was supported by the first author's position as a visiting faculty member at the University of California, Berkeley. We thank Harold Baize for his technical assistance.

REFERENCES

Adams, G. R., Abraham, K. G., & Markstrom, C. A. (1987). The relations among identity development, self-consciousness, and self-focusing during middle and late adolescence. *Developmental Psychology, 23*, 292–297.

Akert, R. M., Cheek, J. M., & Young, M. M. (1989). [Shyness and memories of personal experiences]. Unpublished raw data, Wellesley College.

Alden, L. (1987). Attributional responses of anxious individuals to different patterns of social feedback: Nothing succeeds like improvement. *Journal of Personality and Social Psychology, 52*, 100–106.

Alden, L., & Cappe, R.(1986). Interpersonal process training for shy clients. In W. H. Jones, J. M. Cheek, & S. R. Briggs (Eds.), *Shyness: Perspectives on research and treatment* (pp. 343–355). New York: Plenum.

Allport, G. W. (1937). *Personality: A psychological interpretation*. New York: Holt.

Allport, G. W. (1955). *Becoming*. New Haven, CT: Yale University Press.

Allport, G. W. (1960). The open system in personality. *Journal of Abnormal and Social Psychology, 61*, 301–310.

Anderson, C. A., & Arnoult, L. H. (1985a). Attributional styles and everyday problems in living: Depression, loneliness, and shyness. *Social Cognition, 3*, 16–35.

Anderson, C. A., & Arnoult, L. H. (1985b). Attributional models of depression, loneliness, and shyness. In J. Harvey & G. Weary (Eds.), *Attribution: Basic issues and applications* (pp. 235–279). New York: Academic Press.

Arkin, R. M., Appelman, A. J., & Burger, J. M. (1980). Social anxiety, self-presentation, and the self-serving bias in causal attribution. *Journal of Personality and Social Psychology, 38*, 23–35.

Arkin, R. M., Lake, E. A., & Baumgardner, A. B. (1986). Shyness and self-presentation. In W. H. Jones, J. M. Cheek, & S. R. Briggs (Eds.), *Shyness: Perspectives on research and treatment* (pp. 189–203). New York: Plenum.

Arnold, A. P., & Cheek, J. M. (1986). Shyness, self-preoccupation, and the Stroop color and word test. *Personality and Individual Differences, 7*, 571–573.

Asendorpf, J. B. (1987). Videotape reconstruction of emotions and cognitions related to shyness. *Journal of Personality and Social Psychology, 53*, 542–549.

Baldwin, J. M. (1894). Bashfulness in children. *Educational Review, 8*, 434–441.

Bandura, A. (1982). Self-efficacy mechanism in human agency. *American Psychologist, 37*, 122–147.

Baumeister, R. F., & Scher, S. J. (1988). Self-defeating behavior patterns among normal individuals: Review and analysis of common self-destructive tendencies. *Psychological Bulletin, 104*, 3–22.

Baumgardner, A. H., & Brownlee, E. A. (1987). Strategic failure in social interaction: Evidence for expectancy disconfirmation processes. *Journal of Personality and Social Psychology, 52*, 525–535.

Beck, A. T., & Clark, D. A. (1988). Anxiety and depression: An information processing perspective. *Anxiety Research, 1*, 23–36.

Bell, N. J., Avery, A. W., Jenkins, D., Feld, J., & Schoenrock, C. J. (1985). Family relationships and social competence during late adolescence. *Journal of Youth and Adolescence, 14*, 109–119.

Bem, S. L. (1981). *Bem sex-role inventory professional manual*. Palo Alto, CA: Consulting Psychologists Press.

Berger, C. R. (1980). Self-consciousness and the study of interpersonal interactions: Approaches and issues. In H. Giles, W. P. Robinson, & P. Smith (Eds.), *Language: Social psychological perspectives* (pp. 49–53). Oxford: Pergamon Press.

Blumberg, S. H., & Izard, C. E. (1986). Discriminating patterns of emotions in 10- and 11-year-old children's anxiety and depression. *Journal of Personality and Social Psychology, 51*, 852–857.

Bohrnstedt, G. W., & Felson, R. B. (1983). Explaining the relations among children's actual and perceived performances and self-esteem: A comparison of several causal models. *Journal of Personality and Social Psychology, 45*, 43–56.

Borkovec, T. D., Metzger, R. L., & Pruzinsky, T. (1986). Anxiety, worry, and the self. In L. M. Hartman & K. R. Blankstein (Eds.), *Perception of self in emotional disorder and psychotherapy* (pp. 219–260). New York: Plenum.

Bowlby, J. (1988). *A secure base.* New York: Basic Books.

Breck, B. E., & Smith, S. H. (1983). Selective recall of self-descriptive traits by socially anxious and nonanxious females. *Social Behavior and Personality, 11*, 71–76.

Breckler, S. J. (1984). Empirical validation of affect, behavior, and cognition as distinct components of attitude. *Journal of Personality and Social Psychology, 47*, 1191–1205.

Briggs, S. R. (1985). A trait account of social shyness. In P. Shaver (Ed.), *Review of personality and social psychology* (Vol. 6, pp. 35–64). Beverly Hills, CA: Sage.

Briggs, S. R. (1988). Shyness: Introversion or neuroticism? *Journal of Research in Personality, 22*, 290–307.

Briggs, S. R., & Cheek, J. M. (1986). The role of factor analysis in the development and evaluation of personality scales. *Journal of Personality, 54*, 101–143.

Briggs, S. R., & Cheek, J. M. (1988). On the nature of self-monitoring: Problems with assessment, problems with validity. *Journal of Personality and Social Psychology, 54*, 663–678.

Briggs, S. R., Cheek, J. M., & Jones, W. H. (1986). Introduction. In W. H. Jones, J. M. Cheek, & S. R. Briggs (Eds.), *Shyness: Perspectives on research and treatment* (pp. 1–14). New York: Plenum.

Bruch, M. A. (1989). Familial and developmental antecedents of social phobia: Issues and findings. *Clinical Psychology Review, 9*, 37–47.

Bruch, M. A., Giordano, S., & Pearl, L. (1986). Differences between fearful and self-conscious shy subtypes in background and adjustment. *Journal of Research in Personality, 20*, 172–186.

Buss, A. H. (1962). Two anxiety factors in psychiatric patients. *Journal of Abnormal and Social Psychology, 65*, 426–427.

Buss, A. H. (1980). *Self-consciousness and social anxiety.* San Francisco: Freeman.

Buss, A. H. (1984). A conception of shyness. In J. A. Daly & J. C. McCroskey (Eds.), *Avoiding communication* (pp. 39–49). Beverly Hills, CA: Sage.

Buss, A. H. (1986). A theory of shyness. In W. H. Jones, J. M. Cheek, & S. R. Briggs (Eds.), *Shyness: Perspectives on research and treatment* (pp. 39–46). New York: Plenum.

Buss, A. H., & Plomin, R. (1975). *A temperament theory of personality development.* New York: Wiley-Interscience.

Buss, A. H., & Plomin, R. (1984). *Temperament: Early-developing personality traits.* Hillsdale, NJ: Erlbaum.

Campbell, H. (1896). Morbid shyness. *British Medical Journal, 2*, 805–807.

Cappe, R. F., & Alden, L. E. (1986). A comparison of treatment strategies for clients functionally impaired by extreme shyness and social avoidance. *Journal of Consulting and Clinical Psychology, 54*, 796–801.

Cappella, J. N. (1985). Production principles for turn-taking rules in social interaction: Socially anxious vs. socially secure persons. *Journal of Language and Social Psychology, 4*, 193–212.

Carpentieri, A. M., & Cheek, J. M. (1985). *Shyness and the physical self: Body esteem, sexuality and anhedonia.* Unpublished manuscript, Wellesley College.

Carver, C. S., & Scheier, M. F. (1986). Analyzing shyness: A specific application of broader self-regulatory principles. In W. H. Jones, J. M. Cheek, & S. R. Briggs (Eds.), *Shyness: Perspectives on research and treatment* (pp. 173–185). New York: Plenum.

Caspi, A., Elder, G. H., & Bem, D. J. (1988). Moving away from the world: Life-course patterns of shy children. *Developmental Psychology, 24*, 824–831.

Cheek, J. M. (1979). *Shyness and sociability.* Unpublished master's thesis, University of Texas at Austin.

Cheek, J. M. (1982, August). Shyness and self-esteem: A personological perspective. In M. R. Leary (Chair), *Recent research in social anxiety.* Symposium conducted at the meeting of the American Psychological Association, Washington, DC.

Cheek, J. M. (1983). *The revised Cheek and Buss Shyness Scale.* Unpublished manuscript, Wellesley College.

Cheek, J. M. (1985). Toward a more inclusive integration of evolutionary biology and personality psychology [Comment]. *American Psychologist, 40,* 1269–1270.

Cheek, J. M. (1987). Shyness. *1987 Medical and Health Annual* (pp. 497–500). Chicago: Encyclopaedia Britannica.

Cheek, J. M. (1989a). Identity orientations and self-interpretation. In D. M. Buss & N. Cantor (Eds.), *Personality psychology: Recent trends and emerging directions* (pp. 275–285). New York: Springer-Verlag.

Cheek, J. M. (1989b). Love-shy men [Review of *Shyness and love*]. *Contemporary Psychology, 34,* 791–792.

Cheek, J. M., & Briggs, S. R. (in press). Shyness as a personality trait. In W. R. Crozier (Ed.), *Shyness and embarrassment: Perspectives from social psychology.* New York: Cambridge University Press.

Cheek, J. M., & Busch, C. M. (1981). The influence of shyness on loneliness in a new situation. *Personality and Social Psychology Bulletin, 7,* 572–577.

Cheek, J. M., & Buss, A. H. (1981). Shyness and sociability. *Journal of Personality and Social Psychology, 41,* 330–339.

Cheek, J. M., Carpentieri, A. M., Smith, T. G., Rierdan, J., & Koff, E. (1986). Adolescent shyness. In W. H. Jones, J. M. Cheek, & S. R. Briggs (Eds.), *Shyness: Perspectives on research and treatment* (pp. 105–115). New York: Plenum.

Cheek, J. M., & Cheek, B. (1989). *Conquering shyness.* New York: Putnam.

Cheek, J. M., & Hogan, R. (1983). Self-concepts, self-presentations, and moral judgments. In J. Suls & A. G. Greenwald (Eds.), *Psychological perspectives on the self* (Vol. 2, pp. 249–273). Hillsdale, NJ: Erlbaum.

Cheek, J. M., & Melchior, L. A. (1985, August). *Measuring the three components of shyness.* Paper presented at the meeting of the American Psychological Association, Los Angeles.

Cheek, J. M., Melchior, L. A., & Carpentieri, A. M. (1986). Shyness and self-concept. In L. M. Hartman & K. R. Blankstein (Eds.), *Perception of self in emotional disorder and psychotherapy* (pp. 113–131). New York: Plenum.

Cheek, J. M., & Stahl, S. S. (1986). Shyness and verbal creativity. *Journal of Research in Personality, 20,* 51–61.

Cheek, J. M., Tsang, M. E., & Yee, T. (1984, August). *Audience anxiety and shyness as distinct varieties of social anxiety.* Paper presented at the meeting of the Eastern Psychological Association, Baltimore.

Cheek, J. M., & Watson, A. K. (1989). The definition of shyness: Psychological imperialism or construct validity? *Journal of Social Behavior and Personality, 4,* 85–95.

Cheek, J. M., & Zonderman, A. B. (1983, August). Shyness as a personality temperament. In J. M. Cheek (Chair), *Progress in research on shyness.* Symposium conducted at the meeting of the American Psychological Association, Anaheim, CA.

Clark, J. V., & Arkowitz, H. (1975). Social anxiety and self-evaluation of interpersonal performance. *Psychological Reports, 36,* 211–221.

Crozier, W. R. (1979). Shyness as anxious self-preoccupation. *Psychological Reports, 44,* 959–962.

Crozier, W. R. (1981). Shyness and self-esteem. *British Journal of Social Psychology, 20,* 220–222.

Crozier, W. R. (1982). Explanations of social shyness. *Current Psychological Reviews, 2,* 47–60.

Crozier, W. R. (1986). Individual differences in shyness. In W. H. Jones, J. M. Cheek, & S. R. Briggs (Eds.), *Shyness: Perspectives on research and treatment* (pp. 133–145). New York: Plenum.

Curran, J. P., Wallander, J. L., & Fischetti, M. (1980). The importance of behavioral and cognitive factors in heterosexual-social anxiety. *Journal of Personality, 48,* 285–292.

Cutler, B. L., & Cheek, J. M. (1986, March). *The independence of shyness and need for affiliation.* Paper presented at the meeting of the Midwestern Psychological Association, Chicago.

Daly, J. A., & McCroskey, J. C. (Eds.). (1984). *Avoiding communication: Shyness, reticence, and communication apprehension.* Beverly Hills, CA: Sage.

Damon, W., & Hart, D. (1982). The development of self-understanding from infancy through adolescence. *Child Development, 53,* 841–861.

Deffenbacher, J. L., & Hazaleus, S. L. (1985). Cognitive, emotional, and physiological components of test anxiety. *Cognitive Therapy and Research, 9,* 169–180.

Deffenbacher, J. L., Zwemer, W. A., Whisman, M. A., Hill, R. A., & Sloan, R. D. (1986). Irrational beliefs and anxiety. *Cognitive Therapy and Research, 10,* 281–292.

DePaulo, B. M., Dull, W. R., Greenberg, J. M., & Swaim, G. W. (1989). Are shy people reluctant to ask for help? *Journal of Personality and Social Psychology, 56,* 834–845.

DePaulo, B. M., Kenny, D. A., Hoover, C. W., Webb, W., & Oliver, P. V. (1987). Accuracy of person perception: Do people know what kinds of impressions they convey? *Journal of Personality and Social Psychology, 52,* 303–315.

Dissanayake, E. (1988). *What is art for?* Seattle: University of Washington Press.

Edelmann, R. J. (1985). Individual differences in embarrassment: Self-consciousness, self-monitoring, and embarrassibility. *Personality and Individual Differences, 6,* 223–230.

Efran, J. S., & Korn, P. R. (1969). Measurement of social caution: Self-appraisal, role playing, and discussion behavior. *Journal of Consulting and Clinical Psychology, 33,* 78–83.

Elder, J. P., Edelstein, B. A., & Fremouw, W. J. (1981). Client by treatment interactions in response acquisition and cognitive restructuring approaches. *Cognitive Therapy and Research, 5,* 203–210.

Elliott, G. C. (1984). Dimensions of self-concept: A source of further distinctions in the nature of self-consciousness. *Journal of Youth and Adolescence, 13,* 285–307.

Epstein, S. (1980). The self-concept: A review and the proposal of an integrated theory of personality. In E. Staub (Ed.), *Personality: Basic issues and current research* (pp. 81–132). Englewood Cliffs, NJ: Prentice-Hall.

Eysenck, H. J., & Eysenck, S. B. G. (1969). *Personality structure and measurement.* San Diego, CA: Knapp.

Fatis, M. (1983). Degree of shyness and self-reported physiological, behavioral, and cognitive reactions. *Psychological Reports, 52,* 351–354.

Fehr, L. A., & Stamps, L. E. (1979). Guilt and shyness: A profile of social discomfort. *Journal of Personality Assessment, 43,* 481–484.

Fenigstein, A., Scheier, M. F., & Buss, A. H. (1975). Public and private self-consciousness: Assessment and theory. *Journal of Consulting and Clinical Psychology, 43,* 522–527.

Flavell, J. H. (1979). Metacognition and cognitive monitoring: A new area of cognitive-developmental inquiry. *American Psychologist, 34,* 906–911.

Fleming, J. S., & Courtney, B. E. (1984). The dimensionality of self-esteem: II. Hierarchical facet model for revised measurement scales. *Journal of Personality and Social Psychology, 46,* 404–421.

Flett, G. L., Blankstein, K. R., & Boase, P. (1987). Self-focused attention in test anxiety and depression. *Journal of Social Behavior and Personality, 2,* 259–266.

Foley, F. W., Heath, R. F., & Chabot, D. R. (1986). Shyness and defensive style. *Psychological Reports, 58,* 967–973.

Ford, D. H. (1987). *Humans as self-constructing living systems.* Hillsdale, NJ: Erlbaum.

Fox, J. E., & Houston, B. K. (1983). Distinguishing between cognitive and somatic trait and state anxiety in children. *Journal of Personality and Social Psychology, 45,* 862–870.

Franzoi, S. L. (1983). Self-concept differences as a function of private self-consciousness and social anxiety. *Journal of Research in Personality, 17,* 275–287.

Friedman, P. G. (1980). *Shyness and reticence in students.* Washington, DC: National Education Association.

Gilmartin, B. G. (1987). *Shyness and love: Causes, consequences, and treatment.* Lanham, MD: University Press of America.

Girodo, M., Dotzenroth, S. E., & Stein, S. J. (1981). Causal attribution bias in shy males: Implications for self-esteem and self-confidence. *Cognitive Therapy and Research, 5,* 325–338.

Glass, C. R., & Shea, C. A. (1986). Cognitive therapy for shyness and social anxiety. In W. H. Jones, J. M. Cheek, & S. R. Briggs (Eds.), *Shyness: Perspectives on research and treatment* (pp. 315–327). New York: Plenum.

Goldfried, M. R., Padawar, W., & Robbins, C. (1984). Social anxiety and the semantic structure of heterosocial interactions. *Journal of Abnormal Psychology, 93,* 87–97.

Goldsmith, H. H., & Gottesman, I. I. (1981). Origins of variation in behavioral style: A longitudinal study of temperament in young twins. *Child Development, 52,* 91–103.

Gough, H. G., & Heilbrun, A. B. (1983). *The Adjective Check List manual—1983 edition.* Palo Alto, CA: Consulting Psychologists Press.

Gough, H. G., & Thorne, A. (1986). Positive, negative, and balanced shyness: Self-definitions and the reactions of others. In W. H. Jones, J. M. Cheek, & S. R. Briggs (Eds.), *Shyness: Perspectives on research and treatment* (pp. 205–225). New York: Plenum.

Greenberg, J., Pyszczynski, T., & Stine, P. (1985). Social anxiety and anticipation of future interaction as determinants of the favorability of self-presentation. *Journal of Research in Personality, 19,* 1–11.

Greenberg, M. T., & Marvin, R. S. (1982). Reactions of preschool children to an adult stranger: A behavioral systems approach. *Child Development, 53,* 481–490.

Greene, J. O., & Sparks, G. G. (1983). Explication and test of a cognitive model of communication apprehension. *Human Communication Research, 9,* 349–366.

Greenwald, A. G. (1980). The totalitarian ego: Fabrication and revision of personal history. *American Psychologist, 35,* 603–618.

Greenwald, A. G. (1988). A social-cognitive account of the self's development. In D. K. Lapsley & F. C. Power (Eds.), *Self, ego, and, identity* (pp. 30–42). New York: Springer-Verlag.

Greenwald, A. G., Bellezza, F. S., & Banaji, M. R. (1988). Is self-esteem a central ingredient of the self-concept? *Personality and Social Psychology Bulletin, 14,* 34–45.

Guidano, V. F. (1986). The self as mediator of cognitive change in psychotherapy. In L. M. Hartman & K. R. Blankstein (Eds.), *Perception of self in emotional disorder and psychotherapy* (pp. 305–330). New York: Plenum.

Halberstadt, A. G. (1986). Family socialization of emotional expression and nonverbal communication styles and skills. *Journal of Personality and Social Psychology, 51,* 827–836.

Halford, K., & Foddy, M. (1982). Cognitive and social skills correlates of social anxiety. *British Journal of Clinical Psychology, 21,* 17–28.

Hampton, F. A. (1927). Shyness. *Journal of Neurology and Psychopathology, 8,* 124–131.

Hampson, S. E., Goldberg, L. R., & John, O. P. (1987). Category-breadth and social-desirability values for 573 personality terms. *European Journal of Personality, 1,* 241–258.

Hansson, R. O. (1986). Shyness and the elderly. In W. H. Jones, J. M. Cheek, & S. R. Briggs (Eds.), *Shyness: Perspectives on research and treatment* (pp. 117–129). New York: Plenum.

Harris, P. R. (1984a). The hidden face of shyness: A message from the shy for researchers and practitioners. *Human Relations, 37,* 1079–1093.

Harris, P. R. (1984b). Shyness and psychological imperialism: On the dangers of ignoring the ordinary language roots of the terms we deal with. *European Journal of Social Psychology, 14,* 169–181.

Harter, S. (1986). Processes underlying the construction, maintenance, and enhancement of self-concept in children. In J. Suls & A. G. Greenwald (Eds.), *Psychological perspectives on the self* (Vol. 3, pp. 137–181). Hillsdale, NJ: Erlbaum.

Hartman, L. (1983). A metacognitive model of social anxiety: Implications for treatment. *Clinical Psychology Review, 3,* 435–456.

Hartman, L. M. (1986). Social anxiety, problem drinking, and self-awareness. In L. M. Hartman & K. R. Blankstein (Eds.), *Perception of self in emotional disorder and psychotherapy* (pp. 265–282). New York: Plenum.

Hauck, W. E., Martens, M., & Wetzel, M. (1986). Shyness, group dependence, and self-concept: Attributes of the imaginary audience. *Adolescence, 21,* 529–534.

Hill, C. A. (1987). Affiliation motivation: People who need people . . . but in different ways. *Journal of Personality and Social Psychology, 52,* 1008–1018.

Hogan, R. (1976). *Personality theory: The personological tradition.* Englewood Cliffs, NJ: Prentice-Hall.

Hogan, R., & Cheek, J. M. (1983). Identity, authenticity, and maturity. In T. R. Sarbin & K. E. Scheibe (Eds.), *Studies in social identity* (pp. 339–357). New York: Praeger.

Hogan, R., Jones, W. H., & Cheek, J. M. (1985). Socioanalytic theory: An alternative to armadillo psychology. In B. Schlenker (Ed.), *The self and social life* (pp. 175–198). New York: McGraw-Hill.

Hollin, C. R., & Trower, P. (1988). Development and applications of social skills training: A review and critique. In M. Hersen, R. M. Eisler, & P. M. Miller (Eds.), *Advances in behavior modification* (Vol. 22, pp. 165–214). Newbury Park, CA: Sage.

Hope, D. A., & Heimberg, R. G. (1988). Public and private self-consciousness and social phobia. *Journal of Personality Assessment, 52,* 629–639.

Hugdahl, K., & Ost, L.-G. (1985). Subjectively rated physiological and cognitive symptoms in six different clinical phobias. *Personality and Individual Differences, 6,* 175–188.

Ingram, R. E., Cruet, D., Johnson, B. R., & Wisnicki, K. S. (1988). Self-focused attention, gender, gender role, and vulnerability to negative affect. *Journal of Personality and Social Psychology, 55,* 967–978.

Ishiyama, F. I. (1984). Shyness: Anxious social sensitivity and self-isolating tendency. *Adolescence, 19,* 903–911.

Ishiyama, F. I. (1985). "Origins" of shyness: A preliminary survey on shyness-inducing critical experiences in childhood. *The B. C. Counsellor [Journal of the British Columbia School Counsellor], 7*(1), 26–34.

Izard, C. E., & Hyson, M. C. (1986). Shyness as a discrete emotion. In W. H. Jones, J. M. Cheek, & S. R. Briggs (Eds.), *Shyness: Perspectives on research and treatment* (pp. 147–160). New York: Plenum.

Jacklin, C. N., Maccoby, E. E., & Doering, C. H. (1983). Neonatal sex-steroid hormones and timidity in 6–18-month-old boys and girls. *Developmental Psychobiology, 16,* 163–168.

James, W. (1890). *The principles of psychology* (Vols. 1 & 2). New York: Holt.

John, O. P. (1983). *Searching for the people who would gladden the hearts of personality researchers: Moderator effects of self-consciousness and self-monitoring.* Unpublished master's thesis, University of Oregon.

Jones, W. H., & Briggs, S. R. (1984). The self–other discrepancy in social shyness. In R. Schwarzer (Ed.), *The self in anxiety, stress, and depression* (pp. 93–107). Amsterdam: North Holland.

Jones, W. H., & Briggs, S. R. (1986). *Manual for the Social Reticence Scale.* Palo Alto, CA: Consulting Psychologists Press.

Jones, W. H., Briggs, S. R., & Smith, T. G. (1986). Shyness: Conceptualization and measurement. *Journal of Personality and Social Psychology, 51,* 629–639.

Jones, W. H., & Carpenter, B. N. (1986). Shyness, social behavior, and relationships. In W. H. Jones, J. M. Cheek, & S. R. Briggs (Eds.), *Shyness: Perspectives on treatment and research* (pp. 227–238). New York: Plenum.

Jones, W. H., Cheek, J. M., & Briggs, S. R. (Eds.). (1986). *Shyness: Perspectives on research and treatment.* New York: Plenum.

Jung, C. G. (1933). *Modern man in search of a soul.* New York: Harcourt Brace Jovanovich.

Kagan, J., & Moss, H. A. (1962). *Birth to maturity.* New York: Wiley.

Kagan, J., & Reznick, S. J. (1986). Shyness and temperament. In W. H. Jones, J. M. Cheek, & S. R. Briggs (Eds.), *Shyness: Perspectives on research and treatment* (pp. 81–90). New York: Plenum.

Kagan, J., Reznick, J. S., Snidman, N., Gibbons, J., & Johnson, M. O. (1988). Childhood derivatives of inhibition and lack of inhibition to the unfamiliar. *Child Development, 59,* 1580–1589.

Kahle, L. R., Kulka, R. A., & Klingel, D. M. (1980). Low adolescent self-esteem leads to multiple interpersonal problems: A test of social-adaption theory. *Journal of Personality and Social Psychology, 39,* 496–502.

Kaplan, D. M. (1972). On shyness. *International Journal of Psychoanalysis, 53,* 439–453.

Keen, S. (1978). Deliver us from shyness clinics. *Psychology Today, 12*(3), 18–19.

Kelly, L., Phillips, G. M., & McKinney, B. (1982). Reprise: Farewell reticence, good-by apprehension! Building a practical nosology of speech communication problems. *Communication Education, 31,* 211–219.

Kendler, K. S., Heath, A. C., Martin, N. G., & Eaves, L. J. (1987). Symptoms of anxiety and symptoms of depression: Same genes, different environments? *Archives of General Psychiatry, 44,* 451–457.

Kirsch, I. (1986). Response expectancy and phobic anxiety: A reply to Wilkins and Bandura [Comment]. *American Psychologist, 41,* 1391–1393.

Klopf, D. W. (1984). Cross-cultural apprehension research: A summary of Pacific Basin Studies. In J. A. Daly & J. C. McCroskey (Eds.), *Avoiding communication* (157–169). Beverly Hills, CA: Sage.

Lake, E. A., & Arkin, R. M. (1983, August). *Social anxiety and reactions to interpersonal evaluative information.* Paper presented at the meeting of the American Psychological Association, Anaheim, CA.

Lamb, M. E. (1982). Individual differences in infant sociability: Their origins and implications for cognitive development. In H. W. Reese & L. P. Lipsett (Eds.), *Advances in child development and behavior* (Vol. 16, pp. 213–239). New York: Academic Press.

Langer, E. (1978). Rethinking the role of thought in social interaction. In J. H. Harvey, W. Ickes, & R. Kidd (Eds.), *New directions in attribution research* (Vol. 2, pp. 148–173). Hillsdale, NJ: Erlbaum.

Langston, C. A., & Cantor, N. (1989). Social anxiety and social constraint: When making friends is hard. *Journal of Personality and Social Psychology, 56,* 649–661.

Lazarus, P. J. (1982a). Incidence of shyness in elementary-school age children. *Psychological Reports, 51,* 904–906.

Lazarus, P. J. (1982b). Correlation of shyness and self-esteem for elementary school children. *Perceptual and Motor Skills, 55,* 8–10.

Leahy, R. L. (1985). The costs of development: Clinical implications. In R. L. Leahy (Ed.), *The development of the self* (pp. 267–294). New York: Academic Press.

Leary, M. R. (1983). Social anxiousness: The construct and its measurement. *Journal of Personality Assessment, 47,* 66–75.

Leary, M. R. (1986). Affective and behavioral components of shyness. In W. H. Jones, J. M. Cheek, & S. R. Briggs (Eds.), *Shyness: Perspectives on research and treatment* (pp. 27–38). New York: Plenum.

Leary, M. R., & Atherton, S. C. (1986). Self-efficacy, social anxiety, and inhibition in interpersonal encounters. *Journal of Social and Clinical Psychology, 4,* 256–267.

Leary, M. R., Atherton, S. C., Hill, S., & Hur, C. (1986). Attributional mediators of social inhibition and avoidance. *Journal of Personality, 54,* 704–716.

Leary, M. R., & Dobbins, S. E. (1983). Social anxiety, sexual behavior, and contraceptive use. *Journal of Personality and Social Psychology, 45,* 1347–1354.

Leary, M. R., Kowalski, R. M., & Bergen, D. J. (1988). Interpersonal information acquisition and confidence in first encounters. *Personality and Social Psychology Bulletin, 14,* 68–77.

Leary, M. R., Kowalski, R. M., & Campbell, C. D. (1988). Self-presentational concerns and social anxiety: The role of generalized impression expectancies. *Journal of Research in Personality, 22,* 308–321.

Levin, H., Baldwin, A. L., Gallwey, M., & Paivio, A. (1960). Audience stress, personality, and speech. *Journal of Abnormal and Social Psychology, 61,* 469–473.

Lewinsky, H. (1941). The nature of shyness. *British Journal of Psychology, 32*(2), 105–113.

Liebman, W. E., & Cheek, J. M. (1983, August). Shyness and body image. In J. M. Cheek (Chair), *Progress in research on shyness.* Symposium conducted at the meeting of the American Psychological Association, Anaheim, CA.

Liebowitz, M. R., Gorman, J. M., Fyer, A. J., Campeas, R., Levin, A. P., Sandberg, D., Hollander, E., Papp, L., & Goetz, D. (1988). Pharmacotherapy of social phobia: An interim report of a placebo-controlled comparison of phenelzine and atenolol. *Journal of Clinical Psychiatry, 49,* 252–257.

Liebowitz, M. R., Gorman, J. M., Fyer, A. J., & Klein, D. F. (1985). Social phobia: Review of a neglected disorder. *Archives of General Psychiatry, 42,* 729–736.

Maddux, J. E., Norton, L. W., & Leary, M. R. (1988). Cognitive components of social anxiety: An investigation of the integration of self-presentation theory and self-efficacy theory. *Journal of Social and Clinical Psychology, 6,* 180–190.

Mamrus, L. M., O'Connor, C., & Cheek, J. M. (1983, April). *Vocational certainty as a dimension of self-esteem in college women.* Paper presented at the meeting of the Eastern Psychological Association, Philadelphia.

Maroldo, G. K. (1986a). Shyness, boredom, and grade point average among college students. *Psychological Reports, 59,* 395–398.

Maroldo, G. K. (1986b). Shyness and alcohol response expectancy hypothesis—Social situations [Comment]. *American Psychologist, 41,* 1386–1387.

Maslow, A. H. (1942). The dynamics of psychological security–insecurity. *Character and Personality, 10,* 331–344.

McAdams, D. P. (1985). The "imago": A key narrative component of identity. In P. Shaver (Ed.), *Review of personality and social psychology* (Vol. 6, pp. 115–141). Beverly Hills, CA: Sage.

McCroskey, J. C., & Beatty, M. J. (1986). Oral communication apprehension. In W. H., Jones, J. M. Cheek, & S. R. Briggs (Eds.), *Shyness: Perspectives on research and treatment* (pp. 279–293). New York: Plenum.

McDougall, W. (1963). *An introduction to social psychology* (31st ed.). London: Methuen. (1st ed. published 1908; 23rd ed. published 1936).

McEwan, K. L., & Devins, G. M. (1983). Is increased arousal in social anxiety noticed by others? *Journal of Abnormal Psychology, 92,* 417–421.

Mehrabian, A. (1976). Questionnaire measures of affiliative tendency and sensitivity to rejection. *Psychological Reports, 38,* 199–209.

Melchior, L. A., & Cheek, J. M. (1987). [Shyness correlations.] Unpublished raw data, University of Michigan.

Melchior, L. A., & Cheek, J. M. (in press). Shyness and anxious self-preoccupation during a social interaction. *Journal of Social Behavior and Personality.*

Meyer, R. G. (1983). *The clinician's handbook.* Boston: Allyn and Bacon.

Miller, W. R., & Arkowitz, H. (1977). Anxiety and perceived causation in social success and failure experiences: Disconfirmation of an attribution hypothesis in two experiments. *Journal of Abnormal Psychology, 86,* 665–668.

Morris, D. P., Soroker, M. A., & Burruss (1954). Follow-up studies of shy, withdrawn children: I. Evaluation of later adjustment. *American Journal of Orthopsychiatry, 24,* 743–754.

Mosher, D. L., & White, B. B. (1981). On differentiating shame and shyness. *Motivation and Emotion, 5,* 61–74.

Moskowitz, D. S., Ledingham, J. E., & Schwartzman, A. E. (1985). Stability and change in aggression and withdrawal in middle childhood and adolescence. *Journal of Abnormal Psychology, 94,* 30–41.

Murphy, G. (1947). *Personality: A biosocial approach to origins and structure.* New York: Harper.

Nocita, A., & Stiles, W. B. (1986). Client introversion and counseling session impact. *Journal of Counseling Psychology, 33,* 235–241.

Nunnally, J. C. (1978). *Psychometric theory* (2nd ed.). New York: McGraw-Hill.

O'Banion, K., & Arkowitz, H. (1977). Social anxiety and selective memory for affective information about the self. *Social Behavior and Personality, 5,* 321–328.

Patterson, M. L., & Strauss, M. E. (1972). An examination of the discriminant validity of the social avoidance and distress scale. *Journal of Consulting and Clinical Psychology, 39,* 169.

Pervin, L. A. (Ed.). (1989). *Goal concepts in personality and social psychology.* Hillsdale, NJ: Erlbaum.

Phillips, G. M., & Metzger, N. J. (1973). The reticent syndrome: Some theoretical considerations about etiology and treatment. *Speech Monographs, 40,* 220–230.

Phillips, S. D., & Bruch, M. A. (1988). Shyness and dysfunction in career development. *Journal of Counseling Psychology, 35,* 159–165.

Pilkonis, P. A. (1977a). Shyness, public and private, and its relationship to other measures of social behavior. *Journal of Personality, 45,* 585–595.

Pilkonis, P. A. (1977b). The behavioral consequences of shyness. *Journal of Personality, 45,* 596–611.

Pilkonis, P. A., Heape, C., & Klein, R. H. (1980). Treating shyness and other psychiatric difficulties in psychiatric outpatients. *Communication Education, 29,* 250–255.

Pilkonis, P. A., & Zimbardo, P. G. (1979). The personal and social dynamics of shyness. In C. E. Izard (Ed.), *Emotions in personality and psychopathology* (pp. 133–160). New York: Plenum.

Plomin, R., & Daniels, D. (1986). Genetics and shyness. In W. H. Jones, J. M. Cheek, & S. R. Briggs (Eds.), *Shyness: Perspectives on research and treatment* (pp. 63–80). New York: Plenum.

Plomin, R., & Rowe, D. C. (1979). Genetic and environmental etiology of social behavior in infancy. *Developmental Psychology, 15,* 62–72.

Plutarch (1906). Of bashfulness. In *Plutarch's essays and miscellanies.* Boston: Little, Brown.

Read, S. J., & Miller, L. C. (1989). Inter-personalism: Toward a goal-based theory of persons in relationships. In L. A. Pervin (Ed.), *Goal concepts in personality and social psychology* (pp. 413–472). Hillsdale, NJ: Erlbaum.

Richmond, V. P., Beatty, M. J., & Dyba, P. (1985). Shyness and popularity: Children's views. *Western Journal of Speech Communication, 49,* 116–125.

Riley, T., Adams, G. R., & Nielsen, E. (1984). Adolescent egocentrism: The associations among imaginary audience behavior, cognitive development, and parental support and rejection. *Journal of Youth and Adolescence, 13,* 401–417.

Roopnarine, J. L. (1985). Changes in peer-directed behaviors following preschool experience. *Journal of Personality and Social Psychology, 48,* 740–745.

Rosenberg, M. (1979). *Conceiving the self*. New York: Basic Books.

Rushton, J. P. (1988). Race differences in behavior: A review and evolutionary analysis. *Personality and Individual Differences, 9*, 1009–1024.

Russell, D., Cutrona, C., & Jones, W. H. (1986). A trait-situational analysis of shyness. In W. H. Jones, J. M. Cheek, & S. R. Briggs, (Eds.), *Shyness: Perspectives on research and treatment* (pp. 239–249). New York: Plenum.

Santee, R. T., & Maslach, C. (1982). To agree or not to agree: Personal dissent and social pressure to conform. *Journal of Personality and Social Psychology, 42*, 690–700.

Sarason, I. G. (1988). Anxiety, self-preoccupation and attention. *Anxiety Research, 1*, 3–7.

Scarr, S. (1987). Personality and experience: Individual encounters with the world. In J. Aronoff, A. I. Rabin, & R. A. Zucker (Eds.), *The emergence of personality* (pp. 49–78). New York: Springer.

Schalling, D. S. (1975). Types of anxiety and types of stressors as related to personality. In C. D. Spielberger & I. G. Sarason (Eds.), *Stress and anxiety* (Vol. 1, pp. 279–283). Washington, DC: Hemisphere.

Schlenker, B. R., & Leary, M. R. (1982). Social anxiety and self-presentation: A conceptualization and model. *Psychological Bulletin, 92*, 641–669.

Schlenker, B. R., & Leary, M. R. (1985). Social anxiety and communication about the self. *Journal of Language and Social Psychology, 4*, 171–192.

Schroeder, J. E. (1989, April). *Self processes and interpersonal perception*. Paper presented at the meeting of the Western Psychological Association, Reno, NV.

Semin, G. R., Rosch, E., & Chassein, J. (1981). A comparison of the common-sense and "scientific" conceptions of extroversion–introversion. *European Journal of Social Psychology, 11*, 77–86.

Shedlack, S. M. (1987). *The definition and development of shyness*. Unpublished B. A. honors thesis, Wellesley College.

Sigelman, C. K., Carr, M. B., & Begley, N. L. (1986). Developmental changes in the influence of sex-role stereotypes on person perception. *Child Study Journal, 16*, 191–205.

Smith, R. E., & Sarason, I. G. (1975). Social anxiety and the evaluation of negative interpersonal feedback. *Journal of Consulting and Clinical Psychology, 43*, 429.

Smith, T. W., Ingram, R. E., & Brehm, S. S. (1983). Social anxiety, anxious self-preoccupation, and recall of self-relevant information. *Journal of Personality and Social Psychology, 44*, 1276–1283.

Snell, W. E., Jr. (1989). Willingness to self-disclose to female and male friends as a function of social anxiety and gender. *Personality and Social Psychology Bulletin, 15*, 113–125.

Snyder, C. R., & Smith, T. W. (1986). On being "shy like a fox": A self-handicapping analysis. In W. H. Jones, J. M. Cheek, & S. R. Briggs, (Eds.), *Shyness: Perspectives on research and treatment* (pp. 161–172). New York: Plenum.

Stevenson-Hinde, J., & Hinde, R. A. (1986). Changes in associations between characteristics and interactions. In R. Plomin & J. Dunn (Eds.), *The study of temperament: Changes, continuities, and challenges* (pp. 115–129). Hillsdale, NJ: Erlbaum.

Sroufe, L. A. (1985). Attachment classification from the perspective of infant-caregiver relationships and infant temperament. *Child Development, 56*, 1–14.

Swann, W. B., Jr. (1987). Identity negotiation: Where two roads meet. *Journal of Personality and Social Psychology, 53*, 1038–1051.

Teglasi, H., & Hoffman, M. A. (1982). Causal attributions of shy subjects. *Journal of Research in Personality, 16*, 376–385.

Thorne, A. (1989). Conditional patterns, transference, and the coherence of personality across time. In D. M. Buss & N. Cantor (Eds.), *Personality psychology: Recent trends and emerging directions* (pp. 149–159). New York: Springer-Verlag.

Thyer, B. A. (1987). *Treating anxiety disorders*. Newbury Park, CA: Sage.

Traub, G. S. (1983). Correlations of shyness with depression, anxiety, and academic performance. *Psychological Reports, 52*, 849–850.

Turner, R. G. (1977). Self-consciousness and anticipatory belief change. *Personality and Social Psychology Bulletin, 3*, 438–441.

Turner, S. M., & Beidel, D. C. (1985). Empirically derived subtypes of social anxiety. *Behavior Therapy, 16*, 384–392.

Watson, A. K., & Cheek, J. M. (1986). Shyness situations: Perspectives of a diverse sample of shy females. *Psychological Reports, 59*, 1040–1042.

Watson, A. K., & Dodd, C. H. (in press). Communication apprehension and rational emotive therapy: An interview with Dr. Albert Ellis. *Journal of Social Behavior and Personality.*

Watson, D., & Clark, L. A. (1984). Negative affectivity: The disposition to experience aversive emotional states. *Psychological Bulletin, 96*, 465–490.

Watson, D., & Friend, R. (1969). Measurement of social-evaluative anxiety. *Journal of Consulting and Clinical Psychology, 33*, 448–457.

White, S. H. (1965). Evidence for a hierarchical arrangement of learning processes. In L. P. Lipsitt & C. C. Spiker (Eds.), *Advances in child development and behavior* (Vol. 2, pp. 187–220). New York: Academic Press.

Wilson, D. P. (1958). The woman who has not married. *Family Life, 33*(10), 1–2.

Wink, P., & Cheek, J. M. (1989). [Shyness correlations]. Unpublished raw data, University of California, Berkeley.

Wolfe, R. N., Lennox, R. D., & Cutler, B. L. (1986). Getting along and getting ahead: Empirical support for a theory of protective and acquisitive self-presentation. *Journal of Personality and Social Psychology, 50*, 356–361.

Wright, M. B. (1930). Shyness. *Psyche, 11*, 32–42.

Wurf, E., & Markus, H. (1983, August). *Cognitive consequences of the negative self.* Paper presented at the meeting of the American Psychological Association, Anaheim, CA.

Zimbardo, P. G. (1977). *Shyness.* Reading, MA: Addison-Wesley.

Zimbardo, P. G., Pilkonis, P., & Norwood, R. (1975). The social disease called shyness. *Psychology Today, 8*, 69–72.

Zimbardo, P. G., & Radl, S. (1981). *The shy child.* New York: McGraw-Hill.

II

Social Anxiety in Childhood: Developmental and Clinical Perspectives

"Social Anxiety" in Infancy
Stranger and Separation Reactions

Ross A. Thompson and Susan P. Limber

Consider the following vignette:

> Brian, an 8-month-old infant, crawled briskly into his family's living room and stopped when he reached the middle of the floor. He paused to scan, with a sober expression, the faces of the unfamiliar adults surrounding him until he viewed his mother's smiling demeanor, at which time he broke into an animated grin and an explosive cackle. During the next half hour, Brian played happily at his mother's feet while adult conversation continued. On one occasion, his mother left the room briefly to prepare refreshments. When he later looked up to discover his mother missing, Brian's happy play deteriorated into anguished sobs until his mother returned. It took a few additional minutes of comfort before he was ready to return to play again. At the end of the meeting, one of the adults stooped down to Brian and asked cheerily, "How ya doin', big fella?" Brian looked up at him with a serious expression for a moment. Then he turned to his mother with loud sobs.

Students of early development have long been interested in the nature of stranger and separation reactions in infancy. To some theorists, the onset of stranger wariness and separation distress are the hallmarks of important transitions in psychosocial functioning, signaling the beginning of new modes of self-understanding and relations with others (e.g., Mahler, Pine, & Bergman, 1975; Spitz, 1965). To other theorists, these behaviors indicate emergent cognitive skills which change the infant's appraisal of social situations (e.g., Kagan, Kearsley, & Zelazo, 1978). Individual differences in stranger and separation reactions are measured to index variations in the security of parent–infant attachment (Ainsworth, Blehar, Waters, & Wall, 1978; Lamb, Thompson, Gardner, & Charnov, 1985), cross-cultural differences in child-rearing practices (e.g., Chisholm, 1981; Konner, 1972), and aspects of the child's temperament or behavioral style (see Rothbart and Alansky, Chapter 4, this volume). In many respects, the study of stranger and separation reactions integrates diverse developmental processes relevant to early socioemotional growth.

Ross A. Thompson and Susan P. Limber • Department of Psychology, University of Nebraska, Lincoln, Nebraska 68588-0308.

The study of stranger wariness and separation distress is also important for its practical value. Developmentalists' growing awareness of the diversity of the social experiences of infants and young children has contributed to an interest in how infants respond to strangers of various ages and in diverse contexts (Batter & Davidson, 1979). Current controversies concerning the effects of early day-care experience on emotional development focus on the impact of repeated separations from parents on a young infant's capacity to form secure emotional attachments (see Belsky, 1988; Clarke-Stewart, 1988; Thompson, 1988). In clinical research, the appraisal of early reactions to strangers and separation experiences has contributed to a better understanding of the psychosocial sequelae of maltreatment (Cicchetti, in press), parental psychopathology (e.g., Zahn-Waxler, Cummings, Iannotti, & Radke-Yarrow, 1984), and other risk factors for child disorders.

In some respects, the term "social anxiety" is a misnomer as a conceptual rubric for summarizing research in this area. At the same time that babies are beginning to exhibit stranger wariness and/or separation distress, they also exhibit a broadened capacity for *positive* reactions to strangers and other social partners (e.g., Rheingold & Eckerman, 1973), and their skills at regulating and coping with emotional distress are increasing (Thompson, in press). Thus the traditional emphasis on the emergence of social *anxiety* at this time is potentially misleading, and our use of this term in quotation marks in the title of this chapter reflects our skepticism that it tells the whole story of how infants' reactions to strangers and separation experiences are changing during the first year. In many respects, however, this variability in infant behavior makes the study of these reactions more interesting and exciting, because it provides a window into the diverse processes influencing early socioemotional growth, and the variable pathways that individual growth can assume.

We will try to convey some of this excitement in the discussion which follows. We begin with a summary of the diverse theoretical perspectives which have been applied to the study of stranger and separation reactions in infancy, reflecting efforts to understand why infants begin to exhibit wariness toward strangers and separation distress during the second half of the first year of life. We also propose a new way of portraying these socioemotional reactions which builds upon and extends these theoretical views and provides an orienting framework for the rest of the chapter. Following this, we turn to detailed reviews of the research pertinent to each phenomenon, and we attempt to describe both what is known and what is unknown about these socioemotional phenomena. Finally, we outline directions for future inquiry.

THEORETICAL PERSPECTIVES

Most theories of early development offer explanations for the emergence of stranger wariness and separation distress during the first year, and there is considerable diversity in the kinds of explanations they provide. This review of theoretical viewpoints highlights the influences which are emphasized by each perspective, as well as their relative strengths and weaknesses in providing a useful, comprehensive explanation.

Psychoanalytic Viewpoints

The perspective which traditionally has been most influential in explaining the emergence of stranger and separation reactions in infancy is the psychoanalytic perspective. In this view, stranger wariness and separation distress are important markers of transitional processes in personality development which emerge according to a biomaturational timetable. They reflect significant changes in intrapsychic organization which affect self-awareness, emotional attachments, ego functioning, relations with others, and other socioemotional processes. In this respect, therefore, stranger and separation reactions are significant markers of the broader changes in personality functioning which underlie these reactions.

One influential psychoanalytic formulation was proposed by Spitz (e.g., 1965), who argued that the growth of stranger anxiety at about 8 months of age indicates the emergence of the second organizer of the psyche, reflecting a new transition in ego development. (The first organizer, at about 3 months, is revealed in the emergence of the social smile, and the third organizer, shortly after the beginning of the second year, is reflected in the child's use of the word "no.") Spitz's use of the term "organizer" to describe these transitions in ego development is informative, since he believed that ego processes of perception, attention, cognition, and memory, as well as object relations, are progressively reorganized by each transition. In particular, according to Spitz, the growth of evocative or recall memory provides the foundation for stranger anxiety by enabling the child to retrieve an internalized image of the mother with which to compare the stranger. Anxiety results from distress over mother's absence, according to Spitz, and thus this explanation of stranger anxiety also explains the growth of separation distress. Under normal rearing conditions (e.g., involving adequate and responsive maternal care) the emergence of this psychic organizer is highly predictable: Spitz called it the "eight-month anxiety."

Another representative of the psychoanalytic perspective is Mahler (1974; Mahler, Pine, & Bergman, 1975), who has explored the development of psychological individuation in infancy. According to Mahler, this psychological "birth" requires a transition from the normal autism of early infancy through a symbiotic relation to the mother on to the psychological differentiation of self and other, which is achieved late in the third year. Both stranger and separation reactions derive from the psychological changes occurring during this separation–individuation process. Mahler proposes, for example, that increases in separation distress are normative both during the early subphases of separation–individuation (when the child is experiencing a dawning awareness of psychological separateness) as well as during later phases (when perceptions of psychological isolation provoke ambivalent reactions to being physically separated from the mother). Thus Mahler argues—almost uniquely among developmental theorists—for normative *fluctuations* in the occurrence of separation distress over the first 3 years of life, rather than a simple linear increase and subsequent decline.

Like Spitz, Mahler views these transitions in psychological individuation as significant reorganizers of a variety of ego processes in young children. Along the way, the quality of the infant–mother relationship affects the emergence of anxious responses to strangers and separations. For example, Mahler proposes that infants who have established confidence in the symbiotic relation with the mother will experience considerably less anxiety in the presence of strangers, compared to infants with less confidence.

These psychoanalytic viewpoints offer provocative ways of embedding stranger and separation reactions into a broader network of psychological changes occurring during the early years of life. There is no doubt that the onset of separation distress and stranger wariness coincide with other important socioemotional and personality changes: the consolidation of attachment relationships, the emergence of rudimentary social expectations, the development of notions of object and person permanence, and the emergence of rudimentary concepts of personal effectance (to name a few) (see Lamb & Bornstein, 1987). Establishing the nature of the connections between these developmental phenomena remains a more challenging task, however, and many researchers are unsatisfied with psychoanalytic viewpoints because of the abstractness of the intervening processes and the difficulties encountered in studying them empirically and verifying them unequivocally. Moreover, the fact that infants exhibit anxiety not only in the presence of strangers and during separations but also when faced with heights, looming stimuli, and other events suggests that other processes—not directly tied to the infant–mother bond—may also be relevant to these socioemotional phenomena. Alternative formulations provide better explanations for what these other processes might be.

Evolutionary Approaches

An alternative perspective regards infancy within the context of human evolution and seeks explanations for separation and stranger reactions within the adaptational demands of species survival (Bowlby, 1969, 1973; 1980; Freedman, 1974; Hinde, 1974). From an evolutionary view, it is biologically adaptive for infants to develop wary reactions to unfamiliar adults and to protest separations from care givers, because doing so increases the likelihood of their survival to maturity and subsequent reproductive success. The distress reactions engendered by separations and strangers summon the parent, who is likely to provide protection, nurturance, and comfort. Developmental theorists with an evolutionary orientation argue that it is not coincidental that stranger wariness and separation distress emerge developmentally at about the time that infants become capable of independent locomotion, since this is when infants are likely to wander away or have greater unsupervised contact with other adults (infants also acquire fear of heights at about this time). These theorists also point out that separation distress can be observed in the young of other species, and thus it is not a uniquely human attribute (e.g., Rajecki, Lamb, & Obmascher, 1978). In general, therefore, the evolutionary perspective focuses on "ultimate" explanations for the emergence of stranger and separation reactions, based on the view that infants are biologically predisposed to develop emotional responses which protect them from danger and promote their survival.

As noted earlier, infants respond to strangers with positive as well as negative reactions, and this would appear to be problematic for an evolutionary perspective. However, the evolutionary analysis of stranger and separation reactions has been elaborated by the introduction of the *behavioral systems perspective* to theorizing in this area (Ainsworth, 1973; Bischof, 1975; Bowlby, 1969; Bretherton & Ainsworth, 1974). The behavioral systems perspective posits that infantile reactions can be analyzed in terms of four organized response systems, each of which has biologically adaptive value in promoting the baby's survival and development, and which are thus partly an outcome of evolutionary processes (see Bretherton & Ainsworth, 1974; Lamb & Bornstein, 1987). One of these—the attachment behavioral system—fosters the development of strong emotional bonds between infants and familiar care givers who can provide nurturance and protection, and these attachments are reflected in the baby's preferential signaling and proximity-seeking efforts. Another system is called the fear-wariness system, which promotes the infant's avoidance or escape from threatening or alarming conditions. The attachment and fear-wariness behavioral systems are closely linked, because in alarming circumstances the infant not only tries to escape but also seeks contact with attachment figures. A third system—the affiliative system—is also organized around the baby's reactions to unfamiliar persons, but in nonstressful circumstances. In such conditions, infants may *seek* social contact with strangers because adults are interesting and engaging sources of stimulation and learning and, at times, may also be nurturant and protective. From an evolutionary perspective, contact with mature conspecifics who are not attachment figures may promote the infant's survival and development in this manner. Finally, the fourth system is called the exploratory system, and it fosters the baby's learning and competence in the object world.

As several theorists have noted, these organized behavioral systems interact continuously as they influence infant behavior (Ainsworth, 1973; Bischof, 1975; Bowlby, 1969; Bretherton & Ainsworth, 1974). In nonthreatening circumstances, for example, exploratory and affiliative interest is typically quite high, while fear/wariness is low. If the infant becomes alarmed or distressed, however, exploratory and affiliative interest declines precipitously, and the attachment system is activated at a high level. Similarly, if a stranger approaches the baby sociably, both the fear-wariness and affiliative systems may become activated, and this can be manifested in shy or coy responses. In this manner, therefore, infant reactions may be guided by the interplay among multiple behavioral systems (see Greenberg and Marvin, 1982, for a provocative application of this approach to the analysis of young children's interactions with strangers).

While the behavioral systems perspective adds useful depth to this evolutionary analysis, and helps explain infants' emotionally complex reactions to strangers, it remains subject to a common shortcoming in biological analyses of socioemotional development. While the evolutionary approach helps to explain *why*—in terms of the evolutionary demands on our species—infants develop negative reactions to strangers and separations, it is unhelpful in describing *how* these socioemotional phenomena emerge developmentally. What are the constituent processes, in other words, by which infants acquire these socioemotional reactions at the ages they do? Furthermore, in its focus on normative processes, the evolutionary approach is unsuccessful in explaining the bases for individual differences in infants' reactions to strangers or separation experiences. To explain how these reactions develop in the first year of life, and why individual differences can be seen, developmental researchers have turned to other approaches which focus on the proximate—rather than ultimate (i.e., evolutionary)—causes of early behavior.

Socialization Approaches

Proximate causes relate to the more immediate developmental or situational bases for individual behavior, and among these are the actions of social partners. Socialization approaches to the study of separation and stranger reactions focus on how the infant's emotional reactions are shaped by the social environment.

There are several ways in which these reactions may be socialized during the first year. First, they may come under the control of reinforcement processes. Gewirtz (1972: Gewirtz & Nogueras, 1988) has argued, for example, that infants develop attachments to care givers who establish "positive stimulus control" over the infant's behavior—that is, who become evocative, discriminative, and/or reinforcing stimuli for the baby, partly because of their association with events or experiences the infant finds rewarding (see also Cairns, 1966). According to Gewirtz, separation distress may occur when the infant is involuntarily deprived of this reinforcement source, and thus behaviors which were previously rewarded are rewarded no longer. Similarly, Gewirtz and Nogueras (1988) have proposed that variations in infant separation distress may be affected by the mother's contingent responsiveness to the onset of distress (e.g., by returning, reassuring the child, providing affection, etc.). Infants may exhibit greater separation distress when their mothers have reinforced distress responses in the past by comforting or reassuring the child. Extending this analysis, it is arguable that variations in stranger wariness are also affected by the infant's prior learning history, especially the frequency of rewarding or unrewarding experiences with unfamiliar adults in the past.

Second, stranger and separation reactions may be socialized by observational learning processes. By 10 months of age, infants have become acute observers of parental behavior, and some theorists argue that the emotional reactions of care givers to unfamiliar or unexpected events may alter the infant's own appraisal of these events through a process called "social referencing" (Campos & Stenberg, 1981; Klinnert, Campos, Sorce, Emde, & Svejda, 1983). Thus when a parent regards a stranger with wariness, the infant's own emotional response to the stranger may become more fearful through observation of the care giver. Similarly, parents who anxiously depart may contribute to the baby's distress response because the infant can observe the parent's worried expression prior to separation.

A third way in which stranger and separation reactions may be socialized is through the control of experience by social agents. In other words, the breadth of a baby's prior experiences with strangers and separations is significantly shaped by the opportunities provided by care givers (e.g., through extrafamilial care, interaction with neighbors and friends, play groups, etc.). How a child reacts to strangers and separations may be influenced by the sheer amount of prior exposure the child has had to these experiences, although theorists disagree over their specific effects (e.g., does a 1-year-old's regular experiences with strangers heighten or reduce stranger wariness?). As noted earlier, much of the current controversy over the effects of early day-care experience concerns whether daily separations from the mother undermine a secure attachment relationship (Belsky, 1988) or have negligible effects (Clarke-Stewart, 1988). In these ways, the parents' control over the child's experiences with strangers and separations can significantly socialize the baby's reactions to these events.

Finally, stranger and separation reactions may be socialized in more indirect ways. For example, some theorists have argued that a secure mother–infant attachment fosters the development of social skills and social expectations in infants which contribute to more positive, sociable encounters with unfamiliar adults (e.g., Thompson & Lamb, 1983). In this case, socialization experiences pertain to the parent–infant relationship, with indirect influences on the nature of the baby's reactions to strangers.

Taken together, socialization approaches to the study of stranger and separation reactions provide useful explanations of how the social environment shapes a child's emotional reactions, and in our later review of pertinent research we highlight a number of findings which relate to these formulations. The socialization approach is especially useful for understanding the origins of individual differences in the intensity of stranger fear or separation distress. This approach is weakest, however, in providing a *developmental* analysis, because it is not clear how social influences alone would contribute to the emergence of these reactions during the specific period in the second half of the first year, when they typically occur. It is not apparent, in other words, that care givers alter their behavior significantly enough to account for developmental changes in stranger reactions at this time, and the reinforcing value of the parent does not change markedly enough to account for the emergence of separation distress at the half-year point. For a more thorough developmental analysis, theorists have looked at the changes which occur in a child's cognitive skills during the first year.

Cognitive-Developmental Perspectives

Several theorists argue that developmental changes in stranger and separation reactions are based on changes in a child's cognitive skills. For example, Stayton, Ainsworth, and Main (1973), among others, have argued that a concept of object or person permanence (i.e., the cognitive awareness that people continue to exist independently of perceptual awareness) is a prerequisite not only for the development of attachments to care givers but also for true separation distress (see also Ainsworth, 1973; Bowlby, 1969). In other words, only a baby who has a cognitive awareness that mother is *somewhere else* when she is not present is likely to protest being separated in order to provoke her return. Prior to this time, separation distress may arise simply because of the absence of social stimulation when mother is away (see Lester, Kotelchuck, Spelke, Sellers, & Klein, 1974, for supportive evidence). Schaffer (1966) has proposed a similar argument relating the development of person–object permanence to the emergence of stranger fear. However, the evidence concerning the latter formulation is mixed (Brossard, 1974; Paradise & Curcio, 1974; Scarr & Salapatek, 1970).

Another cognitive-developmental perspective emphasizes the infant's ability to interpret incongruous or discrepant events. Encounters with unfamiliar adults and separations from care givers are incongruous insofar as they face the baby with a social situation which is different from familiar or accustomed experiences. Developmental changes in the baby's cognitive ability to interpret such events may provide one basis for the emotional reactions which follow. In an early formulation, for example, Hebb (1946, 1949) argued that perceived discrepancies between a novel event and cognitive representations of familiar events produce arousal which, under some conditions, may be manifested in a fear response.

Kagan (1974; Kagan et al., 1978) and McCall (McCall & McGhee, 1977) modified Hebb's formulation to propose that fear or distress results directly from failure of the child's efforts to assimilate or understand the discrepancy between novel events and the child's representations (or schemata) of familiar events. When there is little discrepancy between novel events and familiar schemata, little distress results because these novel events are easily understood. When there is moderate discrepancy, the child devotes considerable effort to resolving the incongruity. If this effort is successful, excitement and pleasure may result; if unsuccessful, the child may become distressed. Finally, if the discrepancy between the novel and familiar is very great, there will be little distress because the child does not even try to assimilate that event to familiar schemata. Thus an inverted U-shaped curve is proposed to describe the relation between discrepancy and the potential for distress.

From a developmental analysis, therefore, discrepancy or incongruity theories propose that the cognitive prerequisites for stranger wariness or separation distress are (1) a capacity to spontaneously generate internalized representations of familiar care givers and familiar events, (2) an ability to retain these representations in memory and compare them with current circumstances, and (3) according to Kagan (1974; Kagan et al., 1978), an additional ability to spontaneously generate hypotheses to explain apparent discrepancies. According to Kagan, these cognitive capacities are functional by the age of 7 or 8 months. Stranger wariness thus results from discrepancies between the stranger's demeanor and that of the mother (or another familiar care giver); separation distress is thought to derive from discrepancies between perceptions of mother's absence and familiar representations of her company. According to this view, these distress reactions subside later in infancy as the baby acquires additional cognitive capacities which contribute to a more refined understanding of stranger and separation experiences (e.g., a capacity to understand and remember maternal assurances of return, etc.).

Cognitive-developmental explanations like these provide intriguing portrayals of the links between intellectual development and socioemotional responsiveness by suggesting that there are certain cognitive prerequisites to social discriminations. In identifying these constituents, these theorists provide the most developmentally oriented explanation of the emergence of stranger and separation reactions in the first year. However, there remain substantial problems with these approaches. First, the actual links which exist between cognitive capacities and socioemotional functioning may be more indirect and complex than those proposed by such theories, and some research findings disconfirm the direct links hypothesized by these formulations (see Campos & Stenberg, 1981). Second, discrepancy theories are imprecise concerning the factors which influence how successfully infants can resolve the apparent incongruity produced by a stranger or a separation episode, and theorists may underestimate how complex this evaluation process can be. As we shall see below, for example, a variety of factors influence whether infants respond in a friendly or fearful manner to strangers, and discrepancy theories are unclear concerning their role in the infant's generation of hypotheses to resolve the incongruity.

Third, and finally, discrepancy theories are difficult to verify empirically except in terms of *post hoc* explanations: it is very difficult, in other words, to make predictions of infants' emotional responses based on *a priori* determinations of the degree of discrepancy produced by a novel person or event. Perhaps for these reasons, theorists like Sroufe (1977; Sroufe, Waters, & Matas, 1974) and Lewis and Michalson (1983) have amended discrepancy theory to argue that the degree of discrepancy can alert the child and perhaps also account for the intensity of the emotional response, but the kind of emotion which ensues depends on other aspects of the child's evaluation of the situation (e.g., the stranger's behavior, the context of the separation, etc.).

Summary

Taken together, these alternative theoretical perspectives alert us to important constituents of the development of stranger and separation reactions in infancy, and that these reactions are part of a broader network of developmental changes in psychological functioning. As cognitive-developmental theorists have pointed out, they are affected by significant changes in the baby's cognitive capacity to interpret the appearance of a stranger or a separation from the mother. As psychoanalytic theorists have noted, their emergence may also derive from broader developmental changes in understanding self and other, and they are linked to processes of attachment, affiliation, and exploration (as the behavioral systems perspective also suggests). Individual differences in the intensity of stranger wariness and separation distress are also complexly determined, and as socialization theorists have indicated, they can be affected by both immediate and longer-term social influences in the child's environment.

What is lacking is a more comprehensive, integrative perspective within which these various influences can be understood, and this is an important task for future theorists. We propose that such a formulation should begin by regarding the infant as a relatively complex processor of information, not only concerning a discrepant event itself (i.e., a stranger or separation episode), but also its broader context: the presence or absence of attachment figures, for example, as well as the familiarity of the physical setting, emotional cues from other social partners, antecedent events, and other factors (see also Clarke-Stewart, 1978; Sroufe, 1977). Not only exogenous variables but also endogenous influences enter into this analysis: the baby's temperament or behavioral style, experiential background, and short-term organismic condition (e.g., fatigue) assume significant roles in the child's evaluation of separations or strangers.

From this perspective, therefore, it is not the experience of separation or an encounter with a stranger alone which directs the child's emotional response, but also elements of the situational and organismic context. Within this informal information-processing analysis, we propose that the onset of stranger and separation reactions is attributable not only to the cognitive changes outlined above, but also to developmental changes in the capacity of working (or short-term) memory and the speed and efficiency of the appraisal processes involved in working memory which increasingly enable infants, over the course of the first year, to detect incongruous situations and to quickly evaluate them in a more sophisticated and complex fashion (cf. Case, 1984, 1985). Contrary to a younger baby, who can only appraise situations in a global manner, evaluate them in light of an impoverished range of stimulus elements, who is less likely to relate current conditions to an experiential history, and is a slower, less efficient information processer, the 9- to 12-month-old is capable of a more refined, discriminating appraisal which spontaneously draws upon prior experiences and quickly integrates these en route to a more complex (often multidimensional) emotional response. These changes in memory processing, capacity, and efficiency are also the reason for the progressive waning of distress reactions with increasing age, as the young child becomes capable of appraising situations involving strangers and separations in a more sophisticated manner, encompassing new elements in the appraisal process (e.g., verbal interactions with care givers, an elaborated analysis of the stranger's behavior, symbolic means of staying in contact with care givers, etc.), employing self-regulatory and coping strategies, and reassessing other elements which previously provoked wariness or distress, but which are appraised differently now.

In short, we suggest that our existing knowledge of the bases of stranger and separation reactions in infancy can best be integrated within a portrayal of the infant as an information-processing organism, in which increasingly more complex aspects of the situation become appraised in a more refined and efficient manner with increasing age. Developmental changes occur not only in how specific elements of the situation are interpreted, but also in how they are integrated in shaping the child's socioemotional reactions. With this approach in mind, we now turn to a detailed review of the extensive research literature concerning stranger reactions in infancy. Following this, we discuss the more limited research on separation reactions, and then offer new directions for future inquiry.

Stranger Reactions in Infancy

Research into stranger reactions has a long history, partly due to the psycho-analytic legacy of interest beginning in the early part of this century. As a consequence, there is a voluminous research literature concerned with describing the responses of infants to unfamiliar adults, their developmental course, and the factors which influence individual differences in stranger reactions. The analysis of this research begins, however, with a number of conceptual and methodological concerns which underlie work in this area.

Conceptual and Methodological Issues

What Kinds of Reactions?

Developmental researchers have used a variety of terms to describe how infants typically respond to the approach of an unfamiliar adult. Two of the earliest referred to this response as *shyness* (Gesell, Ilg, & Ames, 1943). However, descriptors with more negative and intensive connotations have been preeminent, including *terror* (Koupernik and Daily, cited in Decarie, 1974), *fear* (e.g., Scarr & Salapatek, 1970; Schaffer, 1966), *anxiety* (e.g., Benjamin, 1961; Brody & Axelrad, 1971; Spitz, 1950, 1965), and *distress* (e.g., Gaensbauer, Emde, & Campos, 1976). Although Spitz (1950, 1965) carefully distinguished anxiety from fear based on differences in their psychological origins, most researchers have tended to use these terms interchangeably. In addition, a number of researchers have used the term *wariness* in their discussions of stranger reactions (e.g., Bretherton & Ainsworth, 1974; Bronson, 1972; Bronson & Pankey, 1977; Schaffer, 1974; Schaffer, Greenwood, & Parry, 1972), with most regarding wariness as a less extreme emotional response than fear, or as the response which is apparent during the period when the stranger is being appraised by the baby prior to a full-blown emotional response (e.g., Schaffer, 1974).

Of course, infants often respond positively to strangers, and recent studies of stranger reactions have departed from earlier research by using descriptive terms with a positive valence. Thus stranger reactions are now commonly described as *sociable, accepting,* or *friendly* (e.g., Clarke-Stewart, Umeh, Snow, & Pederson, 1980; Rheingold & Eckerman, 1973; Thompson & Lamb, 1982, 1983). Clearly, studies which define the phenomenon as stranger "sociability" are likely to differ significantly from those which focus on stranger fear or wariness: the kinds of behaviors which are studied, how they are evaluated, and the interpretation of individual differences are likely to differ considerably, and this variability in orientation can help explain some of the inconsistency in research findings described below. On the other hand, it is informative to find that researchers studying stranger reactions have used descriptive terms which span the continuum of valence and intensity, because this reflects the complexity of the infant responses they are studying. Since infants respond with *both* sociability and wariness to unfamiliar adults (see Figure 1), perhaps it is appropri-

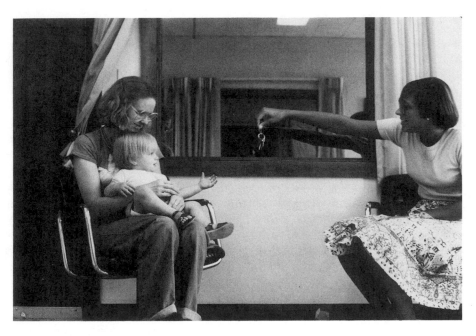

FIGURE 1. Infants often respond to strangers with a mixture of wary and sociable behaviors. This child looks to the stranger and raises his hand to accept her toy, but he simultaneously grasps mother's arm and leans back into her lap. (Photograph courtesy of Ross A. Thompson)

ate that researchers have used diverse descriptive terms to portray these reactions.

How to Measure These Reactions?

Given the variability in infant responses to strangers, researchers have employed an equally broad range of behavioral and autonomic indices to assess these responses.

Behavioral Measures. Behavioral measures used in studies of stranger reactions include: global evaluations of the baby's behavior (e.g., shy, cautious, etc.), facial expressions of emotion (e.g., cryface, sobering, frowning, pouting, smiling), visual orientation toward the stranger (e.g., prolonged gazing, gaze aversion), head movements in the stranger's presence (e.g., turning away, hiding face in mother's lap, turning to mother), locomotor behavior (e.g., approaching stranger, avoiding stranger, retreating to mother), global motor reactions (e.g., drawing back from the stranger, initiating contact), cessation of movement (e.g., freezing, quieting), and vocal reactions (e.g., laughing, crying, whimpering, fussing) (see Figure 2). In assessing infants' reactions, some researchers use a multimeasure strategy, commonly including at least one measure of facial expression, one measure of vocal behavior, and one measure of motor behavior (e.g., Morgan & Ricciuti, 1969; Scarr & Salapatek, 1970).

Since infants often mingle positive and negative responses in their encounters with strangers, the manner in which behavioral measures are recorded can significantly influence researchers' conclusions concerning stranger reactions. Most behavioral measures are unidimensional: that is, stranger reactions are appraised on a single positive-to-negative continuum, with the baby's response summarized globally by a single rating along this continuum. Few behavioral measures permit multidimensional or independent evaluations of *both* positive and negative reactions, even though these measures may better reflect the complex quality of infant responsiveness (see Bretherton, 1978, for an example). It may be difficult to summarize on a unidimensional measure, for example, the reactions of an infant who greets the arrival of a stranger with a smile and a proffered toy, but who immediately retreats to mother. On a multidimensional measure, however, these positive and negative reactions can be independently rated so a finer-grained assessment of infant behavior is possible.

In their review of research on stranger reactions, Rheingold and Eckerman (1973) argued that prudent researchers should consider only the most obvious and self-evident behavioral indicators of a positive or negative reaction to the stranger (e.g., crying, smiling, active avoidance, etc.). In their view, milder or more subtle behavioral indicators, such as staring or cessation of movement, may not be discriminating indices of stranger wariness because such behaviors occur in a wide variety of situations and in response to familiar as well as unfamiliar persons. In their response to this critique, Sroufe (1977) and Waters (Waters, Matas, & Sroufe, 1975) argued that an examination of milder fear reactions is necessary to clarify inconsistencies in research findings concerning the

FIGURE 2. Stranger reactions can be indexed by multiple behavioral measures, including facial expressions indicating wariness or distress, gaze aversion, drawing back from the stranger, and vocal reactions (e.g., crying or fussing). (Photograph courtesy of Ross A. Thompson)

frequency of negative responses to strangers and their developmental course: often infants show only mild, wary reactions, but these may nevertheless be reliable indicators of negative reactions to strangers. Furthermore, they noted that these subtle behavioral indicators can be used validly if they are carefully recorded in relation to the stranger's behavior, and used convergently with other behavioral indicators of fear and distress. In the Waters *et al.* (1975) study, for example, convergent measures of heart rate were used in an attempt to validate the significance of subtle behavioral indicators of stranger wariness (e.g., averted gaze, "wary brow", etc.) which might otherwise be difficult to interpret.

Autonomic Measures. Like Waters and his colleagues, a number of researchers have used measures of heart rate to assess infants' emotional responses to unfamiliar adults (e.g., Boccia & Campos, 1984; Campos, Emde, Gaensbauer, & Henderson, 1975; Skarin, 1977; Sroufe *et al.*, 1974). The use of heart rate is based on extensive research with adults and infants indicating that cardiac acceleration accompanies negative emotional arousal (see Thompson & Frodi, 1984, for a review of the infancy literature). However, heart rate accelerations are multi-determined responses: they accompany not only distress reactions but also experiences of positive affect and heightened motor activity. Consequently, most researchers have not used cardiac measures as sole dependent measures, but rather as convergent measures of infants' emotional responses in which concurrent behavioral measures can confirm inferences derived from heart rate data (Thompson & Frodi, 1984).

Another autonomic measure with some applications to the study of stranger reactions is the electroencephalogram (EEG). Although current views of cerebral lateralization no longer distinguish so simply between the "emotional" right hemisphere and the "rational" left hemisphere of the brain, some theorists now regard the left hemisphere as dominant with respect to approach behavior and the right hemisphere more strongly related to withdrawal or avoidance (see Davidson & Fox, 1988; Fox & Davidson, 1984; Kinsbourne & Bemporad, 1984). Applying this interpretation, Fox and Davidson (1987) measured relative levels of left- and right-frontal activation in EEG recordings of 10-month-old infants during stranger-approach, mother-approach, and mother-separation conditions. They found that patterns of cortical activation generally paralleled behavioral indicators of distress: during the separation episode, for example, infants who cried exhibited greater relative activation in the right-frontal lobe compared to noncriers. Thus like cardiac data, EEG measures can often provide convergent psychophysiological indices of underlying arousal when infants are approached by an unfamiliar adult, or separated from care givers.

Where to Study These Reactions?

Infants, like adults, are sensitive to their surroundings, and the familiarity of the setting can influence how infants respond to strangers. Most research on stranger reactions has been conducted in laboratories where greater control over environmental influences and more sensitive behavioral and autonomic measures can be obtained. A smaller number of studies have occurred in the infants' homes (e.g., Bronson, 1972; Sroufe *et al.*, 1974), and one researcher assessed stranger reactions in a shopping mall (Ferrari, 1981). The importance of the research setting is underscored by the results of studies which have compared stranger reactions in home versus laboratory settings (Skarin, 1977; Sroufe *et al.*, 1974). Not surprisingly, infants responded more positively in the familiar home setting than in an unfamiliar laboratory.

The setting in which stranger reactions is assessed is also important for the generalizability of research findings. Although infants are seldom in laboratories, they frequently encounter strangers in their homes. Perhaps even more useful are studies which examine stranger reactions in the extrafamilial settings where infants commonly encounter strangers. Interestingly, the only study to do so (Ferrari, 1981) found that infants showed primarily affiliative reactions to strangers in a shopping mall with their mothers present, and relatively few instances of fear and anxiety. Our understanding of stranger wariness would benefit from future studies conducted in a wider variety of extrafamilial settings which would permit more ecologically valid conclusions concerning these reactions.

What Procedures to Use?

Whether research occurs at home or in a laboratory, researchers have used a wide variety of procedures to appraise stranger reactions in infants. In some studies, the behavior of strangers has been highly standardized to reduce variations in infant responses attributable to individual differences in stranger behavior (e.g., Campos *et al.*, 1975; Scarr & Salapatek, 1970; Schaffer, 1966; Waters *et al.*, 1975). Typically these standardized procedures involve a series of brief episodes which include an entry period (stranger appears immobile in the doorway, smiling and talking to the baby), an approach (stranger slowly walks toward the baby, continuing to smile and talk), physical contact (commonly involving the baby being picked up by the stranger), and a withdrawal period (when the stranger returns the baby to mother and slowly walks out of the room). In these procedures, maternal behavior is also carefully controlled, and interaction between mother and stranger is minimized to limit these possible confounding influences on the infant's reaction to the stranger.

Other researchers allow much greater flexibility in the stranger's behavior (and maternal behavior) to permit interactions with the baby which seem more natural and are tuned to the individual infant's responses (e.g., Bretherton, 1978). Although such procedures reduce the comparability of infant–stranger interactions across a sample of babies, they have the advantage of permitting observations of infant responses to unfamiliar adults who are not behaving as strangely as they do in more standardized procedures. This more flexible approach yields findings which may be more generalizable to how infants typically react to strangers, because unfamiliar adults seldom act toward infants in the kind of regimented fashion typical of some studies. Moreover, as Bretherton (1978) has noted, these procedures also elicit more affiliative responses from infants, because strangers behave in ways which are responsive to cues from the baby indicating wariness or sociability. Strangers are thus less likely to intrude quickly or abruptly, or establish physical contact before the infant is ready, compared to the behavior of strangers in more standardized procedures.

Other kinds of procedural variations may also influence infants' reactions to strangers. When a baby is immobilized in an infant seat, for example, the child is more likely to respond with fear and distress than when she is freely mobile and can independently change the distance between herself and the stranger or seek proximity to a care giver (e.g., Bretherton, 1978; Bretherton & Ainsworth, 1974). Infants are more likely to be distressed in the presence of a stranger who looms over them compared to one who approaches at eye level (Weinraub & Putney, 1978). And the presence or absence of a familiar care giver also has a powerful effect on infants' reactions to strangers (Campos et al., 1975; Morgan & Ricciuti, 1969; Skarin, 1977). In short, it is possible to significantly influence infants' stranger reactions through the design of procedures which either permit friendly sociability or elicit manifest fear. These procedural variations account for some of the diversity in research findings in this area, but they also highlight the care which researchers must take in designing procedures to appraise stranger reactions in infants without significantly biasing infant response tendencies.

What Constitutes a Stranger?

As suggested above, a number of researchers are concerned that infants' reactions to strangers may not derive solely from the adult's unfamiliarity, but also from the strange behavior of the adult (Clarke-Stewart, 1978; Rafman, 1974; Rheingold, 1974). In procedures which require that the stranger act in a highly standardized fashion, infants may respond fearfully because of the adult's stilted or peculiar actions. Although this problem is somewhat remedied when greater flexibility is allowed in the stranger's behavior, this criticism underscores the importance of regarding the stranger not as a unidimensional "independent variable" in the research context, but as an interactive partner who presents the baby with a range of stimuli to which the infant responds (Clarke-Stewart, 1978). As we shall note in our review of research below, many attributes of the stranger—such as gender, intrusiveness, and visual perspective—influence the baby's reactions. As a consequence, the stranger is actually a multistimulus event to which a baby responds in a summary fashion, integrating various attributes of the stranger (as well as the context and other factors) in his response. Viewed in this way, stranger reactions are considerably more complex than they initially appear when the stranger is regarded as a unidimensional event.

Developmental Changes in Stranger Reactions

Longstanding research interest in stranger reactions in infancy is attributable, in part, to theoretical views which regard these reactions as significant developmental markers or biomaturational milestones (e.g., Mahler *et al.*, 1975; Spitz, 1965). Until the 1970s, there was a general concensus among developmentalists that infants universally experience a period of heightened fear or wariness of unfamiliar adults (Horner, 1980). In the mid-1970s, however, new viewpoints emerged that questioned the universality of this developmental transition.

Perhaps the most vehement critics of traditional theories were Rheingold and Eckerman (1973), who argued that research evidence does not support the view of stranger anxiety as a developmental milestone and suggested that this phenomenon may not even exist. They criticized previous research in this area as methodologically flawed, in which studies inadequately operationalized and measured infant responses and used procedures which confounded stranger reactions, situational stresses, and distress due to separation from the care giver. Moreover, they pointed out that existing research provided inconsistent findings concerning the age of onset of stranger distress and its normative developmental course, and they presented findings from their own laboratory (and those of others) indicating that fewer than half the infants at any age exhibited outright fear of strangers. They noted that affiliative responses toward strangers are at least as common as fearful ones, although sociability was seldom studied because of the preeminent theoretical orientation toward stranger anxiety. In sum, Rheingold and Eckerman (1973) raised both theoretical and empirical objections to the stranger anxiety construct, and they challenged researchers to approach the development of stranger reactions more carefully and objectively.

This critique catalyzed further research and theoretical work, and although most current developmentalists probably do not fully accept Rheingold and Eckerman's (1973) conclusions, this critique has contributed to a broader view of the development of stranger reactions in infancy. Few theorists argue strongly today that stranger anxiety is, in the strict sense, a biomaturationally timed developmental milestone, and most acknowledge both the importance of affiliative responses and the significance of the situational influences on stranger reactions. This means that stranger reactions are currently viewed as more complex developmental phenomena than earlier views had portrayed them. On the other hand, several longitudinal studies (e.g., Campos et al., 1975; Emde, Gaensbauer, & Harmon, 1976; Skarin, 1977) have confirmed a developmental shift toward greater stranger wariness in the second half year of life, while commentators (e.g., Sroufe, 1977) have argued that Rheingold and Eckerman overemphasized the significance of affiliative responses and underestimated the importance of milder negative (e.g., wary) reactions displayed by infants toward strangers. Taken together, the developmental study of stranger reactions has moved from an early theoretical legacy emphasizing stranger anxiety as a fixed developmental milestone to current views which underscore both the multi-determined quality of stranger reactions and their variability among infants of any age.

Descriptive Developmental Trends

These current views are well supported by the empirical evidence. A number of studies examining stranger reactions have used either cross-sectional or longitudinal methodologies: the latter approach is more sensitive to developmental change (Gaensbauer *et al.*, 1976), while the former is less susceptible to biasing influences due to repeated testing. Taken together, however, they have placed the average age of onset of stranger wariness between 6 and 9 months of age, and the peak of wary or fearful reactions occuring between 9 and 12 months (e.g., Campos *et al.*, 1975; Emde *et al.*, 1976; Gaensbauer *et al.*, 1976; Morgan & Ricciuti, 1969; Ricciuti, 1974; Scarr & Salapatek, 1970; Schaffer, 1966; Schaffer & Emerson, 1964; Skarin, 1977; Tennes & Lampl, 1964). Even though these are broad ranges, researchers have had even more difficulty determining when wary or fearful reactions begin to decline developmentally. Some researchers describe a decline in fearful responses at 11–14 months (Scarr & Salapatek, 1970; Tennes & Lampl, 1964), although several indicate that a second peak of fearfulness occurs between 18 and 24 months of age (Mahler *et al.*, 1975; Scarr & Salapatek, 1970), with a subsequent decline later in the third year. This second peak is less well substantiated by research evidence than the first, but it suggests that negative reactions to strangers may not show linear changes with increasing age, but instead fluctuate as additional developmental advances introduce new appraisals of unfamiliar adults (e.g., in Mahler's theory, the growth of psychological individuation). It is partly due to the possibility of normative developmental fluctuations in stranger wariness, as well as the broad range of individual differences among infants, that researchers have varied so much in their estimates of the normative onset, peak, and decline in these reactions.

Although these descriptive findings are informative, they are based on aggregated cross-sectional or longitudinal data and may cause us to underestimate the extent of individual variability in stranger reactions among infants of any age. As Rheingold and Eckerman (1973) pointed out and as researchers in this area have acknowledged, while some infants experience an extended period of heightened sensitivity to strangers, others avoid strangers only on rare occasions or during a brief period of time (e.g., Harmon, Morgan, & Klein, 1977), and some show no apparent wariness of strangers at all. Interestingly, the evidence concerning the consistency of individual differences in stranger reactions is mixed, with some researchers indicating that infants who are wary at one age will tend to be so on a later occasion (Gaensbauer *et al.*, 1976; Scarr & Salapatek, 1970), and others indicating much less consistency in individual differences over time (Schaffer, 1966). As a consequence, the study of developmental changes in stranger reactions has focused also on individual variability and its origins among infants. We now turn to a survey of this research literature.

Influences on Stranger Reactions

Because an unfamiliar adult presents a baby with a multistimulus event, and because that event occurs in a complex situational context, there are many influences on how infants respond to strangers. The extensive research on these influences—most focused on infants who were 9 to 24 months of age—reveals the complexity of the baby's appraisal of stranger encounters.

Characteristics of the Infant

Among these influences are several which arise endogenously from the infant herself. These include the baby's temperamental characteristics and other biogenetic influences, previous experiences, family size and birth order, the quality of the mother–infant relationship, gender, and organismic condition.

Temperament. Developmental researchers have studied the association between aspects of infant temperament (commonly appraised via parent-report questionnaires) and measures of stranger reactions. Although researchers have studied a common range of temperamental attributes, usually drawn from Thomas and Chess's temperamental formulation (see Thomas, Chess, Birch, Hertzig, & Korn, 1963), they have not always derived consistent results. For example, Scarr and Salapatek (1970) found that infants with a temperamentally low threshold of response, poor adaptability, negative mood, low activity level, and low incidence of approach behaviors were more likely to exhibit fear of strangers. Using some of the same measures, Paradise and Curcio (1974) replicated the association between stranger fear and low approach tendencies; however, they did not find the predicted links between fear and temperamental measures of mood. Harmon and colleagues (1977) noted that infants in their sample who were high on fussiness and general irritability were most avoidant of strangers, while Stevenson and Leavitt (1980) discovered that infants who were most sociable had a temperamentally low activity level (contrary to Scarr & Salapatek, 1970), a greater tendency to approach new stimuli, and showed greater distractability. However, Morgan, Levin, and Harmon (1975) found no associations between stranger responsiveness and measures of adaptability and sensitivity. Interestingly, in a longitudinal study, Thompson and Lamb (1982) found different patterns of associations between temperament and stranger sociability at different ages. At 12½ months, only one of six temperamental subscales— fear—was significantly and negatively associated with stranger sociability; by contrast, at 19½ months, temperamental measures of fear, activity level, and distress to limitations (i.e., anger) were negatively associated with sociability, and temperamental smiling and laughter was positively associated with sociability.

These results suggest that the infants who are most likely to be fearful of strangers tend to be temperamentally most reactive, more negative in mood, less adaptable, tend not to approach new stimuli, and are in general more fearful of the unfamiliar. These conclusions are hardly surprising, but provide support for the view that temperamental individuality assumes an important role in infants' responses to unfamiliar persons. The inconsistency in the results of the studies reported above probably derives both from a near-exclusive reliance on various parent-report measures of temperament (in which parents may also experience social-desirability motives when responding) as well as from variations in how stranger reactions were measured in different studies.

Future studies in this area should benefit from a recognition that nearly all researchers have studied temperamental influences within a main-effects model, that is, hypothesizing that intrinsic characteristics of the child directly affect how the child reacts to strangers. It is equally likely—although at present untested—that temperament also has indirect influences on stranger reactions by affecting parent–child interaction and other aspects of early socioemotional experiences which themselves influence stranger reactions. If, for example, infants generalize to strangers some of the social skills and expectations they acquire during interactions with familiar care givers (cf. Thompson & Lamb, 1983), then temperamental characteristics of the child may influence stranger reactions indirectly by affecting the quality and style of parent–child interaction. Moreover, some temperamental attributes may be influential in certain kinds of stranger encounters (e.g., in an unfamiliar setting with an intrusive stranger), but not in others (e.g., stranger interacts at a distance and mother is present). Thus, temperamental influences on stranger reactions may be considerably more complex than they are presently portrayed.

Other Biogenetic Influences. Temperamental characteristics are commonly viewed as having constitutional origins, although they are also influenced by environmental demands (cf. Lerner & Lerner, 1983). A number of researchers have studied more directly whether individual differences in stranger reactions are strongly heritable by examining (1) whether identical twin pairs are more similar on measures of stranger reactions than are fraternal twin pairs and (2) whether children who have been adopted are more similar to their biological (rather than adoptive) parents on measures of sociability and reactions to unfamiliar people. In general, these studies indicate that individual differences in stranger reactions are significantly influenced by hereditary factors (see Plomin, 1986, for a review).

For example, Plomin and Rowe (1979) observed 1½- to 2-year-old infant twin pairs together in their homes when a male stranger was present along with the mother. When each baby's behavior toward each adult was analyzed across a standard series of interactive episodes, they found that identical twins behaved significantly more similarly to the stranger than did fraternal twins, especially during their initial encounters with the stranger. By contrast, identical and fraternal twins did not differ in their reactions toward the mother, nor in their stranger reactions after the male adult had become more familiar. Plomin and Rowe (1979) concluded that hereditary factors have a greater influence on individual differences in social responding to unfamiliar persons than to familiar persons, a conclusion which is supported by several other studies in this area (see Plomin, 1986). Although this conclusion is well founded, it is important to recognize that the total amount of variability in stranger reactions which is accounted for by hereditary influences remains rather small. Clearly, genetic influences interact with the child's environmental experiences and background to affect stranger reactions in complex ways.

Previous Experience with Strangers. Among these environmental experiences is the sheer amount of the baby's previous contact with strangers. It would seem self-evident that infants who have had extensive experience with strangers would react differently than those with little prior contact—but how? Does heightened experience with strangers sensitize infants to unfamiliar people and result in greater fearfulness? Does it instead reduce infants' wariness? Interestingly, each hypothesis has been advanced to predict the effects of previous experience on infants' stranger reactions, and each hypothesis has received some support in the derivative research.

Schaffer (1966), for example, found a significant positive correlation between the number of people whom the child regularly encountered and the onset age of stranger reactions: infants with a broad range of prior social experiences exhibited stranger wariness at later ages compared to infants with a more limited experiential history. But a number of researchers have noted no significant associations between stranger reactions and the extent of the baby's prior experience with strangers or unfamiliar peers (Beckwith, 1972; Bronson, 1972; Harmon et al., 1977; Morgan & Ricciuti, 1969; Ricciuti, 1974; Stevenson & Leavitt, 1980; Thompson & Lamb, 1982).

Another way of examining the influence of prior social experience is to compare infants who differ more markedly in their care-giving conditions. In cross-cultural studies of infant development, for example, researchers have found that infants raised in industrialized Western cultures display less intense stranger anxiety than infants in tribal or Third World societies, such as the Zhun/twa (Konner, 1972) and the Ganda (Ainsworth, 1977). These differences are commonly attributed to the greater experience of Western infants with unfamiliar adults (see also Chisholm, 1981, for a similar interpretation of within-culture differences among the Navajo). Other studies have examined the reactions of infants in institutions who interact with many different unfamiliar people. Several researchers have noted that infants in these settings are less upset by strangers than are home-reared babies (Provence & Lipton, 1962; Rheingold, 1961; but see Tizard & Tizard, 1971).

Taken together, these studies alert us to the fact that when examining the effects of social experience on stranger reactions, the *degree* of variability in these experiences is probably determinative. In certain tribal societies, infants normatively have little contact with adults outside of the immediate family or group, and this experiential background is likely to make a dramatic difference when these infants are compared with middle-class Western infants. By contrast, comparing middle-class infants who have day-care experience with those who are home reared involves a more subtle difference in experiential background: whether in day care or home reared, these infants are nevertheless likely to have had considerable prior contact with unfamiliar adults. Thus, the effects of prior social experience on stranger reactions may be much more apparent when marked differences in experiential history are considered. Moreover, the sheer amount of prior contact with strangers may be less influential than whether infants have found these interactions to be pleasant or unpleasant.

Family Size and Birth Order. In a similar vein, several researchers have studied whether family size or birth order affects stranger reactions. There is some evidence that birth order is influential. Schaffer (1966) found that firstborn children evinced stranger fear about 7 weeks earlier than did later-born children, although Clarke-Stewart and colleagues (1980) found no associations between birth order and stranger reactions. Collard (1968) compared the stranger reactions of firstborn infants with those of infants in two sibling groups: (1) infants who had siblings less than 5 years old and (2) infants who had considerably older siblings. She noted that firstborns and infants with much older siblings showed greater wariness of strangers than did infants with younger sibs, and she suggested that the difference may be due to the number of young persons in the child's immediate environment (see Decarie, 1974). However, the studies which have examined the effects of family size on stranger reactions have yielded contradictory findings. While Schaffer (1966) noted that the number of children in the family correlated positively with the age of onset of stranger anxiety, Morgan and Ricciuti (1969) found no significant differences between infants in large and small families. Thus, the differences between firstborn and later-born children may not be due to variations in family size but instead to how these children are treated by parents, although further research is required to replicate and extend these findings.

Mother–Infant Relationship. Another experiential influence concerns the quality or security of the mother–infant relationship. Although earlier theorists within the psychoanalytic tradition argued that infants with strong parental attachments were likely to show earlier and more intense stranger anxiety (e.g., Freedman, 1961; Spitz, 1950), contemporary attachment theorists argue that infants with secure attachments will react more positively to strangers than will insecurely attached infants (e.g., Main & Weston, 1981; Thompson & Lamb, 1983). The latter believe that securely attached infants are likely to generalize their feelings of trust and confidence in mother to their initial encounters with unfamiliar adults. Moreover, when the care giver is present, confidence in her accessibility makes infants more confident when interacting with strangers.

In general, the research evidence has tended to support attachment theory. Clarke-Stewart and colleagues (1980) reported that infants who responded more positively to strangers had mothers who were responsive and positive in their interactions with the child, and Stevenson and Lamb (1979) likewise reported that sociable infants had sociable mothers. Five studies have directly examined the links between the security of mother–infant attachment and stranger reactions. Main and Weston (1981) discovered that a majority of insecurely attached infants exhibited "conflict behavior" while interacting with an unfamiliar clown in mother's presence at 12 months, while this behavior was uncommon among securely attached infants. Main (1983) also found that securely attached 1-year-olds displayed greater playfulness, cooperation, and positive emotion toward an unfamiliar adult at 21 months in an independent sample. Thompson and Lamb (1983), in a short-term longitudinal study, found that at both 12½ and 19½ months the infants who were most sociable toward a stranger were securely attached, although this finding was not subsequently replicated by Lamb, Hwang, Frodi, and Frodi (1982) with a Swedish sample, nor by Frodi (1983) with a sample of premature and full-term infants. The apparent links between a secure attachment and stranger sociability were further elucidated by Thompson and Lamb (1983), who noted that when the security of attachment remained consistent from 12½ to 19½ months, ratings of stranger sociability were highly correlated over this period, but when attachment security changed over the interim, sociablity scores were nonsignificantly correlated.

Thus it appears that securely attached infants exhibit diminished wariness of strangers, although some researchers have not found this to be true. Whether this association is due to the infant's use of social skills with the stranger which were initially learned in mother–infant interaction, or to the generalization of positive social expectations from the attachment relationship, or to the confidence derived from mother's presence—or some combination of these—remains to be elucidated by future research. It is important to note that in all of the attachment studies reviewed above, stranger reactions were assessed in mother's presence. Thus, future studies examining attachment and stranger reactions in the mother's absence may help to determine the importance of the care giver's immediate presence and support to this association.

Gender. A number of researchers have examined whether gender differences influence stranger reactions among infants, but there is no conclusive evidence to indicate that males and females differ in any systematic fashion. Although some studies have revealed trends in the direction of suggesting that girls manifest stranger anxiety earlier and with greater intensity, these findings were generally nonsignificant and, when taken with other studies finding no gender differences (Bretherton & Ainsworth, 1974; Emde *et al.*, 1976; Skarin, 1977) or that girls tended to be *more* sociable toward strangers (Clarke-Stewart *et al.*, 1980), the most confident conclusion is that there are no reliable gender differences in stranger reactions.

Short-Term Organismic Condition. Although enduring characteristics of the infant—such as temperament, prior experience, and the quality of the mother–infant relationship—likely influence stranger reactions, it is important to recognize that more transient influences also play a role. Among these are short-term organismic conditions, such as the baby's level of fatigue, hunger, or stress, which can bias the child's disposition to react in a positive or negative manner to an unfamiliar adult. Perhaps because wise researchers expend considerable effort to control for such influences in the design of research studies (e.g., by scheduling research sessions for periods in the baby's daily routine when the infant is likely to be rested, well fed, and alert), there has been no systematic research examining how these organismic conditions influence stranger reactions. Nevertheless, they must be included in any comprehensive portrayal of the bases of infants' sociable or wary responses.

Conclusion. As this review of research concerning the role of child characteristics on stranger reactions suggests, all infants do not approach an encounter with a stranger the same way. Children differ substantially according to their temperamental attributes and other biogenetic influences, their experiential histories (including the quality of their relationships with familiar care givers), and short-term conditions which affect their responses to unfamiliar adults. For this reason, the study of stranger reactions must consider these contributors to individual differences in responsiveness as well as other factors which normatively contribute to infants' sociable or wary reactions to unfamiliar adults.

Characteristics of the Stranger

In considering normative influences, researchers have devoted considerable attention to attributes of the stranger which may positively or negatively bias infants' responses. These attributes include the stranger's gender, physical characteristics, behavior, and familiarity to the baby.

Gender. Does it make a difference to infants if the stranger is male or female? Research indicates that it may, although the evidence is mixed. A number of studies indicate that infants react more positively toward female strangers (Belkin & Routh, 1975; Skarin, 1977; Weisberg, 1975) and that the stranger's gender becomes more influential over the first year (Morgan & Ricciuti, 1969), although some researchers have found no differences according to the stranger's gender (Cohen & Campos, 1978; Goulet, 1974; Lewis & Brooks, 1974; Ross, 1975). Clarke-Stewart (1978) has suggested that these discrepant findings may derive from whether male and female strangers were allowed to behave differently when interacting with infants. In studies which constrain the actions of the stranger, sex differences have been minimal. By contrast, when strangers are provided greater flexibility in their behavior, the stranger's gender has had a greater influence on infants' reactions. This difference may be due to the fact that most women interact with infants in the verbally oriented, low-key style which is likely to facilitate infants' friendly responses, while the typical masculine interaction style is more abrupt, intrusive, and arousing, and this style tends to elicit wary or fearful responses (Thompson, 1983). Consequently, the influence of the stranger's gender may be most apparent in studies which permit strangers to interact with the infant in gender-typical ways.

Physical Characteristics of the Stranger. Other physical characteristics of the stranger may also be influential, including the stranger's age and the physical size of the unfamiliar partner. Several researchers have discovered that infants react less fearfully to unfamiliar children than to unfamiliar adults (Greenberg, Hillman, & Grice, 1973; Lewis & Brooks, 1974). This could be due to the physical stature of the partner or to the stranger's facial configuration (children have more rounded facial features than adults). To tease apart these influences, Brooks and Lewis (1976) presented infants with three strangers: a 5-year-old child, a female adult, and a female midget (who was approximately the same size as the child but with an adult facial configuration). They found that infants reacted differentially to all three types of strangers, responding more positively to children than adults but orienting more intently to partners of small rather than large stature. Their findings thus indicated that *both* physical stature and facial configuration were influential. However, stature may not assume so influential a role when adults within the normal range are compared: Weinraub and Putney (1978) discovered that tall (over 6 feet) and short (5½ feet) strangers did not elicit different reactions from infants.

It is worth remembering (as Clarke-Stewart, 1978, reminds us) that differences in the physical characteristics of strangers are typically accompanied by behavioral differences as well. Clarke-Stewart notes that when children are included as strangers in research studies, their behavior is probably less constrained than are the actions of adults. Although the researchers in these studies devoted considerable effort to standardizing the behavior of children and adults alike, it seems likely that the natural spontaneity and animation of preschool children may have fostered infants' positive reactions to them. As a consequence, studies of the effects of the stranger's physical characteristics underscore the fact that, as a multistimulus event, the stranger presents the baby with behavioral characteristics which are likely to have a similarly important influence on the infant's responses.

Behavior. In her own review of the effects of the stranger's behavioral characteristics, Clarke-Stewart (1978) distinguished between three aspects of the stranger's behavior: (1) the stranger's affective tone, (2) the mode of behavior, and (3) the "style" of behavior.

Not surprisingly, the affective tone, or mood, of the stranger can significantly influence the baby's response. In her own research, Clarke-Stewart (1978) noted that "nice" strangers (i.e., those who played with the child in a positive, cooperative manner) elicited significantly more positive responses from 2½-year-olds than "nasty" strangers (i.e., those who played in a demanding and uncooperative manner). Similar results have been obtained for older children (Morris & Redd, 1975). Importantly, the stranger's affective tone can also have significant *indirect* effects on the child by altering how the stranger interacts with a third party, such as the child's care giver. Several studies indicate that an infant's willingness to interact with a stranger can be influenced by the reactions of the mother to the stranger (Feinman & Lewis, 1983; Feiring, Lewis, & Starr, 1984; but see Clarke-Stewart, 1978). This suggests that stranger reactions are affected, in part, by the child's observations of the reactions of trusted adults, and we return to this idea in our subsequent discussion of situational influences on stranger reactions.

The stranger's mode of behavior concerns the manner in which the stranger interacts with the baby, including whether the stranger looks at, talks with, plays with, or physically touches the infant. In general, infants react in a more positive manner to strangers who themselves act positively, provided the stranger is not highly intrusive. More specifically, infants respond more sociably toward strangers who interact rather than ignore them, and who play rather than just look at them (Bretherton, 1978; Clarke-Stewart, 1978; Eckerman & Rheingold, 1974; Ross & Goldman, 1977). However, as earlier noted, infants prefer strangers who interact with them distally rather than proximally (Morgan & Ricciuti, 1969; Roedell & Slaby, 1977; Scarr & Salapatek, 1970), and intrusive behaviors such as touching and patting the baby tend to elicit wary and fearful behaviors (see Figure 3; Ainsworth, 1973; Bronson, 1972; Campos *et al.*, 1975; Clarke-Stewart, 1978; Lewis & Brooks, 1974; Morgan & Ricciuti, 1969; Schaffer, 1966; Tennes & Lampl, 1964; Waters *et al.*, 1975). Indeed, Morgan and Riccitui (1969) noted that from 4 to 12 months of age, infants became progressively more negative to the proximal, intrusive phases of the stranger encounter. Even the baby's visual orientation can influence the degree of psychological intrusiveness experienced during a stranger encounter: infants respond more negatively to strangers who loom over them rather than approaching at eye level (Weinraub & Putney, 1978).

The influence of the stranger's mode of behavior may overlap with stylistic influences. As earlier indicated, some researchers standardize the stranger's behavior in order to heighten comparability from one research session to the next, while others provide greater flexibility to foster the stranger's responsiveness to infant cues. Consequently, strangers vary in the "naturalness" of their behavior toward the baby, as well as on other stylistic features such as vigor, tempo, and playfulness. A number of studies indicate that children react more positively to less vigorous overtures from a stranger (e.g., 3-year-olds prefer "cuddlers" to "ticklers"; see Weisberg, 1975), enjoy greater playfulness from the stranger (Bretherton, 1978), prefer slower, more gradual modes of approach (Ainsworth, 1973; Ricciuti, 1974; Ross & Goldman, 1977; Trause, 1977), and prefer strangers who act more "naturally" (Clarke-Stewart, 1978). The effects of the stranger's interactive style can also affect infant behavior more complexly. Clarke-Stewart (1978), for example, noted that 30-month-olds were more responsive when the stranger adopted an outgoing, stimulating style, but children took more initiative when the stranger adopted a less active interactive style.

In general, these findings suggest that two characteristics of the stranger's behavior are influential in infants' reactions to them. The first is contingency: whether the stranger acts in a manner which is responsive to the infant's cues and signals. Contingency may help to account for why infants prefer interactive rather than passive partners, and why strangers who behave in a highly standardized, stilted fashion elicit greater wariness. When social partners are contingently responsive, the infant's own sense of personal agency in the situation is reinforced, and a large body of research suggests that the exercise of personal agency, even at young ages, has positive socioemotional consequences and contributes to the baby's increased responsiveness in the situation (see Ford & Thompson, 1985, for a review). Consistent with this view, Levitt (1980) found that strangers whose appearance was earlier contingent on the infant's behavior received more positive reactions from infants than did strangers who were noncontingent.

This leads to the second important characteristic of the stranger's behavior: how it defines the range of response options for the baby. Like adults, infants prefer situations which provide them a variety of alternatives for responding, and strangers who move quickly and proximally constrain the baby's response options, which increases wariness and fear. By contrast, strangers whose actions

FIGURE 3. A stranger who interacts proximally and intrusively—such as picking up and holding the baby—tends to elicit greater wariness in an infant. (Photograph courtesy of Ross A. Thompson)

are more gradual, low-key, and distal provide the infant with greater flexibility in responding: the infant can decide whether to approach, remain at a distance, or retreat to mother (see Figure 4).

Taken together, these characteristics illustrate the fact that stranger reactions are not simply a function of whether an adult is unfamiliar but depend also on the adult's attributes and behavior. Indeed, altering these behavioral characteristics can make the same person either attractive or frightening to a baby. Infants are likely to respond sociably when the stranger acts positively and playfully toward the baby and others, interacts distally with the infant without intruding, responds contingently to infant cues, approaches the baby slowly and in a gradual, natural fashion, and thus gives the infant a range of response options. By contrast, infants are likely to fear the same stranger who acts negatively or ignores the child, moves quickly and abruptly to initiate proximal interaction, touches the baby without an invitation to do so, and in other ways limits the child's options. Unfortunately, as many care givers will attest, the latter characteristics frequently resemble the initiatives of relatives or family friends when greeting a baby!

Familiarity. Although a familiarized stranger may no longer be legitimately considered a "stranger," a number of researchers have demonstrated that infants become less fearful and more affiliative when permitted even small amounts of familiarization time with a strange adult (Bretherton, 1978; Levitt, 1980; Ross, 1975; Smith, Eaton, & Hindmarch, 1982; Sroufe et al., 1974; but see Eckerman & Whatley, 1975; Ross & Goldman, 1977, and Trause, 1977). Sroufe and his colleagues (1974), for example, noted that even familiarization periods as brief as 3 minutes diminished the amount of fearful behavior displayed toward a stranger.

Conclusion. These findings contribute to the conclusion that, as a multistimulus event, an unfamiliar adult presents the baby with a variety of stimuli which may affect the child's response in complex ways. A "stranger" is a multifaceted event, and characteristics of the stranger may simultaneously evoke sociable and wary reactions (and thus infants sometimes react in a shy or coy manner). The multidimensional quality of the stranger helps, therefore, to account for the complexity of infant responses.

Characteristics of the Situation

It is important to remember that a stranger encounter occurs in a situational context which may also influence stranger reactions. As noted earlier, the familiarity of the context (e.g., whether the research is conducted in the home or a laboratory) can significantly influence how infants react to a stranger (e.g., Skarin, 1977; Sroufe et al., 1974). Moreover, Rheingold (1969) noted that fearful behavior in a laboratory setting can be reduced by permitting the infant sufficient time to become accustomed to the lab in the mother's presence (see also Sroufe et al., 1974). But the influence of the situational context is significantly broader than just the familiarity of the setting, and it includes the effects of

FIGURE 4. A stranger who interacts sociably from a distance increases the baby's response options: the infant can decide whether to approach or remain away from the stranger. (Photograph courtesy of Ross A. Thompson)

antecedent events, the mother's proximity, and the kinds of cues the child receives from the care giver. We now turn to a discussion of these influences.

Antecedent Events. An encounter with a stranger does not occur in a psychological vacuum, and preceding events can significantly bias infants to respond either positively or negatively to an unfamiliar person. In studies of attachment using the Strange Situation procedure, for example, researchers have found that 12-month-olds respond more negatively to the stranger following a maternal-separation episode compared to their reactions preceding the separation (e.g., Ainsworth *et al.*, 1978; see also Emde *et al.*, 1976). In the only other empirical test of the influence of antecedent events, Sroufe and his colleagues (1974) presented 6- and 10-month-old infants with mother-and-stranger-mask conditions in counterbalanced order. For half the infants, a stranger called to the infant, covered her face with a human-looking mask, and leaned toward the baby on two occasions, and then the mother repeated this procedure; for the remaining half of the infants, the mother preceded the stranger. Sroufe and his colleagues found clear evidence for sequence effects among the 10-month-olds: infants responded more positively to the stranger when they first perceived the mother wearing the mask than when the stranger appeared first. The sequence effect was not apparent, however, among the 6-month-olds. These findings suggest that with increasing age, infants' stranger reactions are likely to be biased by the effects of preceding events like these on the infant's evaluation of the stranger.

Maternal Proximity. Consistent with the formulations of attachment theory described above, the mother's presence provides infants with a "secure base" which fosters more positive, sociable interactions with strangers (Ainsworth & Bell, 1970; Campos *et al.*, 1975; Corter, 1973; Emde *et al.*, 1976; Gaensbauer *et al.*, 1976; Greenberg & Marvin, 1982; Morgan & Ricciuti, 1969; Skarin, 1977; Trause, 1977; Waters *et al.*, 1975). Moreover, even the distance of infant to mother is influential: Morgan and Ricciuti (1969) reported that after 8 months of age, infants exhibited greater stranger anxiety when placed several feet away compared to being held in mother's arms (see also Bronson, 1972). The important factor in these findings may be the psychological availability of the care giver and the extent to which infants perceive that she is accessible. In support of this view, Sorce and Emde (1981) found that in the presence of a stranger, infants whose mothers were preoccupied with reading a newspaper responded significantly less positively compared to the infants of nonreading mothers who visually monitored the child's behavior.

Social Referencing. One reason the mother's psychological availability is important to infants is that they derive significant cues from her expressions about how to respond to the stranger. Developmental researchers have noted that, after 6 months of age, infants look to care givers and other trusted adults when they encounter uncertain or ambiguous circumstances, and researchers believe that infants do so to obtain information about how to respond. They call this phenomenon *social referencing,* and they argue that it constitutes an important influence on infants' behavioral and emotional reactions. In studies of social referencing, for example, infants have been observed to inhibit exploratory activity when mothers exhibit fearful or anxious facial expressions, but to be more positive and outgoing when mothers look pleasant and supportive (see Campos & Stenberg, 1981; Feinman, 1985; Klinnert et al., 1983, for reviews).

Consistent with social referencing phenomena, infants look to their mothers during stranger encounters (Bronson, 1972; Schaffer, 1971; Sorce & Emde, 1981; Sorce, Emde, & Frank, 1982), and the emotions mothers display have a significant influence on infants' subsequent reactions to the stranger. Boccia and Campos (1984), for example, noted that infants smiled more at strangers when their mothers exhibited joyful rather than worried expressions while being referenced by their offspring (see Figure 5). Similarly, Feinman and Lewis (1983) discovered that infants whose mothers spoke positively (rather than neutrally) about a stranger offered more toys to the stranger. The quality or security of the mother–infant relationship can also influence how infants reference the mother. Dickstein, Thompson, Estes, Malkin, and Lamb (1984) found that social referencing varied with the security of attachment in ways which reflected variations in the security provided by the mother's presence.

Conclusion

As this extensive review of research indicates, infants' stranger reactions reflect a surprisingly complex range of influences which arise from characteristics of the child, attributes of the stranger and the stranger's behavior, and the situational and psychological context in which this encounter occurs. Many of these influences are enduring (e.g., the child's temperament, biogenetic influences, etc.), some change over long periods (e.g., the infant's experiential history, the quality of the infant–mother relationship, etc.), while other influences are transient (e.g., short-term organismic condition) or situational (e.g., the stranger's behavior, characteristics of the setting, etc.). Most importantly, these influences not only affect stranger reactions in a direct, main-effects fashion, but they also interact complexly in their effects. The most temperamentally sociable child, for example, is unlikely to respond as positively toward a stranger when tired or hungry, or when the stranger behaves intrusively, as she does when the stranger's behavior is more gradual and low-key. However, this child is likely to be, on the whole, more outgoing than a child with different temperamental attributes. Understanding the complexity of these interactive influences, and their relative strengths in predicting stranger reactions, remains one of the most significant challenges facing developmental researchers in this area of research.

The study of stranger reactions has also revealed the complexity of the information processing which occurs during an infant's immediate encounter with an unfamiliar adult. Contrary to traditional views that it is the unfamiliarity of the adult *per se* which constitutes the basis for stranger anxiety or fear, researchers' current recognition of the diversity of infant responses to strangers and their complex origins has contributed to a new appreciation of the sophistication of the baby's appraisal of this event. To be sure, not all of the influences

Figure 5. Infants who can observe positive emotional cues from their care givers often respond more sociably to strangers than do infants whose care givers are more negative or fearful. In this picture, the mother's positive demeanor derives from her friendly conversation with the stranger. (Photograph courtesy of Ross A. Thompson)

outlined above are consciously apperceived or effortfully integrated. Nevertheless, the baby's capacity—short of a year of age—to integrate information concerning the familiarity of the adult partner with data concerning the stranger's behavior and characteristics, contextual demands and options, and cues from trusted care givers in responding to the stranger has contributed to a new, more complex view of the appraisal processes underlying socioemotional responses in infancy (see Thompson, in press).

Separation Reactions in Infancy

Compared with stranger reactions, considerably less research has been devoted to elucidating the origins and developmental course of infants' reactions to separations from their care givers. This may be due, in part, to the fact that research in this area has been considerably less controversial, with less confrontation between conflicting theoretical models. Nevertheless, the research in this area warrants a similar appreciation of the complexity of infants' appraisal processes in evaluating and integrating diverse organismic and situational influences. Just as stranger reactions do not derive merely from the perception of an unfamiliar adult, separation reactions are not simply a by-product of being apart from the care giver.

Conceptual and Methodological Issues

Conceptual Issues

At the outset, it is important to recognize that the study of separation reactions has focused on infants' *involuntary* separations from their care givers. These do not constitute the entire range of separation experiences in infancy, because with the growth of locomotor skills at the middle of the first year, infants commonly initiate voluntary separations from their care givers to explore new objects or settings (Rheingold & Eckerman, 1970, 1971). These self-initiated separations are typically nonstressful when the baby can reestablish physical or psychological contact at will (e.g., through looking back to the adult), and the distance from the care giver that infants will roam increases with the child's age (Rheingold & Eckerman, 1971). We will not comment further concerning self-initiated separations in infancy, but their common occurrence indicates that it is not separation *per se* which distresses infants, but rather involuntary separation from the care giver.

Separations also vary in their duration, from those lasting only a few minutes to separations lasting several weeks or more, often because of the hospitalization of either the child or the parent. Long-term separations have been of considerable interest to developmental and child-clinical psychologists because they reveal aspects of both attachment and detachment processes, they reflect the child's long-term efforts to cope with the emotions deriving from the separation experience, and they are relevant to practical problems of assisting children when such separations occur (see Bowlby, 1973, and Dunn, 1977, for reviews of this research). By contrast, short-term separations of several minutes or a few hours are experienced much more commonly (e.g., when children are in day care, left with a babysitter, or parents are briefly inaccessible at home), and study of this phenomenon can indicate the bases for developmental changes in naturally occurring separation reactions, the reasons for individual differences in these reactions, and the factors which contribute to increments or decrements in separation distress. Because the study of short-term separations provides greater insight into the factors which influence these normative developmental experiences of young children, they are the focus of the research review of this section.

Reactions to separation should be distinguished from reunion responses, although investigators commonly measure both. However, as students of infant–parent attachment have shown, the amount of distress exhibited during a separation episode does not enable researchers to accurately predict how the baby will greet the parent's subsequent arrival, although there are some links between the two (Thompson, Connell, & Bridges, 1988; Thompson & Lamb, 1984; see Ainsworth et al., 1978, and Lamb et al., 1985, for reviews). Some infants who exhibit intense separation distress respond with positive emotion and proximity-seeking efforts when the parent returns; others show angry, resistant behavior, and still others respond with marked passivity (Ainsworth et al., 1978). Because reunion behavior is a more valid and reliable indicator of the quality or security of the infant–parent relationship, attachment theorists have increasingly emphasized reunion over separation behavior in their assessments of attachment security. For other theoretical questions, however, a focus on separation reactions is more appropriate, and these constitute the concern of this research review.

Finally, some researchers distinguish between "separation distress" and "departure protest" (e.g., Kagan et al., 1978; Weinraub & Lewis, 1977). For these researchers, departure protest is defined as the child's distress when the mother is leaving; separation distress concerns the child's emotional response after mother has left the room. While the two are related both conceptually and empirically (e.g., a child who protests departure is also likely to show separation distress), there are important reasons for distinguishing them. For example, Kagan and his colleagues (1978) note that departure protest may depend cognitively on the child's capacity to predict a future event (related to the acquisition of an understanding of cause–effect relations)—that is, mother's absence—while this capacity is not essential to separation distress. Moreover, some children who protest the mother's departure settle comfortably after she has left, suggesting that emotional reactions to the *process* of leave-taking may be different from reactions to the *state* of separation (Weinraub & Lewis, 1977). Perhaps for these reasons, neither Weinraub and Lewis (1977) nor Gershaw and Schwarz (1971) found strong relations between the child's responses to departure and separation. However, because few researchers have operationally distinguished between the two, our review of research concerning separation reactions discusses research studies in which departure protest and separation distress are combined in measures of infants' behavior.

Methodological Issues

As we discovered to be true in the study of stranger reactions, the *context* in which an infant is separated from the care giver is an important influence on the child's response. Is the child left with a familiar and trusted partner, a stranger, or all alone? Does the separation occur in a familiar environment (e.g., at home) or an unfamiliar one? How far away is the care giver? Is the care giver's departure abrupt, gradual, or undisclosed until the infant happens to realize that the adult is absent? In some studies, for example, the child experiences a prolonged sequence of brief episodes involving permutations of separation episodes, stranger episodes, and episodes involving one or more care givers (sometimes in the presence of a stranger) (e.g., Fleener & Cairns, 1970; Fox, 1977; Kotelchuck, 1976; Lester *et al.*, 1974; Ross, Kagan, Zelazo, & Kotelchuck, 1975; Spelke, Zelazo, Kagan, & Kotelchuck, 1973). Added to these are considerations pertaining to the duration of the separation, the child's organismic state, and the influence of preceding events. As we shall see in the discussion of relevant research below, when these contextual and other influences have been specifically studied, in most cases they have had a significant influence on the child's separation reactions. Unfortunately, the studies in this area are uneven in the amount of relevant procedural detail researchers provide, and consequently it is sometimes difficult to determine the precise circumstances to which the baby responded in any specific separation episode.

Contrary to the study of stranger reactions, students of separation reactions employ univalent response measures which only index the quality or intensity of the child's distress response to separation. Although most researchers measure separation reactions by recording the amount of crying the child exhibits, some have used additional measures as convergent indices. These include measures of play behavior in the care giver's absence (e.g., Feldman & Ingham, 1975; Fox, 1977; Kotelchuck, 1976; Lester *et al.*, 1974; Maccoby & Feldman, 1972; Ross *et al.*, 1975; Weinraub & Lewis, 1977), search behavior and other active efforts to recover the adult (see Figure 6; e.g., Ainsworth *et al.*, 1978; Gershaw & Schwarz, 1971; Kotelchuck, 1976; Lester *et al.*, 1974; Maccoby & Feldman, 1972; Ross *et al.*, 1975), and the amount of the child's speech and movement in the room (Cox & Campbell, 1968; Feldman & Ingham, 1975). Perhaps because there is little ambiguity concerning the interpretation of these behavioral measures (e.g., distressed infants typically quit playing and search for the adult during separation episodes), autonomic measures have been infrequently used in studies of separation reactions (see Fox & Davidson, 1987, for one example using EEG).

Developmental Changes in Separation Reactions

In a number of studies of infants of various ages (using cross-sectional or longitudinal methodologies) and in various cultural contexts, the age of onset

FIGURE 6. The baby's search behaviors are a common index of separation reactions. (Photograph courtesy of Ross A. Thompson)

and the developmental course of distress reactions to separation episodes provide a picture of surprising consistency (Ainsworth, 1977; Emde *et al.*, 1976; Fleener & Cairns, 1970; Kagan, 1976; Kagan *et al.*, 1978; Kotelchuck, 1976; Lester *et al.*, 1974; Maccoby & Feldman, 1972; Ricciuti, 1974; Schaffer & Emerson, 1964; Stayton *et al.*, 1973; Tennes & Lampl, 1964). In general, infants show few signs of separation distress prior to 6½ to 7 months of age (but with a broad range of onset ages, from approximately 5 to 12 months), after which there is a linear increase in the proportion of infants exhibiting distress during separation episodes. The peak is usually reached just prior to or shortly after the end of the first year (between 10 and 18 months) with a subsequent decline in separation distress reactions.

This pattern of developmental change has been noted with fathers as well as with mothers (e.g., Kotelchuck, 1976; Schaffer & Emerson, 1964; but see Lester *et al.*, 1974); infants also protest separations from regular nonparental care givers (Fox, 1977). Interestingly, researchers who have examined the consistency of individual differences in separation protest across several months have found little consistency in these differences (Coates, Anderson, & Hartup, 1972; Kagan *et al.*, 1978; Maccoby & Feldman, 1972; but see Hyson & Izard, 1985). In other words, infants who protest separation at one age do not reliably tend to do so at a later age. Moreover, there is little support for a link between the occurrence of stranger wariness and separation distress: infants who show heightened fear in the presence of a stranger do not tend also to protest separations, even though these socioemotional phenomena show parallel patterns of developmental change (Emde *et al.*, 1976; Kagan *et al.*, 1978).

Influences on Separation Reactions

Because of these inconsistencies, researchers have been interested in what factors can account for individual differences in separation reactions observed among infants of a given age. Included among their investigations have been studies of the roles of infant gender and birth order, experiential background, the parent–infant relationship, immediate contextual influences, the parent's departure behavior, and other influences which may either intensify or diminish separation distress. (Do most of these influences sound familiar to the reader?)

Infant Gender and Birth Order

Although researchers sometimes hypothesize that female infants may be somewhat more prone to separation distress because of gender differences in how parents treat infants, two studies found exactly the opposite: boys cried more during separations (Feldman & Ingham, 1975; Tennes & Lampl, 1964). However, a much larger number of studies has found no gender differences in separation reactions (Fleener & Cairns, 1970; Fox, 1977; Hyson & Izard, 1985; Kotelchuck, 1976; Lester *et al.*, 1974; Maccoby & Feldman, 1972; Schaffer & Emerson, 1964; Weinraub & Lewis, 1977), indicating that it is probably wise to conclude that gender differences are negligible. In a similar manner, although Fox

(1977) found that firstborns exhibited greater separation distress in a study of infants on Israeli kibbutzim, neither Kagan *et al.* (1978), Corter, Rheingold, and Eckerman (1972) nor Schaffer & Emerson (1964) found any effects of birth order, suggesting that this variable also assumes little role in separation reactions.

Experiential Background

It is reasonable to expect that infants who have had considerably greater prior experience with routine separations from care givers would respond differently than infants who rarely experience separations. However, an understanding of the effects of experiential background on separation reactions remains elusive. In studies of the effects of day care, for example, researchers sought to determine whether infants who experienced routine separations from their parents in the context of day care responded with more or less distress to experimental separation episodes. In general, they found few differences between day-care and home-reared children in separation distress (see Belsky, 1988, and Clarke-Stewart & Fein, 1983, for reviews), even though day-care infants tend to respond differently upon reunion with their care givers (Belsky, 1988). Thus, routine separations in the context of day care do not heighten or diminish separation distress. Interestingly, Tulkin (1973) reported that infants of employed working-class mothers cried significantly less during experimental separation episodes compared with nonemployed working-class mothers, although he found no overall differences when he compared infants from working-class and middle-class families.

When more extreme variations in prior experience are compared, there is greater evidence that experiential background can influence separation reactions. Tizard and Tizard (1971), for example, compared 2-year-olds in a long-term residential nursery with home-reared children of the same age, and found that the nursery-reared children showed greater separation distress (and more wariness of strangers) than did the home-reared children. They attributed these differences to the fact that although the nursery-reared children experienced a broader range of social contacts than did home-reared children, they less commonly encountered the kinds of separation experiences and stranger interactions which were assessed by researchers and were thus more vulnerable to being distressed by them. The same interpretation has tended to characterize cross-cultural studies of separation reactions: despite great consistency in the developmental unfolding of separation distress responses noted above, infants in cultural settings which permit greater prior experience with brief separations tend to respond with less distress compared with infants in other cultures who have little prior experience of this kind (e.g., Ainsworth, 1977; Lester *et al.*, 1974; Miyake, Chen, & Campos, 1985; see Super, 1981, for a review). As Ainsworth (1977) has suggested, the infant's experiential background can contribute either to the development of social expectations that separations are common and that mother will return promptly or to expectations providing less confidence in the care giver's accessibility.

Thus, as we discovered to be true with stranger reactions, variations in experiential background within the normal range for American middle-class families do not seem to be associated with differences in separation distress. When more marked experiential differences are considered, however, infants with greater amounts of prior separation experience appear to respond with less distress to experimental separation episodes.

Parent–Infant Relationship

For many years, students of infant–parent attachment regarded the intensity of separation distress as a significant index of the strength of the attachment bond (e.g., Maccoby & Masters, 1970). As noted earlier, however, contemporary attachment theorists now focus on the nature of the infant's postseparation reunion responses as a more valid and reliable index of the security of infant–parent attachment (see Ainsworth et al., 1978). Perhaps for this reason, those investigators who have examined the links between separation distress and indices of the quality of the mother–infant relationship have not generally found strong links between them. Only a few of Schaffer and Emerson's (1964) measures of the mother–infant relationship were related to their index of separation distress, and Fleener and Cairns (1970) similarly found no association between maternal responsiveness to the infant's crying and measures of separation distress. Consequently, contrary to earlier views, there do not appear to be strong links between separation distress intensity and the nature of the mother–infant relationship (see, however, Thompson & Lamb, 1984, and Thompson et al., 1988).

Interestingly, there is some evidence that with respect to father–infant relationships, separation distress intensity may be negatively correlated with the degree of paternal involvement with the child (Spelke et al., 1973; see also Kotelchuck, 1976): infants with highly involved fathers tended to protest separation from them *less* than did infants with less involved fathers. Perhaps highly involved fathers foster confidence in offspring that they will return shortly; however, since these findings are somewhat counterintuitive, they should be interpreted cautiously until independently replicated.

Contextual Influences

An infant's gender and birth order, experiential background, and relationship with parents reflect relatively enduring characteristics which can influence separation reactions. Added to these are more transient contextual influences which may either diminish or intensify separation distress. Children respond with greater distress, for example, when the mother leaves them alone or with a stranger than when left in the company of the father (Cohen & Campos, 1978; Kotelchuck, 1976; Ross et al., 1975), siblings (Blurton Jones & Leach, 1972), or a regular nonparental care giver (Fox, 1977). The company of a stranger during a separation episode reduces distress for some children, while increasing it for others (see Figure 7; Ainsworth & Bell, 1970; Ainsworth & Wittig, 1969). Separation distress is greater in an unfamiliar laboratory environment than at home (Ross et al., 1975). At home, greater distress occurs when mother departs

FIGURE 7. For some infants, a stranger's presence reduces separation distress; for others, it increases distress. (Photograph courtesy of Ross A. Thompson)

through an atypical exit (e.g., a closet door) rather than a familiar one (Litten-berg, Tulkin, & Kagan, 1971), suggesting that the incongruity of the circum-stances can heighten separation reactions. In the laboratory, the availability of a novel, interesting toy during the separation period diminishes infant distress compared to conditions in which a familiar toy is unavailable (Corter *et al.*, 1972; Gershaw & Schwarz, 1971). Finally, Passman's studies indicate that infants and young children can effectively use security objects to foster their coping with separation episodes. Passman and Longeway (1982), for example, found that 2-year-olds who were given a clear photograph of their mothers during separation episodes played longer than those who had blurred, indistinct photographs.

Parental Departure Style

Among the most important of these contextual influences is the manner in which the care giver departs. Weinraub and Lewis (1977) observed mothers' spontaneous behavior while departing from their 2-year-olds in a laboratory separation episode and noted considerable diversity in their departure styles: some mothers slipped out unobtrusively, most mothers told the child they were leaving and would return, and some mothers provided more elaborated instruc-tions to offspring. These variations in departure style were related to children's separation distress: offspring were more likely to cry when mothers slipped out without explanation, but they cried less when mothers provided explanations and instructions to foster the child's understanding of the separation experience (see also Blurton Jones & Leach, 1972). The duration of verbal explanations may also be important, since Adams and Passman (1981) found that, in fostering the child's ease during separation, briefer, more direct verbal descriptions of the impending absence and return were more successful than lengthy, repetitive explanations. Field, Gewirtz, Cohen, Garcia, Greenberg, and Collins (1984) also found that children in nursery school were more likely to protest parental depar-ture when the parent used distraction techniques while leaving.

Thus, parents who provide the infant or young child with a cognitive struc-ture for interpreting the separation experience foster the child's coping with the separation. The effectiveness of verbal explanations during parental departures also varies with the age of the child: older children are likely to benefit from more sophisticated verbal instructions than are younger toddlers and infants. Marvin and Greenberg (1982) noted, for example, that when they were ques-tioned during a separation episode, 4-year-olds exhibited a more objective, less egocentric perspective toward mother's absence than did 3-year-olds, and they speculated that this difference may be related to the greater intellectual skills of the older child in understanding and using the verbal departure explanation provided by their mothers.

Conclusion

In the study of separation reactions, we find that it is not being apart from the care giver alone which reliably predicts an infant's emotional response, but rather the separation experience in conjunction with a particular situational and organismic context. Separations which are self-initiated, are brief in duration, occur in a familiar setting and in the company of a trusted adult, and which provide a structure for the child's coping through the provision of security objects or a verbal explanation during departure are less likely to provoke distress than are separations which are involuntary and long-term, occur in an unfamiliar environment, and are abrupt and unexpected. Several other factors which we earlier found to be influential in stranger reactions—such as the child's temperament and the effects of antecedent events—have not been studied in relation to separation reactions, but they would likely also play an important role in separation reactions.

Thus we again discover that an infant's reactions to social events are the result of a complex information-processing analysis of the event and its context, encompassing a surprising variety of internal as well as situational influences. While increasing researchers' appreciation of the sophistication of the baby's appraisal processes, this research literature also has important practical implications. Since separation experiences are common and inevitable for most infants in our society, an understanding of the contextual factors which either increase or diminish separation distress in infants and young children can assist children's coping with these experiences.

CONCLUDING COMMENTS: DIRECTIONS FOR FUTURE INQUIRY

In this review of research on "social anxiety" in infancy, we have discovered that even very young children are capable of remarkably competent appraisals of social situations involving encounters with unfamiliar adults and separations from care givers, and their emotional reactions to these events reflect an assessment not only of the immediate event but also of its broader situational context, and takes into consideration endogenous influences within the child (e.g., temperament, organismic condition, etc.) as well. This extensive research literature has been guided by diverse theoretical perspectives, but it contributes most to a view of the young child as a surprisingly sophisticated information processor who, with increasing age, becomes capable of appraising various aspects of social situations with greater speed and efficiency, yielding emotional responses which are more discriminating, multidimensional, and responsive to diverse influences in the social surround. Developmental changes in stranger and separation reactions arise partly because of the increasing capacity and efficiency of working memory, which enables the older infant to appraise social situations more quickly, relate this appraisal to an experiential history, and integrate this information en route to a socioemotional response. It is partly because of this emergent portrayal of the infant and toddler that earlier theoretical views which emphasized the growth of stranger anxiety and separation distress as simple biomaturational processes have been rejected in favor of views which underscore the multidimensionality of the infant's appraisal processes. This view has, in turn, increased developmentalists' appreciation of the intellectual sophistication of the infant and toddler and of the cognitive processes underlying early socioemotional behavior.

Although existing research yields considerable insight into the nature of stranger and separation reactions, this review has also highlighted a range of unanswered questions which remain for future study. In addition to these, several broader issues remain unexplored and merit the attention of developmental investigators. One of these issues concerns the waning of stranger wariness and separation distress with increasing age. Although a variety of theoretical perspectives address the emergence of stranger and separation reactions during the first 2 years, these viewpoints are surprisingly silent about why negative reactions decrease in frequency and intensity after 24 months of age. The research reviewed above suggests some reasons, however. With increasing age, for example, children become capable of understanding social situations with greater sophistication and skill, and they can draw upon a broader experiential background and emergent representational abilities to appraise these situations differently. During separation episodes, preschoolers can remain confident in mother's return by spontaneously recalling her departure explanations, remembering prior experiences of separation and reunion, and using comforting self-talk to cope with her absence. During stranger encounters, they can draw upon a broader range of social skills (including language) with which to interact with unfamiliar adults; they know that not all strangers pose threats; and they possess a greater repertoire of strategies for summoning assistance when confronted with an unfamiliar person. Together with their increased cognitive skills at appraising such social situations, these emergent capabilities better equip the young child to approach stranger and separation experiences with greater self-confidence and self-control.

One important difference between the young preschooler and the infant or toddler is that the older child possesses a broader repertoire of emotional regulatory strategies, and this undoubtedly also contributes to the waning of manifest expressions of stranger or separation distress. The study of emotional regulation, and how it can account for developmental changes as well as individual differences in stranger and separation reactions, constitutes a second critically important research agenda for this field. Although the preschooler has greater knowledge of emotional regulatory strategies which can be deliberately used in arousing conditions (e.g., distraction, self-talk and other self-comforting behaviors, etc.), we know surprisingly little about how these regulatory strategies develop and their influence in emotionally arousing situations. Moreover, the origins of individual differences in regulatory styles or strategies have also received little attention, despite their importance to an understanding of personality and social functioning in the early years (Thompson, in press). In this regard, it is noteworthy that nearly all researchers have studied stranger and separation reactions only with regard to dependent indices of distress or wariness, without pursuing further an analysis of how infants and young children cope with the negative arousal which is provoked by a stranger encounter or a separation episode. What do infants do during separation episodes, for example, and how is this related to fluctuations in their distress during mother's absence? Greater attention to the emergence and functioning of emotional reg-ulatory strategies throughout the early years would better contribute to an un-derstanding of how infants and young children can cope with these naturally occuring social experiences.

A third and final area of much-needed further research concerns the infor-mation-processing bases of emotional reactions to strangers and separation ex-periences. We have argued throughout this review that some of the develop-mental changes in stranger and separation reactions researchers have observed may derive from the increased complexity, speed, and efficiency of working memory during the early years (Case, 1984, 1985). The efficiency of information processing is a significant constituent of emotional reactions, because most affec-tive reactions require both an increase in organismic arousal and, for many, an "arousal jag" which precipitates the subjective experience of emotion (cf. Berlyne, 1960, 1969). When organisms require considerable time to process and integrate their perceptions of situational events, organismic arousal may be dampened and the arousal jag diminished, resulting in more subdued emotional reactions. Thus, one reason why younger infants tend to show diminished stranger and separation reactions may be that they require greater time to in-terpret and integrate information concerning their current circumstances, and when these circumstances change, further processing is required. As a conse-quence, emotional arousal may be diminished, distracted, or subdued.

In our research, we have studied the temporal and intensive features of the emotional reactions of different infant populations during stranger encounters and separation episodes to examine some of the information-processing constit-uents of these socioemotional behaviors. In one study, Thompson, Cicchetti, Lamb, and Malkin (1985) compared the emotional reactions of Down syndrome infants during the Strange Situation procedure with those of two groups of normal infants. One group was approximately the same chronological age as the Down syndrome babies, while the other normal group was approximately the same mental age. As earlier noted, the Strange Situation is commonly used to index variations in the security of infant–parent attachment, and it involves repeated encounters with a female stranger as well as two brief separations from the mother (see Ainsworth et al., 1978). When facial and vocal measures of emotion were compared, the Down syndrome infants evinced less intense sepa-ration reactions, longer latencies to their onset, briefer recoveries, and a dimin-ished range and lability of responding compared with each group of normal infants. Comparisons of their reactions to strangers showed similar differences. Thompson and his colleagues (1985) suggested that the more subdued emo-tional reactions and flattened socioemotional variability of the Down syndrome infants could be attributable both to physiological differences (i.e., the bio-chemical functioning of Down syndrome infants contributes to more subdued organismic activation) and cognitive information-processing factors: the cog-nitive retardation of Down syndrome infants contributes to a slower and less efficient processing of social events.

More recently, we have examined developmental changes in the temporal and intensive features of emotional reactions to stranger and separation episodes throughout the first year. Infants at 6, 9, and 12 months of age experienced a period of mother–infant play and subsequently were exposed to a standard, graduated stranger-approach sequence while seated on their mothers' laps. Following another play period, mother left the room so their separation responses could be observed. From ratings of both facial and vocal reactions, there were clear developmental changes in the quality of emotional responding in this longitudinal sample: with increasing age, infants not only showed greater amounts of stranger wariness and separation distress (as expected), but they also responded more quickly, and with greater intensity and persistence. In addition, during the stranger encounters, the rise-time in emotional reactions also increased, perhaps reflecting the older infant's continued appraisal of the unfamiliar adult. Taken together, the developmental changes we observed seem to reflect important links between the speed and efficiency of the child's processing of social conditions and the emotional responses which ensue. They suggest that with increasing age, infants are capable of appraising social circumstances more quickly, monitoring them more efficiently, and responding to changing circumstances with greater efficiency than younger infants, and this is reflected in their emotional behavior.

Thus while much is known about the nature of separation and stranger reactions in infancy, there remains a considerable research agenda for future study. Part of what continues to motivate researchers in this area is that the study of these socioemotional behaviors provides a valuable window into broader aspects of early emotional and personality development. As we look closely at a young child's reactions to these commonly occuring social events, we gain greater insights into how the child is constituted as a socioemotional being.

References

Adams, R. E., Jr., & Passman, R. H. (1981). The effects of preparing two-year-olds for brief separations from their mothers. *Child Development, 52,* 1068–1070.

Ainsworth, M. D. S. (1973). The development of infant–mother attachment. In B. Caldwell & H. Ricciuti (Eds.), *Review of child development research* (Vol. 3, pp. 1–94). Chicago: University of Chicago Press.

Ainsworth, M. D. S. (1977). Infant development and mother–infant interaction among Ganda and American families. In P. H. Leiderman, S. R. Tulkin & A. Rosenfeld (Eds.), *Culture and infancy: Variations in the human experience* (pp. 119–149). New York: Academic Press.

Ainsworth, M. D. S., & Bell, S. M. (1970). Attachment, exploration, and separation: Illustrated by the behavior of one-year-olds in a strange situation. *Child Development, 41,* 49–67.

Ainsworth, M. D. S., Blehar, M. C., Waters, E., & Wall, S. (1978). *Patterns of attachment.* Hillsdale, NJ: Erlbaum.

Ainsworth, M. D. S., & Wittig, B. A. (1969). Attachment and exploratory behavior of one-year-olds in a strange situation. In B. M. Foss (Ed.), *Determinants of infant behavior IV* (pp. 111–136). London: Methuen.

Batter, B. S., & Davidson, C. V. (1979). Wariness of strangers: Reality or artifact? *Journal of Child Psychology and Psychiatry, 20,* 93–109.

Beckwith, L. (1972). Relationships between infants' social behavior and their mothers' behavior. *Child Development, 43,* 397–411.

Belkin, E. P., & Routh, D. K. (1975). Effects of presence of mother versus stranger on behavior of three-year-old children in a novel situation. *Developmental Psychology, 11*, 400.

Belsky, J. (1988). The "effects" of infant day care reconsidered. *Early Childhood Research Quarterly, 3*, 235–272.

Benjamin, J. D. (1961). Some developmental observations relating to the theory of anxiety. *American Psychoanalytic Association Journal, 9*, 652–668.

Berlyne, D. E. (1960). *Conflict, arousal and curiosity.* New York: McGraw-Hill.

Berlyne, D. E. (1969). Laughter, humor and play. In G. Lindzey & E. Aronson (Eds.), *Handbook of social psychology* (2nd ed., Vol. 3, pp. 795–852). Reading, MA: Addison-Wesley.

Bischof, N. (1975). A systems approach toward the functional connections of attachment and fear. *Child Development, 46*, 801–817.

Blurton Jones, N., & Leach, G. M. (1972). Behaviour of children and their mothers at separation and greeting. In N. Blurton Jones (Ed.), *Ethological studies of child behaviour* (pp. 217–247). Cambridge: Cambridge University Press.

Boccia, M. L., & Campos, J. J. (April, 1984). *Maternal emotional signalling: Its effect on infants' reaction to strangers.* Paper presented to the meeting of the Society for Research in Child Development, Detroit.

Bowlby, J. (1969). *Attachment and loss: Vol. 1. Attachment.* London: Hogarth.

Bowlby, J. (1973). *Attachment and loss: Vol. 2. Separation.* London: Hogarth.

Bowlby, J. (1980). *Attachment and loss: Vol. 3. Loss.* London: Hogarth.

Bretherton, I. (1978). Making friends with one-year-olds: An experimental study of infant–stranger interaction. *Merrill-Palmer Quarterly, 24*, 29–51.

Bretherton, I., & Ainsworth, M. D. S. (1974). Responses of one-year-olds to a stranger in a strange situation. In M. Lewis & L. Rosenblum (Eds.), *The origins of fear* (pp. 131–164). New York: Wiley.

Brody, S., & Axelrad, S. (1971). Maternal stimulation and social responsiveness of infants. In H. R. Schaffer (Ed.), *The origins of human social relations* (pp. 195–215). London: Academic Press.

Bronson, G. W. (1972). Infants' reactions to unfamiliar persons and novel objects. *Monographs of the Society for Research in Child Development, 37* (Serial No. 148).

Bronson, G. W., & Pankey, W. B. (1977). On the distinction between fear and wariness. *Child Development, 48*, 1167–1183.

Brooks, J., & Lewis, M. (1976). Infants' responses to strangers: Midget, adult, and child. *Child Development, 47*, 323–332.

Brossard, M. D. (1974). The infant's conception of object permanence and his reactions to strangers. In T. G. Decarie (Ed.), *The infant's reaction to strangers* (pp. 97–116). New York: International Universities Press.

Cairns, R. B. (1966). Attachment behavior of mammals. *Psychological Review, 73*, 409–426.

Campos, J. J., Emde, R. N., Gaensbauer, T., & Henderson, C. (1975). Cardiac and behavioral interrelationships in the reactions of infants to strangers. *Developmental Psychology, 11*, 589–601.

Campos, J. J., & Stenberg, C. R. (1981). Perception, appraisal and emotion: The onset of social referencing. In M. Lamb & L. Sherrod (Eds.), *Infant social cognition: Empirical and theoretical considerations* (pp. 273–314). Hillsdale, NJ: Erlbaum.

Case, R. (1984). The process of stage transition: A neo-Piagetian view. In R. J. Sternberg (Ed.), *Mechanisms of cognitive development* (pp. 19–44). New York: Freeman.

Case, R. (1985). *Intellectual development: A systematic reinterpretation.* New York: Academic Press.

Chisholm, J. S. (1981). Residence patterns and the environment of mother–infant interaction among the Navajo. In T. M. Field, A. M. Sostek, P. Vietze, & P. H. Leiderman (Eds.), *Culture and early interactions* (pp. 3–19). Hillsdale, NJ: Erlbaum.

Cicchetti, D. (in press). The organization and coherence of socioemotional, cognitive, and representational development: Illustrations through a developmental psychopathology perspective on Down syndrome and child maltreatment. In R. A. Thompson (Ed.), *Socioemotional development. Nebraska Symposium on Motivation* (Vol. 36). Lincoln, NE: University of Nebraska Press.

Clarke-Stewart, K. A. (1978). Recasting the lone stranger. In J. Glick & K. A. Clarke-Stewart (Eds.), *The development of social understanding* (pp. 109–176). New York: Gardner Press.

Clarke-Stewart, K. A. (1988). "The 'effects' of infant day care reconsidered" reconsidered: Risks for parents, children, and researchers. *Early Childhood Research Quarterly, 3*, 293–318.

Clarke-Stewart, K. A., & Fein, G. G. (1983). Early childhood programs. In P. H. Mussen (Ed.), *Handbook of child psychology: Vol. II. Infancy and developmental psychobiology* (pp. 917–999). New York: Wiley.

Clarke-Stewart, K. A., Umeh, B. J., Snow, M. E., & Pederson, J. A. (1980). Development and prediction of children's sociability from 1 to 2½ years. *Developmental Psychology, 16*, 290–302.

Coates, B., Anderson, E. P., & Hartup, W. W. (1972). The stability of attachment behaviors in the human infant. *Developmental Psychology, 6*, 231–237.

Cohen, L. J., & Campos, J. J. (1978). Father, mother, and stranger as elicitors of attachment behaviors in infancy. *Developmental Psychology, 10*, 146–154.

Collard, R. R. (1968). Social and play responses of first-born and later-born infants in an unfamiliar situation. *Child Development, 39*, 325–334.

Corter, C. M. (1973). A comparison of the mother's and a stranger's control over the behavior of infants. *Child Development, 44*, 705–713.

Corter, C. M., Rheingold, H. L., & Eckerman, C. O. (1972). Toys delay the infant's following of his mother. *Developmental Psychology, 6*, 138–145.

Cox, F. N., & Campbell, D. (1968). Young children in a new situation with and without their mothers. *Child Development, 39*, 123–131.

Davidson, R. J., & Fox, N. A. (1988). Cerebral asymmetry and emotion: Developmental and individual differences. In S. Segalowitz & D. Molfese (Eds.), *Developmental implications of brain lateralization* (pp. 191–206). New York: Guilford.

Decarie, T. G. (1974). Manifestations, hypotheses, data. In T. G. Decarie (Ed.), *The infant's reaction to strangers* (pp. 7–55). New York: International Universities Press.

Dickstein, S., Thompson, R. A., Estes, D., Malkin, C., & Lamb, M. E. (1984). Social referencing and the security of attachment. *Infant Behavior and Development, 7*, 507–516.

Dunn, J. (1977). *Distress and comfort*. Cambridge, MA: Harvard University Press.

Eckerman, C. O., & Rheingold, H. (1974). Infants' exploratory responses to toys and people. *Developmental Psychology, 2*, 255–259.

Eckerman, C. O., & Whatley, J. L. (1975). Infants' reactions to unfamiliar adults varying in novelty. *Developmental Psychology, 11*, 562–566.

Emde, R. N., Gaensbauer, J. J., & Harmon, R. J. (1976). Emotional expressions in infancy: A biobehavioral study. *Psychological Issues, 10*, Monograph 37.

Feinman, S. (1985). Emotional expression, social referencing, and preparedness for learning in early infancy—mother knows best, but sometimes I know better. In G. Zivin (Ed.), *The development of expressive behavior* (pp. 291–318). New York: Academic Press.

Feinman, S., & Lewis, M. (1983). Social referencing at ten months; A second-order effect on infants' responses to strangers. *Child Development, 54*, 878–887.

Feiring, C., Lewis, M., & Starr, M. D. (1984). Indirect effects and infants' reaction to strangers. *Developmental Psychology, 20*, 485–491.

Feldman, S. S., & Ingham, M. E. (1975). Attachment behavior: A validation study in two age groups. *Child Development, 46*, 319–330.

Ferrari, M. (1981). An observation of the infant's response to strangers: A test for ecological validity. *Journal of Genetic Psychology, 139*, 157–158.

Field, T., Gewirtz, J. L., Cohen, D., Garcia, R., Greenberg, R., & Collins, K. (1984). Leave-takings and reunions of infants, toddlers, preschoolers, and their parents. *Child Development, 55*, 628–635.

Fleener, D. E., & Cairns, R. B. (1970). Attachment behaviors in human infants: Discriminative vocalization on maternal separation. *Developmental Psychology, 2*, 215–223.

Ford, M. E., & Thompson, R. A. (1985). Perceptions of personal agency and infant attachment: Toward a life-span perspective on competence development. *International Journal of Behavioral Development, 8*, 377–406.

Fox, N. A. (1977). Attachment of kibbutz infants to mother and metapelet. *Child Development, 48*, 1228–1239.

Fox, N. A., & Davidson, R. J. (1984). Hemispheric substrates of affect: A developmental model. In N.

A. Fox & R. J. Davidson (Eds.), *The psychobiology of affective development* (pp. 353–381). Hillsdale, NJ: Erlbaum.

Fox, N. A., & Davidson, R. J. (1987). Electroencephalogram assymmetry in response to the approach of a stranger and maternal separation in 10-month-old infants. *Developmental Psychology, 23,* 233–240.

Freedman, D. G. (1961). The infant's fear of strangers and the flight response. *Journal of Child Psychology and Psychiatry, 2,* 242–248.

Freedman, D. G. (1974). *Human infancy: An evolutionary perspective.* Hillsdale, NJ: Erlbaum.

Frodi, A. (1983). Attachment behavior and sociability with strangers in premature and fullterm infants. *Infant Mental Health Journal, 4,* 13–22.

Gaensbauer, T. J., Emde, R. N., & Campos, J. J. (1976). "Stranger" distress: Confirmation of a developmental shift in a longitudinal sample. *Perceptual and Motor Skills, 43,* 99–106.

Gershaw, N. J., & Schwarz, J. C. (1971). The effects of a familiar toy and mother's presence on exploratory and attachment behaviors in young children. *Child Development, 42,* 1662–1666.

Gesell, A., Ilg, F. L., & Ames, L. B. (1943). *Infant and child in the culture of today.* New York: Harper and Row.

Gewirtz, J. L. (1972). Attachment, dependence, and a distinction in terms of stimulus control. In J. L. Gewirtz (Ed.), *Attachment and dependency* (pp. 179–215). Washington, DC: Winston.

Gewirtz, J. L., & Nogueras, M. (April, 1988). *Do infant protests/distress during maternal departures and separations have a learned basis?: How mothers contribute to their children's separation difficulties.* Paper presented at the meeting of the International Conference on Infant Studies, Washington, DC.

Goulet, J. (1974). The infant's conception of causality and his reactions to strangers. In T. G. Decarie (Ed.), *The infant's reactions to strangers* (pp. 59–96). New York: International Universities Press.

Greenberg, D. J., Hillman, D., & Grice, D. (1973). Infant and stranger variables related to stranger anxiety in the first year of life. *Developmental Psychology, 9,* 207–212.

Greenberg, M. T., & Marvin, R. S. (1982). Reactions of preschool children to an adult stranger: A behavioral systems approach. *Child Development, 53,* 481–490.

Harmon, R. J., Morgan, G. A., & Klein, R. P. (1977). Determinants of normal variation in infants' negative reactions to unfamiliar adults. *Journal of the American Academy of Child Psychiatry, 16,* 670–683.

Hebb, D. O. (1946). On the nature of fear. *Psychological Review, 53,* 259–276.

Hebb, D. O. (1949). *The organization of behavior.* New York: Wiley.

Hinde, R. A. (1974). *The biological bases of human social behaviour.* New York: McGraw-Hill.

Horner, T. M. (1980). Two methods of studying stranger reactivity in infants: A review. *Journal of Child Psychology and Psychiatry, 21,* 203–219.

Hyson, M. C., & Izard, C. E. (1985). Continuities and changes in emotion expressions during brief separation at 13 and 18 months. *Developmental Psychology, 21,* 1165–1170.

Kagan, J. (1974). Discrepancy, temperament, and infant distress. In M. Lewis & L. Rosenblum (Eds.), *The origins of fear* (pp. 229–248). New York: Wiley.

Kagan, J. (1976). Emergent themes in human development. *American Scientist, 64,* 186–196.

Kagan, J., Kearsley, R. B., & Zelazo, P. R. (1978). *Infancy: Its place in human development.* Cambridge, MA: Harvard University Press.

Kinsbourne, M., & Bemporad, B. (1984). Lateralization of emotion: A model and the evidence. In N. A. Fox & R. J. Davidson (Eds.), *The psychobiology of affective development* (pp. 259–291). Hillsdale, NJ: Erlbaum.

Klinnert, M. D., Campos, J. J., Sorce, J. F., Emde, R. N., & Svejda, M. (1983). Emotions as behavior regulators: Social referencing in infancy. In R. Plutchik & H. Kellerman (Eds.), *Emotion: Theory, research and experience: Vol. 2. Emotions in early development* (pp. 57–86). New York: Academic Press.

Konner, M. J. (1972). Aspects of the developmental ethology of a foraging people. In N. Blurton Jones (Ed.), *Ethiological studies of child behaviour* (pp. 285–304). Cambridge: Cambridge University Press.

Kotelchuck, M. (1976). The infant's relationship to the father: Experimental evidence. In M. E. Lamb (Ed.), *The role of the father in child development* (pp. 329–344). New York: Wiley.

Lamb, M. E., & Bornstein, M. H. (1987). *Development in infancy: An introduction* (2nd Ed.). New York: Random House.

Lamb, M. E., Hwang, C. P., Frodi, A., & Frodi, M. (1982). Security of mother– and father–infant attachment and its relation to sociability with strangers in traditional and nontraditional Swedish families. *Infant Behavior and Development, 5,* 355–367.

Lamb, M. E., Thompson, R. A., Gardner, W., & Charnov, E. L. (1985). *Infant–mother attachment.* Hillsdale, NJ: Erlbaum.

Lerner, J. V., & Lerner, R. M. (1983). Temperament and adaptation across life: Theoretical and empirical issues. In P. B. Baltes & O. G. Brim (Eds.), *Life-span development and behavior* (Vol. 5, pp. 197–231). New York: Academic Press.

Lester, B. M., Kotelchuck, M., Spelke, E., Sellers, M. J., & Klein, R. E. (1974). Separation protest in Guatemalan infants: Cross-cultural and cognitive findings. *Developmental Psychology, 10,* 79–85.

Levitt, M. J. (1980). Contingent feedback, familiarization, and infant affect: How a stranger becomes a friend. *Developmental Psychology, 16,* 425–432.

Lewis, M., & Brooks, J. (1974). Self, other, and fear. In M. Lewis & L. A. Rosenblum (Eds.), *The origins of fear* (pp. 195–227). New York: Wiley.

Lewis, M., & Michalson, L. (1983). *Children's emotions and moods.* New York: Plenum.

Littenberg, R., Tulkin, S. R., & Kagan, J. (1971). Cognitive components of separation anxiety. *Developmental Psychology, 4,* 387–388.

Maccoby, E. E., & Feldman, S. S. (1972). Mother-attachment and stranger-reactions in the third year of life. *Monographs of the Society for Research in Child Development, 37,* (Serial No. 146).

Maccoby, E., & Masters, J. C. (1970). Attachment and dependency. In P. H. Mussen (Ed.), *Carmichael's manual of child psychology* (3rd Ed., pp. 73–157). New York: Wiley.

Mahler, M. S. (1974). Symbiosis and individuation: The psychological birth of the human infant. *The Psychoanalytic Study of the Child, 29,* 89–106.

Mahler, M., Pine, F., & Bergman, A. (1975). *The psychological birth of the human infant.* New York: Basic Books.

Main, M. (1983). Exploration, play, and cognitive functioning related to infant–mother attachment. *Infant Behavior and Development, 6,* 167–174.

Main, M., & Weston, D. R. (1981). The quality of the toddler's relationship to mother and to father: Related to conflict behavior and the readiness to establish new relationships. *Child Development, 52,* 932–940.

Marvin, R. S., & Greenberg, M. T. (1982). Preschoolers' changing conceptions of their mothers: A social-cognitive study of mother–child attachment. In D. Forbes & M. T. Greenberg (Eds.), *Children's planning strategies* (pp. 47–60). San Francisco: Jossey-Bass.

McCall, R. B., & McGhee, P. E. (1977). The discrepancy hypothesis of attention and affect in infants. In I. C. Uzgiris & F. Weizmann (Eds.), *The structuring of experience* (pp. 179–210). New York: Plenum.

Miyake, K., Chen, S., & Campos, J. J. (1985). Infant temperament, mother's mode of interaction, and attachment in Japan: An interim report. In I. Bretherton & E. Waters (Eds.), *Growing points of attachment theory and research. Monographs of the Society for Research in Child Development, 50* (Serial No. 209), 276–297.

Morgan, G. A., Levin, B., & Harmon, R. J. (1975). Determinants of individual differences in infants' reactions to unfamiliar adults. *JSAS Catalog of Selected Documents in Psychology, 5,* 277 (Ms. No. 1006).

Morgan, G. A., & Ricciuti, H. N. (1969). Infants' responses to strangers during the first year. In B. M. Foss (Ed.), *Determinants of infant behavior IV* (pp. 253–272). London: Methuen.

Morris, E. D., & Redd, W. H. (1975). Children's performance and social preference for positive, negative, and mixed adult–child interactions. *Child Development, 46,* 525–531.

Paradise, E. B., & Curcio, F. (1974). Relationship of cognitive and affective behaviors to fear of strangers in male infants. *Developmental Psychology, 10,* 476–483.

Passman, R. H., & Longeway, K. P. (1982). The role of vision in maternal attachment: Giving 2-year-olds a photograph of their mother during separation. *Developmental Psychology, 18,* 530–533.

Plomin, R. (1986). *Development, genetics, and psychology.* Hillsdale, NJ: Erlbaum.

Plomin, R., & Rowe, D. C. (1979). Genetic and environmental etiology of social behavior in infancy. *Developmental Psychology, 15,* 62–72.

Provence, S., & Lipton, R. C. (1962). *Infants in institutions.* New York: International Universities Press.

Rafman, S. (1974). The infant's reaction to imitation of the mother's behavior by the stranger. In T. G. Decarie (Ed.), *The infant's reaction to strangers* (pp. 117–148). New York: International Universities Press.

Rajecki, D. W., Lamb, M. E., & Obmascher, P. (1978). Toward a general theory of infantile attachment: A comparative review of aspects of the social bond. *The Behavioral and Brain Sciences, 3,* 417–464.

Rheingold, H. L. (1961). The effect of environmental stimulation upon social and exploratory behavior in the human infant. In B. M. Foss (Ed.), *Determinants of infant behavior I* (pp. 143–170). New York: Wiley.

Rheingold, H. L. (1969). The effect of a strange environment on the behavior of infants. In B. M. Foss (Ed.), *Determinants of infant behavior IV* (pp. 137–166). London: Methuen.

Rheingold, H. L. (1974). General issues in the study of fear. In M. Lewis & L. Rosenblum (Eds.), *The origins of fear* (pp. 249–254). New York: Wiley.

Rheingold, H. L., & Eckerman, C. O. (1970). The infant separates himself from his mother. *Science, 168,* 78–83.

Rheingold, H. L., & Eckerman, C. O. (1971). Departures from the mother. In H. R. Schaffer (Ed.), *The origins of human social relations* (pp. 73–78). London: Academic Press.

Rheingold, H. L., & Eckerman, C. O. (1973). Fear of the stranger: A critical examination. In H. W. Reese (Ed.), *Advances in child development and behavior* (Vol. 8, pp. 185–222). New York: Academic Press.

Ricciuti, H. N. (1974). Fear and the development of social attachments in the first year of life. In M. Lewis & L. A. Rosenblum (Eds.), *The origins of fear* (pp. 73–106). New York: Wiley.

Roedell, W. C., & Slaby, R. G. (1977). The role of distal and proximal interaction in infant social preference formation. *Developmental Psychology, 13,* 266–273.

Ross, G., Kagan, J., Zelazo, P., & Kotelchuck, M. (1975). Separation protest in infants in home and laboratory. *Developmental Psychology, 11,* 256–257.

Ross, H. S. (1975). The effects of increasing familiarity on infants' reactions to adult strangers. *Journal of Experimental Child Psychology, 20,* 226–239.

Ross, H. S., & Goldman, B. D. (1977). Infants' sociability toward strangers. *Child Development, 48,* 638–642.

Scarr, S., & Salapatek, P. (1970). Patterns of fear development during infancy. *Merrill-Palmer Quarterly, 16,* 53–90.

Schaffer, H. R. (1966). The onset of fear of strangers and the incongruity hypothesis. *Journal of Child Psychology and Psychiatry, 7,* 95–106.

Schaffer, H. R. (1971). Cognitive structure and early social behaviour. In H. R. Schaffer (Ed.), *The origins of human social relations* (pp. 247–262). London: Academic Press.

Schaffer, H. R. (1974). Cognitive components of the infant's response to strangeness. In M. Lewis & L. Rosenblum (Eds.), *The origins of fear* (pp. 11–24). New York: Wiley.

Schaffer, H. R., & Emerson, P. E. (1964). The development of social attachments in infancy. *Monographs of the Society for Research in Child Development, 29* (Serial No. 94).

Schaffer, H. R., Greenwood, A., & Parry, N. H. (1972). The onset of wariness. *Child Development, 43,* 165–175.

Skarin, K. (1977). Cognitive and contextual determinants of stranger fear in six- and eleven-month-old infants. *Child Development, 48,* 537–544.

Smith, P. K., Eaton, L., & Hindmarch, A. (1982). How one-year-olds respond to strangers: A two-person situation. *Journal of Genetic Psychology, 140,* 147–148.

Sorce, J. F., & Emde, R. N. (1981). Mother's presence is not enough: Effect of emotional availability on infant exploration. *Developmental Psychology, 17,* 737–745.

Sorce, J. F., Emde, R. N., & Frank, M. (1982). Maternal referencing in normal and Down's Syndrome infants: A longitudinal study. In R. N. Emde & R. Harmon (Eds.), *Attachment and affiliative systems* (pp. 281–292). New York: Plenum.

Spelke, E., Zelazo, P., Kagan, J., & Kotelchuck, M. (1973). Father interaction and separation protest. *Developmental Psychology, 9,* 83–90.

Spitz, R. A. (1950). Anxiety in infancy: A study of its manifestations in the first year of life. *International Journal of Psycho-Analysis, 31,* 138–143.

Spitz, R. A. (1965). *The first year of life.* New York: International Universities Press.

Sroufe, L. A. (1977). Wariness of strangers and the study of infant development. *Child Development, 48,* 731–746.

Sroufe, L. A., Waters, E., & Matas, L. (1974). Contextual determinants of infant affective response. In M. Lewis & L. Rosenblum (Eds.), *The origins of fear* (pp. 49–72). New York: Wiley.

Stayton, D. J., Ainsworth, M. D. S., & Main, M. B. (1973). Development of separation behavior in the first year of life: Protest, following, and greeting. *Developmental Psychology, 9,* 213–225.

Stevenson, M. B., & Lamb, M. E. (1979). Effects of infant sociability and the caretaking environment on infant cognitive performance. *Child Development, 50,* 340–349.

Super, C. M. (1981). Behavioral development in infancy. In R. H. Munroe, R. L. Munroe, & B. B. Whiting (Eds.), *Handbook of cross-cultural human development* (pp. 181–270). New York: Garland STM Press.

Tennes, K. H., & Lampl, E. E. (1964). Stranger and separation anxiety. *Journal of Nervous and Mental Disease, 139,* 247–254.

Thomas, A., Chess, S., Birch, H. G., Hertzig, M. E., & Korn, S. (1963). *Behavioral individuality in early childhood.* New York: New York University Press.

Thompson, R. A. (1983). The father's case in child custody disputes: The contributions of psychological research. In M. E. Lamb & A. Sagi (Eds.), *Fatherhood and family policy* (pp. 53–100). Hillsdale, NJ: Erlbaum.

Thompson, R. A. (1988). The effects of infant day care through the prism of attachment theory: A critical appraisal. *Early Childhood Research Quarterly, 3,* 273–282.

Thompson, R. A. (in press). Emotion and self-regulation. In R. A. Thompson (Ed.), *Socioemotional development. Nebraska Symposium on Motivation* (Vol. 36). Lincoln, NE: University of Nebraska Press.

Thompson, R. A., Cicchetti, D., Lamb, M. E., & Malkin, C. (1985). Emotional responses of Down syndrome and normal infants in the Strange Situation: The organization of affective behavior in infants. *Developmental Psychology, 21,* 828–841.

Thompson, R. A., Connell, J. P ., & Bridges, L. J. (1988). Temperament, emotion, and social interactive behavior in the Strange Situation: A component process analysis of attachment system functioning. *Child Development, 59,* 1102–1110.

Thompson, R. A., & Frodi, A. M. (1984). The sociophysiology of infants and their caregivers. In W. M. Waid (Ed.), *Sociophysiology* (pp. 87–113). New York: Springer-Verlag.

Thompson, R. A., & Lamb, M. E. (1982). Stranger sociability and its relationships to temperament and social experience during the second year. *Infant Behavior and Development, 5,* 277–287.

Thompson, R. A., & Lamb, M. E. (1983). Security of attachment and stranger sociability in infancy. *Developmental Psychology, 19,* 184–191.

Thompson, R. A., & Lamb, M. E. (1984). Assessing qualitative dimensions of emotional responsiveness in infants: Separation reactions in the Strange Situation. *Infant Behavior and Development, 7,* 423–445.

Tizard, J., & Tizard, B. (1971). The social development of two-year-old children in residential nurseries. In H. R. Schaffer (Ed.), *The origins of human social relations* (pp. 147–163). London: Academic Press.

Trause, M. A. (1977). Stranger responses: Effects of familiarity, stranger's approach, and sex of infant. *Child Development, 48,* 1657–1661.

Tulkin, S. R. (1973). Social class differences in attachment behaviors of ten-month-old infants. *Child Development, 44,* 171–174.

Waters, E., Matas, L., & Sroufe, L. A. (1975). Infants' reactions to an approaching stranger: Description, validation, and functional significance of wariness. *Child Development, 46,* 348–356.

Weinraub, M., & Lewis, M. (1977). The determinants of children's responses to separation. *Monographs of the Society for Research in Child Development, 42* (Serial No. 172).

Weinraub, M., & Putney, E. (1978). The effects of height on infants' social responses to unfamiliar persons. *Child Development, 49,* 598–603.

Weisberg, P. (1975). Developmental differences in children's perferences for high- and low-arousing forms of contact stimulation. *Child Development, 46,* 975–979.

Zahn-Waxler, C., Cummings, E. M., Iannotti, R. J., & Radke-Yarrow, M. (1984). Young offspring of depressed parents: A population at risk for affective problems. In D. Cicchetti & K. Schneider-Rosen (Eds.), *Childhood depression* (pp. 81–105).San Francisco: Jossey-Bass.

4

Temperament, Behavioral Inhibition, and Shyness in Childhood

Mary K. Rothbart and Jennifer Alansky Mauro

One of the major advances of science in this century has been our increased understanding of the molecular basis of the genetic code. In the same century, advances in the neurosciences and in the employment of behavioral genetic techniques have allowed psychologists to consider more seriously the possibility of biologically based contributions to personality dispositions. These individual differences, called *temperament*, have proven to be of increasing interest and importance to students of socioemotional development. McCall (in Goldsmith *et al.*, 1987) has recently synthesized current definitions of temperament as

> relatively consistent, basic dispositions inherent in the person that underlie and modulate the expression of activity, reactivity, emotionality, and sociability. Major elements of temperament are present early in life, and those elements are likely to be strongly influenced by biological factors. As development proceeds, the expression of temperament increasingly becomes more influenced by experience and context. (p. 524)

If we are to accept the reality of early temperamental differences in activity, reactivity, emotionality, and sociability, we would expect them to contribute strongly to the development of social fear; indeed, during the period of infancy, we would expect measures of fear in social situations to be strongly reflective of early temperamental dispositions.

In this chapter, we explore the constructs of behavioral inhibition, shyness, fear, and social anxiety that can be seen to overlap with components of temperament during the period of early childhood. We then relate these constructs to dimensions of temperamental variability. Theoretical and measurement issues in the study of behavioral inhibition and shyness are then discussed, and research on the early development of these dispositions is reviewed. We then consider biological perspectives on behavioral inhibition and shyness, including animal

---

Mary K. Rothbart and Jennifer Alansky Mauro • Department of Psychology, University of Oregon, Eugene, Oregon 97403.

models and developmental behavioral genetics approaches. Finally, we attempt to relate early individual differences in temperament to the development of childhood psychopathology.

Kagan, Reznick, and Snidman (1986) define *behavioral inhibition* as "the tendency to display or not to display an initial period of inhibition of speech and play, associated with a retreat to a target of attachment, when the child encounters an unfamiliar or challenging event" (p. 54). As the name of this construct suggests, Kagan *et al.* define behavioral inhibition strictly in behavioral, not physiological, terms, although they have related it to underlying physiology. The construct of behavioral inhibition has to date been applied to temperamental individual differences in early childhood, as seen between the ages of 14 months and 5 years.

In the construct of *shyness*, on the other hand (Jones, Cheek, & Briggs, 1986), the situation or context is not so general as to include all novel and challenging conditions but is constrained to include only social stimulation. Definitions of shyness also usually add an element of felt discomfort to elements of behavioral inhibition. Thus, Briggs and Smith (1986) define shyness as "discomfort and inhibition in the presence of others" (p. 629). Buss (1985) also includes discomfort and inhibition in his definition of shyness, and he adds that shyness may also include withdrawal, reticence, inhibition of speech and gestures (similar to the definition of behavioral inhibition given above) fear, feelings of vulnerability, lowered self-esteem, and arousal of the autonomic nervous system.

When Buss considers arousal of the autonomic nervous system to be a defining aspect of shyness, his definition includes all three of the major response systems often identified in definitions of *fear*: "Fear is commonly thought of as a valid reaction to genuine threat that involves at least 3 response systems: a) overt behavioral expressions, b) covert, subjective feelings and thoughts, and c) physiological activity" (Graziano, DeGiovanni, & Garcia, 1979, p. 805).

When we now consider definitions of *social anxiety*, we note that important cognitive components are added to the elements we have already listed:

> This condition is characterized by heightened physiological arousal when in social situations, a fear of negative evaluation by others, a high likelihood of negative expectations regarding the ability to interact with others and in some cases, deliberate avoidance of the threatening situations. (Beidel, Turner, & Dancu, 1985, p. 109)

Reviewing these definitions, we can identify four sets of related responses to novelty and social challenge: the first is behavioral, including inhibition of speech, gestures, and motor activity, and sometimes withdrawal. Behavioral aspects are included in definitions of all of these constructs. The second set includes negative emotional reactions. These are not included in the definition of behavioral inhibition (although sometimes they are included in the operationalization of behavioral inhibition; see the discussion of this research below), but they are included in all other constructs. The third set includes physiological arousal, especially arousal of the autonomic nervous system or its sympathetic branch, which is again not included in the explicit definition of the behavioral inhibition construct (although often studied along with behavioral inhibition) but is included in all other constructs. The fourth set comprises responses that are cognitive, including expectations of negative evaluation from others or from the self, and this set appears to be unique to the social anxiety construct. We may thus identify a kind of ordinal scale of social inhibition and anxiety constructs based upon the response systems involved, with social anxiety seen as the most inclusive, shyness and fear as intermediary, and behavioral inhibition as the most narrow. On the basis of the context for anxiety, however, fear and behavioral inhibition are more general constructs than shyness and social anxiety; both fear and behavioral inhibition include reactions to events going beyond social situations.

We can now consider dimensions of temperament that may be related to one or more of these sets of responses. Relevant temperamental dimensions would include behavioral inhibition, originally observed by Schaffer (1974) as wariness in infants' behavioral reactions to novelty during the last half of the first year of life. Whereas a 5-month-old infant approaches novel objects rapidly and impulsively, by 8 months of age, the infant may approach a novel object only slowly or with some hesitancy, or not at all (see also Rothbart, 1988b). Another relevant temperamental disposition is Thomas and Chess' (1977) construct of approach–withdrawal, defined as

> the nature of the initial response to a new stimulus, be it a new food, new toy or new person. Approach responses are positive, whether displayed by mood expression (smiling, verbalizations, etc.) or motor activity (swallowing a new food, reaching for a new toy, active play, etc.). Withdrawal reactions are negative, whether displayed by mood expression (crying, fussing, grimacing, verbalizations, etc.) or motor activity (moving away, spitting new food out, pushing new toy away, etc.) (p. 21)

This construct is quite similar to that of fear, as employed by Rothbart (1981; Rothbart & Derryberry, 1981) and Goldsmith and Campos (1982). The major difference is that Rothbart and Goldsmith and Campos employ a separate construct for smiling and laughter or joy, rather than including this dimension with the fear construct, as do Thomas and Chess.

To the extent that the constructs of behavioral inhibition, shyness, fear, and social anxiety also include felt or expressed negative affect, we would expect the child's general distress proneness or negative emotionality to be related to them (Bates, 1987, 1989; Buss & Plomin, 1984; Rothbart, 1989a). Finally, we might expect that individual differences in attentional control (the shifting and focusing of attention) would affect both the child's soothability when experiencing social distress and the more cognitive aspects of anxiety, but we would not expect it to match the constructs directly. Temperamental individual differences in flexibility and control of attention are important both in their influence upon recovery from negative emotion (soothability) in infancy (Rothbart, 1989a), and in their relationship to the individual's ability to shift away from a negative focus in adolescence and adulthood (Derryberry & Rothbart, 1988; Mathews & MacLeod, 1986). These temperamental characteristics may be seen to be biologically based, and at least for the dimensions of negative emotionality and behavioral inhibition, they show considerable longitudinal stability once they have appeared in development (Buss & Plomin, 1984; Rothbart, 1989a).

Given this degree of overlap across dimensions of temperament and social fearfulness, we now discuss the early development of behavioral inhibition and shyness, assuming that these constitute early assessments of temperament as well as social fear. We will not discuss the development of negative emotionality and attention directly, because one of us has reviewed them in detail elsewhere (Rothbart, 1989a).

BEHAVIORAL INHIBITION

The most extensive research done on behavioral inhibition in young children has been the longitudinal work begun by Cynthia Garcia-Coll with 21-month-old infants and continued by Kagan and his colleagues. Since this work constitutes the major corpus of research available on behavioral inhibition, we review it here in detail. This detailed exposition will also allow us to discuss differences in Kagan et al.'s use of the behavioral inhibition construct as the child grows older.

In Garcia-Coll, Kagan, and Reznick's (1984) initial report, extreme groups of 21-month-old children on a dimension of inhibition to unfamiliarity were identified. A large sample of 305 infants was first screened by asking the children's mothers to describe their child's reaction in eight settings (meeting unfamiliar children, visiting the doctor, etc.). Children reported as showing withdrawal to four or more of these situations were considered as candidates for falling into the behaviorally inhibited category; children who approached in seven or more situations were considered as candidates for being behaviorally uninhibited. These inhibited and uninhibited children, as seen by their mothers, were then brought into the laboratory for further assessment as they engaged in free play, separation from the mother, interaction with a strange adult, and exposure to a novel toy (a robot). Indices of inhibition in the laboratory included withdrawal, clinging to the mother, crying, inhibition of play, facial and vocal expressions of distress, and extended latency to approach a novel person or object. Infants who displayed nine or more of these behaviors were classified as behaviorally inhibited; those who displayed two or fewer as uninhibited. The inhibited group included 33 children (11% of the original sample); the uninhibited group included 38 children (12% of the original sample). Heart and respiration rate of each child was also monitored while the child was exposed to a series of familiar and unfamiliar slides, linguistic phrases, and environmental sounds. Inhibited children by the behavioral criterion were found to have higher and more stable heart rates than their uninhibited peers.

These extreme groups of infants were again observed at a little under 3 years (31 months) of age (Kagan et al., 1984). At 31 months, the children were observed at home while engaged in free play, in play with an unfamiliar peer, and while listening to a story accompanied by slides. Most of the variables scored for the home and peer episodes involved the latency and frequency of approaches to a novel person or object. A moderate correlation was found between the infants' behavior in the laboratory at 21 months and their behavior at home ($r = .39$) and with an unfamiliar peer ($r = .66$) at 31 months. Kagan *et al.* reported some stability over time for inhibition, especially in predicting children's behavior with the unfamiliar peer, but this finding should be interpreted with caution, because the sample had been reduced to only 21 children for the peer interaction measure. No relation between inhibition and heart rate was found at 31 months, and no stability across time was found for heart rate. On the basis of these data, Kagan *et al.* (1984) argued that between the ages of 2 and 4 years, the child's reaction to an unfamiliar peer becomes a more appropriate index of behavioral inhibition than exposure to unfamiliar toys, settings, or adults. At least as operationalized, then, the behavioral inhibition construct becomes constrained by social setting to become more like a shyness construct.

The longitudinal sample was next assessed when they were 4 years old (Kagan *et al.*, 1984). Kagan *et al.* (1986) argue that between 4 and 6 years, behavioral inhibition can be best measured in a variety of settings: inhibited children are expected to continue to be cautious around others and quick to retreat from unfamiliar settings. In addition, however, they may become concerned with others' evaluations of them, which might result in reluctance to attempt difficult cognitive tasks or a tendency to direct frequent glances at individuals in the position of evaluating the child. Note that by age 4, the assessments are thus moving toward assessments of social evaluation anxiety. At 4 years, Kagan *et al.* asked the children and their parents to make two visits to the laboratory and to participate in a number of cognitive tasks while heart rate was monitored. Assessment now stressed children's reactions to cognitively challenging or difficult stimuli, and children were observed matching familiar figures, engaging in memory tasks, constructing a car from blocks, and taking several subtests of a commonly used IQ test. Tasks were chosen because they were expected to challenge most of the children, and coding included number of glances to the mother and examiner, number of times the child failed to answer a question, and gross motor movements. Children were also exposed to a story accompanied by slides about a fearful and fearless child, and to a series of slides depicting both active and passive scenes, with the amount of time spent looking at active versus passive stimuli being recorded.

Peer play episodes used were similar to earlier assessments, with measures of latency to approach objects or the other child, proximity to the mother, and frequency of staring at the other child combined to form an inhibition index and an uninhibited index. During the cognitive tasks, children in the inhibited group had more stable and higher heart rates and showed fewer gross motor movements. They also looked more frequently at the examiner and refused to answer more questions than their uninhibited peers (Kagan *et al.*, 1984). The inhibited group also had a higher frequency of fears, nightmares, sleeplessness, and constipation, according to maternal interview. This group looked at passive pictures longer and talked about them more than for active pictures. It should be noted that although Kagan *et al.* (1984) might have expected the behaviorally inhibited children to have been especially concerned about adult evaluation, there was little evidence of this.

Stability of inhibition classification between 21 months and 4 years was most strong if the infants had steady heart rates and had been classified as being inhibited at 21 months. If the children were classified as being inhibited at 21 months, but did not have steady heart rates, then the likelihood of them being classified as inhibited at 4 years was smaller.

The most recent follow-up of this longitudinal sample was done when the children were 5½ years old (Reznick *et al.*, 1986). As at the 4-year assessment, heart and respiration rates were monitored during difficult cognitive tasks, subjects played with an unfamiliar peer, and there was a maternal interview. In addition, pupil dilation during selected cognitive tasks, willingness to perform physically risky behaviors such as walking a balance beam and climbing bars, and two school observations were added to this phase of assessment. In school observations, amount and type of interaction of the subject with other children in the classroom were coded.

Variables from peer play, lab, school observations, risk avoidance episodes and number of looks at the examiner in the cognitive tasks were combined to form an inhibition index used in some of the analyses. Reznick *et al.* (1986) found stability for inhibition classification in that 78% of those children classified as inhibited at 21 months remained in that category at age 5, even though a number of quite different assessments of behavioral inhibition were used at the latter time.

The inhibition group as determined at 21 months also had more stable heart rates at 5½ years on all episodes in the laboratory, and they also had increased pupil dilation. Pupil dilation was unrelated to current inhibition or earlier heart rate stability, however. The consistent relation between heart rate stability and inhibition was also seen as reflecting consistency in the structure of behavioral inhibition across age.

In an attempt to replicate Kagan *et al.*'s findings from the longitudinal sample, Reznick, Gibbons, Johnson, & McDonough (1990) studied a sample of infants who did not represent extremes of inhibition, but constituted a normative sample. Infants in this sample were assessed at 14, 20, and 32 months of age. At 14 and 20 months, infants participated in a number of laboratory episodes, six of which focused on inhibition. Infants at first played in the laboratory, followed by the experimenter hanging a dog mask in the corner of the room (used only at 14 months). Later, a stranger entered the room and eventually tried to hand a toy to the child. The final two episodes involved an alarm clock being set off in the room while the child was playing and the child being shown a large toy robot.

At 14 and 20 months, infants were scored on behaviors later grouped into two categories, approach–withdrawal and negative affect (cry or fret). The negative affect variable was found to be positively correlated with inhibition at 14 months and 20 months, but it did not separately predict inhibition at 20 months. In addition, a composite index of inhibition and negative affect was no more accurate at predicting future inhibition than the inhibition index alone, and the negative affect component was therefore dropped from the analysis. Play sessions at 32 months included three children (one inhibited, one uninhibited, one neither, as determined at the earlier ages) of the same gender who played together for 30 minutes. Latency to leave the parent, touch a toy, enter a plastic tunnel and approach another child, frequency of approaching another child, taking an object away from a child, entering the tunnel, and entering another child's territory were coded. In addition, duration of staring at a child and proximity to the parent were coded as well as the total amount of time spent in social interaction with another child.

Having eliminated distress from the operationalization of the construct, Reznick *et al.* define inhibition as "emphasizing vulnerability to the uncertainty caused by unfamiliar events that cannot be assimilated easily," and they stress that the term represents "the construct of interest, rather than shyness, fearfulness or timidity." As in Kagan's work, Reznick *et al.* believe that inhibition can best be shown by one set of behaviors at one age and another set of behaviors at another age. Thus at 14 months, inhibition may be best demonstrated by general fear items, such as exposing the child to a dog mask, and at 32 months by placing the child in a social setting with an unfamiliar peer. The eliciting stimuli (and the consequent behavior) change over development.

Approximately 15% of this sample could be classified as being inhibited. The variables scored as inhibited at 14 and 20 months (proximity to parent, latency to touch toy, etc.) posed a problem for determining an uninhibited group for 32 months, however, in that frequency distributions did not allow for this classification. This problem was solved by using variables (time playing with the peer, approaches to the peer, etc.) that had a more normal distribution than time in proximity to parent or latency to touch a toy. The measure thus became more one of uninhibited behavior than of inhibition.

In addition to exploring the relationship between inhibition and other aspects of temperament, this study sought to replicate Kagan *et al.*'s findings on the stability of inhibition. When data from only the two extreme groups were examined, the correlations across age for inhibition indexes were .68 between 14 and 20 months, .71 between 20 and 32 months, and .66 between 14 and 32 months. The stability correlations for the entire sample ranged from .06 to .39, and Reznick *et al.* argue that there is greater stability if the child is more extreme on the inhibition measure. As a replication, it is important to note that the episodes in this study were not identical to those used by Kagan and that the inhibition indexes differed between ages of assessment and between studies. Children in extreme groups were also more likely to drop out of the sample, thus reducing the sample size as well as possibly biasing the composition of the groups.

ISSUES IN THE ASSESSMENT OF BEHAVIORAL INHIBITION

Two important issues in the assessment of behavioral inhibition are, first, whether distress is to be included in the construct and, second, whether behavioral inhibition refers to only a small, extreme group of children (categorical assessment) or to a dimension on which a general sample of children can be ordered (dimensional assessment). The distress question is important, because its resolution has implications for whether behavioral inhibition can be seen to be similar to the constructs of fear and shyness, which include distress. This issue may in part be related to methodological issues. Shyness is often assessed in adults (Cheek & Buss, 1981; Jones, Briggs, & Smith, 1986), and adults can be asked whether they experience feelings of discomfort when introduced to strangers. In an infant, frank distress expressions in the presence of a novel person or object can also be coded, and distress often accompanies the child's withdrawal from the person or inhibition of approach (Sroufe, 1979). By the time the child is 32 months old, however, there may be little direct expression of distress, while at the same time the child may be feeling discomfort that we are unable to measure. We cannot assess these internal states in the toddler because, to date, self-report on emotion is not a viable assessment technique at this age.

In our research, we have developed a care giver report measure, the Children's Behavior Questionnaire, which assesses shyness as well as other temperamental characteristics for children age 3 to 7 years (Rothbart, 1988a). Our shyness scale includes items assessing children's latency to approach other people and their apparent comfort or discomfort in situations where they might need to approach others. For this scale, items assessing latency to approach were positively correlated with items dealing with discomfort. Similarly, in developing the Infant Behavior Questionnaire (IBQ; Rothbart, 1981) Fear scale, another care giver report measure, we had originally attempted to develop two scales, one assessing children's negative affect to novelty or challenge, and the other, children's latency to approach novel persons or objects. We could not develop enough items to assess these dimensions separately with acceptable internal reliability, but the two classes of items were positively related to each other and, once we combined them, it was possible to develop a scale with good internal reliability (Rothbart, 1981). Again, the two sets of items, latency and negative affect, were positively correlated.

Thus, in the IBQ, mothers' observations of frank distress were positively related to the child's latency to approach; in the Children's Behavior Questionnaire, mothers' judgments of their child's discomfort in novel social situations were also positively related to latency to approach. Finally, for a small sample of longitudinal subjects assessed with the IBQ during infancy and followed up at age 7, early mother ratings of fear at 6, 10, and 13 months (but not at 3 months) were significantly positively correlated with mothers' later ratings of shyness. In our work, then, as well as in other research assessing fear in humans (Goldsmith & Campos, 1982) and in nonhuman primates (Higley & Suomi, in press), inhibition and distress *can* be combined to form a single construct. This view is, of course, quite different from the position taken by Reznick *et al.* (in press), who would wish to characterize behavioral inhibition in terms of interest rather than as a fear-related dimension. Nevertheless, Reznick *et al.'s* own findings for infants at both 14 and 20 months were that inhibition and distress were positively correlated.

Another approach to methodological problems in assessing discomfort in toddlers might be to use psychophysiological measures such as Galvanic Skin Response, which have been associated with ratings of fear (Buck, 1988), concurrently with measures of behavioral inhibition. In this regard, Kagan, Reznick, and Snidman (1987) have already found that measures of sympathetic nervous system function, such as high heart rate, which might be taken as indicants of fear reactions, are positively related to inhibition. We will see below that in studies with rhesus monkeys using a behavioral inhibition paradigm, the construct has alternatively been called timidity or anxiety (Higley & Suomi, 1989). Researchers using an animal model thus also include negative affect within the construct under study. We would argue that duration of interest may be a temperamental dimension worth studying, but that research results on the behavioral inhibition construct suggest that it is related to distress and should be seen as having close ties to constructs of shyness and social fear.

A second issue in the assessment of behavioral inhibition has to do with whether the construct is only applicable to a group of 10 to 15% of the children at the two extremes of the measure (categorical assessment), or whether the dimension can be applied to the complete range of children. In Thomas and Chess' (1977) approach–withdrawal construct and our (Rothbart & Derryberry, 1981) and Goldsmith and Campos' (1982) fear dimension, we would expect the construct to apply to the full range of infants and young children. One kind of evidence that would support the use of behavioral categories would be evidence of distributions that are bi- or trimodal, with extreme groups of children forming separate distributions at the extremes of the population. We have not seen such evidence put forward, and since our own data do not suggest the existence of separate diagnostic groups, we feel more comfortable applying the construct to the general population of children.

SHYNESS AND SOCIAL ANXIETY

Arnold Buss (1980, 1985, 1986) has made an important contribution to our understanding of the development of shyness and behavioral inhibition. In his theory of the development of shyness, he posits two kinds of shyness: one is seen to develop early, and this he calls fearful shyness. The second kind is later-developing and is called self-conscious shyness. Early-developing shyness is similar to the behavioral inhibition described above, assuming, however, that we can continue to include its distress component. In Buss' theory, this fearful shyness is seen to develop during the last half of the first year, to wane over time for most young children, but for some children to persist. Buss argues that later in development, fearful shyness is demonstrated not in overt distress, but "by the inhibition of speech and behavior interactions that are typical of adult shyness" (Buss, 1985, p. 40). Buss also argues that fearful shyness will later become a kind of social anxiety where the person becomes distressed at being evaluated when meeting others.

Buss then describes later-developing shyness, called self-conscious shyness, as being characterized by sensitivity, inhibition or disorganization of social behavior when the individual is exposed to the scrutiny of others. Buss suggests that this kind of shyness emerges around the age of 5 years, when mothers begin to regularly report instances of social embarrassment in their children (Buss, Iscoe, & Buss, 1979). He suggests that this self-conscious shyness may result from the association between being scrutinized and being criticized or ridiculed, and by a person's feelings of being different or conspicuous by reason of race, gender, or other characteristics. He suggests that self-conscious shyness is especially likely to be elicited in formal contexts where the person is interacting with a high-status individual.

Conceptually, we have some difficulty in distinguishing the social anxiety aspect of early-appearing (fearful) anxiety as described by Buss from his later-appearing self-conscious shyness. It would be conceptually simpler, we think, to include social anxiety related to evaluation with the construct of self-conscious rather than fearful shyness, and to see self-conscious shyness (including evaluation apprehension) as developing later than infancy, at a time when the child has become sensitive to the evaluations of others.

Buss further suggests that self-conscious shyness develops when the child has attained an "advanced, cognitive" self (Buss, 1985, p. 43). Research in social cognition suggests that children's concept of self as enduring over time and across situations and as including inherent personal qualities (personality traits) does not develop in our society until ages 7 to 9 (Rholes & Ruble, 1984; Rotenberg, 1982). Thus, the kind of self-consciousness seen in children at age 5 may be related to their sensitivity to criticism, but it also may not require a high level of cognitive sophistication in thinking about the self. Nevertheless, when this sophistication develops, we expect that children would become increasingly vulnerable to negative feelings related to their self-worth, and this appears to be the case (Harter, 1983).

For our understanding of the relation between temperament and social anxiety, Buss' two varieties of shyness are of special interest because the first, fearful shyness, would be seen as temperamentally based. Of the two varieties of shyness, it is relatively early appearing and does not seem to have been influenced by the experience of criticism, as does self-conscious shyness. It is also very similar to Thomas and Chess' (1977) approach–withdrawal dimension and our (Rothbart, 1981) and Goldsmith and Campos' (1984) dimension of fear. The later-developing, self-conscious shyness as described by Buss would be seen more as an aspect of personality than temperament. It is presumably strongly determined by experience, and it is related to a cognitive structure, the representation of self, that would be seen to go beyond the domain of temperamental differences.

A retrospective study in which college students' self-report of their current and previous shyness was investigated has provided some support for Buss' theory (Cheek, Carpentieri, Smith, Rierdan, & Koff, 1986). Students reported whether they now considered themselves shy, and whether there had been a previous time in their lives when they considered themselves to be shy. Of the subjects in this study, 43% reported current shyness, 41% reported previous but not current shyness, and 16% reported they had never considered themselves shy. Among the currently shy students, 45% reported they first became shy before the age of 6, while among the currently not-shy students, only 21%

reported early shyness. Cheek *et al.* take this finding as support for Buss' theory, suggesting that early-appearing shyness, as might be expected of a temperamentally related dimension is more developmentally stable than later appearing shyness.

To the extent that fearful shyness is temperamentally based, we also need to consider the specificity of shyness (and behavioral inhibition) to social as opposed to nonsocial stimuli. Buss (1986) argues that fearful shyness is different from other fears in that it is a social anxiety. To what extent is fear of people independent of other fears or from a general temperamental dimension of fearfulness?

During childhood, we have addressed the question of the relationship between social and nonsocial fear by assessing both shyness and nonsocial, general fearfulness in the Children's Behavior Questionnaire, a parent report instrument (Rothbart, 1988a). In a sample of 235 subjects age 3–7 years, including a large group of children who were twins, we have found a low but significant correlation (r = .18) between the two scales. For a sample of 80 singleton 6–7 year olds, the correlation between the scales was moderate in size (r = .36). We have also developed a self-report temperament questionnaire which we have used with a sample of over 90 early adolescents (Capaldi & Rothbart, 1988). This measure also assesses shyness in a scale separate from general fearfulness. Again, the two scales are positively correlated (r = .48). This early adolescence scale is of special interest, because it allowed us to gather self-reports from subjects about their own felt shyness, and we also administered a highly abbreviated version of the adolescent shyness scale and adapted it to parent's independent report. This allowed us to compare the two scale scores, parent-report and self-report, with one another. The two scales indeed proved to be positively correlated with each other (r = .46).

In a further development of our adult temperament measure (Derryberry & Rothbart, 1988), we have also separated out shyness from general nonsocial fear items and, as in parents' reports for young children and early adolescents' self-report, have found them to be positively correlated for a sample of 90 college students. Thus, in general, our results suggest that shyness and nonsocial fearfulness are positively related, and that temperamentally, shyness may be seen as one manifestation of a general tendency toward fearfulness. The most useful way to think about social fear or shyness might be to say that although we might think about it as being related to general fear, it is also possible to assess it separately, depending on the research questions we are interested in addressing (Rothbart, 1989b).

Unlike the constructs of behavioral inhibition, shyness, and social fear, social anxiety and Buss' later-developing self-conscious shyness, with their cognitive and evaluative content, may be said to be nontemperamental. Thus, although a predisposition to negative emotionality may lead a child to frequently experience negative affect in the presence of others and thus to develop negative expectancies about others and about the child's ability to deal with them, it is also possible that a child temperamentally low in susceptibility to distress may develop negative expectancies and self-evaluations. These may result from frequent negative experiences when others express criticism or dissatisfaction with the child. It is also possible that children who have a great deal of difficulty shifting attention away from a negative focus may be predisposed toward anxiety. In this case, individual differences in the focusing and shifting of attention would make a contribution to children's susceptibility to anxiety.

BIOLOGICAL MODELS FOR BEHAVIORAL INHIBITION

Ever since the pioneering work of Calvin Hall (1936), it has been suggested that a rat's ambulatory activity and defecation in an open (novel) field is a measure of that animal's reactivity or emotionality. King and Appelbaum (1973) have determined, however, that the measures of rat emotionality that show decrements over time (as would be expected when the animal becomes more familiarized to the setting and hence less fearful of its novelty or strangeness) are not general activity and defecation, but instead include time to emerge from the home cage and time to traverse the runway to the field. These measures show strong similarity to the nondistress aspects of the construct of behavioral inhibition.

Behavioral inhibition has also been studied using the rhesus monkey as a model, although sometimes the process studied has been called anxiety (Suomi, 1984, 1986), timidity, or reactivity (Higley, & Suomi, 1989). Measures of behavioral inhibition, timidity, or reactivity in rhesus monkeys assess fearfulness or anxiety in novel or challenging situations and behavioral withdrawal in social interaction. Specific measures have included maintenance of proximity to an attachment object (Suomi, 1983), latency to approach stimuli in a novel situation, initiation of interaction with unfamiliar individuals (Thompson, Higley, Byrne, Scanlan & Suomi, 1986), and assessments of anxiety (oral behaviors, handwringing and self-clasping, immobility, huddling, and distress vocalizations) to social separation (Mineka, Suomi, & DeLizio, 1981; Suomi, Kraemer, Baysinger & De-Lizio, 1981). These measures correspond to the assessments of behavioral inhibition in human children, with the exception of the anxious behaviors to social separation.

Suomi and his associates, like Kagan *et al.* (1986), have suggested that the indicators of anxiety in rhesus monkeys tend to change over age. For the monkeys, signs of anxiety during separation are the indicators most frequently found in infancy (Higley & Suomi, 1989). Later, behavioral withdrawal, flight, and immobility in novel or challenging situations is seen relatively more often in highly reactive monkeys. Thompson *et al.* (1986) found that ratings of fearfulness and consolability when exposed to a novel room during the first month predicted reactions to unfamiliar peers and objects in a novel room at 4 months, with monkeys who were more reactive at the younger age later showing longer latency to explore the room and objects in it, a longer time in close proximity to their surrogate mother, and more time observing the peer monkey exploring the room.

Neonatal ratings of fearfulness and consolability also predicted ratings of despair during a social separation when the animals were 6 months old (Becker, Suomi, Marra, Higley, & Brogan, 1984), and Higley and Suomi (1989) have suggested that there may also be a correlation in humans between behavioral inhibition and susceptibility to depressive reactions. Higley (1985) has also reported that measures of fearfulness and anxiety in the home cage (oral behaviors, clasping, and immobility) showed stability from 9 months (rhesus monkey infancy) to 18 months (childhood) to 30 months (early adolescence), and he found a positive correlation between signs of anxiety in infancy and behaviors indicative of despair at adolescence.

Just as rodents have been bred for reactivity in open field tests (Blizard, 1981), Suomi and his colleagues have also bred rhesus monkeys high and low in behavioral inhibition. In one study, these high- and low-inhibited animals were then cross-fostered to mothers high and low in maternal skills. Whereas there were no main effects or interactions for rearing conditions of the monkeys, the animals who had been bred for behavioral inhibition later showed less exploration and more stereotypical movement in a separation situation, more ventral–ventral proximity when placed in a living unit with peers, and more initiation of aggression to other group members (Champoux & Suomi, 1986; Suomi, Champoux, Higley, Scanlan, & Schneider, 1986).

Although evidence for rearing effects was not found for this highly selected sample, there is also suggestive evidence that rearing conditions may influence behavioral inhibition in infant rhesus monkeys (Higley & Suomi, 1989). Peer-raised monkeys, who spent their first month in a nursery with or without a surrogate mother and who were then housed in groups of four infants without adults, showed high levels of inhibition in comparison with mother-reared infants. Thus, at a time when monkeys raised with mothers were showing much less of their early ventral clinging, peer monkeys continued to show extended clinging (Chamove, Rosenblum, & Harlow, 1973; Harlow, 1969; Hirsch, Higley & Suomi, 1986), often continuing this behavior into their second and third years (Higley, 1985). These behaviors are especially likely to occur with the appearance of a stranger or the occurrence of novel sounds in the home cage. Higley, Danner, and Hirsch (1988) have also found that in an adaptation of Ainsworth's Strange Situation to rhesus monkeys, peer-reared infants are more likely to remain close to a favorite peer and to explore the environment and interact with the stranger less.

Thus the rhesus monkey studies of behavioral inhibition also provide evidence for a biologically based predisposition that shows considerable stability across the life span. In addition, correlations between behavioral inhibition and separation anxiety and later susceptibility to depression suggest the possibility that this variable may also be related to depression in humans as well.

BEHAVIORAL GENETICS APPROACHES

Traits related to shyness, such as sociability, extraversion, and emotionality, have been studied extensively in the behavior genetics literature, with moderate heritability for these factors found throughout the life span (see reviews in Buss & Plomin, 1984; Plomin & Daniels, 1986). However, shyness itself has received less attention in behavior genetics studies. The few studies that have examined a genetic component of shyness have varied greatly in their definition of shyness, and many rely on questionnaires with very few items, or questionnaires designed to measure constructs other than shyness as their source of data. In the majority of twin studies conducted, correlations for shyness ratings between monozygotic twins are consistently higher than those between dizygotic twins. These studies typically employ parent-report questionnaires or interviews, often using the Emotionality, Activity, Sociability and Impulsivity (EASI) sociability scale. As the child approaches adolescence, the self-report Cattell 16 PF Scale is most often used.

The most extensive study in this literature is the Colorado Adoption Project (CAP) carried out by Plomin and his associates (Daniels & Plomin, 1985; Plomin & DeFries, 1985)). The sample included over 200 infants between the ages of 12 and 24 months, from both adoptive and nonadoptive families. Infant shyness was assessed by a five-item sociability scale on the Colorado Childhood Temperament Inventory. The sociability scale on the Colorado Childhood Temperament Inventory consists of items ranging from general sociability (child is very sociable, makes friends easily, is friendly with strangers) to behavioral inhibition (takes a long time to warm up to strangers) and shyness (child tends to be shy). In addition, each parent filled out the Cattell 16 PF Scale including a shyness factor and a second-order extraversion factor, as well as the sociability scale from the EASI questionnaire on both themselves and their spouses. Finally, the Family Environment Scale (FES) and Home Observation for Measurement of the Environment (HOME) were used to assess the infant's home environment.

Results from this project indicated that both genetic and socialization variables played a role in the origin of infant shyness. Perhaps the most exciting result found by the CAP was a significant correlation between biological mothers' shyness and sociability and their infants' shyness at 24 months, a correlation found for both adoptive and nonadoptive families. The finding for adoptive families is especially impressive since the biological parents' self-report was filled out before the birth of the child, and the child's ratings were filled out by their adoptive parents over 24 months later. This relationship was found at 24 months, but not at 12 months. The inability to discover a relationship between infant shyness at 12 months and maternal personality may be due to behavioral and emotional developmental changes that occur in the child between the first and second year of life. This finding suggests the presence of a genetic component for shyness in young children, and it also indicates the genetic comparability between infant shyness and low sociability in the adults' self-report.

For both adoptive and nonadoptive families, parental ratings of infant shyness were also found to be related to mothers' self-reports of shyness, low sociability, and introversion, thereby suggesting the influence of shared home environment. In particular, a Personal Growth factor from the FES Cohesion Scale was found to be related to infant shyness. Families who score high on this factor are active in cultural events, like to learn new things, and are involved in a number of recreational and social events. This finding is in agreement with an "exposure to novelty" hypothesis put forward by Schaffer (1966) and by Kagan, Kearsley, and Zelazo (1977). The exposure to novelty hypothesis suggests that shy mothers do not expose themselves or their infants to novel situations, thereby reinforcing shy tendencies in the children. This link was found for both adoptive (shared environment only) and nonadaptive (shared biological and environmental factors) families, suggesting that family environment must account for some of the resemblance between parent and infant shyness.

JEFFREY GRAY'S MODEL FOR BEHAVIORAL INHIBITION

Gray's (1971, 1982) biologically based model of temperament, mostly developed from results of animal research, includes three constructs that are very relevant to a discussion of behavioral inhibition and shyness in childhood. Gray has identified two orthogonal temperamental dimensions of behavioral inhibition (anxiety) and behavioral activation (impulsivity). Increasing levels of proneness to anxiety, or behavioral inhibition, identified at the physiological level with the action of the septal-hipocampal system, are seen in Gray's theory to reflect the person's sensitivity to novelty, to signals of nonreward and punishment, and to innate fear stimuli. Increasing levels of behavioral activation, or impulsivity, on the other hand, identified at the physiological level with the medial forebrain bundle, are seen to reflect higher proneness to respond to signals of reward or nonpunishment. An additional temperamental variable, neuroticism, or proneness to distress, is seen to be a function of the operation of the arousal due to both activation and inhibition.

In situations where a child's responses have resulted solely in reward, individual differences in approach will depend upon the strength of the behavioral activation system (BAS). In situations where a child's responses have resulted solely in punishment, or when there is a new or fear-inducing stimulus, individual differences will depend upon the strength of the behavioral inhibition system (BIS). In situations where children's approach responses have been alternately rewarded and punished or where both aspects of reward and punishment are present, as in the child's meeting of a stranger, whether an approach will occur will be a function of the operation of both the BAS and the BIS. Thus, children with low activating tendencies may be unlikely to show rapid approach, even when they are not very susceptible to behavioral inhibition. On the other hand, children who are high on both activation and inhibition tendencies would be expected to show rapid approach under circumstances of familiarity and nonthreat, but they might be highly inhibited under conditions of punishment, novelty, or threat. These children would be expected to be especially variable in their behavior, depending upon conditions of novelty–familiarity, challenge, or punishment. Gray's model allows for the important possibility that children can have both approach and inhibition tendencies.

Research by Schaffer and his colleagues and in our own laboratory also suggests that approach tendencies are clearly present by 6 months of age, but that there will be increasing development of a behavioral inhibition system during the last half of the first year of life. Thus Schaffer (1974) argues that the important change occurring in the third quarter of the first year of life is not the onset of avoidance responses in young children but rather the onset of inhibition of children's approach responses.

Schaffer and his colleagues (Schaffer, Greenwood, & Perry, 1972) conducted a longitudinal study in which 20 children were observed monthly from 6 to 12 months in their responses to unfamiliar stimuli. Even at 6 months, children showed by their looking times that they could differentiate between novel and familiar objects. However, at 6 months, the infants approached unfamiliar objects "impulsively and immediately" (Schaffer, 1974, p. 14). At 8 months and beyond, however, latency to reach and grasp was clearly influenced by familiarity. Infants now showed hesitations, sometimes but not always accompanied by distress and/or avoidance. When these older infants made contact with the object, it was likely to be done cautiously.

In a longitudinal study, we have also found increases in infants' latency to reach and grasp toys that are unfamiliar and intense (sound and movement producing) from 6½ to 10 months of age (Rothbart, 1988b). We have also found that individual differences in latency to approach low-intensity stimuli are relatively stable from 6½ to 10 months and beyond to 13½ months of age; that is, some children approach objects much more rapidly than other infants, a sign of individual differences in behavioral activation or Gray's BAS. Individual differences in latency to approach high-intensity stimuli (Gray's BIS) do not show relative stability across this age period. These findings are congruent with the interpretation that behavioral inhibition to intense and unfamiliar stimuli is developing across this age period. They also suggest that individual differences in approach as assessed under conditions unlikely to elicit behavioral inhibition (safe and familiar circumstances) can be observed both before and after the developmental onset of behavioral inhibition and that they show stability from 6½ months.

Considering now the question of the developmental stability of individual differences in shyness and behavioral inhibition past 13½ months, Reznick *et al.* (in press), using somewhat different stimuli and observing different inhibitory responses, have found some stability of behavioral inhibition from 14 months to later ages. In long-term studies of longitudinal stability, variables closely related to behavioral inhibition and shyness have also frequently emerged from tests for stability of multiple personality measures. Thus Honzik (1965) has noted that Fels Longitudinal Study subjects showed stability from early childhood to adulthood for girls and from middle childhood to adulthood for boys on "social interaction anxiety" versus "spontaneity" (Kagan & Moss, 1962).

In addition, Tuddenham (1959) found the greatest longitudinal stability among his personality measures for variables connoting "spontaneity" versus "inhibition" in subjects 14 to 33 years from the Oakland Growth Study; Bronson (1972) reported stability on "introversion" versus "extraversion" and "excessive reserve" versus "spontaneity" from 21 months to 18 years; and Bayley and Schaeffer (1963) reported their most stable dimension from birth to 18 years to be "active, extraverted" versus "inactive, introverted" behavior. Stability of individual differences in shyness has also been reported in clinical judgments of a group of children from ages 7 through 14 (Macfarlane, Allen, & Honzik, 1954), in peer ratings of shyness of children between the third grade and the fifth grade (Coie & Dodge, 1983), and in teachers' ratings of shyness of children between ages 10 and 13 (Backteman & Magnusson, 1981). Finally, in a follow-up study of subjects from the Berkeley Guidance Study (Macfarlane *et al.*, 1954) seen 30 years later, shy boys, in comparison with those less shy, were found to have delayed entry into marriage, parenthood, and a stable career, and shy girls to have followed a more traditional female role of rearing children and homemaking, with either no work history or work terminated at marriage or childbirth (Caspi, Elder, & Bem, 1988).

BEHAVIORAL INHIBITION, SHYNESS, AND PSYCHOPATHOLOGY IN CHILDREN

The DSM-III-R (APA, 1987) includes disorders in which anxiety plays a prominent role as falling within the classification of anxiety disorders. For children, these disorders primarily consist of separation anxiety, avoidant disorder, overanxious disorder, phobic disorder, panic disorder, and obsessive–compulsive disorder. Each of these disorders has its own unique set of specific symptoms and level of impairment. However, they share the characteristic of an abnormally high level of anxiety. Unfortunately, virtually no studies have investigated the prevalence of these disorders in the general population. Instead, researchers have chosen to concentrate their efforts on fears commonly found in childhood at nonpathological levels (e.g., Lapouse & Monk, 1959).

One group of children who may have a connection to behavioral inhibition is a group labeled "socially withdrawn." These children are typically identified by their low rates of interactions with peers. Early studies seemed to suggest that these children were at no risk for developing any behavior problems or peer rejection. However, recent studies have indicated otherwise. Rubin (1985) demonstrated that socially isolated children were less dominant in their peer interactions and reported negative self-perceptions of their social, cognitive, physical, and general attributes. Poor academic achievement has also been shown to be related to extreme withdrawal according to teacher report (Green, Vosk, Beck, & Forehand, 1981). Numerous factor-analytic studies using parent and teacher report have indicated that there is an anxious–withdrawn dimension of child behavior, suggesting that social withdrawal may be related to other dimensions such as depression and anxiety (Rubin, 1985). This possibility is further reinforced by the longitudinal studies by Suomi and his colleagues of behavioral inhibition, separation distress, depression, and anxiety in rhesus monkeys, discussed above (Higley & Suomi, in press). The primate research suggests that research relating behavioral inhibition to problems of separation and depression would be of great interest.

The relationship between social withdrawal and behavioral problems was recently investigated by Strauss, Forehand, Smith, & Frame (1986). A sample of socially withdrawn and socially outgoing second- through fifth-grade students were selected on the basis of teacher and peer report. The children were given a number of self-report measures, including self-concept, depression, and anxiety scales. The teachers filled out a behavior checklist on each child, and peers submitted sociometric ratings. When compared to socially outgoing peers, socially withdrawn children were found to have more internalizing problems and more disrupted relationships with peers. Specifically, withdrawn children were described by their peers as being less well liked, more disliked, and less enjoyable as playmates. Furthermore, these children reported more depressive symptoms and higher rates of anxiety. Taken together, these findings suggest that socially withdrawn children may be at risk for developing affective or anxiety disorders and at risk of being rejected by peers.

In relating later anxiety-related behavior problems to early temperamental characteristics, Bates and his colleagues have attempted to predict the development of behavior problems from early negative emotionality in infancy. In this work, reviewed by Bates (1987), a difficult temperament in infancy (defined as frequent and intense expressions of negative affect) predicted both internalizing and externalizing problems as seen by the mother when the subjects were later assessed at 3–6 years. Additionally, early unadaptability to novel persons and situations as assessed by parent report in the Infant Characteristics Questionnaire at age 6 months predicted later anxiety problems, but not acting-out problems (the latter were related to early activity management problems). These results suggest that early temperamental predispositions to fearfulness may contribute to later problems, but more observational research will be needed in this area. The topic of temperament and behavior problems is an important one, and additional longitudinal research in this area is much needed.

Summary

In this chapter we have suggested that some of the components of the constellation of behavioral dimensions, including behavioral inhibition, shyness, and social anxiety, have their roots in temperamental dispositions. These dispositions are seen to be especially related to inhibited or withdrawing behavior and autonomic reactivity to novelty and challenge. We have also suggested that, as evidenced in situations where both rewarding and novel or challenging stimuli are present, latency to approach the stimulus will be a function of two temperamental dimensions, behavioral activation and inhibition, rather than only one, behavioral inhibition. More cognitive aspects of social anxiety are seen to extend beyond the domain of temperament to include cognitive representations of self and others. Thus an individual not predisposed to social fear may come to experience social anxiety due to the experience of extensive criticism from others. There is currently some evidence to suggest that early fearfulness will be predictive of later social anxiety (and possibly susceptibility to depression), but much more longitudinal research is needed in this area.

REFERENCES

American Psychiatric Association (1987). *Quick reference to the diagnostic criteria from DSM-III-R (3rd Ed.)*. Washington, DC: Author.

Backteman, G., & Magnusson, D. (1981). Longitudinal stability of personality characteristics. *Journal of Personality, 49*, 148–160.

Bates, J. E. (1987). Temperament in infancy. In J. D. Osofsky (Ed.), *Handbook of infant development* (pp. 1101–1149). New York: Wiley.

Bates, J. E. (1989). Application of temperament constructs. In G. D. Kohnstamm, J. Bates, & M. K. Rothbart (Eds.), *Temperament in childhood* (pp. 321–355). Chichester: Wiley.

Bayley, N., & Schaefer, E. E. (1963). Consistency of maternal and child behavior in the Berkeley Growth Study. *American Psychologist, 18*, No. 7.

Becker, M. S., Suomi, S. J., Marra, L., Higley, J. D., & Brogan, N. (1984). Developmental data as predictors of depression in infant rhesus monkeys. *Infant Behavior and Development, 7*, 26.

Beidel, D. C., Turner, S. M., & Dancu, C. V. (1985). Physiological, cognitive, and behavioral aspects of social anxiety. *Behaviour Research and Therapy, 23*, 109–117.

Blizard, D. A. (1981). The Maudsley reactive and nonreactive strains: A North American perspective. *Behavior Genetics, 11*, 469–489.

Briggs, S. R., & Smith, T. G. (1986). The measurement of shyness. In W. H. Jones, J. M. Cheek, & S. R. Briggs (Eds.), *Shyness* (pp. 47–60). New York: Plenum.

Bronson, W. C. (1972). The role of enduring orientations to the environment in personality development. *Genetic Psychology Monographs, 86*, 3–80.

Buck, R. (1988). *Human motivation and emotion* (2nd ed.). New York: Wiley.

Buss, A. H. (1980). *Self-consciousness and social anxiety*. San Francisco: Freeman.

Buss, A. H. (1985). Two kinds of shyness. In R. Schwarzer (Ed.), *Self-related cognitions in anxiety and motivation* (pp. 65–75). Hillsdale, NJ: Erlbaum.

Buss, A. H. (1986). A theory of shyness. In W. H. Jones, J. M. Cheek, & S. R. Briggs (Eds.), *Shyness* (pp. 39–46). New York: Plenum.

Buss, A. H., Iscoe, I., & Buss, E. H. (1979). The development of embarrassment. *Journal of Psychology, 103*, 227–230.

Buss, A. H., & Plomin, R. (1984). *Temperament: Early developing personality traits*. Hillsdale, NJ: Erlbaum.

Capaldi, D., & Rothbart, M. K. (1988). *Development and validation of an adolescent temperament measure*. Unpublished manuscript, University of Oregon.

Caspi, A., Elder, G. H., & Bem, D. J. (1988). Moving away from the world: Life-source patterns of shy children. *Developmental Psychology, 24*, 824–831.

Champoux, M., & Suomi, S. J. (1986, November). *Adaptation to a social group by rhesus monkey juveniles differing in infant temperament*. Paper presented at the meeting of the International Society for Developmental Psychobiology, Annapolis, MD.

Chamove, A. S., Rosenblum, L. A., & Harlow, H. F. (1973). Monkeys (*Macaca mulatta*) raised only with peers: A pilot study. *Animal Behavior, 21*, 316–325.

Cheek, J. M., & Buss, A. H. (1981). Shyness and sociability. *Journal of Personality and Social Psychology, 41*, 330–339.

Cheek, J. M., Carpentieri, A. M., Smith, T. G., Rierdan, J., & Koff, E. (1986). Adolescent shyness. In W. H. Jones, J. M. Cheek, & S. R. Briggs (Eds.), *A sourcebook on shyness: Research and treatment* (pp. 105–115). New York: Plenum.

Coie, J. D., & Dodge, K. A. (1983). Continuities and changes in children's social status: A 5-year longitudinal study. *Merrill-Palmer Quarterly, 29*, 261–282.

Daniels, D., & Plomin, R. (1985). Origins of individual differences in infant shyness. *Developmental Psychology, 21*, 118–121.

Derryberry, D., & Rothbart, M. K. (1988). Arousal, affect, and attention as components of temperament. *Journal of Personality and Social Psychology, 55*, 953–966.

Garcia-Coll, C. T., Kagan, J., & Reznick, J. S. (1984). Behavioral inhibition in young children. *Child Development, 55*, 1005–1019.

Goldsmith, H. H., & Campos, O. (1982). Toward a theory of infant temperament. In R. Emde & R. Harmon (Eds.), *Attachment and affiliative systems* (pp. 161–193). New York: Plenum.

Goldsmith, H. H., Buss, A. H., Plomin, R., Rothbart, M. K., Thomas, A., & Chess, C. (1987). Roundtable: What is temperament? Four approaches. *Child Development, 58,* 505–529.

Gray, J. A. (1971). *The psychology of fear and stress.* New York: McGraw-Hill.

Gray, J. A. (1982). *The neuropsychology of anxiety.* New York: Oxford University Press.

Graziano, A. M., DeGiovanni, I. S., & Garcia, K. A. (1979). Behavioral treatment of children's fears: A review. *Psychological Bulletin, 86,* 804–830.

Green, K. D., Vosk, B., Forehand, R., & Beck, S. (1981). An examination of differences among sociometrically identified accepted, rejected, and neglected children. *Child Study Journal, 11,* 117–124.

Hall, C. S. (1936). Emotional behavior in the rat: III. The relationship between emotionality and ambulatory activity. *Journal of Comparative Psychology, 22,* 365–374.

Harlow, H. F. (1969). Age-mate or peer affectional system. In D. S. Lehrman, R. A. Hinde, & E. Shaw (Eds.), *Advances in the study of behavior.* London: Academic Press.

Harter, S. (1983). Developmental perspectives on the self-system. In P. H. Mussen (Ed.), *Handbook of child psychology: Vol. IV, Socialization, personality and social development* (pp. 275–386). New York: Wiley.

Higley, J. D. (1985). *Continuity of social separation behaviors in rhesus monkeys from infancy to adolescence.* Unpublished doctoral dissertation, University of Wisconsin, Madison.

Higley, J. D., Danner, G. R., & Hirsch, R. M. (1988). Attachment in rhesus monkeys reared either with only peers or with their mothers as assessed by the Ainsworth strange situation procedure. *Infant Behavior and Development, 11,* 139.

Higley, J. D., & Suomi, S. (1989). Temperamental reactivity in nonhuman primates. In G. D. Kohnstamm, J. Bates, & M. K. Rothbart (Eds.), *Temperament in childhood* (pp. 153–167). Chichester: Wiley.

Hirsch, R. M., Higley, J. D., & Suomi, S. J. (1986, November). *Growing-up without adults: The effect of peer-only rearing on daily behaviors in rhesus monkeys.* Paper presented at the meeting of the International Society for Developmental Psychobiology, Annapolis, MD.

Honzik, M. P. (1965). Prediction of behavior from birth to maturity (book review). *Merrill-Palmer Quarterly, 11,* 77–88.

Jones, W. H., Briggs, S. R., & Smith, T. G. (1986). Shyness: Conceptualization and measurement. *Journal of Personality and Social Psychology, 51,* 629–639.

Jones, J. M., Cheek, J. M., & Briggs, S. R. (1986). *Shyness.* New York: Plenum.

Kagan, J., Kearsley, R. B., & Zelazo, P. R. (1977). The effects of infant day care on psychological development. *Educational Quarterly, 1,* 109–142.

Kagan, J., & Moss, H. A. (1962). *Birth to maturity.* New York: Wiley.

Kagan, J., Reznick, J. S., Clarke, C., Snidman, N., & Garcia-Coll, C. (1984). Behavioral inhibition to the unfamiliar. *Child Development, 55,* 2212–2225.

Kagan, J., Reznick, J. S., & Snidman, N. (1986). Temperamental inhibition in early childhood. In R. Plomin & J. Dunn (Eds.), *The study of temperament: Changes, continuities and challenges* (pp. 53–67). Hillsdale, NJ: Erlbaum.

Kagan, J., Reznick, J. S., & Snidman, N. (1987). The physiology and psychology of behavioral inhibition in children. *Child Development, 58,* 1459–1473.

King, D. L., & Appelbaum, J. R. (1973). Effect of trials on "emotionality" behavior of the rat and mouse. *Journal of Comparative and Physiological Psychology, 85,* 186–194.

Lapouse, R., & Monk, M. A. (1959). Fears and worries in a representative sample of children. *American Journal of Orthopsychiatry, 29,* 803–818.

Macfarlane, J., Allen, L., & Honzik, M. P. (1954). *A developmental study of the behavior problems of normal children between twenty-one months and fourteen years.* Berkeley: University of California Press.

Mathews, A. M., & Macleod, C. (1986). Discrimination of threat cues without awareness in anxiety states. *Journal of Abnormal Psychology, 93,* 131–138.

Mineka, S., Suomi, S. J., & DeLizio, R. (1981). Multiple separations in adolescent monkeys: An opponent-process interpretation. *Journal of Experimental Psychology: General, 110,* 56–85.

Plomin, R., & Daniels, D. (1986). Genetics and shyness. In W. H. Jones, J. M. Cheek, & S. R. Briggs (Eds.), *Shyness* (pp. 63–80). New York: Plenum.

Plomin, R., & DeFries, J. C. (1985). *Origins of individual differences in infancy: The Colorado Adoption Project*. New York: Academic Press.

Reznick, J. S., Gibbons, J., Johnson, M., & McDonough, P. (in press). Behavioral inhibition in a normative sample. In S. Reznick (Ed.), *Perspectives on behavioral inhibition*. Chicago: University of Chicago Press.

Reznick, J. S., Kagan, J., Snidman, N., Gersten, M., Baak, K., & Rosenberg, A. (1986). Inhibited and uninhibited children: A follow-up study. *Child Development, 57*, 660–680.

Rholes, W. S., & Ruble, D. N. (1984). Children's understanding of dispositional characteristics of others. *Child Development, 55*, 550–560.

Rotenberg, K. J. (1982). Development of character constancy of self and other. *Child Development, 53*, 505–515.

Rothbart, M. K. (1981). Measurement of temperament in infancy. *Child Development, 52*, 569–578.

Rothbart, M. K. (1988a). *The Children's Behavior Questionnaire*. Unpublished instrument, University of Oregon.

Rothbart, M. K. (1988b). Temperament and the development of inhibited approach. *Child Development, 59*, 1241–1250.

Rothbart, M. K. (1989a). Temperament and development. In G. D. Kohnstamm, J. Bates, & M. K. Rothbart (Eds.), *Temperament in childhood* (pp. 187–248). Chichester: Wiley.

Rothbart, M. K. (1989b). Temperament in childhood: A framework. In G. D. Kohnstamm, J. Bates, & M. K. Rothbart (Eds.), *Temperament in childhood* (pp. 59–73). Chichester: Wiley.

Rothbart, M. K., & Derryberry, D. (1981). Development of individual differences in temperament. In M. E. Lamb & A. L. Brown (Eds.), *Advances in developmental psychology, Volume I* (pp. 37–86). Hillsdale, NJ: Erlbaum.

Rubin, K. H. (1985). Socially withdrawn children: An "at risk" population? In B. Schneider, K. H. Rubin, & J. Ledingham (Eds.), *Children's peer relations: Issues in assessment and intervention* (pp. 125–140). New York: Springer-Verlag.

Schaffer, H. R. (1966). The onset of fear of strangers and the incongruity hypothesis. *Journal of Child Psychology and Psychiatry, 1*, 95–106.

Schaffer, H. R. (1974). Cognitive components of the infant's response to strangeness. In M. Lewis & L. A. Rosenblum (Eds.), *The origins of fear* (pp. 11–24). New York: Wiley.

Schaffer, H. R., Greenwood, A., & Perry, M. H. (1972). The onset of wariness. *Child Development, 43*, 165–175.

Sroufe, L. A. (1979). Socioemotional development. In J. D. Osofsky (Ed.), *Handbook of infant development* (pp. 462–516). New York: Wiley.

Strauss, C. C., Forehand, R., Smith, K., & Frame, C. L. (1986). The association between social withdrawal and internalizing problems of children. *Journal of Abnormal Child Psychology, 14*, 525–535.

Suomi, S. J. (1983). Social development in rhesus monkeys: Consideration of individual differences. In A. Oliverio & M. Zappella (Eds.), *The behavior of human infants* (pp. 71–92). New York: Plenum.

Suomi, S. J. (1984). The development of affect in rhesus monkeys. In N. A. Fox & R. J. Davison (Eds.), *The psychobiology of affective development* (pp. 119–159). Hillsdale, NJ: Erlbaum.

Suomi, S. J. (1986). Anxiety-like disorders in young nonhuman primates. In R. Gittelman (Ed.), *Anxiety disorders of childhood* (pp. 1–23). New York: Guilford.

Suomi, S. J., Champoux, M., Higley, J. D., Scanlan, J. M., & Schneider, M. (1986, July). *Infant temperament and maternal influences on rhesus monkey biobehavioral ontogeny*. Paper presented at the eleventh Congress of the International Primatological Society, Gottingen, FRG.

Suomi, S. J., Kraemer, G. W., Baysinger, C. M., & DeLizio, R. D. (1981). Inherited and experimental factors associated with individual differences in anxious behavior displayed by rhesus monkeys. In D. F. Klein & J. Rabkin (Eds.), *Anxiety: New Research and changing concepts* (pp. 179–200). New York: Raven Press.

Thomas, A., & Chess, S. (1977). *Temperament and development*. New York: Brunner/Mazel.

Thompson, W. W., Higley, J. D., Byrne, E. A., Scanlan, J. M., & Suomi, S. J. (1986, November).

Behavioral inhibition in nonhuman primates: Psychobiological correlates and continuity over time. Paper presented at the meeting of the International Society for Developmental Psychobiology, Annapolis, MD.

Tuddenham, R. D. (1959). The constancy of personality ratings over two decades. *Genetic Psychology Monographs, 60,* 3–29.

5

Socially Withdrawn
and Isolated Children

RONALD J. PRINZ

OVERVIEW

The term *social withdrawal* can be found frequently in the clinical literature on adults and children over several decades. Social withdrawal, as a symptom or a condition, denotes either a disruption to social relations or failure to interact with others. Applied to children, social withdrawal has multiple connotations that include avoidance of children's play activities, low interaction rate across settings, exclusion by peers, poor social skills, unpopularity, shyness, loneliness, and feelings of alienation or rejection. However, most children who might be considered socially withdrawn or isolated do not fit all of these descriptors, nor are all these dimensions highly correlated in the general child population. It is this diversity of conceptualization that plagues the definitional, assessment, etiological, and treatment research on childhood social withdrawal and isolation.

CONCEPTUALIZATION OF SOCIAL WITHDRAWAL AND ISOLATION

The standard classification system published by the American Psychiatric Association (APA) contains clinical categories that incorporate symptoms of childhood social withdrawal and isolation. However, the precise definitions and categorization have changed across editions of the diagnostic system. DSM-II (APA, 1968) included only one diagnostic category pertaining to childhood social withdrawal—Withdrawing Reaction of Childhood or Adolescence—that was characterized by seclusiveness, detachment, sensitivity, shyness or timidity, and a general inability to form close relationships. DSM-III (APA, 1980) replaced Withdrawing Reaction of Childhood or Adolescence with other categories. In an

---

RONALD J. PRINZ • Department of Psychology, University of South Carolina, Columbia, South Carolina 29208.

early draft of DSM-III, Shyness Disorder and Introverted Disorder of Childhood were added, but the final version dropped both of these in favor of Avoidant Disorder of Childhood or Adolescence. The latter category requires a persistent and excessive shrinking from contact with strangers, desire for affection and acceptance, generally positive familial relations, and avoidant behavior sufficiently prominent to interfere with peer relationships and social functioning. DSM-III also included a general category for children and adults called Adjustment Disorder with Withdrawal, which refers to social withdrawal as a reaction to a known psychosocial stressor (e.g., death of a close relative). DSM-III-R (American Psychiatric Association, 1987) retained Avoidant Disorder in basically the same form as the earlier version. In addition, problematic peer relations are noted for three other childhood disorders in DSM-III-R: (1) Overanxious Disorder—concern about social acceptance; (2) Attention-deficit Hyperactivity Disorder—inappropriate behavior with peers, and in severe cases significant impairment of peer relations; and (3) Oppositional Defiant Disorder—in severe cases major impairment in functioning with peers.

The current clinical taxonomy does not reflect the range of variation observed in empirical work on children's peer relations. For example, DSM-III-R makes no distinction between (1) children who are timid and reticent to participate in social activities but are not disliked by peers and (2) children who are actively rejected by peers and become isolated as a result. Perhaps clinical classification systems do not reflect this level of distinction because the significance and stability of such subgroups have not yet been completely established.

Researchers from different spheres, including clinical and developmental psychology, have not reached a concensus as to the basis for defining particular social isolate populations. At least three major dimensions have been suggested. The first is overall interaction rate. Children can be selected on the basis of very low interaction rates with other children. This conceptualization makes no assumption about how the children arrived at a low interaction rate or what is currently preventing them from interacting. This view is also consistent with the general public's notion of a socially isolated child, namely, one who plays by him- or herself and fails to join in with the other children.

The second conceptualization pertains to children's social status. Classroom peers choose to interact with some children and not with others. Peer selection, which can be reasonably assessed with sociometric methodology, is one basis on which to profile children. The pertinent social status groups for this discussion include children who are identified as highly disliked and hence rejected by peers, and children who are neither liked nor disliked by peers but are essentially passed over or neglected.

A third basis for defining childhood social isolation is level of social skills. Overall interaction rate fails to take into account quality of interaction. Children with inadequately developed social skills may interact frequently but ineffectively with other children and hence might be cut off for all practical purposes from other children.

These three dimensions—rate of interaction, social status, and social skillfulness—can be used to define and select children whom we might call socially withdrawn or isolated. There are inherent contradictions among these dimensions, and there is overlap as well. For example, a child who acts inappropriately with peers but nevertheless makes repeated attempts to interact would probably not exhibit a low rate of interaction, and yet such a child may feel very isolated nonetheless. In this situation, social skillfulness and perhaps social status would characterize this child as socially isolated, but rate of interaction would not. On the other hand, a child who also never developed adequate social skills and who has been severely rebuffed by other children might choose to avoid interacting with others and as a result exhibit a low rate of interaction. In this case, all three dimensions are synchronized. As a third illustrative case, a child may choose to play alone and yet be socially accepted by peers and have some degree of social competence. In this situation, rate of interaction would identify this child as a social isolate, whereas peer-group status and social competence would not. Lack of sufficient correspondence among these three dimensions, not to mention an unknown relationship with the formal clinical classification system, underscores the heterogeneity and conceptual problems associated with the pursuit of clearly defined subpopulations of socially inadequate children.

For purposes of this chapter, the term *social isolation* will be used as a generic one to refer to children with social adjustment problems. The use of this expression is not meant to restrict the discussion to children who exhibit low rates of interaction with peers. Isolation can be considered in the more general, connotative sense in that all of the children under study or treatment either feel alienated from other children, are ignored by their classmates, are actively ostracized by their classmates, or are literally isolated due to lack of interaction with others.

ASSESSMENT METHODS

Assessment measures for socially isolated, withdrawn, or rejected children fall into three major categories: (1) peer evaluation methods, which include sociometric measures and peer assessment instruments; (2) observational measures; and (3) nonpeer informant measures, which include instruments based on teacher, parental, and self-evaluations.

Peer Evaluation

Sociometric Assessment

The most commonly cited measure in the clinical research literature on childhood social isolation is the peer sociometric, which has been used in description, subject selection, and treatment outcome assessment. Sociometry in its purest form is the study of human networks and preferences within those networks. In application, sociometric instruments are employed to determine who likes whom or who chooses whom as a friend, playmate, or workmate.

The most widely adopted sociometric method used in studies of socially isolated or rejected children is the one refined by Coie, Dodge, and their colleagues (Coie & Dodge, 1983; Coie, Dodge, & Coppotelli, 1982; Coie & Kupersmidt, 1983). Using a class roster as a guide, each child in the class nominates three classmates whom they like most (LM) and three classmates whom they like least (LL). LM and LL nominations are totaled separately for each nominee. After transforming LM and LL into standardized scores within the children's grade level and school, each child is categorized using a set scheme. Rejected children are defined as those with a high number of LL nominations and a low number of LM nominations (LM $-$ LL less than one SD below the mean; LM $<$ mean; LL $>$ mean). Neglected children have a low quantity of both types of nominations (LM $+$ LL less than one SD below the mean; LM $<$ mean; LL $<$ mean). These groups are contrasted with three other groups: popular (high LM, low LL), average (mid-range on both dimensions), and controversial (high LM, high LL).

The methodology used by Coie and Dodge, adapted by others as well (Krehbiel & Milich, 1986), has distinctive features that are important to consider in applying sociometric assessment. First, the system of data interpretation is two-dimensional in accounting for social impact and preference, as Peery (1979) has recommended. Impact, which refers to the extent to which children catch the attention of their peers, is operationalized as the sum of positive and negative nominations. Preference, which refers to choice of friends and playmates, is defined as positive nominations minus negative nominations. By this scheme, children with low preference and high impact are viewed as rejected, and children with low preference and low impact are considered neglected, although Peery (1979) labeled the latter group "isolated."

A second consideration in the Coie and Dodge method is gender of peer nominators. Coie and Dodge (1983) base their sociometric computations on the nominations by same-sex and opposite-sex classmates because they have found the composite score more stable than one based on same-sex classmates alone. Foster, Bell-Dolan, and Berler (1986) have noted that same-sex and both-sex sociometrics do not yield the same results, particularly in selecting extreme-group membership. However, limiting the sociometric to half the class (or less) undermines the stability of the resulting score and creates other problems.

Third, the nomination method depends on a restricted or fixed choice procedure in that peers must nominate three and only three classmates for each dimension. After standardization across hundreds of children and many classrooms, the restricted nomination procedure may work fine for its intended purposes. However, the procedure might distort the true state of affairs for individual children in specific circumstances, such as in larger classes or when a small number of children collect a disproportionate share of either positive, negative, or both types of nominations. Even though the scores are standardized across classrooms, the fixed-choice sociometric practically ensures that every class will generate some children who would be labeled rejected or neglected. The implicit assumption is that every class probably has rejected and neglected children, an assumption that probably holds for many classrooms but may not hold for all. Since classroom assignment is not always randomly determined, it is conceivable that some classes are made up entirely of children who are at least minimally accepted by their peers. While this does not pose a serious problem for group research, it may for clinical assessment of individual children who might in some circumstances be mislabeled as neglected by a sociometric measure. An alternative method, the unrestricted- or unlimited-choice procedure, could remedy the problem for individual assessments. A child who receives no nominations at all despite unlimited number of nominations by each peer undoubtedly fits the neglected status category. The unrestricted nomination procedure may create additional variance that makes cross-classroom comparisons difficult, although standardization across classrooms within a particular grade and school could address this issue. A third procedure, the roster and rating procedure, permits children to rate their preferences for each classmate and thus ensures that every class member gets deliberate and presumably equal consideration.

A fourth and final consideration regarding the Coie–Dodge sociometric methodology is that the derived scores and social status classifications are relatively stable over time (Coie & Dodge, 1983). Rejected and neglected classifications are not inadvertent in nature. The stability of these categories is desirable in selecting children for studying these problems and for treatment. However, the stability of these categories makes them less amenable for use as outcome measures. There are two obstacles to overcome. The first is that reputation is slow to change. Even when children begin to change their behavior in positive ways, peers might not change their attributions and perceptions so quickly. A second problem is the fixed-choice aspect of the sociometric itself. Suppose that a child who previously received no positive nominations and had no friends in the class manages to befriend one or two classmates. However, when the sociometric is administered a second time, these two classmates would have to drop one of their previous nominations in order to make room for a nomination of their new friend. Furthermore, going from no friends to one friend is a major change that would not make much of a dent in the sociometric score. Consequently, this type of sociometric does not make a good short-term index of improvement or response to treatment. However, the Coie–Dodge sociometric method serves well as a selection measure, a predictor of later adjustment, and a long-term (e.g., 2- or 3-year follow-up) outcome measure.

One other sociometric method is worth noting. The paired comparison sociometric, in which photographs of each possible classmate dyad are paired and children are asked to choose a preference for a playmate in each case, has some useful features (McConnell & Odom, 1986). The method can be used with a broad age range, including preschool children. The procedure works well with smaller groups as well as larger ones, in contrast to nomination sociometrics which break down with smaller classes. The paired comparison method also ensures that every child is carefully considered, that the children are basing their preferences on actual recognized faces rather than on names which they may or may not recognize, and that the method can be administered to children who do not know how to read. Because it is individually administered, the paired comparison method circumvents some of the group stigmatizing behavior that sometimes occurs when sociometrics are being administered in a classroom. There are some disadvantages to this method, however. The procedure is extremely time consuming because pictures of all class members need to be taken, each child has to be interviewed individually, and the number of needed comparisons is large. For example, a class of 25 yields 276 dyadic comparisons that have to be administered to each child.

Peer Assessment

Peer sociometric methods concentrate on children's social preferences as a means of determining social status of each child. Peer assessment measures, by contrast, permit peers to indicate characteristics that they ascribe to the children being evaluated. Peer assessment measures generally provide richer description than sociometric measures and allow the profiling of how a child is perceived. Peer assessment is illustrated by the approaches for two different instruments, the Pupil Evaluation Inventory and the Revised Class Play.

The Pupil Evaluation Inventory (PEI; Pekarik, Prinz, Liebert, Weintraub, & Neale, 1976), which consists of 35 items describing social, antisocial, and asocial behaviors, is administered in classrooms using an unrestricted nomination procedure. The PEI contains three consistent factors—aggression, withdrawal, and likability—obtains acceptable internal consistency and test–retest reliability, and demonstrates some evidence of validity (Pekarik *et al.*, 1976; Weintraub, Prinz, & Neale, 1978). The instrument has been used in descriptive research as well as in treatment research as an outcome measure (McConnell & Odom, 1986). Information obtained from the PEI augments the data obtained from sociometric measures. For example, Cantrell and Prinz (1985) administered the PEI and other instruments to a sample of 492 children in Grades 3 to 6 and found that peer assessment added significant information. The degree to which classmates rejected a given child (sociometrically defined) was strongly correlated ($r = .72$, $p < .001$) with peer-rated aggression on the PEI. While teachers rated rejected children higher on aggression, it is the peers' attribution of aggression that explained their basis for rejecting the children so identified.

A second approach to peer assessment is exemplified by the Revised Class Play (RCP; Masten, Morison, & Pellegrini, 1985; Rubin & Cohen, 1986). In its current form, the RCP is a restricted nomination instrument consisting of 15 positive and 15 negative behavioral roles for a hypothetical play. Children nominate up to three classmates for each role. The instrument factors into three subscales: aggressive/disruptive, sensitive/isolate, and sociable/leader. There is support for reliability and validity of the instrument as a measure of children's perceptions (albeit possibly distorted) of their classmates' personal and social characteristics (Rubin & Cohen, 1986). A particular advantage of the RCP over other instruments is that the revised version includes sufficient assessment of positive social competence dimensions. This is important because the absence of a negative evaluation on other instruments does not mean that the evaluated child has achieved a normative level of social competence.

Behavioral Observation

Sociometric and peer assessment measures only tap social functioning indirectly in terms of impact on peers. In contrast, behavioral observation methods assess what children actually do in social situations. Observational methods used with socially isolated or rejected children fall basically into three categories: rate of interaction, qualitative aspects of interaction, and sequential interaction.

The simplest observational strategy with isolated children is to determine how often they interact with other children in free-play situations. Much of the initial treatment research for childhood social isolation focused on rate of interaction as an outcome measure as well as a basis for selection of children for treatment (Wanlass & Prinz, 1982). Although rate of interaction offers a straightforward measure that can be reliably tallied, there are concerns that the dimension is not as clinically important as one might presume (Asher, Markell, & Hymel, 1981). Disturbed peer relations has been implicated as an early precursor of adolescent and adult maladjustment (Cowen, Pederson, Babigian, Izzo, & Trost, 1973; Janes & Hesselbrock, 1978; Roff, Sells, & Golden, 1972; Watt & Lubensky, 1976), but low interaction rate has not been the way this construct was operationalized. As La Greca and Stark (1986) pointed out, neither the predictive nor concurrent validity have been established for rate of interaction as a measure of social maladjustment. Low interaction rate has not been shown to lead to later problems. Furthermore, some children who exhibit low rates of interaction are accepted by their peers, have attained a reasonable level of social competence when they do choose to interact, and are not experiencing distress (Coie, 1985; Foster & Ritchey, 1979; Krantz, 1982).

A more useful but more difficult observational approach, extending beyond overall interaction rate, is to code quality of interaction. How a child interacts with peers may be more important than how often. Qualitative observation of positive and negative social behaviors provides a more precise description of children's social adjustment. The observation system developed by Hartup, Glazer, and Charlesworth (1967), which has received frequent use, illustrates the kind of behaviors that investigators have assessed. Positive behavioral categories in the Hartup *et al.* (1967) system, which are really ways of providing reinforcement, included giving positive attention/approval, giving affection and personal acceptance, submission, and token giving, while negative dimensions included noncompliance, interference, derogation, and attack. The advantage of this type of observational coding is that the proportions of positive and negative behaviors can be compared, which leads to a more meaningful understanding of social maladjustment. The system also allows examination of reciprocal and nonreciprocal relationships between children. How children treat a target child can be just as telling, if not more so, than the kinds of behaviors the target child emits. A criticism of this observational coding system pertains to limitations in assessing skills. Because of the general summary categories, the Hartup *et al.* (1967) system might not be sensitive to the treatment acquisition of specific social skills (LaGreca & Stark, 1986). For example, a child who increased his or her rate of positive behaviors after going through an intervention program might do so at inappropriate moments or in ways that are ineffective.

Other investigators have focused on different observational targets. With respect to positive dimensions, Ladd (1981) focused on children's offering of support to peers, Bierman and Furman (1984) observed conversational skills, and Cooke and Apolloni (1976) included sharing, compliments, positive physical contact, and smiling in their observational code. Some investigators have focused on molecular behaviors rather than global dimensions. For example, in analyzing assertiveness, Bornstein, Bellack, & Hersen (1977) observed eye contact, number of verbal requests, and speech duration.

Negative behaviors are particularly important in understanding and characterizing rejected children. Aggressive, disruptive, and aversive classes of behavior are commonly cited in observational coding of rejected children's styles (La Greca & Stark, 1986). One of the most significant lines of research related to aggressive behavior in rejected children has been conducted by Dodge (Dodge, 1983; Dodge, Schlundt, Schocken, & Delugach, 1983). Dodge (1983) has successfully implemented a play-group methodology in which he places elementary school children who were previously unacquainted in a small play group that meets on eight occasions for an hour each time. The children are carefully selected from classrooms so that each play group contains a previously rejected child as well as children from other social status categories. Dodge (1983) found that children who came to be rejected by members of the play group had been observed to exhibit higher rates of aggressive and aversive behaviors than the other members of the group. In other words, the aggressive and aversive behaviors were instrumental in causing peer rejection. Consequently, observational systems that are aimed at capturing significant dimensions of rejected, withdrawn, and isolated children's behavior need to contain not only positive aspects of interaction but also clearly specified negative behaviors in order to pinpoint a child's contribution to his or her lack of acceptance.

Another observational consideration is worth noting. Most observational coding systems used with isolated or rejected children are based on nonsequential summaries of each category. While this approach is useful for some purposes, such as selecting children with high rates of negative interaction, there are limitations. Children's social behavior is best interpreted in a contextual manner that takes into account the interactive nature of their behavior. Some investigators have applied sequential observation strategies to this population. Dodge (Dodge, 1983; Dodge et al., 1983) applied a sequential code to videotaped interactions of his play groups and was able to identify successful and unsuccessful peer-group entry strategies and also detect how specific negative and neutral behaviors were consequated by peers. In a sequential analysis of preschoolers' behavior, Tremblay, Strain, Hendrickson, and Shores (1981) were able to identify effective and ineffective behaviors in terms of which ones met with positive peer responses. Finally, Gottman (1983) used sequential observation to better understand the development of friendship patterns. Sequential systems of observation tend to be more difficult and costly to implement than summary-frequency systems, but the benefits in situations where contextual interpretations are needed may outweigh the liabilities.

Other Informants

In addition to peer and observational assessment, investigators have relied on other informants, namely teachers, parents, and the target children themselves, for clinically significant data about isolated and rejected children. Teacher and parent rating scales have been reviewed by Barkley (1988) with regard to general child psychopathology and by Hops and Greenwood (1988) with respect to assessment of social skills deficits. Teacher behavioral rating scales are particularly useful for summarizing problematic and nonproblematic areas of functioning because preschool and elementary school teachers are exposed to frequent samples of a child's social behavior in the classroom, in the hallway, in the lunchroom, and on the playground. For adolescents, teachers typically have a briefer exposure period that is limited primarily to classroom behavior, which constrains the validity of teacher ratings for the older age group. Parental ratings provide more of a supplemental rather than primary source of data bout peer relations. Parents seldom get sufficient opportunity to observe their child's social behavior in school, although their observations about interactions at home with siblings and playmates and in the neighborhood might provide valuable insights for the clinical assessor.

Four instruments in particular are noted here. The Child Behavior Checklist (Achenbach & Edelbrock, 1983), which is one of the most widely used rating instruments for children, is especially useful because there are parallel parent and teacher versions. The instrument is age and gender normed and has a number of dimensions of pertinence to social isolation and rejection, including social withdrawal, aggression, and social competence. The Walker Problem Behavior Identification Checklist (Walker, 1983), which also can be completed by parents or teachers, is designed primarily for preschool and elementary-school-age children. The instrument factors into five scales: immaturity, disturbed peer relations, withdrawal, distractability, and acting out. As Hops and Greenwood (1988) have noted, the instrument has been shown to have adequate psychometric properties and to have particular utility as an outcome measure when treating socially withdrawn children. Two other instruments, the Social Interaction Rating Scale and the Social Behavior Rating Positive Scale, were developed specifically for use with isolate and rejected populations and have utility because of brevity and specificity as screening and change-monitoring measures (see Hops & Greenwood, 1988).

Additional informants regarding peer relations and related domains are the target children themselves. After a several year drought during which time investigators relied on general "self-esteem" measures to tap child perceptions, a number of specific and useful child-report instruments have emerged. Hymel and Franke (1985) have carefully reviewed several such instruments as they pertain particularly to peer relations. The following instruments are recommended for each particular domain: Loneliness Questionnaire (Asher & Wheeler, 1985); an unnamed instrument with social anxiety, social avoidance, and negative peer attitudes subscales (Hymel & Franke, 1985); the Perceived Competence Scale for Children (Harter, 1982); and the Children's Action Tendency Scale for assessment of assertiveness (Deluty, 1979). Self-perception instruments might not corroborate peer, observational, and teacher data, but the perspective is important nonetheless. When peer relations problems are indicated but the child denies such problems, the basis for denial needs to be identified. On the other hand, when children see themselves as unliked, unhappy, or socially incompetent despite behavioral data to the contrary, then the origins of their perceptions need to be uncovered.

INTERVENTION STRATEGIES

Unidimensional Approaches

In many studies conducted during the 1960s and 1970s, investigators targeted for intervention children who exhibited low interaction rates (Wanlass & Prinz, 1982). The intervention methods, which were typically unidimensional and uncomplicated in nature, grouped into four categories: symbolic modeling, contingent reinforcement, peer socialization, and structured activities.

Symbolic modeling focused on showing successful social encounters to socially isolated children via films. The films depicted children initiating social interaction in different settings and experiencing positive consequences from peers. Symbolic modeling as a procedure was intended to convey social competencies and to reduce fear of peer interaction. As a one-shot intervention, modeling produced some changes in interaction but yielded generally mixed results (Gottman, 1977; Keller & Carlson, 1974; O'Connor, 1969, 1972). Symbolic modeling alone is not recommended as a primary intervention for isolated and/or rejected children. However, because modeling is an important part of learning, it should be infused into social skills training programs in order to optimize impact. Additionally, showing films as a way of modeling positive peer interaction is an appropriate prevention strategy for classroom use, particularly if it is followed by a teacher-led discussion and a subsequent free-play period in which to apply what was observed.

Reinforcement procedures were also used as a strategy for increasing interactions of socially isolated children. Proponents of operant approaches assumed that isolated children's social behavior had not been strengthened sufficiently through reinforcement or else the children had been reinforced inadvertently either for asocial behavior or for interacting exclusively with adults. Reinforcement interventions typically involved contingent application of teacher attention, praise, food, or token reinforcers for any social approaches or responses with peers in the naturalistic setting (playground, classroom, lunch area), while withholding reinforcement when the children engaged in nonsocial behavior. In studies such as the one conducted by Walker, Greenwood, Hops, and Todd (1979), short-term experimental control of interactions rates was readily demonstrated. Reinforcement approaches were particularly effective with pre-school children who were timid and needed additional incentive to overcome their reticence. Social interaction did not always maintain when reinforcement interventions were halted, suggesting that more comprehensive programming is needed. A strict reinforcement approach assumes that the children have the necessary prerequisite skills to interact effectively but simply need encourage-ment. This approach might not prove effective with children who have developed inappropriate interaction styles and have become isolated as a result of peer rejection.

Another unidimensional approach centers around peer socialization meth-ods. Some investigators (e.g., Furman, Rahe, & Hartup, 1979) attempted to increase social interaction particularly in preschool children by enlisting other children as socialization agents. Dyadic play sessions were conducted in which each isolate was paired with a peer who was trained to initiate interaction in a positive manner. Generalization to group settings was the goal and was typically achieved on a short-term basis (Wanlass & Prinz, 1982). As an adjunct strategy, or in situations where the child does not have severe social deficits, peer so-cialization is a useful strategy because it permits timid children to engage in social interaction within a controlled and less threatening setting. When there is marked social inadequacy, the child would presumably need more training than peer socialization methods provide. However, dyadic and other contrived play-group situations offer an excellent way for children to practice skills that they are acquiring in training.

There is a collection of approaches loosely referred to as structured activities that has been applied to childhood social isolation. By altering environmental characteristics and activities, investigators assumed that the demands from the social milieu would alter children's social behavior. Approaches in this category primarily included teacher-structured activities, such as reading stories to the children and having them assume character roles, having isolate children pass out candy to their classmates, or conducting a class skit (e.g., Chennault, 1976; Rucker & Vincenzo, 1970; Strain & Wiegerink, 1976). Other such interventions included providing toys designed for social play or prompting children to use outdoor play equipment that facilitated interaction. Overall, the structured ac-tivities approaches offered mild interventions that increased interaction rates for some children, but they are not the treatments of choice for children with more severe deficits. However, structured group activities provide a useful strategy to augment more individualized and intensive training approaches; the activities are easily integrated into classrooms, can be applied to several children simul-taneously, and serve a preventive function.

Social Skills Training Programs

The forerunner to more comprehensive social skills training programs was the systematic use of coaching. In its purest form, coaching refers to the presenta-tion of instructions during a practice session. In application to childhood social isolation, treatment researchers augmented coaching with behavioral rehearsal, feedback about performance, and reinforcement during training sessions. The predominant feature in coaching is that it involves the teaching of social skills presumed to be important in children's successful interactions with peers. Unlike the unidimensional approaches described earlier, coaching has been used in studies that went beyond simply targeting rate of interaction. Several investigations (e.g., Gottman, Gonso, & Schuler, 1976; Ladd, 1981; Oden & Asher, 1977) targeted sociometric status as an outcome variable and focused on quality of interaction within the intervention. Coaching has generally proven to be an effective intervention method (Wanlass & Prinz, 1982), particularly borne out by Oden and Asher (1977), who found significant improvement in social status at 1-year follow-up compared with two control groups.

Coaching has been applied mostly to mid-elementary school and older children because the cognitive development necessary to understand and benefit from the procedures constrains applicability to younger populations. Coaching approaches vary greatly with respect to number, form and structure of sessions, duration of treatment, and the specific behaviors actually trained. Coaching has been used to train friendship-making skills such as greeting, joining in others' activities, or inviting others to play, cooperation, general participation, conversational skills, sharing, complimenting, and offering support to peers (see Wanlass & Prinz, 1982). By contrast, Bornstein, Bellack, and Hersen (1977) focused on more molecular behaviors, such as eye contact and loudness of speech, in training of assertive skills.

Treatment approaches have evolved into social skills training packages designed to improve functioning in multiple areas. Without stopping to test every component, clinical researchers have proceeded to amalgamate multiple procedures into integrated programs that are relatively well delineated and testable. Three such programs are described here.

Hops and his colleagues developed a program called Procedures for Establishing Effective Relationship Skills (PEERS) for socially deficit children (see Hops, Finch, & McConnell, 1985). The program contains four basic components: (1) social skills tutoring of initiating, responding to initiations by other children, maintaining interactions, complimenting and praising, and sharing; (2) a token reinforcement system for social interaction at recess, with rewards shared by the child's entire class; (3) teacher-orchestrated cooperative tasks between the target child and selected classmates; and (4) daily prompting and reinforcing of child's and peers' social behavior on the playground by the program consultant. The program has been demonstrated to yield positive changes (i.e., rate and quality of social interaction) for severely withdrawn children (Hops, Walker, & Greenwood, 1979; Hops et al., 1985).

In contrast to the PEERS program, Bierman's (1986a,b) approach to social skills training was markedly different. Bierman formed triads consisting of two socially accepted children and one socially rejected child. Coached by an adult, each triad was required to make a videotaped film over 10 half-hour sessions. During those sessions, children were trained in three conversational skills: (1) sharing information about oneself and one's feelings, (2) asking others about themselves and their feelings, and (3) making leadership bids via giving suggestions, advice, and invitations. Procedurally, each skill was explained, children generated and discussed examples of the skill, the skill was practiced in group conversations and activities, and the children actually made a film during the last three sessions. Coaches identified and praised skill performance, encouraged group members to self-evaluate, and guided discussions toward topics related to increasing skill performance. In comparison to a peer-experience condition that controlled for triadic interaction and adult support, the children trained in social skills made significant improvements in naturalistic assessments of conversational skills and positive peer response (Bierman, 1986a,b).

A third approach has been developed by Michelson and his colleagues (Michelson & Mannarino, 1986; Michelson & Wood, 1980). In their earlier work, Michelson and Wood (1980) tested a multifaceted social skills training program that involved 16 hours of training, school-based implementation, and an intensive protocol using instructions, coaching, modeling, behavioral rehearsal, prepared scripts for assertive responses and role-played reactions, discussions, and homework assignments. Topics of intervention included giving and receiving compliments and complaints, refusing unreasonable demands, requesting favors, asking why, expressing empathy, requesting behavior change from others, standing up for one's rights, initiating and maintaining conversations, dealing with authority figures, and related issues. Michelson and Wood (1980) found significantly greater classroom-based improvement in skills for the social skills condition in comparison to control conditions.

In a revised format, Michelson and Mannarino (1986) implemented a social skills training regimen that added interpersonal problem solving as a deliberate cognitive component. Skills were ordered in an hierarchical fashion to allow overall shaping. This treatment package was even more intense than the first program and included more explicit definitions and modeling of each target behavior. Outcome data are pending for this program. Both programs are particularly noteworthy for selecting training modules based on social validation of target behaviors.

SIGNIFICANT ISSUES

Choosing Target Behaviors

A nagging issue in this area is: Which behaviors should be targeted for intervention? There is general concensus that focusing the intervention on increasing the rate of social interaction to the exclusion of other goals does not make sense. However, there is not a concensus as to which behaviors to target. The choice of targets depends first on which subgroup the child belongs to. For example, isolated children with neglected rather than rejected social status need to learn how to successfully enter group activities, to overcome any fears about participation, to assert themselves in situations where they might be mistreated or overlooked, and to make and maintain friendships. Rejected children need to learn how to reduce noxious and inappropriate behavior, to approach others in positive ways, to exhibit self-control, to reinforce and support peers, to converse in positive ways, and to replace self-defeating cognitions with more self-efficacious ones.

Within the two general subgroups and across developmental levels, there is still considerable variability from child to child. Despite a large social skills research literature, we have not yet discriminated critical from noncritical skills and behaviors necessary for attaining social acceptance and competence.

Mixed Samples

Given the state of classification for the various subgroups of children with disturbance in peer relations, it is likely that many of the treatment approaches have been applied to what amounts to mixed samples. Investigations that select on the basis of social status are likely to target a population of children who vary considerably with respect to type and degree of social skills deficits. Similarly, selection on the basis of skill deficits likely yields a sample varying in social acceptance and status. When interventions are tested on mixed samples, there is a danger that moderately positive findings will be overgeneralized to all subgroupings of socially disturbed children. Consequently, it is recommended that interventions be evaluated with homogeneous samples with respect to social status and skill deficits. Furthermore, the definitions of the subpopulation to whom the intervention applies need to be tailored to each particular age group. Preschoolers need basic instruction in sharing, playing cooperatively, interacting calmly, and overcoming shyness. Elementary school children need to acquire conversation skills, friendship-making skills, and self-control skills, and to learn how to better match social behaviors to situations. Adolescents probably need similar skills but on a more advanced plane that takes into account more complex and demanding situations encountered by the older group.

Anxiety, the Neglected Construct

Occasionally, clinicians will come across a child who is highly anxious and also socially isolated. Such a child may anticipate rejection or negative evaluation by peers or at least perceive the likelihood of such a state of affairs even if other children are not actively rejecting the child. A fear of social interaction may serve to promote self-imposed social isolation in such children, with avoidance of social situations being negatively reinforced through the reduction of anxiety arousal. Despite the clinical folklore on anxious children who are socially isolated, as well as the compelling logic of such a scenario, the construct of anxiety has seldom been systematically investigated in etiological or treatment studies of isolated or rejected children. For example, in a review of 34 pre-1982 studies of treatment for childhood social isolation, Wanlass and Prinz (1982) found that only one study noted that anxiety was a characteristic of the children in the treated sample. Most likely, anxiety was not assessed in the treatment studies. However, it is conceivable that anxiety was assessed by some of the investigators but did not emerge as a significant distinguishing feature for the treated sample and consequently was not reported. Alternatively, groups of children being treated for social isolation or rejection may in fact contain only a small subgroup of children who are measurably anxious.

Anxiety has not been totally ignored by investigators interested in childhood social isolation. Strauss, Forehand, Smith and Frame (1986) examined the association between internalizing problems, including anxiety, and social withdrawal in a sample of 120 second through fifth graders. Compared with children whom teachers characterized as socially outgoing, low-frequency interactors (also identified by teachers) reflected significantly greater self-reported anxiety on the Revised Children's Manifest Anxiety Scale. Not surprisingly, the low-frequency interactors were also rated significantly higher with respect to the anxiety–withdrawal scale of the Revised Behavior Problem Checklist.

When peers rather than teachers identified the target groups, anxiety failed to emerge as a discriminator. Cantrell and Prinz (1985) compared 39 rejected, 29 neglected, and 39 accepted children (Grades 3 through 6) and found that the anxiety scale on the teacher version of the Child Behavior Checklist failed to discriminate among the three groups for boys or girls. In this study, social status was derived from peer evaluations and was validated by the fact that teachers characterized the rejected group as significantly more unpopular and socially withdrawn than the other two groups. Taken together, the Strauss *et al.* (1986) and Cantrell and Prinz (1985) studies suggest that neither social status category, rejection, nor social neglect is synonymous with social anxiety, but that there are some children identified as social isolates who do in fact report anxiety.

We do not know what comes first for anxious and withdrawn children, the anxiety or the social isolation. Fearful children conceivably could avoid social interaction from an early age and maintain their avoidance over time. Conversely, children who experience social rejection or maltreatment may in turn develop anxiety as a secondary reaction.

The treatment literature of isolated or rejected children essentially does not address the anxiety construct in a direct manner. The early studies that described interventions with low-interacting preschoolers may have implicitly operationalized anxiety via avoidance, which in turn was defined as a low rate of social initiations. For the most part, however, investigators have focused on social skills deficits, cognitive variables that are presumed to promote rejection-causing behaviors, and social–environmental interventions that promote pro-social behaviors. Anxiety reduction methods have not been an integral part of the interventions, perhaps because most of the children being treated were not characterized as socially anxious.

Future Interventions

Research and treatment on childhood social isolation has come a long way in the past 20 years and is likely to continue to improve at a rapid rate. We might expect to see a more tailored fit between intervention strategy and individual child. Interventions can vary along at least three dimensions: target variables, procedures, and settings. Interventions which assume that all children in a given subgroup start with the same deficits and assets and thus need the same type of assistance are likely to attain only partial success. An alternative strategy is to conceive of a small collection of interventions that permit systematic branching as a function of each child's profile. This individualization would be particularly pertinent in the case of target variables but would also apply to procedures and settings to some degree. Procedures refer to the actual operations, independent of specific target behaviors, that are included in the intervention, such as the use and amount of coaching, feedback, behavior rehearsal, *in vivo* practice, dyadic socialization experiences, reinforcement, cognitive instruction, and modeling. Settings, which can also be tailor picked, include the more traditional locations such as therapy room, group meeting room, and classroom, but they could also encompass less used locations such as the playground, the artificially contrived play group, a child's backyard or home, or somewhere in the neighborhood.

To improve the match between treatment strategy and target child, more subtle distinctions among subgroups will need to be accomplished. A subgroup matrix would conceivably account for such variables as social status (rejected, neglected, accepted), interaction rate (low, average, high), anxiety level (problematic, nonproblematic), aggressiveness, and specific categories of social skills deficits. The dual matrices of intervention components and target children will hopefully evolve and progress concurrently as treatment in this area continues to improve.

REFERENCES

Achenbach, T. M., & Edelbrock, C. (1983). *Manual for the Child Behavior Checklist and Revised Child Behavior Profile.* Burlington, VT: Department of Psychiatry, University of Vermont.

American Psychiatric Association. (1968). *Diagnostic and statistical manual of mental disorders* (2nd ed.). Washington, DC: Author.

American Psychiatric Association. (1980). *Diagnostic and statistical manual of mental disorders* (3rd ed.). Washington, DC: Author.

American Psychiatric Association. (1987). *Diagnostic and statistical manual of mental disorders* (3rd ed., revised). Washington, DC: Author.

Asher, S. R., Markell, R. A., & Hymel, S. (1981). Identifying children at risk in peer relations: A critique of the rate-of-interaction approach to assessment. *Child Development, 52,* 1239–1245.

Asher, S. R., & Wheeler, V. A. (1985). Children's loneliness: A comparison of rejected and neglected peer status. *Journal of Consulting and Clinical Psychology, 53,* 500–505.

Barkley, R. A. (1988). Child behavior rating scales and checklists. In M. Rutter, A. H. Tuma, & I. S. Lann, *Assessment and diagnosis in child psychopathology* (pp. 113–155). New York: Guilford.

Bierman, K. L. (1986a). Process of change during social skills training with preadolescents and its relation to treatment outcome. *Child Development, 57,* 230–240.

Bierman, K. L. (1986b). The relation between social aggression and peer rejection in middle childhood. In R. J. Prinz (Ed.), *Advances in behavioral assessment of children and families* (Vol. 2, pp. 151–178). Greenwich, CT: JAI Press.

Bierman, K. L., & Furman, W. (1984). The effects of social skills training and peer involvement on the social adjustment of preadolescents. *Child Development, 55,* 151–162.

Bornstein, M. R., Bellack, A. S., & Hersen, M. (1977). Social skills training for unassertive children. *Journal of Applied Behavior Analysis, 10,* 183–195.

Cantrell, V. L., & Prinz, R. J. (1985). Multiple perspectives of rejected, neglected, and accepted children: Relations between sociometric status and behavioral characteristics. *Journal of Consulting and Clinical Psychology, 53,* 884–890.

Chennault, M. (1967). Improving the social acceptance of unpopular educable mentally retarded pupils in special classes. *American Journal of Mental Deficiency, 72*, 445–458.

Coie, J. D. (1985). Fitting social skills intervention to the target group. In B. H. Schneider, K. H. Rubin, & J. E. Ledingham (Eds.), *Children's peer relations: Issues in assessment and intervention* (pp. 92–109). New York: Springer-Verlag.

Coie, J. D., & Dodge, K. A. (1983). Continuities and changes in children's social status: A five-year longitudinal study. *Merrill-Palmer Quarterly, 29*, 261–281.

Coie, J. D., Dodge, K. A., & Coppotelli, H. (1982). Dimensions and types of social status: A cross-age perspective. *Developmental Psychology, 18*, 557–571.

Coie, J. D., & Kupersmidt, J. B. (1983). A behavioral analysis of emerging social status in boys' groups. *Child Development, 54*, 1400–1416.

Cooke, T. P., & Apolloni, T. (1976). Developing positive social-emotional behaviors: A study of training and generalization effects. *Journal of Applied Behavior Analysis, 9*, 65–78.

Cowen, E. L., Pederson, A., Babigian, H., Izzo, L. D., & Trost, M. A. (1973). Long-term follow-up of early detected vulnerable children. *Journal of Consulting and Clinical Psychology, 41*, 438–446.

Deluty, R. H. (1979). The Children's Action Tendency Scale: A self-report measure of aggressiveness, assertiveness and submissiveness in children. *Journal of Consulting and Clinical Psychology, 47*, 1061–1071.

Dodge, K. A. (1983). Behavioral antecedents of peer social status. *Child Development, 54*, 1386–1399.

Dodge, K. A., Schlundt, D. C., Schocken, I., & Delugach, J. D. (1983). Social competence and children's sociometric status: The role of peer group entry strategies. *Merrill-Palmer Quarterly, 29*, 309–336.

Foster, S. L., Bell-Dolan, D., & Berler, E. S. (1986). Methodological issues in the use of sociometrics for selecting children for social skills research and training. In R. J. Prinz (Ed.), *Advances in behavioral assessment of children and families* (Vol. 2, pp. 227–248). Greenwich, CT: JAI Press.

Foster, S. L., & Ritchey, W. L. (1979). Issues in the assessment of social competence in children. *Journal of Applied Behavior Analysis, 12*, 625–638.

Furman, W., Rahe, D. F., & Hartup, W. W. (1979). Rehabilitation of socially withdrawn preschool children through mixed-age and same-age socialization. *Child Development, 50*, 915–922.

Gottman, J. (1977). The effects of a modeling film on social isolation in preschool children: A methodological investigation. *Journal of Abnormal Child Psychology, 5*, 69–78.

Gottman, J. M. (1983). How children become friends. *Monographs of the Society for Research in Child Development, 48* (Serial No. 201).

Gottman, J., Gonso, J., & Schuler, P. (1976). Teaching social skills to isolated children. *Journal of Abnormal Child Psychology, 4*, 179–197.

Harter, S. (1982). The perceived competence scale for children. *Child Development, 53*, 87–97.

Hartup, W. W., Glazer, J. A., & Charlesworth, R. (1967). Peer reinforcement and sociometric status. *Child Development, 38*, 1017–1024.

Hops, H., Finch, M., & McConnell, S. (1985). Social skills deficits. In P. H. Bornstein & A. E. Kazdin (Eds.), *Social skills deficits* (pp. 543–598). Homewood, IL: Dorsey Press.

Hops, H., & Greenwood, C. R. (1988). Social skill deficits. In E. J. Mash & L. G. Terdal (Eds.), *Behavioral assessment of childhood disorders* (2nd ed., pp. 263–314). New York: Guilford.

Hops, H., Walker, H. M., & Greenwood, C. R. (1979). PEERS: A program for remediating social withdrawal in school. In L. A. Hamerlynck (Ed.), *Behavioral systems for the developmentally disabled: I. School and family environments* (pp. 48–86). New York: Bruner/Mazel.

Hymel, S., & Franke, S. (1985). Children's peer relations: Assessing self-perceptions. In B. H. Schneider, K. H. Rubin, & J. E. Ledingham, *Children's peer relations: Issues in assessment and intervention* (pp. 75–91). New York: Springer-Verlag.

Janes, C. L., & Hesselbrock, V. M. (1978). Problem children's adult adjustment predicted from teacher's ratings. *American Journal of Orthopsychiatry, 48*, 300–309.

Keller, M. F., & Carlson, P. M. (1974). The use of symbolic modeling to promote social skills in preschool children with low levels of social responsiveness. *Child Development, 45*, 912–919.

Krantz, M. (1982). Sociometric awareness, social participation, and perceived popularity in preschool children. *Child Development, 53*, 376–379.

Krehbiel, G. G., & Milich, R. (1986). Issues in the assessment and treatment of socially rejected children. In R. J. Prinz (Ed.), *Advances in behavioral assessment of children and families* (Vol. 2, pp. 249–270). Greenwich, CT: JAI Press.

Ladd, G. W. (1981). Effectiveness of a social learning method for enhancing children's social interaction and peer acceptance. *Child Development, 52,* 171–178.

La Greca, A. M., & Stark, P. (1986). Naturalistic observations of children's social behavior. In P. S. Strain, M. J. Guralnick, & H. M. Walker (Eds.), *Children's social behavior: Development, assessment, and modification* (pp. 181–214). New York: Academic Press.

Masten, A. S., Morison, P., & Pellegrini, D. S. (1985). A revised class play method of peer assessment. *Developmental Psychology, 21,* 523–533.

McConnell, S. R., & Odom, S. L. (1986). Sociometrics: Peer-referenced measures and the assessment of social competence. In P. S. Strain, M. J. Guralnick, & H. M. Walker (Eds.), *Children's social behavior: Development, assessment, and modification* (pp. 215–286). New York: Academic Press.

Michelson, L., & Mannarino, A. (1986). Social skills training with children: Research and clinical application. In P. S. Strain, M. J. Guralnick, & H. M. Walker (Eds.), *Children's social behavior: Development, assessment, and modification* (pp. 373–406). New York: Academic Press.

Michelson, L., & Wood, R. (1980). A group assertive training program for elementary school children. *Child Behavior Therapy, 2,* 1–9.

O'Connor, R. D. (1969). Modification of social withdrawal through symbolic modeling. *Journal of Applied Behavior Analysis, 2,* 15–22.

O'Connor, R. D. (1972). Relative efficacy of modeling, shaping and the combined procedures for modification of social withdrawal. *Journal of Abnormal Psychology, 79,* 327–334.

Oden, S., & Asher, S. R. (1977). Coaching children in social skills for friendship making. *Child Development, 48,* 495–506.

Peery, J. C. (1979). Popular, amiable, isolated, rejected: A reconceptualization of sociometric status in preschool children. *Child Development, 50,* 1231–1234.

Pekarik, E. G., Prinz, R. J., Liebert, D. E., Weintraub, S., & Neale, J. M. (1976). The Pupil Evaluation Inventory: A sociometric technique for assessing children's social behavior. *Journal of Abnormal Child Psychology, 4,* 83–97.

Roff, M., Sells, B., & Golden, M. M. (1972). *Social adjustment and personality development in children.* Minneapolis: University of Minnesota Press.

Rubin, K. H., & Cohen, J. S. (1986). The Revised Class Play: Correlates of peer assessed social behaviors in middle childhood. In R. J. Prinz (Ed.), *Advances in behavioral assessment of children and families* (Vol. 2, pp. 179–206). Greenwich, CT: JAI.

Rucker, C. N., & Vincenzo, F. M. (1970). Maintaining social acceptance gains made by mentally retarded children. *Exceptional Children, 36,* 679–680.

Strain, P. S., & Wiegerink, R. (1976). The effects of sociodramatic activities on social interaction among behaviorally disordered preschool children. *Journal of Special Education, 10,* 71–75.

Strauss, C. C., Forehand, R., Smith, K., & Frame, C. L. (1986). The association between social withdrawal and internalizing problems of children. *Journal of Abnormal Child Psychology, 14,* 525–535.

Tremblay, A., Strain, P. S., Hendrickson, J. M., & Shores, R. E. (1981). Social interactions of normal preschool children. *Behavior Modification, 5,* 237–253.

Walker, H. M. (1983). *Walker Problem Behavior Identification Checklist* (2nd ed. Los Angeles, CA: Western Psychological Services.

Walker, H. M., Greenwood, C. R., Hops, H., & Todd, N. (1979). Differential effects of reinforcing topographic components of free play social interaction: Analysis and systematic replication. *Behavior Modification, 3,* 291–321.

Wanlass, R. L., & Prinz, R. J. (1982). Methodological issues in conceptualizing and treating childhood social isolation. *Psychological Bulletin, 92,* 39–55.

Watt, N. F., & Lubensky, A. (1976). Childhood roots of schizophrenia. *Journal of Abnormal Psychology, 85,* 363–375.

Weintraub, S., Prinz, R. J., & Neale, J. M. (1978). Peer evaluations of the competence of children vulnerable to psychopathology. *Journal of Abnormal Child Psychology, 6,* 461–473.

6

School Phobia and Separation Anxiety

Thomas H. Ollendick and Neville J. King

Introduction

Attempts to both understand and modify the fears and phobias of children have a long and rich history in clinical psychology and psychiatry (Freud 1909/1963; Hall, 1897; Jones, 1924; Watson & Rayner, 1920). School phobia, the particular focus of this chapter, has not been as widely studied until recently, however. Of course, school phobia, as with other child behavior disorders, can be approached from a number of theoretical and clinical perspectives (Morris & Kratochwill, 1983). In this chapter, we review the current status of school phobia from a learning-based perspective. Rather than index all of the literature or issues in the area (see reviews by Atkinson, Quarrington & Cyr, 1985; Blagg, 1987; Hersov, 1977; Hersov & Berg, 1980; Ollendick & Mayer, 1984), our objective is to provide an overview of school phobia. Following a description of school phobia, we highlight diagnostic, etiological, assessment, and intervention issues. Recent years have witnessed a resurgence of interest in school phobia, especially the relationship between school phobia and separation anxiety. In addressing these issues, the complexity of school phobia will be apparent, along with meaningful directions for clinicians and researchers.

At this stage, it is necessary to differentiate the excessive and maladaptive fears of children from those which are mild and transitory. Children display many fears over the course of development (cf. Angelino, Dollins, & Mech, 1956; Angelino & Shedd, 1953; Jersild & Holmes, 1935; Lapouse & Monk, 1959; Mac-Farlane, Allen, & Honzik, 1954), most of which are short lived and considered to be a part of normal development (Bamber, 1974; Bauer, 1976; Ollendick, 1979). Children's fears become more problematic, however, when they are excessive, persist over time, and produce significant discomfort for the child (Graziano,

Thomas H. Ollendick • Department of Psychology, Virginia Polytechnic Institute and State University, Blacksburg, Virginia 24061.   Neville J. King • Faculty of Education, Monash University, Clayton, Victoria 3168, Australia.

DeGiovanni, & Garcia, 1979; King, Hamilton, & Ollendick, 1988; Morris & Kratochwill, 1983). These fears are customarily referred to as *clinical fears* or *phobias*. The following characteristics typify children's phobias: (1) they are out of proportion to the demands of the situation, (2) they cannot be explained or reasoned away, (3) they are beyond voluntary control, (4) they lead to avoidance of the feared situation, (5) they persist over an extended period of time, (6) they are unadaptive, and (7) they are not age or stage specific (Marks, 1969; Miller, Barrett, & Hampe, 1974).

It appears that many children experience difficulties in school adjustment and that a minority at least find school to be highly aversive (cf. King *et al.*, 1989; Mitchell & Shepherd, 1967; Moore, 1966; Ollendick, Matson, & Helsel, 1985). Children who evince school phobia, however, are behaving in ways that are unrealistic, inappropriate, and persistent. This unwarranted fear leads to a refusal to voluntarily attend school and subsequent avoidance of the school situation. Although this definition may appear straightforward and applicable to children with a phobia of school, several theoretical and practical issues become apparent as we examine school phobia.

DESCRIPTION

The clinical features of school phobia have been described by many authorities (e.g., Blagg, 1987; Hersov, 1977; McDonald & Shepherd, 1976). The child's refusal to attend school along with excessive anxiety about school are the most obvious indications of school phobia. Despite the efforts of parents and teachers, regular school attendance breaks down for these children. Hersov (1977) aptly observed that

> The problem often starts with vague complaints of school or reluctance to attend, progressing to total refusal to go to school or to remain in school in the face of persuasion, entreaty, recrimination and punishment by parents and pressure from teachers, family doctors and educational welfare officers. The behaviour may be accompanied by overt signs of anxiety or even panic when the time comes to go to school, and most children cannot even leave home to set out for school. Many who do, return home halfway there, and some children once at school rush home in a state of anxiety. Many children insist that they want to go to school and prepare to do so but cannot manage it when the time comes. (pp. 458–459)

Pressure on the child to attend school usually elicits somatic complaints such as nausea, headache, abdominal pain, sore throat, fevers, and so forth. Noncompliance, temper tantrums, and crying are common responses to parental efforts aimed at getting the child off to school. These anxiety symptoms and aggressive behaviors tend to disappear once the child has been assured that school attendance is no longer required (McDonald & Shepherd, 1976). A few school-phobic children become depressed and withdrawn and may threaten suicide (Blagg, 1987). Typically, these children stay at home through the day under the care of their mother or another person known to the family. Whereas an acute onset is more often seen in young children, it appears that older children and adolescents undergo a more insidious development of school phobia (Hersov, 1977). Episodes of school phobia are frequently triggered by significant changes in the child's life. These precipitating events include, for example, a change of class or school, traumatic or disappointing experiences at school, prolonged absence from school because of illness, and the death of a friend or relative (Hersov, 1960b; Ollendick & Mayer, 1984).

School-phobic children should not be confused with another group of children who refuse to attend school for reasons unrelated to anxiety. These youths are usually not at home throughout the school day and may in fact engage in lying, stealing, cheating, and destructive behaviors. This problem is usually referred to as "truancy" and will not be elaborated upon further here (see Blagg, 1987; Hersov & Berg, 1980).

The characteristics of school-phobic children deserve brief commentary, as certain findings are contrary to what is frequently assumed. While boys outnumber girls for most types of child behavior disorders (Ollendick & Hersen, 1983; Quay & Werry, 1979), school phobia tends to be equally common in both sexes (Berg, Nichols, & Pritchard, 1969; Blagg, 1979; Johnson, 1979; Kennedy, 1965). School phobia can occur throughout the entire range of school years, but it appears there are major peaks at certain ages. Ollendick and Mayer (1984) concluded that school phobia is more likely to occur between 5–6 years and 10–11 years of age. Somewhat similarly, others have observed major peaks at 5–6 years, 11–12 years and 13–14 years (Blagg, 1979; Blagg & Yule, 1984). While it might be expected that school phobia would predominate in children of lower intellectual ability or those who show learning disabilities, this has not been found. Certain findings suggest that the majority of school phobics are of average or above average intelligence and demonstrate a high standard of school work (Goldberg, 1953; Rodriguez, Rodriguez, & Eisenberg, 1959; Warren, 1948). However, it has been pointed out that such findings may be a function of selection bias (Blagg, 1987). In fact, school phobics show a normal distribution of intelligence and include children with learning difficulties (Blagg & Yule, 1984; Chazan, 1962; Hampe, Noble, Miller, & Barrett, 1973; Miller, Barrett, Hampe & Noble, 1972a). In summary, school phobia occurs primarily in younger children and is evident in both girls and boys. As well, children of varying levels of intelligence and diverse levels of academic achievement are equally prone to school phobia.

School phobia is a child behavior disorder that is significant for several reasons. Of course, persistent nonattendance at school raises questions regarding the child's social and educational development. According to Hersov, "long-continued absence may lead to educational backwardness, with far-reaching effects upon social and educational adjustment in later school life and adulthood" (1960a, p. 130). Here, it may be argued that our concern for school phobia is an expression of middle-class values about the role of education in society. Nonetheless, school attendance is mandatory, and there are legal pressures against persistent absenteeism. School phobia has also been of concern clinically because of its possible relationship to agoraphobia and other adult fears (Berg, 1976; Berg, Marks, McGuire & Lipsedge, 1974; Gittelman & Klein, 1985; Hallam,

1978). Possibly reflecting the educational and clinical significance of the problem, school phobia has been strongly represented in the professional literature. In reviewing the behavioral studies on all childhood fears since 1924, Graziano and DeGiovanni (1979) found that 86% addressed school phobia.

The incidence of school phobia has proved difficult to estimate as in the case of children's phobias in general. As might be expected, the incidence of school phobia depends on the criteria used to define it. For example, Kennedy (1965) estimated the incidence of school phobia to be 1.7% of school-aged children. Burke and Silverman (1987) concluded that school phobia is seen in approximately 5% of all clinic-referred children and occurs in 1% of all school-aged children. Further, it has been suggested that the incidence of school phobia may be increasing. For example, Eisenberg (1958) noted the incidence to have risen from 3 cases per 1,000 to 17 cases per 1,000 over an 8-year period. While it is difficult to determine whether the incidence of school phobia is increasing over the years, it is true that youngsters with this condition are regularly referred to clinics for assessment and treatment.

Diagnostic Issues

Historically, the term *school phobia* was introduced by psychoanalytic-oriented clinicians who called for a close examination of the mutual anxiety between mother and child arising from "poorly resolved early dependency" (Johnson, Falstein, Szurek & Svendsen, 1941). Other Freudian workers had described this form of school avoidance as "psychoneurotic truancy" and a manifestation of the "mother following syndrome" (Broadwin, 1932; Partridge, 1939). Thus, these early accounts of school phobia posited that the child suffered from "deep-seated neuroses of the obsessional type." School-phobic children were said to be obsessed by thoughts of harm or death to their mother. Only by returning home from school could the child be assured that no tragedy had befallen the mother and that she was all right. From this perspective, school phobia was viewed as a form of clinical anxiety, precipitated by fear of leaving home rather than fear of school *per se*. In fact, Johnson and her co-workers (Estes, Haylett, & Johnson, 1956) later coined the term *separation anxiety* to provide a diagnostic label that more accurately reflected the locus of pathology from their psychodynamic perspective. The child's fear of school was said to mask what was in large part the child's anxiety about leaving mother, as well as mother's anxieties about separating from the child.

As Ollendick and Mayer (1984) point out, this early work is of more than historical importance. Given these developments, early attention centered upon examination of parent–child relationships and their subsequent impact on school phobia. As a result, considerable definitional and diagnostic problems became evident. Is the child's "phobia" due to separation anxiety from mother or to a real fear of some aspect of the school situation? Is the child afraid to leave home or to go to school? Or both? The resolution of these issues in each case is of extreme importance because of the need to determine whether treatment should be directed primarily toward returning the child to school, to resolving parent–child relationships in the home, or both (Yates, 1970).

Identifying the precipitants of school phobia would appear to be a valuable step toward the resolution of this diagnostic confusion. In a study of 50 cases of school refusal, Hersov (1960b) found that the most common precipitating factor was changes to a new school (19 cases). The death, departure, or illness of a parent (usually the mother) precipitated school refusal in 9 cases. An illness, accident, or operation which led to the child being hospitalized or staying at home was a precipitating factor in 5 cases. However, no clear precipitating factor could be found in 17 cases. The children were also asked why they refused to attend school. The most common explanation was fear of some harm to mother while the child was at school. The other explanations offered by the children included fear of a strict, sarcastic teacher; fear of ridicule, bullying, or harm from other children; and fear of academic failure. In addition, fears about menstruation in girls and concerns about puberty and masturbation were evident in boys.

Ollendick and Mayer (1984) reported that of 37 school-phobic children they had seen in their clinic, 13 cases were judged as primarily due to "separation" problems, 15 appeared to be related to fears of specific aspects of the school situation (e.g., new school, failure, examinations, showers, teachers), and the remaining 9 occurred following absence from school due to illnesses and associated anticipatory anxiety about returning to school. Further, several of these cases shared elements of the above three primary categories; for example, it was not uncommon for a child to express fear of mother's health and a fear of entering a new school (or grade) following relocation. Collectively, these findings suggest that while separation anxiety is a salient factor, it may play a more limited role in school phobia than thought heretofore.

In fact, the findings of a recent study suggest that separation anxiety should be differentiated from school phobia (Last, Francis, Hersen, Kazdin, & Strauss, 1987). Using diagnostic criteria specified in the *Diagnostic and Statistical Manual of Mental Disorders* (DSM-III; American Psychiatric Association, 1980), Last *et al.* (1987) compared the clinical and associated features of the two disorders. Whereas separation anxiety disorder is given in DSM-III and its revision, this is not the case for school phobia. Consequently, the children with a phobia of school were diagnosed as having a phobic disorder (simple or social). These researchers found that children with separation anxiety disorder generally were female, prepubertal, and from families of lower socioeconomic status, whereas children with school phobia tended to be male, postpubertal, and from higher socioeconomic backgrounds.

Many of the children under study had at least one concurrent disorder of which overanxious disorder was most prominent. Almost all of the children with separation anxiety disorder (92%) had a concurrent disorder, compared to 63% of the school-phobic children. Not unexpectedly, children with separation anxiety disorder were less likely to exhibit school refusal than children with school phobia. There were no significant differences between the groups on the State–Trait Anxiety Inventory for Children, the Children's Manifest Anxiety Scale or the Revised-Fear Survey Schedule for Children. However, children with separation anxiety disorder reported more specific fears on average than children with school phobia (18 and 11 fears, respectively). Focusing on maternal psychiatric illness, it was found that the majority of mothers in the separation anxiety disorder and school phobia groups had a lifetime history of at least one anxiety disorder, with generalized anxiety disorder being most prominent. The researchers concluded that the "results from our investigation indicate that separation anxiety disorder and school-phobic disorder differ on a number of dimensions, thus supporting the use of DSM-III criteria for differentially diagnosing the two anxiety disorders" (Last et al., 1987, p. 656).

Although school phobia has a variety of causes and can be differentiated from separation anxiety disorder, it is necessary to develop an agreed-upon set of *explicit* criteria for diagnostic and treatment purposes. For our own clinical and research purposes, we recommend the guidelines set forth by Berg et al. (1969):

1. Severe difficulty attending school often resulting in prolonged absence.
2. Severe emotional upset, including excessive fearfulness, temper outbursts, or complaints of feeling ill when faced with the prospect of going to school.
3. Staying at home with knowledge of the parent when the youngster should be at school.
4. Absence of antisocial characteristics such as stealing, lying, and destructiveness.

These criteria maintain the distinction between school truancy, which is often associated with conduct disorders, and school phobia, which is frequently associated with anxiety disorders (Ollendick & Hersen, 1983; Quay & Werry, 1979), a distinction first offered by Broadwin (1932) and Partridge (1939). Further, the criteria call for evidence of prolonged absence, excessive fearfulness, somatic complaints, and adamant refusal to attend school—all characteristics which are commonly observed in school-phobic children. What is equally important, the criteria do not prejudge etiology; rather, they allow for a multiplicity of causal patterns. In our own work, we have elaborated upon these criteria by operationalizing prolonged absence as at least 2 weeks in duration and by employing self-report, other-report, and behavioral indices of fear. It is noted that other workers have also adopted these diagnostic criteria (e.g., Baker & Wills, 1979; Blagg & Yule, 1984).

In addition to these primary features which characterize all school-phobic children, several authors have described associated features which may help to delineate various subtypes of school phobia. Coolidge, Hahn, and Peck (1957) first offered a distinction between two basic subtypes of school phobia: neurotic and characterological. This distinction, repeated by these same investigators (Waldfogel, Coolidge, & Hahn, 1957), was later adopted by other workers (e.g., Kahn & Nursten, 1962; Kennedy, 1965). In essence, it discriminates between what has come to be known as Type I and Type II school phobias. Type I, or the neurotic variety, is characterized by the following features (Kennedy, 1965): (1) the present episode is the first; (2) Monday onset, following an illness the previous Thursday or Friday; (3) an acute onset; (4) more prevalent in early elementary grades; (5) concern about death; (6) mother's physical health in question—or at least child fears so; (7) generally good communication between parents; (8) mother and father well adjusted; (9) father involved in household management and child rearing; and (10) parents easy to work with and have basic understanding of what child is experiencing. In contrast, Type II, or characterological phobia, is characterized by an obverse pattern: gradual, insidious onset in an older child in whom death themes are not present and whose parents are considerably more difficult to work with, showing little insight into the child's behavior. As is apparent from characteristics of both Type I and Type II school phobia, emphasis is placed upon neuroticism in the child and faulty parenting as general characteristics.

In contrast, Hersov (1960b) has identified a different set of subtypes based on family relationships. In this schema, three subtypes are delineated: Type I: mother is overindulgent, father is passive, and child is demanding at home but passive in school; Type II: mother is overcontrolling, father is passive, and child is obedient at home but timid in school; and Type III: mother is overindulgent, father is firm, and the child is wilful at school but friendly at home. In a similar vein, Weiss and Cain (1964) identified two basic subtypes: an overdependent child with an overprotective mother (Type I) and an overdependent child with a rejecting mother (Type II). Although differences exist among these systems of classification, it appears that the neurotic type of Coolidge et al. (1957) is conceptually similar to Kennedy's (1965) Type I, Hersov's (1960b) Type I and Type II, and Weiss and Cain's (1964) Type I. Similarly, the characterological type of Coolidge et al. is like Kennedy's Type II, Hersov's Type III, and Weiss and Cain's Type II. The primary distinction resides in whether the proposed systems are dealing with basic personality characteristics of the child (Coolidge et al., 1957; Kennedy, 1965) or with the constellation of family relationships (Hersov, 1960b; Weiss & Cain, 1964).

Although these subtypes have been reported frequently in the literature, there are little or no data available regarding their reliability, validity, or clinical utility. For example, while Kennedy (1965) found the distinction between Type I and Type II school phobia to be differentially predictive of child–parent characteristics and treatment outcome, Berg et al. (1969) failed to support such distinctions. Further, in a comparison between school-phobic children and their parents, on the one hand, and a matched group of nonphobic but neurotic youngsters and their parents, on the other, Waldron (1976) reported that although children who were phobic differed on certain dimensions (e.g., more dependent and inhibited), parents of the two groups of children did not. Thus, differential parent characteristics were not substantiated, casting doubt on the validity of delineating subtypes on the basis of parental characteristics alone. Clearly, more research is required before the reliability and validity of subtyping can be established and before such conceptual distinctions can be meaningfully used in clinical practice. Certainly, our own experience suggests that these children and their parents do not present themselves as neat and packaged subtypes. Individual differences in the factors which precipitate and maintain school-avoidance behavior are so diverse that interventions based on a thorough assessment may be more successful than those based on diagnostic categories offered to date (King *et al.*, 1988).

Etiology

The development and maintenance of school phobia is an intriguing question about which there is much controversy but little empirical data. Most attempts to account for school phobia have relied upon psychoanalytic and behavioral models. From a psychoanalytic perspective, children's phobias are symptomatic of underlying disturbances, as exemplified in the legendary case of little Hans (Freud 1909/1963). More specifically, psychoanalytic theory suggests that school phobia is the result of an unresolved mother–child dependency relationship which leads to anxiety in both child and mother when separation is imminent. This heightened anxiety occurs because the child is basically "disturbed" and lives in a family characterized by "disturbed" relationships. As we noted earlier, Johnson and her coworkers (Johnson *et al.*, 1941; Waldfogel *et al.*, 1957) proposed that school phobia was due to "deep-seated neurosis of the obsessional type" and that fear of school represented a form of displacement of anxiety from its real source (separation from other) to a source more palatable to the child (the school). Further, from this perspective, the mother of the school-phobic child was thought to unconsciously support the child's fear by strongly sympathizing with complaints about school. The mother herself was thought to view school as an impersonal and unpleasant place, and indirectly communicated the message that she wished the child to remain at home with her. From this perspective, school phobia was, and continues to be, viewed as a clinical variant of separation anxiety. It will be recalled from the previous section that separation anxiety is not *the* cause of school phobia: heterogeneity rather than homogeneity prevails (Atkinson *et al.*, 1985; Ollendick & Mayer, 1984). Additionally, a number of more general criticisms have been made of the psychoanalytic theory of children's phobias (see, for example, Bandura, 1969; Eysenck, 1965; Rachman & Costello, 1961; Wolpe & Rachman, 1960).

Taking a behavioral perspective, we view school phobia as a *learned* response that has been judged to be maladaptive. The challenge is to understand the causal processes in a clinically meaningful way. To this end the principles of classical, operant, and vicarious conditioning have been employed (King *et al.*, 1988; Miller *et al.*, 1974; Ollendick & Mayer, 1984). Such principles have been used to account for problems in separation as well as specific fears about the school situation itself. For example, Yates (1970) acknowledged the potential importance of mother–child relationships and separation anxiety. Since parents act as strong reinforcers for children during the preschool years, the children see them as a refuge to which they may return when they feel frightened or uncertain. Feelings of anxiety about separation may be both prompted and reinforced by a mother (or father) who is overly concerned about the safety of her child. Consequently, many children will feel some anxiety in separation from the mother when first attending school. Whether or not this anxiety develops into a fear of school will depend on the availability of reinforcers in the school, which effectively compete with anxiety reactions, and on the response of the mother to the fears of the child. Hence, the genesis of a school phobia may be complexly determined by one or more of the following factors: "separation anxiety leading to overdependence on the home as a safe refuge; insufficient rewards or actual anxiety-arousing experiences at school; and possibly, of course, actual traumatic events at school" (Yates, 1970, p. 152). This influential account of school phobia signifies that behavioral formulations can accommodate separation anxiety. Even if separation anxiety is not a contributing factor, conditioning principles are still useful in understanding the development and maintenance of school phobia.

Classical conditioning principles are frequently invoked to account for trauma-induced phobias in children. Illustratively, some children may become school phobic following actual traumatic events at school, such as being teased and bullied by peers. Following several unpleasant incidents of this nature, the child becomes afraid of the peers responsible for these actions. However, the child's fears may also generalize to other children at school. Consequently, a major aspect of school life has become extremely anxiety provoking, and the child turns to avoidance as a means of coping. Refusing to go to school produces conflict at home, but this is not nearly as aversive as the prospect of being bullied at school. As well, the child's phobia of school may intensify even in the absence of further trauma. Eysenck (1979) believes that several factors (e.g., brief exposures to the conditioned stimulus) may facilitate "incubation" of this kind. Thus, brief exposures to school, as sometimes happens in unsuccessful efforts at school return, may produce an even more frightened child. Assuming the validity of the construct (see Bersh, 1980; Eysenck, 1979), the extent to which incubation occurs in school phobia remains to be determined. Nevertheless, it is well established that certain cases of school phobia are acquired through this conditioning process (e.g., Lazarus & Abramovitz, 1962, Lazarus, Davison, & Polefka, 1965; Miller, 1972).

Vicarious conditioning principles may also be an influence in the development of school phobia. For children constantly exposed to peers and siblings who are afraid of school, there is the potential for acquiring a similar fear through observational learning (e.g., Hersen, 1970). Additionally, the child's parents may be poor coping models evinced by their nervousness and anxiety where school matters and teachers are concerned. The precise mechanisms by which children acquire phobias through observational learning is unknown, although arousal level, attention to the model, identification with the model, and possible consequences of such behavior may be important factors (Bandura, 1969). The transmission of fear-inducing information by parents and others is another factor in the vicarious acquisition of children's phobias (Rachman, 1977). In discussing their own experiences about school, for example, parents and older siblings may inadvertently convey the impression that schools are places to be feared. Although children's fears are frequently similar to those of their parents (Bandura & Menlove, 1968; Hagman, 1932; Windheuser, 1977), it is believed that vicarious conditioning may not be as powerful as direct conditioning in phobia acquisition (Emmelkamp, 1982; Rachman, 1977).

Operant conditioning principles provide us with useful insights into the acquisition of school phobia as shown by Ollendick and Mayer (1984). For example, some children make negative statements about school and how bad they feel at school, and they subsequently opt to stay home instead of going to school. Parents and significant others in the child's environment may inadvertently reinforce such statements and behaviors, thereby contributing to the child's desire to avoid school. Under these circumstances, the child probably does not possess an excessive fear of school but has found it simply more reinforcing at home (parental attention and affection). Of course, the child's reluctance to go to school may be genuine and reflect what the child perceives as a punishing environment (perceived criticism and academic failure). The child who is continuously subject to ridicule and criticism from peers or teachers may have legitimate problems. On the other hand, the child's complaints can be exaggerated. In such cases, the child learns that parents are overly sensitive to such complaints and that they respond with much attention. Thus, a little "fear" leads to intense and frequent responses from significant others. The more fear and avoidance behavior the child displays, the more attention he or she receives. An analysis of this kind is supported by several case investigations (e.g., Ayllon, Smith, & Rogers, 1970; Hersen, 1970).

Regardless of the derivation of a child's phobia of school, it may be compounded by the child's academic and social inadequacies. Our clinical experience suggests that often school-phobic children find it difficult to cope at school, with many worries about classwork and social interactions. Aversive experiences at school can be a function of the child not having the requisite skills to cope with the demands placed upon him or her. Ross (1981) illustrates how academic skill deficits contribute to school refusal:

> Afraid of school and therefore avoiding it, a girl falls behind the school work and then fears returning even more because in going back to school she might encounter academic failure. Conversely, a boy who is not doing well academically may find school so aversive that he refuses to go there, whereupon the extended absence results in even greater academic retardation. (p. 252)

Whereas Ross discusses academic skill deficits as a crucial factor in school phobia, social skill must also be taken into consideration. Oftentimes school-phobic children lack the necessary social skills and self-confidence needed to mix with other children, and approach their teacher(s), in an appropriate manner. A child with these difficulties must inevitably suffer many negative consequences given that social skills are necessary for most aspects of school life.

Having identified the various sources of conditioning in the development of school phobia, the complexity of these processes must be emphasized. Not all children develop school phobia, despite the fact that many children have similar learning histories. Therefore, children who acquire school phobia must be *susceptible* to conditioning influences. Eysenck (1957, 1967) saw this susceptibility mainly in the individual's personality. Accordingly, school phobia is more likely to develop in children who are introverted and endowed with a labile autonomic nervous system (neuroticism; Rachman, 1968). Another predisposing factor may be the degree of stress experienced by the child at the time of conditioning. The accumulation of stressful events may disinhibit or potentiate mild fear states and lead to the development of conditioned fear (Lovibond, 1966). In other words, school phobia is more readily conditioned in children who are functioning under stress. In perusing the charts of children with excessive fears, Poznanski (1973) observed that

> the children with excessive fears tended to have the onset of their fears associated with a definite historical event. For example, one child witnessed the slaughtering of a pet cow, another child connected the onset of fears with watching the Kennedy funeral on TV while a third child's fears were associated with a brother's being sent to Vietnam. (p. 432)

These findings led Poznanski to conclude that preexisting stress is an important factor in the acquisition of phobias: "Most of the children who were excessively fearful seemed to have more than the usual amount of anxiety prior to the onset of the excessive fears, and a mild situational stress precipitated a more open display of fears and anxiety" (p. 432). Obviously, more needs to be known about the factors that predispose children to develop a phobia of school.

Furthermore, the conditioning process itself is likely to be interactive in the development and maintenance of school phobia. For example, a child already upset by a death in the family suffers a traumatic experience at school (classical conditioning), observes another child's fear behavior of school (vicarious conditioning), and receives an inordinate amount of attention for the phobic behavior (operant conditioning). Typically, the child's perception of school becomes negative; school is believed to be a frightening place in which it is impossible to cope. From a social learning theory perspective, school phobia can be due to traumatic experiences, observational learning, instruction, or reinforcement; but the final common pathway entails the learned expectations children have about their inability to cope with school. Once established, these "efficacy expectations" can be self-initiated or activated by the environment, producing autonomic arousal and/or escape–avoidance behavior (Wilson & O'Leary, 1980). A major attraction of social learning theory is the emphasis upon the reciprocity between the individual and the environment. Unlike traditional conditioning theories that assume unidirectional causality (i.e., the environment acting upon the individual), social learning theory acknowledges the interaction between behavior, cognitive and other internal events, and the external environment. It is to be hoped that more attention will be given to social learning theory by those interested in the development of an integrated model of school phobia.

ASSESSMENT

Consistent with current thinking about child behavioral assessment (Mash & Terdal, 1981; Ollendick & Hersen, 1984), we advise a multimethod approach to the behavioral assessment of school phobia. Nowadays, child behavioral assessment involves the use of behavioral interviews, ratings forms and checklists, traditional standardized instruments, behavioral observations, physiological instruments, and so forth. Collectively, these varied sources of information help us obtain a complete picture of the child and the treatment context (Ollendick & Hersen, 1984). It is not always possible or necessary to use all assessment strategies. The specific assessment methods used depend on the nature of the referral question and the time and resources available to the clinician. Because of their specific relevance to the behavioral assessment of school phobia, we examine the behavioral interview, rating forms, and behavioral observations.

Behavioral Interviews

The behavioral interview has three primary purposes: (1) to establish a positive relationship with the child and his or her care givers, (2) to obtain specific information about the phobic behavior and its antecedents and consequent conditions, and (3) to determine the larger social and cultural context in which the behavior occurs. The development of a positive relationship helps to increase the likelihood of the child and his or her family willingly and honestly sharing their concerns so that accurate information can be obtained (Lazarus, 1971; Truax & Carkhuff, 1967). Basic helping skills, including empathy, warmth, and genuineness, together with a sense of humor, help facilitate rapport and make the interview a less threatening experience for both child and care givers.

In working with children and their families, special problems may arise during the interview because of the child's limited verbal abilities (especially younger children), frequent fear of strangers (i.e., "doctors"), and embarrassment about "the problem." Oftentimes parents, as well as clinicians, ignore, or at least fail to attend to, the child's own observations. Statements like "he's too young to know what's really going on" and "let's not discuss it in front of her, it will probably only make matters worse" unnecessarily prevail. In our own practice, we routinely interview the child (regardless of age) *prior* to requesting parents and teachers to complete ratings forms, or prior to observing the child in the home or school setting. We use this procedure for ethical reasons and to obtain the explicit cooperation of the child (Ollendick & Cerny, 1981; Ollendick & Mayer, 1984).

When interviewing young children, it is frequently necessary to simplify questions to make them concrete and specific. Such a strategy requires skill and patience; skill in using words the child will understand and patience in clarifying and restating questions until they are understood. In those cases where the child is seemingly unable to describe the fear-producing events, instructing the child to imagine what goes on when he or she is afraid may be helpful. Such a procedure was used by Smith and Sharpe (1970) in their assessment of a school-phobic child. The child was asked to imagine in minute detail a school day, from the time he woke up to his return home from school. He was assisted in this process by specific questions about concrete events, such as what he was wearing, whom he was with, and where he was. During this process he was carefully observed for behavioral indices of fear: flushing of the skin, increased body movements, vocal tremors, and crying. Based on this process, it was surmised that certain school classes produced greatest anxiety. In particular, the child apparently was afraid of being called on in these classes and being made fun of by his teacher and peers. This procedure was also helpful in ruling out separation from mother as a source of intense anxiety; visualizing leaving mother evoked no indices of anxiety, a finding later confirmed by parents and by direct observation.

In general, a thorough interview should examine the early precursors to the school phobia, current antecedent and consequent conditions, and topographical features (frequency, intensity, and duration). The child's history and anxieties need exploration, along with the specific aspects of the family and school situations and previous treatments. For greater detail concerning these issues, the reader is referred to the comprehensive assessment plan developed by Blagg (1987). As well, Blagg provides advice on many practical issues such as the location and organization of interviews. Interestingly, he suggests that the child and parents be interviewed in the school with the onus on the parents to get the child to school (by force if necessary) for the interview. A number of practical advantages are seen to be associated with this tactic. For example, it minimizes parent and child collusion from the beginning, demonstrates the parent's desire to get the child to school under protest and ability to act as an escort, and gives information on whether the child's problem is largely that of separation from mother and leaving home or a phobic avoidance of school. Blagg recommends that once at school, the child, parents, and teacher be interviewed separately. Following the development of rapport and the understanding of individual perspectives, the parties can be brought together for a group discussion. Blagg has found that setting aside a whole morning to interview all parties—separately and in groups—is more cost effective than a series of shorter and tightly timed sessions over several weeks. In these initial interviews Blagg believes that the harsh realities of the situation should be impressed on parents, including the legal requirements concerning school attendance and the complications of prolonged absenteeism.

The information derived from clinical interviews may be problematic regarding its reliability and validity. For example, how accurate is the parental report that prior to the current display of school phobia their child had *never* refused to attend school? Two precautions should be made. First, the retrospective recollections by parent or child may be distorted (e.g., Chess, Thomas, & Birch, 1966). As well, parents may inaccurately recall certain behavior problems in accordance with popular theories. Obviously this may have a bearing on the clinical utility of information derived from the interview. For example, the parent who is familiar with the theory that school phobia is *really* a form of separation anxiety could "recall" events in support of this hypothesis. Second, although the reliability and validity of general recollections are suspect, parents and children are reliable and accurate reporters of current and specific information about problematic behaviors (e.g., Herjanic, Herjanic, Brown, & Wheatt, 1975). Thus specification of precise behaviors and circumstances is likely to produce more reliable and valid information.

Rating Instruments

There are many rating instruments that may be used to assess fear and anxiety in children (see reviews by Barrios, Hartmann, & Shigetomi, 1981; King *et al.*, 1988; Ollendick & Mayer, 1984). The advantages to these instruments include being able to compare the child's responses with those of other children. Normative comparisons of this nature help determine the developmental appropriateness of the child's behavior. These ratings can be used as outcome measures to determine treatment efficacy. When used for this purpose, they must be administered prior to intervention, at postintervention, and at follow-up intervals to assess both specific and generalized behavior change. A further potential advantage of administering these rating forms is that it may help show that specific school-return and anxiety reduction procedures (e.g., systematic desensitization, emotive imagery) are related to "subtypes" of school phobia as determined by the pattern of responding on these scales. In the use of rating forms there are times when the child may give a self-report, whereas at other times the assessment has to rely on other-report (Ollendick & Francis, 1988).

The major self-report instruments of fear and anxiety include the Children's Manifest Anxiety Scale (Castaneda, McCandless, & Palermo, 1956), the State–Trait Anxiety Inventory for Children (Spielberger, 1973), and the Fear Survey Schedule for Children (Scherer & Nakamura, 1968). Both the Children's Manifest Anxiety Scale (Reynolds & Richmond, 1978, 1979) and the Fear Survey Schedule for Children (Ollendick, 1983; Ollendick *et al.*, 1985; Ollendick, King, & Frary, 1989) have been revised. Despite the good reliability and validity, little research on school phobia has included these measures of fear. However, the Revised-Fear Survey Schedule for Children (FSSC-R) has been used to discriminate between school-phobic children and non-school-phobic children matched for sex, age, IQ, and socioeconomic status. It was found that the mean level of fear (Total Fear Score) was significantly greater in school-phobic children. In addition, specific fear items differentiated school-phobic youngsters whose etiology appeared to be related to separation (e.g., death, getting lost) from those whose etiology appeared to be due to specific aspects of school or recent illness (e.g., taking a test, sharp objects, being teased). However, there was no difference between the two subgroups on overall level of self-reported fear (Ollendick, 1983; Ollendick & Mayer, 1984). Recently, the FSSC-R has been used to differentiate among anxiety disorders (Last *et al.*, 1987) and to examine the presence of fear in the offspring of adult anxiety disorder patients (Turner, Beidel, & Costello, 1987).

For many reasons it may not be possible for the child to complete a self-report instrument. For example, age-related constraints, intellectual disability, or lack of cooperation may be serious obstacles to the completion of rating scales by children. Hence, rating scales have been developed for completion by the child's parents or teacher (other-report). Foremost of these is the Louisville Fear Survey Schedule for Children (Miller, Barrett, Hampe, & Noble, 1972b). This is an 81-item inventory that requires a rating on a 3-point scale: no fear, normal or reasonable fear, and unrealistic fear. A critical issue is the extent to which the ratings of care givers correspond to the perceptions of children. In a study by Bondy, Sheslow, and Garcia (1985), the same fear survey schedule was administered to a group of children and their parents. From this investigation, it appears that children's self-reports correlate with their mothers' estimates of the highest-rated fears. However, mothers' overall estimates of their children's general fearfulness were significantly correlated only with their daughters fearfulness, not with their sons.

The rating forms developed for teachers and parents may be quite simple but nonetheless useful for clinical and research purposes. For example, Gittelman-Klein and Klein (1973) used a rating form in the assessment of school return. In response to the question "How well has the child being doing for the past week?" the parent was required to rate the child on a 7-point scale (ranging from "Attends classes regularly" to "Complete school refusal"). Rating forms have the potential advantage of assessing the adjustment of the child in school return. While treatment programs appear to be very effective on attendance criteria, more needs to be known about the process of school return. The impact of "forced return" procedures on the child's behavior at home and school is a particular concern that lends itself to assessment via the use of rating forms. Of course, reliability and validity would have to be demonstrated before their routine clinical use could be endorsed. To conclude, rating forms (both self-report and other-report) are potentially valuable sources of information that deserve closer scrutiny and, if found to be psychometrically sound, more use in the assessment of school phobia. No parent checklist, teacher checklist, or child self-report measure has so far been developed specifically for school phobia or separation anxiety, however.

Behavioral Observations

The hallmark of behavioral assessment is the direct observation of the child's behavior in the setting in which it occurs. In this tradition, assessment has ranged from unobtrusive observation in the child's home or school to direct observation in the laboratory (Lick & Katkin, 1976). Such observation provides a direct sample of the child's behavior and thus is the least inferential of data collection methods (Goldfried & Kent, 1972). In behavioral observation systems, a behavior or set of behaviors that are indicative of anxiety are operationally defined, observed, and recorded in a systematic fashion.

Illustratively, Neisworth, Madle, and Goeke (1975) conducted a behavioral assessment of a young girl's separation anxiety in a preschool setting. When left at school, she began to cry, sob, and scream until her mother returned to retrieve her. These behaviors (crying, screaming, and sobbing) were operationally defined, and their intensity and duration were monitored in the preschool setting throughout baseline, treatment, and follow-up phases. Treatment, based on differential reinforcement and shaping procedures, was highly successful. More importantly, for our purposes here, school avoidance behavior (labeled separation anxiety) was defined as a set of observable behaviors. These fearful behaviors occurred only in school where mother, as well as the preschool staff, found it difficult to endure the child's distress without attending to her. Neisworth *et al.* (1975) indicated that records and additional observations supported the notion that this attention played a role in the maintenance and development of "separation anxiety." Thus, in this case, specific behaviors were identified and observed; further, these observations suggested a specific treatment based on the antecedent (preschool setting only) and consequent (attention) conditions under which the behaviors occurred. Typically, school-phobic children have stopped attending school by the stage they are assessed by specialists. Nonetheless, behavioral observations of the child in the school setting are advised as soon as the child returns to school. At school it is likely the child will be highly anxious and require much support. Hence, behavioral observations can provide information on the child's specific fear behavior as well as the negative and positive influences on adjustment to school.

Behavioral observations in the home also provide valuable assessment information on the child's school phobia and controlling antecedent and consequent events. Such observations may be directed at the various stages of the "behavior chain" at which school refusal becomes evident. For example, Ayllon et al. (1970) instigated systematic behavioral observations in the home of a school-phobic girl who had been absent from school for a prolonged period of time. In this case, mother left for work approximately 1 hour after the girl (Valerie) and her siblings were to set off for school. Although her siblings went to school on time, Valerie was observed to sleep late and then to "cling" to mother until she left for work. "Valerie typically followed her mother around the house, from room to room, spending approximately 80 per cent of her time within 10 ft of her mother. During these times, there was little or no conversation" (Ayllon et al., 1970, p. 128). Upon leaving for work, mother took Valerie to a neighbor's apartment to stay until she returned from work (mother had long abandoned any hope of Valerie's going to school). When mother left the neighbor's apartment, Valerie would follow. Observations indicated that this pattern continued with Valerie "following her mother at a 10-foot distance." Frequently, mother had to return Valerie to the neighbor's apartment. This daily pattern was usually concluded with mother "literally running to get out of sight of Valerie" so that she would not follow her into traffic.

At the neighbor's apartment, observations revealed that Valerie was free to do whatever she pleased for the remainder of the day. As noted by Ayllon et al., "Her day was one which would be considered ideal by many grade children— she could be outdoors and play as she chose all day long. No demands of any type were made on Val" (p. 129). Since Valerie was not attending school, the authors arranged a simulated school setting to determine the extent of fear associated with academically related materials. Much to their surprise, Valerie exhibited little or no fear in the presence of these materials. Based on these observations, the authors hypothesized that Valerie's refusal to attend school was maintained by attention from mother and pleasant and undemanding characteristics of the neighbor's l., behavioral observations led directly to a specific and effective intervention.

Although not mentioned in the studies just described, behavioral observations can also help identify the extent to which poor household rules and routines contribute to school refusal (antecedent events). Further compounding the problem, parents may lack instruction-giving competencies with their child. In fact, Forehand and McMahon (1981) outline five types of commands that can lower compliance in children. These include long chains of commands, vague commands, question commands, "let's" commands, and commands followed by a rationale or other verbalizations. Obviously, antecedent events as significant as these need to be identified in the assessment of school phobia.

As with other types of assessment, behavioral observation procedures must possess adequate reliability and validity before their routine use can be endorsed. Although early behaviorists tended to accept behavioral observation data on the basis of their deceptively simple surface validity, more recent investigators have enumerated a variety of problems related to their use (e.g., Johnson & Bolstad, 1973; Kazdin, 1979). Among these issues are the complexity of the observation code, observer bias, observer drift, and the reactive nature of the observation process itself. It is beyond the scope of this chapter to address these issues. Suffice it to indicate, however, that when these issues are adequately controlled for, direct observation is a welcome complement to behavioral interviews and rating forms. In our work with school-phobic children, we have attempted to incorporate all three sources of information: behavioral interviews, behavioral ratings, and behavioral observations.

INTERVENTION

Despite fundamental theoretical differences, both psychodynamic and behavioral approaches to school phobia place emphasis on the child's return to school as the primary criterion of successful intervention (e.g., Ayllon et al., 1970; Eisenberg, 1958). As noted by the psychodynamically oriented Eisenberg (1958), it is

> essential that the paralyzing force of the school phobia on the child's whole life be recognized. The symptom itself serves to isolate him from normal experience and makes further psychological growth almost impossible. If we do no more than check this central symptom, we have nonetheless done a great deal. (p. 718)

While behaviorally oriented clinicians might disagree with Eisenberg's labeling of school phobia as a *symptom* (an overt expression of some underlying conflict), they would hardly disagree with his conclusion. In this section, behaviorally based strategies that are commonly used in achieving this goal will be described. Conceptually, these strategies parallel the causal processes thought to be present in school phobia and are based on the principles of classical, operant, and vicarious conditioning (Ollendick & Mayer, 1984). However, the overall rationale for the behavioral treatment of school phobia is *exposure* to the feared stimulus. As will become evident, behavioral strategies are fundamentally exposure-based in the arrangement of therapeutic tasks and advice to parents. The emphasis placed on exposure or confrontation is of course consistent with contemporary accounts of phobia reduction (King et al., 1989; Marks, 1969, 1975).

Classical Conditioning

Treatments based on classical conditioning principles have utilized two primary strategies for fear reduction: counterconditioning and extinction. During counterconditioning procedures, specific feared stimuli are presented in the presence of stimuli which elicit responses incompatible with anxiety. In this manner, anxiety is counterconditioned and the individual is said to acquire a competing response, most frequently the relaxation response. During extinction, on the other hand, the conditioned fear stimuli are repeatedly presented in the absence of the original unconditioned stimuli. In this manner, the individual learns that there is really nothing to be afraid of and the anxiety response is said to dissipate.

The best known counterconditioning procedure is systematic desensitization, a fear-reduction technique developed by Wolpe (1958). Customarily, three steps are involved in systematic desensitization: teaching progressive relaxation to the client, constructing a stimulus hierarchy of anxiety-evoking situations ("anxiety hierarchy"), and counterimposing the anxiety scenes with relaxation. Usually the fear-provoking stimuli are presented imaginally while the individual is relaxed. For example, Lazarus (1960) successfully applied systematic desensitization to a school-phobic girl. The girl developed multiple symptoms following three traumatic experiences of death (a school friend drowned, a playmate died suddenly, and she witnessed a man killed in a motorbike accident). She was afraid of being separated from her mother, had nightmares, and was enuretic. Using a 7-item hierarchy of fears relating to separation from the mother, the child underwent imaginal desensitization over five treatment sessions which resulted in school return.

When conducting systematic desensitization, it is possible for the exposures to be carried out *in vivo* rather than relying on the child's imaginal abilities. Illustratively, Garvey and Hegrenes (1966) have reported the successful treatment of a 10-year-old school-phobic boy using *in vivo* desensitization. The child's school refusal was precipitated by an illness which followed the Christmas holidays. When he thought about going to school in the morning he became frightened and often vomited. He was described as being highly strung, sensitive, and preoccupied with high-level performance. Concerns about his mother and the prospect of losing her were also expressed. After 6 months of traditional psychotherapy he felt more confident but was still unable to return to school. The 10-step desensitization procedure in this case was carried out in the school environment. School officials were informed of the procedure and were very cooperative. Since it was known that the child could tolerate going by the school in a car, the first step consisted of sitting in the car in front of the school with the therapist. The remaining 9 steps in the anxiety hierarchy were as follows: (2) getting out of the car and approaching the curb; (3) going to the footpath; (4) going to the top of the steps; (5) going to the door of the school; (6) entering the school; (7) approaching the classroom with the teacher present; (8) sitting in the classroom with the teacher present; (9) sitting in the classroom with the teacher and one or two classmates; and (10) sitting in the classroom with the full class present. This procedure was carried out over consecutive days, including Saturdays and Sundays. The amount of time spent each day ranged from 20 to 40 minutes. After 20 consecutive treatments, the child resumed a normal school routine with no return of the symptoms noted during a 2-year follow-up.

A *combination* of imaginal and real-life systematic desensitization is also possible in the treatment of school phobia. Miller (1972) presented the case of a 10-year-old boy with multiple fears that responded to imaginal and *in vivo* desensitization. He was afraid of separation from his mother, his own death, and the school situation. Approximately 8 weeks before treatment he had been criticized by a teacher, and he subsequently refused to attend school. The subject's fears were treated separately using systematic desensitization. He was trained in muscular relaxation over three 20-minute sessions, with candy and verbal praise being used to reinforce the relaxation response. Separation anxiety was successfully treated by working through a hierarchy of imaginal scenes related to distance from his mother. Desensitization to imagined scenes of dying was unsuccessful, as the subject was unable to experience the anxiety in relation to these scenes. For this problem, the child was instructed to phone the therapist at night when he experienced anxiety. Each time the subject called, instructions to relax were given over the telephone. After about 6 weeks the boy no longer reported fears of dying. The subject's fear of the school situation was then tackled. A hierarchy of scenes was constructed involving a distance continuum (being a block from school, standing in front of school, walking into the classroom, etc.). After desensitization to these scenes in imagination, the subject reported less school-related anxiety and agreed to gradually return to the classroom. For the next week he was required to walk to school, stand at the front door, and then return home. He was instructed to apply muscle relaxation if he experienced anxiety. The length of time the subject spent near school (and subsequently in the classroom) was gradually increased. By the fifth week after initial reentry, normal school attendance was achieved. Follow-ups at three-months and 18-months revealed the maintenance of all behavior changes.

Emotive imagery is a variant of systematic desensitization that has been used with children. Lazarus and Abramovitz (1962) describe emotive imagery as "those classes of imagery which are assumed to arouse feelings of self-assertion, pride, affection, mirth, and similar anxiety-inhibiting responses" (p. 191). Rather than muscular relaxation being used as the anxiety inhibitor, feelings of "positive affect" are employed to counter anxiety. An exciting story involving the child's hero images might be told, with school-related scenes being interwoven at various points in hierarchical order. Of central importance are the child's hero images, usually from television, fiction, or a fantasy from the child's imagination, and identifications which accompany these. When using imagery techniques with children, Rosenstiel and Scott (1977) caution that imagery scenes should be tailored to the age of the child and maintain that treatment ought to incorporate existing fantasies and cognitions. They also suggest that the nonverbal cues supply important information about the treatment process and that the language used by children about their images should be utilized in treatment. In view of the current emphasis on matching therapy with the age-related cognitive and verbal abilities of children, emotive imagery is a treatment option of considerable interest. Lazarus and Abramovitz (1962) report a case of an 8-year-old girl referred for treatment because of nocturnal enuresis and school phobia, which had been precipitated by a series of emotional upsets in the classroom. Emotive imagery was introduced and featured Noddy as the child's hero image. Noddy was a truant who responded fearfully to the school setting. A hierarchy of assertive problems in the school setting was encountered in emotive imagery. The school-phobic symptoms were extinguished after four sessions, with the bedwetting disappearing within 2 months. The child continued to improve over an unspecified follow-up period, despite an "unsympathetic teacher."

Although numerous case studies have utilized systematic desensitization and its variants, there is a dearth of controlled evaluations on this treatment approach to school phobia. However, the relative efficacies of systematic desensitization and traditional psychotherapy compared to waiting-list control were evaluated in a study by Miller et al. (1972a). The target phobias comprised mainly school phobia (69%) and fear of storms, the dark, and domestic animals. Both systematic desensitization and psychotherapy groups received 24 sessions of individual treatment over a 3-month period. Muscle relaxation training and construction of fear hierarchies were completed during the first four sessions of the systematic desensitization group. In the following sessions, the child was instructed to imagine progressively greater fear-eliciting stimuli while remaining relaxed. When all items of the hierarchy could be imagined without fear, an *in vivo* assessment was scheduled. If the results of this assessment were negative, imaginal desensitization was resumed. In the psychotherapy group, young children were seen for play therapy, while older children were seen for interview therapy. Both older and younger children were encouraged to explore their hopes, fears, and dependency needs. Additionally, the children were "encouraged to examine and formulate both behavioral strategies for coping with stress and the affect accompanying these efforts" (p. 271). Further, intervention with families of children in this group was essentially the same as for children in the systematic desensitization group: "Where parent–child interaction patterns appeared to reinforce fear behavior, behavior therapy principles were employed to restructure contingency schedules, for example, eliminating television during school hours for a school phobic who stayed home" (p. 271). Thus, the "psychotherapy" treatment contained many factors of "behavioral" treatment, even though children did not specifically undergo systematic desensitization. The child's fear was evaluated by a clinician and by two other-report instruments completed by the parents: The Louisville Behavior Checklist (Miller, Barrett, Hampe, & Noble, 1971) and the Louisville Fear Survey for Children (Miller et al., 1972b). The evaluations were completed prior to treatment, following treatment, and at a 6-week follow-up. Parents of children in the two treatment groups reported a greater reduction in fear in their children than did parents in the waiting-list group; the two treatment groups did not differ, however. Moreover, the clinician's evaluation failed to support parental judgments and, in fact, revealed no differences among the three groups at posttreatment or follow-up. Unfortunately, behavioral observations of the children were not reported, and as a consequence it is difficult to determine the reliability and validity of the findings. Had such a measure been included, one would be in a better position to answer the question about the comparative efficacies of these strategies.

As already indicated, there are several fear-reduction techniques that utilize the classical conditioning principle of extinction. Extinction of the fear response is said to occur as the result of continuous presentation of the fear-producing stimuli in the absence of the actual feared stimuli. *In vivo* desensitization without relaxation training (see above) can be considered an extinction procedure. Flooding, also an *in vivo* procedure, involves the school-phobic child being forced to attend school despite protests. Implosion, a variant of flooding, is carried out in the individual's imagination; in addition, it frequently involves extremely intense (exaggerated) scenes of a psychodynamic nature. Smith and Sharpe (1970) employed implosive therapy with a 13-year-old school-phobic boy. He had been absent from school for 60 days prior to treatment. The school-phobic symptoms included extreme anxiety, inability to eat breakfast, chest pains, and trembling and crying when at school. His phobic symptoms developed after a 3-week absence from school due to illness. Neither tranquilizers, force, punishment, nor bribes could induce the boy to return to school. The assessment procedure indicated that mathematics and literature classes were the probable sources of intense anxiety, especially when called on in class or when unable to answer the teacher's questions. Consequently, nine scenes were constructed around the hypothetical anxiety-arousing cues. The boy was seen for six consecutive daily sessions of implosive therapy. Each scene was presented until a visible reduction in anxiety was observed. The seventh scene involving the literature class entailed the following description:

> The patient is ordered to his literature classroom by the principal. The room is dark and strange, and the chairs have been pushed to the sides of the room. Students begin silently filing into the room. It is too dark to identify them. Tension grows as Billy wonders what will happen. The students encircle him, pressing ever closer, and begin to murmur "Crazy Bill" and "stupid, stupid, stupid." They then begin to jostle and strike him. (Smith & Sharpe, 1970, p. 241)

The first session was extremely anxiety provoking and physically exhausting. At the conclusion of the first implosive therapy session, the boy was directed to attend his anxiety-provoking mathematics class the next day. Following the second and third sessions, he was told to attend half-day sessions of school. After the fourth session, he was directed to school on a full-time basis. A 13-week follow-up indicated that he continued to attend school regularly with no reported anxiety. Despite the fact that implosive therapy is less time consuming than desensitization treatments, it has not become popular among behavioral practitioners (see King *et al.*, 1988). Further, it has not been systematically evaluated.

Vicarious Conditioning

Vicarious conditioning principles have been utilized in the treatment of child behavior disorders including fears and phobias (see reviews by Graziano *et al.*, 1979; King *et al.*, 1988). Here the emphasis is on the role of observational learning or modeling in behavior change (e.g., Bandura, 1969). Essentially, modeling entails demonstrating nonfearful behavior in the anxiety-producing situation and showing the child an appropriate response for handling the feared stimuli. Thus anxiety is reduced and skills are learned by the child. As avoidance behavior for phobic children may be a function of excessive anxiety *and* not knowing what specific behaviors are required, modeling serves a crucial function in this respect. Three types of modeling have been used with children: video-modeling, live modeling, and participant modeling. Video-modeling entails the child observing a graduated series of videos in which a model exhibits progressively more intimate interaction with the feared object or setting, whereas live modeling consists of having the child observe a live model engage in graduated interactions with a live feared object or participate in real-life situations that are anxiety provoking. On the other hand, participant modeling requires the child to observe another person interact fearlessly with the anxiety-producing object–situation and then perform the appropriate behavior with the physical and psychological support of the therapist. A clear ordering of effectiveness is evident from the research findings on modeling: video-modeling is least effective, live modeling is intermediate, and participant modeling is most effective (see review by Ollendick, 1979).

Unfortunately, accounts of modeling procedures as the primary treatment for school phobia are virtually nonexistent (Ollendick & Mayer, 1984). Nonetheless, modeling procedures appear to be used indirectly in school-return programs. For example, in interventions that use *in vivo* desensitization or successive approximations, the child is usually accompanied to school by either a parent, therapist, or therapist's assistant (e.g., Ayllon *et al.*, 1970; Garvey & Hegrenes, 1966; Lazarus *et al.*, 1965; Tahmisian & McReynolds, 1971). Although not specified, it is likely that the child attends to the coping behaviors of the accompanying individual as they make a graduated reentry to school. Even when the child is part of a rapid treatment program, there is likely to be a positive modeling effect since parents and others are encouraged to display "calm, firm behavior" (Blagg, 1977, 1987). Once the child's initial fears of entering the classroom are overcome, and the attendance is more regular, the child is able to observe and learn from the behavior of peers.

Illustratively, Tahmisian and McReynolds (1971) utilized a school-approach hierarchy in the treatment of Carol, a 13-year-old school-phobic girl. Prior to implementation of *in vivo* desensitization, Carol had been seen by a social worker and had also been prescribed tranquilizers. Both were reported to be ineffective, and she had been absent from school on 80 consecutive days. In this study, parents accompanied the client in executing the following steps:

First week:
1. Walk around school after classes are dismissed 15 minutes, accompanied by parent
2. Same as Step 1, alone
3. Same as Step 1, 30 min, accompanied by parent
4. Same as Step 1, 30 min, alone
5. Same as Step 1, 60 min, alone
Second week:
6. Walk around school while classes are in session for 30 min, accompanied by parent

    7. Same as Step 6, alone
    8. Same as Step 6, 60 min, alone
    9. Attend first class period (60 min), with parent in hall
10. Same as Step 9, parent in car
Third week:
11. Attend first class period (60 min), parent gone
12. Attend class periods (160 min), alone
13. Attend 3 class periods (180 min), alone
14. Attend class all morning, alone
15. Attend class all day, alone

Carol was attending school normally by the end of the third week of treatment and reported that she was no longer afraid. A 4-week follow-up indicated that her school attendance was still regular.

As can be seen, the parent was faded out of the stimulus situation intermittently rather than at the termination of treatment. Thus, while the child had the opportunity to model herself on the parent's behavior, she also had the opportunity to perform each step in the hierarchy alone. This would be particularly important if being alone was a salient cue within the complex of fear stimuli. In addition, periodic removal of the adult model helped prevent Carol's performance from becoming contingent on the presence of an adult.

The most explicit application of modeling in the treatment of school phobia has been reported by Esveldt-Dawson, Wisner, Unis, Matson, and Kazdin (1982). Hospitalized on a psychiatric intensive care unit, the subject was a 12-year-old girl with a phobia of school and extreme fear of unfamiliar males, following alleged sexual molestation by her grandfather. Behaviors associated with her presenting problems included avoidance of school and unfamiliar men, diminished ability to interact with peers, and multiple somatic complaints. Treatment focused on decreasing several inappropriate behaviors (stiffness in bodily posture and nervous mannerisms) and the strengthening of appropriate behaviors (eye contact, appropriate affect and gestures). The key aspect of treatment was participant modeling; this involved the therapist modeling specific behaviors and subsequent practice by the child. Combined with the use of feedback and social reinforcement, this procedure was applied to a variety of anxiety-provoking situations related to school and unfamiliar males. Marked changes in the target behaviors occurred when treatment was introduced in a multiple-baseline design. Generalization beyond the persons and situations in training were evident from the use of global ratings. Follow-up contacts with the girl suggested that the gains were reflected in school attendance and social interactions in everyday situations. Thus, despite the complexities of the case, participant modeling was very useful in helping the girl overcome her phobias of school and unfamiliar males.

There are many issues that have to be considered for the optimal use of modeling with school-phobic children. With regard to factors that facilitate response acquisition, attention must be given to model characteristics (e.g., competence at task), observer characteristics (e.g., general level of cognitive functioning) and modeling presentation characteristics (e.g., single versus multiple models). To enhance performance, the therapist needs to consider incentives for performance and factors that enhance generalization. A full discussion of "modeling enhancers" is beyond the scope of the chapter (see King et al., 1988; Perry & Furukawa, 1980). As more attention is given to the finer points of modeling in the treatment of school phobia, we are optimistic about its potential utility, particularly in view of its effectiveness with other childhood anxieties and phobias (Graziano et al., 1979; Ollendick, 1979).

Operant Conditioning

In contrast to procedures derived from classical and vicarious conditioning, strategies based on the principles of operant conditioning make no assumption about the necessity to reduce or eliminate anxiety. Rather, operant procedures assume that simple acquisition of approach responses to the anxiety-producing situations is sufficient. In the treatment of school phobia, strategies based on the operant model attempt to increase the reinforcement value of school attendance (e.g., increased peer acceptance, teacher and parental approval) as well as decrease the reinforcement value of staying at home (e.g., withdrawal of parental attention, prohibiting the watching of television). Using a shaping procedure, full-time school attendance can be established via a series of graduated approximations. This is similar to the *in vivo* extinction procedures described earlier, omitting relaxation training. Usually the therapist has the child carry out a tolerable school-related morning task (e.g., visit school at normal starting time without going into school) and builds up from this point until satisfactory school attendance is achieved. On the other hand, the therapist can have the child start with a school-related afternoon task (e.g., sitting in on the last class) and work backwards in increasing the amount of time spent at school until full-time school attendance occurs. Until "natural" consequences (i.e., good grades, improved peer relations) associated with regular school attendance are realized by the school-phobic child, material or social reinforcers in the form of preferred activities and social praise may be required. The administration of reinforcers has varied in terms of who administers them and how frequently they are administered. The clinical utility of operant procedures is evident from numerous case reports of contingency management being successfully applied at home and/or school (e.g., Ayllon et al., 1970; Brown, Copeland, & Hall, 1974; Cooper, 1973; Hersen, 1970; Tahmisian & McReynolds, 1971; Vaal, 1973).

The now classic study on the operant approach to school phobia is that reported by Ayllon et al. (1970). The case involved an 8-year-old girl who had gradually stopped attending school in the second grade, with this refusal continuing on into the third grade. Whenever the mother attempted to take her to school, she threw such violent temper tantrums that it was impossible to take her to school. A 10-day baseline was taken in which behavioral observations were made in the child's home and a neighbors home. The child's principal and teachers were also interviewed.

Four distinct procedures were used in treatment. The first procedure entailed the prompting–shaping of school attendance. The subject was taken to school by the therapist's assistant toward the end of the school day. Each day she was taken to school progressively earlier. Although progress was made to the stage where she would remain in school all day without the presence of the assistant, she still refused to get dressed in the morning and walk to school with her three siblings. Thus, the problem was how to provide sufficient motivation to ensure her leaving for school. The second procedure entailed withdrawal of social reinforcers upon failure to leave for school. As the subject was able to spend one hour with her mother after her siblings had gone to school, the mother was required to leave for work at the same time the children left for school. Although the mother left for work at the designated time, the subject still refused to go to school, and each day she was taken to a neighbor's apartment. The subject also started to follow her mother to work. The third procedure entailed prompting school attendance combined with a home-based motivational system. This time the mother, rather than the assistant, was responsible for the prompting. A large chart with each child's name and the days of the week was given to the mother. The placement of a star signified one day of going to school on a voluntary basis; five stars indicated perfect attendance for the week and would result in a special treat or outing. Candy was also dispensed for going to school. Under these conditions school attendance improved. The fourth procedure was designed to prompt voluntary school attendance and introduced a mild aversive element for the mother if the subject failed to attend school. The mother now left 10 minutes before the children left for school and met the children at school with a reward. If the subject did not arrive at school with her siblings, the mother had to return home and escort her to school. It was hoped that this inconvenience would prompt the mother into becoming firmer with the subject. Only twice was the mother inconvenienced by school refusal under these conditions. The second incident was very significant:

> As it was raining, it was a considerable inconvenience for Val's mother to have to go back home. Once she reached home she scolded Val and pushed her out of the house and literally all the way to school. As Val tried to give some explanation the mother hit her with a switch. By the time they arrived at school, both were soaking wet. (Ayllon et al., 1970, pp. 134–135)

The home-based motivational system was withdrawn after 1 month, with all of the children continuing to attend school. The subject was successfully treated in 45 days. Academic and social skills improvements were also noted on 6-month and 9-month follow-ups.

The overall treatment strategy described here has several noteworthy strengths. First of all, comprehensive behavioral observations during baseline and treatment were invaluable in selecting and specifying the treatment procedures used. Second, the therapists closely observed Valerie's behavior and were relatively flexible in their approach to treating the problem. Although "school phobia" in this case was defined quite narrowly, the antecedent and consequent events to low school attendance were thoroughly examined and eventually controlled. Finally, altering mother's contingencies, as well as the child's, proved to be instrumental in improving the child's compliance. School refusal was finally brought under control by the mother's use of punishment for staying at home. The use of punishment is rarely reported in the behavioral management of school phobia. Nevertheless, it is a treatment option that can be adopted in conjunction with positive treatment procedures, as this case illustrates. The operant approach to the management of school phobia has so far stressed consequential control (i.e., reinforcement of appropriate behavior and the extinction of inappropriate behavior). Antecedent stimulus control has not been considered, especially as it relates to events in the home. To a certain extent, school phobia can be seen as noncompliant behavior with parental instructions. As suggested by King *et al.* (1988), training parents in antecedent stimulus control procedures, like command giving, would seem a potentially useful strategy. Blagg (1987) agrees that this is pertinent with respect to those school phobics who are omnipotent with ineffectual parents. Forehand and McMahon's (1981) model of helping parents manage noncompliant children seems particularly relevant here. An important part of their program involves training parents to give clear and direct commands to their children. Emphasis is placed upon getting the child's attention, firmness of voice, specific and direct commands, and giving only one command at a time. Parents can be taught to improve their command giving via modeling and behavior rehearsal in a structured learning situation. Helping parents establish rules and organizational procedures related to "getting ready for school" might also be of assistance, especially in families that seem very disorganized with respect to school matters. It is to be hoped that more attention will be given to antecedent stimulus control in the behavioral management of school phobia (King *et al.*, 1988).

It is evident that contingency management procedures are useful in the treatment of school-phobic children. As school-phobic children are usually referred by others, operant strategies serve an important motivating function. We identified several specific components that enhance the utility of these approaches. These components include: (1) conducting a thorough functional analysis *within* the particular setting, (2) procuring cooperation of significant others (e.g., parents, siblings, teachers), and (3) continuing assessment throughout treatment in order to evaluate the need for its continuation or modification. However, practitioners planning to use contingency management with school-phobic children should be aware that some care givers and professionals display negative reactions to these procedures, as they believe them to be manipulative and tantamount to bribery. As with all phobia-reduction procedures, sensitivity and skill are required in the application of operant strategies.

Integrative Treatment

In our own clinical work with school-phobic children, we attempt to design integrative treatment programs incorporating classical, vicarious, and operant conditioning principles. The basic goal is return to school and maintenance of school attendance, despite what we can do or cannot do in other areas of the child's life. Although the goal is school return, this may be achieved by using procedures that involve graduated reentry or steps designed to promote rapid reentry to school. This fundamental issue has to be addressed by all clinicians responsible for the management of school-phobic children. While acknowledging that certain cases may require a deliberately slow and gradual return to school, the more confronting approach appears to have wide acceptance (Blagg, 1987; Kennedy, 1965). The preference for rapid treatment is that it minimizes the chances of secondary gain, which has long been recognized to be the major impediment to the effective treatment of school phobia. It should be emphasized that rapid-treatment programs still reflect an integrative approach to treatment regarding the various conditioning paradigms. Further, the methodological and clinical complexity of treatment should not be underestimated, as we now illustrate.

Kennedy (1965) developed a rapid-treatment program for school-phobic children, entailing forced return to school (flooding). According to Kennedy: "The treatment involved the application of broad learning theory concepts by blocking the escape of the child and preventing secondary gains from occurring. In addition, the child was reinforced for going to school without complaint" (pp. 286–287). In essence, Kennedy's rapid-treatment program for school phobia involves six essential components: good professional public relations, avoidance of emphasis on somatic complaints, forced school attendance, structured interview with parents, brief interview with child, and follow-ups. Of these, the critical feature is forced school attendance. It was advocated that the father take the child to school, where the principal or other staff take an active part in keeping the child in the classroom. However, it appears that there was little necessity for actual physical force in getting school-phobic children back to school: "It is essential to be able to require the child to go to school and to be willing to use any force necessary. In all of the present cases, simply convincing the parents of this necessity, and having them come to a firm decision, has generally been enough" (p. 288).

Kennedy (1965) carried out his rapid-treatment program with 50 Type-I (see previous discussion of Types in "Diagnostic Issues") school-phobic cases over an 8-year period. The age range of the children was 4 to 16 years, although only 10 children were older than 12 years. Of the 50 Type-I school-phobic cases, Kennedy reports that 5 might be considered semicontrols. They were untreated Type-I cases of considerable duration, or were Type-I cases that had been unsuccessfully treated elsewhere. All of the 50 cases responded to the rapid-treatment program with a complete remission of the school-phobic symptoms. The families were followed up 2 weeks and 6 weeks after intervention, and then on an annual basis for 2–8 years. In discussing these results, which are quite outstanding, Kennedy commented that "perhaps what is called Type-I School Phobia is not really a severe phobic attack at all, but borders on malingering of a transient nature which would spontaneously remit in a few days anyway" (p. 289). Taking into account these considerations, Kennedy concludes that the treatment program may accelerate a facilitated remission of what is a serious problem despite its possible transient nature. In the absence of nontreatment controls, however, it is difficult to gauge the effectiveness of Kennedy's rapid-treatment program.

A more detailed account of the rapid treatment of school-phobic children has been reported by Blagg (1977, 1981, 1987). This particular treatment plan stresses early return to school and incorporates:

1. Desensitization of the stimulus through humor and emotive imagery.
2. Blocking the avoidance response through forced school attendance.
3. Maximizing positive reinforcement for school attendance both at home and at school.
4. Extinction of protests, fear reactions, and psychosomatic complaints through contingency management.

Blagg is particularly sensitive to the complexity of school phobia and emphasizes the need to adopt a comprehensive *and* flexible approach to its treatment. Following a careful assessment and the development of a working relationship with the child, family, and school authorities, Blagg suggests a 7-point sequence of events in school return: (1) prepare the parties, (2) confirm the mandate, (3) negotiate areas of change required in the school, (4) negotiate areas of change required in the home, (5) find a suitable escort, (6) discuss the treatment plan with the child, and (7) give support and make follow-up arrangements. Similar to Kennedy (1965), the parents are responsible for escorting the child to school. Blagg suggests that a special effort be made to involve the father, who very often is ineffectual and avoids taking responsibility. When it is apparent the parents will not be able to force the child to attend school because of their anxiety and/or lack of firmness, other escorts have to be considered (close relatives, school teacher, social worker, psychologist). The escort must be able to handle the child's temper tantrums, be supportive but firm with parents, and continue to take the child to school until protest and/or psychosomatic symptoms have passed, even if this takes several weeks. When the child arrives at school, "supervising staff should be warm but firm, ignoring the child's tears and protests but attending to the child when he shows signs of recovering. The child should be integrated into the normal school routine as quickly as possible" (Blagg, 1977, p. 74). On the other hand, it is acknowledged that certain children may find school to be an overwhelming and aversive experience, thus they require a greater level of support. He states that

> with particularly resistant and anxious pupils, who express multiple worries about many lessons, a graded re-introduction to a normal timetable may be necessary. That is, whilst full-time attendance at school is insisted upon, the child may not necessarily be expected to attend every lesson from day one. (Blagg, 1987, p. 150)

In view of the child's absence from school, it is recognized that the child may return to school and find him- or herself to be socially isolated. To help the child along socially "it can be helpful to break the ice by choosing one or two, sensitive, understanding pupils to make a point of shepherding the child around school for the first few weeks" (Blagg, 1987, p. 151). Obviously, many arrangements are possible in forced school attendance. In the final analysis, the clinician probably needs to judge the level of anxiety and disruption that is present so that treatment can be based on the proper combination of operant, vicarious, and respondent practices. This was actually recommended many years ago by Lazarus *et al.* (1965) and more recently by ourselves (King *et al.*, 1988; Ollendick & Mayer, 1984)

In addition to providing comprehensive guidelines on the behavioral management of school phobia, Blagg and Yule (1984) have evaluated the effectiveness of their behavioral prescription. The behavioral treatment approach (BTA) was systematically applied to a series of 30 school-refusal cases referred over a 3-year period. These 30 cases were compared with 16 hospitalized school refusers (HU) and 20 who received home instruction and psychotherapy (HT). The 66 cases involved in the study met diagnostic criteria of school refusal similar to those proposed by Berg *et al.* (1969). Although there was no random allocation to treatment groups, the groups were systematically compared on a range of variables. Most of the children were in the 11- to 16-year age range. There were no statistically significant differences on sex, social-class distribution, intelligence, or reading age. They were very similar with respect to associated symptoms, school- and home-related anxieties, family size, parent attitudes, and employment. Applying Kennedy's criteria, half of the children in the BTA group, three-quarters of the HU group, and one-quarter of the HT groups were classified as Type-II school-refusal. Thus, the three groups were reasonably similar at the start of treatment. Operational criteria were employed to compare treatment results. A child was judged a treatment "success" if he or she returned to full-time schooling without any further problems. Here, one attendance breakdown was allowed, provided that the child quickly responded to booster treatment. A child was classified as a "partial success" if he or she returned to school for at least 1 year but then had attendance breakdowns culminating in school refusal. A child was judged a treatment "failure" if he or she did not return to normal school or returned for less than 3 months but was unresponsive to further treatment. After 1 year of treatment, 93.3% of the BTA group were judged to be successful compared with 37% of the HU group and 10% of the HT group. Attendance rates were also compared for the year prior to follow-up. While 83% of the BTA group were attending school on more than 80% of occasions, this occurred for only 31% of the HU group and for none of the HT group. Five girls did not meet the criterion attendance rate between the end of treatment and follow-up. The girls concerned were over 13 years of age, had low scores on the WISC-R (Verbal), and were classified as Kennedy Type-II cases. Four of these girls had siblings who also had attendance problems, as well as having parents who were far from cooperative during treatment.

The findings of the study highlight a number of points of clinical significance. Despite frequent objections about the behavioral management of school phobia (considered too stressful for the child), the behavioral approach was very effective. Furthermore, it was more effective than hospitalization or home instruction and psychotherapy. The results also indicate that so-called disturbed cases of school phobia can respond to behavioral treatment. This is quite important, as it has become part of clinical mythology that only simple cases of school phobia respond to behavioral intervention. However, it must be acknowledged that the treatment failures of the behavioral approach were classified as Kennedy Type-II cases. Thus, greater difficulty is likely to be encountered with these cases. As well as being effective, it must be emphasized that behavioral treatment was the most economical form of intervention. The average length of

behavioral treatment was 2.53 weeks, compared with 45.3 weeks of hospitalization, and 72.1 weeks for home instruction. As emphasized by the researchers,
this is to say nothing of salary costs, which would be extremely high for those
cases involving hospitalization. Of course, the study is by no means immune to
criticism. Although quite understandable in terms of obligation to provide a
clinical service, a no-treatment control condition was not included. Thus, the
extent to which spontaneous remission accounts for the results can be queried.
Given the differences in outcome between the three groups, however, it does
not seem likely that spontaneous remission is the operative variable in so far as
behavioral treatment is concerned. Another possible criticism is that subjects
were not randomly allocated to the treatment conditions. Thus it can be argued
that easier cases were dealt with in behavioral treatment. This does not appear to
be so in view of the fact that no significant differences were found between the
groups on major subject characteristics. In conclusion, Blagg's work is a significant development in the behavioral management of school phobia. Although
methodological problems are present, it represents the type of clinical-research
study that must be undertaken to verify our treatment procedures (King et al.,
1988).

Finally, as Wolf (1978) and others have noted, the nature of behavioral goals,
interventions, and outcomes are in need of "social validation." For a strategy or
set of strategies as potentially aversive as forced school attendance, it is imperative that we assess the acceptability of these interventions to our clients and
society. Gullone and King (1988) had secondary school students and care givers
rate the acceptability of various treatments that were described in relation to a
case of school phobia. The treatments included: (1) home tuition and psychotherapy, (2) hospitalization, (3) medication, and (4) behavior management (incorporating forced school attendance and other fear reduction procedures). Behavior management and home tuition/psychotherapy received higher ratings on
acceptability than hospitalization or medication. In fact, behavior management
was the most acceptable of all the treatment options. Interestingly, students
were more accepting than care providers of the hospitalization and medication
conditions. Why behavior management was the preferred option is unknown,
although it may be hypothesized that it is seen as the closest of the options to
everyday child-rearing practices. Further research should focus on the various
elements of the behavioral approach, as they may elicit quite different reactions.
While these findings are encouraging, we also need to evaluate the reactions of
actual consumers as well as potential consumers. Certainly we need to be more
aware of social validation issues in the treatment of school phobia and childhood
anxiety disorders in general (see Gullone & King, 1989).

Summary

Although there have been some encouraging findings in the assessment
and treatment of school phobia, we must conclude this chapter by acknowledging that our understanding of school phobia is in need of considerable refine-

ment. Little systematic work has been conducted; rather, investigations in this area have been for the most part sporadic.

School phobia is a complex phenomenon which, historically and into the present, has been subject to definitional and diagnostic confusion. Although the operational guidelines set forth by Berg et al. (1969) are straightforward and seem useful, a majority of studies have not adhered to them; nor, for that matter, have they adhered to any consistent set of criteria. Moreover, efforts to distinguish between "subtypes" of school phobia have encountered major difficulties and are characterized by inconsistent findings. In addition, etiological factors remain incompletely understood. As we have noted, the etiology of school phobia varies from child to child; heterogeneity rather than homogeneity prevails. Children evince school phobia for a number of reasons, including separation anxiety, fear of some aspect of the school situation, and anxiety associated with anticipatory return to school.

From a behavioral perspective, school phobia is acquired according to principles of classical, vicarious, and operant conditioning. Once acquired, it is likely that the phobic behavior is maintained by a complex interactive process involving all of these principles. Sorting out the relevant contributing factors is not an easy task. Nonetheless, assessment designed to ferret out these processes is important, since efficacious treatment is dependent on the information obtained. In this pursuit, we have recommended the utility of a multimethod approach involving behavioral interviews, self-report and other-report test data, and detailed behavioral observations. Based on this information, treatment strategies such as systematic densensitization, participant modeling, and contingency contracting have been set forth and, in general, found to be useful. Still, most of these investigations have been uncontrolled case studies. Although results are promising, they remain to be empirically validated by well-controlled research strategies. The work of Blagg and Yule stand as notable exceptions.

In summary, our review of school phobia raises many questions. Much remains to be accomplished. Even though "the whining schoolboy with his satchel and shining morning face creeping like a snail unwillingly to school" (Shakespeare, As You Like It, Act II) has been with us for a long time, we know precious little about him. For us, this remains an exciting venture; the area appears fertile for systematic and well-controlled research.

REFERENCES

American Psychiatric Association (1980). *Diagnostic and statistical manual of mental disorders* (3rd ed.). Washington, DC: Author.

Angelino, H., Dollins, J., & Mech, E. V. (1956). Trends in the "fears and worries" of school children as related to socio-economic status and age. *Journal of Genetic Psychology, 89,* 263–276.

Angelino, H., & Shedd, C. (1953). Shifts in the content of fears and worries relative to chronological age. *Proceedings of the Oklahoma Academy of Science, 34,* 180–186.

Atkinson, L., Quarrington, B., & Cyr, J. J. (1985). School refusal: The heterogeneity of a concept. *American Journal of Orthopsychiatry, 55,* 83–101.

Ayllon, T., Smith, D., & Rogers, M. (1970). Behavioral management of school phobia. *Journal of Behavior Therapy & Experimental Psychiatry, 1,* 125–138.

Baker, H., & Wills, U. (1979). School phobia: Children at work. *British Journal of Psychiatry, 135,* 561–564.

Bamber, J. H. (1974). The fears of adolescents. *Journal of Genetic Psychology, 125,* 127–140.

Bandura, A. (1969). *Principles of behavior modification.* New York: Holt, Rinehart & Winston.

Bandura, A., & Menlove, F. L. (1968). Factors determining vicarious extinction of avoidance behavior through modeling. *Journal of Personality & Social Psychology, 8,* 99–108.

Barrios, B. A., Hartmann, D. P., & Shigetomi, C. (1981). Fears and anxieties in children. In E. J. Mash & L. G. Terdal (Eds.), *Behavioral assessment of childhood disorders* (pp. 259–304). New York: Guilford Press.

Bauer, D. H. (1976). An exploratory study of developmental changes in children's fears. *Journal of Child Psychology & Psychiatry, 17,* 69–74.

Berg, I. (1976). School phobia in the children of agoraphobic women. *British Journal of Psychiatry, 128,* 86–89.

Berg, I., Nichols, K., & Pritchard, C. (1969). School-phobia—its classification and relationship to dependency. *Journal of Child Psychology & Psychiatry, 10,* 123–141.

Berg, I., Marks, I., McGuire, R., & Lipsedge, M. (1974). School phobia and agoraphobia. *Psychological Medicine, 4,* 428–434.

Bersh, P. J. (1980). Eysenck's theory of incubation: A critical analysis. *Behaviour Research & Therapy, 18,* 11–17.

Blagg, N. (1977). A detailed strategy for the rapid treatment of school phobics. *Behavioural Psychotherapy, 5,* 70–75.

Blagg, N. (1979). *The behavioural treatment of school refusal.* Unpublished Ph.D. thesis, Institute of Psychiatry, University of London.

Blagg, N. (1981). A behavioural approach to school refusal. Behaviour modification in education. *Perspectives, 5,* School of Education, University of Exeter.

Blagg, N. (1987). *School phobia and its treatment.* London: Croom Helm.

Blagg, N. R., & Yule, W. (1984). The behavioural treatment of school refusal—a comparative study. *Behaviour Research & Therapy, 22,* 119–127.

Bondy, A., Sheslow, D., & Garcia, L. T. (1985). An investigation of children's fears and their mothers' fears. *Journal of Psychopathology & Behavioral Assessment, 7,* 1–12.

Broadwin, I. T. (1932). A contribution to the study of truancy. *American Journal of Orthopsychiatry, 2,* 253–259.

Brown, R. E., Copeland, R. E., & Hall, R. V. (1974). School phobia: effects of behavior modification treatment applied by an elementary school principal. *Child Study Journal, 4,* 125–133.

Burke, A. E., & Silverman, W. (1987). The prescriptive treatment of school refusal. *Clinical Psychology Review, 7,* 353–362.

Castaneda, A., McCandless, B. R., & Palermo, D. S. (1956). The children's form of the Manifest Anxiety Scale. *Child Development, 27,* 317–326.

Chazan, M. (1962). School phobia. *British Journal of Educational Psychology, 32,* 200–217.

Chess, S., Thomas, A., & Birch, H. G. (1966). Distortions in developmental reporting made by parents of behaviorally disturbed children. *Journal of the American Academy of Child Psychiatry, 5,* 226–236.

Coolidge, J. C., Hahn, P. B., & Peck, A. L. (1957). School phobia: neurotic crisis or way of life. *American Journal of Orthopsychiatry, 27,* 296–306.

Cooper, J. A. (1973). Application of the consultant role to parent–teacher management of school avoidance behavior. *Psychology in the Schools, 10,* 259–262.

Eisenberg, I. (1958). School phobia: A study in the communication of anxiety. *American Journal of Psychiatry, 14,* 712–718.

Emmelkamp, P. M. G. (1982). Anxiety and fear. In A. S. Bellack, M. Hersen, & A. E. Kazdin (Eds.), *International handbook of behavior modification and therapy* (pp. 349–95). New York: Plenum.

Estes, H. R., Haylett, C. H., & Johnson, A. M. (1956). Separation anxiety. *American Journal of Orthopsychiatry, 10,* 682–95.

Esveldt-Dawson, K., Wisner, K. L., Unis, A. S., Matson, J. L., & Kazdin, A. E. (1982). Treatment of phobias in a hospitalized child. *Journal of Behavior Therapy & Experimental Psychiatry, 13,* 77–83.

Eysenck, H. J. (1957). *The dynamics of anxiety and hysteria.* London: Routledge & Kegan Paul.

Eysenck, H. J. (1965). *Fact and fiction in psychology.* Harmondsworth: Penguin.

Eysenck, H. J. (1967). Single-trial conditioning, neurosis and the Napalkov phenomenon. *Behaviour Research & Therapy, 5,* 63–65.

Eysenck, H. J. (1979). The conditioning model of neurosis. *Behavioural & Brain Sciences, 2,* 155–199.

Forehand, R. L., & McMahon, R. J. (1981). *Helping the non compliant child: A clinician's guide to parent training.* New York: Guilford Press.

Freud, S. (1963). The analysis of a phobia in a five-year-old boy. In *Standard edition of the complete psychological works of Sigmund Freud* (Vol. 10, pp. 37–57). London: Hogarth Press. (Original work published 1909)

Garvey, W. P., & Hegrenes, J. R. (1966). Desensitization techniques in the treatment of school phobia. *American Journal of Orthopsychiatry, 36,* 147–152.

Gittelman, R., & Klein, D. (1985). Childhood separation anxiety and adult agoraphobia. In A. H. Tuma & J. D. Maser (Eds.), *Anxiety and the anxiety disorders* (pp. 321–341). Hillsdale, NJ: Lawrence Erlbaum.

Gittelman-Klein, R., & Klein, D. (1973). School phobia: Diagnostic considerations in the light of imipramine effects. *Journal of Nervous and Mental Disease, 156,* 199–215.

Goldberg, T. B. (1953). Factors in the development of school phobia. *Smith College Studies in Social Work, 23,* 227–248.

Goldfried, M. R., & Kent, R. N. (1972). Traditional versus behavioral personality assessment: A comparison of methodological and theoretical assumptions. *Psychological Bulletin, 77,* 409–420.

Graziano, A. M., & DeGiovanni, I. S. (1979). The clinical significance of childhood phobias: a note on the proportion of child-clinical referrals for the treatment of children's fears. *Behaviour Research & Therapy, 17,* 161–162.

Graziano, A. M., DeGiovanni, I. S., & Garcia, K. A. (1979). Behavioral treatment of children's fears: a review. *Psychological Bulletin, 86,* 804–830.

Gullone, E., & King, N. J. (1988, May). *Acceptability of major treatment models for school phobia: Comparison of adolescent and caregiver perceptions.* Paper presented at the 11th National Conference of the Australian Behaviour Modification Association, Adelaide, S.A.

Gullone, E., & King, N. J. (1989). Acceptability of behavioral interventions: Perceptions of children and caregivers. In M. Hersen, R. Eisler, & P. M. Miller (Eds.), *Progress in behavior modification* (Vol. 24, pp. 132–151). Newbury Park, CA: Sage.

Hagman, E. R. (1932). A study of fears of children of pre-school age. *Journal of Experimental Education, 1,* 110–130.

Hall, G. S. (1897). A study of fears. *American Journal of Psychology, 8,* 147–249.

Hallam, R. S. (1978). Agoraphobia: A critical review of the concept. *British Journal of Psychiatry, 133,* 314–319.

Hampe, E., Noble, H., Miller, L. C., & Barrett, C. L. (1973). Phobic children one and two years posttreatment. *Journal of Abnormal Psychology, 82,* 446–453.

Herjanic, B., Herjanic, M., Brown, F., & Wheatt, T. (1975). Are children reliable reporters? *Journal of Abnormal Child Psychology, 3,* 41–48.

Hersen, M. (1970). Behavior modification approach to a school-phobia case. *Journal of Clinical Psychology, 26,* 128–132.

Hersov, L. A. (1960a). Persistent non-attendance at school. *Journal of Child Psychology & Psychiatry, 1,* 130–136.

Hersov, L. A. (1960b). Refusal to go to school. *Journal of Child Psychology & Psychiatry, 1,* 137–145.

Hersov, L. (1977). School refusal. In M. Rutter & L. Hersov (Eds.), *Child psychiatry. Modern approaches* (pp. 455–486). Oxford: Blackwell.

Hersov, L., & Berg, I. (Eds.). (1980). *Out of school. Modern perspectives in truancy and school refusal.* Chichester: Wiley.

Jersild, A. T., & Holmes, F. B. (1935). *Children's fears.* New York: Teachers College, Columbia University.

Johnson, A. M., Falstein, E. I., Szurek, S. A., & Svendsen, M. (1941). School phobia. *American Journal of Orthopsychiatry, 11,* 702–711.

Johnson, S. B. (1979). Children's fears in the classroom setting. *School Psychology Digest, 8,* 382–396.

Johnson, S. M., & Bolstad, O. D. (1973). Methodological issues in naturalistic observation: Some problems and solutions for field research. In L. A. Hamerlynck, L. C. Handy, & E. J. Mash (Eds.), *Behavior change: Methodology, concepts, and practice* (pp. 325–347). Champaign, IL: Research Press.

Jones, M. C. (1924). A laboratory study of fear: the case of Peter. *Journal of Genetic Psychology, 31,* 308–315.

Kahn, J. H., & Nursten, J. P. (1962). School refusal. *American Journal of Orthopsychiatry, 32,* 707–718.

Kazdin, A. E. (1979). Situational specificity: The two-edged sword of behavioral assessment. *Behavioral Assessment, 1,* 57–75.

Kennedy, W. A. (1965). School phobia: rapid treatment of fifty cases. *Journal of Abnormal Psychology, 70,* 285–289.

King, N. J., Hamilton, D. I., Ollendick, T. H. (1988). *Children's phobias: A behavioural perspective.* Chichester: Wiley.

King, N. J., Ollier, K., Iacuone, R., Schuster, S., Bays, K., Gullone, E., & Ollendick, T. H. (in press). The fears of children and adolescents in Australia: A cross-sectional study using the Revised-Fear Survey Schedule for Children. *Journal of Child Psychology & Psychiatry.*

Lapouse, R., & Monk, M. A. (1959). Fears and worries in a representative sample of children. *American Journal of Orthopsychiatry, 29,* 223–248.

Last, C. G., Francis, G., Hersen, M., Kazdin, A. E., & Strauss, C. C. (1987). Separation anxiety and school phobia: A comparison using DSM-III criteria. *American Journal of Psychiatry, 144,* 653–657.

Lazarus, A. A. (1960). The elimination of children's phobias by deconditioning. In H. J. Eysenck (Ed.), *Behaviour therapy and the neuroses* (pp. 114–122). Oxford: Pergamon Press.

Lazarus, A. A. (1971). *Behavior therapy and beyond.* New York: McGraw-Hill.

Lazarus, A. A., & Abramovitz, A. (1962). The use of "emotive imagery" in the treatment of children's phobias. *Journal of Mental Science, 108,* 191–195.

Lazarus, A. A., Davison, G. C., & Polefka, D. A. (1965). Classical and operant factors in the treatment of a school phobia. *Journal of Abnormal Psychology, 70,* 225–229.

Lick, J. R., & Katkin, E. S. (1976). Assessment of anxiety and fear. In M. Hersen & A. S. Bellack (Eds.), *Behavioral assessment* (pp. 175–206). New York: Pergamon Press.

Lovibond, S. H. (1966). The current status of behavior therapy. *Canadian Psychologist, 7,* 93–101.

MacFarlane, J. W., Allen, L., & Honzik, M. P. (1954). *A developmental study of the behavioral problems of normal children between 21 months and 14 years.* Berkeley: University of California Press.

Marks, I. M. (1969). *Fears and phobias.* New York: Academic Press.

Marks, I. M. (1975). Behavioral treatments of phobic and obsessive–compulsive disorders: a critical appraisal. In M. Hersen, R. M. Eisler, & P. M. Miller (Eds.), *Progress in behavior modification* (Vol. 1, pp. 66–158). New York: Academic Press.

Mash, E. J., & Terdal, L. G. (Eds.). (1981). *Behavioral assessment of childhood disorders.* New York: Guilford Press.

McDonald, J. E., & Sheperd, G. (1976). School phobia: An overview. *Journal of School Psychology, 14,* 291–306.

Miller, L. C., Barrett, C. L., & Hampe, E. (1974). Phobias of childhood in a prescientific era. In A. Davids (Ed.), *Child personality and psychopathology: Current topics* (Vol. 1, pp. 89–134). New York: Wiley.

Miller, L. C., Barrett, C. L., Hampe, E., & Noble, H. (1971). Revised anxiety scales for the Louisville Behavior Checklist. *Psychological Reports, 29,* 503–511.

Miller, L. C., Barrett, C. L., Hampe, E., & Noble, H. (1972a). Comparison of reciprocal inhibition, psychotherapy and waiting list control for phobic children. *Journal of Abnormal Psychology, 79,* 269–279.

Miller, L. C., Barrett, C. L., Hampe, E., & Noble, H. (1972b). Factor structure of childhood fears. *Journal of Consulting & Clinical Psychology, 39,* 264–268.

Miller, P. M. (1972). The use of visual imagery and muscle relaxation in the counterconditioning of a phobic child: a case study. *Journal of Nervous & Mental Disease, 154,* 457–460.

Mitchell, S., & Shepherd, M. (1967). The child who dislikes going to school. *British Journal of Educational Psychology, 37,* 32–40.

Moore, T. (1966). Difficulties of the ordinary child in adjusting to primary school. *Journal of Child Psychology and Psychiatry, 7,* 17–38.

Morris, R. J., & Kratochwill, T. R. (1983). *Treating children's fears and phobias. A behavioral approach.* New York: Pergamon Press.

Neisworth, J. T., Madle, R. A., & Goeke, K. E. (1975). "Errorless" elimination of separation anxiety: a case study. *Journal of Behavior Therapy & Experimental Psychiatry, 6,* 79–82.

Ollendick, T. H. (1979). Fear reduction techniques with children. In M. Hersen, R. M. Eisler, & P. M. Miller (Eds.), *Progress in behavior modification* (Vol. 8, pp. 127–168). New York: Academic Press.

Ollendick, T. H. (1983). Reliability and validity of the Revised Fear Survey Schedule for Children (FSSC-R). *Behaviour Research & Therapy, 21,* 685–692.

Ollendick, T. H., & Cerny, J. A. (1981). *Clinical behavior therapy with children.* New York: Plenum.

Ollendick, T. H. & Francis, G. (1988). Behavioral assessment and treatment of childhood phobias. *Behavior Modification, 12,* 165–205.

Ollendick, T. H., & Hersen, M. (1983). An historical introduction to child psychopathology. In T. H. Ollendick & M. Hersen (Eds.), *Handbook of child psychopathology* (pp. 3–12). New York: Plenum.

Ollendick, T. H., & Hersen, M. (Eds.). (1984). *Child behavioral assessment. Principles and procedures.* New York: Pergamon Press.

Ollendick, T. H., King, N. J., & Frary, R. B. (1989). Fears in children and adolescents. Reliability across gender, age and nationality. *Behaviour Research & Therapy, 27,* 19–26.

Ollendick, T. H., Matson, J. L., & Helsel, W. J. (1985). Fears in children and adolescents: Normative data. *Behaviour Research & Therapy, 23,* 465–467.

Ollendick, T. H., & Mayer, J. A. (1984). School phobia. In S. M. Turner (Ed.), *Behavioral theories and treatment of anxiety* (pp. 367–411). New York: Plenum.

Partridge, J. M. (1939). Truancy. *Journal of Mental Science, 85,* 45–81.

Perry, M. A., & Furukawa, M. J. (1980). Modeling methods. In F. H. Kanfer & A. P. Goldstein (Eds.), *Helping people change* (2nd ed., pp. 131–71). New York: Pergamon Press.

Poznanski, E. O. (1973). Children with excessive fears. *American Journal of Orthopsychiatry, 43,* 428–438.

Quay, H. C., & Werry, J. S. (Eds.). (1979). *Psychopathological disorders of childhood* (2nd ed.). New York: Wiley.

Rachman, S. (1968). *Phobias: Their nature and control.* Springfield, IL: Charles C. Thomas.

Rachman, S. (1977). The conditioning theory of fear acquisition: a critical examination. *Behaviour Research & Therapy, 15,* 375–387.

Rachman, S., & Costello, C. G. (1961). The aetiology and treatment of children's phobias: a review. *American Journal of Psychiatry, 118,* 97–105.

Reynolds, C. R., & Richmond, B. O. (1978). What I think and feel: a revised measure of children's manifest anxiety. *Journal of Abnormal Child Psychology, 6,* 271–280.

Reynolds, C. R., & Richmond, B. O. (1979). Factor structure and construct validity of "What I think and feel": the Revised Children's Manifest Anxiety Scale. *Journal of Personality Assessment, 43,* 281–283.

Rodriguez, A., Rodriguez, M., & Eisenberg, L. (1959). The outcome of school phobia: a follow-up study based on 41 cases. *American Journal of Psychiatry, 116,* 540–544.

Rosenstiel, A. K., & Scott, D. S. (1977). Four considerations in using imagery techniques with children. *Journal of Behaviour Therapy & Experimental Psychiatry, 8,* 287–290.

Ross, A. O. (1981). *Child behavior therapy: Principles, procedures and empirical basis.* New York: Wiley.

Scherer, M. W., & Nakamura, C. Y. (1968). A Fear Survey Schedule for Children (FSS-FC): a factor analytic comparison with manifest anxiety (CMAS). *Behaviour Research & Therapy, 6,* 173–182.

Smith, R. E., & Sharpe, T. M. (1970). Treatment of a school phobia with implosive therapy. *Journal of Consulting & Clinical Psychology, 35,* 239–243.

Spielberger, C. (1973). *Manual for the state–trait anxiety inventory for children.* Palo Alto, CA: Consulting Psychologists Press.

Tahmisian, J. A., & McReynolds, W. T. (1971). Use of parents as behavioral engineers in the treatment of a school phobic girl. *Journal of Counseling Psychology, 18,* 225–228.

Truax, C. B., & Carkhuff, R. R. (1967). *Toward effective counseling and psychotherapy: Training and practice.* Chicago: Aldine.

Turner, S. M., Beidel, D. C., & Costello, A. (1987). Psychopathology in the offspring of anxiety disorders patients. *Journal of Consulting & Clinical Psychology, 55,* 229–235.

Vaal, J. J. (1973). Applying contingency contracting to a school phobic: a case study. *Journal of Behavior Therapy & Experimental Psychiatry, 4,* 371–373.

Waldfogel, S., Coolidge, J. C., & Hahn, P. (1957). Development and management of school phobia. *American Journal of Orthopsychiatry, 27,* 754–780.

Waldron, S., Jr. (1976). The significance of childhood neurosis for adult mental health: A follow-up study. *American Journal of Psychiatry, 133,* 532–538.

Warren, W. (1948). Acute neurotic breakdown in children with refusal to go to school. *Archives of the Disturbed Child,* 266–272.

Watson, J. B., & Rayner, R. (1920). Conditioned emotional reactions. *Journal of Experimental Psychology, 3,* 1–14.

Weiss, M. & Cain, B. (1964). The residential treatment of children and adolescents with school phobia. *American Journal of Orthopsychiatry, 34,* 103–114.

Wilson, G. T., & O'Leary, K. D. (1980). *Principles of behavior therapy.* Englewood Cliffs, NJ: Prentice-Hall.

Windheuser, H. J. (1977). Anxious mothers as models for coping with anxiety. *Behavioral Analysis & Modification, 2,* 39–58.

Wolf, M. M. (1978). Social validity: the case for subjective measurement or how applied behaviour analysis is finding its heart. *Journal of Applied Behavior Analysis, 11,* 203–224.

Wolpe, J. (1958). *Psychotherapy by reciprocal inhibition.* Stanford, CA: Stanford University Press.

Wolpe, J., & Rachman, S. (1960). Psychoanalytic "evidence": a critique based on Freud's case of Little Hans. *Journal of Nervous & Mental Diseases, 131,* 135–148.

Yates, A. J. (1970). *Behavior therapy.* New York: Wiley.

Social Anxiety in Adulthood: Establishing Relationships

Dating Anxiety

Debra A. Hope and Richard G. Heimberg

In the late 1960s and early 1970s, an increasing number of articles began to appear in behavioral journals on the treatment of dating anxiety. This was not a response to a sudden recognition that dating-anxious individuals were desperately in need of treatment, but rather an academic reaction to mounting criticism of analog studies of behavioral techniques which focused on problems such as snake and spider phobias (Bernstein & Paul, 1971; Cooper, Furst, & Bridger, 1969). Dating anxiety, or heterosocial anxiety as it was often called, had a number of characteristics which made it an excellent target behavior for analog behavioral research (Borkovec, Stone, O'Brien, & Kaloupek, 1974): (1) it frequently occurred in psychiatric populations, so it was seen as more worthy of attention than simple phobias; (2) it occurred frequently enough among college students to provide adequate sample sizes; (3) it often involved physiological arousal, which was useful for testing desensitization treatments which were particularly popular at the time; and (4) it caused disruption in the individual's life and, in fact, was identified as a significant problem among college students (Bryant & Trower, 1974). However, Heimberg (1977) argued that the high incidence and amount of distress experienced by dating-anxious college students made dating anxiety among college students worthy of treatment attention in its own right, not just as an analogue to the problems of psychiatric patients. While severe dating anxiety is now considered an example of social phobia (American Psychiatric Association, 1987), we argue that dating anxiety in college students and other normal populations continues to merit attention in its own right.

The Disruptive Effects of Dating Anxiety

The dating-anxious man or woman is a common figure in film, literature, and even comic strips. Who is not familiar with the portrayal of the young man nervously shuffling his feet while trying to ask the young woman of his dreams to go out with him? Often this figure is viewed sympathetically, his distress an

Debra A. Hope and Richard G. Heimberg • Department of Psychology, State University of New York at Albany, Albany, New York 12203.

understandable reflection of the depth of his affection. In fiction he overcomes his internal struggle and wins her hand. If this were the nature of real-life dating anxiety, then it would hardly merit our attention. However, research suggests that dating anxiety does not always result in such happy endings. Instead, because of extreme fear of rejection, the man may never approach the woman.

In addition, dating anxiety is related to difficulties in other important areas of functioning. For example, those who have difficulty in heterosocial situations are also likely to experience difficulty in same-sex interactions. Same-sex interaction partners rated anxious, minimally dating men as more anxious and less skillful than nonanxious, frequently dating men (Himadi, Arkowitz, Hinton, & Perl, 1980). Self-monitoring measures also revealed that the minimally dating men engaged in less frequent interactions with other men and with a fewer number of men. Although there were no differences in this study in same-sex interactions among high and low frequently dating women, in another study, Robins (1986) found that dating anxiety was highly correlated with anxiety in same-sex interactions for both men and women.

Dating anxiety has also been associated with depression, low self-esteem, and nonassertiveness in women (Dow, Biglan, & Glaser, 1985; Greenwald, 1978) and poorer adjustment on the Eysenck Personality Inventory (Eysenck & Eysenck, 1968) in men (Himadi *et al.*, 1980). Masculinity, usually positively correlated with measures of good mental health in both genders (Bassoff & Glass, 1982), was negatively related to dating anxiety in both men and women (Robins, 1986). Not surprisingly, low dating anxiety is also associated with more extensive sexual experience (Leary & Dobbins, 1983). However, even sexually experienced anxious men and women were more anxious about the prospect of engaging in intercourse and had enjoyed recent encounters less than experienced, but nonanxious, subjects. Finally, heterosocial anxiety may actually impair sexual performance in men in that high anxiety tended to be associated with a higher incidence of premature ejaculation and temporary impotence. Anxiety was unrelated to sexual dysfunction among women in this study. These findings for men are particularly intriguing given recent conceptualizations of sexual dysfunction as a form of social phobia (Barlow, 1986; Heimberg & Barlow, 1988).

Thus it appears that the media portrait of heterosocial anxiety is more optimistic than accurate. Dating anxiety may be part of a larger picture of distress and dysfunction in social situations and appears to have an impact on the development of sexual relationships. Logically, it may also reduce the chances of successful adjustment in relationships and therefore continue to exert its influence throughout the life span. Clearly dating anxiety merits attention.

ISSUES IN THE RESEARCH LITERATURE

Definition of Dating Anxiety

Exactly what "dating anxiety" is has never been clearly specified. Furthermore, terminology has changed over the years, and there appears to be considerable overlap between subjects described as "dating anxious," "low-frequency daters," "socially anxious," "shy," and "social phobic." We now examine these different labels and attempt to clarify what will be meant by "dating anxiety" in this chapter.

There are four problems with defining heterosocial adjustment in terms of dating frequency. First, what is considered low-frequency dating in one study (three dates in the last month; Greenwald, 1978) is viewed as high-frequency dating in another study (Klaus, Hersen, & Bellack, 1977). Although there are reports on the average number of dates per month among college students (e.g., $M = 5.58$ in Klaus et al.'s sample), there are no clear guidelines on what is a "normal" dating frequency. Second, reports of dating frequency depend upon how a "date" is defined. For example, does two students meeting in the library to study together constitute a date? In this situation, studying may be the end goal of the interaction, or it may be a means by which two mutually attracted people can become better acquainted. Only the latter circumstance is properly considered a date. Third, simply counting numbers of dates says little about the individual. Consider the case of the very extroverted, popular person who dates 10 different people per month versus the shy, anxious person who repeatedly dates a familiar but incompatible partner due to fear of meeting anyone else. Both individuals might fall into the high-frequency dating category but would likely differ on numerous cognitive, behavioral, and personality variables. Fourth, low-frequency dating is a heterogeneous category. Nondaters may not date because they are fearful of social interaction, because they prefer solitude, because of devotion to a career goal which limits social contact, or because of the unavailability of appropriate partners. Clearly only those falling in the first category are truly "dating anxious."

How does dating anxiety differ from social anxiety? An examination of commonly used measures of social anxiety such as the Social Avoidance and Distress Scale (SADS; Watson & Friend, 1969) indicates that social anxiety includes both dating and nondating situations (being the center of attention, talking to strangers, and performing tasks under scrutiny). Although Leary (1983a) has argued for a distinction between interaction anxiety and performance anxiety, interaction anxiety is a broader category than dating anxiety because it includes anxiety in nondating situations, such as job interviews and talking with authority figures. To make matters more complex, research on social anxiety appears under various titles, including shyness, communication apprehension, and stage fright (Leary, 1983b). However, as will be seen below, much of the research on social anxiety focuses on heterosocial interactions and thus will be relevant to the discussion of dating anxiety.

A similar distinction can be made between dating anxiety and shyness, particularly given that shyness may be indistinguishable from social anxiety on the measurement level (Anderson & Harvey, 1988). Again, shyness is a broader category than dating anxiety, generally including reticence in both dating and nondating situations (Buss, 1980; Leary, 1983b).

Individuals who are severely anxious in dating situations may meet the criteria for social phobia (DSM-III-R; American Psychiatric Association, 1987).

However, social phobia is covered separately in this volume (see Chapter 9 by Scholing and Emmelkamp), and our discussion also includes dating anxiety which does not meet the DSM-III-R restriction for significant interference in social functioning.

In summary, we define dating anxiety as distress associated with interactions with potential romantic partners prior to the development of a full-fledged relationship. This definition includes a subset of individuals who would be classified as low-frequency daters, shy, socially anxious, or social phobic. Therefore, our review includes research from each of these domains.

Generalizability of Dating Anxiety Research

An examination of the available literature on dating anxiety would lead to the conclusion that it is almost exclusively confined to male, heterosexual college students. Although there is evidence that the nature of dating anxiety is different for men and women (e.g., women may be more likely to be deficient in social skills and men more likely to exhibit irrational cognitions; Glasgow & Arkowitz, 1975), research has typically focused on dating anxiety in men. Although there is a growing literature on dating anxiety in women (e.g., Dow et al., 1985; Haemmerlie, 1983), women continue to be underrepresented, or the data for men and women are not analyzed separately. We are also unaware of any studies of dating anxiety among homosexual and bisexual individuals. In fact, the phenomenon is often referred to as "heterosocial anxiety" and the questionnaires used to screen subjects for studies assume heterosexuality. Undoubtedly, some proportion of subjects engaging in role plays and answering questions about interactions with the opposite sex have done so without considering them to be potential romantic/sexual partners. Although one would expect some similarities between same-sex and opposite-sex dating, there are likely many differences as well. Behavior changes resulting from the AIDS epidemic make research on this topic particularly timely (Kelly, St. Lawrence, Hood, & Brasfield, 1988).

The focus on college students has resulted in a lack of attention to dating anxiety in nonstudent groups. Divorced individuals, for example, may return to dating with some trepidation (Canter & Drake, 1983). Given that their initial dating experiences are likely to be blind dates (Petronio & Endres, 1985), they may be thrust into situations like those commonly used to induce dating anxiety in college students (such as sharing a meal with someone one has just met; Curran, Gilbert, & Little, 1976). However, whether their reaction to these situations is similar to that of college students is unknown. Clearly, more research is needed in this area.

THE NATURE OF DATING ANXIETY

Most studies comparing dating-anxious and -nonanxious individuals have found they differ on a number of dimensions, including physiological arousal, overt behavior, cognition, and physical attractiveness. Each of these dimensions has served as the basis for an etiological model of dating anxiety. We will examine these models in light of available research evidence and conclude with a review of the self-presentational model of social anxiety (Schlenker & Leary, 1982).

Conditioned Anxiety and Physiological Aspects of Dating Anxiety

The efficacy of systematic desensitization for dating anxiety (e.g., Bander, Steinke, Allen, & Mosher, 1975; Curran, 1975) suggested that dating anxiety may be a product of classical conditioning. According to the conditioned anxiety model, social interactions may have become cues which elicit physiological arousal as a result of previous pairing with aversive stimuli. The anxiety does not extinguish because anxiety reduction negatively reinforces avoidance of potential dating situations. Thus the model predicts that dating anxiety will be associated with physiological arousal in the feared situation. Unfortunately, there has been little research in this area.

Borkovec and colleagues (1974) reported that anxious and nonanxious men demonstrated similar patterns of heart rate arousal in a heterosocial interaction. Both experienced heart rate acceleration in anticipation of the interaction. Heart rate peaked as the interaction began and then began to decrease. However, anxious men's heart rates were higher at each point. In another study, anxious and nonanxious men's heart rates differed in some role-play situations but not others, although anxious men did have higher peak arousal than nonanxious men (Twentyman & McFall, 1975).

Physiological arousal may also play an indirect role in dating anxiety. Anxious individuals who report physiological arousal in social situations fear it will be seen by others, apparently without justification (McEwan & Devins, 1983). Although there is some evidence for the accuracy of self-report of autonomic arousal among the socially anxious (Borkovec et al., 1974; Johansson & Ost, 1982), there appears to be little relationship between physiological arousal (sampled by heart rate) and behavioral signs of anxiety (Ahern, Wallander, Abrahms, & Monti, 1983). It may be reassuring, yet surprising, to dating-anxious individuals that even though they can feel their heart pound, no one can see it.

Social Skills Deficits and Behavioral Aspects of Dating Anxiety

The social skills deficit model of dating anxiety states that dating-anxious individuals lack appropriate skills to behave effectively in social situations. Consequently, their efforts result in failure and/or rejection by the interaction partner and subsequent anxiety and avoidance of future situations. There have been fairly consistent findings that subjects high and low in dating anxiety can be differentiated on global ratings of social skill, whether those ratings are made by objective observers (Arkowitz, Lichtenstein, McGovern, & Hines, 1975; Twentyman & McFall, 1975), friends (Phibbs & Arkowitz, 1982), or interaction partners (Greenwald, 1977). As will be seen below, attempts at rating specific aspects of social skill, such as eye contact or voice quality, have been met with mixed success.

Arkowitz et al. (1975) examined six behaviors (talk time, number of silences, number of verbal reinforcements, head nods, smiles, and eye contact) and found that in men, high- and low-frequency daters differed only on number of silences, with low-frequency daters having more 10-second silences than high-frequency daters. Greenwald (1977) found that in women, only two of seven specific behavioral measures (subject talk time and eye contact) distinguished high- and low-frequency daters. Dow et al. (1985) found two of nine behaviors (talk time and 4-second pauses) to distinguish between anxious and nonanxious women. In another study, nonanxious men shared conversation time equally with partners in a heterosocial conversation, talking more than anxious men. The anxious men were also more likely to chose negative topics for discussion (Faraone & Hurtig, 1985). Several recent studies have found significant correlations between global ratings of social skill and anxiety and discrete behaviors such as talk time, eye contact, and head and body movements (Conger & Farrell, 1981; Millbrook, Farrell, & Curran, 1986; Wallander, Conger, & Conger, 1985). Increasing sophistication in behavioral assessment may result in greater success at defining the molecular components of social skill.

Why is it so difficult to determine the specific behaviors which comprise global ratings of social skill? First, subjects' behavior in interactions is influenced by their partner's behavior. The social skill and dating experience of each person make a unique contribution to each interaction. Individuals who interact with a low-frequency dater may become less confident in their own social skill (Jaremko, Myers, Daner, Moore, & Allin, 1982), which may result in changes in their own behavior. In fact, Faraone and Hurtig (1985) found that anxious men's verbalizations were less likely to evoke a positive response from female conversation partners than those of nonanxious men. Second, most studies employ simple frequency counts of specific behaviors. It may not be the raw frequency of a behavior that denotes social skill but rather the timing of the behavior (Fischetti, Curran, & Wessberg, 1977; Peterson, Fischetti, Curran, & Arland, 1981) or the content of verbalizations (Leary, Knight, & Johnson, 1987). Finally, there may be more than one way to be socially skillful. Although Conger and colleagues (Conger, Wallander, Conger, & Ward, 1980) found that ratings of specific components of social skill were generally predictive of global ratings, peer judges used different combinations of behaviors to determine competency for different people.

The essential skills for successful dating may be different for men and women, particularly the skills needed to initiate a date. Although asking may be the most effective strategy for a woman to obtain a date with a man (Muehlenhard & McFall, 1981), both men and women prefer that women hint rather than ask directly (Muehlenhard, Koralewski, Andrews, & Burdick, 1986). However, even asking directly may be better than not asking at all. Men who viewed videotapes of a woman who either requested or did not request a date with a man rated the woman who requested the date more positively. They also believed her to be more sexually active which, as the authors point out, could put her at higher risk for date rape, particularly with men who adhere to traditional sex roles (Muehlenhard & Scardino, 1985).

Although analysis of social skill is a complex task, it appears that dating anxiety *is* associated with poorer performance in social interactions. The exact source of the performance deficit is unclear and is likely subject to individual variation. It is important to note that this association does not necessarily mean that social skills deficits are responsible for dating anxiety. It could well be the reverse; that is, dating anxiety may be responsible for impaired social performance.

Cognitive Models of Dating Anxiety

Cognitive models of dating anxiety hypothesize that dating anxiety results from inefficient allocation of limited attentional capacity or from faulty appraisal of the individual's performance and/or of the likelihood of an aversive outcome. Cognitive models attribute apparent social skills deficits associated with dating anxiety to disruptive cognitive processes which interfere with execution of the skills the person possesses. Similarly, overanticipation of negative events results in physiological arousal.

A number of studies have examined the content of high- and low-anxious individuals' thoughts. Anxious people report more negative (Cacioppo, Glass, & Merluzzi, 1979), less positive (Heimberg, Acerra, & Holstein, 1985), and more self-focused (Hope, Heimberg, Zollo, Nyman, & O'Brien, 1987; Johnson & Glass, in press) thoughts than nonanxious people. Furthermore, frequent negative self-statements are associated with lower social skill and higher anxiety as perceived by both heterosocial interaction partners and objective observers (Glass, Merluzzi, Biever, & Larsen, 1982).

As noted above, dating anxiety is sometimes associated with social performance deficits. However, self-ratings of performance may not be very accurate, and deficits may be perceived (and consequently acted upon) where none exist. Clark and Arkowitz (1975) reported that high-anxious men underestimated and low-anxious men overestimated their own performance (compared to judges' ratings) in heterosocial interactions. Both groups accurately perceived others' level of social skill. When anxious subjects were divided into two groups—those with and without social skills deficits—a more complex picture emerged (Curran, Wallander, & Fischetti, 1980). High-anxious, socially skilled subjects underestimated the quality of their performance. Anxious, socially unskilled subjects' ratings were similar to judges' ratings. However, this latter finding may be attributable to floor effects.

The attentional capacity devoted to excessively self-focused or negative cognitions may come at the expense of adequately processing important neutral or positive information. For example, anxious women were less able to recall information about people to whom they had just been introduced (Kimble & Zehr, 1982) or about men with whom they had engaged in a semistructured conversation (Hope, Heimberg, & Klein, in press). Anxious men showed no preference for potential interaction partners with similar attitudes and interests (Heimberg *et al.*, 1985), a phenomenon that has been repeatedly demonstrated in nonanxious populations (Byrne, 1971). In other words, high anxiety was associated with either a failure to detect or to utilize important social information. All three of these studies suggest that dating-anxious individuals may respond inadequately to important social cues, not because they lack the skill or knowledge to make a response (as a skills deficit model hypothesizes), but because they fail to process the relevant cues appropriately.

What are anxious individuals attending to if they are not attending to their partners? Three studies indirectly address that question. Using a depth of processing paradigm, Smith, Ingram, and Brehm (1983) demonstrated that anxious subjects anticipating a heterosocial interaction devoted excessive cognitive processing to information about how they appeared to others. Anxious subjects also selectively recalled negative feedback from others about themselves and their performance (O'Banion & Arkowitz, 1977), suggesting high anxiety may be associated with attention to negative rather than to positive reactions from others in social situations. When anxious and nonanxious individuals received the same feedback from an interaction partner, anxious persons saw the feedback as more negative, felt worse about receiving the feedback, and had a greater expectation of being evaluated negatively compared to nonanxious persons (Smith & Sarason, 1975). Thus it appears that when anxious individuals fail to adequately process information about their partners, they may be overly concerned about negative evaluation, focusing their attention on how they appear to the other person.

Several researchers have examined attributional patterns associated with dating anxiety. Social psychologists have repeatedly demonstrated that people tend to take more responsibility for positive than for negative events, a phenomenon known as the self-serving bias for causal attributions (Miller & Ross, 1975). However, dating-anxious subjects reversed the self-serving bias and took more responsibility for negative and less for positive social outcomes than nonanxious subjects (Teglasi & Hoffman, 1982). Subjects prescreened to be low in social self-esteem, a construct related to social anxiety, also reversed the self-serving attributional bias when making ratings for heterosocial events (Girodo, Dotzenroth, & Stein, 1981). It should be noted that Miller and Arkowitz (1977) failed to find a reversal of the self-serving bias among anxious subjects. However, as we have noted elsewhere (Hope, Gansler, & Heimberg, 1989), that failure may be attributable to the particular methodology they employed.

Leary and colleagues (Leary, Kowalski, & Campbell, 1988) investigated how anxious and nonanxious individuals believe they appear to other people. They asked subjects to rate the impression they would make in three types of interactions ranging from a brief glance through an extended interaction. Compared to nonanxious subjects, anxious subjects thought interaction partners would evaluate them more negatively, regardless of the duration of the interaction and even on traits which could not be evaluated at a brief glance. Interestingly, anxious individuals did not confine their pessimistic ratings to themselves. In fact, they felt that others would be rated equally negatively. But nonanxious subjects reported they would make a *better* impression than other people, suggesting that the "belief that one makes better impressions than others *lowers* anxiety" rather than the lack of confidence increasing anxiety (p. 317, emphasis in original). Leary *et al.* point out that this is similar to a phenomenon that has been recognized among depressed individuals in which they view events more realistically than nondepressed persons (Abramson & Alloy, 1981).

In a similar vein, nonanxious subjects may engage in self-presentational strategies designed to evoke the expected positive impression. Nonanxious subjects who anticipated that their self-statements would be read by a prospective interviewer made their statements more favorable compared to those not expecting an interview or to anxious subjects (Greenberg, Pysczynski, & Stine, 1985).

Although anxious individuals may too readily expect to make poor impressions and take too much responsibility for negative events, they may take advantage of an excuse for poor performance when one is clearly available, a type of self-handicapping strategy. When anxious subjects thought a background noise would interfere with conversation, their pulse rate was lower and their self-ratings of adjectives were as positive as those of nonanxious subjects (Leary, 1986).

Cognitive models of dating anxiety have received substantial support. It appears that anxious individuals may be excessively self-focused and overly concerned about the impression they are making on others. This may interfere with performance in interactions and be mistaken for a social skills deficit. The overconcern is not surprising, given that they have little expectation of making a good impression.

Physical Attractiveness

Given that physical attractiveness relates to interpersonal attraction (Berscheid & Walster, 1973), it has been hypothesized that dating anxiety may result from rejection by potential dating partners due to physical unattractiveness. This model has been supported by evidence that dating-anxious subjects are rated as less attractive than nonanxious subjects (Glasgow & Arkowitz, 1975; Greenwald, 1977). In fact, in his review of the literature on the relationship between physical attractiveness and social skill, Calvert (1988) concluded that physical attractiveness is consistently associated with high-frequency dating and is often the best predictor of social skill. There are three possible explanations for this relationship: (1) Social skill may be one of the many traits attributed to attractive individuals, but they may not actually be more skilled than unattractive individuals. Researchers have found that many positive characteristics, including intellectual competence (Webster & Driskell, 1983) and psychological health (Jones, Hansson, & Phillips, 1978), are attributed to physically attractive people. The same may be true for heterosocial skill and (lack of) anxiety, particularly given that ratings are usually based on direct observation or videotapes of interactions. However, Goldman and Lewis (1977) found that subjects who had telephone conversations with unfamiliar opposite-sex peers rated physically attractive partners as more skilled. (2) Socially skilled, nonanxious people may be viewed as more physically attractive because their competent, relaxed behavior allows them to make a better overall impression. This hypothesis is supported by data showing that individuals are viewed as more attractive when they exhibit positive social behaviors, such as asking questions, than when they do not exhibit such behaviors (Muehlenhard *et al.*, 1986; Muehlenhard & McFall, 1981). Furthermore, since dating anxiety impacts on the behavior of interaction partners (Faraone & Hurtig, 1985; Jaremko *et al.*, 1982), the partners' positive reaction to nonanxious subjects may also influence their perceptions of attractiveness. (3) Physically attractive people may actually be more skilled and less anxious than unattractive people, possibly because they have had more practice in social interactions. Goldman and Lewis's data discussed above support this contention.

We concur with Calvert's (1988) conclusion that much research is needed to clarify the relationship between physical attractiveness and heterosocial skill and anxiety. Most observer and confederate ratings in previous research confound the two constructs. Assessment of physical attractiveness not confounded by aspects of the interaction itself and ratings of heterosocial skill unconfounded by physical attractiveness are needed before this model can be adequately evaluated.

Self-Presentational Model for Dating Anxiety

The four models of dating anxiety—conditioned anxiety, social skill, cognitive, and physical attractiveness—may all describe different subsets of dating-anxious people. In other words, individuals may experience dating anxiety for a variety of reasons. Schlenker and Leary (1982) proposed that the overall dysfunction in social anxiety (and dating anxiety as a specific type of social anxiety) is doubt about whether one will be able to make desired impressions on others. In a recent elaboration of the self-presentational model, as Schlenker and Leary's approach is called, Leary and Atherton (1986) hypothesized that individuals may doubt their ability to engage in successful impression management for two reasons. They may be skeptical that they can perform the required behavior (low self-efficacy expectations) or skeptical that the behavior will result in the desired outcome (low outcome expectations). Furthermore, excessively high standards for successful impression management may be impossible to attain, resulting in doubt that achievement of the desired goal is possible.

Although essentially a cognitive model, the self-presentational approach incorporates all four theories discussed above. Conditioned anxiety may be visible to others or interfere with performance in dating situations. Such difficulties would result in low self-efficacy expectations that one could appear to be an attractive, desirable dating partner. Social skills deficits would also contribute to low self-efficacy expectations. In fact, according to the self-presentational model, one only has to *believe* he or she has inadequate social skills, whether or not that is true (Clark & Arkowitz, 1975), for dating anxiety to occur, because the essential component is *doubt* about whether one can engage in the appropriate behaviors. The cognitive models of dating anxiety discussed above also fit well into the self-presentational framework. Low self-efficacy expectations may reflect a cognitive distortion in which one underestimates his or her impression management skills. Low outcome expectations may be an overestimation of the like-lihood of being rejected by a potential dating partner. Finally, according to the self-presentational model, physically unattractive individuals (or those who be-lieve they are) may become anxious even if they perform adequately, since they fear their physical appearance will prevent them from making the desired impression.

Leary (1988) argues that the essential feature of any successful treatment for dating anxiety is to increase confidence in the ability to engage in successful impression management. Only careful assessment will determine the exact source of a person's presentational concerns, whether it be conditioned anxiety, skills deficits, cognitive dysfunction, or physical unattractiveness. Treatment should then be tailored to address the particular deficit.

ASSESSMENT OF DATING ANXIETY

Given the evidence outlined above that dating anxiety may be attributable to physiological arousal and conditioned anxiety, social skills deficits, cognitive dysfunction, or lack of physical attractiveness, assessment of all four areas may be necessary before implementing treatment. There are several sources which adequately review the various dating-anxiety assessment instruments, including psychometric characteristics, so we do not duplicate that effort here (see Arko-witz, 1977; Becker & Heimberg, 1988). Rather, we take a more clinical approach to assessment of each aspect of dating anxiety.

Technological improvements have made physiological assessment much less cumbersome. Heart rate is the most accessible physiological measure and has been used by most researchers. In our own research on social anxiety we have utilized a portable heart rate monitor (Exersentry III by Respironics, Inc., Model No. 51330), which allows the collection of physiological data during role-played or *in vivo* interactions (see Heimberg, Gansler, Dodge, & Becker, 1987, for a detailed description of the equipment and procedure.)

Given the reactivity of self-report of social skill (Clark & Arkowitz, 1975), behavioral observation is needed to assess this dimension. Although *in vivo* observation is intuitively preferable, the nature of dating interactions makes it excessively intrusive. However, role plays appear to serve quite well. Wessberg, Mariotto, Conger, Farrell, & Conger, (1979) compared role-play interactions to a more naturalistic situation in which male subjects were unobtrusively monitor-ed while engaging in a heterosocial interaction in the experimental waiting room. Although subjects believed the naturalistic situation was more realistic, rank ordering of the judges' ratings for skill and anxiety were similar for the two situations. Several other studies have also supported the validity of role-played interactions (Farrell, Curran, Zwick, & Monti, 1983; Merluzzi & Biever, 1987; Monti, Wallander, Ahern, Abrams, & Monroe, 1983), although this issue re-mains controversial (Becker & Heimberg, 1988; Bellack, 1983).

The decision to assess specific behaviors versus global evaluations of social performance in role-played situations will be influenced by the reasons for col-lecting the data. As noted above, global ratings more consistently distinguish between anxious and nonanxious subjects and are useful for many research purposes. However, global ratings provide little information for planning an individualized social skills training program. In the latter case, evaluation of specific aspects of social skill is essential. Needless to say, this task would be simplified if there were clear data on the components of skilled behavior. However, a number of behaviors do appear to consistently distinguish between anxious and nonanxious subjects. Anxious subjects make insufficient eye contact, pause too often, and do not talk enough or discuss negative topics. Although their results need to be replicated, Faraone and Hurtig (1985) provide an excellent description of the specific conversational skills employed by a nonanxious man. Muehlenhard and colleagues (1986) have identified 21 verbal and 15 nonverbal behaviors that women use to convey interest to men. Both sources provide useful suggestions for clinical assessment.

Assessment of irrational beliefs, negative self-statements, and dysfunctional attributional patterns can be assessed through report of self-statements (e.g., thought listing; Cacioppo et al., 1979) or the Social Interaction Self-Statement Test (SISST; Glass et al., 1982). The SISST requires subjects to rate the frequency of positive and negative self-statements a person may have concerning a heterosocial interaction. Although it was developed with a college population, it also appears to be valid for use with clinical samples (Dodge, Hope, Heimberg, & Becker, 1988).

As noted above, some apparent social skills deficits may be attributable to cognitive deficits. For example, anxiety appears to interfere with attending to information about an interaction partner (Heimberg, Acerra, & Holstein, 1985; Hope, Heimberg, & Klein, in press; Kimble & Zehr, 1982). To determine if lack of knowledge about the partner is attributable to a skill deficit or misallocation of attentional processing capacity, recall should be assessed in anxiety-provoking and neutral situations. Skill deficits should be evident even when the person is not anxious. However, poor performance due to cognitive deficits will disappear as anxiety decreases.

Since lack of physical attractiveness may contribute to an individual's dating anxiety, this dimension should be assessed. Although many aspects of physical appearance are not readily modified, personal hygiene, dress, hair styles, and cosmetic use may be improved. We are unaware of any guidelines for the assessment of physical attractiveness. Intuitively, peer ratings would appear to be preferable since clothing and hair styles are specific to peer groups.

In conclusion, the variable nature of dating anxiety suggests that comprehensive assessment of physiological arousal, social skill, cognitive functioning, and physical attractiveness is needed to adequately determine an individual treatment plan. We now turn to the treatment of dating anxiety.

MODIFICATION OF DATING ANXIETY

Four primary approaches to the treatment of dating anxiety have been evaluated: practice dating, social skills training, systematic desensitization, and cognitive modification. Practice dating is an exposure-based approached which involves having subjects date either confederates or other subjects. Usually no attempt is made to match subjects with partners who have compatible interests or personality characteristics. Consequently, practice dating is extremely inexpensive in that it requires virtually no contact with a therapist and can be administered by clerical staff. Social skills training assumes that dating-anxious individuals do not possess adequate skills to effectively handle social interactions. Therefore, it utilizes some combination of modeling, rehearsal, and feedback to teach the appropriate skills. Systematic desensitization attempts to reduce dating anxiety through the pairing of relaxation and graduated imaginal exposure. Cognitive modification has typically targeted self-statements or irrational beliefs.

Two excellent papers (Arkowitz, 1977; Curran, 1977) review much of the treatment literature, so those efforts are not duplicated here. Our efforts focus on the conclusions drawn from those earlier reviews and a discussion of more recently published studies.

Curran (1977) reviewed studies which examined the efficacy of what he termed "response practice" (practice dating) and "response acquisition" (social skills training). The most extensive study of practice dating compared practice dating with and without feedback from the interaction partner to a delayed treatment control group (Christensen, Arkowitz, & Anderson, 1975). Subjects in the active treatment had dates with six other subjects of the opposite sex. At posttest both treatment groups were more improved than the control group on self-report, self-monitoring, and behavioral measures, with no difference between the two feedback conditions. Unfortunately only half of the practice-dating subjects were available for the 3-month follow-up. However, data for these subjects suggested treatment gains were maintained.

Curran concluded from this and other studies that practice dating appeared to be effective with most subjects, demonstrating increases in dating frequency and decreases in anxiety. However, he noted that practice dating has not been subjected to particularly rigorous tests. Among the design and methodological flaws he noted were: (1) use of volunteer subjects who may have been only minimally distressed; (2) lack of adequate control conditions, with excessive reliance on delayed treatment control groups; (3) inadequate posttreatment follow-up; and (4) inadequate assessment procedures.

Curran's review of the literature on social skills treatments for dating anxiety concluded that social skills training was generally superior to no-treatment and attention-placebo control groups. Comparisons between skills training and systematic desensitization found the two to be equally effective, with an advantage for skills training on some measures and no additional benefit when desensitization was added to skills training. The one study comparing social skills training to cognitive modification (Glass, Gottman, & Shmurak, 1976) found them to be equally effective on most measures. Curran (1977) concluded that "[t]he majority of the studies demonstrated significant therapeutic effects with regard to increased social skills and a reduction of anxiety at posttreatment as measured by both self-report and behavioral indices." (p. 153). Studies which included follow-up data usually reported that treatment gains were maintained. Although these studies were generally more methodologically rigorous than the practice-dating studies, they suffered from some of the same deficiencies in subject selection, assessment, and follow-up. Furthermore, as noted above, definition of the essential elements of social skill has been an elusive endeavor. The selection of targets for social skills training has been largely based on face validity, and it is unclear how or if the particular behaviors are related to dating in the subjects' natural environment.

Arkowitz (1977) reviewed many of the same studies on practice dating and social skills training as Curran. Although he was somewhat more optimistic about the potential efficacy of practice dating, he reached essentially the same conclusion: Both practice dating and social skills training appear to be effective treatments for dating anxiety. However, given the methodological inadequacies of most of the studies, no definitive conclusion can be drawn.

Arkowitz cited three studies which examined systematic desensitization (Curran, 1975; Curran & Gilbert, 1975; Mitchell & Orr, 1974). He concluded that systematic desensitization was superior to waiting-list or attention control groups and as effective as social skills training. Arkowitz also discussed the Glass et al. (1976) study on cognitive modification reviewed by Curran and reported that modifying negative self-talk is at least as effective as social skills training and may be superior in promoting generalization to new situations.

Only a handful of treatment outcome studies for dating anxiety have been conducted since Arkowitz and Curran published their reviews. A series of three studies examined a modified version of practice dating (Haemmerlie, 1983; Haemmerlie & Montgomery, 1982, 1984). One compared social skills training and systematic desensitization (Geary & Goldman, 1978), and two compared cognitive modification to skills training and/or desensitization (Gormally, Varvil-Weld, Raphael, & Sipps, 1981; Heimberg, Madsen, Montgomery, & McNabb, 1980). Haemmerlie and Montgomery (1982) designed a minimal intervention which appears to be quite effective in the treatment of dating anxiety. They prescreened undergraduate men, selecting those who scored one standard deviation above the mean on the Situation Questionnaire, a self-report measure of social anxiety among college males (SQ; Heimberg, Harrison, Montgomery, Madsen, & Sherfey, 1980; Rehm & Marston, 1968), and who reported two or fewer dates in the previous 3 months. Subjects were randomly assigned to the treatment or waiting-list conditions, but they were not informed that they were part of a treatment study and believed themselves to be participating in a study about dyadic interactions. The treatment consisted of two sets of six 12-minute positively biased interactions with 12 different women. The interaction partners received minimal training and were simply instructed to be friendly and initiate conversation. Pre- and posttreatment assessment measures included the Fear of Negative Evaluation Scale (FNE; Watson & Friend, 1969), the Social Avoidance and Distress Scale (SADS; Watson & Friend, 1969), the state portion of the State–Trait Anxiety Inventory (Spielberger, Gorsuch, & Lushene, 1970), and two measures derived from a naturalistic interaction with a female confederate (conversation initiations and personal statements). At 6-month follow-up, two-thirds of the subjects completed the SQ and reported on their number of dates in the previous 3 and 6 months. Subjects who participated in the interactions improved on all measures and differed significantly from the waiting-list control subjects. Improvement was maintained at follow-up, and treated subjects continued to differ from control subjects.

In the second study of the series, Haemmerlie (1983) explored whether expectancy for treatment success influenced the effectiveness of the positively biased interactions treatment. Women scoring in the top 10% on the SQ (modified for college women) served as subjects. They were randomly assigned to either the high- or low-expectancy condition. High-expectancy subjects were told they were to receive a highly effective treatment for their heterosocial anxiety. Low-expectancy subjects were told that the interactions were part of a pretreatment sensitization procedure which would heighten their anxiety. Measures of expected anxiety confirmed the success of the expectancy manipulation. The treatment consisted of twelve 10-minute positively biased heterosocial interactions. At posttest both high- and low-expectancy subjects demonstrated improvement on five of the seven self-report and behavioral measures. Even when subjects expected to become more anxious, they improved on most measures and showed no change on the other two.

The third study of the positively biased interactions treatment (Haemmerlie & Montgomery, 1984) compared that treatment to imaginal exposure and a no-treatment control group among dating-anxious men. Half of the subjects receiving each treatment received either the positive or negative outcome expectancy described above. The imaginal exposure consisted of two 50-minute sessions of imaginal exposure to 30 heterosocial scenes. Dependent measures included the SQ, the State Anxiety Inventory, pulse rate following completion of a distractor task with a female confederate, the Wechsler Digit Span Backwards Test (Wechsler, 1955), and the interpersonal distance between the subject and confederate. A manipulation check again supported the efficacy of the expectancy manipulation. Assessment consisted of pre- to posttreatment comparisons only. Subjects who participated in the biased interactions improved on all measures except the interpersonal distance variable, regardless of expectancy level. Positive expectancy/imaginal exposure subjects improved on the SQ and State Anxiety Inventory, but not on digit span, pulse rate, or interpersonal distance. Negative expectacy/imaginal exposure and control subjects failed to improve on any measure.

This series of studies suggests that positively biased interactions may be a viable treatment option for dating anxiety. It appears to be more effective than no treatment or imaginal exposure. The one study with follow-up data supports its long-term efficacy and generalization to the subjects' daily lives. These results are particularly intriguing since total treatment time was less than 2½ hours divided between two sessions and required virtually no therapist time or confederate training.

Particularly compared to many of the older studies, the methodology of the first study was quite sound. Subjects were selected on the basis of self-reported social anxiety *and* low-frequency dating. However, since they did not know they were participating in a treatment study, there is no evidence that subjects' dating anxiety caused enough distress or impairment to motivate them to pursue treatment. In the later studies, subjects were informed they would receive treatment, but it is not clear from the reports whether they sought treatment or desired to change their dating anxiety. It is particularly impressive that subjects improved even when they expected to get worse.

The first study raised some some ethical issues regarding informed consent (which the authors acknowledged), since subjects received a treatment without their knowledge which apparently caused long-term changes in their life. In the later studies, all subjects agreed to receive treatment but were not informed until after the fact that the interactions were positively biased. Unfortunately, since follow-up data were not collected in the later studies, it is unclear if informing subjects of the positive nature of the interactions reduced long-term treatment effectiveness, as the authors had suggested in the first article. Clearly this issue must be resolved before this treatment can be extensively utilized in clinical settings, where clients have the right to information about the nature of the treatment.

Geary and Goldman (1978) compared social skills training, systematic desensitization, and a combination of the two to insight-oriented therapy and a waiting-list control. Subjects were undergraduate men who responded to advertisements for free therapy for dating anxiety. Subjects who reported little anxiety or did not wish to increase their dating frequency were disqualified. The treatment consisted of five 50-minute weekly group sessions with two masters-level therapists who both conducted groups in each condition. Assessment measures included the SADS and measures derived from a role play with a female confederate. The role-play measures included respiration and pulse rates at baseline before and after the interaction, self-reported anxiety before and after the interaction, conversation ratings (i.e., subject talk time, number of silences), and a checklist of observable anxiety signs. The SADS was readministered to treated subjects at 6-week follow-up.

Unfortunately, the results are confounded by differential effects for the two therapists across treatments, with one therapist getting the best results with the insight-oriented treatment (which had been conceptualized as an attention control). Following treatment, social skills training subjects were superior on some behavioral measures. They were also less anxious than desensitization subjects in anticipation of the role-played interaction. All treated subjects improved on the SADS, and this improvement was maintained at follow-up with no difference between the treatments. The treatment groups did not differ from each other or from waiting-list subjects on the physiological measures. The authors concluded that there was some evidence that skills training was more effective than the other treatments, particularly in enhancing social skill and reducing anticipatory anxiety. There was no support for the superiority of systematic desensitization, even when combined with skills training. In fact, the combined treatment appeared to reduce the effectiveness of the skills training component, probably by limiting the time devoted to that component.

Geary and Goldman are to be commended for their use of relatively well-qualified therapists, treatment manuals to facilitate treatment integrity, and self-report, physiological, and behavioral assessment. However, the study also presents a number of methodological problems. First, although subjects were selected on the basis of their desire for change in their dating behavior, the authors report no data on their pretreatment anxiety level or dating frequency. Thus it is impossible to evaluate the severity of their dating anxiety. Second, in some aspects, the therapist variable appears to have been the best predictor of treatment outcome, with the more experienced therapist getting better results with the behavioral treatments. This clouds interpretation of the results. Third, it is unfortunate that the follow-up consisted only of self-report measures since some of the most interesting posttreatment effects were seen on the behavioral measures.

Heimberg, Madsen *et al.* (1980) compared systematic desensitization, social skills training, structured homework with cognitive restructuring, and an assessment control in which subjects self-monitored heterosocial interactions. Undergraduate male subjects who scored one standard deviation above the mean on the Situation Questionnaire, expressed dissatisfaction with current dating behavior, and demonstrated sufficient motivation by attending multiple screening interviews served at subjects. The active treatments consisted of eight weekly 2-hour group sessions conducted by highly trained graduate students. Assessment at pretreatment, posttreatment, and 9-week follow-up included self-monitoring records and questionnaires, as well as pulse rate, self-report, and behavioral measures derived from a role play of a heterosocial interaction.

Subjects in all treatments, including the assessment control, improved and maintained improvement at follow-up. The few differences between groups were not maintained at follow-up.

The findings of Heimberg and colleagues are disconcerting in that relatively intensive behavioral treatments did not add significantly to the gains made by the assessment control subjects, apparently as a result of the reactivity of self-monitoring (Kazdin, 1974). The authors point out that the treatment effects may have been minimized by the failure to match subjects to specific treatments.

Gormally *et al.* (1981) compared cognitive restructuring, social skills training, and the combination of the two to a waiting-list control condition. Subjects were college men who responded to advertisements for a social skills program. Those who had fewer than 12 dates in the last 6 months, had two or fewer in the last month, and wished to change their dating behavior were included in the study. Male graduate students conducted nine 90-minute weekly group treatment sessions. Assessment measures included attainment of individual goals for number of dates and of male and female friends, self-monitoring logs, the Survey of Heterosexual Interactions (SHI; Twentyman & McFall, 1975), self-report scales of maladaptive cognitions, and measures derived from two behavioral tasks—telephoning a woman and a role-played conversation with a female confederate. Follow-up assessment at 5 months posttreatment consisted of a structured interview conducted by interviewers blind to treatment condition.

Across measures, subjects in all treatments improved and were superior to the waiting list. Improvement appeared to have been maintained at follow-up.

There was little difference between treatments, with the exception that cognitive procedures produced more cognitive change. However, skills training did not produce superior effects on social skills measures.

This study was well designed, with the exception of limited follow-up data. Although the dating frequency criteria were quite liberal, subjects did express a desire to change their dating behavior. Although the cognitive treatment may have been more effective on some measures, it also had the highest number of drop-outs, many of whom appear to have been identified as particularly withdrawn.

In summary it appears that all four treatments—practice dating, social skills training, systematic desensitization, and cognitive modification—are effective for dating anxiety. However, any conclusions must be tempered with the notation that many of the methodological problems noted by Curran (1977) and Arkowitz (1977) are also present in the later studies. For example, the severity of subjects' dating anxiety is not consistent across studies, with some using very liberal criteria such as up to two dates in the last month (Gormally et al., 1981). Follow-ups have tended to be short and limited in scope.

Perhaps the question that has been addressed least by researchers is the mechanism(s) by which the treatments produce their effect. All four procedures have some element of exposure, and all involve some skill rehearsal. Is there one common mechanism, or do different treatments work with different types of individuals? As noted previously (e.g., Arkowitz, 1977; Heimberg, Madsen et al., 1980), there is a need for studies matching treatment to individuals' deficits, that is, social skills training for those with social skills deficits and cognitive modification for those with dysfunctional cognitive patterns. Possibly all four treatments appear to be approximately equal in effectiveness because subjects with different causes for dating anxiety are grouped together. Or, as Leary (1988) suggested, all four treatment strategies may increase individuals' confidence that they can achieve self-presentational goals, either by making the goals more realistic or by increasing self-efficacy beliefs. These two hypotheses are not mutually exclusive and both merit exploration.

We now turn to a case example to illustrate cognitive-behavioral assessment and treatment of dating anxiety. The case demonstrates the crippling impact dating anxiety can have on an individual's life and furthers our contention that it is an area well worth study.

CASE EXAMPLE

The Treatment

The dating-anxious client described below received cognitive-behavioral group therapy as part of a study on the treatment of social phobia (Heimberg, in press; Heimberg, Becker, Goldfinger, & Vermilyea, 1985; Heimberg et al., in press). The treatment is based on Beck's cognitive therapy (e.g., Beck & Emery, 1985) and consists of three components: cognitive restructuring, in-group exposure to anxiety-provoking situations, and homework for *in vivo* exposure. The groups consist of six clients meeting DSM-III-R criteria for social phobia and male–female cotherapist teams. Groups meet for 2 hours, once a week, for 12 weeks. Early sessions are devoted to teaching cognitive coping skills, including identifying dysfunctional automatic thoughts, recognizing cognitive distortions in those thoughts, and developing rational responses to cope with automatic thoughts in anxiety-provoking situations. The remainder of treatment focuses on practicing the cognitive coping skills by using them in individualized role plays in the group and during assigned homework. Each role play serves as a behavioral experiment, focusing on one or two automatic thoughts.

The Client

Jim was a 36-year-old white male who had never married. Although he experienced some anxiety in almost any conversation, he was more anxious when speaking with women and sought treatment primarily for dating anxiety. Jim had a well-paying blue-collar job but had chosen to work the night shift because it required less interpersonal contact. He had been involved in two relationships, neither of which had been particularly satisfying. From Jim's report it appeared that he and the women had not been compatible, but he had tried to continue the relationships for fear that he would be unable to find anyone else. He described a history of depression and met DSM-III-R criteria for dysthymic disorder, which appeared to be secondary to his anxiety disorder. Prior to treatment his social life consisted almost exclusively of meeting women at bars after drinking heavily to reduce his anxiety. There were two other situations in which he could potentially interact with women—a community college class and a health club. During the initial cognitive exercises it became apparent that Jim's automatic thoughts were characterized by two primary cognitive distortions (Burns, 1980): fortune telling ("I won't be able to come up with anything to say." "She won't like me.") and all-or-nothing thinking ("I don't say the right things." "There is no use talking to her because she is married/not my type/etc.").

The Course of Treatment

Jim's first exposure in the group was a role play of initiating a conversation with a woman in his class at the community college. The female cotherapist served as the role-play partner and, since it was Jim's first exposure, was generally facilitative of the conversation. As is typical of group members, Jim reported a variety of automatic thoughts in anticipation of the role play. Cognitive restructuring exercises focused on the thought "I won't be able to come up with anything to say." With the therapists' and group members' help, he identified this as fortune telling and developed the rational response "I'll probably be able to say at least one thing." He agreed that the goal for the exposure would be to make three statements. At 1-minute intervals during the exposure, the male cotherapist prompted Jim for a rating (higher ratings indicate more anxiety) on the 1–

100 Subjective Units of Discomfort Scale (SUDS; Wolpe & Lazarus, 1966) and had him repeat his rational response aloud. As shown in Panel 1 of Figure 1, Jim's SUDS started at 50, decreased slightly during the first minute, then increased until the end of the conversation. He exceeded his goal with seven statements that were not answers to questions. This success bolstered his confidence in his rational response by providing evidence that, despite extreme anxiety, he would be able to say something. His homework for that week was to say hello and one more thing to a woman in his class.

During postexposure processing, Jim reported an automatic thought of which he had been previously unaware. He indicated he was primarily concerned that if there were a silence in the conversation he would not be able to break it and would become extremely anxious. This thought served as the basis for the next exposure.

The second exposure was a conversation with a woman at the health club. The same role player was used, but she was less facilitative and agreed not to

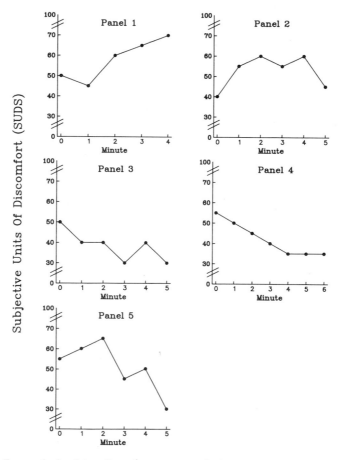

FIGURE 1. Anxiety ratings for exposures during treatment sessions.

break the silence first if one occurred. The primary automatic thought was "If there is a silence, I won't be able to start the conversation again." Based on his experience in the previous exposure, Jim developed the rational response that "I can probably come up with *something* to say." He set his goal to break the silence if one occurred. During the first 2 minutes Jim was able to carry the conversation but with increasing anxiety (see Figure 1, Panel 2). Near the beginning of minute 3, a silence developed and continued for approximately 2 minutes until Jim resumed the conversation in minute 5. The therapists feared that Jim would use the extended silence as evidence supporting his automatic thought. However, during the postexposure processing, it became apparent that he had used the role play to conduct his own behavioral experiment. He indicated that soon after the silence began, he thought of something to say. However, he refrained from speaking because he wanted to test how anxious he would become if his worst fear happened and the silence became extended. Once he realized his SUDS would not go above 60, he resumed the conversation and his anxiety quickly decreased. His homework that week was to start conversations with three women and to find out the name of the woman from his class with whom he had been conversing for previous homework.

Because Jim reported substantial success in conversations between sessions, the third exposure focused on a more difficult situation—asking a woman for a date. Even before entering the situation Jim was anticipating that she would turn him down because "I'm not good enough for her." Closer examination revealed that he usually had no evidence that he was inadequate or a woman was better than him on any of the dimensions he defined as important because most could not be evaluated until they were better acquainted (e.g., honesty, sincerity, being a good friend). Armed with the rational response "I have no evidence she is better than me," he set the goal of asking a woman at the health club to have lunch. He easily met the goal by having made arrangements for the date by the end of the second minute. The remainder of the exposure then became a heterosocial conversation. The homework assignment that week was to ask the woman he had been conversing with to have coffee after class. Her acceptance was not required for successful completion of the assignment. Anxiety prevented him from fulfilling the assignment the first week. However, reiteration of his rational response and encouragement of the other group members led to successful completion the next week.

As can be seen in Panel 3 of Figure 1, Jim's SUDS pattern for the third exposure differed dramatically from earlier exposures. His highest anxiety occurred initially, followed by rapid habituation. He reported that since he was less worried about silences, the hardest part of a conversation was getting out the first few words. The fourth exposure addressed initiating conversations.

Jim's self-analysis of his difficulty starting conversations was that he had a skills deficit—"I don't know what to say to start a conversation." The group was quick to disagree with this analysis by pointing out that they had observed him successfully initiating many conversations, both in the context of exposures and with other group members. It became evident that Jim was engaging in a cognitive distortion called "emotional reasoning" (Burns, 1980). Because he felt awkward and unskilled, he assumed that he appeared anxious and performed poorly. Thus his rational response became "Feelings don't equal reality." In other words, "Just because I feel anxious and awkward doesn't mean it shows or that I won't be able to perform."

Initiating a conversation is a short, specific event. Once the conversation has started, it becomes a new situation and one in which Jim had become quite comfortable. In order to give repeated exposure to initiation, the therapists had group members stand alone and in pairs around the room. Jim approached each "station" and started a conversation. Once the conversation was underway, one of the therapists instructed him to move to the next conversation. The goal was to start each conversation and say a couple of things. During the 6-minute exposure, Jim started six conversations, with his anxiety decreasing each of the first 4 minutes before leveling off (Figure 1, Panel 4). His homework was to start a conversation with someone, preferably a woman, with whom he would not normally talk everyday.

One of the consequences of Jim's long social isolation was that there were few places he could meet appropriate dating partners. Therefore he decided to join a singles' outdoor recreation group. Attendance at the first meeting presented a much more difficult social situation than he had previously approached. As his final exposure, the group role played a portion of the club meeting in which Jim would approach two women who were discussing an upcoming camping trip. Once again Jim's automatic thoughts centered around his lack of skill. He used as evidence difficulty he had had attempting similar situations years before. Thus in addition to the rational response developed for the last exposure ("Feelings don't equal reality"), the group helped him see that he was selectively attending to past difficulties while ignoring recent successes. This was summarized as "That was another life." His goal was to talk to the two women for a few minutes.

Given that this was the last exposure for Jim within the context of the group, it was designed to give him success in a very difficult situation. Talking to two women was more difficult for Jim than talking to one. The role players were seated, quite engrossed in their conversation. Jim had to wait nearly 2 minutes before having a reasonable opening to break into the conversation. The difficulty of the situation is reflected in the high SUDS ratings (Figure 1, Panel 5). However, once he had entered the conversation near the end of the second minute, his anxiety again followed a general downward trend.

Before, after, and 6-months after treatment Jim completed extensive assessment procedures, including an evaluation by an independent assessor, ratings on a fear and avoidance hierarchy, self-report questionnaires, and an individualized behavioral test. The latter consisted of a 3-minute anticipatory phase in which the subject hears a description of the upcoming situation and a 4-minute videotaped performance phase. Jim's behavioral test situation was a conversation with two women he had just met at a party. Trained research assistants served as role players. The independent assessor rating is a 0–8 phobic-severity rating scale (Watson & Marks, 1971). A rating of 4 indicates definite distress and interference in social and occupational functioning. As shown in Table 1, Jim was rated as quite

TABLE 1. Assessment Data for a Dating-Anxious Male Receiving
Cognitive-Behavioral Group Therapy

	Pretreatment	Posttreatment	6-month follow-up
Phobic severity	7	3	2
SADS	22	14	16
FNE	26	15	2
Hierarchy[a]			
Fear	65.00	27.50	21.25
Avoidance	62.50	17.50	19.37
Concern for evaluation	63.75	24.38	35.62

Note. SADS = Social Avoidance and Distress Scale. FNE = Fear of Negative Evaluation
Scale.
[a]Scores are means for eight situations related to dating anxiety.

impaired at pretreatment, but not so at posttreatment. Continued improvement
was noted at the 6-month follow-up. Jim also showed improvement on the SADS
and FNE, with particularly dramatic improvement on the latter. Eight of ten items
from Jim's fear and avoidance hierarchy were relevant to dating anxiety and were
rated on 0–100 scales for fear, avoidance, and concern about being evaluated
(higher ratings indicate greater fear, avoidance, or evaluative concern). Jim's
hierarchy situations ranged from talking to an unfamiliar attractive woman in the
presence of other people (pretreatment fear = 90) to attending a movie with a date
(pretreatment fear = 50). The mean for each scale at each assessment point is
presented in the lower portion of Table 1.

SUDS ratings for the behavioral test situation are presented in Figure 2.
Note that prior to treatment Jim's SUDS showed the steadily increasing pattern
also evident in the first treatment exposure. However, following treatment and
at follow-up assessment, he reported reduced anticipatory anxiety with further
reductions during the actual performance. Although there is no definitive evidence, it appears that Jim's self-designed experiment to test the effects of extended silence (second exposure) dramatically altered his anxiety pattern. Anticipating that his anxiety would decrease once the anxiety-provoking situation has
been entered may have facilitated the reduction of avoidance demonstrated on
the hierarchy items.

On a more personal assessment note, Jim reported to his therapist at 6-month
follow-up that he had been dating a woman for a few months and they were
discussing marriage. He indicated that he realized after treatment that he needed
to keep practicing his skills by dating regularly rather than waiting for the perfect
woman to come along. His current partner was one of these "practice" dates, with
greater attraction developing after they became more acquainted. Thus it was
essentially a cognitive intervention, recognizing the error in dismissing potential
partners on the basis of first appearances, that resulted in a successful
relationship.

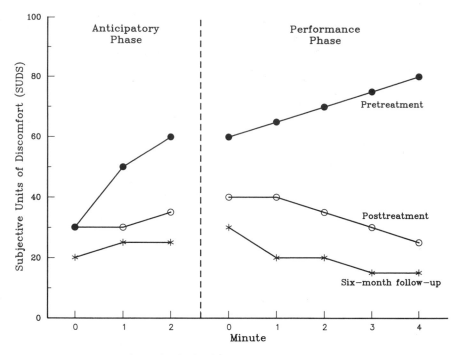

Figure 2. Anxiety ratings for individualized behavioral test at pretreatment, posttreatment, and 6-month follow-up.

Summary and Conclusions

Dating anxiety is a potentially serious problem which may impact nondating aspects of the person's life and have serious long-term consequences. Clearly it is worthy of consideration on its own, not just as an analogue to anxiety disorders research.

A variety of deficits are associated with dating anxiety, at least in some individuals. These include excessive physiological arousal, poor social skill, cognitive dysfunctions such as inappropriate allocation of attentional capacity and self-defeating attributional strategies, and, possibly, a lack of physical attractiveness.

Several different treatments appear to be effective for dating anxiety, with no clear evidence for superiority of any one approach. Social skills training has been consistently successful, and the addition of cognitive interventions may enhance generalization to new situations. There are very few studies employing cognitive treatments, but the initial data appear promising. While effective in most studies, systematic desensitization was usually outperformed by other treatments on at least a few measures. Therefore, it may not be the treatment of choice for most cases. Practice dating, in general, and exposure to positively biased interactions, in particular, are of special interest because a minimal intervention (in terms of client and therapist time) produced very impressive results.

Several aspects of dating anxiety appear to be particularly fertile ground for future research:

1. The role of physical attractiveness in dating anxiety remains unclear. As noted above, this can be partially attributed to the overlap between social skill and attractiveness, at least on the measurement level. Are attractive people more socially skilled? Are socially skilled people more attractive? Better measures of social skill, of physical attractiveness, and of the impact of one upon the other need to be developed. Calvert (1988) offers some excellent methodological and statistical suggestions to approach this problem.

2. The time has come to stop viewing dating anxiety as a problem attributable to only a single type of deficit. Future researchers should take a multidimensional approach to the assessment of dating anxiety, examining physiological, cognitive, and behavioral aspects and physical appearance.

3. More treatment outcome research is needed to refine current methods and develop new ones. However, a number of issues that have plagued past research require attention. These include adequate screening and definition of the target population. Selection criteria based solely on dating frequency are inadequate. A combination of self-reported anxiety, low dating frequency, and a desire to change dating patterns may define those who are truly "dating anxious." Second, more long-term follow-up is needed to adequately evaluate the various treatment approaches. Third, excessive reliance on waiting-list control groups should be avoided. Comparison to attention-control procedures and other active treatments is essential to adequately evaluate treatment efficacy. One of the practice-dating approaches may serve well in this capacity since these approaches are quite economical to administer.

4. As noted above, the majority of the dating anxiety research employs heterosexual male college students as subjects. Virtually no research exists on noncollegiate populations even though divorced or widowed individuals returning to dating may experience substantial dating anxiety. Perhaps dating anxiety should be addressed in high school or junior high, when dating usually begins. Also, attending a college or university automatically provides many opportunities for socializing not available to people in other settings. Dating-anxious people in their late teens and early twenties who do not attend college may face unique difficulties meeting appropriate partners with whom they can practice overcoming their anxiety. Although the situation has improved in recent years, dating anxiety in women needs more attention. A better definition of social skill for women is particularly needed. Given the void of current research, studies on dating anxiety in gay and lesbian individuals is essential if clinicians are to adequately serve these populations.

5. Much of the research on dating anxiety has focused on the initiation phase of dating relationships, but the impact of interpersonal anxiety after the relationship has started also merits attention. Three areas may be of particular interest. First, initiating or refusing sexual activity may be anxiety provoking and result in dissatisfying intimate relationships (Leary & Dobbins, 1983). Second, since social anxiety is associated with unassertiveness (e.g., Greenwald, 1978), conflicts within the relationship may go unresolved or be resolved inadequately.

Finally, how does dating anxiety impact termination of a relationship? Our clinical data suggest anxious individuals may stay in poor relationships out of fear they will be unable to find another partner. These data should be followed up with carefully controlled studies.

REFERENCES

Abramson, L. Y., & Alloy, L. B. (1981). Depression, nondepression, and cognitive illusions: A reply to Schwartz. *Journal of Experimental Psychology: General, 110,* 436–447.

Ahern, D. K., Wallander, J. L., Abrams, D. B., & Monti, P. M. (1983). Bimodal assessment in a stressful social encounter: Individual differences, lead-lag relationships, and response styles. *Journal of Behavioral Assessment, 5,* 317–326.

American Psychiatric Association. (1987). *Diagnostic and statistical manual of mental disorders* (3rd ed., revised). Washington, DC: Author.

Anderson, C. A., & Harvey, R. J. (1988). Discriminating between problems in living: An examination of measures of depression, loneliness, shyness, and social anxiety. *Journal of Social and Clinical Psychology, 6,* 482–491.

Arkowitz, H. (1977). Measurement and modification of minimal dating behavior. In M. Hersen, R. Eisler, & P. Miller (Eds.), *Progress in behavior modification* (Vol. 5, pp. 1–61). New York: Academic Press.

Arkowitz, H., Lichtenstein, E., McGovern, K., & Hines, P. (1975). The behavioral assessment of social competence in males. *Behavior Therapy, 6,* 3–13.

Bander, K. W., Steinke, G. V., Allen, G. J., & Mosher, D. L. (1975). Evaluation of three dating-specific treatment approaches for heterosexual dating anxiety. *Journal of Consulting and Clinical Psychology, 43,* 259–265.

Barlow, D. H. (1986). Causes of sexual dysfunction: The role of anxiety and cognitive interference. *Journal of Consulting and Clinical Psychology, 54,* 140–145.

Bassoff, E. S., & Glass, G. V. (1982). The relationship between sex roles and mental health: A meta-analysis of twenty-six studies. *Counseling Psychologist, 10,* 105–122.

Beck, A. T., & Emery, G. (1985). *Anxiety disorders and phobias: A cognitive perspective.* New York: Basic Books.

Becker, R. E., & Heimberg, R. G. (1988). Behavioral assessment of social skill. In M. Hersen & A. S. Bellack (Eds.), *Behavioral assessment: A practical handbook* (3rd ed., pp. 365–395). New York: Pergamon Press.

Bellack, A. S. (1983). Recurrent problems in the behavioral assessment of social skill. *Behaviour Research and Therapy, 21,* 29–41.

Bernstein, D. A., & Paul, G. L. (1971). Some comments on therapy analogue research with small animal "phobias." *Journal of Behavior Therapy and Experimental Psychiatry, 2,* 225–237.

Berscheid, E., & Walster, E. (1973). Physical attractiveness. In L. Berkowitz (Ed.), *Advances in experimental social psychology* (Vol. 7, pp. 158–215). New York: Academic Press.

Borkovec, T. D., Stone, N. M., O'Brien, G. T., & Kaloupek, D. G. (1974). Evaluation of a clinically relevant target behavior for analogue outcome research. *Behavior Therapy, 5,* 503–513.

Bryant, B., & Trower, P. E. (1974). Social difficulty in a student sample. *British Journal of Educational Psychology, 44,* 13–21.

Burns, D. D. (1980). *Feeling good: The new mood therapy.* New York: William Morrow.

Buss, A. H. (1980). *Self-consciousness and social anxiety.* San Francisco: Freeman.

Byrne, D. (1971). *The attraction paradigm.* New York: Academic Press.

Cacioppo, J. T., Glass, C. R., & Merluzzi, T. V. (1979). Self-statements and self-evaluations: A cognitive-response analysis of heterosocial anxiety. *Cognitive Therapy and Research, 13,* 249–262.

Calvert, J. D. (1988). Physical attractiveness: A review and reevaluation of its role in social skill research. *Behavioral Assessment, 10,* 29–42.

Canter, D., & Drake, E. (1983). *Divorced parents and their children: A guide for mental health professionals.* New York: Springer.

Christensen, A., Arkowitz, H., & Anderson, J. (1975). Practice dating as treatment for college dating inhibitions. *Behaviour Research and Therapy, 13,* 321–331.

Clark, J. V., & Arkowitz, H. (1975). Social anxiety and the self-evaluation of interpersonal performance. *Psychological Reports, 36,* 211–221.

Conger, J. C., & Farrell, A. D. (1981). Behavioral components of heterosocial skills. *Behavior Therapy, 12,* 41–55.

Conger, A. J., Wallander, J. L., Conger, J. C., & Ward, D. (1980, November). *Peers as judges of social competence: They do pay attention.* Presented at the annual meeting of the Association for the Advancement of Behavior Therapy, New York.

Cooper, A., Furst, J. B., & Bridger, W. H. (1969). A brief commentary on the usefulness of studying fears of snakes. *Journal of Abnormal Psychology, 74,* 413–414.

Curran, J. P. (1975). Social skills training and systematic desensitization in reducing dating anxiety. *Behaviour Research and Therapy, 13,* 65–68.

Curran, J. P. (1977). Skills training as an approach to the treatment of heterosexual-social anxiety: A review. *Psychological Bulletin, 84,* 140–157.

Curran, J. P., & Gilbert, F. S. (1975). A test of the relative effectiveness of a systematic desensitization program and an interpersonal skills training program with date anxious subjects. *Behavior Therapy, 6,* 510–521.

Curran, J. P., Gilbert, F. S., & Little, L. M. (1976). A comparison between behavioral replication training and sensitivity training approaches to heterosexual dating anxiety. *Journal of Counseling Psychology, 23,* 190–196.

Curran, J. P., Wallander, J. L., & Fischetti, M. (1980). The importance of behavioral and cognitive factors in heterosexual-society anxiety. *Journal of Personality, 48,* 285–292.

Dodge, C. S., Hope, D. A., Heimberg, R. G., & Becker, R. E. (1988). Evaluation of the Social Interaction Self-Statement Test with a social phobic population. *Cognitive Therapy and Research, 12,* 211–222.

Dow, M. G., Biglan, A., & Glaser, S. R. (1985). Multimethod assessment of socially anxious and nonanxious women. *Behavioral Assessment, 7,* 273–282.

Eysenck, H. J., & Eysenck, S. B. G. (1968). *Manual: Eysenck Personality Inventory.* San Diego: Educational and Industrial Testing Service.

Faraone, S. V., & Hurtig, R. R. (1985). An examination of social skill, verbal productivity, and Gottman's model of interaction using observational methods and sequential analyses. *Behavioral Assessment, 7,* 349–366.

Farrell, A. D., Curran, J. P., Zwick, W. R., & Monti, P. M. (1983). Generalizability and discriminant validity of anxiety and social skills ratings in two populations. *Behavioral Assessment, 6,* 1–14.

Fischetti, M., Curran, J. P., & Wessberg, H. W. (1977). Sense of timing: A skill deficit in heterosexual-socially anxious males. *Behavior Modification, 1,* 179–194.

Geary, J. M., & Goldman, M. S. (1978). Behavioral treatment of heterosexual social anxiety: A factorial investigation. *Behavior Therapy, 8,* 971–972.

Girodo, M., Dotzenroth, S. E., & Stein, S. J. (1981). Causal attribution bias in shy males: Implications for self-esteem and self-confidence. *Cognitive Therapy and Research, 5,* 525–338.

Glasgow, R., & Arkowitz, H. (1975). The behavioral assessment of male and female social competence in dyadic heterosexual interactions. *Behavior Therapy, 6,* 488–498.

Glass, C. R., Gottman, J. M., & Shmurak, S. H. (1976). Response-acquisition and cognitive self-statement modification approaches to dating-skills training. *Journal of Counseling Psychology, 23,* 520–526.

Glass, C. R., Merluzzi, T. V., Biever, J. L., & Larsen, K. H. (1982). Cognitive assessment of social anxiety: Development and validation of a self-statement questionnaire. *Cognitive Therapy and Research, 6,* 37–55.

Goldman, W., & Lewis, P. (1977). Beautiful is good: Evidence that the physically attractive are more socially skillful. *Journal of Experimental Social Psychology, 3,* 125–130.

Gormally, J., Varvil-Weld, D., Raphael, R., & Sipps, G. (1981). Treatment of socially anxious college men using cognitive counseling and skills training. *Journal of Counseling Psychology, 28,* 147–157.

Greenberg, J., Pysczynski, T., & Stine, P. (1985). Social anxiety and anticipation of future interaction as determinants of the favorability of self-presentation. *Journal of Research in Personality, 19,* 1–11.

Greenwald, D. P. (1977). The behavioral assessment of differences in social skill and social anxiety in female college students. *Behavior Therapy, 8,* 925–937.

Greenwald, D. (1978). Self-report assessment in high- and low-dating college women. *Behavior Therapy, 9,* 297–299.

Haemmerlie, F. M., (1983). Heterosocial anxiety in college females: A biased interactions treatment. *Behavior Modification, 7,* 611–623.

Haemmerlie, F. M., & Montgomery, R. L. (1982). Self-perception theory and unobtrusively biased interactions: A treatment for heterosocial anxiety. *Journal of Counseling Psychology, 29,* 362–370.

Haemmerlie, F. M., & Montgomery, R. L. (1984). Purposefully biased interactions: Reducing hetero-social anxiety through self-perception theory. *Journal of Personality and Social Psychology, 47,* 900–908.

Heimberg, R. G. (1977). Comment on "Evaluation of a clinically relevant target behavior for analog outcome research." *Behavior Therapy, 8,* 492–493.

Heimberg, R. G. (in press). Cognitive therapy for social phobia. In A. S. Bellack & M. Hersen, (Eds.), *Comparative handbook of treatments of adult disorders.* New York: Wiley.

Heimberg, R. G., Acerra, M. C., & Holstein, A. (1985). Partner similarity mediates interpersonal anxiety. *Cognitive Therapy and Research, 9,* 443–453.

Heimberg, R. G., & Barlow, D. H. (1988). Psychosocial treatments for social phobia. *Psychosomatics, 29,* 27–37.

Heimberg, R. G., Becker, R. E., Goldfinger, K., & Vermilyea, J. A. (1985). Treatment of social phobia by exposure, cognitive restructuring and homework assignments. *Journal of Nervous and Mental Disease, 173,* 236–245.

Heimberg, R. G., Dodge, C. S., Hope, D. A., Kennedy, C. R., Zollo, L., & Becker, R. E. (in press). Cognitive behavioral treatment of social phobia: Comparison to a credible placebo control. *Cognitive Therapy and Research.*

Heimberg, R. G., Gansler, D., Dodge, C. S., & Becker, R. E. (1987). Convergent and discriminant validity of the Cognitive-Somatic Anxiety Questionnaire in a social phobic population. *Behavioral Assessment, 9,* 379–388.

Heimberg, R. G., Harrison, D. F., Montgomery, D., Madsen, C. H., Jr., & Sherfey, J. A. (1980). Psychometric and behavioral analyses of a social anxiety inventory: The Situation Question-naire. *Behavioral Assessment, 2,* 403–415.

Heimberg, R. G., Madsen, C. H., Jr., Montgomery, D., & McNabb, C. E. (1980). Behavioral treat-ments for heterosocial problems: Effects on daily self-monitored and roleplayed interactions. *Behavior Modification, 4,* 147–172.

Himadi, W. G., Arkowitz, H., Hinton, R., & Perl, J. (1980). Minimal dating and its relationship to other social problems and general adjustment. *Behavior Therapy, 11,* 345–352.

Hope, D. A., Gansler, D. A., & Heimberg, R. G. (1989). Attentional focus and causal attributions in social phobia: Implications from social psychology. *Clinical Psychology Review, 9,* 49–60.

Hope, D. A., Heimberg, R. G., & Klein, J. F. (in press). Social anxiety and the recall of interpersonal information. *Journal of Cognitive Psychotherapy: An International Quarterly.*

Hope, D. A., Heimberg, R. G., Zollo, L. J., Nyman, D. J., & O'Brien, G. T. (1987, November). *Thought listing in the natural environment: Valence and focus of listed thoughts among socially anxious and nonanxious subjects.* Presented at the annual meeting of the Association for the Advancement of Behavioral Therapy, Boston.

Jaremko, M. E., Myers, E. J., Daner, S., Moore, S., & Allin, J. (1982). Differences in daters: Effects of sex, dating frequency, and dating frequency of partner. *Behavioral Assessment, 4,* 307–316.

Johannsson, J., & Ost, L. G. (1982). Perception of autonomic reactions and actual heart rate in phobic patients. *Journal of Behavioral Assessment, 4,* 133–143.

Johnson, R. L., & Glass, C. R. (in press). Heterosocial anxiety and direction of attention in high school boys. *Cognitive Therapy and Research.*

Jones, W. H., Hansson, R. O., & Phillips, A. L. (1978). Physical attractiveness and judgments of psychopathology. *Journal of Social Psychology, 105,* 79–84.

Kazdin, A. E. (1974). Reactive self-monitoring: The effects of response desirability, goal setting, and feedback. *Journal of Consulting and Clinical Psychology, 42,* 704–716.

Kelly, J. A., St. Lawrence, J. S., Hood, H. V., & Brasfield, T. L. (1988). Behavioral intervention to reduce AIDS risk activities. *Journal of Consulting and Clinical Psychology, 57*, 60–67.

Kimble, C. E., & Zehr, H. D. (1982). Self-consciousness, information load, self-presentation and memory in a social situation. *Journal of Social Psychology, 118*, 39–46.

Klaus, D., Hersen, M., & Bellack, A. (1977). Survey of dating habits of male and female college students: A necessary precursor to measurement and modification. *Journal of Clinical Psychology, 33*, 369–375.

Leary, M. R. (1983a). Social anxiousness: The construct and its measurement. *Journal of Personality Assessment, 47*, 66–75.

Leary, M. R. (1983b). *Understanding social anxiety: Social, personality and clinical perspectives.* Beverley Hills, CA: Sage.

Leary, M. R. (1986). The impact of interactional impediments on social anxiety and self-presentation. *Journal of Experimental Social Psychology, 22*, 122–135.

Leary, M. R. (1988). A comprehensive approach to the treatment of social anxiety: The self-presentational model. *Phobia Practice and Research Journal, 1*, 48–57.

Leary, M. R., & Atherton, S. C. (1986). Self-efficacy, social anxiety, and inhibition in interpersonal encounters. *Journal of Social and Clinical Psychology, 4*, 256–267.

Leary, M. R., & Dobbins, S. E. (1983). Social anxiety, sexual behavior, and contraceptive use. *Journal of Personality and Social Psychology, 45*, 1347–1354.

Leary, M. R., Knight, P. D., & Johnson, K. A. (1987). Social anxiety and dyadic conversation; A verbal response analysis. *Journal of Social and Clinical Psychology, 5*, 34–50.

Leary, M. R., Kowalski, R. M., & Campbell, C. D. (1988). Self-presentational concerns and social anxiety: The role of generalized impression expectancies. *Journal of Research in Personality, 22*, 308–321.

McEwan, K. L., & Devins, G. M. (1983). Is increased arousal in social anxiety noticed by others? *Journal of Abnormal Psychology, 92*, 417–421.

Merluzzi, T. V., & Biever, J. (1987). Role-playing procedures for the behavioral assessment of social skills: A validity study. *Behavioral Assessment, 9*, 361–377.

Millbrook, J. M., Farrell, A. D., & Curran, J. P. (1986). Behavioral components of social skills: A look at subject and confederate behaviors. *Behavioral Assessment, 8*, 203–220.

Miller, D. T., & Ross, M. (1975). Self-serving biases in the attribution of causality: Fact or fiction? *Psychological Bulletin, 82*, 213–225.

Miller, W. R., & Arkowitz, H. (1977). Anxiety and perceived causation in social success and failure experiences: Disconfirmation of an attribution hypothesis in two experiments. *Journal of Abnormal Psychology, 86*, 665–668.

Mitchell, K. R., & Orr, F. E. (1974). Note on treatment of heterosexual anxiety using short-term massed desensitization. *Psychological Reports, 35*, 1093–1094.

Monti, P. M., Wallander, J. L., Ahern, D. K., Abrams, D. B., & Monroe, S. M. (1983). Multi-modal measurement of anxiety and social skills in a behavioral role-play test: Generalizability and discriminant validity. *Behavioral Assessment, 6*, 15–25.

Muehlenhard, C. L., Koralewski, M. A., Andrews, S. L., & Burdick, S. A. (1986). Verbal and nonverbal cues that convey interest in dating: Two studies. *Behavior Therapy, 17*, 404–419.

Muehlenhard, C. L., & McFall, R. M. (1981). Dating initiation from a woman's perspective. *Behavior Therapy, 12*, 682–691.

Muehlenhard, C. L., & Scardino, T. J. (1985). What will he think? Men's impressions of women who initiate dates and achieve academically. *Journal of Counseling Psychology, 32*, 560–569.

O'Banion, K., & Arkowitz, H. (1977). Social anxiety and selective attention for affective information about the self. *Social Behavior and Personality, 5*, 321–328.

Peterson, J., Fischetti, M., Curran, J. P., & Arland, S. (1981). Sense of timing: A skill deficit in heterosocially anxious women. *Behavior Therapy, 12*, 194–201.

Petronio, S., & Endres, T. (1985). Dating and the single-parent: Communications in the social network. *Journal of Divorce, 9*, 83–105.

Phibbs, J. A., & Arkowitz, H. (1982). Minimal dating, assertiveness, and depression. *Behavioral Counseling Quarterly, 2*, 100–110.

Rehm, L. P., & Marston, A. R. (1968). Reduction of social anxiety through modification and self-reinforcement: An instigation therapy technique. *Journal of Consulting and Clinical Psychology, 32,* 565–574.

Robins, C. J. (1986). Sex-role perceptions and social anxiety in opposite-sex and same-sex situations. *Sex Roles, 14,* 383–395.

Schlenker, B. R., & Leary, M. R. (1982). Social anxiety and self-presentation: A conceptualization and model. *Psychological Bulletin, 92,* 641–669.

Smith, R. E., & Sarason, I. G. (1975). Social anxiety and the evaluation of negative interpersonal feedback. *Journal of Consulting and Clinical Psychology, 43,* 429.

Smith, T. W., Ingram, R. E., & Brehm, S. S. (1983). Social anxiety, anxious self-preoccupation, and recall of self-relevant information. *Journal of Personality and Social Psychology, 44,* 1276–1283.

Spielberger, C. D., Gorsuch, R. W., & Lushene, R. E. (1970). *State–trait anxiety inventory.* Palo Alto, CA: Consulting Psychologists Press.

Teglasi, H., & Hoffman, M. H. (1982). Causal attributions of shy subjects. *Journal of Research in Personality, 16,* 376–385.

Twentyman, C. T., & McFall, R. M. (1975). Behavioral training of social skills in shy males. *Journal of Consulting and Clinical Psychology, 43,* 384–395.

Wallander, J. L., Conger, A. J., & Conger, J. C. (1985). Development and evaluation of a behaviorally referenced rating system for heterosocial skills. *Behavioral Assessment 7,* 137–153.

Watson, D., & Friend, R. (1969). Measurement of social-evaluative anxiety. *Journal of Consulting and Clinical Psychology, 33,* 448–457.

Watson, J. P., & Marks, I. M. (1971). Relevant and irrelevant fear in flooding: A crossover study of phobic patients. *Behavior Therapy, 2,* 275–295.

Webster, W., & Driskell, J. E. (1983). Beauty as status. *American Journal of Sociology, 89,* 140–165.

Wechsler, D. (1955). *Wechsler Adult Intelligence Scale manual.* New York: The Psychological Corporation.

Wessberg, H. W., Mariotto, M. J., Conger, A. J., Farrell, A. D., & Conger, J. C. (1979). Ecological validity of role plays for assessing heterosocial anxiety and skill of male college students. *Journal of Consulting and Clinical Psychology, 47,* 525–535.

Wolpe, J., & Lazarus, A. A. (1966). *Behavior therapy techniques.* Oxford: Pergamon Press.

8

Loneliness and Social Anxiety

WARREN H. JONES, JAYNE ROSE, AND DANIEL RUSSELL

A great deal of recent research in psychology has focused on the role of close personal relationships in behavior and experience. For example, topics such as social support, friendship, jealousy, marriage, and divorce have received increasing attention in recent years. Such research has extended our appreciation of the centrality of personal relationships while also verifying the relevance of close relationships to a wide variety of psychological and other processes, including, for example, physical and mental health.

One part of the focus on relationships has involved the common problem of loneliness. Surveys indicate that as much as 25% of the adult population in the United States report having felt intensely lonely during the past 2 weeks (Bradburn, 1969). In addition, loneliness is a common presenting complaint among clients of telephone counseling services, college psychological clinics, and marital counseling services (e.g., Rosenbaum & Rosenbaum, 1973). The importance of loneliness is also indicated in its connection to a wide variety of emotional, behavioral, and social problems. These include substance abuse, suicide, anxiety, and vulnerability to health problems.

Another substantial body of literature has developed focusing on social anxiety. Although it has appeared under a variety of labels—shyness, communication apprehension, embarrassment, shame—such research shares with the literature on loneliness an emphasis on the subjective experience of emotional distress in actual or anticipated social situations (cf. Buss, 1980; Schlenker & Leary, 1982).

Given that both loneliness and social anxiety concern subjectively defined and experienced problems in interactions with other people in social situations, one might expect a substantial overlap in the empirical and theoretical literature pertaining to these areas. Indeed, studies of their statistical relationship have consistently yielded correlations of .40 or greater (Anderson & Arnoult, 1985; Cheek & Busch, 1981; Jones, Freemon, & Goswick, 1981; Moore & Schultz, 1983).

WARREN H. JONES • Department of Psychology, University of Tulsa, Tulsa, Oklahoma 74104. JAYNE ROSE • Department of Psychology, Augustana College, Rock Island, Illinois 61204.   DANIEL RUSSELL • Graduate Program in Hospital and Health Administration, College of Medicine, University of Iowa, Iowa City, Iowa 52242.

However, little attention has been paid to the common theoretical structures underlying these concepts.

One purpose of this chapter is to review that part of the loneliness literature of greatest relevance to the phenomenon of social anxiety. First, issues concerning the definition and measurement of loneliness are addressed, followed by a discussion of the psychological and social characteristics and processes that are related to self-reported loneliness. A second purpose is to discuss convergence and problems in the theoretical and empirical linkages between loneliness and social anxiety.

REVIEW OF THE LONELINESS LITERATURE

Definition and Measurement Issues

As often happens in psychological research, loneliness has been defined differently by various scholars. However, Peplau and Perlman (1982) have noted that three themes underlie virtually all definitions of loneliness. First, by definition, loneliness results from deficiencies in the lonely person's social relationships. Second, loneliness is ultimately conceptualized as an internal and subjective psychological experience and is therefore not identical to physical isolation or solitude. Third, most theories define loneliness as an unpleasant and distressing psychological condition which, at least initially, stimulates efforts to overcome it.

Similarly, there have been several approaches to the measurement of loneliness, including Q-sort methodology (Eddy, 1961), rating scales (e.g., Rubenstein & Shaver, 1982; Russell, Peplau, & Cutrona, 1980), single-item measures (e.g., Berg, Mellstrom, Persson, & Svanborg, 1981), and projective techniques (Krulik, 1978). Despite the diversity of available measures, the most frequently used measure of loneliness has been the UCLA Loneliness Scale (Russell, 1982; Russell et al., 1980; Russell, Peplau, & Ferguson, 1978). This measure contains 20 items assessing experiences related to loneliness (e.g., dissatisfaction with one's relationships, feeling left out). The words lonely and loneliness do not appear in any of the items.

Assessments of the adequacy of the UCLA Scale as a measure of loneliness have strongly supported its reliability and validity (Russell, 1982). However, recently it has been simplified to facilitate its use in non-college student populations (see Figure 1; Russell & Cutrona, 1988). The changes have involved simplifying the wording of the items and rewording statements into questions, thereby improving the readability of the items. As was the case with earlier versions, psychometric analyses support the quality of this version of the scale (Russell, Kao, & Cutrona, 1987; Russell & Cutrona, 1988). Internal consistency (coefficient alpha) estimates of .89 to .94 have been obtained in mail survey studies of teachers and nurses, and interview studies of the elderly. Its construct validity has been established by significant relationships with other measures of mental health status (e.g., depression, life satisfaction) and nonsignificant rela-

Instructions:

The following statements describe how people sometimes feel. For each statement, please indicate how often you feel the way described by writing a number in the space provided. Here is an example:

　　How often do you feel happy?

If you never felt happy, you would respond "never"; if you always feel happy, you would respond "always."

Never	Rarely	Sometimes	Always
1	2	3	4

*1.　How often do you feel that you are "in tune" with the people around you?

2.　How often do you feel that you lack companionship?

3.　How often do you feel that there is no one you can turn to?

4.　How often do you feel alone?

*5.　How often do you feel part of a group of friends?

*6.　How often do you feel that you have a lot in common with the people around you?

7.　How often do you feel that you are no longer close to anyone?

8.　How often do you feel that your interests and ideas are not shared by those around you?

*9.　How often do you feel outgoing and friendly?

*10.　How often do you feel close to people?

11.　How often do you feel left out?

12.　How often do you feel that your relationships with others are not meaningful?

13.　How often do you feel that no one really knows you well?

14.　How often do you feel isolated from others?

*15.　How often do you feel you can find companionship when you want it?

*16.　How often do you feel that there are people who really understand you?

17.　How often do you feel shy?

18.　How often do you feel that people are around you but not with you?

*19.　How often do you feel that there are people you can talk to?

*20.　How often do you feel that there are people you can turn to?

Scoring:

Items that are asterisked should be reversed (i.e., 1-4, 2-3, 3-2, 4-1), and the scores for each item then summed together. Higher scores indicate greater degrees of loneliness.

FIGURE 1. UCLA Loneliness Scale (Version 3)

tionships with measures of physical health status (e.g., symptom reports, functional abilities; see Russell *et al.*, 1987). Discriminant validity has been demonstrated through analyses showing that social support and loneliness, although highly correlated, are distinct, separable constructs that are differentially related to other variables (Russell*et al.*, 1987). The discriminant validity of earlier versions of the scale has also been demonstrated (Russell *et al.*, 1980; Weeks, Michela, Peplau, & Bragg, 1980).

All versions of the UCLA Loneliness Scale yield a single, global index of loneliness. Such unidimensional scales conceptualize loneliness as a unitary phenomenon that varies only in intensity. This approach assumes that regardless of the cause of loneliness, the basic experience of individuals who are lonely would be essentially the same. By contrast, a multidimensional approach conceives of various types of loneliness that cannot be accurately represented by a global index. Such a view suggests that the subjective experiences of loneliness for a new college student and a recent widow would not be comparable; therefore, different scales are necessary to adequately assess different types of loneliness.

In a study designed to address this issue, Russell, Cutrona, Rose, and Yurko (1984) investigated Weiss' (1974) hypothesis that there are two distinct types of loneliness. Weiss suggested that emotional loneliness is experienced by a person who lacks a close, intimate attachment to another person (e.g., the recent widow), whereas social loneliness results from a person not being integrated into a network of friends who share interests and activities (e.g., the new college student). Results of the study revealed that social and emotional loneliness are indeed different in some respects. For example, on the UCLA Loneliness Scale, emotionally lonely individuals were more likely to report that there was no one for them to turn to and that no one knew them well, whereas individuals identified as socially lonely indicated that they were not a part of a group of friends and did not have much in common with others. However, social and emotional loneliness also shared a common core of experiences possibly characteristic of all varieties of loneliness. For example, although social and emotional lonely persons differed significantly on 6 of the UCLA items, significant differences were not observed on the remaining 14 items. Overall scores on the UCLA Loneliness Scale were found to correlate equally ($r = .42$) with the measures of social and emotional loneliness. This suggests that loneliness—at least as measured by the UCLA Scale—may be most accurately conceptualized as a unitary construct with an underlying common core of experiences, but which sometimes results in modestly differing patterns of experience.

Another criticism of the UCLA Loneliness Scale concerns its failure to distinguish between state and trait loneliness. *State* loneliness may be defined as temporary and situationally caused, whereas *trait* loneliness is seen as chronic and persisting beyond the interpersonal circumstances which may have initiated it. Studies that incorporate this distinction have demonstrated that it is an empirically and theoretically useful one (Cutrona, 1982; Gerson & Perlman, 1979; Jones, Cavert, Snider, & Bruce, 1985; Shaver, Furman, & Buhrmester, 1985). For example, Cutrona (1982) found that chronically lonely students perceived their loneliness to be due to enduring personality traits. By contrast, students who overcame their loneliness attributed the experience to a wide variety of environmental, as well as personal, factors. Therefore, whether loneliness will be a temporary state or an enduring trait may be influenced by an individual's beliefs about the situation and why he or she is lonely in the first place. Unfortunately, many studies have relied on ad hoc procedures for distinguishing between state and trait loneliness, suggesting the need for additional research directed toward the development of loneliness instruments that simultaneously yield measures of state and trait loneliness.

To summarize, although many definitions of loneliness have been proposed, they consistently emphasize that loneliness is a subjective dissatisfaction with one's relationships. Approaches to assessment have differed in terms of whether loneliness is defined and measured as unidimensional or multidimensional, and whether or not the distinction between state and trait loneliness is contained in the measurement strategy. However, the majority of published research has used the UCLA Loneliness Scale—which conceptualizes loneliness as a unitary construct—and there is considerable empirical support for doing so.

Psychological Characteristics and Processes

Much of the research on loneliness has been devoted to identifying the psychological concommitants of loneliness, that is, the states and traits with which it is associated. For example, considerable research has compared measures of loneliness with measures of self-concept, attitudes, personality, and emotion, particularly the latter two domains. These studies not only provide evidence regarding the characteristics of individuals who are most likely to become lonely and something about what it is like to be lonely, but they also provide indirect evidence of some of the predisposing and determining factors in the development of loneliness.

Self-Attitudes

One of the most frequently reported correlates of self-reported loneliness is low self-esteem, with several studies indicating substantial covariation between the two variables (Jones et al., 1981; Russell et al., 1980). Rubenstein and Shaver (1982) reported a significant positive correlation between loneliness and a derived factor entitled self-deprecation among adult respondents, and Goswick and Jones (1982) found coefficients in excess of .70 between loneliness and a factor labeled "inferiority feelings" among both high school and college students. There is also evidence that loneliness is more strongly related to social aspects of self-esteem as compared to other domains of self-reflection such as personal self, moral-ethical self, or physical self (Goswick & Jones, 1981). Furthermore, as would be expected, self-esteem is more strongly related to chronic than to transitory or situational loneliness (Jones, Cavert et al., 1985; Wilbert & Rupert, 1986).

Evidence suggests that the relationship between loneliness and self-esteem is stable and fundamental. For example, the correlation between the two remains significant even when the effects of other personality and social network variables are statistically controlled (Carpenter, Hansson, Rountree, & Jones, 1984), and their covariation has been reported in studies involving a wide variety of populations (cf. Peplau & Perlman, 1982).

Emotions

Another extensive pattern of relationships has been reported with respect to loneliness and various emotional states and traits (Hansson, Jones, Carpenter, & Remondent, 1986; Jones, Carpenter, & Quintana 1985; Loucks, 1980; Moore & Schultz, 1983; Perlman, Gerson, & Spinner, 1978; Russell *et al.*, 1978). Research has indicated direct correlations with such emotional and quasi-emotional variables as tension, fatigue, confusion, boredom, restlessness, emptiness, hopelessness, and helplessness, and inverse correlations with vigor, energy, and morale. In addition, loneliness is strongly associated with the experience of depression and anxiety.

Studies have also supported the expected association between loneliness and emotional arousal as reflected in emotionality scales and composite scores on the Profile of Mood States (Loucks, 1980). Even though the strong correlations between loneliness and emotional variables may suggest that loneliness is "nothing but" emotional arousal, there is evidence to suggest the discriminant validity of the construct of loneliness, at least as measured by some scales (Russell *et al.*, 1980). For example, Bragg (1979) compared college students who were lonely and depressed, lonely but not depressed, or neither lonely nor depressed. He found that persons who were lonely without being depressed tended to be distressed specifically about the interpersonal aspects of their lives, whereas those who were both lonely and depressed tended to be distressed with respect to a wider array of personal issues. Additional support of the distinction between loneliness and general emotional arousal is provided by Weeks *et al.* (1980). They analyzed longitudinal data using a structural equation procedure, concluding that loneliness and depression are highly related but not identical constructs.

In summary, loneliness has been found to be a construct distinct from other psychological concepts. However, it is closely associated with being depressed, anxious, and having low self-esteem. Longitudinal studies are needed to more accurately identify potential causal relationships among these variables.

Social Characteristics and Processes

Loneliness refers to the status and quality of an individual's relationships, and, quite naturally, much of the research on loneliness has involved assessments of the frequency and satisfaction with which respondents engage in various kinds of interpersonal activities. A smaller body of literature focuses further on specific interpersonal and conversational behaviors in which participants reporting various levels of loneliness engage.

Relational Status and Satisfaction

Loneliness has been found to be inversely related to self-reported quantitative measures of social relationships, such as the number of both casual and intimate friends, having a steady dating or romantic partner, and the size and density of one's social support network among various populations (Jones, Carpenter, & Quintana, 1985; Jones & Moore, 1987; Levin & Stokes, 1986; Russell *et al.*, 1980; Stokes, 1985). Not surprisingly, greater loneliness is associated with being single, divorced, separated, and widowed, and there is evidence that among the widowed the more recent the loss and the longer the prior marriage, the greater the loneliness (Bahr & Harvey, 1979; Kivett, 1979).

Another quantitative variable, frequency of contact, has also been found to be inversely related to loneliness among college students, adolescents, and the elderly (Arling, 1976, Bahr & Harvey, 1979; Berg *et al.*, 1981; Brennan, 1982; Cutrona, 1982; Evans, 1983; Kivett, 1979; Russell *et al.*, 1987). Furthermore, loneliness is often directly correlated with the self-report of spending time alone and more frequently engaging in putative "social" activities (e.g., eating) by oneself (Hoover, Skuja & Cosper, 1979; Russell *et al.*, 1980). Finally, lonely people are more likely to report living alone and having problems with significant others (Berg *et al.*, 1981; Rook, 1984).

However, some studies have failed to find statistically significant relationships between quantitative measures of social interaction and loneliness (Austin, 1983; Baum, 1982; Berg *et al.*, 1981; Carpenter *et al.*, 1984; Hoover *et al.*, 1979). Thus, although loneliness is generally related to the self-reported amount and frequency of social contact, research indicates that it is neither perfectly nor always related. Differences in results apparently depend on variations in loneliness instruments, measures of social contact, and the characteristics of the samples tested (e.g., differences in age, culture, gender, relational norms; cf. Russell *et al.*, 1987).

In addition, it is also quite likely that frequency or amount of contact is not as critical as the quality of the interpersonal contact one has. In this regard, research on these variables has produced significant inverse relationships involving satisfaction with overall levels of interpersonal contact, satisfaction with contact with family and parents, helpfulness of the network, and closeness to parents, siblings, and friends (Brennan, 1982; Carpenter *et al.*, 1984; Cutrona, 1982; Evans, 1983; Franzoi & Davis, 1985; Jones, Carpenter, & Quintana, 1985; Schultz & Saklofske, 1983; Williams & Solano, 1983). Studies that have compared the amount of variance in loneliness scores explained by qualitative as compared to quantitative variables have demonstrated in every instance that the qualitative measures account for a larger proportion of the variance in loneliness scores (e.g., Cutrona, 1982; Jones, Carpenter, & Quintana, 1985).

Several studies have examined the relationship between loneliness and social contact more directly and precisely by requesting participants to record in diaries various aspects of their interactions with others immediately or soon after the occurrence of the interaction. In some instances, "beepers" have been used to signal the times at which respondents are to record what they are doing at that moment, including whether or not they were with someone or alone, their mood, whether they wished to be doing something different, and so on. Such research has produced several interesting findings. First, when alone, both adolescents and adults were more likely to report feeling lonely, and this was particularly true for adolescent and single adults who found themselves alone on Friday and Saturday evenings (Larsen, Csikszetmihalyi, & Graef, 1982). However, several studies have failed to produce significant correlations between loneliness and the average number of interactions per day or the amount of time spent with others (Hecht & Baum, 1984; Jones, 1981; Wheeler, Reis, & Nazlek, 1983). Instead, most of the significant findings have involved the quality of the interaction or various characteristics of one's interactional partners. For example, loneliness has been found to be inversely related to degree of acquaintance with one's partner and the emotional quality of the interaction (Jones, 1981). From this perspective, then, loneliness appears to have less to do with how often or how long one interacts with others as it does with characteristics of the persons with whom one interacts.

To summarize, numerous studies have demonstrated that measures of loneliness are related to social contact, marital status, and satisfaction with one's social relationships. However, the connection is more complex than was initially expected. In general, the key to the association between self-reported loneliness and social contact appears to be the quality of the social relationship (i.e., the degree of satisfaction of the participant) and the context in which the contact occurs.

Relational Stress

Jones and his colleagues (Jones, Cavert et al., 1985) have conducted a series of studies investigating the situations and events associated with loneliness, termed *relational stress*. Results indicated that the experience of relational stress predicts loneliness concurrently as well as 2 months later. Analyses suggested that the external determinants of loneliness tend to consist of one of four kinds of events and situations: (1) emotional threats to relationships (e.g., arguments, failure), (2) social isolation (e.g., few friends, being left out); (3) social marginality (e.g., being with strangers or others with whom one has little in common), and (4) romantic conflict (e.g., romantic breakups). Additional research indicated that these events and situations are threatening and contribute to the development of loneliness for four reasons. First, as is the case with stress generally, such situations and events are unpleasant but difficult to predict or control. Second, relational stress situations tend to be experienced relatively infrequently—perhaps preventing the development of effective coping strategies—and last a relatively long time when they occur. Third, although relational stress apparently increases the desire to affiliate with others, at the same time it is paradoxically associated with the increased use of coping strategies which do not include other people. Finally, relational stress increases feelings of dissimilarity from others.

Interpersonal Perceptions of Self and Others

There is considerable evidence to suggest that lonely persons subscribe to negativistic, cynical, and pessimistic views of people and relationships. For example, measures of loneliness have been inversely correlated with self-reported measures of acceptance of others; beliefs in the trustworthiness, altruism, and favorability of human nature; belief in a just world; and feelings of acceptance from one's family, friends, and other relationships. They have been directly correlated with measures of hostility and alienation (Jones et al., 1981; Wittenberg & Reis, 1986). However, a more direct way of assessing loneliness in a social context is to examine its connections with the kinds of impressions formed by others in response to lonely persons as well as the typical interpersonal perceptions of lonely persons. In so doing it is important to distinguish between such perceptions occurring among strangers who participate in laboratory interactions and perceptions among persons who share on-going and more important relationships with one another. Evidence regarding self and other perceptions among strangers is examined first, followed by perceptions within relationships of greater intimacy and duration.

Strangers

Several studies assessing interpersonal perceptions and loneliness have used the same basic paradigm (Bell, 1985; Jones et al., 1981; Jones, Sansone, & Helm, 1983; Solano, Batten, & Parish, 1982). College student participants who do not know one another are placed in dyads or groups and given instructions to hold conversations on a particular topic or to get acquainted for a brief period of time. After these conversations, participants are requested to rate themselves and their partners (or fellow group members) on several relevant dimensions (e.g., quality of the interaction, interpersonal attraction, friendliness). In some instances, the degree of knowledge gained about the partner is assessed, as well as the desire for continued interactions or friendship. Also, in some instances, metaperceptions (e.g., participants' views of partners' views) are also assessed.

Such data may be examined from each of two perspectives: (1) the association between loneliness and ratings given, which might be called observer effects, and (2) the association between loneliness and ratings received, which may be called target effects. For observer effects, several studies have demonstrated that high- as compared to low-lonely participants tend to rate themselves negatively following laboratory interactions with strangers. Specifically, lonely participants are more likely to rate themselves as having been less honest, open, warm, and friendly in both dyadic and group settings (Jones et al., 1981, 1983). These findings are consistent with research on self-esteem and self-reported social skill correlates of loneliness. Also, in these studies loneliness has been associated with more negative metaperceptions, often termed "reflected self-ratings" (i.e., a participant's rating of how his or her partner or fellow group members will rate him or her), along the same dimensions. Similarly, Bell (1985) found that high-lonely participants expected their partners to be less interested in continued interactions with them. Consistent with the pessimistic and hostile attitudes associated with loneliness, high-lonely as contrasted with low-lonely participants tend to rate their partners more negatively, in some cases indicating less interest in continued interactions with their partners, less interpersonal attraction for partners, and less interest in developing a friendship with their partner (Bell, 1985; Jones *et al.*, 1981, 1983). In other words, following brief interactions with strangers, lonely persons rate themselves and their fellow participants negatively, and they expect negative ratings if not outright rejection from their fellow participants.

Results regarding target effects have been somewhat less consistent, although statistically significant results have always been in the expected direction. Jones and his colleagues found only modest support for the expectation that the partners of lonely participants in these studies would rate them more negatively (Jones *et al.*, 1981, 1983). Specifically, in one study, high- as compared to low-lonely participants were rated by their fellow group members as likely to rate themselves lower on friendliness, interpersonal attractiveness, and leadership. But these results were obtained for analyses following 2 days of acquaintance and were not replicated in a subsequent assessment after 2 months of interaction. Similarly, Sloan and Solano (1984) found no differences in communication satisfaction among partners of lonely as compared to partners of not-lonely participants, and Chelune, Sultan, and Williams (1980) found no significant relationships between confederates' ratings of participants' social skill and participants' self-rated loneliness.

On the other hand, Bell (1985) reported several inverse target correlates of loneliness. In addition, Spitzberg and Canary (1985) found that partners rated lonely participants as less socially competent, and Solano *et al.* (1982) reported that partners rated lonely participants as "more difficult to get to know." Also, Gerson and Perlman (1979) found that transient loneliness was related to accuracy in emotional expressiveness. Finally, Ayers (1986) found that dyads consisting of two lonely participants as compared to not-lonely dyads gave lower ratings of mutual interpersonal attraction, although in this instance, it is not clear whether this was a target or an observer effect.

A more consistent pattern regarding target effects has emerged with respect to metaperceptions (i.e., partners' ratings of how a participant will rate him- or herself). Partners of lonely participants rate them as "liking themselves less" and as rating themselves lower on relevant dimensions such as friendliness (Jones *et al.*, 1983) and as "less interested in future interactions" (Bell, 1985).

Ongoing Relationships

Only a few studies have examined interpersonal perceptions in the context of ongoing relationships, and almost all of these investigations have focused on target effects. Furthermore, these studies generally indicate stronger correlations between self-ratings of loneliness and the perceptions of significant others. For example, among children, loneliness was inversely related to ratings of one's desirability as a playmate, popularity choices, and social sensitivity (Asher & Wheeler, 1985; Marcoen & Brumagne, 1985). Among college students, loneliness has been found to be inversely correlated with ratings of roommate's social skills, disclosure, positive attributes, social self-esteem, and friendship (Williams & Solano, 1983; Wittenberg & Reis, 1986).

To summarize, in initial interactions with strangers, loneliness is related to more negative appraisals of self, others, and the expectation of rejection. Loneliness is also related to the ratings received but only for certain dimensions (especially ratings of social skill). In on-going and more important relationships, lonely persons are rated as less attractive and less skilled. Furthermore, we may extrapolate from the abundance of data on loneliness and relational satisfaction that lonely persons view their on-going relationships more negatively; there is some empirical evidence supporting this contention (Jones & Moore, 1987).

Social Skills and Social Behavior

There is considerable evidence that loneliness is related to social skill and confidence. For example, loneliness is highly related to measures of shyness and social anxiety and inversely related to extraversion and sociability (Jones & Carpenter, 1986; Moore & Schultz, 1983; Stokes, 1985) Similarly, loneliness is inversely related to the various skills involved in dating, conflict resolution, and social initiation as well as likability (Moore & Schultz, 1983; Wittenberg & Reis, 1986). Also, loneliness consistently correlates positively with communication apprehension and sensitivity to rejection, and inversely with measures of communication competence (Bell, 1985; Russell et al., 1980; Zahaki & Duran, 1982).

Less consistent results have been found for studies investigating other social skills. Several researchers have reported inverse correlations between loneliness and self-reported measures of social risk taking (Moore & Schultz, 1983). Although measures of assertiveness usually show modest but significant inverse correlations with loneliness, nonsignificant correlations have also been reported (e.g., Carpenter et al., 1984; Jones, Carpenter, & Quintana, 1985).

A similar pattern of low inverse correlations with occasional nonsignificant results has also been reported with respect to associations between loneliness, empathy, and its various components, such as empathic concern and perspective taking (Davis, 1983). In one instance, a gender difference in the relationship between loneliness and perspective taking was reported, in which the correlation for female adolescents was statistically significant, whereas the association for male adolescents was unreliable (Franzoi & Davis, 1985).

Related to the issue of social skills is that of social behavior. In an earlier review (Jones, 1982), it was noted that virtually no studies had been reported directly comparing loneliness and actual social or conversational behavior, despite many speculations and hypotheses regarding the overt consequences of loneliness and the obvious relevance of social behavior for understanding loneliness. Perhaps part of the difficulty is the lack of an experimental paradigm by which some form of loneliness could be produced in controlled laboratory situations. Although several studies have now been published, this area of loneliness research still suffers from a relative lack of productivity and standardization of procedures.

However, there is now some evidence suggesting that loneliness is related to certain conversational behaviors which occur during laboratory interactions with strangers. For example, in such settings, high- as compared to low-lonely college students have been found to talk less, ask fewer questions, change the topic more frequently, respond more slowly, and attend less to their interaction partners (Bell, 1985; Jones, Hobbs, & Hockenbury, 1982; Sloan & Solano, 1984). Although such results were initially conceptualized as deficiencies in social skill (e.g., Jones et al., 1982), more recently Vitkus and Horowitz (1987) have provided evidence suggesting that lonely individuals actually do have the knowledge necessary to act in socially appropriate ways, but they adopt passive and ineffective roles in social interactions with strangers and judge their own interpersonal behavior negatively.

Examinations of loneliness in the context of laboratory paradigms and hypothetical manipulations have also been used, and somewhat more successfully, in the search for reliable behavioral correlates of loneliness. In general, lonely persons appear to behave in a manner that deviates from the norm. For example, in two separate studies of responses to the influence of others, a gender by loneliness interaction was observed (Hansson & Jones, 1981). Specifically, high-lonely male participants conformed to and modeled others significantly less than both low-lonely men and women, whereas high-lonely women modeled and conformed to a greater degree. This apparent tendency of lonely persons to engage in social behaviors at variance with normative expectations has been found with respect to self-disclosure as well (Chelune et al., 1980; Solano et al., 1982). For example, Solano et al. (1982) found that high- as contrasted with low-lonely participants tended to select less intimate topics on which to disclose personal information to opposite-sex strangers as compared to same-sex strangers in an acquaintanceship exercise, a pattern of disclosure at variance with normative data among college students.

In addition, high- as contrasted with low-lonely participants have been found to be less willing to engage in social comparison with similar others regarding their opinions on controversial topics (Hansson & Jones, 1981), to provide fewer and less effective solutions to hypothetical interpersonal as compared to noninterpersonal problems (Horowtiz, French, & Anderson, 1982), and to more frequently use coercive power strategies as opposed to referent power strategies in response to hypothetical scenerios calling for attempts to influence others (Gerson & Perlman, 1979). Check, Perlman, and Malamuth (1985) also found that high- as compared to low-lonely males administered higher levels of aversive noise to a critical and rejecting female confederate. Finally, Gerson and Perlman (1979) reported that participants classified as situationally lonely were less accurate encoders of expressive affect than either chronically lonely or nonlonely participants.

In summary, several social skills and behaviors have been investigated as they relate to loneliness. Generally, lonely persons have been found to have poorer skills and to behave in less socially appropriate ways than nonlonely persons. However, not all studies support such conclusions. A distinction that may help to clarify this area is whether lonely people actually lack social knowledge and abilities or whether they do have the abilities, but fail to use them appropriately when called for by the situation.

LINKAGES BETWEEN LONELINESS AND SOCIAL ANXIETY

At the conceptual level loneliness and social anxiety appear closely related. Various definitions of both constructs generally emphasize emotional distress resulting from subjective evaluations in socially relevant situations. For example, shyness has been defined as discomfort and inhibition in the presences of others, where these reactions derive directly from the social nature of the situation (Jones, Briggs, & Smith, 1986). Similar to loneliness, shyness has been conceptualized as both an emotional state (e.g., Izard, 1977) and a dispositional trait (Crozier, 1979), and as both a unitary construct (Jones *et al.*, 1986) and one which may be decomposed into types of shyness (e.g., Buss, 1986). At a broader level of analysis, social anxiety is often regarded as a collection of specific reactions (e.g., shyness, embarrassment, communication apprehension, shame) and as both a trait and a state (cf. Buss, 1980).

Empirically, the apparent convergence between the constructs of loneliness and social anxiety is also extensive. Evidence from a variety of studies support five general conclusions regarding the interface between loneliness and social anxiety. First, measures of loneliness are consistently related to measures of specific forms of social anxiety, especially shyness but also including communication apprehension, shame, and embarrassability, and with social anxiety assessed more globally (Jones *et al.*, 1981). Researchers have reported correlations between loneliness and shyness ranging from .40 to .51 (Anderson & Arnoult, 1985; Cheek & Busch, 1981; Jones, Carpenter, & Quintana, 1985; Jones *et al.*, 1986).

Second, the pattern of associations between loneliness and other self-reported variables denoting emotion, personality, and adjustment bear striking similarity to results from studies examining these processes in relation to various forms of social anxiety. Once again, this is especially true in the case of shyness. For example, similar to loneliness, shyness when conceptualized as a dispositional variable is strongly related to negative affective and cognitive variables (e.g., depression, anxiety, hostility, low self-esteem, alienation; Cheek, Melchior, & Carpentieri, 1987; Crozier, 1979; Jones & Russell, 1982).

Third, as with loneliness, shyness has been related to variables suggesting inhibited and less satisfactory interpersonal involvements, such as fewer friends, lower dating frequencies, and lower relational satisfaction (e.g., Jones & Carpenter, 1986; Jones & Russell, 1982). Not surprisingly, individuals scoring higher on measures of shyness are more likely to be rated as unfriendly, less poised, and less relaxed (Cheek & Buss, 1981; Jones *et al.*, 1986; Pilkonis, 1977).

Fourth, the behavioral correlates of social anxiety suggest ineffective interpersonal styles and therefore resemble the general pattern of overt manifestations of loneliness, although perhaps less so than is the case with self-reported variables. To illustrate, persons high in shyness and other forms of social anxiety show slower speech latencies, fewer facial expressions, gaze aversion, and nervous self-manipulations (e.g., Cheek & Buss, 1981; Daly, 1978; Pilkonis, 1977).

Finally, although the literature on the situational contribution to loneliness is far less extensive than the comparable focus on situational factors in social anxiety, there is again at least a modest convergence. For example, similar to social anxiety, state loneliness appears to arise in social situations of consequence, where the individual in question feels incapable of responding appropriately to the demands of the situation.

Given similar conceptualizations and the extensive overlap in empirical correlates between loneliness and social anxiety, one is tempted to conclude that these two constructs simply reflect different aspects of the same basic process. However, several points argue against such a conclusion. For one thing, although reported correlations between measures of loneliness and social anxiety are typically in the .30 to .50 range, the corresponding proportion of variance shared by these constructs is approximately 16 to 25%. Although these values are statistically significant, they are moderate, leaving a large amount of the variance in each measure unexplained by the other and, hence, unique. Furthermore, in an extensive investigation of frequently used measures of shyness, Jones et al. (1986) found that each measure was more highly related to other shyness measures than to loneliness, thereby suggesting the distinctiveness of the measures of each construct. This study also reported that the intercorrelations among the shyness scales were higher than the associations between the shyness scales and several additional constructs, such as introversion and sociability. Finally, there is at least some evidence from longitudinal studies that shyness precedes and more strongly predicts subsequent loneliness than vice versa (Jones, Cavert, et al., 1985). Thus, there is sufficient empirical evidence on which to base the conclusion that, although strongly related, shyness and loneliness are distinct constructs. Furthermore, it is reasonable to assume that loneliness is also distinguishable from other forms of social anxiety in that measures of these constructs are typically less strongly and extensively related to loneliness.

But if they are distinct, what accounts for the frequently reported statistical relationship between loneliness and measures of social anxiety? As an initial answer to this question, we propose the following conceptual model linking the two constructs. First, as indicated above, numerous studies have found that socially anxious persons (particularly dispositionally shy persons) tend to hold negative opinions and perceptions of themselves with respect to their interpersonal abilities. They tend to rate their performance in interpersonal interactions more negatively and to be less satisfied with that performance than individuals who score lower on measures of shyness (e.g., Jones & Briggs, 1984). Such critical self-evaluations are likely to lead one to limit and restrict one's social efforts to acquire and maintain social contacts.

Leary (1982) labeled these "disaffiliative behaviors," and they include nonverbal behaviors such as poor eye contact, as well as fewer attempts to initiate or sustain conversation, particularly with strangers and acquaintances with whom one is uncomfortable. Such behaviors result in shy persons having fewer social interactions, which means that they will have fewer opportunities to succeed interpersonally and hence to perceive themselves as adequate in this domain of experience. In addition, research indicating that the reticent behavior of shy persons is often misperceived as "snobbishness" or disinterest in interaction suggests that potentially available others may also restrict interpersonal approaches toward persons who are shy. Thus, fewer interpersonal opportunities— whether the result of the shy person's disaffiliative behaviors or others' reactions to misperceived reticence—would be expected to increase the likelihood of loneliness directly, especially as such patterns of experience begin to crystalize into chronic ruminations of interpersonal inadequacy.

Second, social anxiety may lead to loneliness, particularly when it is accompanied by a strong motivation to affiliate with others. For example, Cheek and Buss (1981) demonstrated that shyness and sociability (defined as the degree of interest in interacting with others) are distinct concepts and that considering an individual's standing with respect to both dimensions allowed for more accurate predictions of their overt interpersonal behavior than did considering either dimension alone. Specifically, shy people who were high on sociability spent significantly less time talking and had poorer eye contact with strangers in laboratory conversations than non-shy participants. Furthermore, in comparing participants who scored high in both shyness and sociability with participants who were high on shyness but low on sociability as well as participants who scored low on shyness, members of the first group were significantly more tense, inhibited, and unfriendly, and they engaged in more self-manipulative behaviors (e.g., touching their face with their hands) as compared to the latter two groups.

Consequently, the next step in our model concerns the comparison of the individual's actual level of interpersonal contact and involvement with their desired level. Presumably for persons high in shyness and other forms of social anxiety, the actual level of social participation is relatively low due to their tendency toward disaffiliative behaviors. However, whether this translates into loneliness for any given individual may depend on the desired level of contact. By definition, individuals who are high in sociability would most likely desire more contact and involvement. Therefore, for these individuals who are also shy, the discrepancy between actual and desired contact would be large, resulting in greater loneliness. On the other hand, individuals who are less sociable would have less desire for social contact and involvement, and therefore greater consistency between their desired and actual levels of contact. This would, presumably, result in their being less vulnerable to loneliness despite their shyness. Based on this portion of the model, we would predict that, although the majority of lonely people are shy, not all shy people are lonely.

It is also likely that shyness and loneliness are related in another way. Many persons first report experiencing loneliness after a change in lifestyle or circumstance which disrupts their network of friends and companions. For example, adults losing their spouse through death or divorce often find themselves excluded from social networks which are often formed on a "couple-companionate" basis (e.g., Lopata, 1969). Similarly, young adults leaving an environment of friends and family with whom they feel comfortable and with whom they have associated for years often feel lost and bewildered on large college campuses where they have few friends (e.g., Cutrona, 1982). The difficulty in rising to these challenges is even greater for shy and socially anxious individuals, who may find themselves having to depend on their own social skills and "network building strategies," perhaps for the first time in their lives. Thus, in addition to being mediated by the match between desired and actual social contact, the degree of association between social anxiety and loneliness may also depend upon the nature of the interpersonal environment. Familiar environments containing friends and family who encourage and facilitate interpersonal involvements and the development of new friends may constrain the emergence of loneliness among socially anxious persons. By contrast, new, unfamiliar, and particularly threatening social environments may increase the likelihood of loneliness among these individuals.

One final issue that should be addressed by any model attempting to link social anxiety and loneliness is whether the disruption in mutually satisfying relationships associated with loneliness is chronic or acute. Jones, Carpenter, & Quintana (1985) factor analyzed a large number of self-reported personality and attitudinal variables previously found to be associated with loneliness and then compared the resultant factor scores with scores on the UCLA Loneliness Scale using an hierarchical regression procedure. Two factors appeared to be strongly and equally (inversely) related to loneliness, in terms of the proportion of variation in loneliness scores that was explained. One composite variable included positively loaded scales such as masculinity and assertiveness and negatively loaded variables such as shyness and social anxiety. The second factor contained variables such as empathy, self-esteem, self-disclosure, femininity, and trust, all of which were positively loaded. This basic pattern of results has been replicated by Wittenberg and Reis (1986). It is reasonable to assume that these two factors emerge as related to loneliness because they converge on two complementary sets of skills and attitudes necessary at different points in the sequence of developing a relationship. Initial interactions with strangers often require abilities and dispositions which enhance meeting people and working past the discomfort and awkwardness of interacting with someone one hardly knows. Thus, being outgoing, self-assured, and free from inhibitory social anxieties such as shyness would be expected to contribute positively to the initial development of a relationship. By contrast, more intimate interactions place a premium not so much on such instrumental behaviors as they do on such factors as sensitivity, taking the perspective of one's partner, listening, and openness. Furthermore, it is possible that lacking one set of skills is associated with acute loneliness, whereas lacking the other set of skills may be associated with chronic loneliness. Although additional research is needed to verify these speculations, this line of reasoning is also consistent with research on the relationship between loneliness and androgyny (Avery, 1982).

We would further assume that loneliness occurs in socially anxious persons because of a greater tendency on their part to make internal, stable, and uncontrollable attributions for their self-perceived interpersonal failures (Anderson & Arnoult, 1985). Specifically, as with individuals scoring high in loneliness, high social anxiety is associated with perceiving one's distress as due to something about oneself that will not change and about which one can do little or nothing. This leads shy and socially anxious persons to see themselves as ineffective and the future as bleak, as far as social interactions are concerned. Such attitudes and feelings would also presumably increase their social anxiety regarding subsequent opportunities for social involvement, thereby keeping the cycle engaged.

In conclusion, an examination of the relevant literature suggests that the constructs of loneliness and social anxiety share basic features of conceptualization as well as both direct and indirect empirical connections. It is our contention that available studies do not indicate that the two constructs reduce to the same basic phenomenon, but instead suggest that they are linked in predictable and theoretically interesting ways. Additional research is, of course, necessary to fully examine the model proposed above. Beyond this, however, there is an important reason for investigating further the linkages between loneliness and social anxiety. It is possible that the most important consequences of social anxiety lie beyond the immediate discomfort experienced in social situations. Specifically, it is clearly unpleasant to feel shy, embarrassed, and otherwise emotionally aroused in social situations, but it is even more devastating when the propensity for such emotions begins to interfere with the development and maintenance of a network of casual and intimate relationships.

REFERENCES

Anderson, C. A., & Arnoult, L. H. (1985). Attributional style and everyday problems in living: Depression, loneliness and shyness. *Social Cognition, 3*, 16–35.

Arling, G. (1976). The elderly widow and her family, neighbors and friends. *Journal of Marriage and the Family, 38*, 757–768.

Asher, S. R., & Wheeler, V. A. (1985). Children's loneliness: A comparison of rejected and neglected peer status. *Journal of Consulting and Clinical Psychology, 53*, 500–505.

Austin, B. A. (1983). Factorial structure of the UCLA Loneliness Scale. *Psychological Reports, 53*, 883–889.

Avery, A. W. (1982). Escaping loneliness in adolescence: The case for androgyny. *Journal of Youth and Adolescence, 11*, 451–459.

Ayers, J. (1986). *Loneliness and interpersonal communication patterns.* Unpublished manuscript, Washington State University.

Bahr, H. M., & Harvey, C. D. (1979). Correlates of loneliness among widows bereaved in a mining disaster. *Psychological Reports, 44*, 367–385.

Baum, S. K. (1982). Loneliness in elderly persons: A preliminary study. *Psychological Reports, 50*, 1317–1318.

Bell, R. A. (1985). Conversational involvement and loneliness. *Communication Monographs, 52*, 218–235.

Berg, S., Mellstrom, D., Persson, G., & Svanborg, A. (1981). Loneliness in the Swedish aged. *Journal of Gerontology, 36*, 342–349.

Bradburn, N. (1969). *The structure of psychological well-being.* Chicago: Aldine.

Bragg, M. (1979). *A comparative study of loneliness and depression.* Unpublished doctoral dissertation, University of California, Los Angeles.

Brennan, T. (1982). Loneliness at adolescence. In L. A. Peplau & D. Perlman (Eds.), *Loneliness: A sourcebook of current theory, research and therapy* (pp. 269–290). New York: Wiley-Interscience.

Buss, A. H. (1980). *Self-consciousness and social anxiety.* San Francisco: Freeman.

Buss, A. H. (1986). A theory of shyness. In W. H. Jones, J. M. Cheek, & S. R. Briggs (Eds.), *Shyness: Perspectives on research and treatment* (pp. 39–46). New York: Plenum.

Carpenter, B. N., Hansson, R. O., Rountree, R., & Jones, W. H. (1984). Relational competence and adjustment in diabetic patients. *Journal of Social and Clinical Psychology, 1,* 359–369.

Check, J. V. P., Perlman, D., & Malamuth, N. M. (1985). Loneliness and aggressive behavior. *Journal of Social and Personal Relationships, 2,* 243–252.

Cheek, J. M., & Busch, C. M. (1981). The influence of shyness on loneliness in a new situation. *Personality and Social Psychology Bulletin, 7,* 572–577.

Cheek, J. M., & Buss, A. H. (1981). Shyness and sociability. *Journal of Personality and Social Psychology, 41,* 330–339.

Cheek, J. M., Melchior, L. A., & Carpentieri, A. M. (1987). Shyness and self-concept. In L. M. Hartman & K. R. Blankstein (Eds.), *Perception of self in emotional disorder and psychotherapy* (pp. 150–171). New York: Plenum.

Chelune, G. J., Sultan, F. E., & Williams, C. L. (1980). Loneliness, self-disclosure and interpersonal effectiveness. *Journal of Counseling Psychology, 27,* 462–468.

Crozier, W. R. (1979). Shyness as a dimension of personality. *British Journal of Social and Clinical Psychology, 18,* 121–128.

Cutrona, C. E. (1982). Transition to college: Loneliness and the process of social adjustment. In L. A. Peplau & D. Perlman (Eds.), *Loneliness: A sourcebook of current theory, research and therapy* (pp. 291–309). New York: Wiley-Interscience.

Daly, S. (1978). Behavioral correlates of social anxiety. *British Journal of Social and Clinical Psychology, 18,* 121–128.

Davis, M. H. (1983). Measuring individual differences in empathy: Evidence for a multidimensional approach. *Journal of Personality and Social Psychology, 44,* 113–126.

Eddy, P. D. (1961). *Loneliness: A discrepancy with the phenomenological self.* Unpublished doctoral dissertation, Adelphi College, New York.

Evans, R. L. (1983). Loneliness, depression and social activity after determination of legal blindness. *Psychological Reports, 52,* 603–608.

Franzoi, S. L., & Davis, M. H. (1985). Adolescent self-disclosure and loneliness: Private self-consciousness and parental influence. *Journal of Personality and Social Psychology, 48,* 768–780.

Gerson, A. C., & Perlman, D. (1979). Loneliness and expressive communication. *Journal of Abnormal Psychology, 88,* 258–261.

Goswick, R. A., & Jones, W. H. (1981). Loneliness, self-concept and adjustment. *Journal of Psychology, 107,* 237–240.

Goswick, R. A., & Jones, W. H. (1982). Components of loneliness during adolescence. *Journal of Youth and Adolescence, 11,* 373–384.

Hansson, R. O., & Jones, W. H. (1981). Loneliness, cooperation and conformity. *Journal of Social Psychology, 115,* 103–108.

Hansson, R. O., Jones, W. H., Carpenter, B. N., & Remondent, J. (1986). Loneliness and adjustment to old age. *International Journal of Aging and Human Development, 24,* 41–53.

Hecht, D. T., & Baum, S. K. (1984). Loneliness and attachment patterns in young adults. *Journal of Clinical Psychology, 40,* 193–197.

Hoover, S., Skuja, A., & Cosper, J. (1979). Correlates of college students' loneliness. *Psychological Reports, 44,* 1116.

Horowtiz, L. M., French, R. De S., & Anderson, C. (1982). The prototype of a lonely person. In L. A. Peplau & D. Perlman (Eds.), *Loneliness: A sourcebook of current theory, research and therapy* (pp. 183–205). New York: Wiley-Interscience.

Izard, C. E. (1977). *Human emotions.* New York: Plenum.

Jones, W. H. (1981). Loneliness and social contact. *Journal of Social Psychology, 113,* 295–296.

Jones, W. H. (1982). Loneliness and social behavior. In L. A. Peplau & D. Perlman (Eds.), *Loneliness: A sourcebook of current theory, research and therapy* (pp. 238–252). New York: Wiley-Interscience.

Jones, W. H., & Briggs, S. R. (1984). The self-other discrepancy in social shyness. In R. Schwarzer (Ed.), *The self in anxiety, stress and depression* (pp. 93–107). Amsterdam: North Holland.

Jones, W. H., Briggs, S. R., & Smith, T. G. (1986). Shyness: Conceptualization and measurement. *Journal of Personality and Social Psychology, 51,* 629–639.

Jones, W. H., & Carpenter, B. N. (1986). Shyness, social behavior and relationships. In W. H. Jones, J. M. Cheek, & S. R. Briggs (Eds.), *Shyness: Perspectives on research and treatment* (pp. 227–238). New York: Plenum.

Jones, W. H., Carpenter, B. N., & Quintana, D. (1985). Personality and interpersonal predictors of loneliness in two cultures. *Journal of Personality and Social Psychology, 48,* 1503–1511.

Jones, W. H., Cavert, C. W., Snider, R. L., & Bruce, T. (1985). Relational stress: An analysis of situations and events associated with loneliness. In S. Duck & D. Perlman (Eds.), *Understanding personal relationships* (pp. 221–242). London: Sage.

Jones, W. H., Freemon, J. A., & Goswick, R. A. (1981). The persistence of loneliness: Self and other determinants. *Journal of Personality, 49,* 27–48.

Jones, W. H., Hobbs, S. A., & Hockenbury, D. (1982). Loneliness and social skill deficits. *Journal of Personality and Social Psychology, 42,* 682–689.

Jones, W. H., & Moore, T. L. (1987). Loneliness and social support. *Journal of Social Behavior and Personality, 2,* 145–156.

Jones, W. H., & Russell, D. (1982). The Social Reticence Scale: An objective instrument to measure shyness. *Journal of Personality Assessment, 46,* 629–631.

Jones, W. H., Sansone, C., & Helm, B. (1983). Loneliness and interpersonal judgments. *Personality and Social Psychology Bulletin, 9,* 437–441.

Kivett, V. R. (1979). Discriminators of loneliness among the rural elderly: Implications for intervention. *The Gerontologist, 19,* 108–115.

Krulik, T. (1978). *Loneliness in school age children with chronic life-threatening illness.* Unpublished doctoral dissertation, University of California, San Francisco.

Larsen, R., Csikszetmihalyi, M., & Graef, R. (1982). Time alone in daily experience: Loneliness or renewal? In L. A. Peplau & D. Perlman (Eds.), *Loneliness: A sourcebook of current theory, research and therapy* (pp. 40–53). New York: Wiley-Interscience.

Leary, M. R. (1982). Social anxiety. In L. Wheeler (Ed.), *Review of personality and social psychology* (Vol. III, pp. 97–120). Beverly Hills, CA: Sage.

Levin, I., & Stokes, J. P. (1986). An examination of the relation of individual differences variables to loneliness. *Journal of Personality, 54,* 201–217.

Lopata, H. Z. (1969). Loneliness: Forms and components. *Social Problems, 17,* 248–261.

Loucks, S. (1980). Loneliness, affect and self-concept: construct validity of the Bradley Loneliness Scale. *Journal of Personality Assessment, 44,* 142–147.

Marcoen, A., & Brumagne, M. (1985). Loneliness among children and young adolescents. *Developmental Psychology, 21,* 1025–1031.

Moore, D., & Schultz, N. R. (1983). Loneliness at adolescence. Correlates, attributions and coping. *Journal of Youth and Adolescence, 12,* 95–100.

Peplau, L. A., & Perlman, D. (1982). (Eds.). *Loneliness: A sourcebook of current theory, research and therapy.* New York: Wiley-Interscience.

Perlman, D., Gerson, A. C., & Spinner, B. (1978). Loneliness among senior citizens: An empirical report. *Essence, 2,* 239–248.

Pilkonis, P. A. (1977). The behavioral consequences of shyness. *Journal of Personality, 45,* 566–611.

Rook, K. S. (1984). The negative side of social interaction: Impact on psychological well-being. *Journal of Personality and Social Psychology, 46,* 1097–1108.

Rosenbaum, J., & Rosenbaum, V. (1973). *Conquering loneliness.* New York: Hawthorn Books.

Rubenstein, C. M., & Shaver, P. (1982). The experience of loneliness. In L. A. Peplau & D. Perlman (Eds.), *Loneliness: A sourcebook of current theory, research and therapy* (pp. 206–223). New York: Wiley-Interscience.

Russell, D. (1982). The measurement of loneliness. In L. A. Peplau & D. Perlman (Eds.), *Loneliness: A sourcebook of current theory, research and therapy* (pp. 81–104). New York: Wiley-Interscience.

Russell, D., & Cutrona, C. E. (1988). *Development and evolution of the UCLA Loneliness Scale.* Unpublished manuscript, University of Iowa.

Russell, D., Cutrona, C. E., Rose, J., & Yurko, K. (1984). Social and emotional loneliness: An examination of Weiss' typology of loneliness. *Journal of Personality and Social Psychology, 46,* 1313–1321.

Russell, D., Kao, C., & Cutrona, C. E. (1987, June). *Loneliness and social support: Same or different constructs?* Paper presented at the Iowa Conference on Personal Relationships, Iowa City.

Russell, D., Peplau, L. A., & Cutrona, C. E. (1980). The revised UCLA Loneliness Scales: Concurrent and discriminant validity evidence. *Journal of Personality and Social Psychology, 39,* 472–480.

Russell, D., Peplau, L. A., & Ferguson, M. (1978). Developing a measure of loneliness. *Journal of Personality Assessment, 42,* 290–294.

Schlenker, B. R., & Leary, M. R. (1982). Social anxiety and self-presentation: A conceptualization and model. *Psychological Bulletin, 92,* 641–669.

Schultz, B. J., & Saklofske, D. H. (1983). Relationship between social support and selected measures of psychological well-being. *Psychological Reports, 53,* 847–850.

Shaver, P., Furman, W., & Buhmester, D. (1985). Transition to college: Network changes, social skills, and loneliness. In S. Duck & D. Perlman (Eds.), *Understanding personal relationships* (pp. 193–220). London: Sage.

Sloan, W. W., Jr., & Solano, C. H. (1984). The conversational style of lonely males with strangers and roommates. *Personality and Social Psychology Bulletin, 10,* 293–301.

Solano, C. H., Batten, P. G., & Parish, E. A. (1982). Loneliness and patterns of self-disclosure. *Journal of Personality and Social Psychology, 43,* 524–531.

Spitzberg, B. H., & Canary, D. J. (1985). Loneliness and relationally competent communication. *Journal of Social and Personal Relationships, 2,* 387–402.

Stokes, J. (1985). The relationships of social network and individual difference variables to loneliness. *Journal of Personality and Social Psychology, 48,* 981–990.

Vitkus, J., & Horowitz, L. M. (1987). Poor social performance of lonely people: Lacking a skill or adopting a role? *Journal of Personality and Social Psychology, 52,* 1266–1273.

Weeks, D. G., Michela, J. L., Peplau, L. A., & Bragg, M. E. (1980). The relation between loneliness and depression: A structural equation analysis. *Journal of Personality and Social Psychology, 39,* 1238–1244.

Weiss, R. S. (1974). The provisions of social relationships. In Z. Rubin (Ed.), *Doing unto others* (pp. 17–26). Englewood Cliffs, NJ: Prentice-Hall.

Wheeler, L., Reis, H., & Nazlek, J. (1983). Loneliness, social interaction, and sex roles. *Journal of Personality and Social Psychology, 45,* 943–955.

Wilbert, J. R., & Rupert, P. A. (1986). Dysfunctional attitudes, loneliness and depression in college students. *Cognitive Therapy and Research, 10,* 71–77.

Williams, J. G., & Solano, C. H. (1983). The social reality of feeling lonely: Friendship and reciprocation. *Personality and Social Psychology Bulletin, 9,* 237–242.

Wittenberg, M. T., & Reis, H. T. (1986). Loneliness, social skills, and social perception. *Personality and Social Psychology Bulletin, 12,* 121–130.

Zahaki, W. R., & Duran, R. L. (1982). All the lonely people: The relationship among loneliness, communicative competence and communication anxiety. *Communication Quarterly, 30,* 202–209.

IV

Social Anxiety in Adulthood: Clinical Perspective

9

Social Phobia

Nature and Treatment

AGNES SCHOLING AND PAUL M. G. EMMELKAMP

INTRODUCTION

Temporary distress in social situations is familiar to most people. For example, for many people, speaking or performing in public is associated with trembling of the voice and hands, heartpounding, dry mouth, and sweating. An essential characteristic in these situations is the fear of scrutiny by other people. However, most people do not feel incapacitated by these fears and may even see the associated arousal and alertness as conducive to their performance.

A relatively small group of individuals feels hindered by the distress to such an extent that they apply for treatment. Many of these people qualify for the diagnosis social phobia, which is distinguished from the "normal" distress mentioned above by the *intensity* of the fears and *avoidance* of the situations in which the fears arise. Although social phobia is a rather prevalent disorder, relatively few studies on social anxiety have used real patients, in contrast with the numerous analog studies that deal with dating anxiety, speech anxiety, and assertiveness problems (reviewed by Emmelkamp, 1982; Scott, Himadi, & Keane, 1983).

The purpose of this chapter is to describe the clinical features, assessment, and treatment of social phobia. After defining social phobia, the prevalence, clinical features, and etiology of social phobia are described. The clinical value of various assessment procedures are discussed, including self-report of fear, cognitive measures, psychophysiological assessment, and behavioral measures. Finally, the chapter deals with psychopharmacological and psychological treatment of social phobia. The emphasis throughout is on severe social phobia rather than on social anxiety as studied in analog studies.

AGNES SCHOLING AND PAUL M. G. EMMELKAMP • Department of Clinical Psychology, University of Groningen, Academic Hospital, 9713 EZ Groningen, The Netherlands.

DEFINITION OF SOCIAL PHOBIA

Before the introduction of DSM-III (American Psychiatric Association [APA], 1980), little agreement existed among researchers about the definition of social phobia. The classification schemes most commonly used at that time, the 9th edition of the International Classification of Diseases (World Health Organization, 1978) and DSM II, both recognized only one category for phobias, "phobic syndrome" and "phobic neurosis," respectively.

Marks & Gelder introduced the term *social phobia* in 1966, and they defined it to include "fears of eating, drinking, shaking, blushing, writing, or vomiting in the presence of other people." According to them the essential feature of the syndrome was a fear of seeming ridiculous to other people. Since that time a number of studies were published that dealt with some sort of interpersonal anxiety. However, the names used to describe the "syndrome" differed, as did clinical features that characterized it.

Amies, Gelder, and Shaw (1983) defined social phobia as unreasonable anxiety experienced by a person when in the company of other people, usually increasing with the degree of formality of the situation and the extent to which the person feels under scrutiny, and accompanied by a desire to avoid the situations in which it is experienced.

According to Nichols (1974) social phobics are characterized by a sensitivity to disapproval and criticism, low self-evaluation, rigid concepts of appropriate social behavior, negative fantasy-producing anticipatory anxiety, increased awareness of scrutiny from others, and an exaggerated interpretation of the sensory feedback related to tension or embarrassment.

Edelmann (1985) distinguished embarrassment from other forms of social anxiety, such as audience anxiety, shyness, and shame. In his opinion there are crucial differences between the various forms of social anxiety, but they share a common element of either a perceived or an anticipated discrepancy between one's self-presentation and one's standard for self-presentation.

Falloon, Lloyd, and Harpin (1981) make a distinction between "specific" and "generalized" social phobia. Specific social phobia refers to a phobia for a very specific social situation (for example, eating in public). When fears are generalized (e.g., difficulties with initiating conversations or participating in group activities) the term general social phobia is used.

Since 1980, with the appearance of DSM-III, social phobia has been described as a separate syndrome among the anxiety disorders. In DSM-III, it was defined as a persistent, irrational fear of a situation in which the individual is exposed to possible scrutiny by others, in which he or she may act in a way that will be embarrassing, combined with a strong desire to avoid those situations. Beyond this, the person had to recognize his or her fear as unreasonable. An important problem with the definition according to DSM-III is the notion that "generally, an individual only has *one* social phobia." This implies that the description in fact refers only to a very specific group of patients, namely, those people with, for example, fear of eating in public, of using public lavatories, or of writing in the presence of others. Clinical practice, however, indicates that many individuals report a much more generalized and pervasive fear, especially those individuals that have suffered from the disorder since late childhood or early adolescence. According to DSM-III criteria, these cases often meet criteria for avoidant personality disorder, which is characterized by hypersensitivity to criticism or potential rejection, an unwillingness to enter into social situations unless unusually strong guarantees of uncritical acceptance are provided, social withdrawal despite a desire for social interaction, and low self-esteem.

In the most recent edition of the manual (DSM-III-R; APA, 1987), the definitions of both social phobia and avoidant personality disorder have been changed in some respects.

The diagnosis of social phobia is based on the following seven criteria:

1. A persistent fear of one or more situations in which the person is exposed to possible scrutiny by others. Essential is the fear to act in a way that will be embarrassing or humiliating.
2. The fear may not have any relation to another Axis-I or -III disorder (if present). This criterion states that fear of trembling caused by Parkinson's disease is not social phobia. In case panic disorder is also present, the fear of having a panic attack in social situations is not diagnosed as social phobia.
3. Exposure to the phobic stimulus almost invariably provokes an anxiety response.
4. Mostly, the situation is avoided or, if not possible, is endured with intense anxiety.
5. As a consequence of the avoidance behavior, problems exist in occupational functioning or in usual social relationships.
6. The individual has to recognize his or her fears as unreasonable or excessive.
7. If the person is under 18, the disorder does not meet criteria for avoidant disorder of childhood/adolescence. (DSM-III-R, pp. 351–353)

The most important difference between the definitions from DSM-III and DSM-III-R is that the DSM-III-R definition also applies to individuals that fear almost all social situations and show marked avoidance behavior, in contrast with DSM-III, where such complaints are diagnosed as avoidant personality disorder. In such cases the additional "generalized type" is given in DSM-III-R.

Social Phobia and the Other Anxiety Disorders

Two studies have compared social phobics with other anxiety disorders on symptom profiles.

Turner, McCann, Beidel, and Mezzich (1986) divided patients into three groups. One consisted of the phobic disorders (12 social phobics and 32 simple phobics), one of the anxiety states (9 patients with generalized anxiety, 9 with panic disorder, and 9 obsessive–compulsives), while agoraphobics with or without panic attacks formed the third group (18 patients). All patients were diagnosed according to DSM-III criteria. On each of the eight measures employed the results showed differences between the anxiety states and the phobic states, thereby providing support for the distinction made. The agoraphobia group resembled the anxiety group more than it did the phobic group. The phobic patients reported less anxiety, less avoidance and distress, less fear of negative evaluation, and less depression. Since 75% of the phobic group consisted of simple phobics, however, drawing conclusions with respect to social phobia seems premature.

Cameron, Thyer, Nesse, and Curtis (1986) examined symptom profiles of patients with DSM-III anxiety disorders and reported that the results support the grouping of all disorders into one general diagnostic category of "anxiety disorders," because the differences between them were small. Interestingly, they found simple phobia to be a relatively distinct disorder, and social phobia in many respects to show more similarity with agoraphobia than with simple phobia. In general, the simple phobic patients reported the least distress and anxiety symptoms.

According to DSM-III-R, several diagnoses are mutually exclusive, but in reality the distinction is sometimes difficult to make. Most common problems still seem to arise with the differential diagnoses of avoidant personality disorder (Axis II) and panic disorder (Axis I).

Social Phobia versus Panic Disorder

As mentioned above, according to DSM-III-R, social phobia and panic disorder may coexist, but the social phobia is not allowed to be related to the fear of having a panic attack. However, one of our male patients experienced a sudden panic attack when in the classroom, 8 years ago, when some remarks were made about his being involved with a girl. At that moment he was totally in panic, resulting in sweating, blushing, and heart palpitations. Since that first time, he has been very afraid of having another panic attack in social situations. In this case, it is difficult to decide which diagnosis is the primary one, since outside of social situations, he does not have panic attacks at all.

Liebowitz, Gorman, Fyer, and Klein (1985) made a useful distinction between "primary social phobics" (no history of spontaneous panic attacks) and "secondary social phobics" (with social avoidance being the result of panic attacks). In their opinion primary social phobics fear scrutiny or evaluation by others; their anxiety is confined to such situations or anticipation of such situations. Secondary social phobics have panic attacks in a variety of *non*social situations, and they tend to fear or avoid situations in which easy or unobtrusive exit is difficult. Thus, an important question seems to be whether the feelings of panic more often develop in (anticipation of) social situations than in situations of being (left) alone.

Results of a study by Munjack, Brown, and McDowell (1987) corroborate the distinction between primary and secondary social phobics as made by Liebowitz *et al.* Although patients with panic disorder and social phobia both report anxiety in social situations, the nature of the fears in both groups was found to be quite different, as assessed with the SCL-90R (Derogatis, 1977). Panic patients reported significantly more somatic complaints than social phobics, while interpersonal sensitivity was found to be higher in social phobics than in patients with panic disorder.

Social Phobia versus Avoidant Personality Disorder

In contrast with DSM-III, in which a definition of social phobia was excluded if problems in social situations are due to personality disorders (e.g., avoidant personality disorder), in DSM-III-R both diagnoses may coexist. Although the definition is changed in the way that individuals with strongly generalized fears and avoidance behavior can be classified as social phobics, this does not solve the problem.

Avoidant personality disorder is characterized by social discomfort, fear of negative evaluation, and timidity, beginning by early childhood. Seven criteria are given, of which at least four must be fulfilled. These criteria state that the individual:

1. Is easily hurt by criticism or disapproval.
2. Has no close friends or confidants (or only one) other than first-degree relatives.
3. Is unwilling to get involved with people unless certain of being liked.
4. Avoids social or occupational activities that involve significant interpersonal contact (e.g., refuses a promotion that will increase social demands).
5. Is reticent in social situations because of a fear of saying something inappropriate or foolish, or of being unable to answer a question.
6. Fears being embarrassed by blushing, crying or showing signs of anxiety in front of other people.
7. Exaggerates the potential difficulties, physical dangers, or risks involved in doing something ordinary but outside his or her usual routine. (DSM-III-R; APA, 1987, pp. 352–353)

Thus, six out of seven of the criteria are clearly related to social phobia of the generalized type.

It has been argued that the diagnosis avoidant personality disorder is to be reserved for those individuals who show a relatively stable, lifelong pattern of avoidance of social situations. In general, this may be a useful distinction between personality disorders (Axis II) and the more temporary phobic disorders (Axis I), but if we look at DSM-III-R information about age of onset and duration of social phobia, this distinction may be of little help. In DSM-III-R, age of onset of social phobia is considered to be late childhood or early adolescence, an observation that is confirmed in several studies (e.g., Amies et al., 1983; Marks & Gelder, 1966; Ost, 1987; Solyom, Ledwidge, & Solyom, 1986). Thus, the disorder is found to be chronic.

Heimberg, Dodge, and Becker (1987) suggest that both diagnoses may be distinguished by the desire the person has to confront the difficult social situation and to engage in social relationships. In their view persons that don't want to mix with others and have accepted their avoidance behavior as a comfortable if unfulfilling lifestyle are to be diagnosed as avoidant personality disorder, while social phobics keep trying to enter the feared social situations or relationships. However, this is not in accordance with DSM-III-R, in which it is stated that people with avoidant personality disorder do yearn for affection and acceptance. In contrast, a lack of desire for social involvement is a central characteristic in the diagnosis of schizoid personality disorder.

Greenberg and Stravynski (1983) described a sample of 46 patients whose main complaint was a difficulty in initiating and maintaining conversations, especially with strangers of the opposite sex, at parties and at other social meetings. The majority were single men who reported problems in social relationships since the second decade of their life. Agoraphobics and social phobics, classified according to DSM-III criteria, were excluded. The distinction between social phobics and these patients was based on the very early development of the problems. The authors suggest that the group of 46 patients all had avoidant personality disorder, which, in their view, has consequences for treatment. They suggest that avoidant personality disorder possibly would benefit more from social skills training, while social phobics need anxiety reduction.

To date, only one study has been carried out to clarify the distinction between both diagnoses. Turner, Beidel, Dancu, and Keys (1986) assessed the clinical manifestations of social phobia in a sample of 21 social phobics. Moreover, individuals with a diagnosis of social phobia were compared with persons with avoidant personality disorder. Diagnoses were based on several interviews, and a diagnosis of avoidant personality disorder excluded a diagnosis of social phobia. Patients did *not* meet criteria for any other DSM-III diagnosis. Their results show that social phobia is a chronic and pervasive disorder, and, contrary to DSM-III notions, affects a variety of life areas and produces significant emotional distress. It was found that 90% of the social phobics could mention at least two different situations in which they experienced significant distress, and 45% reported anxiety in at least three different situations. Those individuals with avoidant personality disorder were found to be more sensitive interpersonally and to exhibit significantly poorer social skills than the social phobics did. They also showed significantly higher social distress and avoidance behavior.

The results seem to suggest that it is possible to discriminate between both groups. However, in this study the decision rules of DSM-III were followed in that *no* diagnosis of social phobia was given once the criteria for the diagnosis avoidant personality disorder were fulfilled. In DSM-III-R, however, both diagnoses may coexist. This implies that persons in the sample of avoidant personality disorder ($n=8$) in fact were at least "mixed diagnoses," and according to the new definition even may be called social phobics. On psychophysiological and cognitive variables *no* differences were found between both groups.

Individual Differences and Subtypes

In DSM-III-R, under the diagnosis social phobia no explicit distinction is made between several subtypes. Only a suggestion is given toward a difference between persons with a relatively specific social phobia (as described in the previous definition of DSM-III) and individuals with more generalized fears (generalized type).

However, social phobic patients form a rather heterogeneous group, and they may differ from each other in many respects. For example, some individuals who demonstrate a lot of somatic symptoms, like sweating, blushing, increased heart rate, or shortness of breath, nevertheless function well in diverse areas and hardly avoid difficult situations. Others show marked deficits in social skills, report distressing thoughts without strong physiological symptoms, and have developed generalized avoidance behavior to such an extent that they have become completely socially isolated.

In our view, several dimensions are involved in social phobia. These include:

- Socially skilled versus unskilled
- Low versus high psychophysiological arousal
- Rational versus irrational style of thinking
- One or two specific fears versus generalized social fears
- (Almost) no avoidance versus generalized avoidance
- Fear in familiar versus unfamiliar situations
- Fear in groups versus fear in situations with one other person
- Presence or not of fear for the somatic symptoms as such (e.g., "My only problem is my trembling; if I could be sure never to tremble again there would be no problem at all")

Only a few researchers have tried to distinguish subtypes (Table I reviews those studies).

Before we take a closer look at the results reported, it has to be noted that almost all studies, apart from that of Mersch, Emmelkamp, Bögels, and Van der Sleen (1989), suffered from the same methodological problem: the distinction in subtypes is based on a median split of the data. In addition, in those studies that used volunteers or students, it is possible that in fact the whole group consisted of nonanxious subjects, when compared with patients.

Socially Skilled versus Unskilled. Trower, Yardley, Bryant, and Shaw (1978) made a distinction between primary social failures versus secondary social failures, a distinction based on assumptions about the etiology of the social problems. The main problem of primary failures was supposed to be a lack of social skills due to faulty socialization. On the contrary, secondary failure was considered to be a consequence of other kinds of psychopathology, resulting from biochemical, cognitive, or dynamic disturbance.

Low versus High Arousal. In an analog study by Fremouw, Gross, Monroe, and Rapp (1982) with socially anxious volunteers, some evidence was found for the typologies given by Borkovec (1976) and Davidson and Schwartz (1976). Both typologies are alike in that they use a physiological reaction dimension. The difference between them lies in the second dimension: while Borkovec assumes

Table 1. Subtypes and Individual Characteristics among Social Phobics

Authors	Population (number of subjects)	Subtypes indiv. characteristics	Results
Trower et al. (1978)	Outpatients diagnosed neurotic or abnormal personalities (40)	Socially unskilled (primary) vs. socially phobic (secondary)	Partial support for existence of primary failures, *no* support for secondary failures
Fremouw et al. (1982)	Speech and socially anxious psychology students (58)	Subjects ranking on 2 dimensions: physiological arousal and self-report (cognitions or autonomic perception), resulting in 4 groups	Support for the existence of 3 of 4 groups. *Not identified*: high on physiology, low on self-report. Largest subtype: low on physiology, high on self-report.
Ost et al. (1981)	Outpatients, major complaint anxiety in a wide range of social situations (40)	Subjects ranking on 2 dimensions (social behavior and physiological arousal) yielding 2 types: behavioral reactors (16) vs. physiological reactors (16)	Treatment results partly corroborate the distinction made
Shahar & Merbaum (1981)	Volunteers reporting high interpersonal anxiety and a serious desire for treatment (54)	Subjects ranking on 2 dimensions (physiological reactivity and autonomic perception). 2 of the 4 groups used: strong reactors/perceivers and weak reactors/strong perceivers	Differential treatment effects only found on a limited number of measures
Turner & Beidel (1985)	Socially anxious (26) and non-socially anxious (26) individuals	2 subtypes both characterized by negative cognitions but differing in physiological arousal	80% of subjects could be classified into 2 empirically derived subtypes
Jerramalm et al. (1986)	Outpatients, major complaint anxiety in a wide range of social situations (43)	Subjects ranking on 2 dimensions (cognitions and physiological arousal) yielding 2 types: cognitive reactors (19) vs. physiological reactors (19)	Only a few differential treatment effects observed, maybe due to chance
Mersch et al. (1989)	Socially phobic patients (76)	Subjects ranking on 2 dimensions (cognitions and social behavior) yielding 2 types: cognitive reactors (19) vs. behavioral reactors (19)	No differential treatment effects observed

this to be perception of autonomic reactions, Davidson and Schwartz use a cognitive anxiety dimension, including worry and irrational thoughts. Based on cluster analyses, Fremouw *et al.* determined the number of groups and the major dimensions of the two samples of subjects. The data in this study support the existence of three of the four subgroups. For both typologies most individuals were to be characterized as high on the self-report measure (cognition or autonomic perception) in combination with low scores on the physiological reaction. One subgroup was not identified: those individuals with strong physiological reaction and low scores on self-report.

Turner and Beidel (1985) used independent criterion scores on blood pressure and on a cognitive measure during a performance task to divide socially anxious subjects into subgroups. They reported that more than 80% of the subjects could be placed in two of the four cells: all subjects were characterized by high levels of negative cognitions, but they differed in their scores on physiological reaction. Considering the fact that only blood pressure was used for assessing the physiological reaction, and only one measure for the cognitive component, it would be useful to replicate such studies with more comprehensive measures.

Blushing and Trembling. There are some other possible subtypes. At our department we regularly see people who complain of only one problem: blushing, sweating, or trembling in social situations. Often they assure us that, if they could be sure they would never blush or tremble again, the problem would be completely solved. First impressions of these patients as a distinct subgroup suggest that they may indeed show some differences from other social phobics; for example, in general they appear to be relatively highly educated, they often show eminent social skills, and many of them do not seem to feel socially anxious in other situations. Many of them share a rather strong need "to have everything under control." The relationship between the fear of blushing or trembling and more general social anxiety is not totally clear. Differentiating these persons from other social phobics may have important consequences for treatment.

Dysmorphophobia. A related group may be patients with dysmorphophobia. This diagnosis is given to individuals who are preoccupied with some imagined bodily defect. If a slight physical anomaly is present, the person's concern is grossly excessive. The term does not apply to patients who have an organic basis for their preoccupations. Examples of the disturbance include: being convinced that one has hair on one's face, body, and legs that causes people to stare and laugh; complaints of disfiguring facial skin or hair loss, or disfigured nose or mouth; preoccupation with the idea that other people notice one's body odor. Conditions that are not considered dysmorphophobia are anorexia nervosa (the conviction of being too fat) and transsexualism. The relationship between the disorder and social phobia is unclear. In DSM-III-R, body dysmorphic disorder is classified among the somatoform disorders, and not among the phobic disorders. However, dysmorphophobics may feel restricted in many social situations and often show considerable avoidance.

Hardy and Cotterill (1982) investigated whether this disorder is related to obsessive–compulsive disorder. Dysmorphophobic patients were found to be more depressive than psoriasis patients, who in turn were more depressive than the controls. Both patient groups showed equally elevated obsessional symptom scores compared to controls, but their scores were lower than those of an obsessional neurotic group. The hypothesis that dysmorphophobia is part of an obsessional state was not confirmed in this study. The relationship with social phobia has not yet been investigated, but clinical cases suggest that there is a clear relationship. Marks and Mishan (1987) reported that in four of their five cases social avoidance and anxiety arose from the dysmorphophobia and remitted as the disorder improved.

EPIDEMIOLOGY

In early childhood, school phobia (which may be related to social fears) is the main phobic condition referred for treatment; in adolescence social fears are the most common. Fears of blushing and fears of being looked at peaked in girls on the average about 2 years earlier than in boys (Abe & Masui, 1981).

Costello (1982) found in a community survey that mild social fears are common, but severe social phobias are not. Other data with respect to the epidemiology of social phobia come from the Epidemiologic Catchment Area program's inquiry into the lifetime prevalence of specific psychiatric disorders in the community (Robins, et al., 1984). Interviews were held with over 9,000 persons from large general population samples: New Haven, Connecticut; Baltimore, Maryland; and St. Louis, Missouri. The lifetime prevalence of a disorder is stated as the proportion of persons in a representative sample of the population who have ever experienced that disorder up to the date of assessment. The lifetime prevalence of phobic disorders ranged from 7.8% (New Haven) to 23.3% (Baltimore). Unfortunately, the prevalence of social phobia was not reported separately.

Myers et al. (1984) focused on the prevalence rates for the 6-month period immediately preceding the interview in the Epidemiologic Catchment Area program. The 6-month prevalence rates for social phobia were 2.2% in Baltimore and 1.2% in St. Louis. In both sites the prevalence of agoraphobia was higher (5.8% and 2.7%, respectively). In primary care settings social phobics are also less common than agoraphobics (Burns, 1980). In clinical settings social phobia is the third most common anxiety disorder in Western (Amies et al., 1983; Di Nardo, O'Brien, Barlow, Waddell, & Blanchard, 1983) and Eastern countries (India: Raguram & Bhide, 1985).

CHARACTERISTICS OF SOCIAL PHOBIA

Age of Onset

The first study in which information was given about age of onset of social phobia was published in 1966 (Marks & Gelder, 1966). Since that time, several studies have addressed the same issue. The results of these studies are summarized in Table 2.

The table shows that social phobic complaints generally started between the ages of 15 and 20 years, some years later than is mentioned in DSM-III-R. The onset of social phobia is earlier than that of agoraphobia, but later than that of simple phobia.

In the Amies *et al.* study, age of onset varied from 5 to 45 years; in the study of Ost, from 6 to 40 years. Most patients first noticed their problems between 10 and 14 years, followed by the group where onset was between 15 and 19 years. Taken together, about 70% of the patients reported that their social phobia started between 10 and 19 years.

We have some serious doubts with respect to establishing the reliability of the age of onset of social phobia, based upon our own experiences with social phobics. Most of our patients are hardly able to say when the first symptoms developed. Often the answer is something like: "I realized that I was different from other children and felt uncomfortable among them when I was about 14 or 15, but, when I look back at it now, I think I have always been a shy, silent person." In such cases the disorder presumably was present long before the individual was able to reflect upon him- or herself as a social person. One can state that those patients should be diagnosed as suffering from Avoidant Personality Disorder. However, we have the impression that many of them are very much alike the "real" social phobics, who firstly experienced anxiety during adolescence or later. Further, adolescence for most people is associated with considerable uncertainties in social contacts. In the stage theory of Erickson (1968), basic components are postulated for each of eight stages a person has to go through in life. The fifth phase, that of adolescence, is characterized by the themes of identity and identity confusion, the following phase, that of young adulthood, by intimacy versus isolation. This implies that the building of social relationships becomes important in this period and that feelings of distress are a normal part of it. According to Elkind (1967), the adolescent is egocentric and is acting before an "imaginary audience," believing that other people are preoccupied with his or her appearance and behavior in the same way as he or she is. So, presumably, most "normal" persons have the same sorts of conflicts and feelings in adolescence (at least the authors had) but do not acquire social phobia.

TABLE 2. Age of Onset of Different Phobic Disorders

	Social phobia		Agoraphobia		Simple phobia	
Marks & Gelder (1966)	19	(25)	24	(84)		
Shafar (1976)	20	(20)	32	(68)		
Amies *et al.* (1983)	19	(87)	24	(57)		
Thyer *et al.* (1985)	16	(42)	27	(115)	16	(152)
Persson & Nordlund (1985)	21	(31)	27	(37)		
Solyom *et al.* (1986)	17	(47)	25	(80)	13	(72)
Ost (1987)	16	(80)	28	(100)		

Note. Mean age of onset in years. Number of subjects is given in parentheses.

Sex Differences

The results with regard to sex differences among social phobics are inconclusive. Percentages of male patients in various studies are summarized in Table 3.

The data in the reviewed studies vary from 35 to 60% male. In the Myers *et al.* (1984) study, the 6-month prevalence of social phobia ranged from 0.9 to 1.7% for males, and from 1.5 to 2.6% for females, suggesting that more females suffer from the disorder. There is no doubt that, in contrast with agoraphobia and the simple phobias, social phobia is common in both men and women.

It is possible that, due to sex-role differences, men may fear different social situations than women. To our knowledge, no studies have addressed this issue.

Duration of the Fears

According to DSM-III-R, social phobia is considered to be chronic. This is confirmed by data from Turner, Beidel, *et al.* (1986). In their sample of 21 social phobics, the mean number of years that they experienced distress in social situations was 20.9, with a range of 5–46 years. Actual avoidance behavior on the average started 15.3 years prior to assessment, ranging from 0–46 years.

Social Class

On the average, social phobics have a better education, belong to a higher social class, and less often report current economic problems than agoraphobic patients (Amies *et al.*, 1983; Persson & Nordlund, 1985; Solyom *et al.*, 1986). In addition, the Amies *et al.* (1983) study pointed out that, in contrast to agoraphobics, 33% of the social phobics were from a higher social class than their parents, which suggests that social phobia may be (partly) the result of uncertainties related to social behavior in "higher" social classes.

Marital Status

Social phobics are less often married than agoraphobics, which is not surprising in view of their problems in social relationships. Amies *et al.* (1983) found

TABLE 3. Sex Differences in Different Phobic Disorders

	Social phobia (%)	Agoraphobia (%)	Simple phobia (%)
Marks & Gelder (1966)	40 (25)	13 (84)	
Shafar (1976)	45 (20)	13 (68)	
Amies *et al.* (1983)	60 (87)	14 (57)	
Thyer *et al.* (1985)	48 (42)	19 (115)	
Solyom *et al.* (1986)	53 (47)	14 (80)	22 (72)
Ost (1987)	35 (80)	13 (100)	20 (190)

Note. Percentages of male patients. Total number of patients is given in parentheses.

that 7% of the social phobics were married, in contrast with 32% of the agora-phobics. In the Persson and Nordlund study (1985) the percentages of married patients were 25% and 50% for social phobics and agoraphobics, respectively. Solyom *et al.* (1986) reported that 58% of the social phobics, 78% of the agorapho-bics, and 71% of the simple phobics were married.

Kinds of Situations Feared

Although the fears of social phobics are essentially the same, that is, the fear of being evaluated and criticized by other people, the situations that evoke anxiety differ. Amies *et al.* (1983) report that in their sample of social phobics the most distressing situation was "being introduced to unfamiliar people," fol-lowed by "meeting people in authority." Next were situations in which the individual felt observed by others (e.g., using the telephone, receiving visitors at home). The most disturbing situation in the Persson and Nordlund (1985) study was eating with others (48%), being in groups—whether or not being urged to speak (48%), and being watched while working (4%). As common forms of the disorder, Heimberg, Dodge, and Becker (1987) mention fear of conversing, par-ticularly in a heterosexual situation or with a person in authority, and fear of asserting oneself.

The Turner, Beidel, *et al.* (1986) study pointed out that the most difficult situation was formal speaking; 81% of their patients reported distressing feel-ings in this situation, while 71% avoided it. Informal speaking was the next most difficult (76% distress, 57% avoidance). Other difficult situations were eating, drinking, and writing in public.

Behavior

With regard to behavior of social phobics generally, two components are to be distinguished: social skills and avoidance behavior. Some studies have dem-onstrated that socially anxious persons are rated as significantly more poorly skilled than nonanxious persons when global measures are used (Arkowitz, Lichtenstein, McGovern, & Hines, 1975; Twentyman & McFall, 1975). However, with respect to specific social skills (e.g., eye contact and total speaking time), results are less conclusive (McFall, 1982; Monti *et al.*, 1984).

With respect to differences in avoidance behavior between social phobics and nonanxious persons, no observational data are available, but some studies used diaries for gathering information. For example, Dodge, Heimberg, Nyman, and O'Brien (1987) employed a behavioral diary for comparing daily heterosocial interactions of students in their natural environment. They found that high-anxious students participated in fewer interactions than low-anxious students, which may be the result of stronger avoidance tendencies. However, total and mean duration of interactions did not differ between groups.

Cognitions

Recent cognitive-behavioral research has isolated a number of differences between socially anxious and nonanxious persons. Social anxiety is characterized by anxious self-preoccupation (Smith, Ingram, & Brehm, 1983). It has been shown that socially anxious persons endorse a high frequency of negative self-statements (Glass, Merluzzi, Biever, & Larsen, 1982) and negatively evaluate the quality of their social performance (Arkowitz, 1977; Edelmann, 1985). Further, socially anxious persons have also been found to be preoccupied with the evaluation of others. Smith *et al.* (1983) demonstrated that anxious self-preoccupation occurred only in a socially evaluative situation.

Social phobics report a number of anticipatory thoughts. Partly, these thoughts are centered around the possibility of showing somatic symptoms in social situations, symptoms that will reveal their distress to other people (e.g., "What if I stutter (blush/sweat/tremble)" (Persson & Nordlund, 1985). This is in contrast with anticipatory thoughts of agoraphobics that deal with the possibility of losing control, fainting, or even dying.

Somatic Symptoms and Psychophysiological Reactions

Compared with nonanxious individuals, socially anxious persons demonstrate significant increases in heart rate and blood pressure during behavioral tasks such as conversation with an opposite-sex confederate and impromptu speech, but during an interaction with a same-sex confederate, no differences on physiological measures between the groups are found (Turner, Beidel, & Larkin, 1986).

It has been shown that the somatic symptoms as experienced by social phobics differ in some respects from those of agoraphobics. Amies *et al.* (1983) found that social phobics complained of blushing and twitching of the muscles, while agoraphobics reported weakness in the limbs, difficulty in breathing and dizziness or faintness. No differences were found between groups in palpitations, tense muscles, dry throat, trembling, and sweating. Similar results were reported by Solyom *et al* (1986), with social phobics complaining of blushing, tremor, and stammering while agoraphobics complained of panic dyspnea and tachycardia.

Restrictions in Daily Life Caused by the Fears

According to DSM-III-R, social phobia "is rarely, in itself, incapacitating," but this is not in line with our clinical experience. Liebowitz *et al.* (1985) found that many social phobic individuals (we suspect especially those that can be characterized as "generalized type") experienced problems in a wide range of areas. With a few social phobics their anxiety leads to inferior or incomplete education. This is illustrated by several of our patients who deliberately went to a school with only boys or only girls because they felt very uncomfortable around the opposite sex. Other problems caused by the fears are inability to work, lack of career advancement, and difficulty in establishing a relationship or marriage. A limited number of social phobics are totally housebound and even unable to use the telephone or see visitors.

Turner, Beidel, *et al.* (1986) pointed out that 85% of the patients felt restricted in school or academic functioning because they were afraid to speak in class or to join clubs or athletic teams; the fears prevented them from being elected to leadership positions, and they missed better grades due to nonparticipation in classroom discussions. A larger amount of the patients (92%) reported significant impairment in occupational functioning. Normal social functioning was restricted in 69%, while 50% of the unmarried individuals were dissatisfied with their heterosexual functioning.

Concomitant Fears

A considerable amount of social phobics mentioned other, nonsocial phobic situations. In the Turner, Beidel, *et al.* (1986) study, 33% reported at least one other fear, most commonly fear of heights and of small animals. A similar figure was reported by Cerny, Himadi, and Barlow (1984). Few social phobics have panic attacks in nonsocial situations, but most do have panic attacks in social situations (Barlow, 1985). Comorbidity data reported by the same research group showed that 48% of the social phobics received an additional diagnosis, most often depression (Barlow, 1985).

Alcohol and Anxiolytic Drug Usage

Socially anxious individuals may be predisposed toward excessive drinking because of alcohol's ability to reduce tension.

Turner, Beidel, *et al.* (1986) found that 52% of their social phobics had at least one alcoholic beverage per week, an observation we do not expect to differ from the data reported by normals. However, 50% of the subjects intentionally used alcohol prior to attending a social event, and 46% used alcohol while at a party to feel more sociable. These data are somewhat difficult to interpret, since, as far as we know, no study has compared alcohol use of normals and social phobics. We expect the main difference between both groups to be found on "anticipatory drinking." An extreme example is that of a 23-year-old man, treated by us. This patient was unable to leave the house unless he had consumed at least 12 bottles of beer.

Amies *et al.* (1983) compared alcohol use of social phobics and agoraphobics and found that 20% of the former group took alcohol in excess, compared to 7% of the latter group. A number of studies have investigated the prevalence of social phobia among alcoholics. Weiss and Rosenberg (1985) found only two social phobics among a sample of 84 alcoholics. In contrast, Mullaney and Trippett (1979) found that 23% of alcoholics had disabling social phobia. Apart from the patients who qualified for the diagnosis of social phobia, another 33% were diagnosed as "borderline social phobics" because they reported distress in social situations but did not show marked avoidance behavior. The age of onset of the phobic symptoms preceded the development of alcohol problems. Smail, Stockwell, Canter, and Hodgson (1984), found that 39% of a sample of 60 alcoholics had suffered from social phobia during their last typical drinking period. Chambless, Cherney, Caputo, and Rheinstein (1987) reported that 40% of alcoholics suffered from anxiety disorders, half of them being social phobics. Nearly two-thirds of the social phobics admitted using alcohol to control anxiety. Although it seems that many socially anxious persons use alcohol as an anxiety reducer, which eventually may result in alcohol dependence, results at present are inconclusive. Patients in the Chambless et al. (1987) study did not acknowledge a causal connection between the anxiety disorder and the onset of alcoholism. Thus, the evidence to date suggests a link between alcohol abuse and social phobia, but the etiological significance is unclear.

Information about the abuse of anxiolytic drugs in social phobia is scarce. Of the subjects in the Turner, Beidel, et al. (1986) study, 52% used these type of drugs to relieve anxiety, while 13.3% reported using drugs prior to attending a social event. In the study by Amies et al. (1983), drug dependence was minimal among social phobics.

ETIOLOGY

Conditioning and Vicarious Learning

The two-stage theory of fear acquisition (Mowrer, 1960) has been influential but has recently come under attack. Clinical observations have shown that this theory is untenable as a uniform theory for the development of clinical phobias (Emmelkamp, 1982). Although the *classical conditioning paradigm* can explain the development of phobias after a traumatic experience, this paradigm is inadequate in explaining the *gradual* development of social phobias, as often appears to be the case (Amies et al., 1983). Ost and Hugdahl (1981) found that 58% of social phobics acquired their phobia as a result of a conditioning experience. They based their conclusion, however, on only two questions in a questionnaire. These two questions do not allow such conclusions to be drawn, since social phobics were only asked whether they could remember if their anxiety started in a *specific* situation. An affirmative answer to such questions does not necessarily mean that classical conditioning is involved. As noted elsewhere (Emmelkamp, 1982), the occurrence of traumatic incidents in the history of a phobic patient, which is in some way related to the development of the phobia, is by itself insufficient evidence that classical conditioning can be held responsible for the acquisition of fear. Further, many persons experience traumatic incidents in social situations *without* subsequently developing a social phobia.

The second stage of the two-stage theory of fear conditioning that holds that *avoidance leads to anxiety reduction* and thus strengthens the avoidance behavior has not been experimentally studied on (social) phobics. However, social phobics usually relate that this is indeed the case.

Another possibility is that social fears are acquired through *vicarious learning*. According to this paradigm, observing others experiencing anxiety in social situations might lead to fear of those situations in the observer. One of our patients, an orthodox religious person, became socially anxious after having observed her father publicly confessing a sin in a full church. Indirect evidence in favor of a vicarious learning interpretation comes from a study by Windheuser (1977), who found a significant similarity of fears reported by mothers and their phobic children, including social phobics. Bruch, Heimberg, Berger and Collins (1988) found that the parents of social phobics avoided social situations themselves, but Ost and Hugdahl (1981) found that in only 12% of their social phobics was vicarious learning responsible for the development of the phobia. It should be noted, however, that a relationship between fears of parents and children can also be the result of processes other than vicarious learning, for example, informational processes, genetic influences, or similar traumatic experiences.

The Skills-Deficits Hypothesis

The skills-deficits hypothesis holds that anxiety experienced in social situations is the result of inadequate handling of these situations. Results of studies investigating whether socially anxious persons are less skillful and less socially competent than nonanxious individuals are inconclusive (Arkowitz, 1977; Beidel, Turner, & Dancu, 1985; Dow, Biglan, & Glaser, 1985). Studies on clinically socially anxious subjects suggest that social skills deficits are of less importance in the etiology of social anxiety than once thought (Edelmann, 1985; Newton, Kindness, & McFadyen, 1983). This suggests that individuals experience social anxiety not because they are unable to behave in a socially competent manner *per se*, but because they *believe* that they are socially inadequate. In a similar vein, Hartman (1983) has argued that the social inadequacy of socially anxious people may be the result of a difference in the attentional focus of high and low socially anxious persons during interpersonal encounters. The socially anxious person is impaired by the effort to divide attention between internal cues (self-deprecatory thinking and perception of autonomic arousal) and external cues in the social situation, while nonanxious persons concentrate on the interpersonal interaction only.

Cognitive Factors

Other influential theories concerning social phobia have been proposed by cognitively oriented clinicians. In their view anxiety reactions in social situations are mediated by faulty cognitions.

Several studies indicate that irrational beliefs are related to social anxiety (Golden, 1981; Goldfried & Sobocinski, 1975; Gormally, Sipps, Raphael, Edwin, & Varvil-Weld, 1981; Sutton-Simon & Goldfried, 1979). These studies are of questionable relevance, because none of them investigated the thoughts of social phobics. More recently, Sanderman, Mersch, van der Sleen, Emmelkamp, and Ormel (1987) and Mizes, Landolf-Fritsche, and Grossman-McKee (1987) found irrational beliefs associated with social anxiety in social phobics. While the results of these studies might indicate that such irrational beliefs are causally related to anxiety evocation in social situations, it is equally plausible that increased emotional arousal in certain situations sensitizes individuals to certain irrational expectancies.

Biological Factors

In the classical conditioning theory of fear acquisition, the importance of biological factors is neglected. Studies conducted by Lader and his coworkers (Lader, 1967; Lader & Mathews, 1968; Lader & Wing, 1966) demonstrated that social phobics evidenced a chronic state of overarousal which was comparable to that of agoraphobics and individuals with anxiety states. Although Lader and Mathews (1968) ascribe a causative role to the high level of arousal in the development of social phobia, the high arousal level could also be a result of the phobia.

A number of studies have investigated the contribution of a genetic component in anxiety disorders. It is now a well-established finding that there is a higher family prevalence of anxiety disorders than would be expected by chance (Torgersen, 1988). The only study on social phobics was reported by Reich and Yates (1988), who found a higher incidence of social phobic family probands among social phobics than among panic patients and normals. However, results of such family studies have to be qualified. First, such studies provide only meager evidence of a genetic disposition, since environmental factors can account equally well for the differences found. Second, there is a serious risk of overdiagnosis when doing family studies in an unblind fashion.

If it is observed that monozygotic twins are more similar than dizygotic twins with regard to anxiety, it is usually considered to be evidence of a genetic contribution, while differences in dizygotic twins are considered to be the result of differences in environmental factors. Several studies found a higher concordance in anxiety for monozygotic twins than for dizygotic twins (Torgersen, 1988), but studies with social phobics are lacking. However, twin studies by Torgersen (1979) and Rose and Dilto (1983) found some support for a genetic contribution to social fears in normals.

Marks (1986) reported that blood-injury phobics had the strongest family history of all anxiety disorders, which suggests that blood-injury phobia may originate in a genetically determined autonomic response. Marks (1986) suggested that some social phobias (e.g., blushing) may also arise from autonomic specificities under genetic control: ". . . when anxious, those with labile blood flow in the cheeks might blush more readily than others, and so be liable to become phobic about blushing" (p. 3).

While there is some evidence that hereditary factors are involved in anxiety disorders, the lack of research with social phobics precludes the drawing of any conclusion. It should be noted, however, that genetic research may be irrelevant to the question of what kind of therapy (biochemical or psychological) is the best choice (Torgersen, 1988).

Parental Attitudes

Atypical parental characteristics have frequently been suggested as antecedents to phobic disorders. For instance, it has been suggested that phobic subjects are extremely dependent and that parental, (not necessarily affectionate) overprotective involvement and lack of care may account for the development of a phobic disorder in the child. These suggestions, however, have mainly been based on clinical observations or experimental studies without controls.

Buss (1980) hypothesized that social anxiety ("shyness") resulted from experiences in childhood and adolescence that foster excessive social-evaluative concerns. According to Buss such hypersensitivity to social-evaluative stimuli may be due to childrearing practices. Parker (1979) made an attempt to investigate the perceived parental attitudes and behavior of social phobic and agoraphobic patients; both groups scored their parents as less caring and as more overprotective than did normal controls. Further analyses revealed that parental rearing practices for social phobics may have differed from those for agoraphobics: "Social phobics scored both parents as low on care and high on overprotection, while agoraphobics differed from controls only in lower maternal care" (Parker, 1979, p. 559). However, in Parker's study, the subjects who constituted the experimental groups had been treated some 5–7 years previously for agoraphobia or social anxiety, without the researcher having established whether these were still the predominant disorders. Parker (1979) suggested that a child exposed to parental characteristics of low care and overprotection, which inhibit the development of a satisfying parent–child bond, might subsequently experience greater difficulty in interpersonal situations: ". . . parental overprotection, by restricting the usual developmental process of independence, autonomy and social competence, might further promote any diathesis to a social phobia" (p. 559).

Arrindell, Emmelkamp, Monsma, and Brilman (1983) also investigated the parental characteristics of phobics. Social phobics (as did simple phobics) scored their parents as low on emotional warmth or care and high on rejection and overprotection, in contrast with agoraphobics, who scored their parents as low on emotional warmth and only their mothers as rejecting. Thus, insufficiency of parental care was found to be more strongly related to social phobia than to agoraphobia.

Bruch et al. (1988) investigated whether parental attitudes influenced social-evaluative threat in phobics. In contrast with agoraphobics, social phobics perceived their parents as having isolated them from social events, as being excessively concerned with the opinion of others, and as being less sociable as a family. In addition, social phobics reported greater social fears and inhibition during adolescence and reported having had fewer dating partners than agoraphobics.

In sum, although all three studies into parental attitudes are limited by their retrospective nature, the results are consistent. Lack of warmth and rejection in combination with overprotection may be precursors of the social-evaluative concern characteristic of social phobia. More definite conclusions can be drawn only when prospective studies have been carried out.

ASSESSMENT

Three-System Approach

It has become commonplace to consider anxiety as a constellation of three different response channels: (1) verbal-cognitive, (2) behavior-motoric, and (3) psychophysiological. The multimethod approach is based on the notion that these three channels are partly independent (discordance) and may change independently from each other in the course of therapy (desynchrony).

There are, indeed, a number of studies that demonstrate that the intercorrelations among (1) self-report scales, (2) behavioral measures, and (3) psychophysiological indices are typically low (Emmelkamp, 1982; Williams, 1985). Self-reports of fear generally correlate moderately with avoidance behavior, but only modestly with autonomic indices (Rachman, 1978). Results of studies into concordance of the three systems of anxiety are difficult to interpret, since often only mildly fearful individuals were used. In clinically severe reactions a greater concordance between the response systems was found (Craske and Craig, 1984; Sallis, Lichstein, & McGlynn, 1980).

The notion of the "triple response mode" has been criticized on methodological grounds (Cone, 1979; Emmelkamp, 1982; Hugdahl, 1981). Cone (1979) called attention to basic flaws in the methodology of studies that investigated relationships among systems: "Research has varied both method of assessment and content area when computing correlations" (p. 87). For example, self-report can consist of such different statements as "I feel heart palpitations" or "I would like to run away." The former self-statement is more likely to be related to heart rate, whereas the latter is probably associated with behavioral indices. However, self-report of anxiety has usually been considered to refer to the "cognitive channel," thus neglecting the specific content of the self-statements. This lack of consistency concerning the definition of the cognitive component is problematic since it makes comparisons between various studies intending to measure the relationship between components difficult. In a similar vein, Hugdahl (1981) has noted that the "cognitive component" may mean at least three different things. The first conceptualization of the cognitive component is that the subject has perceived his or her autonomic arousal and cognitively relabeled it as anxiety. Further, the cognitive component may mean worrying and brooding about the forthcoming fear-provoking event and, finally, the cognitive component may refer to "the thinking style" of the phobic patient when confronted with the phobic stimulus.

To summarize, lack of concordance between the different response systems is at least partly a function of methodological inadequacies associated with the measurement of the different "channels." As noted by Cone (1979): ". . . the conclusions of response system independence (e.g., Lang, 1971) are premature and . . . a sorting out of behavior method confounds would lead to different interpretations" (p. 80).

Assessment of social phobics can be accomplished by several kinds of instruments: (semi) structured interview schedules; self-report measures concerning somatic symptoms, behavioral reactions or cognitive processes; direct behavioral measures; and psychophysiological measures. In the next section a brief overview is given of some commonly used instruments with social phobics.

Interview Schedules

Interview schedules can be general, covering a wide range of psychiatric disorders, or aim more specifically at anxiety disorders. In this category only one instrument is regularly used with social phobics, the Anxiety Disorders Interview Schedule (ADIS). This instrument was developed by Di Nardo *et al.* (1983) and later revised (ADIS-R; Di Nardo *et al.*, 1985). The ADIS-R is aimed at making differential diagnoses among the DSM-III-R anxiety disorder categories, providing brief descriptions of both DSM-III and DSM-III-R criteria. This instrument assesses affective disorders and allows screening for psychosis, substance abuse, and somatoform disorders. When administered by trained interviewers, completion takes about 2 hours. Barlow (1985) studied reliability and comorbidity of the anxiety disorder categories using the ADIS. The interrater agreement was quite high for social phobia (kappa = .91). Thus, experienced clinicians generally do not have difficulty in diagnosing social phobia, in contrast with some other anxiety disorders (e.g., simple phobia) and personality disorders, where reliability figures are generally lower. Interrater reliability of the revised version has yet to be determined.

Self-Report Measures

There are several fear questionnaires that may be used for the assessment of social phobic patients. These can be divided into two groups: *general anxiety and fear questionnaires,* which in clinical practice are particularly useful since they provide information on a wide range of specific phobic situations, and *anxiety and fear questionnaires, that specifically deal with social phobic problems.*

Commonly used general instruments are the Fear Survey Schedule (FSS-III; Wolpe & Lang, 1964), the Fear Questionnaire (FQ; Marks & Matthews, 1979), the Cognitive-Somatic Anxiety Questionnaire (CASQ; Schwartz, Davidson, & Goldman, 1978), the Willoughby Personality Schedule (WPS; Turner, DiTomasso, & Murray, 1980), and the Lehrer–Woolfolk Symptom Questionnaire (Lehrer & Woolfolk, 1982). Instruments that mainly deal with social phobic symptoms are the Social Avoidance and Distress Scale (SADS; Watson & Friend, 1969), the Fear of Negative Evaluation Scale (FNE; Watson & Friend, 1969), the Social Phobia and Anxiety Inventory (SPAI; Turner, Beidel, Dancu, & Stanley, 1989), and the Social Interaction Self Statement Test (SISST, Glass *et al.*, 1982).

Apart from the distinction between general and specific fear questionnaires, another distinction is that between "single-factor" and "multiple-factor" questionnaires. This refers to the fact, mentioned above, that anxiety is not a unitary, unidimensional phenomenon. Factor analyses have pointed out that anxiety symptoms can be grouped along several dimensions that are relatively independent—described roughly as somatic, cognitive, and behavioral anxiety (Barrett, 1972; Lehrer & Woolfolk, 1982). In single-factor questionnaires only one dimension of anxiety responses is covered (e.g., somatic symptoms experienced in a phobic situation). In contrast, in multiple-factor instruments, two or three dimensions are represented.

The Fear Survey Schedule (FSS)

The FSS has been used clinically and experimentally in various forms for over 20 years and has enjoyed considerable prestige among behavior therapists and researchers as a measure of phobic anxiety. This instrument lists 76 fear items that are common in phobic patients. Cognitions and somatic symptoms are excluded. Factor analysis revealed five interpretable factors that to a high degree were generalizable across phobic and nonphobic populations: (1) social anxiety; (2) agoraphobia; (3) fears related to bodily injury, death, and illness; (4) fears of sexual and aggressive scenes; and (5) fear of harmless animals (Arrindell, Emmelkamp, & van der Ende, 1984). Scale reliability for the subscales (Cronbach's coefficient α) were all very high.

The Fear Questionnaire (FQ)

Another general inventory is the Fear Questionnaire (FQ; Marks & Mathews, 1979). This form includes the most common 15 phobias and 5 associated anxiety–depression symptoms found in clinical practice. The phobia score is composed of (1) agoraphobia, (2) social fears, and (2) blood and injury fears. The subscale Social Anxiety consists of the items eating or drinking with other people, being observed or stared at by others, meeting people in authority, receiving criticism, and speaking to a group. The dimension represented is avoidance behavior, and no items refer to cognitions or somatic symptoms. Arrindell *et al.* (1984) factor analyzed the scores on the FQ of various phobic and nonphobic samples and found that *all* items *a priori* hypothesized to load on their respective factors were found to do so in a meaningful fashion; most of the items evidenced very high ($\geq$ .70) loadings on their theoretically related factor and only moderate, and in most cases low ($\leq$ .20), loading on their unrelated counterparts. The FQ was found to possess acceptable temporal stability over a 1-year period. However, the Anxiety-Depression subscale evidenced very low stability, which might be due to the episodic nature of panic attacks and depressed mood. It should be noted, however, that findings from this study and a study by Michelson and Mavissakalian (1983) indicate that small to moderate decreases occur over both relatively short (5–10 weeks) and relatively long (13 months) periods of time (if there have been no interventions).

The Cognitive-Somatic Anxiety Questionnaire (CASQ)

The CASQ consists of two subscales, cognitive and somatic anxiety, each represented by seven items that are rated on a 5-point scale. The cognitive subscale deals with tendencies to worry, tendencies to experience anxiety-provoking thoughts, and with concentration difficulties. The somatic subscale includes physical symptoms of anxiety as well as their effects on behavior.

Some studies investigated the psychometric properties of the CASQ. The originally described subscales (Schwartz *et al.*, 1978) were closely replicated in the results of factor analysis revealing two factors (Delmonte & Ryan, 1983). Internal consistency of the subscales appeared to be satisfactory in a sample of normal volunteers (α = .81 for the somatic subscale, α = .85 for the cognitive subscale). A recent study examined the convergent and discriminant validity of the CASQ with social phobic patients (Heimberg, Gansler, Dodge, & Becker,

1987). Ratings of social phobics were compared with ratings of normals, college students, and patients with chronic pain complaints, reported in studies by De Good, Buckelew, and Tait (1985), Tamaren, Allen, and Carney (1985), and Schwartz *et al.* (1978). It was found that the social phobics on the average had somewhat higher scores on the cognitive subscale than the students and normals, with the chronic pain group reporting the lowest scores. On the somatic subscale the averages of social phobics and college students were equally high, while again the pain patients obtained the lowest scores. Due to the fact that statistical tests of significance could not be conducted because no standard deviations were known for the other groups, the clinical relevance of these findings is unclear. In contrast to the study of Tamaren *et al.* (1985), in which a nonsignificant and small correlation ($r=.26$) between both subscales was found, Heimberg *et al.* (1987) found a significant correlation ($r=.56$), suggesting that somatic and cognitive anxiety as represented here are not independent. One of the conclusions is that more effort has to be spent on developing independent, othogonal subscales prior to using the CASQ as a predictive tool (Heimberg *et al.*, 1987).

The Willoughby Personality Schedule (WPS)

The Willoughby Personality Schedule was developed in 1932 (Willoughby, 1932) for assessing common areas of neurotic reactivity. The majority of the 25 items cover social anxieties in particular. This inventory was hardly used for decades, revised in 1973 (Wolpe, 1973), and only recently have studies employed the original or revised version for assessing social phobics. Factor analysis (Turner *et al.*, 1980) yielded three common factors, labeled "hypersensitivity to interpersonal stress," "labile affect," and "fear of criticism," accounting for 40%, 6.8%, and 4.8% of the variance, respectively.

Studies with regard to discriminant validity have shown that the WPS is able to correctly classify 88% of control subjects and social phobics. In contrast, another study pointed out that the WPS did not discriminate between high- and low-assertive psychiatric patients (Eisler, Miller, & Hersen, 1973), casting doubt on its validity as a measure of assertiveness.

Willoughby (1934) reports a split-half reliability coefficient of .91 and a test–retest correlation of .89. For the revised instrument, coefficient alpha for internal consistency was .82 (Turner *et al.*, 1980). In view of its satisfactory psychometric properties, further research with the WPS as a predictive tool is desirable.

The Lehrer–Woolfolk Symptom Questionnaire

Lehrer and Woolfolk (1982) constructed a questionnaire by drawing and adapting items from the Minnesota Multiphasic Inventory (MMPI) and the Spielberger State–Trait Anxiety Inventory (STAI), supplemented with items based on their own experiences. The choice of their items was based on the hypothesized existence of three orthogonal factors representing three types of anxiety: somatic, cognitive, and behavioral avoidance. After several studies, each with different versions of the list, and subsequent factor analyses, a 36-item inventory remained, consisting of those items which loaded more than or equal to .5 on one of the three rotated factors in the previous study. The somatic dimension is represented by 16 items, such as "I can't catch my breath," "I experience chest pains," and "my stomach hurts." The majority of the 9 items of the behavioral subscale refer to avoidance of social situations; for example, "I try to avoid starting conversations" and "I pass by school friends, or people I know but have not seen for a long time, unless they speak to me first." Finally, examples of the 11 items of the cognitive subscale are, "I am concerned that others might not think well of me" and "I have to be careful not to let my real feelings show."

In two studies, mainly dealing with student samples, the reliability of the subscales appeared to be quite satisfactory (in the first study α ± .85 for all subscales, in the second study α ± .91). Validity of the subscales was examined with normals and with a sample of 67 nonpsychotic neurotic outpatients of psychotherapists. Only items that, according to a t test, discriminated between the students and the patients were included in a principal components analysis. Because no information is given about these clients in terms of DSM-III-R, the relevance of these findings for social phobic populations remains unclear.

Social Avoidance and Distress Scale (SADS) and Fear of Negative Evaluation Scale (FNE)

The SADS (consisting of 28 items) and FNE (30 items) are two separate instruments that specifically deal with social anxiety, each covering different areas. Because in most studies they are used in combination, we discuss them together. They were developed by Watson & Friend in 1969, and since that time, the SADS, designed to measure avoidance of and distress experienced in social situations, and the FNE, covering apprehension about and avoidance of negative evaluation by others, have become the best known and certainly the most widely used instruments for assessment of social anxiety. The items of both questionnaires were based on student statements about social situations. In many studies a cutoff score on the SADS was used to divide subjects into "socially anxious" versus "nonanxious" or "highly anxious" versus "moderately anxious" groups (Beidel, Turner & Dancu, 1985; Cacioppo, Glass, & Merluzzi, 1979; Edelmann, 1985; Kanter & Goldfried, 1979; McCann, Woolfolk, & Lehrer, 1987; Turner et al., 1986). In other studies it was used as a measure of treatment effectiveness (Butler, Cullington, Munby, Amies, & Gelder, 1984; Hall & Goldberg, 1977; Heimberg, Becker, Goldfinger, & Vermilyea, 1985; Marzillier, Lambert, & Kellett, 1976; Stravynski, Marks, & Yule, 1982).

Considering the popularity of these instruments, it is somewhat surprising that few studies have examined their psychometric properties, especially their discriminative and predictive validity with patient groups. Watson and Friend (1969) used both questionnaires only with student groups and found a test–retest reliability of $r = .68$ (SADS) and .78 (FNE). Turner, McCanna, and Beidel (1987) used the SADS and the FNE with a heterogeneous group of 206 patients to examine its ability to discriminate between various anxiety disorders according to DSM-III. They found moderately high correlations with the State–Trait Anxiety Inventory, the Beck Depression Inventory and the SCL-90R General Symptom Index. However, it was shown that both the SADS and the FNE did not differentiate social phobics from other phobic patients, although the mean scores of the former group were somewhat higher than those of the other groups. This implies that the instrument is suitable for assessing emotional distress, but that it may not be able to distinguish between social phobics and other phobic patients (Turner *et al.*, 1987).

Social Phobia and Anxiety Inventory (SPAI)

More recently, Turner, Beidel, Dancu, and Stanley (1989) have developed a new self-report measure of social phobia. It was designed to more precisely match DSM-III-R criteria for social phobia. It consists of 32 items, and there is an additional 13-item agoraphobia subscale in the questionnaire. Test–retest reliability over a 2-week period in a nonclinical sample was high ($r = .86$), and internal consistency as measured by Cronbach's alpha was also good (.96). Students who were socially phobic scored higher than those who were not, and a clinical sample of social phobics scored still higher. The SPAI was also able to discriminate social phobics from other patient groups with different anxiety disorders. Social phobics scored higher than either patients with panic disorders with or without agoraphobia and patients with obsessive–compulsive disorder. In another study, Beidel, Borden, Turner, and Jacob (1989) reported that scores on the SPAI in a clinic sample of social phobics were moderately but significantly correlated with behavioral measures of cognitive and somatic distress in social situations and avoidance of specific social situations.

Cognitive Measures

Given the recent interest in cognitive therapy procedures for anxiety disorders, there has been surprisingly little attention paid to the development of cognitive assessment methods for phobic patients. In general, with cognitive assessment a distinction has to be made in assessment of more general belief systems versus assessment of self-statements: more immediate cognitions which are experienced in specific (phobic) situations. It has been shown that with social phobics both categories do not correlate at all (Sanderman *et al.*, 1987), implying that they refer to different thought contents or processes.

A questionnaire such as the Rational Behavior Inventory (Shorkey & Whiteman, 1977) is an example of the first category and is not particularly suited to assess cognitions associated with specific social phobic situations. For measurement of self-statements several instruments have been developed. In this section we discuss only an instrument with particular relevance to social phobia, namely, the Social Interaction Self-Statement Test (Glass *et al.*, 1982).

The Rational Behavior Inventory (RBI) is a 37-item questionnaire measuring irrational beliefs as defined by Ellis (1962). The total score, a composite of 11 subscales, yields an overall index of rationality. The subscales are: (1) catastrophizing, (2) guilt, (3) perfectionism, (4) need for approval, (5) caring and helping, (6) blame and punishment, (7) inertia and avoidance, (8) independence, (9) self-downing, (10) projected misfortune, and (11) control of emotions. Recently the psychometric properties of the RBI have been evaluated with diverse populations: two community samples ($n = 327$) and a social phobic patient group ($n = 74$) (Sanderman et al., 1987). Results indicate that internal consistency is low for most subscales, which casts doubt on their utility. Test–retest results have been found to be satisfactory. The RBI scores of the social phobics changed significantly during cognitive treatment, indicating that the questionnaire is suitable as an outcome measure for cognitive therapy (Mersch, Bogels, Van der Sleen, & Emmelkamp, 1987).

With regard to measurement of self-statements Clark (1988) follows a categorization proposed by Kendall and Hollon (1981), in which four categories are discriminated: (1) recording methods (e.g., think aloud while in the phobic situation); (2) production methods (e.g., thought listing) in which subjects retrospectively produce their thoughts during a preceding interval; (3) sampling, which involves verbalization of current thoughts when cued by a random signal; and (4) endorsement approaches, in which the individual gets a list with predetermined items and has to indicate whether or not he or she had that thought.

An example of the latter approach is the Social Interaction Self-Statement Test (SISST) developed by Glass et al. (1982). This 30-item questionnaire measures the frequency of positive (facilitative) and negative (inhibitory) self-statements in social situations. This instrument has been used with high and low socially anxious women and psychology students (Glass et al., 1982), with psychiatric outpatients (Merluzzi, Burgio, & Glass, 1984) and with a social phobic population (Dodge, Hope, Heimberg, & Becker, 1988). The last study showed that negative, but not positive, self-statement scores were related to self-report measures of depression and anxiety. No relations were found between physiological or anxiety measures and self-statements during role playing of a personal relevant situation. Interestingly, the SISST was able to discriminate between "private social phobics" (with primary fear for social interactions) and "public social phobics" (primary fear for performing in public).

Behavioral Measures

Assessment of behavior in the phobic situations can be useful in many respects. Due to the discordance of the three anxiety response channels as mentioned above, it is very well possible that changes on self-report measures are not reflected in changes in overt behavior. Second, appropriate assessment of behavior prior to therapy can yield useful information with regard to the most preferable strategy. However, behavioral assessment is accompanied by a lot of methodological problems, especially with regard to the validity of the data produced. It is still an open question whether the behavior of social phobics shows observable differences when compared with that of normals, and whether there is a relationship between the experience of anxiety in social situations and behavior in social situations. Many studies have tried to answer this question, but most of them suffer from serious methodological problems. The majority of them were analog studies, so generalization to clinical populations is questionable. A more critical objection is that all studies used laboratory situations. In contrast with agoraphobia, in which it is possible and relatively easy to assess the behavioral and somatic symptoms in the phobic situation in reality, with social phobia this is more difficult to accomplish. The use of behavioral measures in laboratory situations is based on the assumption that behavior in these situations is quite similar to real-life behavior. However, it has been pointed out that behavior in these tests may be only minimally related to social anxiety (Trower *et al.*, 1978). Additionally, there is increasing evidence that role-played behavior does not accurately represent the behavior shown in more realistic settings (Bellack, Hersen, & Lamparski, 1979; McNamara & Blumer, 1982). Finally, a related problem of role playing is that the behavior of the patient is assessed in only one or a few standard situations, which ignores the fact that a situation that is relevant for one patient may be trivial for another and vice versa. Social phobia often is highly situation specific and idiosyncratic. This implies that standardization, an essential condition in science, is difficult. More fundamental, however, is the fact that social phobics' fears often arise in situations with particular relevance for the individual, situations in which the person has "something to lose." Many individuals at our department report that they do not have many problems when confronted either with strangers or with very familiar persons, but with the group in between: those too familiar to say nothing, but not familiar enough to feel at ease. To assess their behavior when confronted with their most difficult "stimuli" would require involvement of those kind of people in a behavioral test. Even were this possible in the laboratory, the situation would be substantially different from real life.

An examination of the previous studies of behavioral assessment yields two types of role plays, to be characterized roughly as "structured" and "unstructured." In the structured methods the subject is confronted with descriptions of several social situations, situations which are considered to cover a number of important social skills. One of the most standardized and evaluated instruments, the Social Situations Interactions Test (SSIT; Monti, Wallander, Ahern, Abrams, & Munroe, 1983) consists of situations with regard to different social skills (e.g., reacting to critical remarks about delivered work, accepting compliments, being offended by a family member, introducing oneself to a stranger of the opposite sex, and using assertive behavior in a restaurant).

Coding Systems for Behavioral Assessment

Several kinds of behavioral ratings are possible with behavioral measures, varying from very global to very specific. With global measures, also called macro measures, scores are given on several dimensions of the behavior of the subject. Most commonly, judgments are made on social skills and observable distress or anxiety on (semi)continuous scales. With the use of specific, or micro, measures a number of specific behavior components are measured, using frequency counts and/or duration. Caballo, Catena, and Buala (1987) presented a review of 90 studies that used molecular behavioral components. They discriminated between four categories—nonverbal components, paralanguage/vocal components, verbal components, and mixed components—each of them consisting of a large number of behavioral items. Commonly used nonverbal components were gaze/eyecontact (78% of the reviewed studies), response latency (48%), smiles (37%), and gestures (34%). The most frequently used paralanguage component was loudness of voice (43%), followed by talk time (37%) and response duration (31%). With regard to verbal components, most studies used skills such as requests of behavior change, compliance content, praise content, asking questions, and liking content.

Advantages of global ratings of social skills and/or social anxiety are that they are easier to obtain than moleculair measures and seem to have a greater ecological validity. Wallander, Conger, and Ward (1983) showed that training of raters only slightly enhanced the interrater-reliability, implying that untrained peer judges can be used just as well as trained assistants. However, with regard to treatment the molar measures lack sufficient specificity to help sort which behavior needs to be targeted for change, and which specific treatment (e.g., social skills training) should be chosen. On the other hand, molecular measures may be too specific and, beyond this, give no information about the "adequacy" of the observed behavior, so that clinical relevance is limited. Measures based on frequency counts or duration may be less useful for direct application in therapy than measures about the impression a patient makes on other people. Actually, these measures may not be related to each other. For example, talking too much may be equally inappropriate as talking not enough. Another skill with particular relevance to adequate social behavior seems to be timing of responses, which may be as important as the response itself. A quantitative method of assessment is not able to do justice to the reciprocal nature of social interactions (Boice, 1982). Although specific behavioral components can be assessed reliably, studies of micromeasures have produced inconsistent results. While some studies revealed specific behavioral differences between several groups (Conger & Farrell, 1982; Dow, Glaser, & Biglan, 1981; Kupke, Hobbs, & Cheney, 1979), results of others were inconclusive (Arkowitz et al., 1975; Twentyman & McFall, 1975).

In recent studies, attempts have been made to combine the advantages of macro and micro level, a compromise that has received the name "midi-level" measurement. Monti et al. (1984) summarize the differences between midi and micro assessment. Remarkable differences exist in the way in which they are measured (on a rating scale versus frequency/duration counts) and in the fact that midi-levels allow for qualitative judgments by trained clinical raters. Finally, midi-level categories were derived from theories on human ethology (Boice, 1982). In the study of Monti et al. (1984), nine categories of midi-level behaviors were chosen: extremity movements, self-manipulation, facial expression, posture, orienting, gestures, voice, speech rate/pressure, and sense of timing. All behaviors were rated according to an 11-point Likert-type scale, ranging from *not anxious at all* to *extremely anxious*. Results with patient groups showed that all midi-level measurements were reliable and convenient to use, and that they were all correlated with ratings of global anxiety.

To date at least two coding systems at midi-level have been developed and evaluated: the Behavioral Referenced Rating System of Intermediate Social Skills (BRISS; Wallander, Conger, & Conger, 1985), revised by Farrell, Rabinowitz, Wallander, & Curran (1985), and the Intermediate Level Social Skills Assessment Checklist (ILSSAC; Farrell *et al.*, 1985), derived from the same pool of items as the BRISS. Both systems differ in rating procedure: the BRISS is rated on a Likert scale, the ILSSAC on Thurstone scales. Examples of BRISS scales are use of head, use of facial expression, speech delivery, conversation content, personal conversational style and partner-direct behavior. The ILSSAC consists of the same scales, but each of them is represented by a number of items. For instance, items of the conversation content scale are variety of topics covered, uninteresting topics most of the time, and knowledgeable about topics most of the time. In general, both systems showed high interrater reliability and internal consistency, while strong relationships were found between global ratings at the one side and molecular ratings at the other.

Behavioral Approach/Avoidance Tests

Some studies attempted to measure avoidance behavior rather than social skills. The Behavioral Approach/Avoidance Test (BAT) is not a specific instrument but an assessment strategy which can be used in different ways. With social phobics generally an individually tailored list of difficult social situations is constructed. The subject is asked to rate each situation on difficulty, thereby making a hierarchy. For BAT assessment, each item of the list, starting with the easiest one, is described, and the subject is asked whether this item could be attempted. The position in the hierarchy of the item completed and a rating of anxiety experienced when this item is undertaken are usually recorded (Mattick & Peters, 1988; Mattick, Peters, & Clarke, 1988; Shaw, 1979). Theoretically, physiological measures could be taken during the behavioral test, but this has not yet been done with social phobics. Reliability and validity of this measure is unknown. Further, a number of disadvantages preclude its clinical use, the most important being that such a test is difficult and expensive to implement when an independent observer has to accompany the patient in the phobic situation. If not, then this measure can better be considered as a self-report rather than as a pure behavioral measure.

Psychophysiological Measures

Few studies have used psychophysiological measures with social phobics, but reliability and validity of such measures is questionable. Results from a study by Arena, Blanchard, Andrasik, Cotch, & Myers (1983) cast serious doubts upon the reliability of psychophysiological measures. Heart rate was found to be not quite reliable and skin conductance appeared completely unreliable over time. To quote Arena *et al.*: "If subjects can one day respond with a heart rate of 65 beats per minute to a stressful stimulus and the next day respond with a heart rate of 124 beats per minute, what clinical utility is a psychophysiological measure?". Holden and Barlow (1986) assessed the reliability and validity of heart rate as a measure of anxiety in agoraphobia during an *in vivo* standardized behavioral avoidance test. The test–retest reliability for heart rate was low. In addition, not only phobics but also *non*phobic control were found to improve over the course of time on heart rate! Results by Arena *et al.* (1983) and Holden and Barlow (1986) suggest a cautious use of physiological assessment with phobic patients.

At present, there is little reason to recommend psychophysiological assessment as routine practice with social phobics. Although a few recent studies suggest that such psychophysiological indices may have prognostic utility (Jerremalm, Jansson, & Ost, 1986; Ost, Jerremalm, & Johansson, 1981), results at present are far from conclusive, and the lack of reliability and validity of the measures used suggest caution in the interpretation of the results from these studies. Turner, Beidel, and Larkin (1986) found that psychophysiological arousal (heart rate and blood pressure) was differentially mediated by specific social interactions. Apart from the methodological issues discussed above, there are also theoretical issues that limit the applicability of psychophysiological measurement. For instance, heart rate, a measure which is now widely used in treatment research studies may reflect other processes than fear. Several studies in the area of social anxiety indicate that *non*socially anxious subjects react with increased heart rate when they have to deliver a speech. For example, Lang, Levin, Miller and Kozak (1983) found that snake phobics generated an equally marked heart rate change during speech exposure as speech-anxious subjects. As Lang *et al.* note, the cardiovascular demand required by a speech task is so pronounced that it may mask any evidence of an affective component in this system.

It may be worthwhile to investigate the utility of other physiological measures than those currently used. Tyrer and Lader (1976) have suggested that physiological measurement directly concerned with cerebral functions (resting electroencephalogram and averaged evoked potentials) may be better correlates of anxiety than heart rate, but studies with social phobics to support this claim are lacking.

Psychophysiological indices can only be recommended as measures when they can be reliably measured over time and are found to discriminate between social phobics and normal subjects when confronted with the phobic situation. And even then, it is questionable whether these measures would significantly add information to what is much more easily obtained by behavioral measures and self-report of anxiety, including self-report of awareness of physiological arousal. In sum, using psychophysiological assessment is very time consuming and costly with questionable reliability and validity.

Treatment of Social Phobia

Psychopharmacological Treatment

Although most social phobics do take psychopharmacological drugs, the effects of these drugs for this specific disorder have hardly been investigated.

The following types of drugs will be discussed: benzodiazepines, MAO inhibitors and beta-blockers. Trycyclic antidepressants have not yet been evaluated with social phobics.

Benzodiazepines

Benzodiazepines (e.g., diazepam) are presumable most commonly prescribed for social phobics, although to the best of our knowledge the effects with this category of patients have never been assessed in a controlled study. One study using volunteers with musical performance anxiety as subjects found diazepam inferior to the beta-blocker nadolol. Actually, diazepam was found to slightly impair performance. Apart from case studies (Lydiard, Laraia, Howell, & Ballenger, 1988), alprazolam (Xanax) has not yet been evaluated with social phobics. Alprazolam is known to produce serious dependency problems. In a study by Fyer et al. (1987), over half of the patients were unable to stop taking alprazolam when requested. In addition, nearly all patients experienced panic attacks after drug discontinuation. In another study (Lydiard, Laraia, Ballenger, & Howell, 1987), one-third of the patients became depressed after taking alprazolam. Given the lack of research and the dependency problems associated with long-term use of benzodiazepines, the automatic prescription of these drugs does not seem to be justified.

MAO Inhibitors

A number of studies with mixed phobics evaluated the effects of MAO inhibitors (phenelzine), but these contained heterogeneous samples, including other phobics (most often agoraphobics) (Mountjoy, Roth, Garside, & Leitch, 1977; Solyom et al., 1973; Solyom, Solyom, LaPierre, Pecknold, & Morton, 1981; Tyrer, Candy, & Kelly, 1973). Generally, small but significant effects were found for phenelzine, which need to be qualified in several ways. First, most studies instructed patients to expose themselves in vivo between treatment sessions. Thus, the effects of phenelzine have not been assessed independently of the effects of exposure in vivo. Second, discontinuation of medication generally leads to relapse (Solyom et al., 1973; Tyrer et al., 1973). Third, the serious side effects associated with the interaction of this type of drug with foods containing high concentration of amines preclude its widespread use. Finally, conclusions with respect to social phobia are not warranted, since the results were not reported separately for the different types of phobias.

Beta-Blockers

It has been suggested that beta-adrenergic blocking agents are useful in the treatment of anxiety disorders when somatic manifestations of anxiety are prominent. Thus, beta-blockers are of particular interest with social phobics who experience many somatic symptoms, including palpitations, sweating, trembling, and blushing. Not surprisingly, the majority of drug studies with social anxiety have evaluated the effects of various beta-blockers with these patients.

In Table 4, results of clinically relevant studies are summarized. All studies compared a beta-blocker with either placebo or some other type of drug. In the studies on stage fright, volunteers with musical performance anxiety were treated. Only two studies (Falloon *et al.*, 1981; Liebowitz *et al.*, 1985) involved real social phobic patients. As shown in Table 4, all beta-blockers given in a single dose before performance were found to be more effective than placebo. However, results of beta-blockers when regularly administered with clinically social phobics are inconclusive. In the study by Falloon *et al.* (1981), propanolol was no more effective than placebo. Liebowitz *et al.* (1985) found no difference between atenolol and phenelzine (MAOI), but the lack of a placebo control group and methodological confounds (open study, no random assignment) preclude the drawing of conclusions. Beta-blocking drugs are contraindicated in patients with bronchial asthma, patients who are prone to hypoglemic reactions, and patients with congestive heart failure and brachycardia (Noyes, 1988). In sum, there is little evidence yet that psychopharmacological drugs are effective in the treatment of social phobia.

Psychological Treatment

Historical Perspective

In the early days of behavior therapy, it was assumed that anxiety must be inhibited before avoidance behavior can be reduced. This assumption is based on the two-stage theory of Mowrer (1960). In Mowrer's view, classically conditioned fear motivates avoidance behavior, which leads to a reduction of fear and a strengthening of the avoidance behavior (negative reinforcement). According to this theory, anxiety and avoidance are causally linked, and avoidance behavior should be reduced as soon as anxiety is eliminated. However, the two-stage theory of learning is now untenable as a uniform theory for the functioning of phobic behavior (Emmelkamp, 1982).

Systematic desensitization is aimed at changing the classically conditioned fear. In systematic desensitization patients are first trained in muscular relaxation and then move gradually up a hierarchy of anxiety-arousing situations while remaining relaxed. Although desensitization may be applied either in imagination or *in vivo*, most studies involved the imaginal variant. According to Wolpe (1963), "there is almost invariably a one-to-one relationship between what the patient can imagine without anxiety and what he (or she) can experience in reality without anxiety." However, patients who have been successfully desensitized in imagination nevertheless become anxious when confronted with the phobic situation *in vivo* (e.g., Agras, 1967; Barlow, Leitenberg, Agras, & Wincze, 1969).

Flooding therapies are derived from the work of Stampfl (Stampfl & Levis, 1967) on implosive therapy. The therapist tries to maximize anxiety throughout treatment, which eventually leads to "extinction." Sessions are continued until a significant reduction in anxiety is achieved. As in the case of systematic desensitization, it is assumed that if anxiety is inhibited, the avoidance behavior will

TABLE 4. Summary of Studies on Drugs in Social Anxiety

Study	Disorder	Population[a]	N	Drug type	Design	Conclusions[b]
Brantigan et al. (1982)	Stage fright	V	29	(1) propanolol[c] (40 mg) (2) placebo	Double-blind Crossover	1 > 2
Falloon et al. (1981)	Social phobia	P	12	(1) propanolol (160–320 mg) (2) placebo	Double-blind Between-group	1 = 2
James et al. (1977)	Stage fright	V	24	(1) oxprenolol[c] (40 mg) (2) placebo	Double-blind Crossover	1 > 2
James et al. (1983)	Stage fright	V	30	(1) pindolol[c] (5 mg) (2) placebo	Double-blind Crossover	1 > 2 on anxiety 1 = 2 on performance
James & Savage (1984)	Stage fright	V	33	(1) nadolol[c] (40 mg) (2) dizaepam[c] (2 mg) (3) placebo	Double-blind Crossover	1 > 2 & 3
Liden & Gottfried (1974)	Stage fright	V	15	(1) alprenolol[c] (50 & 100 mg) (2) placebo	Double-blind Between-group	1 > 2
Liebowitz et al. (1985)	Social phobia	P	21	(1) atenolol (50–100 mg) (2) phenelzine (60–90 mg)	Open study Between-group	1 = 2 Patients not randomized Results not assessed blindly
Neftel et al. (1982)	Stage fright	V	22	(1) atenolol[c] (100 mg) (2) placebo	Double-blind Between-group	1 = 2 > 2 on anxiety 1 = 2 on performance

[a]V = volunteers; P = patients.
[b]1 > 2, treatment 1 superior to treatment 2; 1 = 2, treatment 1 equally as effective as treatment 2.
[c]single dose before performance.

change accordingly. For a detailed discussion of implosive and flooding procedures the reader is referred to Emmelkamp (1982).

In the early days of *exposure in vivo*, guidelines for conducting treatment were derived from implosion and flooding theory. It was thought to be essential that anxiety should be maximized during exposure *in vivo* before extinction or habituation could occur. In the first controlled study that included flooding *in vivo* with phobic patients (Marks, Boulougouris, & Marset, 1971), therapists tried to evoke anxiety deliberately. However, subsequent studies indicate that the inclusion of horrifying stimuli during flooding in imagination does not enhance the effectiveness of this procedure. Rather, it seems that flooding without such cues is more effective (Emmelkamp, 1982). Hafner and Marks (1976) compared exposure *in vivo* with high anxiety to exposure *in vivo* with low anxiety. In the high-anxiety condition, the therapist tried to induce anxiety by statements such as: "Imagine yourself feeling worse and worse, giddy, sweaty, nauseated, as if you are to vomit any moment. You fall to the floor half-conscious; people gather round you; someone calls for an ambulance." Although patients in the high-anxiety condition experienced more anxiety during treatment than patients in the low-anxiety condition, *no* differences in improvement were found between both conditions. Thus, deliberately inducing anxiety during exposure *in vivo* did not enhance improvement.

According to operant theory, reinforcement of approach behavior will lead to an increase in that behavior. Leitenberg and his colleagues have investigated the effects of positive social reinforcement on the approach behavior of phobic patients. This procedure has been called *shaping*, successive approximation, or reinforced practice. In contrast with imaginally based procedures, such as systematic desensitization and flooding, the avoidance behavior is changed directly; this eventually may lead to a decrease of anxiety (Leitenberg, Agras, Butz, & Wincze, 1971). However, this approach has not been evaluated with social phobics.

Generally, three models are distinguished to explain the maintenance of social phobic complaints. The *skills-deficit model* asserts that social anxiety results from a lack of social skills within the patients behavioral repertoire, for example, through faulty socialization processes. According to this model, the appropriate goal of treatment should be to teach patients the skills they lack. A lot of patients, however, show adequate social skills, but feel restricted in social situations by anxiety that has become conditioned to interpersonal settings. According to *the conditioned-anxiety model*, the principal goal of treatment should be the direct reduction of social anxiety and avoidance through procedures aimed at anxiety reduction. Finally, *the cognitive inhibition* model suggests that maladaptive cognitions rather than skills deficit or conditioned anxiety are responsible for the problems in social situations. The emphasis on various aspects of social anxiety has led to a number of different strategies: systematic desensitization, flooding and exposure *in vivo* for focusing on anxiety reduction modeling and behavior rehearsal for social skills training, and several cognitive procedures like rational-emotive therapy and self-instructional training for altering the negative cognitions.

In the last 20 years several studies have been published in which the treatment of socially anxious subjects is described. However, implications of these findings for treatment of social phobics are often unclear, due to the fact that (1) most studies did not deal with patient groups but with students or community residents and (2) in those studies that did use real patients, samples consisted of various psychiatric diagnoses, including other anxiety disorders and personality disorders. Since introduction of social phobia in DSM-III, more homogenous samples have been treated, but until now controlled studies with this group are still limited. However, drawing of conclusions is preliminary, firstly because of the methodological problems associated with some of the studies; secondly because, compared with the number of studies, variability among them is considerable (Heimberg, 1989; Emmelkamp & Scholing, 1989). Table 5 summarizes results of studies with clinically socially-anxious or social phobic patients.

Systematic Desensitization (SD)

Several studies in the 1970s have evaluated the effects of SD with social phobic patients (Hall & Goldberg, 1977; Marzillier *et al.*, 1976; Shaw, 1979; Trower *et al.*, 1978; van Son, 1978). In general, only limited clinical improvements were achieved. In a study by Gelder *et al.* (1973) with a mixed sample of phobics, it was noticed that desensitization appeared to lead to a particularly poor response in the social phobics. Results of studies dealing with real patients contrast with those using analog populations. In the latter studies desensitization has consistently been found to be effective in the treatment of social anxiety, but with social phobic patients this strategy is of limited value.

Flooding

Only one study examined the effect of flooding in comparison with those of desensitization and social skills training with social phobics (Shaw, 1979). Patients in all conditions showed some improvement, while no differences between the treatment strategies were found. Results are somewhat difficult to interpret since no control group was included, and most of the outcome measures were not validated (5-point rating scales). Considering these results and the fact that flooding is a very upsetting treatment strategy for the patient, we advise against its use with social phobic patients.

Social Skills Training

Principles and Components of Social Skills Training. Anxiety experienced in social situations may be the result of inadequate handling of these situations. A patient may lack the skills to initiate conversations or to handle him- or herself in groups. If it is assumed that such lack of social skills provokes anxiety, then anxiety may be overcome through social skills training. Common ingredients of skills training are instruction of appropriate skills, modeling by the therapist or, in a group, by other patients, behavior rehearsal by means of role playing, and practicing newly learned skills in the patients natural environment.

TABLE 5. Studies Comparing Treatment Effectiveness on Social Phobics

Study	Population and problem	N	Treatment[a]	Therapy	Sessions[b]	Length of follow-up	Results[c]
Argyle et al. (1974)	Difficulties in mixing with other people	16	(1) SST (2) Psychotherapy (3) No-treatment (crossover)	Individual	6 × 60 18 × 60	6 weeks 12 months	1 and 2 > 3 in improving interpersonal behavior. 1 = 2 at posttest. 1 > 2 at 6-week follow-up.
Marzillier et al. (1976)	Both social anxiety and social skills deficits	21	(1) SD (2) SST (3) Waiting list	Individual	15 × 45	6 months	1 = 2 = 3 in anxiety reduction, improving clinical adjustment. 2 > 1 and 3 in improving social lives.
Hall & Goldberg (1977)	Socially anxious patients	30	(1) SD (2) SST	Individual	9 × ?	3 months	1 = 2 in improving social anxiety. 2 > 1 in improving problem behavior. 1 > 2 in improving participation.
Falloon et al. (1977)	Social skills deficits (18 social phobics)	51	(1) Discussion (2) SST (3) SST + homework	Group	10 × 75	16 months (range, 12–24)	3 > 2 > 1
Trower et al. (1978)	Social inadequacies (20) Social phobics (20)	40	(1) SD (2) SST	Individual	10 × 75–90 10 × 90–105	6 months	Social inadequacies, 2 > 1. Social phobics, 1 = 2.
Van Son (1978) Study I	Social inadequacies	52	(1) SD (2) SST (3) SD + SST (4) SST + SD (5) SST (6) Waiting list	Individual Group	12 × 60 12 × 150	1 month	1 = 2 = 3 = 4 = 5 = 6

Study	Diagnosis	N	Treatment		Sessions	Follow-up	Results
... Study II		17	(1) SD (2) SST (3) Waiting list	Individual	12 × 60	1 month	2 > 1 and 3
Shaw (1979)	Social phobics	30	(1) SD (2) Flooding (3) SST	Individual	10 × 60 10 × 60 10 × 75	6 months	1 = 2 = 3
Ost et al. (1981)	Outpatients with major problem social anxiety in a wide range of social situations: behavioral reactors (16) vs. physiological reactors (16)	40	(1) AR (2) SST	Individual	10 × 60	—	Behavioral reactors: 2 > 1 on 6 out of 10 measures. Physiological reactors: 1 > 2 on 3 out of 10 measures.
Stravynski et al. (1982)	Socially dysfunctional outpatients	22	(1) SST (2) SST + COG	Individual Group	12 × 90	6 months	1 = 2 at any time on all measures.
Butler et al. (1984)	Social phobics (DSM-III)	45	(1) EXP (2) EXP + AM (3) Waiting list	Individual	7 × 60 weekly	6 months	At posttest: 1 and 2 > 3. 2 > 1 on cognitive measures. At 6-month follow-up: 2 > 1 on other measures.
Alström et al. (1984)	Social phobics	42	B B + prolonged EXP B + relaxation B + supportive t.	Individual	9 ×	9 months	1 = 3 2 and 4 > 1 and 3 2 > 4 on global rating
Emmelkamp, Mersch, Vissia, & v.d. Helm (1985)	Social phobics (DSM-III)	34	EXP RET SIT	Group	6 × 150 weekly	1 month	at PT: 1 = 2 = 3 on anxiety 1 > 2, 3 on pulse rate 2, 3 > 1 on cognitive measures
Heimberg et al. (1985)	Social phobics (DSM-III)	7	Combination of EXP and CR	Group	14 × 90	3/6 months	No comparison between strategies. Significant improvements on all measures.

(continued)

TABLE 5. (Continued)

Study	Population and problem	N	Treatment[a]	Therapy	Sessions[b]	Length of follow-up	Results[c]
Jerremalm et al. (1986)	Outpatients with major problem anxiety in a wide range of social situations: cognitive reactors (19) vs. physiological reactors (19)	43	(1) AR (2) SIT (3) Waiting list	Individual	10 × 60 weekly	—	Physiological reactors: 1 = 2. Cognitive reactors: 2 > 1 on 4 of 11 measures.
Mersch et al. (1989)	Social phobics (DSM-III-R): cognitive reactors (19) behavioral reactors (19)	74	(1) SST (2) COG	Group	8 × 150 weekly	Not yet available	No differential effects found.
Mattick & Peters (1988)	Social phobics (DSM-III)	51	(1) EXP (t.g.) (2) EXP + COG	Small group	6 × 120 2 weekly	3 months	2 > 1 on endstate functioning, increasing behavioral approach, decreasing self-rated avoidance.
Mattick et al. (1988)	Social phobics (DSM-III)	43	(1) EXP (t.g.) (2) COG (3) EXP (t.g.) + COG	Group	6 × 120 2 weekly	3 months	At posttest: 1 and 3 > 2 on BAT. At follow-up: 3 > 2 = 1. No differences on self-report.
Scholing & Emmelkamp (1989)	Social phobics (DSM-III-R)	9	(1) EXP-RET-SST (2) RET-SST-EXP (3) SST-EXP-RET (4) RET-EXP-SST (5) SST-RET-EXP (6) EXP-SST-RET	Individual	3 × (6 × 60)	1 month	All treatment strategies comparable results. In general largest improvement after first treatment phase.

[a]AM = anxiety management, AR = applied relaxation, B = basal therapy, Bat = behavioral approach test, COG = cognitive therapy, COMB = combination, EXP (t.g.) = exposure in vivo (therapist-guided), FU = follow-up, RET = rational emotive therapy, SD = systematic desensitization, SIT = self-instructional training, SST = social skills training, PT = posttest, SM = stress management.

[b]a > b = Treatment a superior to treatment b.

Empirical Results of Social Skills Training. There is some evidence that, at least for a number of social phobics, skills training leads to beneficial effects. However, the evidence in favor of this approach is far from conclusive. Several studies could not find consistent differences between systematic desensitization and social skills training (Hall & Goldberg, 1977; Shaw, 1976; Trower *et al.*, 1978), while other studies demonstrated the superiority of social skills training above systematic desensitization (Marzillier *et al.*, 1976; von Son, 1978) and group psychotherapy (Falloon, Lindley, McDonald, & Marks, 1977).

Although it is assumed that the effective component of skills training is acquisition of adequate skills, it is still unclear whether this is indeed the way it works. At first, social phobics and normals may not differ in their behavioral competence *per se*, but in their evaluation of their own performance: social phobics (wrongly) consider themselves as less socially competent than normals. Second, it should be noted that exposure *in vivo* may account for part of the effects achieved with social skills training. It is quite possible that modeling is superfluous with most social phobics and that the essential therapeutic ingredients are repeated behavior rehearsal *in vivo* (exposure) in the group and the structured homework practice involving real-life rehearsal in feared situations. Further studies are needed to solve this issue.

Exposure in Vivo

Principles of Exposure In Vivo. Graduated exposure *in vivo* has proved to be an effective method of reducing phobic reactions (Emmelkamp, 1982). It is based on the principle that fearful subjects try to avoid situations that evoke anxiety reactions and that this avoidance behavior is reinforced by anxiety reduction, thereby maintaining the phobic reaction. In exposure treatment the individual is stimulated to enter fearful situations again, given the rationale that although in the beginning anxiety will increase, with long enough exposure it eventually will decrease. In exposure treatment it is essential for the individual to stay in the difficult situation until the anxiety indeed diminishes. It is also important that the fearful situations gradually become more difficult (more anxiety provoking). Examples of exposure assignments for social phobics are the following:

1. Go to a hi-fi store (not in a department store) and let a clerk inform you extensively about color TV sets. Inquire about the advantages and disadvantages of the different makes, the longevity, the price and guarantee, etc.
2. Go to a supermarket and buy one article, hold the right amount of money in your hand and ask another customer if you could go first at the checkout counter. If the answer is "no," try again at another counter.
3. Go to a travel agency and inquire about trips to Portugal for a certain period of time previously decided upon. You want to go as cheaply as possible. Ask, for example, whether it is possible to travel by charter flight without having to take an all-inclusive trip.
4. Go to an established record shop and ask one of the assistants for

medieval music. Select one record from this category and ask to listen to it. Listen to a part of it. Do not buy anything.

5. Visit a busy department store with a clock section. Set off at least one of the alarm clocks. Do not buy it.
6. Buy a piece of cheese in a busy shop and ask if you may taste it first.
7. Ask a number of people in the street where they bought their coat, bag, tie, etc.
8. Go into a bar and start a conversation with a stranger.
9. Invite one of your neighbors to have a drink at your home.
10. Go to a bar and ask to use the phone. Only use the phone; do not order anything.
11. Enter a shoe store. Ask someone to help you. Try on at least five pairs of shoes, but do not buy any.
12. Stand in line at the supermarket and give the person in front of you a compliment.
13. Go into a store and change a 20-dollar bill and a 5-dollar bill for two 10s and five 1s. Do not buy anything.
14. Walk in a straight line through a busy street. Do not step aside for anyone and look passersby straight in the eyes.
15. During coffee break at work tell fellow employees something about a book you've read or a movie you've seen. Ask other people whether they read/saw it too and what their opinion was.
16. Gather information about different kinds of clubs (sports, aerobics, astrology, photo clubs, stage clubs, etc.) and ask whether it is possible to come for an introductory lesson. Visit a club that seems interesting to you.

Butler (1985, 1989) discussed a number of difficulties of exposure-*in-vivo* treatment with social phobia, that are summarized here: (1) Most social situations are very unpredictable (mainly because of the social interaction processes involved), which makes it almost impossible to specify the nature and difficulty of exposure tasks in advance; (2) Many social situations have an intrinsic time limit, thus patients are often not exposed long enough for anxiety reduction to occur. Introducing oneself to other people or being criticized by others are examples of such situations; (3) Many social phobic patients report that they avoid relatively few situations, but nevertheless stay anxious; (4) In contrast with agoraphobia, where the central fear is losing control or fainting, social phobics fear negative evaluation from others. While exposure provides evidence to agoraphobics that their fears do not come true, social phobics still lack information about the impression they make on other people, despite the exposure to the social situations.

These findings have important implications for exposure treatment with social phobics. First, instead of formulating just one hierarchy of difficult situations, it may be more appropriate to make several hierarchies, each centered around one common theme (e.g., working while observed by others, informal contacts with other people, or heterosexual situations). These hierarchies can be exercised separately, one by one, but in most cases it will be more practical and effective to combine them. Second, instead of stressing the importance of staying *long enough* in the situation for the anxiety to decrease, the emphasis in some cases should be placed on entering situations *frequently* enough for anxiety reduction to occur. In the same way, strong emphasis has to be placed on the *amount of practice* instead of the *difficulty of each task.*

Although social phobics may not avoid social situations *per se,* clinical practice points out that they show more subtle avoidance behavior *in* the situation: they behave in such a way that they prevent themselves from being the center of attention and from being criticized. Examples of such behavior are: sitting back in a group, not asking questions in a meeting, and excusing oneself when there is no reason for it. Continuous talking may be another way to hold control over the situation and prevent other people from asking difficult questions. This implies that, prior to specifying tasks for exposure hierarchies, very detailed information has to be gathered about more subtle avoidance behavior, by asking what the individual especially fears in social situations and what he or she does to preclude this from occurring. Fear of negative evaluation by others may be reduced by exposure to criticism, for example, in group therapy or by assignments to behave ridiculously. However, this may be unethical, impractical, and may not be necessary. According to Butler (1985), "fear of negative evaluation is more likely to be reduced by a demonstration that it does not occur than by exposure to criticism" (p. 655).

Empirical Results with Exposure in Vivo. The number of studies that evaluated effectiveness of exposure *in vivo* without addition of other strategies is limited. As was mentioned above, in several studies in which social skills training was applied, several exposure elements were included too, so that in fact a combined treatment was given, especially in group treatments.

Falloon *et al.* (1981) reported a pilot study with 16 socially anxious outpatients. Treatment was aimed at maximizing rehearsal in real-life settings and was conducted in small groups, each consisting of two patients and one nonprofessional therapist. After behavior rehearsal of problem situations at the clinic, the same behavior was repeatedly rehearsed in real-life situations. Results of this (time-intensive) 4-week program were similar to that achieved with social skills training conducted over a 10-week period (Falloon *et al.*, 1977).

Emmelkamp, Mersch, Vissia, and van der Helm (1985) compared (1) exposure *in vivo,* (2) rational-emotive therapy, and (3) self-instructional training with socially anxious outpatients. Treatment was conducted in small groups. In the exposure-*in-vivo* sessions, patients had to confront their feared situations in the group. For example, patients who were afraid of blushing had to sit in front of others with an open-necked blouse until anxiety dissipated. Others who feared that their hands would tremble had to write on the blackboard and to serve tea to the group. All patients had to give speeches in front of the group. An important part of treatment consisted of actual exposure in real social situations in the town center. Patients had to perform a number of difficult assignments, such as making inquiries in shops and offices, speaking to strangers, or visiting bars. Specific examples have been given above. Role playing was not applied.

Each of the three therapeutic procedures resulted in significant decrements in anxiety at posttesting, which were either maintained or improved upon at follow-up. In contrast to the result of studies with agoraphobics, where exposure *in vivo* was found to be significantly superior to cognitive interventions, the results with social phobics do not reveal many significant differences. Interestingly, only the cognitive treatment revealed significant changes in cognitions as measured by the Irrational Beliefs Test, thus demonstrating the construct validity of the cognitive treatment. Different effects found after the various treatments suggest that the treatments did not produce gains solely due to a placebo effect. Exposure was found to lead to a significant reduction in pulse rate, which is in line with an explanation of the effects of exposure in terms of habituation. On the other hand, exposure did not lead to a change in irrational cognitions, while the irrational beliefs did improve after cognitive treatment. Thus, changes in dependent measures were restricted to those consonant with the treatment approach.

Butler *et al.* (1984) compared effectiveness of exposure, either alone or in combination with anxiety management. All patients were social phobics according to DSM-III (persons with avoidant personality disorder were excluded). Patients were randomly assigned to the two treatment conditions or the waiting-list control group. The (individual) treatment consisted of seven weekly sessions. Exposure was self-controlled, and patients had to practice homework assignments for 1 hour a day. In the anxiety management, patients learned to control their symptoms of anxiety by relaxation, distraction, and rational self-talk, following the training as described by Suinn and Richardson (1971). The amount of exposure was equal in both treatment conditions, the remaining time in the exposure-alone condition being filled up with nonspecific associative therapy. The results at posttest show that both treatment groups were improved significantly in comparison with the control group. At posttest, the combination of exposure and anxiety management showed significantly more improvement only on the more cognitive measures, while at follow-up similar differences between both groups were found on the majority of the other self-report measures. Although these results seem to support the use of a combination of several techniques, it has to be noted that the effects of adding anxiety management procedures were not substantial and only reached significance at 6-months follow-up. This may be due to several factors, including the small numbers of patients and the brevity of the treatment.

Mattick *et al.* (1988) investigated the effects of (1) therapist-guided exposure *in vivo*, (2) cognitive therapy, and (3) a combination of these two techniques. All three treatments proved to be more effective than a waiting-list condition. At posttest there were few significant differences between the three treatment groups. Results corroborate the results of the Emmelkamp *et al.* (1985) study in that exposure and cognitive therapy were found to be equally effective. Interestingly, at posttest there was a superiority for both the exposure treatment and the combined procedure on the behavioral test. However, at 6-months follow-up the combined procedure had maintained its improvement on this measure, the cognitive group had made further improvement, while the exposure group had deteriorated. These last findings were not paralleled by a worsening on self-report measures.

In a partial replication of this study (Mattick & Peters, 1988), the combined treatment procedure was again found to be superior to exposure alone. Interestingly, in both studies a change between pretest and posttest on fear of negative evaluation predicted outcome at follow-up. Thus, the results of the studies by Mattick *et al.* suggest that the thought pattern of social phobics must change for improvements to endure. An integrative treatment approach addressing both the irrational beliefs of these patients and their avoidance behavior looks promising.

Scholing and Emmelkamp (1989) evaluated the effects of exposure *in vivo*, cognitive therapy, and assertive training in a within-subject design with nine social phobics. Thus, patients received all three treatments, but in a different order. Each treatment was applied during six sessions spread over 4 weeks. Periods of 4 weeks without treatment elapsed between the various treatment phases. No single treatment appeared superior to the others, but each treatment enhanced the effect of the other treatments, which suggests that a combination of various techniques should be considered.

Cognitive Therapy

Some Remarks about Cognitive Therapy with Social Phobics. The use of cognitive strategies within the treatment of social phobics has increased recently. Several variants of cognitive therapy (for example, rational emotive therapy, self-instructional training, and anxiety-management procedures) were used in experimental studies, the results of which have been discussed above. At this point, only some general remarks about the application of these strategies will be made. According to the definition of social phobia in DSM-III-R, the fear of negative evaluation plays a central role. Butler (1989) distinguishes the following four sets of concerns: (1) developing intimate relationships, (2) more general personal acceptability or social worth, (3) contact with people in authority, and (4) performance in public. We feel that one major concern should be added, namely, concern about showing bodily symptoms like blushing, trembling, or sweating in social situations. This concern may be associated with all kinds of social situations. An important central feature of the concern about showing bodily symptoms is a vicious circle in which the symptoms are exacerbated as a consequence of negative anticipatory thoughts. During treatment, attention should be paid to this point, such as by correcting nonrealistic treatment goals (e.g., "I must never blush or tremble again") and by explaining the vicious circle.

Combination of Different Treatment Strategies

In some of the studies described above the effectiveness of a combination of treatment strategies (exposure and cognitive therapy) was compared to that of a singular treatment.

Several studies investigated a combination of social skills training and cognitive therapy. This package was found to result in significant clinical improvements as compared to no-treatment control (Kindness & Newton, 1984). However, the addition of cognitive techniques to social skills training did not enhance the effectiveness of social skills training (Frisch, Elliott, Atsaides, Salva, & Denney, 1982; Hatzenbühler & Schröder, 1982; Stravynsky, Marks, & Yule, 1982), but it is questionable whether the subjects in these studies were truly socially phobic or just socially inadequate. Considering the results with real social phobics in the Butler *et al.* (1984) and the Mattick *et al.* (1988) studies, the evidence for use of combined procedures is not totally conclusive. Differences may be significant but small. Replication of those studies with larger samples and longer treatments are necessary. In view of the heterogeneity of the social phobics, a comparison between a standard combination of treatment strategies and a combination based on functional analysis of the problem for each individual would be worthwhile.

Individual Response Patterns

The clinical studies discussed so far grouped all socially anxious patients together and ignored the role of individual differences. Three clinical studies with social phobics have been located to date that attempted to identify optimal matches between patient and treatment procedure. A research strategy that underlines the importance of individual characteristics of clients is found in experimental designs that examine the interaction between treatment factors and individual characteristics.

Ost *et al.* (1981) divided socially anxious outpatients into two groups showing different response patterns: behavioral and physiological reactors. Within each group, half of the patients were randomly assigned to treatment that focused on the behavioral component (social skills training) while the other half received treatment that primarily focused on the physiological component (applied relaxation). Applied relaxation was taught as a coping response that was applied *in vivo* in role-play situations. Further, patients received homework assignments to apply the relaxation in anxiety-arousing situations. Thus an active ingredient of this procedure involved exposure *in vivo*. It was hypothesized that patients who were treated with a method that matched their response pattern would achieve better results than the group treated with the other method. The results generally supported the hypothesis.

In another study (Jerremalm *et al.*, 1986), socially anxious patients were classified into cognitive reactors and physiological reactors. Here the hypothesis that matching treatment (cognitive therapy, in the form of self-instructional training, and applied relaxation) to the individual response pattern would increase treatment effectiveness was not corroborated. Cognitive reactors improved to the same extent with both treatment procedures; for physiological reactors, no differential effectiveness of the procedures was shown. Mersch, Bögels, Emmelkamp, and Van der Sleen, (1989) divided social phobics into (1) behavioral reactors, and (2) cognitive reactors. Behavioral reactors were patients whose main deficit was in the area of social skills, as rated by independent raters from a videotaped interaction test (the SSIT; Curran, 1982). Cognitive reactors were primarily characterized by dysfunctional cognitions, as measured by the Rational Behavior Inventory (RBI). Half of the patients in each condition received social skills training, whereas the other half received cognitive therapy. It was hypothesized that skills training would be superior for behavioral reactors and cognitive therapy would produce better results for the cognitive reactors. Contrary to expectation, both treatments were about equally effective.

In sum, both cognitive therapy, exposure *in vivo*, and social skills training have shown promise as treatment procedures for social phobics. When social phobics do possess the necessary social skills, a combination of exposure *in vivo* and cognitive therapy seems to be the treatment of choice. When social phobics lack the necessary social skills, treatment may focus first on the teaching of appropriate skills and then other procedures may be added if necessary.

Group Therapy versus Individual Therapy

Especially with social phobia, group therapy may have some marked advantages. First, group treatment provides a continuous exposure to a group—for many social phobics one of the most difficult situations. Second, since many social phobics are convinced that their fears are uncommon and exclusively theirs, sharing their fears with others may be very beneficial. Some patients notice that, compared with other people, their own problems in fact are not as heavy as they thought they were. Third, group therapy requires less therapist time than individual therapy, thus it is more efficient. Finally, specific treatment effects can be enhanced by calling in assistance of other group members. In exposure groups, other group members can be used to arrange difficult social situations. Examples of group exposure exercises are: getting compliments from everyone in the group, being criticized by others, being observed by all group members until anxiety decreases, and the like. When self-controlled exposure outside the group is applied, patients can perform tasks together prior to doing them alone. With social skills training, a group provides different models of social skills that can be observed and imitated. With cognitive therapy, patients have a possibility to check whether their fear of negative evaluation is realistic or not.

Group therapy also has a number of disadvantages. One of them is the impossibility of doing enough justice to the individual problems. Meeting other people with the same problems can also have negative effects: some patients may get the impression that even in a group of people with the same fears, they are the most anxious, or they are the ones with the worst skills. Another problem with group therapy is that for the patient it is more time consuming, which can be a reason to drop out prematurely.

Direct comparison between group and individual treatment is scarce. In studies by Linehan, Walker, Bronheim, Haynes, and Yerzeroff (1979) and van Son (1978), group and individual assertion therapy were compared. The results did not reveal differences between treatments.

The selection of patients for groups is very important. Excessive social anxiety often inhibits the proper application of therapeutic exercises in the groups.

For example, a number of social phobics find it very distressing to close their eyes in the group, as is typically done during self-instructional and relaxation training. In rational-emotive therapy groups, patients have to bring in their homework into the group. This usually consists of written self-analyses of emotional problems, which are discussed and corrected, if necessary, by other group members and the therapist. Patients with an excessive fear of failure find this very difficult and are inclined to avoid possible criticism in the group by not doing their homework analyses at all. In such cases, it may be better to start treatment individually and proceed later to group therapy when the patient can more adequately cope with these anxieties.

Group cohesion is held to be an important factor in contributing to the outcome of group therapy, but this issue has been ignored almost completely by behavior therapists. To date, two studies (Falloon, 1981; Rose, 1981) have investigated this particular issue with social phobics, but results are inconclusive. Although Falloon (1981) found a relationship between group cohesion and anxiety reduction, this finding does not necessarily mean that group cohesion was causal in effecting the favorable outcome. The relationship can also be the other way around, with the patients' ratings of cohesion being reflections of their overall satisfaction with treatment.

Group cohesion does not necessarily have to enhance improvement. Some social phobics experience high levels of group cohesion as threatening. Such patients may feel forced by group pressure to do activities against their will, which may lead to dropping out of treatment. Further studies are needed to investigate under which conditions group cohesion is therapeutic and under which conditions it is not.

The number of patients that participate in a group varies from study to study and is partially dependent on the availability of suitable patients. Generally, six to eight patients seem to be a workable number, enabling each individual to participate actively in the group activities. With smaller numbers, dropouts may cause serious problems. As to duration of the group therapy, time-limited groups are preferred to "open" groups. Prolonging the therapy after a certain number of sessions does not seem to add substantially to treatment outcome. Time limitation provides a motivating condition that may enhance treatment effectiveness. A second advantage of time-limited groups is that patients are better prepared to function independently from the therapist and the group. Finally, time-limited groups are organized like an adult education program. Such an educational approach, emphasizing the role of homework assignments, requires a more active participation from the individual group members than in more traditional group therapies (Emmelkamp & Kuipers, 1985).

Concluding Remarks and Future Directions

Research into social phobia is still in its infancy, which is not surprising given the fact that social phobia was first acknowledged as a separate disorder in

1980 (DSM-III). There are still a number of definitional problems, which have been outlined in this chapter. Further research is needed into the diagnostic validity of the social phobia concept and to establish whether this is indeed a separate disorder or merely a more severe variant of social anxiety, as the present authors believe. In our view, social phobia is closer to normal anxiety than, for instance, agoraphobia or obsessive–compulsive disorder. On the other hand, the demarcation with several personality disorders, especially Avoidant Personality and Schizoid Personality Disorders, is still a problem. This may be partly a consequence of the fact that two separate dimensions that are important for assessment are not sufficiently disconnected, namely, severity of symptoms (ranging from mild to severe) and number of situations in which these are provoked (ranging from one—with specific social phobias—to many—with generalized social phobia). Besides, we think that it would be helpful to change the definition of Avoidant Personality Disorder by stressing more the tendency to generalized avoidance rather than avoidance limited to social contacts.

Further, the relationship among various anxiety disorders needs to be studied. Results of one research group (Barlow, 1985) demonstrate a considerable overlap among the various anxiety disorder categories. In our view, rather than consider each as a distinct category, anxiety disorders are better viewed as lying along a continuum. The actual clinical diagnosis depends on the predominant feature in a particular patient.

Social phobia, which is often associated with depression, may exist independently from the depressive disorder, it may precede the depressive disorder, or it may be the result of the depressive disorder. Unfortunately, research in this area is lacking. This is clearly an issue that deserves further study.

The etiology of social phobia is largely unknown. At present both biological and social-learning formulations have something to offer, but the results of the few empirical studies that have been conducted are far from conclusive. Although a possible contribution of genetic factors cannot be ruled out, nothing is known about what exactly is inherited. Genetic research indicates only that some people have a higher inherited proneness to anxiety, not why this is so (Torgersen, 1988). However, even if genetic factors are involved, environmental factors are presumably of much more importance. Although research into parental characteristics of social phobics suggests that a specific (rejecting and overprotective) parental style may be related to the development of social phobia, prospective studies are needed before more definite conclusions can be drawn.

To date, firm conclusions with respect to the value of psychopharmacological treatment of social phobia cannot be drawn, due to the lack of research in this area. Although there is some evidence that beta-blockers may have something to offer when anxiety is related to a specific situation (performance anxiety), all controlled studies involved volunteers rather than patients.

More evidence is available that psychological treatments are beneficial for social phobics. Research in the past few years suggests that a combination of cognitive therapy and exposure *in vivo* can be an effective treatment for social phobics who have adequate social skills. When such skills are lacking, training in such skills seems tantamount. To date, research has established the short-term effectiveness of cognitive-behavioral programs, but long-term follow-up studies are lacking. Another important issue involves prognostic variables. As we have outlined in this chapter, it is a myth that all social phobics are alike. Future studies may profit from distinguishing among various subtypes of social phobics; it may be worthwhile to investigate whether specific subtypes do better or worse with specific treatments. Clinically, other important prognostic variables seem to be the presence of personality disorder(s) and depressive disorder in addition to social phobia. Further studies into such prognostic variables are greatly needed.

Another area that deserves further study is the therapeutic relationship. A few studies have investigated the impact of the therapeutic relationship on the outcome of behavior therapy with anxiety disorders (Emmelkamp, 1986), but only one study was relevant with respect to social phobia (Ford, 1978). In the latter study, therapist qualities accounted for more variance in treatment outcome than therapy type.

To conclude, although recent developments in the area of social phobia are promising, there is a great deal to be accomplished to enable a proper understanding of etiological processes and to devise efficient and effective treatment for social phobics.

REFERENCES

Agras, W. S. (1967). Transfer during systematic desensitization therapy. *Behaviour Research & Therapy, 5,* 193–199.

American Psychiatric Association (1980). *Diagnostic and statistical manual of mental disorders* (3rd ed.). Washington, DC: Author.

American Psychiatric Association (1987). *Diagnostic and statistical manual of mental disorders* (3rd ed., revised). Washington, DC: Author.

Abe, K., & Masui, T. (1981). Age-sex trends of phobic and anxiety symptoms in adolescents. *British Journal of Psychiatry, 138,* 297–302.

Amies, P. L., Gelder, M. G., & Shaw, P. M. (1983). Social phobia: A comparative clinical study. *British Journal of Psychiatry, 142,* 174–179.

Arena, J. G., Blanchard, E. B., Andrasik, F., Cotch, J., & Myers, J. K. (1983). Reliability of psychophysiological assessment. *Behaviour Research & Therapy, 21,* 447–460.

Arkowitz, H. (1977). The measurement and modification of minimal dating behavior. In M. Hersen, R. M. Eisler & P. M. Miller (Eds.), *Progress in behavior modification* (Vol. 5, pp. 1–57). New York: Academic Press.

Arkowitz, H., Lichtenstein, E., McGovern, K., & Hines, P. (1975). The behavioral assessment of social competence in males. *Behavior Therapy, 6,* 3–13.

Arrindell, W. A., Emmelkamp, P. M. G., & van der Ende, J. (1984). Phobic dimensions: I. Reliability and generalizability across samples, gender and nations. *Advances in Behavioral Research & Therapy, 6,* 207–254.

Arrindell, W. A., Emmelkamp, P. M. G., Monsma, A., & Brilman, E. (1983). The role of perceived parental rearing practices in the aetiology of phobic disorders: A controlled study. *British Journal of Psychiatry, 143.* 183–187.

Barlow, D. H. (1985). The dimensions of anxiety disorders. In A. H. Tuma & J. D. Maser (Eds.), *Anxiety and the anxiety disorders* (pp. 479–500). Hillsdale, NJ: Lawrence Erlbaum.

Barlow, D. H., Leitenberg, H., Agras, W. S., & Wincze, H. (1969). The transfer gap in systematic desensitization: An analogue study. *Behaviour Research & Therapy, 7,* 191–197.

Barratt, E. S. (1972). Anxiety and impulsiveness. Toward a neuropsychological model. In A. Spielberger (Ed.), *Anxiety: Current trends in theory and research* (Vol. 1, pp. 195–227). New York: Academic Press.

Beidel, D. C., Borden, J. W., Turner, S. M., & Jacob, R. G. (1989). The Social Phobia and Anxiety Inventory: Concurrent validity with a clinic sample. *Behaviour Research & Therapy, 27*(5), 573–576.

Beidel, D. C., Turner, S. M., & Dancu, C. V. (1985). Psychological, cognitive and behavioral aspects of social anxiety. *Behavior Research & Therapy, 23,* 109–117.

Bellack, A. S., Hersen, M., & Lamparski, D. (1979). Role-play tests for assessing social skills: Are they valid? Are they useful? *Journal of Consulting and Clinical Psychology, 47,* 335–342.

Boice, R. (1982). An ethological perspective on social skills research. In I. P. Curran & P. M. Monti (Eds.), *Social skills training: A practical handbook for assessment and treatment* (pp. 374–396). New York: Guilford Press.

Borkovec, T. D. (1976). Physiological and cognitive processes in the regulation of anxiety. In G. E. Schwartz & D. Shapiro (Eds.), *Consciousness and self regulation: Advances in research* (Vol. 1, pp. 261–312). New York: Plenum.

Brantigan, C. O., Brantigan, T. A., & Joseph, N. (1982). Effect of beta blockade and beta stimulation on stage fright. *American Journal of Medicine, 72.* 88–94.

Bruch, M. A., Heimberg, R. G., Berger, P., & Collins, T. A. (1988). Parental and personal origins of social evaluative threat: Differences between social phobics and agoraphobics. Unpublished manuscript.

Burns, L. (1980). The epidemiology of fears and phobias in general practice. *Journal of Internal Medicine Research, 8,* 1–7.

Buss, A. H. (1980). *Self-consciousness and social anxiety.* San Francisco: Freeman.

Butler, G. (1985). Exposure as a treatment for social phobia: Some instructive difficulties. *Behaviour Research & Therapy, 23,* 651–657.

Butler, G. (1989). Issues in the application of cognitive and behavioral strategies to the treatment of social phobia. *Clinical Psychology Review, 9,* 91–106.

Butler, G., Cullington, A., Munby, M., Amies, P., & Gelder, M. (1984). Exposure and anxiety management in the treatment of social phobia. *Journal of Consulting and Clinical Psychology, 52,* 642–650.

Caballo, V. E., Catena, A., & Buela, G. (1987). *Behavioral components of social skills.* European Congress of Behavior Therapy, Amsterdam.

Cacioppo, J. T., Glass, C. R., & Merluzzi, T. V. (1979). Self-statements and self-evaluations: A cognitive-response analysis of social anxiety. *Cognitive Therapy & Research, 3,* 249–262.

Cameron, O. G., Thyer, B. A., Nesse, R., & Curtis, G. C. (1986). Symptom profiles of patients with DSM-III anxiety disorders. *American Journal of Psychiatry, 143,* 1132–1137.

Cerny, J. A., Himadi, W. G., & Barlow, D. H. (1984). Issues in diagnosing anxiety disorders. *Journal of Behavioral Assessment, 6,* 301–330.

Chambless, D. L., Cherney, J., Caputo, G. C., & Rheinstein, B. J. G. (1987). Anxiety disorders and alcoholism: A study with inpatient alcoholics. *Journal of Anxiety Disorders, 1,* 29–40.

Clark, D. A. (1988). The validity of measures of cognition: A review of the literature. *Cognitive Therapy & Research, 12,* 1–20.

Cone, J. D. (1979). Confounded comparisons in triple response mode assessment research. *Behavioral Assessment, 1,* 85–95.

Conger, J. C., & Farrell, A. D. (1982). Behavioral components of heterosocial skills. *Behavior Therapy, 12,* 41–55.

Costello, C. G. (1982). Fears and phobias in women: A community study. *Journal of Abnormal Psychology, 91,* 280–286.

Craske, M. G., & Craig, K. D. (1984). Musical performance anxiety: The three systems model and self-efficacy theory. *Behaviour Research & Therapy, 22,* 267–280.

Curran, J. P. A. (1982). A procedure for the assessment of social skills: The Simulated Social Interaction Test. In: J. P. Curran & P. M. Monti (Eds.), *Social skills training: A practical handbook for assessment and treatment.* New York: Guilford Press.

Davidson, R. J., & Schwartz, G. E. (1976). The psychology of relaxation and related states. A multiprocess theory. In D. I. Mostofski (Ed.), *Behavioral control and modification of physiological activity.* New York: Prentice-Hall.

De Good, E. D., Buckelew, S. P., & Tait, R. C. (1985). Cognitive-somatic anxiety response patterning in chronic pain patients and nonpatients. *Journal of Consulting & Clinical Psychology, 53,* 137–138.

Delmonte, M. M., & Ryan, G. M. (1983). The Cognitive-Somatic Anxiety Questionnaire (CSAQ): A factor analysis. *British Journal of Clinical Psychology, 22,* 209–212.

Derogatis, L. R. (1977). *Scl-90 Administration, scoring and procedures manual 1 for the R(evised) version and other instruments of the psychopathology rating scale series.* Baltimore, MD: Clinical Psychometrics Research Unit, Johns Hopkins University School of Medicine.

Di Nardo, P. A., Barlow, D. H., Cerny, J. A., Vermilyea, B. B., Himadi, W. G., & Waddell, M. T. (1985). *Anxiety Disorders Interview Schedule Revised (ADIS-R).* Albany, NY: Center for Stress and Anxiety Disorders.

Di Nardo, P. A., O'Brien, G. T., Barlow, D. H., Waddell, M. T., & Blanchard, E. B. (1983). Reliability of DSM-III anxiety disorder categories using a new structured interview. *Archives of General Psychiatry, 40,* 1070–1075.

Dodge, C. S., Heimberg, R. G., Nyman, D., & O'Brien, G. T. (1987). Daily heterosocial interactions of high and low socially anxious college students: A diary study. *Behavior Therapy, 18,* 90–96.

Dodge, C. S., Hope, D. A., Heimberg, R. G., & Becker, R. E. (1988). Evaluation of the Social Interaction Self Statement Test with a social phobic population. *Cognitive Therapy & Research, 12,* 211–222.

Dow, M. G., Biglan, A., & Glaser, S. R. (1985). Multimethod assessment of socially anxious and socially unanxious women. *Behavioral Assessment, 7,* 273–282.

Dow, M. G., Glaser, S. R., & Biglan, A. (1981). The relevance of specific conversational behaviors to ratings of social skill: An experimental analysis. *Journal of Behavioral Assessment, 3,* 233–242.

Edelmann, R. J. (1985). Dealing with embarrassing events: Socially anxious and non-socially anxious groups compared. *British Journal of Clinical Psychology, 24,* 281–288.

Eisler, R. M., Miller, P. M., & Hersen, M. (1973). Components of assertive behavior. *Journal of Clinical Psychology, 29,* 295–299.

Elkind, D. (1967). Egocentrism in adolescence. *Child Development, 38,* 1025–1034.

Ellis, A. (1962). *Reason and emotion in psychotherapy.* New York: Lyle-Stuart.

Emmelkamp, P. M. G. (1982). *Phobic and obsessive–compulsive disorders: Theory, research and practice.* New York: Plenum.

Emmelkamp, P. M. G. (1986). Behavior therapy with adults. In S. L. Garfield & A. E. Bergin (Eds.), *Handbook of psychotherapy and behavior change* (pp. 385–442). New York: Wiley.

Emmelkamp, P. M. G., & Kuipers, A. C. M. (1985). Behavioral group therapy for anxiety disorders. In D. Upper & M. Ross (Eds.), *Handbook of behavioral group therapy* (pp. 443–471). New York: Plenum.

Emmelkamp, P. M. G., & Scholing, A. (1989). Behavioral treatment for simple and social phobics. In G. D. Burrows, R. Noyes, & M. Roth, *Handbook of anxiety, Vol. 4: The treatment of anxiety.* Amsterdam: Elsevier Science Publishers. In press.

Emmelkamp, P. M. G., Mersch, P. P., Vissia, E., & van der Helm, M. (1985). Social phobia: A comparative evaluation of cognitive and behavioral interventions. *Behavior Research & Therapy, 23,* 365–369.

Erickson, E. H. (1968). *Identity: Youth and crisis.* New York: Norton.

Falloon, I. R. H. (1981). Interpersonal variables in behavioral group therapy. *British Journal of Medical Psychology, 54,* 133–141.

Falloon, I. R. H., Lindley, P., McDonald, R., & Marks, I. M. (1977). Social skills training of out-patient groups: A controlled study of rehearsal and homework. *British Journal of Psychiatry, 131,* 599–609.

Falloon, I. R. H., Lloyd, G. G., & Harpin, R. E. (1981). The treatment of social phobia. *Journal of Nervous and Mental Disease, 169,* 180–184.

Farrell, A. D., Rabinowitz, J. A., Wallander, J. L., & Curran, J. P. (1985). An evaluation of two formats for the intermediate-level assessment of social skills. *Behavioral Assessment, 7,* 155–171.

Ford, J. D. (1978). Therapeutic relationship in behavior therapy: An empirical analysis. *Journal of Consulting & Clinical Psychology, 46,* 1302–1314.

Fremouw, W., Gross, R., Monroe, J., & Rapp, S. (1982). Empirical subtypes of performance anxiety. *Behavioral Assessment, 4,* 179–193.

Frisch, M. B., Elliott, C. H., Atsaides, J. P., Salva, D. M., & Denney, D. R. (1982). Social skills and stress management training to enhance patients interpersonal competencies. *Psychotherapy: Theory, Research and Practice, 19,* 349–358.

Fyer, A. J., Liebowitz, M. R., Gorman, J. M., Campeas, R., Levin, A., Davies, O., Goetz, D., & Klein, D. F. (1987). Discontinuation of Alprazolam treatment in panic patients. *American Journal of Psychiatry, 144,* 303–308.

Gelder, M. G., Bancroft, J. H. J., Gath, D. H., Johnston, D. W., Mathews, A. M., & Shaw, P. M. (1973). Specific and non-specific factors in behaviour therapy. *British Journal of Psychiatry, 123,* 445–462.

Glass, C. R., Merluzzi, T. V., Biever, J. L., & Larsen, K. H. (1982). Cognitive assessment of social anxiety: Development and validation of a self-statement questionnaire. *Cognitive Therapy & Research, 6,* 37–55.

Golden, M. (1981). A measure of cognition within the context of assertion. *Journal of Clinical Psychology, 37,* 253–262.

Goldfried, M. R., & Sobocinski, D. (1975). The effect of irrational beliefs on emotional arousal. *Journal of Consulting and Clinical Psychology, 43,* 348–355.

Gormally, J., Sipps, G., Raphael, R., Edwin, D., & Varvil-Weld (1981). The relationship between maladaptive cognitions and social anxiety. *Journal of Consulting and Clinical Psychology, 39,* 300–301.

Greenberg, D., & Stravynski, A. (1983). Social phobia: A letter. *British Journal of Psychiatry, 143,* 526.

Hafner, R. J., & Marks, I. M. (1976). Exposure in vivo in agoraphobics: Contributions of diazepam, group exposure, and anxiety evocation. *Psychological Medicine, 6,* 71–88.

Hall, R., & Goldberg, D. (1977). The role of social anxiety in social interaction difficulties. *British Journal of Psychiatry, 131,* 610–615.

Hardy, G. E., & Cotterill, J. A. (1982). A study of depression and obsessionality in dysmorphophobic and psoriatic patients. *British Journal of Psychiatry, 140,* 19–22.

Hartman, L. M. (1983). A metacognitive model of social anxiety: Implications for treatment. *Clinical Psychology Review, 3,* 435–456.

Hatzenbühler, L. C., & Schröder, H. E. (1982). Assertiveness training with outpatients: The effectiveness of skill and cognitive procedures. *Behavioral Psychotherapy, 10,* 234–252.

Heimberg, R. G. (1989). Cognitive and behavioral treatments for social phobia: A critical analysis. *Clinical Psychology Review, 9,* 107–128.

Heimberg, R. G., Becker, R. E., Goldfinger, K., & Vermilyea, J. A. (1985). Treatment of social phobia by exposure, cognitive restructuring and homework assignments. *Journal of Nervous and Mental Disease, 173,* 236–245.

Heimberg, R. G., Dodge, C. S., & Becker, R. E. (1987). Social phobia. In L. Michelson & M. Ascher (Eds.), *Cognitive-behavioral assessment and treatment of anxiety disorders* (pp. 280–309). New York: Guilford Press.

Heimberg, R. G., Gansler, D., Dodge, C. S., & Becker, R. E. (1987). Convergent and discriminant validity of the Cognitive-Somatic Anxiety Questionnaire in a social phobic population. *Behavioral Assessment, 9,* 379–388.

Himadi, W. A., Boice, R., & Barlow, D. H. (1985). Assessment of agoraphobia: Triple response measurement. *Behaviour Research & Therapy, 3,* 311–323.

Holden, A. E., & Barlow, D. H. (1986). Heart rate and heart rate variability recorded in vivo in agoraphobics and non-phobics. *Behavior Therapy, 17,* 26–42.

Hugdahl, K. (1981). The three-systems model of fear and emotion: A critical examination. *Behaviour Research & Therapy, 19,* 75–85.

James, I. M., Burgoyne, W., & Savage, I. T. (1983). Effect of pindolo on stress-related disturbances of musical performance. *Journal of the Royal Society of Medicine, 76,* 194–196.

James, I. M., Griffith, D. N. W., Pearson, R. M., & Newby, P. (1977). Effect of oxprenolol on stage-fright in musicians. *Lancet, 2*, 952–954.

James, I., & Savage, I. (1984). Nadolol, diazepam and placebo for anxiety in musicians. *American Heart Journal, 108*, 1150–1155.

Jerremalm, A., Jansson, L., & Ost, L. G. (1986). Cognitive and physiological reactivity and the effects of different behavioral methods in the treatment of social phobia. *Behavior Research & Therapy, 24*, 171–180.

Jones, R. (1968). *A factored measure of Ellis' irrational beliefs system with personality adjustment correlates.* Unpublished dissertation, Texas Technical College.

Kanter, N. J., & Goldfried, M. R. (1979). Relative effectiveness of rational restructuring and self-control desensitization in the reduction of interpersonal anxiety. *Behavior Therapy, 10*, 472–490.

Kendall, P. C., & Hollon, S. D. (1981). Assessing self-referent speech: Methods in the measurement of self-statements. In P. C. Kendall & S. D. Hollon (Eds.). *Assessment strategies for cognitive-behavioral interventions* (pp. 85–118). New York: Academic Press.

Kindness, K., & Newton, A. (1984). Patients and social skills groups: Is social skills training enough? *Behavioral Psychotherapy, 12*, 212–222.

Kupke, T. E., Hobbs, S. A., & Cheney, T. H. (1979). Selection of heterosocial skills—I. Criterion related validity. *Behavior Therapy, 10*, 327–335.

Lader, M. H. (1967). Palmar conductance measures in anxiety and phobic states. *Journal of Psychosomatic Research, 11*, 271–281.

Lader, M. H., & Mathews, A. M. (1968). A physiological model of phobic anxiety and desensitization. *Behaviour Research & Therapy, 6*, 411–421.

Lader, M. H., & Wing, L. (1966). *Physiological measures, sedative drugs, and morbid anxiety, 6*, 411–421.

Lang, P. J. (1971). The application of psychophysiological methods to the study of psychotherapy and behavior modification. In A. E. Bergin & S. L. Garfield (Eds.), *Handbook of psychotherapy and behavior change* (pp. 75–125). New York: Wiley.

Lang, P. J., Levin, D. N., Miller, G. A., & Kozak, M. J. (1983). Fear behavior, fear imagery, and the psychophysiology of emotion: The problem of affective response integration. *Journal of Abnormal Psychology, 92*, 276–306.

Lehrer, P. M., & Woolfolk, R. L. (1982). Self-report assessment of anxiety: Somatic, cognitive and behavioral modalities. *Behavioral Assessment, 4*, 167–177.

Leitenberg, H., Agras, S., Butz, R., & Wincze, J. (1971). Relationship between heart rate and behavioral change during the treatment of phobias. *Journal of Abnormal Psychology, 78*, 59–68.

Liden, S., & Gottfried, C. G. (1974). Beta-blocking agents in the treatment of catecholamine-induced symptoms in musicians. *Lancet, 2*, 529.

Liebowitz, M. R., Gorman, J., Fyer, A., Campeas, R., Levin, A., Davies, S., & Klein, D. F. (1986). Psychopharmacological treatment of social phobia. *Journal of Clinical Psychopharmacology, 6*, 93–98.

Liebowitz, M. R., Gorman, J. M., Fyer, A. J., & Klein, D. F. (1985). Social phobia: Review of a neglected anxiety disorder. *Archives of General Psychiatry, 42*, 729–736.

Linehan, M. M., Walker, R. O., Bronheim, S., Haynes, K. F., & Yerzeroff, H. (1979). Group vs. individual assertion training. *Journal of Consulting and Clinical Psychology, 47*, 1000–1002.

Lydiard, R. B., Laraia, M. T., Ballenger, J. C., & Howell, E. F. (1987). Emergence of depressive symptoms in patients receiving Alprazolan for panic disorder. *American Journal of Psychiatry, 5*, 664–665.

Lydiard, R. B., Laraia, M. T., Howell, E. F., & Ballenger, J. C. (1988). Alprazolam in the treatment of social phobia. *Journal of Clinical Psychiatry, 49*, 17–19.

Marks, I. M. (1969). *Fears and phobias.* London: Heinemann.

Marks, I. M. (1986). Genetics of fear and anxiety disorders. *British Journal of Psychiatry, 149*, 406–418.

Marks, I. M., Boulougouris, J., & Marset, P. (1971). Flooding versus desensitization in the treatment of phobic patients. *British Journal of Psychiatry, 119*, 353–375.

Marks, I. M., & Gelder, M. G. (1966). Different ages of onset in varieties of phobias. *American Journal of Psychiatry, 123*, 218–221.

Marks, I. M., & Mathews, A. M. (1979). Brief standard self-rating for phobic patients. *Behaviour Research and Therapy, 17*, 59–68.

Marks, I. M., & Mishan, J. (1988). Dysmorphophobia: A pilot study of behavioural treatment in disturbed bodily perception. *British Journal of Psychiatry, 152,* 674–678.

Marzillier, J. S., Lambert, C., & Kellett, J. (1976). A controlled evaluation of systematic desensitization and social skills training for socially inadequate psychiatric patients. *Behaviour Research & Therapy, 14,* 225–238.

Mattick, R. P., & Peters, L. (1988). Treatment of severe social phobia: Effects of guided exposure with and without cognitive restructuring. *Journal of Consulting and Clinical Psychology, 56,* 251–260.

Mattick, R. P., Peters, L., & Clarke, J. C. (1988). Exposure and cognitive restructuring for social phobia: A controlled study. *Behavior Therapy, 20*(1), 3–8.

McCann, B. S., Woolfolk, R. L., & Lehrer, P. M. (1987). Specificity in response to treatment: A study of interpersonal anxiety. *Behaviour Research & Therapy, 25,* 129–137.

McFall, R. M. (1982). A review and reformulation of the concept of social skills. *Behavioral Assessment, 4,* 1–33.

McNamara, J. R., & Blumer, C. A. (1982). Role playing to assess social competence. *Behavior Modification, 6,* 519–549.

Merluzzi, T. V., Burgio, K. L., & Glass, C. R. (1984). Cognition and psychopathology: An analysis of social introversion and self-statements. *Journal of Consulting and Clinical Psychology, 52,* 1102–1103.

Mersch, P. P. A., Bögels, S. M., Van der Sleen, J., & Emmelkamp, P. M. G. (1987). Social phobia: Patient characteristics and the effects of behavioral and cognitive interventions. In W. Huber (Ed.), *Progress in psychotherapy research* (pp. 188–201). Louvain-la-Neuve: University Press.

Mersch, P. P. A., Emmelkamp, P. M. G., Bögels, S. M., & Van der Sleen, J. (1989). Social Phobia: Individual response patterns and the effects of behavioral and cognitive interventions. Behaviour Research & Therapy, 27, 4, 421–434.

Michelson, C. (1984). The role of individual differences, response profiles and treatment consonance in anxiety disorders. *Journal of Behaviour Assessment, 6,* 349–367.

Michelson, L., & Mavissakalian, M. (1983). Temporal stability of self-report measures in agoraphobia research. *Behaviour Research and Therapy, 21,* 695–698.

Mizes, J. S., Landolf-Fritsche, B., & Grossman-Mc Kee, D. (1987). Patterns of distorted cognitions in phobic disorders: An investigation of clinically severe simple phobics, social phobics and agoraphobics. *Cognitive Therapy & Research, 11,* 583–592.

Monti, P. M., Boice, R., Fingeret, A. L., Zwick, W. R., Kolko, D., Munroe, S., & Grunberger, A. (1984). Midi-level measurement of social anxiety in psychiatric and non-psychiatric samples. *Behaviour Research and Therapy, 22,* 651–660.

Monti, P. M., Wallander, J. L., Ahern, D. K., Abrams, D. B., & Munroe, S. M. (1983). Multimodal meausrement of anxiety and social skills in a behavioral role-play test: Generalizability and discriminant validity. *Behavioral Assessment, 6,* 15–25.

Mountjoy, C. Q., Roth, M., Garside, R. F., & Leitch, I. M. (1977). A clinical trial of phenelzine in anxiety depressive and phobic neuroses. *British Journal of Psychiatry, 131,* 486–492.

Mowrer, O. H. (1960). *Learning theory and behavior.* New York: Wiley.

Mullaney, J. A., & Trippett, C. J. (1979). Alcohol dependence and phobias: Clinical description and relevance. *British Journal of Psychiatry, 135,* 563–573.

Munjack, D. J., Brown, R. A., & McDowell, D. E. (1987). Comparison of social anxiety in patients with social phobia and panic disorder. *Journal of Nervous and Mental Disease, 175,* 49–51.

Myers, J. K., Weissman, M. J., Tischler, G. L., Holzer, C. E., Leaf, P. J., Orvaschel, H., Anthony, J. C., Boyd, J. H., Burke, J. D., Kramer, M., & Stoltzman, R. (1984). Six-month prevalence of psychiatric disorders in three communities. *Archives of General Psychiatry, 41,* 959–967.

Neftel, K. A., Adler, R. H., Kappell, L., Rossi, M., Dolder, M., Kaser, H. E., Bruggesser, H. H., & Vorkauf, H. (1982). Stagefright in musicians: A model illustrating the effect of beta blockers. *Psychosomatic Medicine, 44,* 461–469.

Newton, A., Kindness, K., & McFadyen, M. (1983). Patients and social skills groups: Do they lack social skills? *Behavioural Psychotherapy, 11,* 116–126.

Nichols, K. A. (1974). Severe social anxiety. *British Journal of Medical Psychology, 47,* 301–306.

Noyes, R. (1988). Beta-adrenergic blockers. In C. G. Last & M. Hersen (Eds.), *Handbook of anxiety disorders* (pp. 445–459). New York: Pergamon Press.

Ost, L.-G. (1987). Age of onset in different phobias. *Journal of Abnormal Psychology, 96,* 3, 223–229.
Ost, L.-G., & Hugdahl, K. (1981). Acquisition of phobias and anxiety response patterns in clinical patients. *Behaviour Research & Therapy, 19,* 439–447.
Ost, L.-G., Jerremalm, A., & Johansson, J. (1981). Individual response patterns and the effects of different behavioral methods in the treatment of social phobia. *Behaviour Research and Therapy, 19,* 1–16.
Parker, G. (1979). Reported parental characteristics of agoraphobics and social phobics. *British Journal of Psychiatry, 135,* 555–560.
Persson, G., & Nordlund, C. L. (1985). Agoraphobics and social phobics: Differences in background factors, syndrome profiles and therapeutic response. *Acta Pychiatrica Scandinavica, 71,* 148–159.
Rachman, S. (1978). *Fear and courage.* San Francisco: Freeman.
Raguram, R., & Bhide, A. (1985). Patterns of phobic neurosis: A retrospective study. *British Journal of Psychiatry, 147,* 557–560.
Robins, R. N., Helzer, J. E., Weissman, M. M., Orvaschel, H., Gruenberg, E., Burke, J. D., & Regier, D. A. (1984). Lifetime prevalence of specific psychiatric disorders in three sites. *Archives of General Psychiatry, 41,* 949–958.
Rose, S. D. (1981). How group attributes relate to outcome in behavior group therapy. *Social Work Research and Abstracts, 16,* 25–29.
Rose, R. J., & Dilto, W. B. (1983). A developmental-genetic analysis of common fears from early adolescence to early adulthood. *Child Development, 54,* 361–368.
Sallis, J., Lichstein, K., & McGlynn, F. (1980). Anxiety response patterns: A comparison of clinical and analogue populations. *Journal of Behaviour Therapy and Experimental Psychiatry, 11,* 179–183.
Sanderman, R., Mersch, P. P., van der Sleen, J., Emmelkamp, P. M. G., & Ormel, J. (1987). The Rational Behavior Inventory (RBI): A psychometric evaluation. *Person. Individ. Diff., 8,* 561–569.
Scholing, H. A., & Emmelkamp, P. M. G. (1989). Social phobia: An analysis in single cases. In P. M. G. Emmelkamp, W. T. A. M. Everaerd, F. W. Kraaimaat & M. J. M. van Son (Eds.), *Fresh perspectives on anxiety disorders* (Vol. 4, pp. 213–220). Amsterdam: Swets en Zeitlinger.
Schwartz, G. E., Davidson, R. J., & Goldman, D. J. (1978). Patterning of cognitive and somatic processes in the self-regulation of anxiety: Effects of meditation vs. exercise. *Psychosomatic Medicine, 40,* 321–328.
Scott, R. R., Himadi, W., & Keane, T. M. (1983). A review of generalization in social skills training. In M. Hersen, R. M. Eisler, & P. M. Miller (Eds.), *Progress in behavior modification* (Vol. 15, pp. 113–172). New York: Academic Press.
Shafar, S. (1976). Aspects of phobic illness. A study of 90 personal cases. *British Journal of Medical Psychology, 49,* 221–236.
Shahar, A., & Merbaum, M. (1981). The interaction between subject characteristics and self-control procedures in the treatment of interpersonal anxiety. *Cognitive Therapy and Research, 5,* 221–224.
Shaw, P. (1979). A comparison of three behaviour therapies in the treatment of social phobias. *British Journal of Psychiatry, 134,* 620–623.
Shorkey, C. T., & Whiteman, V. L. (1977). Development of the Rational Behavior Inventory: Initial validity and reliability. *Educational and Psychological Measurement, 37,* 527–534.
Smail, P., Stockwell, T., Canter, S., & Hodgson, R. (1984). Alcohol dependence and phobia anxiety states: I. A prevalence study. *British Journal of Psychiatry, 144,* 53–57.
Smith, T. W., Ingram, R. E., & Brehm, S. S. (1983). Social anxiety, anxious self-preoccupation, and recall of self-relevant information. *Journal of Personality and Social Psychology, 44,* 1276–1283.
Solyom, L., Heseltine, G. F., McClure, D. J., Solyom, C., Ledwidge, B., & Steinberg, S. (1973). Behaviour therapy versus drug therapy in the treatment of phobic neurosis. *Canadian Psychiatric Association Journal, 18,* 25–31.
Solyom, C., Ledwidge, B., & Solyom, C. (1986). Delineating social phobia. *British Journal of Psychiatry, 149,* 464–470.
Solyom, C., Solyom, L., La Pierre, Y., Pecknold, J. C., & Morton, L. (1981). Phenelzine and exposure in the treatment of phobias. *Journal of Biological Psychiatry, 16,* 239–248.
Stampfl, T. G., & Levis, D. (1967). Essentials of implosive therapy: A learning-theory-based psychodynamic behavioral therapy. *Journal of Abnormal Psychology, 72,* 496–503.

Stravynski, A., Marks, I., & Yule, W. (1982). Social skills problems in neurotic outpatients. *Archives of General Psychiatry, 39,* 1378–1385.

Suinn, R. M., & Richardson, F. (1971). Anxiety management training: A non-specific behaviour therapy program for anxiety control. *Behavior Therapy, 2.* 498–510.

Sutton-Simon, K., & Goldfried, M. R. (1979). Faulty thinking patterns in two types of anxiety. *Cognitive Therapy and Research, 3,* 193–203.

Tamaren, A. J., Allen, W., & Carney, R. M. (1985). Assessment of cognitive and somatic anxiety: A preliminary validation study. *Behavioral Assessment, 7.* 197–202.

Thyer, B. A., Parrisch, R. T., Curtis, G. C., Nesse, R. M., & Cameron, O. G. (1985). Ages of onset of DSM-III anxiety disorders. *Comprehensive Psychiatry, 26*(2), 113–122.

Torgersen, S. (1979). The nature and origin of common phobic fears. *British Journal of Psychiatry, 134,* 343–351.

Torgersen, S. (1988). Genetics. In C. G. Last & M. Hersen (Eds.), *Handbook of anxiety disorders* (pp. 159–170). New York: Pergamon Press.

Trower, P., Yardley, K., Bryant, B., & Shaw, P. (1978). The treatment of social failure: A comparison of anxiety reduction and skills-acquisition procedures on two social problems. *Behaviour Modification, 2,* 41–60.

Turner, S. M., & Beidel, D. C. (1985). Empirically derived subtypes of social anxiety. *Behavior Therapy, 16,* 384–392.

Turner, S. M., Beidel, D. C., Dancu, C. V., & Keys, D. J. (1986). Psychopathology of social phobia and comparison to avoidant personality disorder. *Journal of Abnormal Psychology, 95*(4), 389–394.

Turner, S. M., Beidel, D. C., Dancu, C. V., & Stanley, M. A. (1989). An empirically derived inventory to measure social fears and anxiety: The Social Phobia and Anxiety Inventory. *Psychosocial Assessment: A Journal of Consulting and Clinical Psychology, 1,* 35–40.

Turner, S. M., Beidel, D. C., & Larkin, K. T. (1986). Situational determinants of social anxiety in clinic and nonclinic samples: Physiological and cognitive correlates. *Journal of Consulting and Clinical Psychology, 54,* 523–527.

Turner, R. M., DiTomasso, R., & Murray, M. R. (1980). Psychometric analysis of the Willoughby Personality Schedule. *Journal of Behavior Therapy & Exp. Psychiatry, 11,* 185–195.

Turner, S. M., McCann, B. S., Beidel, D. C., & Mezzick, J. E. (1986). DSM-III classification of the anxiety disorders: A psychometric study. *Journal of Abnormal Psychology, 95*(2), 168–172.

Turner, S. M., McCanna, M., & Beidel, D. C. (1987). Validity of social avoidance and distress and fear of negative evaluation scales. *Behavioral Research & Therapy, 25,* 113–117.

Turner, R. M., Meles, D., & DiTomasso, R. (1983). Assessment of social anxiety: A controlled comparison among social phobics, obsessive–compulsives, agoraphobics, sexual disorders and simple phobics. *Behavior Research and Therapy, 21*(2), 181–183.

Twentyman, C. T., & McFall, R. M. (1975). Behavioral training of social skills in shy males. *Journal of Consulting and Clinical Psychology, 43,* 384–395.

Tyrer, P., Candy, J., & Kelly, D. (1973). A study of the clinical effects of phenelzine and placebo in the treatment of phobic anxiety. *Psychopharmacology, 32,* 237–254.

Tyrer, P. J., & Lader, M. H. (1976). Central and peripheral correlates of anxiety: A comparative study. *Journal of Nervous and Mental Disease, 162,* 99–104.

van Son, M. J. M. (1978). Sociale vaardigheidstherapie bij bloosproblemen en slaapproblemen. In M. J. M. van Son, *Sociale vaardigheidstherapie, gedragstherapie en sociaal gedrag.* Amsterdam: Swets & Zeitlinger.

Wallander, J. L., Conger, A. J., & Conger, J. C. (1985). Development and evaluation of a behaviorally referenced rating system for heterosocial skills. *Behavioral Assessment, 7,* 137–153.

Wallander, J. L., Conger, A. J., & Ward, D. G. (1983). It may not be worth the effort! Trained judges global ratings as a criterion measure of social skills and anxiety. *Behavior Modification, 7,* 139–150.

Watson, D., & Friend, R. (1969). Measurement of social evaluative anxiety. *Journal of Consulting & Clinical Psychology, 33,* 448–459.

Weiss, K. J., & Rosenberg, D. J. (1985). Prevalence of anxiety disorders among alcoholics. *Journal of Clinical Psychiatry, 46,* 3–5.

Williams, S. L. (1985). On the nature and measurement of agoraphobia. In M. Hersen, R. M. Eisler,

& P. M. Miller (Eds.), *Progress in behavior modification* (Vol. 19, pp. 109–144). New York: Academic Press.

Willoughby, R. R. (1932). Some properties of the Thurstone Personality Schedule and a suggested revision. *Journal of Social Psychology, 3,* 401–424.

Willoughby, R. R. (1934). Norms for the Clark–Thurstone Inventory. *Journal of Social Psychology, 5,* 91–97.

Windheuser, H. J. (1977). Anxious mothers as models for coping with anxiety. *Behavioural Analysis and Modification, 1,* 39–58.

Wolpe, J. (1973). *The practice of behavior therapy.* New York: Pergamon Press.

Wolpe, J., & Lang, P. J. (1964). A Fear Survey Schedule for use in behavior therapy. *Behaviour Research and Therapy, 2,* 27–30.

World Health Organization (1977, 1978). *Manual of the International Statistical Classification of Diseases, Injuries and causes of death,* 9th revision, Vol. 1/2. Geneva.

10

Social Skills, Social Anxiety, and Cognitive Factors in Schizophrenia

Robert K. Heinssen, Jr., and Carol R. Glass

Introduction

Above all, human beings are social creatures. We are born into social environments, we discover and explore the world through social discourse, and we come to know ourselves through interpersonal experience. Social interaction is so basic to our nature that individuals unable to relate normally may appear alien and lacking in some essential human quality. Disturbed social functioning represents a great human tragedy, since social dysfunction often results in estrangement from society, with limited opportunities for participation, self-discovery, and contribution. This tragedy is central to schizophrenia, which is characterized by pervasive interpersonal anxiety, impaired social behavior, and withdrawal from human relationships.

The social disability of schizophrenia is well established and is believed to play a pivotal role in the pathogenesis and course of the disorder (Brady, 1984; Goldsmith & McFall, 1975; Hersen & Bellack, 1976b; Liberman, 1982; Morrison & Bellack, 1984). Evidence suggests that many adult schizophrenic patients exhibited maladaptive patterns of interpersonal functioning in childhood (Lewine, Watt, & Freyer, 1978; Lewine, Watt, Prentky, & Freyer, 1980), and poor social competence almost invariably predates the illness (Strauss, Kokes, Klorman, & Sacksteder, 1977; Zigler & Phillips, 1961, 1962). Isolation, withdrawal, and emotional detachment are identified as prominent prodromal symptoms (American Psychiatric Association, 1987), and heightened anxiety, poor performance, and avoidance characterize the interactions of schizophrenics during both the psychotic and nonpsychotic phases of the illness (Serban, 1975; Strauss, Carpenter, & Bartko, 1974). Residual interpersonal difficulties are currently considered evidence of the negative syndrome or defect state (Andreasen, 1982) and play a significant role in determining the quality of a patient's posthospital adjustment

Robert K. Heinssen, Jr. • Chestnut Lodge Research Institute, 500 West Montgomery Avenue, Rockville, Maryland 20850.   Carol R. Glass • Department of Psychology, Catholic University of America, Washington, DC 20064.

and the likelihood of eventual relapse (Bellack, Turner, Hersen, & Luber, 1984; Hogarty *et al.*, 1986; Wallace & Liberman, 1985). Thus, social incompetence limits opportunities for social support, enrichment, and intimacy throughout the schizophrenic's life, affecting long-term adjustment in interpersonal, occupational, and psychopathologic domains (Beels, Gutwirth, Berkeley, & Struening, 1984; Gleser & Gottschalk, 1967; McCelland & Walt, 1968; McGlashan, 1986b).

Despite evidence for the poor interpersonal functioning of schizophrenic patients, we do not fully understand the precise nature of their social difficulties (Morrison & Bellack, 1987). Social inadequacy is a complex phenomenon, and a given patient's difficulties may or may not include social anxiety, self-deprecation, or problems with behavioral deficits or excesses (Curran, Miller, Zwick, Monti, & Stout, 1980). Despite the evidence that social inadequacy is multiply determined, the models of social functioning applied to schizophrenia have not adequately shown how these components interact to produce schizophrenics' disordered interpersonal experience. The current chapter addresses this issue by examining how interactions among skill deficiency, cognitive dysfunction, and social anxiety may affect the social performance of schizophrenic patients. After briefly reviewing models of social inadequacy in both nonpsychotic and schizophrenic populations, we discuss how social skill and problem-solving variables have been assessed with schizophrenics and how deficits in each area have been addressed in treatment. The role of social anxiety and dysfunctional cognitions in the interpersonal behavior of schizophrenics is then considered. Finally, we offer a number of directions that appear ripe for further research and clinical consideration.

SOCIAL FUNCTIONING IN NONSCHIZOPHRENIC POPULATIONS

Historically, four major viewpoints have emerged regarding the etiology and maintenance of interpersonal dysfunction. These hypotheses can be labeled the conditioned-anxiety model, the cognitive-evaluative model, the faulty discrimination model, and the skills deficit model (Bellack & Hersen, 1979; Bellack & Morrison, 1985; Curran, 1977). Contemporary models of social functioning draw heavily upon these systems in describing interpersonal behavior, maintaining that poor social performance is influenced by many factors, including heightened social anxiety, disruptive internal dialogue, misappraisal of social situations, and inadequate response or social skills. While the importance of one or another of these variables may be emphasized in a particular theoretical model, it is generally agreed that cognitive, behavioral, and emotional factors interact to determine a person's interpersonal competence.

According to an interactive paradigm, social functioning is both multidimensional and multidetermined. Environmental demands engage a person's social-processing system, prompting responses across emotional, cognitive, and behavioral domains. Numerous scenarios can therefore account for poor interpersonal performance. For example, heightened anxiety could overwhelm an individual, temporarily undermining his or her ability to access appropriate response skills. Anxiety need not be present, however, to produce an incompetent social response. An individual's cognitive-interpretive style could cause one to misjudge social data (e.g., "She's just playing hard to get"), leading to an inappropriate emotional reaction (e.g., "This is great!") and the selection of an inappropriate behavioral response (e.g., "I'll ask her to go out with me"). An impoverished or undifferentiated skills repertoire can also lead to interpersonal problems, as in the case of the adolescent male who correctly perceives the interest of a female peer, experiences enthusiasm as a result, but avoids contact because he does not know how to initiate a conversation. Finally, simultaneous aggravation of the three subsystems is possible, resulting in misappraisal of situational demands, elevated anxiety, and substandard interpersonal performance. A consequence of this situation is withdrawal from social situations and a course of escalating isolation.

Variations of this interactive model have been used to conceptualize interpersonal difficulties in many nonschizophrenic populations, ranging from "analogue" samples of socially anxious college students to cohorts meeting DSM-III-R criteria for social phobia. While similar in certain aspects, the models of social functioning applied to schizophrenia have emphasized particular components of the general paradigm, stressing the importance of the variables most noticeably compromised by the illness.

MODELS OF SOCIAL DISABILITY IN SCHIZOPHRENIA

Two primary conceptual models have been developed to explain social incompetence in schizophrenia. These systems focus primarily on the motoric and information-processing aspects of social functioning, hypothesizing that deficits in these areas account for schizophrenics' impaired interpersonal behavior.

The Topographic Model

Initial efforts to understand the social difficulties of schizophrenic patients were based on topographic, or motor skills, models of social functioning (Morrison & Bellack, 1984). According to this approach, social performance is determined by the interplay of numerous molecular skills that, when emitted together, determine an individual's overall level of social competence (McFall, 1982). Molecular skills can be verbal or nonverbal in nature, and in combination define a person's social skills repertoire. The skills found in these repertoires are numerous, and include conversational abilities (initiating, maintaining, and ending), the paralinguistic features of speech (voice tone, volume, pitch, and pace), nonverbal behaviors (facial expression, body movements, interpersonal distance, gaze), and interactive balance (Morrison & Bellack, 1984). Disorders in molecular skills (in the form of inappropriate deficits or excesses) presumably account for socially inadequate behavior. Consequently, the therapeutic goal of the motor skills model is to identify patients' problematic response skills and then teach them to perform component molecular behaviors more effectively.

Assessing Skills Deficits

Two central questions confront a therapist in designing a social skills training program: which skill deficits account for the patient's poor interpersonal performance, and under which circumstances are these deficits manifested? Pretreatment assessment provides answers to these questions and enables the therapist to individualize treatment goals and specify interventions. In addition to facilitating treatment planning, establishing the parameters of a patient's social problems helps the social skills trainer to evaluate the effectiveness of treatment.

Assessment of interpersonal problems would be straightforward if there were a universally accepted definition of social competence. With such a definition we could construct a "social performance battery" and use this instrument to determine the form of a patient's interpersonal difficulties. Unfortunately, an acceptably comprehensive definition of social competence has proved elusive, and no standardized protocol for assessing social skill currently exists. To date, we lack consensus as to which components of social behavior are critical for effective interpersonal performance. As a result, a wide variety of behaviors have been targeted in motor skills studies with schizophrenics, including eye contact, voice volume, use of physical gestures, speech content, conversational skills, and assertive behaviors (Morrison & Bellack, 1987; Wallace *et al.*, 1980).

Assessment Strategies. Both cross-sectional and longitudinal assessment strategies have been utilized in motor skills investigations. The cross-sectional approach is typical in group comparison studies, where "snap shots" of interpersonal functioning are obtained before and after treatment. A recent investigation by Bellack and his colleagues (Bellack *et al.*, 1984) illustrated the cross-sectional approach. These authors evaluated the efficacy of combining social skills training with day hospital treatment for chronic schizophrenic patients, compared to day hospital treatment alone. All subjects were assessed with a variety of self-report and performance measures before treatment, at the conclusion of treatment, and at a 6-month follow-up. Conversational skills, positive and negative assertive behavior, and social perception variables were evaluated and targeted for intervention. Results indicated greater long-term improvements for patients who received social skills training.

In contrast to the cross-sectional strategy, longitudinal methods are typical in studies utilizing multiple baseline analysis. This procedure involves the observation of several target behaviors over time to determine the frequency and stability of specific social skills. The multiple baseline design has a long and distinguished history in social skills research, and an early study by Hersen and Bellack (1976a) exemplifies the use of this approach. Those authors utilized a multiple baseline strategy to monitor eye contact, speech duration, appropriate affect, assertive requests, and verbal compliance in two male chronic schizophrenics involved in social skills training. Several pretreatment assessment sessions (structured role-play interactions) helped determine subjects' initial competence on each target behavior. Assessment was continued on target behaviors throughout treatment and follow-up periods in order to establish that treatment gains (improvements on each target) were maintained over time.

We feel that longitudinal assessment methods hold important advantages when evaluating social behavior in schizophrenic patients. As Morrison and Bellack (1987) have pointed out, "schizophrenic disorders are not static, but can be best understood from a longitudinal, developmental perspective" (p. 720). As it is likely that the social functioning of schizophrenics fluctuates with the course of illness, interpersonal adjustment should be evaluated from a long-term perspective. Longitudinal assessment strategies, as opposed to cross-sectional procedures, seem best equipped for this task and should be considered when designing social skills programs for schizophrenic patients.

Measures for Motor Skill Assessment. In one of the better assessment and treatment studies of social skills training with psychiatric patients, Goldsmith and McFall (1975) developed a set of 55 problematic interpersonal situations from interviews with patients themselves. These empirically derived situations formed the basis for a self-report inventory of social competence as well as a set of 25 tape-recorded simulated situations (the Interpersonal Behavior Role-Play Test, or IBRT). Using Goldfried and D'Zurilla's (1969) behavioral-analytic model, Goldsmith and McFall derived specific scoring criteria for rating the social effectiveness and competence of responses on the IBRT. These highly relevant problematic social scenarios, which had been drawn from the actual population of interest, were then used to teach patients more effective social behavior. Psychiatric patients (50% schizophrenic) who received social skills training improved significantly more than pseudotherapy and assessment-only control groups, and change generalized to situations not practiced as part of the intervention.

We highly recommend the use of such empirical methods to devise measures tailored to the needs of specific patient populations. In addition, more standardized instruments could also be included for the behavioral assessment of social skill. One such measure is the Simulated Social Interaction Test (SSIT; Curran, 1982), a role-play test consisting of eight brief social interactions, each initiated by a series of confederate prompts delivered in face-to-face interactions. The situations were selected based on factor analytic results from previous research on social anxiety, and they represent a range of social encounters. It is interesting to note that Curran (1982) has found considerable overlap in the situations generated by Goldsmith and McFall's (1975) psychiatric patients and the situational factors on the SSIT. The Behavioral Assertiveness Test (BAT; Eisler, Miller, & Hersen, 1973; Eisler, Hersen, Miller, & Blanchard, 1975) has also been the focus of considerable research. The BAT has good reliability, validity, and utility with hospitalized schizophrenics, and it should be considered if one is interested in assessing the expression of positive and negative assertiveness.

While the BAT is typically scored for judges' molecular (micro) ratings of behavior, such as eye contact, duration of reply, smiles, and gestures, the SSIT yields only subjects' and judges' global (molar) ratings of social anxiety and skill on 11-point scales. Both levels of measurement have various strengths and weaknesses, and both types of data can be valuable (Curran, Farrell, & Grunberger, 1984). A more recent approach to level of measurement that appears to be a promising compromise is the use of intermediate or "midi"-level ratings. Such intermediate coding combines the subjective judgment of global ratings with the focus on specific kinds of behavior seen in molecular approaches. The midi-level rating scales developed by Monti *et al.* (1984) were significantly related to judges' global ratings of skill and anxiety on the SSIT in a study with psychiatric inpatients and day hospital patients. Intermediate rating systems developed by Wallander, Conger, and Conger (1985) and Farrell, Rabinowitz, Wallander, and Curran (1985) may also be of use with inpatient populations.

Social Skills Training

Social skills training, which follows the logic of the skills deficit model, attempts to train patients on the verbal and nonverbal molecular behaviors assumed important for effective social functioning. A response acquisition model (Bandura, 1969) characterizes the skills training approach, with active steps taken to teach social skills absent from the individual's repertoire. Deficient response elements are treated one at a time, according to hierarchies of increasing difficulty (i.e., gaze, posture, and smiling are trained before self-disclosure or conversational skills). Response elements are applied to successively difficult problem situations in a manner that insures successful experiences for the patient. The actual skills training proceeds according to an instructional format and incorporates the techniques of instruction and coaching, behavior rehearsal, corrective feedback, social reinforcement, modeling, and homework assignments (Bellack & Hersen, 1979).

Rationale and Instruction. The purpose of the training is first explained to the patient, emphasizing why it is important to learn a particular social skill. For example, a therapist might state that the reason it is important to look at people when speaking to them is because that is the only way to insure that others are listening and paying attention. Verbal instructions then describe how a particular social skill is performed: "Try to look at me when you answer. If you don't want to look me right in the eye, try to look at my nose."

Behavioral Rehearsal. After providing the treatment rationale and instruction in how to produce socially skilled responses, the therapist presents a social situation for the patient to role-play with either the therapist, a cotherapist role model, or a member of the therapy group. A scenario is described to the patient ("You are standing in line waiting for your medicine and another patient comes up and gets ahead of you in line"); a prompt is delivered by the role model ("You don't care if I go ahead of you, do you?"); and the patient is encouraged to respond.

Feedback and Social Reinforcement. Following the patient's role-play response, the therapist or other group member provides feedback concerning the adequacy of his or her performance. Feedback is presented in a supportive and encouraging manner, emphasizing the successful elements of the patient's response. For example, the therapist might state the following: "That was very good, you were very clear in telling me that you don't like it when people cut ahead of you. You also looked over at me once, which made me pay attention to what you were saying." Additional instructions would follow as the therapist further shapes the patient's response: "Let's try that situation again, and this time try to look me in the eye when you speak to me. That will make your statement even stronger."

Modeling. Certain social skills, such as appropriate gaze or posture, are relatively easy for patients to learn; and verbal instructions, rehearsal, and feedback may be sufficient to bring about positive changes. Other social skills, such as asking follow-up questions in a conversation, are more complex and may not be readily learned through these techniques alone. It is often helpful for the therapist or role model to demonstrate (model) appropriate responses when complex behaviors are being taught. Modeling exercises are based on the patient's previous response to a role-play situation, and they elaborate upon the skill being trained. For example, the therapist might introduce a modeling exercise in the following way: "That was better. This time let me do the work and you relax. Listen to how I answer the woman's question and then ask her about the same thing. 'Yes I do enjoy rock music. What's your favorite type of music?' You see, I didn't just answer her question, but I kept the conversation going by asking her a question too." The patient is then redirected to the role-play situation to further practice his or her response. The sequence of instruction, rehearsal, feedback, modeling, and further rehearsal facilitates the process of response acquisition and is repeated until a particular social skill is mastered.

Homework Assignments. Although patients can be taught new social behavior during training sessions, this does not guarantee that response skills will generalize to the patient's natural environment, or that skills will be maintained in novel social situations. Several studies demonstrate that generalization is not necessarily a by-product of social skills training (Bellack, Hersen, & Turner, 1976; Frederiksen, Jenkins, Foy, & Eisler, 1976; Gutride, Goldstein, & Hunter, 1973; Williams, Turner, Watts, Bellack, & Hersen, 1977). For this reason it is important to include both in vivo training and homework assignments in order to facilitate generalization and maintenance of skills (Bellack & Morrison, 1985; Wallace *et al.*, 1980).

Liberman and his colleagues (Liberman *et al.*, 1984) have recommended assigning specific and verifiable homework tasks between sessions. These authors instructed patients to perform a number of interpersonal tasks each day, such as initiate brief (i.e., 10-minute) conversations with nursing staff, invite family members on recreational outings (museum or movie trips), or interact with community service personnel (e.g., obtain a library card and bring it back as proof). The Liberman *et al.* study demonstrated that when homework assignments are clearly presented, concrete in nature, and easily verified, subjects can follow through to reproduce social skills in new environments.

While behavior rehearsal, corrective feedback, social reinforcement, modeling, and homework assignments are common elements in social skills training,
no standardized treatment protocol exists, and training programs have varied on
several dimensions, including format, frequency of sessions, and length of
treatment.

Training Format. Social skills training has been conducted successfully in
both individual and group formats. Eisler, Bellack, Hersen, and colleagues have
demonstrated that individual training programs are highly effective, and permit
treatment to be maximally tailored to the needs of the patient (Edelstein & Eisler,
1976; Hersen & Bellack, 1976a; Hersen, Turner, Edelstein, & Pinkston, 1975).
While a small-group format may not be as responsive to a particular patient's
needs, there are a number of advantages to this approach. Among these are
opportunities for patients to observe several interpersonal styles, and chances to
relinquish the "patient role" by serving as a role-model participant. Small
groups also permit patients to relax occasionally while other group members
participate in training procedures. This can be an important feature for schizophrenic patients, many of whom react adversely to prolonged emotional stimulation.

Frequency and Duration of Training. A survey of social skills treatment studies
reveals significant diversity in the frequency of training sessions, as well as the
overall length of treatment (Matson, 1980). As yet, there is no consensus as to
how frequently sessions should be scheduled, or how much training constitutes
an adequate trial. Clinical experience indicates that questions about frequency
and duration can be best answered by considering the patient's level of functioning and severity of social disability. For example, many schizophrenic patients
suffer from attentional problems and have difficulty tolerating tasks which require concentrated effort. For these patients it is wise to keep training sessions
relatively brief, so training does not become aversive. Lost treatment time can be
recovered by scheduling sessions often, perhaps as frequently as every day
(Wallace, 1982).

In many schizophrenic patients, particularly chronic schizophrenics, social
dysfunction is pronounced and pervades numerous areas of interpersonal functioning. Long-term training appears necessary for these patients to develop
adequate social skills. Liberman and his colleagues (Liberman, Nuechterlein, &
Wallace, 1982) have stated that a minimum of 6 months may be necessary to
establish clinically relevant changes in the social functioning of schizophrenic
patients, and that it may take as long as 2 to 4 years for clinically significant and
durable results to be achieved. Such a time frame is far longer than that of most
social skills programs, which may be as short as 2 weeks and are rarely longer
than 6 months (Matson, 1980).

Efficacy of the Skills Training Approach

The efficacy of social skills training has been evaluated through single-
subject designs (e.g., reversal designs or multiple baseline analysis) and group

comparisons. Such single-subject studies (Bellack *et al.*, 1976; Edelstein & Eisler, 1976; Hersen & Bellack, 1976a; Hersen *et al.*, 1975; Williams *et al.*, 1977) provide strong evidence of the effectiveness of social skills training with schizophrenic patients. There is ample documentation that specific molecular responses (e.g., eye contact, speech duration, speech disruptions, voice volume and tone, response latency, smiles, posture, and positive and negative assertive behavior) improve in schizophrenic patients exposed to social skills training. In addition, improvements in molecular responding seem to be associated with increases in overall social skill (Hersen & Bellack, 1976a).

It is more difficult to summarize the results of group comparison studies, since these investigations vary considerably in terms of patient characteristics (e.g., accuracy of diagnosis and level of social skills impairment), assessment methodologies, and treatment interventions (Bellack & Morrison, 1985; Curran, Monti, & Corriveau, 1985). It does appear, however, that schizophrenic patients benefit from participation in social skills groups. Group comparisons indicate that treated patients improve on self-report measures of social skill and anxiety, and behavioral measures of social functioning (Field & Test, 1975; Goldsmith & McFall, 1975; Percell, Berwick, & Beigel, 1974; Williams *et al.*, 1977). Consistent with findings from the single-subject research, social skills groups have been shown to facilitate improvement in both molecular responding and overall social performance (Hersen & Bellack, 1976b; Matson, 1980; Morrison & Bellack, 1987; Wallace *et al.*, 1980). However, not every patient responds well to group training (Morrison & Bellack, 1984), indicating that this format may be inappropriate for certain subgroups of schizophrenic patients.

While both single-subject and group comparison studies demonstrate that social skills training influences subjects' posttreatment social performance, there is some controversy as to the clinical significance of these results (Wallace *et al.*, 1980). Specifically, two questions have been raised: First, do the social skills gained during treatment generalize to the patient's natural environment; and second, how durable are treatment gains? Unfortunately, little data currently exist indicating that generalization of skills is an automatic benefit of treatment. Available evidence indicates that treatment results form a "gradient of generalization" (Curran *et al.*, 1985, p. 232), with treatment effects generalizing well to measures similar to training situations, but less consistently to measures dissimilar to those presented in treatment. In other words, social functioning is effective when "real-life" interactions are similar to scenarios practiced during treatment. The more reality diverges from training situations, however, the less effective performance is likely to be. This limits the usefulness of the motor skills approach since it is impossible for any training program to fully anticipate the variety of interpersonal situations which may challenge patients.

Likewise, there is a paucity of data regarding the maintenance of treatment gains over time. This can be attributed to the fact that relatively few investigations with schizophrenic patients include long-term follow-up assessment. Many studies either fail to include a follow-up evaluation (e.g., Frederiksen *et al.*, 1976; Shepherd, 1977; Williams *et al.*, 1977), or report on relatively brief follow-up periods (e.g., Bellack *et al.*, 1976; Hersen & Bellack, 1976a; Hersen *et al.*, 1975; King, Liberman, & Bryan, 1977). As a result, there are currently insufficient data to conclude that social skills training promotes long-term maintenance of behavior change (Curran *et al.*, 1985).

The dearth of empirical data concerning generalization and maintenance effects has encouraged speculation as to procedures that might enhance these aspects of outcome. For example, it has been suggested that social skills programs should routinely include homework assignments and *in vivo* practice sessions as methods of promoting generalization of treatment gains (Bellack & Morrison, 1985). Furthermore, posttreatment "booster sessions" have been suggested as a means of facilitating long-term maintenance of social skills (Curran *et al.*, 1985). Suggestions such as these are consistent with the motor skills hypothesis and do not challenge the theoretical underpinnings of this approach. Other researchers, however, have proposed that the motor skills paradigm may be too limited in focus and that generalization and maintenance issues are best addressed by expanding the scope of the topographic model. One area of expansion that appears particularly relevant for schizophrenic patients is the domain of cognitive functioning.

The Cognitive–Information-Processing Model

The motor skills model did not originally consider the role of cognitive factors in interpersonal performance. This omission has been addressed in several reconceptualizations of the topographic scheme (e.g., McFall, 1982; Morrison & Bellack, 1981; Trower, Bryant, & Argyle, 1978), and a variety of cognitive functions are now considered important determinants of social behavior. Among these are attention, memory, and concept formation (Liberman *et al.*, 1982), affect recognition (Morrison, Bellack, & Mueser, 1988), perceptual skills (Morrison & Bellack, 1981, 1987), social knowledge structures (Liberman *et al.*, 1986), and interpersonal problem-solving abilities (Wallace, 1982, 1984; Wallace *et al.*, 1980). While the addition of cognitive variables has significantly expanded the scope of the topographic model, the importance of molecular motor behaviors remains undisputed. Cognitive theories, however, view response skills as only one link in a complex social-processing chain.

According to the cognitive–information-processing model applied to schizophrenia, effective interpersonal functioning requires successful integration of three types of social skill (Liberman *et al.*, 1986; Wallace, 1982, 1984): accurate reception (recognizing and decoding social data), efficient processing (interpreting incoming stimuli and selecting a response option), and appropriate responding (motoric performance). Each skill system is multifaceted, with numerous subprocesses contributing to interpersonal behavior. For example, a social exchange begins when one party recognizes an interpersonal stimulus. Recognition is a complicated process, however, and depends upon attention and memory functions. An individual must first focus attention long enough for social data to be observed, and once noticed, short-term memory must be intact to retain information for further processing.

Even if attention and memory processes are operating, there is no guarantee that social stimuli will be correctly identified. Deficiencies in affect recognition (e.g., reading facial and body cues, integrating speech content and voice tone) may create a barrier for interpersonal data, causing an afflicted individual to miss subtle social messages. Assuming, however, that a social stimulus has been noticed, stored, and identified, processing continues. The meaning of social data is ascertained by comparing the stimulus to knowledge about appropriate interpersonal behavior which is stored in long-term memory. Once information has been interpreted, problem-solving skills are brought into play: the individual generates response options, evaluates the potential effectiveness of each, and finally selects a response from those available in his or her skills repertoire. Motoric skills are accessed at this point, and the person responds behaviorally.

Not surprisingly, the cognitive–information-processing paradigm contends that many factors (e.g., attentional and/or perceptual difficulties, memory dysfunction, inadequate social knowledge, poor problem-solving skills, ineffective motor responding) potentially contribute to schizophrenics' interpersonal difficulties (Liberman *et al.*, 1982). As a result, the therapeutic goal of the cognitive approach is to first identify the skill system(s) that contribute to the patient's social problems and then develop strategies to overcome any existing deficits.

Assessing Cognitive Processes

Although the information-processing paradigm posits that many cognitive processes are involved in social functioning, more research is needed showing that cognitive deficits directly contribute to poor interpersonal performance (Morrison, 1988; Morrison & Bellack, 1984, 1987). Until recently, cognitive theorists have relied primarily on the findings of experimental psychopathologists to establish links between cognitive functions and schizophrenics' social behavior. (Liberman *et al.*, 1982). Unfortunately, assessment of cognitive–perceptual variables has been generally absent in social skills outcome studies. While the trend is to include attention focusing, social perception, and/or problem-solving training in treatment programs (e.g., Bellack *et al.*, 1984, Liberman *et al.*, 1986; Wallace & Liberman, 1985), we do not know how pervasive these problems are prior to treatment, thereby making it difficult to judge the effectiveness of training. In this regard, development of cognitive treatment strategies has outpaced developments in cognitive assessment methods. Thus, in addition to assessment of basic cognitive abilities, measures of social perception, social judgment, social knowledge, and problem-solving skills should be further explored with schizophrenic populations.

Basic Cognitive Functions. Erickson and Binder (1986) have suggested several easily administered procedures for assessing patients' basic cognitive deficits and current adaptive abilities. Specific neuropsychological tests (Lezak, 1983) are proposed for assessing attention (Serial Sevens, Letter Cancellation, Word Fluency), concentration (Trails A & B, Digit Symbol), memory (Wechsler Memory Scale, Bender-Gestalt Recall, Inglis Paired Associates), abstraction (Proverbs, Similarities, Wisconsin Card Sort), and cognitive flexibility (Trails A vs. Trails B, Stroop Test, Wisconsin Card Sort). It is clear that many of these measures have relevance to the information-processing and problem-solving processes that are assumed to play a role in social functioning. Including such measures in social skills assessments would help to determine the nature and extent of cognitive deficits prior to treatment, and the reactivity of deficits to cognitive retraining.

Social Perception and Social Judgment. As Morrison and Bellack (1981) have argued, poor social functioning may result from a combination of poor social skills (response deficits) *and* from deficits in social perception. While not generally included in outcome studies, experimental evidence suggests that this latter ability, which typically refers to one's ability to decode cues or messages from conversation partners, appears to be especially deficient in schizophrenics and psychiatric patients (Fingeret, Monti, & Paxon, 1985; Monti & Fingeret, 1987). In addition, deficits in social perception skills may be related to inadequate social performance (Eisler, Frederiksen, & Peterson, 1978; Fingeret, Monti, & Paxon, 1983; Morrison, 1988).

The Profile of Nonverbal Sensitivity (PONS; Rosenthal, Hall, Archer, Di-Matteo, & Rogers, 1979) has often been used to assess the ability of psychiatric patients to decode messages from nonverbal information. Subjects are asked to choose the response communicated by a series of nonverbal sequences presented on videotape. Fingeret *et al.* (1985) suggest reading response alternatives aloud rather than presenting them in written form. A recent chapter by Rosenthal and Benowitz (1986) reviewed this literature and concluded that psychiatric patients perform more poorly than nonpsychiatric samples on the PONS.

Another measure of social perception has asked patients to view a series of both skilled and unskilled videotaped social interactions and to rate the social skill or appropriateness of each response. Fingeret and his colleagues (Fingeret *et al.*, 1985; Monti & Fingeret, 1987) have used the situations presented on the SSIT to measure this aspect of social perception. Eisler, Frederiksen, and Peterson (1978) used a similar technique, the Social Alternates Test, in which psychiatric patients were asked to choose the two most effective responses from a list of six which accompanied a number of videotaped assertive situations. These choices consisted of passive, aggressive, and assertive alternatives. Alternate strategies, such as the picture arrangement subtest of the WAIS-R, could also be used to assess social judgment or social knowledge.

A final aspect of perceptual dysfunction in schizophrenia focuses on deficits in facial affect recognition and perceptual judgments of emotion cues. The typical methodology to assess affect recognition (Izard, 1971) is to show subjects a set of photographs depicting a range of emotional expressions and ask them to either identify the emotion or to associate each photo with a printed emotion label card. Walker, Marwit, and Emory (1980) chose the latter response format, since it is likely to be less ambiguous and rely less on vocabulary skills. Walker *et al.* found normals to be significantly better than schizophrenic patients at identifying all emotions. A recent review by Morrison *et al.* (1988) provides an excellent summary of this literature, which should aid in the selection of appropriate measures.

Problem-Solving Strategies. While cognitively based outcome studies have not routinely measured subjects' cognitive abilities (i.e., attention deficits, distractibility, affect recognition, memory), Wallace and his colleagues (Liberman *et al.*, 1986; Wallace & Liberman, 1985) have introduced a technique for measuring social perception and interpersonal problem-solving skills. In this procedure, cognitive variables are assessed as patients participate in role-play exercises. While one patient role-plays a social vignette with a therapist, two other patients observe the interaction. After the role play is completed, the three patients are asked a series of questions to assess receiving skills (e.g., "Who spoke to you? What did ——— say? What was ——— feeling? What were the short- and long-term goals in this situation?") and problem-solving strategies (e.g., "What was the problem in the situation? What is one alternative that you could have used when ——— said ———? What could the other person do if you said that? Would you get your short- and long-term goals by using that alternative?"). Patients' responses are recorded, allowing the therapist to monitor patients' progress in acquiring cognitive skills. In this manner Wallace and Liberman (1985) have reported that social perception and problem-solving "errors" decrease following treatment.

Another approach to assessing problem-solving competency has been described by Hansen, St. Lawrence, and Christoff (1985), who presented a series of problematic interpersonal situations to chronic psychiatric patients (86% schizophrenic) and audiotaped patients' strategies for resolving each dilemma. Patients' solutions were rated by independent judges for the occurrence or nonoccurrence of five problem-solving skills: (1) problem identification, (2) goal definition, (3) solution evaluation, (4) evaluation of alternatives, and (5) selection of a best solution. Hansen and his colleagues evaluated subjects prior to social skills training and found that not only did problem-solving skills occur infrequently in this sample, but that patients scored significantly lower than a social validation cohort (nonpsychiatric volunteers from the community) on the average effectiveness of their problem-solving solutions. Problem-solving skills were successfully modified by training, and posttreatment and follow-up assessments revealed that patients and social validation subjects no longer differed in solution effectiveness. The authors therefore demonstrated both that problem-solving deficits exist prior to treatment and that patients could acquire these skills with training.

Treating Cognitive-Processing Deficits

Attention and Social Perception. It has been speculated that some schizophrenic patients may require direct training of basic cognitive processes as a prerequisite to social skills treatment (Spaulding, Storms, Goodrich, & Sullivan, 1986). For example, Liberman and colleagues (Liberman *et al.*, 1986) have described an attention-focusing procedure for teaching conversational skills. The procedure is intended to place minimal demands on patients' cognitive and information-processing capabilities by presenting brief training sessions (20-

minutes each, twice daily), systematic repetition of training material, graduated prompting, and consistent and immediate reinforcement. The program utilizes a confederate, who serves as the patient's conversational partner, and a trainer, who provides instructions, prompts, and social reinforcement. Confederates open role-play exercises by making a statement to the patient, such as "I went to the movies last night." If the patient makes an appropriate response (e.g., "What did you see?"), the exercise is terminated and reinforcement is provided. If there is no response or an inappropriate response, the trainer delivers a prompt to the patient—"Ask him a question." If the patient still does not ask a question of the confederate, a second prompt is given—"One good question is 'What did you see?' " If the patient still does not ask a question, that prompt is repeated. The trial ends after the third prompt (whether or not a correct response was made), and a new trial is initiated. Liberman et al. (1986) report that the attention-focusing procedure is an effective adjunct to conversational skills training with some schizophrenic patients.

Cognitively based training programs have also incorporated environmental manipulations in an effort to offset schizophrenics' perceptual and attentional deficits (Liberman et al., 1982). Tactics have included minimizing distracting visual and auditory stimuli in the training area, posting graphic charts for clear and simple visual cueing of training procedures, and liberal use of videotaped material (Wallace, 1982). These efforts are intended to facilitate the learning of social skills by minimizing the load placed on the patient's information-processing system. Thus, environmental features are coupled with other "prosthetic" ingredients (i.e., brief and focused training tasks, repetition of instructions to decrease novelty, a slow training pace, low performance demands, and positive performance-contingent feedback) to present a "friendly" learning atmosphere.

Interpersonal Problem-Solving Skills. In addition to attention-focusing strategies and environmental structuring, the cognitive treatment model has emphasized the importance of interpersonal problem solving in social skills training. Wallace (1982) has described a comprehensive program that is designed to teach schizophrenic patients problem-solving skills applicable to the social arenas of hospital, family, peers, and community. Treatment is conducted in a small-group format, with a high therapist to patient ratio. Sessions are scheduled frequently (five mornings each week, 2 hours per session), and place a heavy emphasis on role-playing interpersonal scenes. Up to 120 different scenarios, focusing on instrumental and friendship–dating situations, are presented over a 9-week period. Each role play is videotaped and reviewed in a two-stage process. First, the therapist asks patients specific questions about receiving skills. If a patient answers a receiving question incorrectly, the relevant portion of the situation is reviewed and he or she is asked the question again. Patients are assisted by the therapist if they are unable to provide the correct response on their own, and are prompted to repeat the correct answer in response to further questioning.

After completing receiving questions, the focus of the session shifts to assessing and training problem-solving skills. Patients are asked a series of processing questions that emphasize the following points (Wallace, 1982): (1) interpersonal problems can be broken down into manageable subproblems, (2) response alternatives exist in every social situation, and (3) each alternative response differs in its consequences. Patients are encouraged to role-play alternative responses (e.g., compromise, get angry, repeat your request, ask for assistance) and evaluate the consequences of each. Throughout the processing phase the therapist provides corrective feedback, models alternate behaviors, and generally encourages the development of "flexible" processing skills. Once an effective alternative has been role-played, the focus of the session shifts to assessing and training sending skills. From this point on the training program resembles "traditional" social skills training, with an emphasis on motor skills performance.

Efficacy of the Cognitive–Information-Processing Approach

Although proponents of the cognitive–information-processing perspective have developed elegant theories of social behavior and comprehensive treatments of interpersonal dysfunction (e.g., Liberman, Massel, Mosk, & Wong, 1985; Liberman et al., 1986; Wallace, 1982; Wallace et al., 1980), relatively few studies have examined the additional contributions of interventions aimed at treating cognitive-processing deficits to social skills training with schizophrenics. For example, several recent investigations included social perception training as a component of treatment (Bellack et al., 1984; Hogarty et al., 1986; Wallace & Liberman, 1985). Two of these studies (Bellack et al., 1984; Wallace & Liberman, 1985) reported that patients registered durable improvements on measures of social skill and psychopathology. However, neither study reported specific data indicating that social perception deficits existed prior to treatment, or that social perception skills were learned following training. In addition, no information is reported to document that social perception skills directly enhanced patients' interpersonal performance. Thus, we do not yet know the extent to which social perception training is effective with schizophrenic patients.

Similar conclusions can be drawn regarding the efficacy of adding interpersonal problem-solving components to social skills treatment. This was demonstrated by Hansen et al. (1985), who developed and tested a cognitive training program based on D'Zurilla and Goldfried's (1971) problem-solving model. Treatment was offered to seven chronic psychiatric patients (six were schizophrenic) who were identified at pretreatment assessment as deficient in adaptive problem-solving skills. Skills targeted for training were problem identification, goal definition, solution evaluation, evaluation of alternatives, and selection of a best solution. Training was conducted in a small-group format and employed didactic instruction, modeling, behavioral rehearsal, corrective feedback, and verbal reinforcement. The effectiveness of the training was evaluated with a multiple baseline analysis.

The authors report that subjects were able to learn the problem-solving skills targeted for training, and that some generalization of these skills was observed. While several problem-solving skills were maintained at a 1-month follow-up, only problem identification and goal definition abilities remained improved at 4 months. This suggests that treatment gains were somewhat evanescent. Of greater concern, however, is the fact that patients' interpersonal behavior was not assessed in this investigation. We therefore have no way of ascertaining whether increases in interpersonal problem-solving skills were associated with improvements in social functioning. Thus, the relationship between problem-solving ability and interpersonal competence remains unclear.

Wallace and Liberman (1985) did monitor patients' social behavior in their investigation of interpersonal problem solving with schizophrenics. Twenty-eight schizophrenic patients were randomly assigned to either a problem-solving treatment or "holistic health therapy," a treatment which emphasized physical exercise, meditation, and stress management. The authors report that patients in both conditions registered posttreatment improvements on measures of psychopathology, social skill, and social anxiety. While there were few significant differences between the two groups immediately following treatment, several measures collected at a 9-month follow-up indicated superior functioning for "problem-solving" patients. Ratings of interpersonal performance, appropriateness, and social adjustment suggested that patients in the social skills condition maintained treatment gains, while patients receiving holistic health therapy did not sustain improvements.

The receiving and processing skills of patients in the problem-solving condition improved following 9 weeks of training, and treatment gains were maintained at the 9-month follow-up. "Holistic health" patients, however, did not show any evidence of change on these dimensions. While one might conclude from these results that improvements in cognitive skill are associated with increased behavioral competence, there is no direct causal evidence supporting this assertion. Wallace and Liberman (1985) observed receiving and processing improvements on one measure (Role Play Test of Social Competence; Wallace, 1982) and behavioral changes on another (Confederate Test of Social Skills; Goldsmith & McFall, 1975).

When evaluating the efficacy of the cognitive paradigm it is necessary to remember that cognitive–information-processing models were proposed in response to limitations observed in motor skills studies. Specifically, cognitive strategies were suggested as methods of strengthening generalization and maintenance effects. Without doubt, the cognitive–information-processing model possesses face validity and should be pursued. However, much empirical work is necessary to validate this paradigm. For example, future investigations must (1) document the influence of cognitive-processing deficits on impaired social behavior, (2) demonstrate that cognitive functions change following cognitive process interventions, (3) show that patients apply cognitive strategies *in vivo*, (4) illustrate that changes in cognitive skills are associated with improvements in motor responding, and (5) demonstrate that cognitive process interventions promote greater change in social functioning and greater generalization and maintenance of treatment gains than motor skills approaches alone. Until this work is accomplished, it is best to consider the cognitive–information-processing model a working hypothesis, and not an established fact.

SOCIAL ANXIETY AND DYSFUNCTIONAL COGNITIONS IN SCHIZOPHRENIA

The two preceding sections illustrate how social skills training with schizophrenics has evolved over time. Early efforts at treating socially impaired schizophrenics may have applied conceptual models ill equipped to handle the multiple deficits that characterize the disorder. Proponents of the cognitive–information-processing perspective responded to these limitations by suggesting training programs which addressed schizophrenics' perceptual and cognitive disabilities. By doing so, the cognitive paradigm expanded the conceptual and therapeutic scope of social skills training. It can be argued, however, that this cognitive reformulation was not expansive enough. Surprisingly, the influence of social anxiety and/or dysfunctional thoughts on the interpersonal behavior of schizophrenics has not been adequately addressed in either the topographic or cognitive–information-processing models.

Social Anxiety in Schizophrenia

The influence of social anxiety on interpersonal behavior has been well studied in nonschizophrenic samples, and findings from this literature suggest that anxiety affects social performance in a number of ways. In small doses, social anxiety can facilitate interpersonal behavior by serving as a "cue" to prepare for social encounters. In larger amounts, anxiety can impair and inhibit social behavior by disrupting response skills and contributing to the avoidance of interpersonal situations. Consequently, anxiety reduction is frequently a goal of treatment with nonschizophrenic patients, and measures of social anxiety are routinely included as dependent variables in intervention studies.

The situation is somewhat different in the schizophrenia literature. Although clinical observations suggest that interpersonal anxiety impairs schizophrenics' social behavior (e.g., Liberman, 1982; Liberman et al., 1982; Morrison & Bellack, 1984, 1987), neither the topographic nor cognitive–information-processing models have fully integrated the social anxiety construct into their conceptual system. For example, while Liberman (1982; Liberman et al., 1982) has stated that comprehensive assessment of social dysfunction requires an evaluation of social anxiety, such efforts are rare in studies involving schizophrenic patients. This point is illustrated by Wallace et al. (1980), who reviewed 32 investigations involving social skills training with schizophrenics. Only seven of these studies included social anxiety as a dependent variable. The lack of interest in the social anxiety construct may be unwise, since clinical observation suggests that social anxiety is prevalent in schizophrenia and may play a role in the interpersonal withdrawal observed in the disorder. Furthermore, we speculate that insufficiently treated social anxiety may also account for the uneven treatment gains reported in some studies (e.g., Bellack *et al.*, 1984), as well as the generalization difficulties reported in other investigations.

The Prevalence of Social Anxiety

It is difficult to determine precisely the incidence of social anxiety within schizophrenic populations, since no empirical studies have directly studied this question. Some data, however, suggest that the rate of social anxiety may be substantial. For example, McGlashan (1984b, 1986a) has retrospectively studied the premorbid characteristics of schizophrenic spectrum patients treated at Chestnut Lodge Hospital. High rates of social anxiety were found among schizophrenic (24%), schizoaffective (40%), and schizophreniform (33%) patients in the Chestnut Lodge sample. McGlashan's retrospective methods may have yielded conservative estimates, however. This is suggested by the results reported by Pilkonis and his colleagues (Pilkonis, Feldman, Himmelhoch, & Cornes, 1980), who found that 54% of a "cognitive disorder" cohort (79% schizophrenic) labeled themselves as shy. Group means on measures of social anxiety were moderate for these patients, but substantial within-group variation indicated that a subgroup of patients experienced high levels of interpersonal discomfort.

Other studies indicate that schizophrenic patients appear more anxious during interpersonal encounters than do comparison subjects. Monti and Fingeret (1987) found that schizophrenics exhibited higher levels of social anxiety during social performance tasks than did nonschizophrenic patients or normal controls. Similar results were reported by Fingeret *et al.* (1985), who found that psychiatric patients (41% schizophrenic) were rated as more anxious during social interactions than nonpsychiatric volunteers. Other studies demonstrate that social anxiety relates negatively to social performance (Fingeret *et al.*, 1983; Fingeret *et al.*, 1985; Monti *et al.*, 1984). However, low to moderate correlations among dependent measures indicate that social anxiety and social skill are relatively independent constructs. These findings suggest that the social withdrawal observed in schizophrenia may not be solely attributable to inadequate response skills or cognitive deficits. Phobic avoidance, a consequence of heightened anxiety, may account for the social isolation of at least some schizophrenics.

Assessment of Social Anxiety

Although measures of social anxiety have typically not been included in studies with schizophrenics, one instrument that has been used with a psychiatric population (38% psychotic) is Curran, Corriveau, Monti, and Hagerman's (1980) Social Reaction Inventory (SRI), a revision of Richardson and Tasto's (1976) Social Anxiety Inventory (SAI). Curran *et al.* concluded that the SRI showed utility with this population as a measure of both anxiety experienced and degree of skill or competency reported. The measure had good internal consistency and test–retest reliability, and its factor structure for anxiety replicated that of the SAI.

The majority of patients in Curran *et al.*'s sample, however, were not schizophrenic, and only 10% were inpatients. Asking hospitalized schizophrenics to respond twice to 105 items on 5-point Likert scales could well lead to less than valid results. With schizophrenics, then, we would recommend revising the SRI so that only one or two key questions are selected loading on each of the seven factors or domains of anxiety assessed (e.g., "Someone acts as if they dislike you," "Being interviewed for a job"). These questions could then be presented in an interview format.

Other self-report questionnaires of social anxiety and shyness (see Glass & Arnkoff, 1989) could be considered for use with schizophrenics. The Social Avoidance and Distress (SAD) and Fear of Negative Evaluation (FNE) scales (Watson & Friend, 1969) have been among those most frequently used for research and clinical purposes with nonpsychotics. The SAD has also been employed as an outcome measure in a treatment study with both schizophrenic and nonpsychotic inpatients (Eisler, Blanchard, Fitts, & Williams, 1978). In addition to these 28- and 30-item true–false inventories, Leary's (1983) brief 12-item revision of the FNE and the 9-item Cheek and Buss (1981) Shyness Scale could be explored for use with a schizophrenic population.

Another feasible approach to assessing social anxiety in schizophrenics is through global self-report and judges' ratings of anxiety following role-played interactions. Such ratings, which are obtained from Curran's Simulated Social Interaction Test (SSIT), significantly discriminated between patient and non-patient groups (Curran, 1982; Wessberg et al., 1981). The SSIT, which consists of eight brief social interactions initiated by confederate prompts, appears to be a promising technique for assessing schizophrenics' *in vivo* anxiety during social interactions. In a sense it can be seen as the behavioral equivalent of the SRI, since seven of the eight social situations parallel the seven factors represented on the self-report inventory. The SSIT has the advantage, however, of yielding more objective judges' ratings as well as patients' self-evaluations of their own social anxiety and social skill. These single-item Likert-scale ratings are also more likely to be accessible to schizophrenic subjects than is the lengthy SRI. Both measures have been used to assess outcome in a study comparing social skills and sensitivity training with psychiatric inpatients and day hospital patients (Monti, Curran, Corriveau, DeLancey, & Hagerman, 1980). Both anxiety and skill measures showed greater improvement for subjects who had received social skills training.

Social Anxiety and Treatment "Matching"

As stated earlier, the empirical literature suggests that social skills training is not universally successful in improving patients' social functioning. Results from numerous outcome studies indicate that not all treated patients experience improvements in interpersonal behavior or reductions in social anxiety (e.g., Bellack et al., 1984; Monti et al., 1979; Weinman, Gelbart, Wallace, & Post, 1972). The heterogeneous nature of patient samples and the relative homogeneity of training procedures may explain these mixed results. Specifically, certain "types" of schizophrenics (e.g., unskilled patients) may be well matched to skills-oriented training, while others (e.g., socially anxious patients) may be inadequately served by skills-based programs.

It is likely that schizophrenics vary along several dimensions of interpersonal disability, with every patient displaying a unique profile of social dysfunction. Curran and his colleagues (Curran et al., 1980) have described how this is possible. These authors evaluated the demographic and clinical features of 58 socially deficient psychiatric patients (22% schizophrenic) and reported that few of these patients displayed all of the behavioral, clinical, and social attributes that fit the stereotype of social inadequacy. For example, while some patients reported subjective distress in social situations, others did not. Likewise, some patients were characterized by problems with behavioral deficits or excesses, but these features were not universal. Cognitive difficulties were also variable, with only a subset of patients describing self-deprecatory ideation. These results suggest that socially impaired schizophrenics may not be a homogeneous cohort, and they raise the possibility that specific subgroups of social dysfunction (e.g., response deficit, anxiety disorder, and cognitive dysfunction groups) exist within schizophrenic samples.

The probability of "social dysfunction subtypes" suggests that social skills training may be differentially effective with specific cohorts. For example, we would anticipate that patients with specific behavioral deficits would respond best to response acquisition programs. It is not clear, however, whether such an approach would be most effective for individuals plagued by social anxiety. Investigations with nonschizophrenic subjects indicate that social discomfort may be preceded by anticipatory anxiety and negative thoughts that could directly strengthen avoidance responses (Cacioppo, Glass, & Merluzzi, 1979). Social skills training programs may not diminish the disruptive effects of negative expectations and anticipatory anxiety. If anticipatory anxiety remains untreated, socially anxious individuals may continue to avoid social situations due to heightened arousal and distress *prior* to such interactions. Consequently, anticipatory anxiety may fuel phobic avoidance, leading to the social isolation and withdrawal so characteristic of schizophrenic patients. Furthermore, we speculate that untreated anticipatory anxiety may contribute to the nonsignificant generalization effects observed in many outcome investigations.

An investigation conducted by Monti and his colleagues (Monti et al., 1979) illustrates this point. Thirty psychiatric patients (23% with a "psychotic" diagnosis) were randomly assigned to social skills training, bibliotherapy, and hospital treatment control groups. Assessments of posttreatment social performance (role-play exercises) indicated that patients in skills training improved significantly more than control subjects. However, treated subjects did not report significant decreases in social anxiety. Interestingly, behavioral improvements were not observed on *in vivo* generalization tasks. One possible explanation for these results is that social skills training may not have successfully neutralized the anticipatory anxiety of "anxiety profile" patients. If this were the case, avoidance behaviors may have remained strong, resulting in reluctance to use response skills spontaneously in the natural environment.

Stress Management and Social Anxiety

If social anxiety does play a significant role in the social withdrawal of schizophrenic individuals, anxiety management procedures might assist patients in combatting the limiting effects of anxiety and autonomic arousal. Wallace and his colleagues (Lukoff, Wallace, Liberman, & Burke, 1986; Wallace & Liberman, 1985) report data suggesting this speculation has merit. As described earlier, these researchers randomly assigned 28 schizophrenic patients to either social skills training (SST) or "holistic health therapy" (HHT), a program designed to increase patients' ability to handle stressful life events. The holistic health treatment was a comprehensive stress management package which combined daily yoga, exercise, and meditation sessions with twice weekly stress education, weekly positive imaging sessions, and sessions encouraging the acceptance of psychotic experiences and the building of self-esteem. The HHT program emphasized applying anxiety reduction procedures as a method of coping with subjective distress and autonomic arousal.

After 9 weeks of treatment, both SST and HHT patients showed similar significant decreases in psychopathology (although these gains were maintained better by SST subjects at follow-up). Of greater interest are the results pertaining to social functioning: both SST and HHT patients showed similarly significant improvements on measures of social performance and anxiety immediately after treatment. We speculate that the similar rates of improvement may have resulted from interactions between the treatment condition and subgroup variables. For example, the SST group may have contained a sample of behaviorally impaired patients who responded well to the response acquisition model. Socially anxious patients in this condition may not have fared as well, however, since SST might not be well "matched" to the anxiety subtype. The HHT program may have offered maximum treatment benefits to these patients since anxiety reduction techniques would help to decrease the debilitative effects of anticipatory anxiety and autonomic arousal. Behaviorally impaired individuals in HHT may not have done as well, however, since their particular needs were not addressed by the stress management program. Thus, "mismatches" between patients and treatment may have contributed to the lack of uniform improvement observed in each treatment condition. Likewise, the unexpected success of the HHT program (at least at posttreatment assessment) may have been due to an unplanned, but beneficial, treatment match for socially anxious patients.

Debilitative Thoughts and Cognitions in Schizophrenia

While social anxiety has been underemphasized in schizophrenia, virtually no attention has been paid to the influence of dysfunctional thoughts on the interpersonal performance of schizophrenic patients. Eisler, Frederiksen, and Peterson (1978) offer some support for this approach, finding that unassertive psychiatric patients expected fewer positive or reinforcing consequences for their actions that their assertive peers, and erroneously believed passive responses to be more appropriate. Although a number of studies have attempted to modify cognitive *processes* such as discrimination, attention, and information retrieval (e.g., Adams, Brantley, Malatesta, & Turkat, 1981), we know less about changing the *content* of schizophrenics' distorted thoughts, attitudes, and beliefs. Meichenbaum and Cameron (1973), in perhaps the first study of its kind to focus on psychiatric patients' internal dialogue, found that self-instructional training improved performance on measures of conceptual, attentional, and verbal behavior. Patients learned to recognize cues for emitting task-relevant thoughts and developed a set of self-statements that included self-talk about what they were asked to do, self-instruction when their responses were bizarre or irrelevant, and self-rewarding thoughts.

Irrational Beliefs

In a recent study with a heterogeneous psychiatric population (37% schizophrenic), Monti, Zwick, and Warzak (1986) found that patients exhibited irrational beliefs in a number of areas to a significantly greater extent than did undergraduates in previous research. Irrational beliefs about dependency issues were also significantly related to judges' ratings of social anxiety and skill during role-played social interactions. Monti *et al.* urge further examination of the relationship between cognitive factors and behavioral measures of social anxiety and social skill in this population. Both the original Irrational Beliefs Test (IBT; Jones, 1969) and the revised version employed by Monti *et al.* in their investigation of irrational beliefs in psychiatric patients do not seem particularly appropriate for use with psychotic or schizophrenic patients, however. The 100-item IBT, administered as a self-report questionnaire, would tax these individuals' abilities to the limit. We recommend revising and validating this measure further, by selecting only a few items representative of each irrational belief, rewording the content for greater simplicity and clarity, and presenting these questions orally rather than in inventory format.

Self-Statements

The Social Interaction Self-Statement Test (SISST; Glass, Merluzzi, Biever, & Larsen, 1982) is the most frequently used self-statement measure in both the social anxiety and social phobia literature. This questionnaire, which consists of 15 debilitative or negative thoughts and 15 positive thoughts facilitative to social interaction, was empirically developed and validated with undergraduates. Dodge, Hope, Heimberg, and Becker (1988), in their recent evaluation of the SISST with social phobics, found that negative thoughts were significantly related to social anxiety, public self-consciousness, and fear of negative evaluation. Clinicians' shyness ratings of clinical outpatients have also been found to be significantly correlated with SISST scores. This short self-report measure of positive and negative thoughts appears to be very appropriate for use with a schizophrenic population, although to our knowledge the SISST has never been used in this setting. Changing the response format for each thought from a 5-point scale representing thought frequency to a simple checklist response (yes–no) is recommended if the SISST is to be used with schizophrenic patients.

Videotaped thought reconstruction (Meichenbaum, 1977) also has promise as a measure of self-statements or internal dialogue. Just as the SISST could be administered following a series of role-played social situations, patients could be shown a videotape of their interaction and articulate whatever thoughts were going through their mind during the conversation. Stopping the tape at predetermined points and prompting for responses (e.g., "What were you thinking when he said that?") might aid in the collection of useful and valid information on patients' thoughts.

Cognitive Therapy

In his cognitive therapy groups with young adult chronic patients, Greenwood (1983) has employed cognitive restructuring and stress-inoculation training to change schizophrenics' self-statements as well as core irrational beliefs, maladaptive perceptions, and attributions. He suggests four cognitive distortions that are especially prevalent in this population: (1) selective abstractions and arbitrary inference, where patients scan for "clues" to support global interpretations of danger and threat; (2) dichotomous or all-or-none thinking—seeing oneself or others in absolute terms as all good and powerful or all evil and ineffective; (3) magnification or catastrophizing, so that patients exaggerate the negative consequences of taking risks or trying new behavior; and (4) faulty attributions that over- or underestimate the extent to which patients can control events and their own or others' behavior. Greenwood helps his schizophrenic patients learn to discriminate confirmable reality and more realistic ways of interpreting events from perceived reality, where their distortions may reinforce avoidance, overreaction, or a sense of worthlessness.

It is unfortunate that so little work exists that examines the nature of dysfunctional cognitive content in schizophrenic populations, since an increasing number of therapy interventions and assessment instruments for socially anxious or phobic clients have stressed cognitive factors (Arnkoff & Glass, 1989; Glass & Shea, 1986). We suggest that the assessment of maladaptive thoughts is an important addition to a comprehensive assessment of social functioning in schizophrenia. Assessment techniques such as videotape thought reconstruction, think-aloud tasks, and structured self-statement questionnaires, which have yielded rich information on the nature of social anxiety and social phobia, could be utilized with inpatients to delineate the nature of their dysfunctional thinking styles. Measures of irrational beliefs, attributional style, expectations, self-focused attention, and cognitive schemata could also be considered in order to develop a more complete understanding of schizophrenics' functioning in social situations. Many of these measures could be revised to allow presentation in an interview rather than questionnaire format, thereby increasing their usefulness with schizophrenic patients.

FUTURE DIRECTIONS

The preceding sections have illustrated the heterogeneous nature of social dysfunction in schizophrenia. The topographic and cognitive– information-processing models propose that disturbed cognitive, perceptual, and behavioral processes account for deficient interpersonal behavior. We have suggested that social anxiety, maladaptive internal dialogue, and irrational beliefs also play a significant role, and that the influence of cognitive, affective, and behavioral deficits varies from patient to patient. Consequently, it is likely that each schizophrenic patient possesses a unique profile of social disability, with the factors contributing to social impairment weighted differently for each individual. Some profiles may aggregate into homogeneous subtypes, however. Verifying the existence of independent "social deficit" subgroups could have important ramifications for nosology and treatment planning.

Clinical observation suggests that socially isolated schizophrenics vary significantly in the quality of their withdrawal. For example, some patients display a schizoid orientation, demonstrating a genuine indifference to social relationships. While interpersonal deficits are pronounced in these individuals, they appear to experience minimal discomfort or anxiety in social situations. Indeed, such patients often convey the impression that relationships are unwanted and represent an uninvited imposition. The template for human affiliation appears absent in these cases, with a resulting attenuation of interpersonal consideration, reciprocity, and intimacy.

For other patients isolation seems a defensive maneuver, one intended to minimize interpersonal discomfort. These individuals avoid social contact not due to indifference, but because of heightened fears of negative evaluation and rejection. In other words, in addition to potential social skills deficits, the presence of an internal dialogue concerned with negative expectations may play a role in these patients' social anxiety. Avoidant patients seem "reachable," however, and communicate the impression that human contacts are desirable and potentially rewarding. Although the ability to interact is compromised in these individuals, the potential for relating appears intact. While social withdrawal characterizes these patients, the presence of interpersonal anxiety distinguishes them, and it may portend a different prognosis and outcome.

Tentative support for this hypothesis is provided by further analyses of data from the Chestnut Lodge follow-up study (McGlashan, 1984a). Briefly described, the Chestnut Lodge investigation retrospectively studied the longitudinal clinical profile of patients hospitalized between the years of 1939 and 1975. Application of DSM-III criteria (American Psychiatric Association, 1980) to hospital medical records identified 188 schizophrenic patients; 163 of these individuals were interviewed an average of 15 years after discharge to assess functioning across six domains: living situation at follow-up, further treatment, employment, social activity, psychopathology, and global outcome.

Using baseline sign and symptom data, we identified 96 schizophrenic patients in this data set who were described as socially withdrawn and isolated prior to Chestnut Lodge hospitalization. Thirty-six patients from this sample displayed a schizoid orientation (e.g., flat, constricted affect and an absence of social anxiety). Twenty-six patients were labeled "avoidant" based on a positive history of social anxiety. Males constituted 58% of the Schizoid subgroup and 42% of the Avoidant cohort. Marital status (percent ever married) was similar for the two samples (Schizoid = 25%, Avoidant = 23%), as was age of illness onset (Schizoid = 18.9, Avoidant = 18.5). Premorbid social and occupational functioning was similarly poor for both subgroups.

Significant differences were noted on several diagnostic instruments (Astrachan et al., 1972; Gunderson & Kolb, 1978). Subjects in the Schizoid sample displayed more signs and symptoms of schizophrenia, and Avoidant patients demonstrated significantly more character pathology. Avoidant patients also recorded superior scores on the Chestnut Lodge Prognostic Scale for Chronic Schizophrenia (Fenton & McGlashan, 1987). While long-term functioning was routinely poor for all subjects, several outcome dimensions approached significance, with patients in the Avoidant subgroup having a somewhat better outcome. Avoidant individuals socialized more frequently, were employed more often, and received higher ratings of overall global functioning than their Schizoid counterparts.

These results, especially those pertaining to prognosis and long-term outcome (Guze, 1975), raise the possibility that our Avoidant and Schizoid subtypes may represent different nosological entities. While we recognize that the data supporting this conclusion are only preliminary, our analyses established a consistent trend of superiority for Avoidant patients, in a direction consistent with clinical observations: the "reachable" patients were more likely to eventually form some social and occupational connections, while Schizoid individuals followed an uninterrupted course of asociality. This finding tentatively supports the hypothesis of subtypes of social disability, at least along the Schizoid–Avoidant dimension, and indicates the need for further research in this area.

We have already suggested that a subtyping system might increase the effectiveness of social skills training, since knowledge of subtype would permit the tailoring of interventions to meet an individual patient's needs. Optimal patient–treatment combinations could be ascertained through a systematic program of research that tests several matching schemes. One tactic might involve matching particular patients to specific interventions in order to determine therapeutic benefits. For example, we could test whether anxiety profile patients benefit most from stress-reduction treatments, or if skills deficit patients respond best to social skills training. Other patient–treatment matches are possible, and they can be investigated when other subtypes of social disability are identified.

An alternate matching strategy would involve prescribing a particular sequence of social skills training, depending upon the nature of the patient's social disability. For example, "primary" interpersonal deficits (e.g., attention deficits or inaccurate perception of social data) would be addressed before other problems in the social functioning hierarchy (e.g., problem solving, behavioral responding, interactive balance). Liberman and his colleagues (Liberman et al., 1986) have proposed this strategy for highly distractible patients, suggesting that attentional problems be treated as a precursor to social skills training. Future research may discover that there is indeed a hierarchy of social skills, and that certain subgroups of schizophrenics require active treatment of the principal (attention, social perception, social knowledge) and/or intermediate (dysfunctional thoughts and beliefs, social anxiety, problem solving) components of social functioning before complex behavioral responses can be effectively trained.

To date, results pertaining to subtyping have been quite variable, and independent profiles of skills deficits have yet to be identified within schizophrenic samples (Morrison & Bellack, 1987). However, inadequate experimental methods may account for these results. Obviously, successful subtyping on the social dysfunction dimension can only be achieved through reliable, valid, and comprehensive assessment procedures. This strategy has not always typified the social skills literature pertaining to schizophrenia. We currently lack empirically based assessment protocols that simultaneously survey the spectrum of cognitive, behavioral, affective, and physiological variables commonly associated with interpersonal behavior. In light of this, we propose development of assessment procedures which provide broad, longitudinal evaluation of social functioning in schizophrenia. Important areas for such a protocol include: (1) basic cognitive functions, (2) social perception and social judgment, (3) thoughts, beliefs, and problem-solving skills, (4) social anxiety, (5) autonomic arousal, and (6) behavioral deficits and/or excesses. Potential measures for these domains have already been identified and discussed in this chapter. We believe that such an assessment battery will not only increase our understanding of the social difficulties observed among schizophrenic patients, but will guide our attempts to deliver the most effective treatments possible.

ACKNOWLEDGMENTS. We would like to thank Dr. Thomas H. McGlashan, Dr. Dexter M. Bullard, Jr., and the staff of the Chestnut Lodge Research Institute for their support in the writing of this chapter.

References

Adams, H., Brantley, P., Malatesta, V., & Turkat, I. (1981). Modification of cognitive processes: A case study of schizophrenia. *Journal of Consulting and Clinical Psychology, 49*, 460–464.

Arnkoff, D. B., & Glass, C. R. (1989). Cognitive assessment in social anxiety and social phobia. *Clinical Psychology Review, 9*, 61–74.

American Psychiatric Association. (1980). *Diagnostic and statistical manual of mental disorders* (3rd ed.). Washington, DC: Author.

American Psychiatric Association. (1987). *Diagnostic and statistical manual of mental disorders* (3rd ed., rev). Washington, DC: Author.

Andreasen, N. C. (1982). Negative symptoms in schizophrenia. *Archives of General Psychiatry, 39*, 784–788.

Astrachan, B. M., Harrow, M., Adler, D., Brauer, L., Schwartz, A., Schwartz, C., Tucker, G. (1972). A checklist for the diagnosis of schizophrenia. *British Journal of Psychiatry, 131*, 529–539.

Bandura, A. (1969). *Principles of behavior modification.* New York: Holt, Rinehart & Winston.

Beels, C., C., Gutwirth, L., Berkeley, J., & Struening, E. (1984). Measurement of social support in schizophrenia. *Schizophrenia Bulletin, 10*, 399–411.

Bellack, A. S. & Hersen, M. (Eds.). (1979). *Research and practice in social skills training*. New York: Plenum.

Bellack, A. S., & Morrison, R. L. (1985). Interpersonal dysfunction. In A. S. Bellack, M. Hersen, & A. E. Kazdin (Eds.), *International handbook of behavior modification and therapy* (pp. 277–307). New York: Plenum.

Bellack, A. S., Hersen, M., & Turner, S. M. (1976). Generalization effects of social skills training in chronic schizophrenics: An experimental analysis. *Behaviour Research & Therapy, 14*, 391–398.

Bellack, A. S., Turner, S. M., Hesen, M., & Luber, R. F. (1984). An examination of the efficacy of social skills training for chronic schizophrenic patients. *Hospital and Community Psychiatry, 141*, 333–340.

Brady, J. P. (1984). Social skills training for psychiatric patients, I: Concepts, methods, and clinical results. *American Journal of Psychiatry, 141*, 333–340.

Cacioppo, J. T., Glass, C. R., & Merluzzi, T. V. (1979). Self-statements and self-evaluations: A cognitive-response analysis of heterosocial anxiety. *Cognitive Therapy and Research, 3*, 249–263.

Cheek, J. M., & Buss, A. H. (1981). Shyness and sociability. *Journal of Personality and Social Psychology, 41*, 330–339.

Curran, J. P. (1977). Skills training as an approach to the treatment of heterosexual-social anxiety: A review. *Psychological Bulletin, 84*, 140–157.

Curran, J. P. (1982). A procedure for the assessment of social skills: The simulated social interaction text. In J. P. Curran & P. M. Monti (Eds.), *Social skills training: A practical handbook for assessment and treatment* (pp. 348–373). New York: Guilford.

Curran, J. P., Corriveau, D. P., Monti, P. M., & Hagerman S. B. (1980). Social skill and anxiety. *Behavior Modification, 4*, 493–512.

Curran, J. P., Miller, I. W., Zwick, W. R., Monti, P. M., & Stout, R. L. (1980). The socially inadequate patient: Incidence rate, demographic and clinical features, and hospital and post-hospital functioning. *Journal of Consulting and Clinical Psychology, 48*, 375–382.

Curran, J. P., Farrell, A. D., & Grunberger, A. J. (1984). Social skills: A critique and a rapprochement. In P. Trower (Ed.), *Radical approaches to social skills training* (pp. 16–46). London: Croom Helm.

Curran, J. P., Monti, P. M., & Corriveau, D. P. (1985). Treatment of schizophrenia. In A. S. Bellack, M. Hersen, & A. Kazdin (Eds.), *International handbook of behavior modification and therapy* (pp. 209–242). New York: Plenum.

Dodge, C. S., Hope, D. A., Heimberg, R. G., & Becker, R. E. (1988). Evaluation of the Social Interaction Self-Statement Test with a social phobic population. *Cognitive Therapy and Research, 12*, 211–222.

D'Zurilla, T., & Goldfried, M. (1971). Problem-solving and behavior modification. *Journal of Abnormal Psychology, 78*, 107–126.

Edelstein, B. A., & Eisler, R. M. (1976). Effects of modeling and modeling with instructions and feedback on the behavioral components of social skills. *Behavior Therapy, 7*, 382–389.

Eisler, R. M., Miller, P. M., & Hersen, M. (1973). Components of assertive behavior. *Journal of Clinical Psychology, 29*, 295–299.

Eisler, R. M., Hersen, M., Miller, P. M., & Blanchard, E. B. (1975). Situational determinants of assertive behaviors. *Journal of Consulting and Clinical Psychology, 43*, 330–340.

Eisler, R. M., Blanchard, E. B., Fitts, H., & Williams, J. G. (1978). Social skill training with and without modeling for schizophrenic and non-psychotic hospitalized psychiatric patients. *Behavior Modification, 2*, 147–172.

Eisler, R. M., Frederiksen, L. W., & Peterson, G. L. (1978). The relationship of cognitive variables to the expression of assertiveness. *Behavior Therapy, 9*, 419–427.

Erickson, R. C., & Binder, L. M. (1986). Cognitive deficits among functionally psychotic patients: A rehabilitative perspective. *Journal of Clinical and Experimental Neuropsychology, 8*, 257–274.

Farrell, A. D., Rabinowitz, J. A., Wallander, J. L., & Curran, J. P. (1985). An evaluation of two formats for the intermediate level assessment of social skills. *Behavioral Assessment, 7*, 155–171.

Fenton, W. S., & McGlashan, T. H. (1987). Prognostic scale for schizophrenia. *Schizophrenia Bulletin, 13*, 277–286.

Field, G. D., & Test, M. A. (1975). Group assertiveness training for severely disturbed patients. *Journal of Behavior Therapy and Experimental Psychiatry, 6*, 129–134.

Fingeret, A. L., Monti, P. M., & Paxson, M. A. (1983). Relationships among social perception, social skill, and social anxiety of psychiatric patients. *Psychological Reports, 53,* 1175–1178.

Fingeret, A. L., Monti, P. M., & Paxson, M. A. (1985). Social perception, social performance, and self-perception: A study with psychiatric and nonpsychiatric groups. *Behavior Modification, 9,* 345–356.

Frederiksen, L. W., Jenkins, J. O., Foy, D. W., & Eisler, R. M. (1976). Social-skills training to modify abusive verbal outbursts in adults. *Journal of Applied Behavior Analysis, 9,* 117–125.

Glass, C. R., & Arnkoff, D. B. (1989). Behavioral assessment of social anxiety and social phobia. *Clinical Psychology Review, 9,* 75–90.

Glass, C. R., & Shea, C. A. (1986). Cognitive therapy for shyness and social anxiety. In W. H. Jones, J. M. Cheek, & S. R. Briggs (Eds.), *Shyness: Perspectives on research and treatment* (pp. 315–327). New York: Plenum.

Glass, C. R., Merluzzi, T. V., Biever, J. L., & Larsen, K. H. (1982). Cognitive assessment of social anxiety: Development and validation of a self-statement questionnaire. *Cognitive Therapy and Research, 6,* 37–55.

Gleser, G. C., & Gottschalk, L. A. (1967). Personality characteristics of chronic schizophrenics in relationship to sex and current functioning. *Journal of Clinical Psychology, 23,* 349–354.

Goldfried, M. R., & D'Zurilla, T. J. (1969). A behavioral-analytic model for assessing competence. In C. D. Spielberger (Ed.), *Current topics in clinical and community psychology* (Vol. 1, pp. 151–196). New York: Academic Press.

Goldsmith, J. B., & McFall, R. M. (1975). Development and evaluation of an interpersonal skill-training program for psychiatric patients. *Journal of Abnormal Psychology, 84,* 51–58.

Greenwood, V. B. (1983). Cognitive therapy with the young adult chronic patient. In A. Freeman (Ed.), *Cognitive therapy with couples and groups* (pp. 183–198). New York: Plenum.

Gunderson, J. G., & Kolb, J. E. (1978). Discriminating features of borderline patients. *American Journal of Psychiatry, 135,* 792–796.

Gutride, M. E., Goldstein, A. P., & Hunter, G. F. (1973). The use of modeling and role-playing to increase social interaction among asocial psychiatric patients. *Journal of Consulting and Clinical Psychology, 40,* 408–415.

Guze, S. B. (1975). Differential diagnosis of the borderline personality syndrome. In J. E. Mack (Ed.), *Borderline states in psychiatry* (pp. 69–74). New York: Grune & Stratton.

Hansen, D. J., St. Lawrence, J. S., & Christoff, K. A. (1985). Effects of interpersonal problem-solving training with chronic aftercare patients on problem-solving component skills and effectiveness of solutions. *Journal of Consulting and Clinical Psychology, 53,* 167–174.

Hersen, M. & Bellack, A. S. (1976a). A multiple-baseline analysis of social-skills training in chronic schizophrenics. *Journal of Applied Behavior Analysis, 9,* 239–245.

Hersen, M., & Bellack, A. S. (1976b). Social skills training for chronic psychiatric patients: Rationale, research findings, and future directions. *Comprehensive Psychiatry, 17,* 559–580.

Hersen, M., Turner, S. M., Edelstein, B. A., & Pinkston, S. G. (1975). Effects of phenothiazines and social skills training in a withdrawn schizophrenic. *Journal of Clinical Psychology, 31,* 588–594.

Hogarty, G. E., Anderson, C. M., Reiss, D. J., Kornblith, S. J., Greenwald, D. P., Javna, C. D., & Madonia, M. J. (1986). Family psychoeducation, social skills training, and maintenance chemotherapy in the aftercare treatment of schizophrenia. I. One-year effects of a controlled study on relapse and expressed emotion. *Archives of General Psychiatry, 43,* 633–642.

Izard, C. E. (1971). *The face of emotion.* New York: Appleton-Century-Crofts.

Jones, R. G. (1969). A factored measure of Ellis' irrational belief system with personality and adjustment correlates (Doctoral dissertation, Texas Technological College, 1968). *Dissertation Abstracts International, 29,* 4379–4380. (University Microfilms No. 69-6443)

King, L. W., Liberman, R. P., & Bryan, E. (1977). Personal effectiveness: A structured therapy for improving social and emotional skills. *European Journal of Behavioural Analysis and Modification, 2,* 82–91.

Leary, M. R. (1983). A brief version of The Fear of Negative Evaluation Scale. *Personality and Social Psychology Bulletin, 9,* 371–376.

Lewine, R. R. J., Watt, N. F., & Freyer, J. H. (1978). A study of childhood social competence, adult premorbid competence, and psychiatric outcome in three schizophrenic subtypes. *Journal of Abnormal Psychology, 87*, 294–302.

Lewine, R. R. J., Watt, N. F., Prentky, J. H., & Freyer, J. H. (1980). Childhood social competence in functionally disordered psychiatric patients and in normals. *Journal of Abnormal Psychology, 89*, 132–138.

Lezak, M. D. (1983). *Neuropsychological assessment* (2nd ed.). New York: Oxford University Press.

Liberman, R. P. (1982). Assessment of social skills. *Schizophrenia Bulletin, 8*, 62–83.

Liberman, R. P., Nuechterlein, K. H. & Wallace, C. J. (1982). Social skills training and the nature of schizophrenia. In J. P. Curran & P. M. Monti (Eds.), *Social skills training: A practical handbook for assessment and treatment* (pp. 5–56). New York: Guilford.

Liberman, R. P., Lillie, F., Falloon, I. R. H., Harpin, R. E., Hutchinson, W., & Stoute, B. (1984). Social skills training with relapsing schizophrenics: An experimental analysis. *Behavior Modification, 8*, 155–179.

Liberman, R. P., Massel, H. K., Mosk, M. D., & Wong, S. E. (1985). Social skills training for chronic mental patients. *Hospital and Community Psychiatry, 36*, 396–403.

Liberman, R. P., Mueser, K. T., Wallace, C. J., Jacobs, H. E., Eckman, T., & Massel, H. K. (1986). Training skills in the psychiatrically disabled: learning coping and competence. *Schizophrenia Bulletin, 12*, 631–647.

Lukoff, D., Wallace, C. J., Liberman, R. P., & Burke, K. (1986). A holistic program for chronic schizophrenic patients. *Schizophrenia Bulletin, 12*, 274–282.

Matson, J. L. (1980). Behavior modification procedure for training chronically institutionalized schizophrenics. In M. Hersen, R. M. Eisler, & P. M. Miller (eds.), *Progress in behavior modification* (Vol. 9, pp. 167–204). New York: Academic Press.

McCelland, D. C., & Walt, N. F. (1968). Sex role alienation in schizophrenia. *Journal of Abnormal Psychology, 12*, 217–220.

McFall, R. M. (1982). A review and reformulation of the concept of social skills. *Behavioral Assessment, 4*, 1–33.

McGlashan, T. H. (1984a). The Chestnut Lodge follow-up study: I: Follow-up methodology and study sample. *Archives of General Psychiatry, 41*, 573–585.

McGlashan, T. H. (1984b). The Chestnut Lodge follow-up study: II: Long-term outcome of schizophrenia and the affective disorders. *Archives of General Psychiatry, 41*, 586–601.

McGlashan, T. H. (1986a). The prediction of outcome in chronic schizophrenia: IV: The Chestnut Lodge follow-up study. *Archives of General Psychiatry, 41*, 167–176.

McGlashan, T. H. (1986b). Schizophrenia: Psychosocial treatments and the role of psychosocial factors in its etiology and pathogenesis. In A. J. Frances & R. E. Hales (Eds.), *Annual review of psychiatry* (Vol. V, pp. 96–111). Washington, DC: American Psychiatric Press.

Meichenbaum, D. (1977). *Cognitive-behavior modification.* New York: Plenum.

Meichenbaum, D., & Cameron, R. (1973). Training schizophrenics to talk to themselves: A means of developing self-controls. *Behavior Therapy, 4*, 515–534.

Monti, P. M., & Fingeret, A. L. (1987). Social perception and communication skills among schizophrenics and nonschizophrenics. *Journal of Clinical Psychology, 43*, 197–205.

Monti, P. M., Fink, E., Norman, W., Curran, J., Hayes, S., & Caldwell, A. (1979). Effect of social skills training groups and social skills bibliotherapy with psychiatric patients. *Journal of Consulting and Clinical Psychology, 47*, 189–191.

Monti, P. M., Curran, J. P., Corriveau, D. P., DeLancey, A. L., & Hagerman, S. M. (1980). Effects of social skills training groups and sensitivity training groups with psychiatric patients. *Journal of Consulting and Clinical Psychology, 48*, 241–248.

Monti, P. M., Boice, R., Fingeret, A. L., Zwick, W. R., Kolko, D., Munroe, S., & Grunberger, A. (1984). Midi-level measurement of social anxiety in psychiatric and non-psychiatric samples. *Behaviour Research and Therapy, 22*, 651–660.

Monti, P. M., Zwick, W. R., & Warzak, W. J. (1986). Social skills and irrational beliefs: A preliminary report. *Journal of Behavior Therapy and Experimental Psychiatry, 17*, 11–14.

Morrison, R. L. (1988). Social dysfunction in relation to other schizophrenic symptoms: New findings, new directions. *The Behavior Therapist, 11*, 139–142.

Morrison, R. L., & Bellack, A. S. (1981). The role of social perception in social skill. *Behavior Therapy,* *12,* 69–79.

Morrison, R. L., & Bellack, A. S. (1984). Social skills training. In A. S. Bellack (Ed.), *Schizophrenia:* *Treatment, management and rehabilitation* (pp. 247–279). Orlando, FL: Grune & Stratton.

Morrison, R. L., & Bellack, A. S. (1987). Social functioning of schizophrenic patients: Clinical and research issues. *Schizophrenia Bulletin, 13,* 715–725.

Morrison, R. L., Bellack, A. S., & Mueser, K. T. (1988). Deficits in facial-affect recognition and schizophrenia. *Schizophrenia Bulletin, 14,* 67–83.

Percell, L. P., Berwick, P. T., & Beigel, A. (1974). The effects of assertiveness training on self-concept and anxiety. *Archives of General Psychiatry, 31,* 502–504.

Pilkonis, P. A., Feldman, H., Himmelhoch, J., & Cornes, C. (1980). Social anxiety and psychiatric diagnosis. *Journal of Nervous and Mental Disease, 168,* 13–18.

Richardson, F. C., & Tasto, D. L. (1976). Development and factor analysis of a social anxiety inventory. *Behavior Therapy, 7,* 453–462.

Rosenthal, R., & Benowitz, L. I. (1986). Sensitivity to nonverbal communication in normal, psychiatric, and brain-damaged samples. In P. D. Blanck, R. W. Buck, & R. Rosenthal (Eds.), *Nonverbal communication in clinical context* (pp. 223–257). State College, PA: Pennsylvania State University Press.

Rosenthal, R., Hall, J. A., Archer, D., DiMatteo, M. R., & Rogers, P. L. (1979). *The PONS test manual:* *Profile of nonverbal sensitivity.* New York: Irvington.

Serban, G. (1975). Functioning ability in schizophrenia and normal subjects: Short-term prediction for rehospitalization of schizophrenics. *Comprehensive Psychiatry, 16,* 446–456.

Shepherd, G. (1977). Social skills training: The generalization problem. *Behavior Therapy, 8,* 1008–1009.

Spaulding, W. D., Storms, L., Goodrich, V., & Sullivan, M. (1986). Applications of experimental psychopathology in psychiatric rehabilitation. *Schizophrenia Bulletin, 12,* 560–577.

Strauss, J. S., Carpenter, W. T., & Bartko, J. J. (1974). The diagnosis and understanding of schizophrenia. Part III. Speculation on the processes that underlie schizophrenic symptoms and signs. *Schizophrenia Bulletin, 11,* 61–69.

Strauss, J. S., Kokes, R. F., Klorman, R., & Sacksteder, J. L. (1977). Premorbid adjustment in schizophrenia: Concepts, measures, and implications. Part I. The concept of premorbid adjustment. *Schizophrenia Bulletin, 3,* 182–185.

Trower, P., Bryant, B., & Argyle, M. (1978). *Social skills and mental health.* Pittsburgh, PA: The University of Pittsburgh Press.

Walker, E., Marwitt, S. J., & Emory, E. (1980). A cross-sectional study of emotion recognition in schizophrenics. *Journal of Abnormal Psychology, 89,* 428–436.

Wallace, C. J. (1982). The social skills training project of the mental health clinical research center for the study of schizophrenia. In J. P. Curran & P. M. Monti (Eds.), *Social skills training: A practical handbook for assessment and treatment* (pp. 57–89). New York: Guilford.

Wallace, C. J. (1984). Community and interpersonal functioning in the course of schizophrenic disorders. *Schizophrenia Bulletin, 10,* 233–257.

Wallace, C. J., & Liberman, R. P. (1985). Social skills training for patients with schizophrenia: A controlled clinical trial. *Psychiatry Research, 15,* 239–247.

Wallace, C. J., Nelson, C. J., Liberman, R. P., Aitchison, R. A., Lukoff, D., Elder, J. P., & Ferris, C. (1980). A review and critique of social skills training with schizophrenic patients. *Schizophrenia Bulletin, 6,* 42–63.

Wallander, J. L., Conger, A. J., & Conger, J. C. (1985). Development and evaluation of a behaviorally referenced rating system for heterosocial skills. *Behavioral Assessment, 7,* 137–153.

Watson, D., & Friend, R. (1969). Measurement of social-evaluative anxiety. *Journal of Consulting and Clinical Psychology, 33,* 448–457.

Weinman, B., Gelbart, P., Wallace, M., & Post, M. (1972). Inducing assertive behavior in chronic schizophrenics: A comparison of socioenvironmental, desensitization, and relaxation therapies. *Journal of Consulting and Clinical Psychology, 39,* 246–252.

Wessberg, H. W., Curran, J. P., Monti, P. M., Corriveau, D. P., Coyne, N. A., & Dziadosz, T. H.

(1981). Evidence for the external validity of a social simulation measure of social skills. *Journal of Behavioral Assessment*, *3*, 209–220.

Williams, M. T., Turner, S. M., Watts, J. G., Bellack, A. S., & Hersen, M. (1977). Group social skills training for chronic psychiatric patients. *European Journal of Behavioural Analysis and Modification*, *1*, 223–229.

Zigler, E., & Phillips, L. (1961). Social competence and outcome in psychiatric disorders. *Journal of Abnormal and Social Psychology*, *63*, 264–271.

Zigler, E., & Phillips, L. (1962). Social competence and the process-reactive distinction in psychopathology. *Journal of Abnormal and Social Psychology*, *65*, 215–222.

11

The Nature and Role of Performance Anxiety in Sexual Dysfunction

Timothy J. Bruce and David H. Barlow

Introduction

The area of sexual dysfunction has been an excellent arena for investigations of the means through which anxiety interferes with complex behavioral performance in general and sexual responsivity specifically. Historically, anxiety reduction has been a prominent theme in theories and treatment of sexual dysfunction since the late 1950s and 1960s (Brady, 1966; Lazarus, 1963; Wolpe, 1958). Key to both the conceptual and therapeutic genesis of this approach was Wolpe's (1958) application of systematic desensitization to sexual dysfunction. Today, strands of his influence, such as the concept of reciprocal inhibition, continue to influence current conceptualizations of anxiety, the processes through which it inhibits sexual arousal, and techniques used to reduce its effects. This view was strongly reinforced by the pioneering work of Masters and Johnson (1966, 1970). Evidence of their influence is substantial and includes current nosological classification schemes (cf. DSM-III and DSM-III-R; American Psychiatric Association, 1980, 1987), a common definition of the sexual response cycle (Masters & Johnson, 1966), as well as widely accepted hypotheses of the etiology and maintenance of sexual dysfunction gleaned from their numerous case studies (Masters & Johnson, 1970).

However, despite this foundation, basic research of these formative theories of the etiology and maintenance of sexual dysfunctions accelerated more slowly than the widespread adoption of the treatment techniques developed from them. The point is exemplified by Schiavi (1976), who observed that despite the extensive use of anxiety reduction techniques at this time there were "no studies

Timothy J. Bruce and David H. Barlow • Department of Psychology, State University of New York at Albany, Albany, New York 12203.

of men with erectile dysfunction that have assessed the pattern of autonomic arousal and penile tumescence in response to erotic stimulation" (p. 564). In fact, most research to date has focused on treatment outcome rather than basic investigations of the means through which sexual fear–anxiety interferes with sexual responsivity. Not surprisingly, treatment innovations since Masters and Johnson have been limited largely to slight variations of treatment procedures reflecting clinical inclinations of various sex therapists (e.g., Hartmann & Fithian, 1972; Kaplan, 1981). The success rates of these approaches and commonalities among them have been reviewed many times (e.g., Cooper, 1981; Crown & D'Ardenne, 1982; Kuriansky & Sharpe, 1981; Marks, 1981; Mills & Kilmann, 1982). It appears that with or without variations in the basic approach, approximately one-half to two-thirds of sexually dysfunctional patients will show some improvement. For inhibited sexual excitement (DSM-III), however, the figure can be as low as 30% (Crown & D'Ardenne, 1982). Furthermore, Levine and Agle (1978) pointed out that these "improved" patients with erectile dysfunction are quite unstable in their sexual functioning over time and are certainly not "cured." These more pessimistic results for erectile dysfunction are paralleled by increasing reports from sex therapists of difficulties in replicating the success of Masters and Johnson, even in the area of erectile dysfunction, where some of their highest failure rates were originally reported (e.g., Zilbergeld & Evans, 1980).

More recently, basic research of the relationship between anxiety and sexual arousal has begun to be productive, revealing important implications for both theory and therapy. Much of this research has focused on teasing out the role of specific components of anxiety in disrupting sexual arousal. Results from these lines of investigation have been integrated into our proposed model of sexual dysfunction (Barlow, 1986). This model shares important features with current models of social and other evaluation anxieties emphasizing the interactive role of cognitive interference and autonomic arousal (e.g., Sarason, 1982). In this chapter we discuss each of these several lines of investigation and how they suggest changes in prevailing definitions of anxiety and presumed mechanisms of action. We present the working model of sexual dysfunction drawn from the integration of this research, and highlight the similarities and differences among this model and related theories of performance disruption in other than sexual contexts (e.g., test and social anxiety). Finally, we discuss briefly directions for research in this area and implications of the model for assessment and treatment.

For the most part, the studies to be reviewed utilize paradigms sufficiently similar to allow comparison of the responding of sexually functional (SFs) and sexually dysfunctional subjects (SDs). The term sexually disfunctional refers particularly to males meeting the criteria for Inhibited Sexual Excitement (DSM-III: 302.72; American Psychiatric Association, 1980); although, a few studies reviewed involve female subjects and subjects meeting the criteria for other dysfunctions of the sexual response cycle (e.g., inhibited desire and orgasm). In all cases SDs have been screened for physical etiology and other major psychopathology. SFs have typically been matched to SDs on age, race, and educational level and have been screened for psychopathology as well. In most cases, the experimental conditions utilized in these studies were designed to investigate hypothetical anxiety processes derived from the relevant clinical literature. Results from these investigations indicate, in preliminary fashion, five dimensions on which the responding of SDs and SFs can be meaningfully differentiated. These dimensions include the responding of SDs and SFs to "anxiety induction" procedures, nonsexual distraction, and performance demand manipulations, as well as the quality of affective responding during sexual stimulation and the concordance of different indices of their sexual arousal.

CONCEPTUAL GROUNDWORK

As a launching point, we begin with a brief discussion of the influential work of Wolpe (1958) and Masters and Johnson (1966, 1970), whose theoretical contributions served as a foundation for most subsequent research.

Initial Conceptualizations of Sexual Anxiety

It is not always clear how one or another theorist construes anxiety or the process through which it operates. This has been especially true for sexuality researchers. One method of approaching the study of treatment underpinnings is to examine the techniques built from them. For instance, the use of the intercourse ban and sensate focus (see Masters & Johnson, 1970) suggests that a male's preoccupation with attaining erection is inhibitory to sexual arousal. Similarly, the use of relaxation techniques, designed to reduce physiological arousal, presupposes that this dimension of anxiety is disruptive to sexual arousal.

Fortunately, Wolpe (1958) allowed for more direct analysis of his thinking by specifying both a proposed definition and mechanism of anxiety upon which he based his treatment approach. The mechanism of action through which desensitization therapy restores sexual responsivity is elucidated through the concept of reciprocal inhibition, which Wolpe (1958) described as follows:

> if a response antagonistic to anxiety can be made to occur in the presence of the anxiety-evoking stimuli, so that it is accompanied by a complete or partial suppression of anxiety responses, the bond between the stimuli and the anxiety responses will be weakened. (p. 71)

Working from within this statement, Wolpe defined anxiety as "an autonomic response constellation whose unconditioned response origin is noxious stimulation" (p. 34). Through additional analysis of his descriptions of anxiety responses, it is clear that Wolpe conceptualized anxiety as operative in many response system dimensions (e.g., behavioral, cognitive), but, as indicated, based autonomically or, more precisely, sympathetically. Response constellations "antagonistic to anxiety" (e.g., sexual arousal, relaxation) were classified as such because of their presumed parasympathetic basis. Although it is a common misconception that Wolpe thought of parasympathetic and sympathetic activity as completely mutually inhibitory, he described the reciprocal inhibition process as one operative simultaneously at the autonomic level. More recently, he has reiterated this notion: "reciprocal inhibition implies simultaniety of responses . . . if responses do not overlap in time they cannot be reciprocally inhibitory . . . if they do overlap, reciprocal inhibition of the weaker will occur" (Wolpe, 1978, p. 453).

Thus, sexual dysfunction was thought to be a result of parasympathetic inhibition by an (sympathetically based) anxiety response constellation conditioned to stimuli in the sexual context. Desensitization was designed to re-strengthen the associative bond between the (parasympathetically based) sexual arousal response and sexual stimuli, eventually inhibiting evocation of the anxiety response constellation.

Unfortunately, Masters and Johnson (1970) were not as explicit as Wolpe (1958) in describing an etiological model or mechanism(s) of therapeutic action; consequently, one is left to infer them from a number of sources, including treatment techniques (as indicated above) and statements dispersed throughout their published works.

Masters and Johnson (1966, 1970) generally describe several potential pathways to the onset of sexual dysfunction, including alcohol intoxication, religion-based guilt, and attempts to control premature ejaculation. However, they suggest that these various initiators result in "performance anxiety/fear" within the sexual situation. They described fear of performance in males as follows:

> The impotent male's fear of performance can be described in somewhat general terms. With each opportunity for sexual connection, the immediate and overpowering concern is whether or not he will be able to achieve an erection. Will he be capable of "performing" as a "normal" man? He is constantly concerned not only with achieving, but also with maintaining an erection of quality sufficient for intromission. (1970, pp. 10–11).

These authors link performance fears to the process of spectatoring. They described spectatoring as an attitudinal stance wherein the fearful individual monitors his or her sexual functioning from a third-person perspective, watching for indications of inadequacy or failure. Although these authors did not detail a mechanism(s) of action through which performance fears and spectatoring inhibit sexual arousal, one process implicated is distraction: "fear of inadequacy is the greatest known deterrent to effective sexual functioning, simply because it so completely distracts the fearful individual from his or her natural responsivity" (1970, p. 12). However, it is unclear exactly how Masters and Johnson conceive of the distraction process or how primary it is in that they also suggest that performance fear has a concurrent physiological component, and they seem to suggest that the components of performance fear are inseparable. For example, they state, "men contending with fears of sexual function have distorted this basic natural response pattern to such an extent that they literally break out in cold sweat as they approach sexual opportunity." (Masters & Johnson, 1970, p. 11).

Integration and Summary

Among other observations, one commonality uniting the theories of Wolpe (1958) and Masters and Johnson (1970) is in how they defined anxiety. All appear to characterize sexual anxiety (as well as sexual arousal) as responses which manifest both cognitive and physiological dimensions synchronously. Stated another way, anxiety was defined as an emotional state, characterized by a highly correlated group of cognitive and physiological components. Concerning the mechanisms through which this state inhibits sexual arousal, Wolpe (1958) specifically emphasized the inhibitory role of the sympathetic component of anxiety within the concept of reciprocal inhibition. Accordingly, an integral technique in desensitization therapy is to induce relaxation in temporal contiguity to imaginal sexual stimuli in an effort to strengthen the parasympathetic bond. In more general fashion, Masters and Johnson (1970) implicated the "distracting" nature of performance concerns and concomitant physiological disruption ("distortion") in the inhibition of sexual response. They describe the sexual response as a basic, natural, and (as will be discussed) involuntary response pattern which emerges only under the proper alignment of conditions. Accordingly, Masters and Johnson (1970) include treatment techniques aimed at the reduction of both autonomic and cognitive components of the performance anxiety state (e.g., relaxation, sensate focus).

THE ROLE OF ANXIETY IN SEXUAL RESPONSIVITY

A series of studies drawn from the writings of Wolpe (1958) and Masters and Johnson (1970) has investigated the sexual responding of subjects under conditions designed to induce an anxious state within a sexual context.

Anxiety Induction Studies

One of the first of these laboratory investigations was conducted by Hoon, Wincze, and Hoon (1977). In a test of Wolpe's (1958) concept of reciprocal inhibition, these researchers showed brief film segments of either neutral (travelogue scenes) or noxious content (scenes of automobile accidents) to female SFs. Immediately following each segment, subjects in each group were shown a sexually explicit film segment. As can be seen, these researchers borrowed directly from Wolpe's (1958) definition of anxiety in hypothesizing that the noxious stimuli would evoke sympathetic arousal (defined in part as heart rate increases), while the neutral segments would evoke a parasympathetically dominant state (e.g., relaxation). In accordance with the reciprocal inhibition concept, it was hypothesized that sexual arousal following noxious preexposure would be less relative to neutral preexposure due to sympathetic inhibition of sexual arousal in the former. Surprisingly, results indicated the converse. Sexual arousal (i.e., vaginal blood volume) was higher during the noxious preexposure condition. Interestingly, when the order of presentation was reversed (i.e., erotic preexposure to both neutral and noxious films), sexual arousal was less during the noxious segment. Wolchik et al. (1980) partially replicated these results with male SFs, demonstrating elevated sexual arousal following noxious preexposure.

These results were some of the first to question the assumption that physiologic correlates of anxiety are inhibitory to sexual arousal.

In response to the Hoon et al. (1977) results, Wolpe (1978) described many problems with the preexposure paradigm as a test of reciprocal inhibition. First, he questioned whether exposure to the auto accident segments evoked anxiety as he (Wolpe, 1958) defined it. For example, Hoon et al. were unable to demonstrate differences in heart rate between the neutral and noxious conditions. Wolpe (1978) stated further that even if an anxious state was evoked during noxious preexposure, one could not assume its "perseverative effects" (p. 453); and therefore, relative increases following noxious preexposure could be a response to an "emotional state of relief" (p. 453) signaled by the offset of the accident scenes. He indicated that a better test of reciprocal inhibition is to attempt simultaneous evocation of anxiety and sexual arousal.

Wolpe's points were taken by other researchers who utilized "simultaneous induction paradigms," but whose results were similar. For example, Lange, Wincze, Zwick, Feldman, and Hughes (1981) induced anxiety by subcutaneously injecting male SFs with epinephrine hydrochloride under single-blind control. Results showed that epinephrine and no-epinephrine conditions were associated with equal levels of sexual arousal during a sexually explicit film segment. Again, a secondary result, partially replicating Hoon et al. (1977), was that subjects receiving epinephrine demonstrated shorter latencies to penile flaccidity after film offset; that is, increased sympathetic arousal appears to accelerate penile detumescence when sexual stimuli are absent. These results support the finding from preexposure paradigms in suggesting that increased sympathetic arousal is not necessarily inhibitory to sexual arousal (i.e., while subjects are in the presence of sexual stimuli–a seemingly obvious point to which we will return).

This conclusion has been supported further by Barlow, Sakheim, and Beck (1983), who investigated the hypothesis utilizing a shock-threat paradigm in repeated-measures fashion with young male SFs. Two shock-threat conditions were employed, operationally defining two types of anxiety described in the clinical literature. During the contingent shock condition (CS) subjects were told that there was a 60% chance of receiving a tolerance level electric shock to their wrist if they did not attain the "normal" level of erection attained by previous subjects. During the noncontingent shock-threat condition (NCS) subjects were told their chance of shock was unrelated to any of their responses. These two conditions were compared to a no-shock-threat control (NS). CS was considered to be an operationalization of "performance demand," and it was expected to elicit (inhibitory) performance anxiety such as that described by Masters and Johnson (1970). NCS was designed to elicit generalized "anxiety" and sympathetic arousal in the absence of performance concerns. Results indicated that both shock-threat conditions were associated with significantly higher levels of penile circumference change from baseline related to the control condition (see Figure 1).

Additionally, these researchers indicated that autonomic activity was ele-

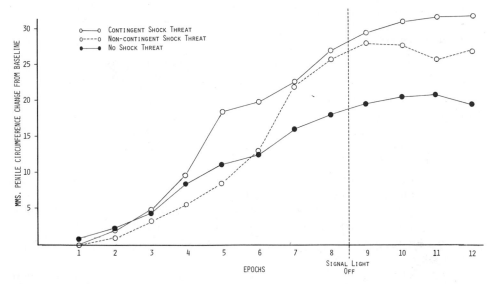

FIGURE 1. Mean penile circumference change in millimeters (MMS) for each 15-second epoch during each of three conditions: no shock threat, noncontingent shock threat, and contingent shock threat. (From "Anxiety Increases Sexual Arousal" by D. H. Barlow, D. K. Sakheim, & J. G. Beck, 1983, *Journal of Abnormal Psychology, 92*, p. 52. Copyright 1983 by the American Psychological Association. Reprinted by permission.)

vated. Extensive debriefings revealed that the contingent shock condition did induce subjects to monitor their level of sexual arousal. Despite the effectiveness of the manipulations, subjects showed facilitation of erection. Taken together, the results of this line of investigation suggest that anxiety, operationalized in a number of ways, either has no directional effect on sexual arousal or facilitates it, but does not inhibit it.

For reasons to be discussed, Beck and Barlow (1984) and Norton and Jehu (1984) raised the possibility that the facilitative effects of anxiety induction procedures may be specific to the young SFs used in these studies. To test this possibility, Beck, Barlow, Sakheim, and Abrahamson (1984) replicated the Barlow *et al.* (1983) study using a clinical sample of male SDs and a matched group of SFs. Results indicated a partial replication of previous findings in that SFs demonstrated significantly more sexual arousal during the NCS than the NS. However, CS did not elevate sexual arousal over NS levels (although again it did not inhibit it). And although the latter finding does not contradict previous results, these authors suggested that this may be related to age differences between the two samples. That is, the previous experiment was conducted with relatively young SFs (mean age: 26), while the mean age of SFs in this study was 38 years old. On the other hand, SDs showed a very different response pattern in evidencing less sexual arousal during NCS and CS compared to NS. These results, which suggest that induced anxiety may affect SDs and SFs differently, raise new questions.

Integration and Summary

Definitional Issues

These results have raised a number of concerns about the role of sexual anxiety as described in the early clinical literature. One of these concerns revolves around the difficulty of defining sexual anxiety as an emotional state which manifests as a highly correlated group of cognitive and physiological components. Not only did initial theories characterize anxiety in this manner (see Masters & Johnson, 1970; Wolpe, 1958), so too have some researchers attempting to induce anxiety. One result of defining sexual anxiety in this manner is the inevitable difficulty in identifying its referents and, similarly, distinguishing this unique state from others. This point is exemplified in part by Beck and Barlow (1984), who observe that "anxiety connotes different meanings for different authors, ranging from inhibitions based on moral sanctions, to generalized discomfort over being sexually intimate to fear over loss of control to spectatoring" (p. 5).

These definitional difficulties with the "unitary view of anxiety" (Beck & Barlow, 1984, p. 5) are more apparent when one applies this approach to the interpretation of results of studies reviewed thus far. For example, it can be argued that the anxiety states associated with erectile facilitation (e.g., Barlow et al., 1983) were not representative of those described in the clinical literature, and dissimilar to those inhibiting erection (e.g., Beck et al., 1984). Many of these arguments rely on outcome to determine if a particular state was evoked (i.e., post hoc circularity) and/or the eventual generation of an unwieldy list of potentially inhibitory emotional states distinguished by subtle connotational distinctions of authors. The utility of such an approach is questionable since attempts to reproduce these states can always be reduced to the argument that they were misrepresentative in one crucial way or another.

These definitional issues are not unique to the study of fear or anxiety in the sexual context (cf. Lang, 1968, 1970; Rachman, 1978). In his discussion of fear, Lang (1968) was one of the first to suggest that this construct involves at least three not necessarily correlated response systems: the behavioral, cognitive, and physiological. Beyond its theoretical justification, the utility of this reconceptualization has also been demonstrated in terms of both its descriptive and predictive validity (e.g., Barlow, 1988; Barlow, Mavissakalian, & Shofield, 1980; Mavissakalian & Barlow, 1981). More recently, Barlow (1988) has reemphasized the usefulness of this definitional approach by providing evidence for distinguishing "anxiety" as a more loosely integrated cognitive-affective structure and "fear" as a highly integrated (synchronous) response constellation.

The Autonomic Component

One obvious consequence of applying this alternative definition of anxiety is that it promotes investigation of the role of each response dimension and their interaction. Results of the studies reviewed above suggest that sympathetic arousal associated with anxiety induction differentially affects the sexual arousal of SFs and SDs, and therefore is not uniformly inhibitory to sexual arousal, as one might prefer of a proposed mechanism of action. In view of this conclusion, several authors have suggested alternative roles for the physiological correlates of anxiety other than an inhibitory one (e.g., Barlow, 1986, Beck & Barlow, 1984; Hoon et al., 1977). Indeed, Beck and Barlow (1984), for example, have presented a fairly diverse clinical and experimental literature suggesting a positive correlation between sexual arousal and experiences of probable sympathetic arousal (e.g., threats of harm, near accidents, electric shock, and other "emotion-inducing" situations). Likewise, many theorists have borrowed from social-psychological research suggesting that "performance" can be facilitated by increased physiological arousal. For example, in his discussion of the differential responding of SFs and SDs to anxiety induction conditions, Barlow (1986) draws parallels to Zillman's (1983) excitation transfer theory, which, in general, predicts the intensification of subsequent emotional experiences as a function of residual sympathetic excitation from preceding emotional reactions. Zillman and his colleagues have suggested that autonomic arousal increases evoked from an unrelated preceding source can be transferred to increase the subsequent experience of sexual arousal (e.g., Cantor, Zillman, & Bryant, 1975). Other researchers, working from Schachter's (1964) missattribution theory, have suggested that autonomic arousal evoked from one source can be missattributed as interpersonal attraction (e.g., Brehm, Gatz, Goethels, McCrimmon, & Ward, 1978; Dutton & Aron, 1974). Hoon et al. (1977), for example, offered a missattributional interpretation of their results.

It is the case that some paradigms used to support both excitation transfer and missattribution theories assume the perseverative effects of preelicited physiological arousal, and therefore are subject to Wolpe's (1978) criticisms of the preexposure paradigm. But results of anxiety induction studies utilizing simultaneous induction procedures support the conclusion that sympathetic arousal, per se, is not inhibitory to sexual arousal. Indeed, while it may be some time before technological advances allow more precise description of both sympathetic and parasympathetic influences on sexual arousal, data using peripheral indices of these systems in male subjects have suggested for some time that both subsystems can be characterized as active, but neither dominant, during sexual arousal (e.g., Wengler, Averill, & Smith, 1968). These authors found that during sexual arousal systolic and diastolic blood pressure changes indicative of both peripheral vasodilation and constriction occurred concurrent with constant heart and respiration rates. They suggest that the changes in pressures can be attributed to the simultaneous activity of both autonomic branches rather than a function of, for example, heart rate changes.

Therefore, it is apparent that results of initial empirical tests of the anxiety constructs upon which most sex therapies are based speak to the utility of applying a multiresponse system approach to the study of anxiety and sexual arousal. Utilizing this approach, the results of studies reviewed thus far suggest that the physiological correlates of induced anxiety, operationalized in several ways, either do not inhibit sexual arousal (Lange et al., 1981; Beck et al., 1984) or facilitate it (Barlow *et al.*, 1983; Beck *et al.*, 1984) in SFs, but inhibit sexual arousal in SDs (Beck *et al.*, 1984). This conclusion is one of five dimensions on which the responding of SFs and SDs is meaningfully differential. Finally, from this convergence of evidence it is suggested that the differential responding of SFs and SDs to anxiety induction may be more usefully construed as differences in cognitive processing than inhibitory autonomic dominance. After presenting the literature examining the influence of cognitive factors on sexual arousal, the specific role of autonomic arousal will be revisited.

THE ROLE OF COGNITION IN SEXUAL RESPONSIVITY

Voluntary Control of Sexual Arousal

One test of cognitive influence on any response is whether it can be manipulated volitionally. Several studies have investigated this hypothesis. It is of interest to note that although Masters and Johnson (1970) suggested that sexual arousal could be inhibited by performance concerns, they rejected the notion that cognitive resources could be used voluntarily to control sexual arousal: "Attainment of an erection is something over which he has absolutely no voluntary control . . . no man can will, wish, or demand an erection" (p. 11). Indeed, these authors asserted that the allocation of attentional resources directed at the enhancement of erection was central to the inhibitory spectatoring process. However, in one of the initial lines of sexuality research, reports indicate that subjects can both enhance and suppress their erectile responses.

Two of the earliest studies in the area showed that subjects could attain erection without the assistance of overt stimulation (Bancroft & Mathews, 1971; Laws & Rubin, 1969). In both studies subjects were instructed to increase sexual arousal through mental means only. Rubin and Henson (1975) reported that SFs could increase their genital response to a film or to fantasy over levels attained to film or fantasy without the instruction to enhance arousal.

Similarly, several studies have shown that subjects can voluntarily suppress erections during overt sexual stimulation (Abel, Barlow, Blanchard, & Mavissakalian, 1975; Beck, Barlow, & Sakheim, 1982; Henson & Rubin, 1971, Laws & Rubin, 1969, Rosen, 1973). Based on debriefing data, subjects in these studies often reported accomplishing erectile suppression through concentration on some nonsexual, off-task foci (e.g., arithmetic manipulations). Interestingly, suppression of erection has also been reported of subjects who were asked to describe verbally the content of the erotic stimuli to which they were attending (Henson & Rubin, 1971). Finally, Beck *et al.* (1982) have demonstrated that both SFs and SDs can suppress erection voluntarily while in the presence of overt sexual stimuli. However, while SFs reported that they were aware of their success in suppressing erection and could confidently report the cognitive strategies used to do so, SDs were neither aware they had suppressed erection nor could they report the strategies used.

The results of voluntary control studies demonstrate that indeed cognitive resources can be harnessed toward the end of increasing or decreasing sexual arousal. They also suggest more specifically that the shifting of attentional resources may be key to voluntary control. This research has prompted more systematic investigations of attentional factors and their effect on sexual arousal.

Attentional Factors

Attentional Resource Allocation

Several studies have investigated the role of attentional resources by utilizing distraction paradigms in which subjects are asked to attend to sexual and nonsexual stimuli simultaneously. The premise of such studies is that attentional resources are limited. As such, the alternative hypothesis of these studies is that nonsexual, task-irrelevant cognitive activities will impair performance (e.g., erection) because they compete with sexual, task-relevant activities for space in the "processing system" (e.g., working memory; see Baddeley & Hitch, 1974).

In a pioneering study within this area, Geer and Fuhr (1976) utilized a dichotic listening paradigm to test the effects of a neutral distracting task on the sexual arousal of SFs. In counterbalanced order, subjects listened to a sexually explicit audiotaped presentation in one ear, while listening simultaneously to number presentations in the other. Four conditions were defined by the cognitive complexity of the distracting task. Complexity was varied by having subjects perform cognitive tasks which increased in the degree of attentional resources necessary for their performance (i.e., acknowledging hearing each number; repeating, or shadowing, the numbers; adding consecutive pairs of numbers; and adding then classifying numbers). Results indicated that the tumescence level in response to sexually explicit stimuli decreased as an approximately linear function of the complexity of distracting tasks. Two other studies (Farkas, Sine, & Evans, 1979; Viglietta, 1982), both as part of larger experiments, replicated the distraction effect using visual sexual stimuli (i.e., sexually explicit film segments) and auditory nonsexual stimuli (i.e., tone presentations and a tape-recorded story presentation, respectively). Furthermore, Becker and Byrne (1988) have demonstrated that an inverse relationship exists between self-reported genital arousal and knowledge of the sexual stimuli (i.e., score on content recall task) within a distraction paradigm, suggesting more directly that shifting from sexual (on-task) to nonsexual (off-task) foci is the mechanism of the distraction process.

Given that SFs and SDs have responded differently under anxiety induction (Beck et al., 1982; Beck et al., 1984), Abrahamson, Barlow, Sakheim, Beck, and Athanasiou, (1985) examined the effects of distraction on these two groups. During the distraction condition, subjects were instructed to view a sexually explicit film segment while listening simultaneously to a taped reading of a passage from a popular novel. Subjects were told that they were going to be asked to recall parts of the passage postsession. Results indicated that under the no-distraction condition both groups attained equal and moderate levels of penile circumference change. During the distraction condition, SFs predictably evidenced significant decrements in erection compared to no-distraction levels, replicating previous findings (e.g., Farkas *et al.*, 1979; Geer & Fuhr, 1976; Viglietta, 1982). On the other hand, SDs evidenced no such decrement in erection during the distraction condition, demonstrating a slight, statistically nonsignificant increment in arousal (see Figure 2).

Therefore, a second dimension on which the responding of SDs and SFs is meaningfully distinguished is their response to neutral, nonsexual distraction. Results from the distraction literature suggest strongly that the sexual arousal of SFs is inhibited by activities which require the reallocation of attentional resources away from stimuli that would ordinarily facilitate their sexual arousal. Moreover, the degree of inhibition appears to be, in part, a function of the degree of this reallocation (Geer & Fuhr, 1976). On the other hand, Abrahamson *et al.* (1985) have demonstrated that SDs show no such distraction effects. At first glance, this latter result would seem counterintuitive; that is, again one might

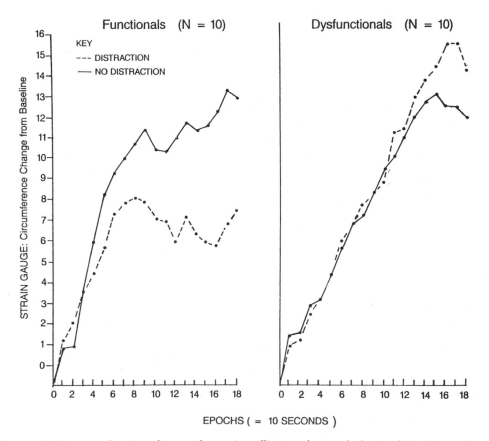

FIGURE 2. Mean penile circumference change in millimeters by epoch during distraction and no distraction: sexually functional (left) versus sexually dysfunctional (right) subjects. (From "Effects of Distraction on Sexual Responding in Functional and Dysfunctional Men" by D. A. Abrahamson, D. H. Barlow, D. K. Sakheim, J. G. Beck, & R. Athanasiou, 1985, *Behavior Therapy, 16*, p. 509. Copyright 1985 by the Association for Advancement of Behavior Therapy. Reprinted by permission.)

not expect the effects of a proposed mechanism of action such as autonomic interruption or, in this case, distraction to vary between populations. However, these researchers suggest that the mechanism of distraction may occur with SDs as it does with SFs, but with a converse effect on sexual arousal. That is, unlike SFs who are distracted from sexual foci, with SDs neutral distraction may reallocate their attentional resources from an off-task focus that would ordinarily inhibit their sexual arousal to attentional foci equally or less inhibitory. Therefore, distracting SDs from one off-task focus to another results in either no change in level of erection or possibly a slight increase in arousal (i.e., disinhibition).

Of course, in examining the "disinhibition hypothesis," it is necessary to recognize that its premise is that SFs and SDs may be responding sexually to different foci of attention in the sexual situation. As noted above, there is wide agreement among clinicians that SDs engage in several cognitive activities which may have a marked effect on sexual arousal. For example, Masters and Johnson (1970) discussed the distracting nature of performance concerns, as well as the restorative effect of sensate focus. Kaplan (1974, 1981) has discussed various distracting thoughts that may interfere with sexual responding reported by many of her clients. These types of hypotheses laid the groundwork for several studies of the effects of these cognitive activities on sexual responding which are reviewed in the next subsection.

Attentional Focus

One line of research within this area has utilized analog manipulations of the oft-noted concept of performance demand (Masters & Johnson, 1970). One of the first in this series of studies chose to manipulate performance demand via an expectancy set manipulation (Farkas et al., 1979). As part of a larger factorial design, these researchers varied high and low demand by informing each group of young SFs that they should expect to become either "quite aroused" or "not . . . very aroused" (p. 27), based on responses of previous subjects. Contrary to expectation, results showed this demand manipulation had no differential effect on penile tumescence.

In what they described as an attempt to improve the Farkas et al. (1979) definition of performance demand, Lange et al. (1981) used an instructional set characterized by an explicit demand to "try to achieve an erection quickly, as fully, for as long as they could" (p. 449). They compared the results of this condition to a no-demand condition defined by the instruction to "focus on sexual enjoyment or pleasure that they might receive" (p. 449). The demand and no-demand condition were described as attempts to operationalize the concepts of spectatoring and sensate focus (Masters & Johnson, 1970), respectively. Despite the changes in definition, the effect of spectatoring was to increase penile responding to levels significantly higher than those of the sensate focus condition at the end of the first 1-minute epoch. This effect washed-out over the remainder of the condition, resulting in equivalent levels between conditions. One noteworthy aside is the similarity of the "spectatoring" instruction used by

Lange *et al.* (1981) to that used in voluntary control studies to enhance erection (Bancroft & Mathews, 1971; Henson & Rubin, 1971; Laws & Rubin, 1969). Again, these combined results indicate that when SFs are "demanded" to enhance erection level, they do. However, the key question is whether SDs may respond differently under these conditions.

This question was addressed directly by Heiman and Rowland (1983), who compared the erectile responding of SFs and SDs under conditions of "high performance demand" and "low performance demand/sensate focus" (p. 108) instructions. High demand was manipulated by instructing subjects to "concentrate on . . . your erection . . . try to maintain it . . . remain an objective observer of your arousal" (p. 108) while listening to a sexually explicit audiotaped presentation. The sensate focus instruction asked subjects to focus instead on pleasurable, nongenital bodily sensations during the erotic presentation. Although these researchers hypothesized that high demand, relative to low demand, would inhibit arousal across both groups, they found differential response patterns between groups. Specifically, SDs demonstrated significantly less tumescence during high- compared to low-demand conditions. SFs demonstrated the converse pattern.

This differential response to demand has also been reported by Abrahamson, Barlow, and Abrahamson (1989), who utilized a genital feedback paradigm to study the effects of both performance-related and non-performance-related stimuli on the sexual responding of SDs and SFs. During each of three conditions, subjects were shown sexually explicit film segments on one monitor and a stimulus presentation on an adjacent monitor. Conditions were defined by the type of stimulus presented on the adjacent monitor, which appeared every 30 seconds for a duration of 3 seconds. During the performance-related condition, the stimulus was live genital feedback. During the non-performance related condition, the stimulus was a line varying in length at each presentation. The third condition was a no-distraction control, during which no stimulus was presented on the adjacent monitor. To assure processing of the respective stimuli, subjects were asked to make a percentage rating of the particular stimulus during each presentation based on predetermined standards for both stimuli. Results from this study replicated previous findings in that SDs evidenced significantly lower penile circumference change under the performance-related feedback condition than SFs under this condition. The finding shows again that performance demand does not necessarily inhibit sexual arousal in SFs, but does in SDs.

Similar results have been reported in studies discussed previously which indicate that demand defined as response to CS (i.e., shock threat contingent on attaining a "normal" erection level) either does not inhibit erection or facilitates it in SFs (Barlow *et al.*, 1983; Beck *et al.*, 1984), but inhibits erection in SDs (Beck *et al.*, 1984). It is of interest to note that just as clinical definitions of performance demand have varied based on the subtle connotational preferences of authors, laboratory operationalizations also share this feature. Despite these differences, all of these studies share at least two commonalities. First, an attempt is made to direct subjects to a particular focus of attention presumed to be inhibitory to sexual arousal (e.g., performance related), and to compare the effects of these manipulations to those of attentional foci presumed to be facilitative or non-inhibitory. Second, the results of these investigations demonstrate reliably the differential responding of SFs and SDs to the presumed inhibitory foci. This response to performance demand conditions is a third dimension of differential responding to distinguish these two groups. Again, the result is that SFs show either no inhibition of erection or facilitation in response to performance demands. SDs, on the other hand, demonstrate erectile inhibition (Abrahamson *et al.*, 1989; Barlow *et al.*, 1983; Beck *et al.*, 1984; Farkas *et al.*, 1979; Heiman & Rowland, 1983; Lange *et al.*, 1981).

Integration and Summary

The attentional resource allocation literature shows that imposing nonsexual, off-task stimuli inhibits sexual arousal in SFs (Abrahamson *et al.*, 1985; Farkas *et al.*, 1979; Geer & Fuhr, 1976; Viglietta, 1982). Theoretically, this effect is a function of the degree to which attentional resources are allocated from sexual (task-relevant) to nonsexual (task-irrelevant) cognitive activities. However, SDs are not distracted when nonsexual stimuli are imposed on their attentional foci, in that they show no decrease in their attained erection level (Abrahamson *et al.*, 1985). This imperviousness to distraction by SDs has led to a disinhibition hypothesis (see Abrahamson *et al.*, 1985), which suggests that when nonsexual stimuli are imposed on SDs, their erection level does not change because they are essentially being distracted from one off-task activity (e.g., performance concerns) to another (e.g., the particular mathematical task being imposed on them in an experimental distraction condition). Theoretically, one could expect an increase in erection levels upon the imposition of alternative stimuli (i.e., disinhibition) if the stimuli imposed was more on-task than those "replaced." As indicated, the disinhibition hypothesis is based on the premise and clinically oft-noted observation that, to their detriment, SDs may selectively attend to nonsexual, task-irrelevant concerns in the sexual context. In turn, this premise is supported by the attentional focus literature which shows that SDs demonstrate an inhibition of sexual arousal in response to various operationalizations of performance demand. SFs show no change in erection or erectile facilitation to these same conditions (Abrahamson *et al.*, 1989; Barlow *et al.*, 1983; Beck *et al.*, 1984; Farkas *et al.*, 1979; Heiman & Rowland, 1983; Lange *et al.*, 1981).

These two bodies of literature converge in that the attentional resource findings highlight the potential role of the subject's attention to the properties of the stimulus field in determining sexual arousal, while the attentional focus literature indicates the importance of their representation of that field (i.e., the meaning derived or appraisal of the field). For example, in discussion of their results Heiman and Rowland (1983) exemplify the latter point in stating that "high demand instructions are not in and of themselves antisexual; thinking about and emotionally reacting to them give them their meaning" (p. 114).

Another empirical example is provided by Beck, Barlow, and Sakheim (1983), who examined the interactive effects of self- versus partner-focus within three levels of partner arousal (high, low, and ambiguous) on the sexual arousal of both SFs and SDs. The key finding in relation to the current discussion is that under conditions depicting a highly aroused partner, SDs showed lower penile circumference change while focusing on the partner than did SFs under this attentional focus (both relative to the self-focus conditions). Abrahamson, Barlow, Beck, Sakheim, and Kelly (1985) replicated these finding using audiotaped erotic stimuli rather than videotapes used in Beck *et al.* (1983). In both studies, subjects reported experiencing increased pressure to become aroused while attending to the highly aroused partner. However, SDs described this thought as unarousing, while SFs found it arousing.

The studies reviewed thus far suggest that the neutral distraction effect as observed in SFs is the prototype of the cognitive process inhibiting sexual arousal. In general, what distinguishes functional from dysfunctional sexual responding is the difference in selective attention and interpretation involved in this process. Beck and Barlow (1984) suggest further that concerns labeled variously as performance demand, fear of inadequacy, spectatoring, and the like, are all forms of situation-specific, task-irrelevant cognitive activities which distract SDs from task-relevant processing of stimuli in the sexual context. Although the nature of the content and process of this differential cognitive activity is just beginning to be understood, two other areas of differential responding between SDs and SFs are providing initial guidance down this avenue of study and are briefly introduced in the next section.

Subjective Reports of Arousal and Affect

Many of the studies reviewed thus far have employed a continuous measure of subjective sexual arousal (Wincze, Venditti, Barlow, & Mavissakalian, 1980) in addition to a genital measure. Others have assessed subjective arousal in poststimulus fashion. In most of the studies these genital and subjective indices of sexual arousal are highly concordant. However, those studies reporting discordance share noteworthy similarities. Studies employing measures of self-reported affect have yielded some interesting results as well. These two sets of findings are reported in the following two subsections.

Subjective Estimates of Arousal

This area of study was prompted, in part, by the hypothesis that the spectatoring concept (see Masters & Johnson, 1970) may be useful for investigating the off-task cognitive activities characteristic of SDs. For example, the most common hypothesis has been that spectatoring (defined as monitoring ones erectile responding, looking for signs of failure) may operate to distract SDs from on-task foci. By this formulation, one might expect SDs to be good estimators of their erectile level.

Sakheim (1984) was one of the first to examine directly the degree of concordance between a continuous measure of estimated and measured erectile responding. As part of this study, he examined this relationship between SDs and

SFs. Results showed that at periods of equivalent levels of penile responding during the viewing of a sexually explicit film, SDs reported lower estimates of erection levels than did SFs. Other studies have also shown that SDs evidence lower correlations between measured and estimated erection than SFs (Abrahamson et al., 1985; Bruce, Cerny, & Barlow, 1986).

Although, these results sound contrary to what one would expect if SDs are spectatoring, the underestimation of arousal level by SDs suggests hypotheses about the selective attention and interpretation process described previously. One possibility in this regard is that through repeated experiences with inhibition of erectile response (e.g., longer latency to tumescence, lower maximum levels of erection), SDs anticipate or expect little to no erectile response. This presumptive stance may preclude them from appraising these cues more directly or positively and, in a sense, fulfill their prophesy. This hypothesis was recently supported by Bruce et al. (1986), who asked SDs and SFs to view a 10-minute sexually explicit film segment while tracking their degree of erection with a precalibrated lever. During the condition subjects could also obtain visual feedback of their genital responding by pushing a signal marker. The feedback appeared for 3 seconds and could be re-obtained throughout the 10-minute film. Results indicated that SFs showed significantly higher erectile levels and penile–lever concordance than did SDs, who showed moderate tumescence and concordance as well as a tendency toward underrating erectile level. Additionally, SFs showed significantly more requests for genital feedback than did SDs, some of whom never requested feedback. A measure of cumulative frequency of requests indicated that neither SFs nor SDs showed a propensity for requesting feedback during particular periods (e.g., during high or low levels of erection). Finally, debriefing data indicated that while SFs requested feedback out of interest and/or curiosity, SDs reported little desire to view the feedback, typically indicating that it would "only confirm what (they) knew" (in reference to their evaluation of inadequate responding).

These results suggest that SDs may be engaged in ruminative, self-deprecating thought concerning the inadequacy of their sexual responding. They do not appear interested in feedback, despite attaining moderate erection in this study. Indeed, when Abrahamson et al. (1989) delivered genital feedback to SDs, they responded with strong negative affect and little to no sexual arousal. SFs, on the other hand, can find performance feedback arousing and will choose to attend to it (see Bruce et al., 1986). They also show positive affect and no decrease in sexual arousal when viewing the feedback is not voluntary (Abrahamson et al., 1989). Sakheim, Barlow, Beck, and Abrahamson (1984) discuss other implications of the spectatoring process.

A similar set of findings has emerged from the distraction literature. Specifically, while several studies have shown inhibition of penile responding in SFs during nonsexual distraction (i.e., Abrahamson et al., 1985; Farkas et al., 1979; Viglietta, 1982), they have also reported that SFs did not indicate a corresponding decrease in their estimates of sexual arousal. In light of the above data suggesting that SDs may underestimate their erection levels, Abrahamson et al. (1985) posit that SFs may tend to overestimate theirs by discounting or ignoring indicators of detumescence. Again, these results, taken together, indicate that SFs and SDs differ in their selective attention and interpretation processes within the sexual context. The concordance studies highlight this process as it pertains to self-directed attention and evaluation of responding. The difference in the concordance between measured and estimated sexual arousal is the fourth area of meaningfully differential responding between SDs and SFs.

Perceived Control and Affect

Several authors (Abrahamson et al., 1985, Barlow, 1986, 1988; Beck & Barlow, 1984) have drawn parallels between the overestimation of erection in SFs and the overestimation of control by nondepressed individuals (Abramson, Seligman, & Teasdale, 1978). By inference, this comparison suggests that SFs and SDs may be differentially susceptible to the affective repercussions of their different perceptions of control. Results from studies including an assessment of perceived control and affect suggest this possibility. For example, results from one study reported within the voluntary control literature (Beck et al., 1982) indicates that SFs may perceive more control over erectile responding in that they confidently report cognitive strategies used to control erection levels. On the other hand, SDs in this study were unaware that they could use strategies to control erectile level.

A few of the studies reviewed previously have included postcondition affective measures such as affective checklists or Likert-type scales. It has been found that SDs typically endorse negative or neutral affective indicators, whereas SFs typically endorse positive affective indicators. (Abrahamson et al., 1985; Heiman & Rowland, 1983). In the Abrahamson et al. (1985) study, the affective measure, which was a factor-analytically derived checklist (Multiple Affective Adjective Checklist, MAACL; Zuckerman & Lubin, 1965), indicated that those adjectives endorsed by SDs were items within the factor labeled depression. Additionally, Abrahamson et al. (1989) reported a condition-specific difference in affective responses of SFs and SDs, wherein SDs reported more negative affect while under the performance-related manipulation. Beck and Barlow (1986) provide supporting evidence of more neutral, disinterested affective responding by SDs and, again, more positive affective responding by SFs.

These results suggest several distinctions in the cognitive and affective responding of SDs and SFs in the sexual situation. Specifically, SDs may presume a low probability that they will become aroused, perceive low control over their responding, and respond with negative or disinterested affect in the sexual situation. On the other hand, SFs presume no difficulty attaining sexual arousal, perceive control over this response, and experience positive affect in these situations.

Barlow (1986) speculates further that the affective differences noted between these groups may predate erectile difficulties, and as such may be as important to etiology as to maintenance of the dysfunction. Preliminary supporting evidence has recently been reported by Jones, Carpenter, Bruce, and Barlow (1987), who showed that SDs and SFs score more "erotophobic" and "erotophilic," respectively, on this dimension, derived from the work of Byrne and his colleagues (e.g., Byrne, 1977, 1983a, 1983b; Byrne, Fisher, Lambert, & Mitchell, 1974) with the Sexual Opinion Survey—a personality scale designed to assess long-term affective responding to a variety of sexual situations. Thus, a fifth dimension of differential responding between SDs and SFs is the combined factor of their perceptions of control and the quality of their affective response to sexual stimuli.

THE INTERACTION OF AUTONOMIC AND ATTENTIONAL FACTORS

If anxiety is conceptualized as being composed of multiple response systems, then the interactive effects of autonomic and cognitive factors can be tested. Recently such investigations suggest, in a preliminary way, how autonomic arousal may differentially affect the sexual arousal of SDs and SFs. Specifically, results of these studies suggest that increased autonomic arousal may facilitate processing of those stimuli to which one is simultaneously attending. For example, Beck, Barlow, Sakheim, and Abrahamson (1987) presented young SFs with sexually explicit audiotaped presentations simultaneous to four levels of noncontingent shock threat (no threat, half tolerance, tolerance, and twice tolerance). Subjects were told both to attend to the sexually explicit presentation and that their attention would be checked poststimulus via a sentence cognition task. Borrowing from Yerkes and Dobson (1908), it was hypothesized that erectile responding would increase as a function of increased autonomic arousal associated with the threat of shock. Erectile levels were expected to lower as shock threat reached high levels (i.e., twice tolerance), thereby resulting in an inverted U-function of penile responding. However, as can be seen in Figure 3, the results indicated that subjects responded in a U-function of penile responding across the four levels of shock threat. Performance on the sentence recognition task, however, followed an inverted U-function across levels.

In interpreting these results, Barlow (1986, 1988) suggests that the increase in induced anxiety facilitated performance as hypothesized, but did so on the sentence recognition task. Accordingly, the decrease in erectile levels was due to a distraction effect. In other words, the sentence recognition task distracted subjects from freely listening to the sexually explicit tape. Autonomic arousal facilitated this distraction effect by facilitating performance on the distracting sentence recognition task. Of course, this interpretation suggests that removing the sentence recognition task would result in increased sexual arousal as originally hypothesized. Indeed, this effect has been suggested by previous studies showing increases in erection in response to shock threat which did not include a sentence recognition task (e.g., Barlow et al., 1983; Beck et al., 1984). Additionally, the possibility that sexually explicit stimuli (i.e., the sentences from the sexually explicit audiotape subjects were asked to recognize) can serve as distractors has been discussed in previous sections. Recall one study in the voluntary control literature which reported that SFs could successfully suppress their erections despite being required to verbalize the content of a sexually explicit

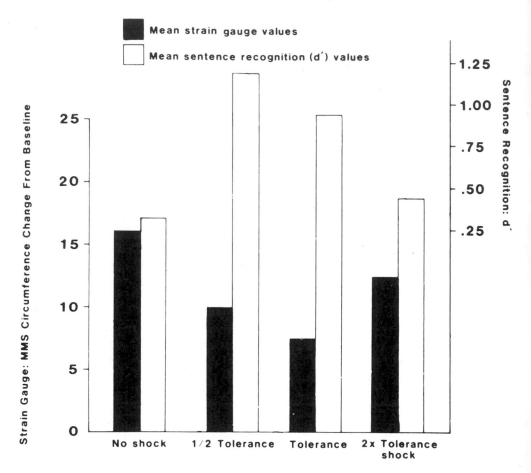

FIGURE 3. Mean penile circumference change in millimeters (MMS) across stimulus duration, and mean sentence recognition values during four shock-threat conditions. (From "Shock Threat and Sexual Arousal: The Role of Selective Attention, Thought Content, and Affective States" by J. G. Beck, D. H. Barlow, D. K. Sakheim, and D. J. Abrahamson, 1987, *Psychophysiology*, 24, p. 169. Copyright 1987 by the Society for Psychophysiological Research, Inc.)

stimulus presentation (Henson & Rubin, 1971). It is possible that the processing of the sexually explicit stimuli is also a "task" that is distracting in a manner similar to the off-task processing by SDs in a sexually explicit context. This possibility prompted a second study.

As suggested, given that the sentence recognition task used in Beck *et al.* (1987) functioned to distract SFs, replication of this study without this task suggests that they would show increased penile responding. Theoretically, this effect would be a function of the facilitative action of autonomic arousal on the on-task attentional foci of SFs. It could also be hypothesized that if autonomic arousal facilitates one's concurrent attentional processing, then SDs should show a decrease in penile responding due to the facilitation of the off-task processing characteristic of them. Results of this replication were recently reported by Jones, Bruce, and Barlow (1986). As hypothesized, SFs responded in an inverted U-function across conditions. SDs also responded as predicted by demonstrating a decrease in erectile responding during shock-threat conditions from the level attained during the no-shock-threat control condition.

Further evidence that autonomic arousal may serve to facilitate one's concurrent focus of attention has also been suggested in results of previously discussed studies by Hoon *et al.* (1977) and Lange *et al.* (1981). For example, in Lange *et al.* (1981) subjects who received epinephrine displayed shorter latencies to detumescence following offset of the sexually explicit stimulus than the no-epinephrine subjects. Hoon *et al.* (1977) found similar results when they followed a sexually explicit film with a noxious one. Again, this hypothesis warrants further study. But it is clear that results from these preliminary studies speak to the importance of further investigations of the interaction between autonomic and attentional factors, and suggest the hypothesis that autonomic arousal may facilitate one's concurrent focus of attention (see Barlow, 1988).

Working Model and Summary

In this section Barlow's (1986) working model of sexual dysfunction will be described, and a summary of the literature reviewed thus far will be integrated into this description. A schematic depiction of the model, to which the reader is referred, can be found in Figure 4.

The model is characterized by its emphasis on the interactive effects of a cognitive interference process and autonomic arousal in determining functional and dysfunctional sexual responding. The processes are conceptualized within a positive and negative feedback loop system. Within the negative feedback loop, the nature of the interaction revolves around a focus on nonsexual, task-irrelevant concerns within a sexual context. The focus becomes increasingly efficient through increases in autonomic arousal. While the same process is posited for functional sexual responding (within the positive feedback loop), the nature of the cognitive activities is task relevant.

The model is drawn from results of investigations reviewed thus far suggesting the differential sexual responding of SFs and SDs on five major dimensions. Moving through the flowchart of the model, the first group of studies suggests that SDs and SFs respond with differential affect in sexual situations. Generally, SFs have been shown to report more positive affect, while SDs report negative or disinterested affect characterized as dysphoric (Abrahamson *et al.*, 1985; Beck & Barlow, 1986; Heiman & Rowland, 1983). Second, while SDs have shown a tendency to underestimate erection level (Abrahamson *et al.*, 1985; Bruce *et al.*, 1986; Sakheim, 1984), SFs show either high correlation between these two indices (e.g., Beck & Barlow, 1986; Bruce *et al.*, 1986; Sakheim, 1984) or will overestimate erection levels despite decrements in its actual level (Abrahamson *et al.*, 1985; Farkas *et al.*, 1979; Viglietta, 1982). Some authors (e.g., Abrahamson *et al.*, 1985; Beck & Barlow, 1984) have related both the over- and underestimation phenomena to possible differences between these groups in

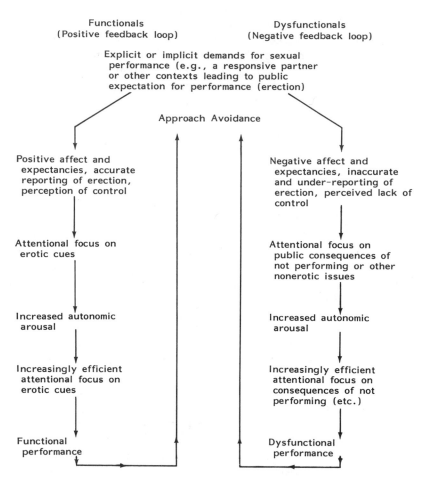

FIGURE 4. Working model of erectile dysfunction. (From "Causes of Sexual Dysfunction: The Role of Anxiety and Cognitive Interference" by D. H. Barlow, 1986, *Journal of Consulting and Clinical Psychology, 54,* p. 146.)

terms of perceptions of control. This suggestion is supported by voluntary control studies in which SFs reported awareness of their erectile suppression and described the mental operations they used to achieve it. On the other hand, SDs did not know if they were successful in suppressing erection, and they reported a lack of awareness of operations used to attempt it (Beck *et al.*, 1982). Third, SDs are not distracted by nonsexual stimulus presentations in that they evidence no decrease in erectile responding under these conditions (Abrahamson *et al.*, 1985); whereas, SFs show inhibition of erection under the same conditions (Abrahamson *et al.*, 1985; Farkas *et al.*, 1979; Geer & Fuhr, 1976; Viglietta, 1982). Fourth, SDs show erectile inhibition in response to a number of instructional sets and stimulus presentations operationalizing performance demand–spectatoring constructs (Abrahamson *et al.*, 1989; Barlow *et al.*, 1983; Beck *et al.*, 1984; Bruce *et al.*, 1986; Heiman & Rowland, 1983); whereas, the sexual arousal of SFs is either unaffected or facilitated by these conditions (Abrahamson *et al.*, 1989; Barlow *et al.*, 1983; Beck *et al.*, 1982, 1984; Bruce *et al.*, 1986; Farkas *et al.*, 1979; Heiman & Rowland, 1983; Henson & Rubin, 1971; Lange *et al.*, 1981; Laws & Rubin, 1969). These results suggest that SFs and SDs may be differentially processing (e.g., attending, appraising) stimuli in the sexual situation. Fifth, increases in autonomic arousal, as a result of varied manipulations, results either in no inhibition of erection or facilitation in SFs (Barlow *et al.*, 1983; Beck *et al.*, 1984; Jones *et al.*, 1986; Lange *et al.*, 1981); whereas, SDs evidence erectile inhibition in response to these conditions (Beck *et al.*, 1984; Jones *et al.*, 1986). These results have led to the hypothesis that increases in autonomic arousal may result in an increasingly efficient processing of those foci to which one is simultaneously attending.

One of the key features of this model is the proposition that a distraction process is the mechanism of action through which many experiences act to inhibit sexual responsivity. This process combined with autonomic arousal leads to the inhibition of sexual arousal by facilitating the distraction effect. Autonomic arousal in and of itself does not disrupt sexual arousal. As such this model shares several similarities with current models of social and other evaluation anxieties emphasizing cognitive interference in performance.

RELATED AREAS OF PERFORMANCE ANXIETY

There are several similarities between the processes proposed to be operative in the maintenance of sexual dysfunction and those hypothesized to maintain other social and evaluative anxieties. For example, on a descriptive level, the nosological category of Social Phobia, as described in the DSM-III and DSM-III-R (American Psychiatric Association, 1980, 1987), shares much in common with our model of sexual dysfunction. Specifically, individuals with social phobia are characterized by concerns of scrutiny, negative evaluation, humiliation, or embarrassment while performing in public. On a theoretical level, several models of the etiology and maintenance of social phobias and other evaluation-based anxieties highlight the primary role of cognitions in causing performance disruption.

One of the most thoroughly researched examples has appeared in the area of test anxiety. It has been known for some time that highly test-anxious students report less confidence in their abilities (Meunier & Reile, 1967), aspire to lower levels of performance (Trapp & Kausler, 1958), and blame themselves more for perceived poor performance (Doris & Sarason, 1955) than do low test-anxious students. More recently, Sarason and his colleagues (Sarason, 1982; Sarason & Stoops, 1978) suggested that cognitive interference, in the form of task-irrelevant thought, is the primary factor disrupting the performance of the highly test-anxious student. Others have proposed similar models of performance disruption in social anxiety (e.g., Schlenker & Leary, 1982) and assertion difficulties (e.g., Schwartz & Gottman, 1976).

Obviously, sexual responding differs from test-taking behavior and other behavioral performances subject to disruption through social anxiety. For example, erectile dysfunction involves a unique physiological response. Nevertheless, the comparisons are made to suggest that cognitive interference is capable of disrupting performance across many response systems (e.g., verbal and motoric behavior, physiological regulation, cognitive problem solving), and that it may be central to performance disruption in evaluation-based anxieties. Similarly, these formulations also suggest that autonomic arousal is not a necessary condition in the disruption process. These findings have also been related recently to theories of anxiety in general, particularly those emanating from emotion theory (Barlow, 1988). This formulation suggests something basic about the nature of anxiety, as a loose cognitive affective structure that is sharply different from more basic discrete emotions such as fear or sadness. In this sense, all anxiety might be social or performance anxiety, with distinction made only on the basis of which specific responses are subject to interference such that it becomes a problem for the individual (in its pathological expression).

FUTURE DIRECTIONS

The model of sexual dysfunction presented in this chapter is a working model which is supported in a preliminary way by the data presented. Many conclusions are based on contrasting data sets from similar but independent experiments. However, these data are encouraging and suggest several areas of future investigation.

One area deserving more study concerns both the content and process of thought involved in the proposed interference process. Currently, we are investigating in depth the neutral distraction effect in SFs and SDs in an attempt to understand more about the process of attentional shifting between on- and off-task thought, the appraisal process determining "on" and "off" task, and potential themes in the content of this cognition. Further study of the differential responding of SFs and SDs to performance demand conditions could be most useful in regards to elucidating the processes of functional and dysfunctional selective attention discussed previously. Factor and cluster analytic investigations of thought content derived in the natural or analog setting might have strong implications not only for theory, but for assessment and treatment as indicated below. Another related area of study includes investigations of affective responding to sexually explicit stimuli. The results in the area of perceived control suggest that new theories of anxiety emphasizing traditional notions of predictability and controllability may have potential relevance to the interference process (Barlow, 1988). False-feedback paradigms may be useful in studying perceived control.

A second general area of study is the interaction of autonomic arousal and attentional processes. Paradigms from experimental cognitive science, including stimulus recognition, dichotomous listening, and reaction time may be useful in investigating the effect of induced autonomic arousal on the processing of a variety of on- and off-task foci between SDs and SFs. For example, we are currently investigating the effect of caffeine-induced arousal on sexual and non-sexual distraction in SFs and SDs.

If support for the model is forthcoming, then there are several assessment and treatment implications. For example, detailed assessment of affective and cognitive functioning in the sexual context may predict the degree of improvement as well as long-term functioning. Elements of treatments successful for clinical and social phobia may provide some useful guidelines for the treatment of sexual dysfunction. For example, more emphasis on cognitive change (e.g., allocation and focus of attention) may improve treatment success; this emphasis combined with the current practice of using performance-based exercises may be the most effective way to improve treatment outcome. Emphasizing anxiety reduction operationalized as decreasing physiological arousal may be unnecessary, or its usefulness, like other techniques, may have to be measured in consideration of the attentional focus of the client. Clearly, these and other hypotheses suggested by the lines of investigation reviewed in the present chapter are testable with relevant implications for sexual dysfunction as well as performance anxiety in other contexts.

REFERENCES

Abel, G. G., Barlow, D. H., Blanchard, E. B., & Mavissakalian, M. (1975). Measurement of sexual arousal in male homosexuals: Effects of instructions and stimulus modality. *Archives of Sexual Behavior, 4,* 623–630.

Abrahamson, D. J., Barlow, D. H., & Abrahamson, L. S. (1989). Differential effects of performance demand and distraction on sexually functional and dysfunctional males. *Journal of Abnormal Psychology, 98,* 241–247.

Abrahamson, D. J., Barlow, D. H., Beck, J. G., Sakheim, D. K., & Kelly, J. P. (1985). The effects of attentional focus and partner responsiveness on sexual responding: Replication and extension. *Archives of Sexual Behavior, 14,* 361–371.

Abrahamson, D. J., Barlow, D. H., Sakheim, D. K., Beck, J. G., & Athanasiou, R. (1985). Effects of distraction on sexual responding in sexual functional and sexually dysfunctional men. *Behavior Therapy, 16,* 503–515.

Abramson, L. Y., Seligman, M. E., & Teasdale, J. D. (1978). Learned helplessness in humans: Critique and reformulation. *Journal of Abnormal Psychology, 87,* 49–74.

American Psychiatric Association. (1980). *Diagnostic and statistical manual of mental disorders* (3rd ed.). Washington, DC: Author.

American Psychiatric Association. (1987). *Diagnostic and statistical manual of mental disorders* (3rd ed., revised). Washington, DC: Author.

Baddeley, H. D., & Hitch, G. (1974). Working memory. In G. H. Bower (Ed.), *The psychology of learning and motivation* (Vol. 8). London: Academic Press.

Bancroft, J. H. J., & Mathews, A. M. (1971). Autonomic correlates of penile erection. *Journal of Psychosomatic Research, 15,* 159–167.

Barlow, D. H. (1988). *Anxiety and its disorders: The nature and treatment of anxiety and panic.* NY: Guilford Press.

Barlow, D. H. (1986). Causes of sexual dysfunction: The role of anxiety and cognitive interference. *Journal of Consulting and Clinical Psychology, 54,* 140–148.

Barlow, D. H., Mavissakalian, M., & Schofield, L. (1980). Patterns of desynchrony in agorophobia. *Behaviour Research and Therapy, 18,* 441–448.

Barlow, D. H., Sakheim, D. K., & Beck, J. G. (1983). Anxiety increases sexual arousal. *Journal of Abnormal Psychology, 92,* 49–54.

Beck, J. G., & Barlow, D. H. (1984). Current conceptualizations of sexual dysfunction: A review and an alternative perspective. *Clinical Psychology Review, 4*, 363–378.

Beck, J. G., & Barlow, D. H. (1986). The effects of anxiety and attentional focus on sexual respond-ing—II: Cognitive and affective patterns in erectile dysfunction. *Behaviour Research and Therapy, 24*, 19–26.

Beck, J. G., Barlow, D. H., & Sakheim, D. K. (1982, August). *Sexual arousal and suppression patterns in functional and dysfunctional men.* Paper presented at the annual convention of the American Psychological Association, Washington, DC.

Beck, J. G., Barlow, D. H., & Sakheim, D. K. (1983). The effects of attentional focus and partner arousal on sexual responding in functional and dysfunctional men. *Behaviour Research and Thera-py, 21*, 1–8.

Beck, J. G., Barlow, D. H., Sakheim, D. K., & Abrahamson, D. J. (1984, November). *Sexual responding during anxiety: Clinical versus non-clinical patterns.* Paper presented at the 18th Annual Convention of the Association for the Advancement of Behavior Therapy, Philadelphia.

Beck, J. G., Barlow, D. H., Sakheim, D. K., & Abrahamson, D. J. (1987). Shock threat and sexual arousal: The role of selective attention, thought content, and affective states. *Psychophysiology, 24*, 165–172.

Becker, M. A., & Byrne, D. (1988). Type A behavior, distraction, and sexual arousal. *Journal of Social and Clinical Psychology, 6*, 478–481.

Berschied, E., & Walter, E. (1978). *Interpersonal attraction* (2nd ed.). Reading, MA: Addison-Wesley.

Brady, J. (1966). Brevital relaxation treatment of frigidity. *Behaviour Research and Therapy, 4*, 71–77.

Brehm, J., Gatz, M., Goethels, G., McCrimmon, W., & Ward, L. (1978). Physiological arousal and interpersonal attraction. *JSAS: Catalog of Selected Documents in Psychology, 8*, 63.

Bruce, T. J., Cerny, J. A., & Barlow, D. H. (1986, November). *Spectatoring operationalized: Its influence on sexually functional and dysfunctional men.* Paper presented at the annual convention of the Associa-tion for the Advancement of Behavior Therapy, Chicago.

Byrne, D. (1977). Social psychology and the study of sexual behavior. *Personality and Social Psychology Bulletin, 3*, 3–30.

Byrne, D. (1983a). The antecedents, correlates, and consequences of erotophobia–erotophilia. In C. M. Davis (Ed.), *Challenges in sexual science* (pp. 53–75). Philadelphia: Society for the Scientific Study of Sex.

Byrne, D. (1983b). Sex without contraception. In D. Byrne & W. A. Fisher (Eds.), *Adolescents, sex, and contraception* (pp. 2–31). Hillsdale, NJ: Erlbaum.

Byrne, D., Fisher, J. D., Lambert, J., & Mitchell, H. E. (1974). Evaluations of erotica: Facts of feelings? *Journal of Personality and Social Psychology, 29*, 111–116.

Cantor, J. R., Zillman, D., & Bryant, J. (1975). Enhancement of experienced sexual arousal in re-sponse to erotic stimuli through misattribution of unrelated residual excitation. *Journal of Person-ality and Social Psychology, 32*, 69–75.

Cooper, A. J. (1981). Short-term treatment of sexual dysfunction: A review. *Comprehensive Psychiatry, 22*, 206–217.

Crown, S., & D'Ardeene, P. (1982). Symposium on sexual dysfunction: Controversies, methods, results. *British Journal of Psychiatry, 140*, 70–77.

Doris, J., & Sarason, S. B. (1955). Test anxiety and blame assignment in a failure situation. *Journal of Abnormal and Social Psychology, 50*, 335–338.

Dutton, D. G., & Aron, A. P. (1974). Some evidence of heightened sexual attraction under conditions of high anxiety. *Journal of Personality and Social Psychology, 30*, 510–517.

Farkas, G. M., Sine, L. F., & Evans, I. M. (1979). The effects of distraction, performance demand, stimulus explicitness, and personality on objective and subjective measures of male sexual arousal. *Behaviour Research and Therapy, 17*, 25–32.

Geer, J. H., & Fuhr, R. (1976). Cognitive factors in sexual arousal: The role of distraction. *Journal of Consulting and Clinical Psychology, 44*, 238–243.

Hartman, W., & Fithian, M. (1972). *Treatment of sexual dysfunction: A bio-psychosocial approach.* Long Beach, CA: Center for Marital and Sexual Studies.

Heiman, J. R., & Rowland, D. L. (1983). Affective and physiological sexual patterns: The effects of instruction on sexually functional and dysfunctional men. *Journal of Psychosomatic Research, 27,* 105–116.

Henson, D. E., & Rubin, H. B. (1971). Voluntary control of eroticism. *Journal of Applied Behavior Analysis, 4,* 37–44.

Hoon, P., Wincze, J., & Hoon, E. (1977). A test of reciprocal inhibition: Are anxiety and sexual arousal in women mutually inhibitory? *Journal of Abnormal Psychology, 86,* 65–74.

Jones, J. C., Bruce, T. J., & Barlow, D. H. (1986, November). *Effects of four levels of "anxiety" on the sexual arousal of sexually functional and dysfunctional men.* Paper presented at the annual convention of the Association for the Advancement of Behavior Therapy, Chicago.

Jones, J. C., Carpenter, K., Bruce, T. J., & Barlow, D. H. (1987, November). *Sexual attitudes and affective responding in sexually functional and dysfunctional men.* Paper presented at the annual convention of the Association for the Advancement of Behavior Therapy, Boston.

Kaplan, H. S. (1974). *The new sex therapy.* New York: Brunner/Mazel.

Kaplan, H. S. (1981). *The new sex therapy: Active treatment of sexual dysfunctions.* New York: Brunner/Mazel.

Kuriansky, J. B., & Shapre, L. (1981). Clinical and research implications of the evaluation of women's group therapy for anorgasmia: A review. *Journal of Sex and Marital Therapy, 7,* 268–277.

Lang, P. J. (1968). Fear reduction and fear behavior: Problems in treating a construct. In J. M. Shlien (Ed.), *Research in psychotherapy* (Vol. 3, pp. 90–102). Washington, DC: American Psychological Association.

Lang, P. J. (1970). Stimulus control, response control, and desensitization of fear. In D. J. Levis (Ed.), *Learning approaches to theraputic behavior change.* Chicago: Aldine.

Lange, J. D., Wincze, J. P., Zwick, W., Feldman, S., & Hughes, P. (1981). Effects of demand for performance, self-monitoring of arousal, and increased sympathetic nervous system activity on male erectile response. *Archives of Sexual Behavior, 10,* 443–463.

Laws, D. R., & Rubin, H. B. (1969). Instructional control of an autonomic response. *Journal of Applied Behavioral Analysis, 2,* 93–99.

Lazarus, A. (1963). The treatment of chronic frigidity by systematic desensitization. *Journal of Nervous and Mental Diseases, 136,* 272–278.

Levine, S. B., & Agle, D. (1978). The effectiveness of sex therapy for chronic secondary psychological impotence. *Journal of Sex and Marital Therapy, 4,* 235–258.

Marks, I. M. (1981). Review of behavioral psychotherapy, II: Sexual disorders. *American Journal of Psychiatry, 138,* 750–756.

Masters, W. H., & Johnson, V. E. (1966). *Human sexual response.* Boston: Little, Brown.

Masters, W., & Johnson, V. (1970). *Human sexual inadequacy.* Boston, Little, Brown.

Mavissakalian, M. R., & Barlow, D. H. (Eds.). (1981). *Phobia: Psychological and pharmacological treatment.* New York: Guilford Press.

Meunier, C., & Reile, B. G. (1967). Anxiety, confidence, and uniformity. *Journal of Personality, 35,* 498–504.

Mills, K. H., & Killman, P. R. (1982). Group treatment of sexual dysfunction: A methodological review of the outcome literature. *Journal of Sex and Marital Therapy, 8,* 259–296.

Norton, G. R., & Jehu, D. (1984). The role of anxiety in sexual dysfunctions: A review. *Archives of Sexual Behavior, 2,* 165–183.

Rachman, S. J. (1978). *Fear and courage.* San Francisco: Freeman.

Rosen, R. C. (1973). Suppression of penile tumescence by instrumental conditioning. *Psychosomatic Medicine, 35,* 509–514.

Rubin, H. B., & Henson, D. E. (1975). Voluntary enhancement of penile erection. *Bulletin of the Psychonomic Society, 6,* 158–160.

Sakheim, D. K. (1984). *Waking assessment of erectile potential: The validation of a laboratory procedure to aid in the differential diagnosis of psychogenic and organic impotence.* Unpublished doctoral dissertation, State University of New York at Albany.

Sakheim, D. K., Barlow, D. H., Beck, J. G., & Abrahamson, D. J. (1984). The effect of an increased awareness of erectile cues on sexual arousal. *Behaviour Research and Therapy, 22,* 51–158.

Sarason, I. G. (1982). *Stress, anxiety, and cognitive interference: Reactions to tests* (Report No. 170-908). Office of Naval Research, Arlington, VA.

Sarason, I. G., & Stoops, R. (1978). Test anxiety and the passage of time. *Journal of Consulting and Clinical Psychology, 46,* 102–109.

Schachter, S. (1964). The interaction of cognitive and physiological determinants of emotional state. In L. Berkowitz (Ed.), *Advances in experimental social psychology.* New York: Academic Press.

Schiavi, R. (1976). Sex therapy and psychophysiological research. *American Journal of Psychiatry, 133,* 562–566.

Schlenker, B. R., & Leary, M. R. (1982). Social anxiety and self-presentation: A conceptualization and model. *Psychological Bulletin, 92,* 641–669.

Schwartz, R. M., & Gottman, J. M. (1976). Toward a task analysis of assertive behavior. *Journal of Consulting and Clinical Psychology, 44,* 910–920.

Trapp, E. P., & Kausler, P. H. (1958). Test anxiety level and goal setting behavior. *Journal of Consulting Psychology, 22,* 31–34.

Viglietta, M. B. (1982). *The effects of anxiety versus distraction on sexual arousal in males.* Unpublished doctoral dissertation, State University of New York at Albany.

Wengler, M., Averill, J., & Smith, D. (1968). Autonomic activity during sexual arousal. *Psychophysiology, 4,* 468–478.

Wincze, J. P., Vendetti, E., Barlow, D. H., & Mavissakalian, M. (1980). The effects of a subjective monitoring task in the physiological measure of genital response to erotic stimulation. *Archives of Sexual Behavior, 9,* 533–598.

Wolchik, S. A., Beggs, V., Wincze, J. P., Sakheim, D. K., Barlow, D. H., & Mavissakalian, M. (1980). The effects of emotional arousal on subsequent sexual arousal in men. *Journal of Abnormal Psychology, 89,* 595–598.

Wolpe, J. (1958). *Psychotherapy by reciprocal inhibition.* Stanford, CA: Stanford University Press.

Wolpe, J. (1978). Comments on "A Test of Reciprocal Inhibition" by Hoon, Wincze, & Hoon. *Journal of Abnormal Psychology, 87,* 452–454.

Yerkes, R. M., & Dodson, J. D. (1908). The relation of strength of stimulus to rapidity of habit-formation. *Journal of Comparative Neurology and Psychology, 18,* 459–482.

Zilbergeld, B., & Evans, M. (1980, August). The inadequacy of Masters and Johnson. *Psychology Today,* pp. 29–43.

Zillman, D. (1983). Transfer of excitation in emotional behavior. In J. T. Cacioppo & R. E. Petty (Eds.), *Social psychophysiology: A sourcebook* (pp. 215–240). New York: Guilford Press.

Zuckerman, M., & Lubin, B. (1965). *Multiple affect adjective checklist.* San Diego, CA: EDITS.

12

Guilt, Shame, and Embarrassment
Cognitive-Behavioral Approaches

ELLEN TOBEY KLASS

INTRODUCTION

The topics of guilt, shame, and embarrassment evoke wide recognition and are everyday experiences. Theorists have suggested adaptive roles for guilt (e.g., Hoffman, 1976; Wright, 1971), shame (e.g., Lewis, 1986), and embarrassment (e.g., Edelmann, 1987). These emotions may encourage self-regulation and socially desirable behavior and also inhibit undesirable conduct. On the other hand, clinical observers have implicated high levels of guilt, shame, and embarrassment in a variety of psychological difficulties. These emotions have bearing on social anxiety in that they have aversive motivational properties and often inhibit social behavior. Moreover, one presumed source of guilt, shame, and embarrassment is interpersonal learning experiences in which violations of norms and standards were met with punishment, especially social rejection and disapproval. (Presumably, even if the potential for these emotions is innate, the particular eliciting stimuli within any culture or subculture are acquired in socialization about violations of specific norms and standards.) In addition, there are striking individual differences both in the specific events that occasion these emotions and also in their pervasiveness.

The central purpose of this chapter is to bring together cognitive-behavioral work pertinent to the treatment of dysfunctional guilt, shame, and embarrassment. Dysfunctional levels of these emotions have been noted in clinical descriptions of problems with excessive inhibition, affective symptoms, and self-regulation. Inappropriate and excessive guilt has been viewed as a psychological

---

ELLEN TOBEY KLASS • Department of Psychology, Hunter College, City University of New York, New York, New York 10021.

problem in its own right (e.g., Wright, 1971). It is a defining symptom of major depressive disorder (American Psychiatric Association, 1987) and is widely viewed as characteristic of patients with obsessive–compulsive disorder (e.g., Rachman & Hodgson, 1980). In posttraumatic stress disorders, despite wide variations in survivors' apparent personal control over the traumatic event, guilt feelings are frequently noted, including guilt for provoking the traumatic incident, for one's actions during it, and for having survived it. Inappropriate guilt has also been described as a feature of pathological grief, and high guilt levels have been viewed as a factor in problems in living, such as assertion difficulties (Jakubowski & Lange, 1978) and strain when adult daughters are their mothers' primary caregivers (Scharlach, 1987).

Shame and embarrassment are central in the phenomenology of social phobia and avoidant personality disorder, with the predominant fear of receiving humiliating negative evaluation by others. Guilt, shame, and embarrassment have been noted as issues for adult children of alcoholics (Brown, 1988) and as part of the clinical picture in eating disorders, although opinions differ on whether these emotions are focused reactions to eating-disordered symptoms (e.g., Fairburn & Cooper, 1984) or are more pervasive (cf. Leitenberg & Rosen, 1988). These emotions have also been linked to sexual deviations and sexual dysfunctions (e.g., LoPiccolo, 1978). Despite these consistent clinical assertions, it should be noted, few controlled studies have assessed guilt, shame, or embarrassment in particular psychopathological conditions. Finally, guilt, shame, and embarrassment are frequently manifested as patients react to the therapist within sessions. Although these within-session experiences can sometimes interfere with treatment, they can also be viewed as *in vivo* behavior samples. As such, they can be a useful medium for assessment and intervention.

DEFINING GUILT, SHAME, AND EMBARRASSMENT

Although lay adults often refer to feelings of guilt, shame, and embarrassment, psychologists have not attained consensus on precise definitions of these terms. For present purposes, the emotions are viewed descriptively in terms of their phenomenology as conscious experiences. *Guilt* involves self-reproach and remorse for one's behavior (thoughts, feelings, and actions), as if one has violated moral principle (Klass, 1987). *Shame* involves a humiliating sense of exposure of central personal inadequacies (Aronfreed, 1968; Buss, 1980), while *embarrassment* involves discomfort with how one appears to others, an upsetting sense that the presented self is receiving negative evaluation (Buss, 1980; Edelmann, 1987). Guilt, shame, and embarrassment, then, are all unpleasant experiences that express discomfort with the self and a sense that one has been found wanting in comparison to some standard. These emotions are not purely affective but involve substantial, though implicit, cognitive appraisal. (Although on this basis it has sometimes been suggested that guilt is not an emotion at all, many recent emotion theorists have viewed cognitive appraisal as intrinsic to most or all emotions; cf. Greenberg & Safran, 1987, pp. 144–167).

With the present definitions, guilt, shame, and embarrassment differ in degree, not kind, on two dimensions—moral weighting and explicit concern with others' opinions. Guilt involves the strongest sense of moral wrongdoing, shames involves some degree of moral concern, and in embarrassment, self-evaluation is usually nonmoral. Explicit concern with others' opinions is most evident in embarrassment, while shame involves a sense of exposure to oneself or significant imagined others, and guilt involves the least explicit concerns with others' opinions. These dimensional definitions of guilt, shame, and embarrassment stand in some contrast to sharp distinctions that have been drawn by others and that have, in my opinion, been problematic. Many theorists have distinguished guilt, shame, and embarrassment by the provocative behaviors that evoke them—interpersonal harm or moral rule violations for guilt, as opposed to failures in external appearance or self-image for shame (Aronfreed, 1968; Buss, 1981; Lewis, 1986) and defects in self-presentation for embarrassment (Edelmann, 1987). As already noted, however, there are extremely wide variations and overlaps in the immediate provocative behaviors for these emotions. Although the feelings in each emotion are *as if* one had morally transgressed, revealed personal inadequacy, or received negative feedback about external image, the individual and outside observers do not need explicitly to view the provocative behavior as meeting one of these criteria for the emotion to be reported. Given the overlap between guilt, shame, and embarrassment, what is the value of retaining the three different terms? Emotion theorists have often asked why there are so many emotional terms when they can be reduced to a small basic set. Differences in the connotations, the texture, of experience conveyed by each term is the usual answer. For clinicians, awareness of the spectrum of negative self-evaluative emotions conveyed by these terms can allow more precise description of patients' difficulties and may encourage effective treatment.

My definitions of guilt, shame, and embarrassment characterize the subjective affective and cognitive components of the emotions but do not specify overt actions or physiological responses. Although the view that emotions are action tendencies with motivational status (Greenberg & Safran, 1987) is compelling, evidence to support distinctive action tendencies for such closely related emotions as guilt, shame, and embarrassment is lacking. (Even the physiological response of blushing in embarrassment has not been consistently found; Edelmann, 1987.) Although associated behaviors do seem to serve to reduce these emotions, it is difficult to link specific behaviors to each emotion. For instance, individuals who feel guilty about having harmed another person may approach victims to make reparation, or avoid them (Freedman, 1970), or redefine their own actions as not harmful (Bandura, 1977). The parameters governing the topographics of behavioral consequences are not yet clear (Klass, 1978). Based on considerations like these, Aronfreed (1968) argued that the pertinent distinctions between guilt and shame reside in their "cognitive housings" rather than in overt behaviors, an analysis equally applicable to embarrassment vis-à-vis guilt and shame.

ASSESSMENT CONSIDERATIONS

When guilt, shame, or embarrassment is a potential clinical target, the question arises as to whether the emotion is maladaptive and intervention ought to be undertaken. As in any cognitive-behavioral therapy, assessment—including antecedents, behaviors, and consequences—can inform this decision. Because many guides to cognitive-behavioral assessment are available (e.g., Goldfried & Davison, 1976), I discuss only additional areas of special import in assessing guilt, shame, and embarrassment.

Antecedents, Behaviors, and Consequences

Cognitive and affective, as well as situational, antecedents of the potentially problematic emotion should be considered. Pertinent cognitive antecedents are not limited to explicit self-statements. As discussed in "Defining Guilt, Shame, and Embarrassment," the individual experiencing these emotions reacts as if an implicit standard has been violated, whether or not he or she can readily identify it. Elucidating these *implicit rules* can help determine if the provocative behavior is consistent with current values, which is essential for both ethical and therapeutic reasons. Since standards, norms, and values are generally implicit, the individual does not need currently to believe that the provocative behavior is unacceptable to feel one of these emotions. An inductive strategy for identifying rules is most useful, starting by asking, "What do you suppose it is about doing _____ that feels _____?" The question can be completed for guilt with "morally wrong," for shame with "humiliating or disgusting," and for embarrassment with "like it looks bad to other people." My approach converges with Safran, Vallis, Segal, and Shaw's (1986) discussion of "vertical" exploration of cognitive processes, in which implicit, organizing principles are sought before intervention is undertaken. Discussion of implicit rules in light of the patient's current values naturally follows (e.g., "How do you feel about that? What are its advantages and disadvantages?"). Discussion can reveal values that the patient feels are invalid but also may suggest that changing the provocative behavior should be considered.

Detailed description of provocative behavior can reveal controlling conditions that treatment ought to address. Patients are sometimes reluctant to discuss specifics of such behavior. Rather than pressing for disclosure, it can be useful to explore anticipations (e.g., "How do you imagine I'd react if you told me what you'd done? How do you suppose you would feel?"). Consequences of both the provocative behavior and of the target emotion should be considered. Anticipated adverse effects of reduced guilt, shame, or embarrassment can support current symptoms, as when bulimics feel that if they were not ashamed of their weight, their eating would be completely uncontrolled and they would become huge. Actions that the patient feels could reduce guilt, shame, or embarrassment are also relevant (J. P. Galst, personal communication, May 21, 1986). Responses may reveal conflicts that therapy ought to address (e.g., "I could stop having the affair, but I don't want to").

The Therapist–Patient Relationship in Assessment and Treatment

In assessment and treatment of guilt, shame, and embarrassment, a nonjudgmental and empathic stance toward the patient's disclosures is extremely important. As a central aspect of assessment that ought to continue throughout therapy, therapists ought to be aware of their own values and monitor potentially interfering reactions to the patient's disclosures. "Should" thoughts (e.g., "He *should* be ashamed of X") may signal overly evaluative reactions. It can be helpful to strive for assessment from the inside out, that is, to account for the end result of feeling guilty, ashamed, or embarrassed from the patient's frame of reference. It ought to be noted that there is wide variation between individuals, subcultures, and ethical schools as to the norm violations that are seen as worthy of these emotions, so that therapists' awareness of their own values is crucial. When therapists have difficulty managing judgmental reactions, I encourage them to seek consultation with colleagues and supervisors.

In-therapy incidents of guilt, shame, and embarrassment can be viewed as *in vivo* behavior samples. As such, they can repay careful attention. The possibility that the therapist's behavior evoked the emotion should be considered. In treatment, in addition to the relief that a benign and accepting therapist may indirectly provide, the therapist–patient relationship affords opportunities for more direct interventions with experiences of guilt, shame, or embarrassment vis-à-vis the therapist. In cognitive-behavioral therapy, such experiences are often provoked by *in vivo* assignments:

> For several weeks, Mr. J. made excuses for not having done exposure practices for his panic attacks. Each time, the therapist pointed out how this impeded progress and encouraged task completion. After several weeks of this pattern, exploration of Mr. J.'s feelings revealed that he had refrained from telling the therapist he was unwilling to do the practices, because she seemed eager and he felt guilty about disappointing her.

One way to deal with such instances is to intervene to reduce the interfering emotion (e.g., explicitly correcting faulty assumptions). Alternatively, the immediate incident can be the basis for a social-learning analysis of factors that support the maladaptive emotion. (See the discussion of social-learning analysis in the "Self-Blame, Control, and Power" section.) In choosing whether to make a social-learning analysis, whether the patient has similar experiences in other relationships is pertinent. If so, social-learning analysis may have more utility and generalizability than otherwise.

Sources of Assessment Data

The clinical interview has great flexibility in gathering information on guilt, shame, and embarrassment, but self-report scales and self-monitoring can also contribute. Therapists who want a systematic profile of the patient's guilt might use my Situational Guilt Scale (SGS; Klass, 1983, 1987), the items of which were empirically generated to represent an array of typical, naturally occurring guilt experiences. To my knowledge, there are no standardized self-report measures of shame. For embarrassment, the rationally derived Fear of Negative Evaluation Scale (Watson & Friend, 1969), a short true–false scale, taps anticipation and fear of others' adverse opinions, though it is not limited to embarrassment. The Embarrassability Scale (Modigliani, 1968) elicits anticipated embarrassment in a set of rationally derived situations; it is available in Edelmann's monograph, along with a literature review (1987, pp. 120–124). Individualized self-monitoring assignments can also be of value. Given the cognitive loading in guilt, shame, and embarrassment, self-monitoring assignments should include thoughts before, during, and after provocative behavior.

Functional Analysis

Assessment should allow a functional analysis of the role of the potentially problematic guilt, shame, or embarrassment in the patient's difficulties—its impact, sources, and relationship to the patient's values. Most cognitive-behavioral theories have not taken absolute positions on the appropriateness of these emotions but rather have relied on the functional analysis to resolve questions about imposing values on patients: The primary criterion for intervention is the impact of the target on the patient's life. The functional analysis can thus inform the therapist as to whether the emotion ought to be viewed as maladaptive and in need of reduction, as well as help guide intervention. Assessment of implicit rule violations can shed light on the patient's values and thus inform these decisions.

GUILT

Guilt involves self-reproach and remorse for one's behavior and expresses a sense of moral wrongdoing. The origins of guilt, normal and maladaptive, have received attention from several cognitive-behavioral theorists. Accounts of treatment methods are scattered but include both interventions for guilt in general and also methods for guilt in the context of specific problem areas. Discussion of treatment is therefore divided into methods for guilt in general and for problem-specific guilt.

Theories of Guilt

Cognitive-behavioral theories of guilt have differed regarding the sources of guilt and the extent to which it is viewed as appropriate. In Wright's social-learning formulation (1971), guilt was seen as a species of anxiety that is first aroused when parents react to children's behavior by conveying hurt and disappointment and by withdrawing love. Behaviors that receive these consequences, whether or not the behaviors are consensually viewed as having moral referents, elicit guilt feelings, as do behaviors that are linked by association or cognitive appraisal. (Aronfreed, 1968, likewise proposed a learning sequence in which socializing agents provide punishment and point out harmful effects on others. Instead of a special role for attachment and threats to it, Aronfreed implicated a generalized state of conditioned anxiety resulting from direct and vicarious punishment. Guilt results when socializing agents label punished behavior in ways that emphasize moral evaluation in terms of harmful interpersonal effects.)

In Wright's (1971) view, within limits guilt plays a constructive role in self-regulation and contributes to the welfare of the individual and society. As therapists, then, we should not always aim to reduce people's guilt, but ought to make this choice based on the quality of the guilt experience, especially the associated distress and the rigidity of standards. Sources of excessive guilt proneness involve threats of rejection from significant others and include parents with high standards who strongly emphasize the personally hurtful aspects of the child's failures to meet these standards; overly intense and exclusive parent–child relationships, which make love withdrawal especially threatening; and difficulties in restoring the relationship with the parent after transgression.

Hoffman's cognitive-affective theory (1976, 1983) also emphasized the role of interpersonal ties in guilt, although there are substantial differences as well. Hoffman viewed guilt as the result of empathic distress that is aroused when one recognizes another person's distress and also makes a cognitive appraisal that one has caused the distress. Hoffman believed that both the affective and cognitive component of this reaction are capacities available from early in life. Guilt was viewed as a prosocial affect that originates in genuine concern for others (rather than in self-interested anxiety) and that motivates constructive actions while deterring harmful ones. When socializing agents activate empathic distress by explaining how the child's action hurts other people (a method that Hoffman called induction), the child feels guilty. Discipline strategies that increase concern for the needs of others, including induction rather than love withdrawal, heighten guilt proneness by drawing on the individual's empathic capacity. Other factors that enhance empathy should also enhance guilt: Hoffman (1977) proposed, for instance, that females are innately more empathic than males and hence are more guilt-prone. Sex differences in empathy may, however, be an artifact of assessment methods (Eisenberg & Lennon, 1983), and the empirical evidence on sex differences in guilt is equivocal (Klass, 1988b).

Hoffman (1976) suggested that guilt feelings without an apparent basis in interpersonal damage or causal responsibility may occur when the individual reads these variables into the experience. More recently, Hoffman (1983) proposed that people may not have to encode experiences explicitly as moral to feel guilty. Instead, guilt and moral perceptions may become organized into schematic information-processing networks, such that recognition of harm is infused with guilt and self-blame ("hot cognition"). Also, the affective response of guilt may be encoded separately, so that guilt is evoked first (e.g., by empathic distress upon observing harm) and cognitions follow, or moral perceptions may be so implicit that guilt can be evoked without conscious awareness of supporting moral perceptions. Clinically relevant aspects of Hoffman's theory include his view that guilt feelings do not need to be logical in the sense of being linked to easily retrievable thoughts; the possibility of affective primacy, such that guilt feelings may guide cognitions rather than the reverse; and the view that guilt is often positive and constructive.

The two contrasting theories of Ellis (1962) and Mowrer (1966) highlight the relevance of values in the psychotherapy of guilt. In one of his most absolute statements, Ellis (1962) asserted that feeling guilty is always irrational because self-derogation is never warranted. Instead, the sense of personal worth ought to be unconditional, and although it is appropriate to recognize and regret wrongdoing, it is never appropriate to devalue oneself and feel guilty. Guilt feelings, then, would always need to be treated as symptoms of faulty thinking, and in every case, reduction of guilt would be the goal.

Mowrer's integrity therapy (1966), on the other hand, asserted that guilt feelings signal real guilt in the sense of actual transgression of valid moral standards. Unresolved guilt means that the patient has not adequately confronted his or her transgression. The correct therapeutic stance is to identify the wrongdoing and encourage the patient to admit personal responsibility, make reparation, and refrain from further immorality. To my knowledge, Mowrer did not discuss circumstances under which guilt might be inappropriate and one's values self-defeating. Rather, guilt was portrayed as an invariably appropriate response, in which the values associated with the guilt-provoking experience are taken as valid. Mowrer's view is welcome in reminding us to consider whether the patient's actions may indeed be immoral by his or her (or our own) standards. However, it seems unlikely that guilt feelings are always warranted and reasonable, especially considering the arbitrary conditions of socialization under which they are often learned and the frequent intensity of their negative functional impact.

Along similar lines as Mowrer's views, Marin's (1981) discussion of combat-related guilt in veterans of the Vietnam War is a powerful indictment of the assumption that guilt is always symptomatic. Marin pointed out that the conduct of the Vietnam War can readily be seen as involving gratuitous violence against civilians, due to both policy and individual transgressions. Veterans with combat guilt may be expressing "the realization that . . . [they have] committed acts with real and terrible consequences" (Marin, 1981, p. 68). Marin eloquently argued for helping people in therapy consider their actions in a moral light. Again, from my point of view, it is indeed important to recognize the reality and seriousness of transgression of central moral values. At the same time, the functional impact of intense guilt, even in the presence of central transgressions, must also be considered. Taking both these aspects into account may sometimes mean that treatment ought to encourage acts of reparation and atonement. Exploration of the patient's values (see "Assessment Considerations") should encourage moral sensitivity on the part of therapists.

Kelly's personal construct theory of guilt (1955, 1969) represents a more structural, rather than content-oriented, viewpoint. In cognitive-behavioral terms, structures (or schemata) are implicit organizing principles that summarize experience and guide perceptions, feelings, and actions (Fiske & Linville, 1980). Structures must be inferred by the observer, and they are not directly accessible to conscious self-report. In Kelly's (1955) personality theory, the organizing structure is the system of personal constructs—the individual's implicit interpretations of the world—which develops through experience and is hierarchically organized in terms of centrality to the self. *Core role constructs* are central self-definitions that express one's sense of self in relation to expectations about significant others. (Thus, despite its reputation as wholly cognitive, personal construct theory held that crucial phenomena are also fundamentally interpersonal). Kelly interpreted specific emotions as the result of particular relationships among constructs. Guilt is the result of perceiving one's behavior as threatening dislodgement from core roles (Kelly, 1955, pp. 502–514, 1969). For instance, implicitly, "Doing X means I'm not a good mother" or "Doing Y indicates I'm a nasty person." There is one restriction: Being a good mother or being a non-nasty person must be a valued part of self-definition—a core role—for these perceptions to trigger guilt. Thus, guilt feelings are not dictated by specific cognitive content (e.g., interpersonal harm, intentionality, or explicit moral rules) but by the perceived relationship of behavior to core roles, readily accounting for guilt-provoking experiences that do not meet clear moral criteria. Guilt proneness does not depend on specific moralizing or discipline but on the interpersonal experiences that have built one's sense of self.

In the personal construct view, feeling guilty always makes sense in that it signals a perceived discrepancy from a core role. (Many core roles have been learned under preverbal and nonverbal contingencies, so they may not be directly accessible to the patient's awareness or conscious choice, and core role discrepancies will usually be implicit. Thus, Kelly's theory, like Hoffman's [1983] work, recognizes nonconscious cognitive appraisal processes.) On the other hand, one needs to examine the impact of the guilt feelings to determine whether guilt needs to be treated. When the therapist concludes that guilt is maladaptive, personal construct treatment would be directed to resolving the core role discrepancy.

Cognitive-behavioral theories of guilt thus have had varied stances on the meaningfulness and functions of this emotion. Wright (1971), Hoffman (1976, 1983), and Kelly (1955, 1969) believed that guilt feelings always make sense in relation to one's past learning history, whether or not they are appropriate to current realities. These theorists also shared the view that, at least at moderate levels, guilt serves positive functions in binding us to other people. Ellis (1963), on the other hand, believed that feeling guilty is illogical and does not have positive social functions at any intensity, while Mowrer (1966) viewed all guilt feelings as valid reactions to one's own provocative behavior. (Readers may wonder why Kohlberg's cognitive-developmental theory of morality has not been reviewed. I have located only one statement of Kohlberg's about guilt: that guilt characterizes persons with lower-level, less autonomous moral reasoning; Kohlberg & Kramer, 1969, p. 114).

General Treatment Methods for Guilt

Kelly's (1955, 1969) view of guilt as the result of perceived discrepancies from core roles (central self-definitions) can provide a useful organization for the array of cognitive-behavioral treatment methods for maladaptive guilt, although endorsement of his causal theory should not be inferred from its use as an organizational device. Interventions with guilt could reduce core role discrepancies by (1) changing the patient's perception of the behavior as discrepant from a core role, (2) changing personal definition of a core role, or (3) changing the actual behavior.

Changing Perceived Role Discrepancies

One set of treatment methods for guilt focuses on changing the patient's evaluation of the guilt-provoking behavior, such that perceived inconsistency with a core role is reduced or eliminated.

Permission-Giving Tactics. Permission-giving is my term for interventions whose major goal is to convey the view that provocative behavior is acceptable. Permission-giving tactics vary in how explicitly the therapist expresses this view, with *direct therapist endorsement* (e.g., "It's human to feel angry") at one extreme. *Therapist-provided information* on typical behavior (e.g., "Most people have sexual fantasies") is also quite direct. Exposure to *other informational sources,* such as suggested readings or encouraging the patient to ask friends about their behavior, can normalize provocative behavior less explicitly. Explanations that stress the *understandability* of provocative behavior can also be permission-giving. For instance, rape victims may be helped with guilt about their apparent acquiescence with attack by the concept of rape-induced paralysis and its possible parallel to tonic immobility (a freezing reaction to attack by a predator; Barlow, 1988, pp. 5–6). *Reframing behavior* involves defining it in a more benign fashion, as by relabeling (e.g., suggesting the patient think of breaking his or her diet as "slipping" rather than "cheating") or by eliciting the patient's ideas on its advantages as well as disadvantages (Beck, Rush, Shaw, & Emery, 1979). Because guilt difficulties often involve stigmatizing problems (e.g., incest, bulimia), *therapy and self-help groups* in which all members share the same problem can be a powerful source of permission. I would recommend that the more explicit types of therapist permission-giving be used sparingly, as when they are repeated in relation to the same provocative behavior, they seem to evoke defensiveness and frustration. Permission-giving tactics are also applicable to shame and embarrassment.

Changing Guilt to Regret. Changing guilt to regret (C. Blanchard, personal communication, September 19, 1987) involves a detailed review of the context of the guilt-provoking behavior, followed by reframing the patient's actions in a more benign light. This technique is especially relevant when guilt-provoking behavior cannot be undone. The detailed review should focus on the specific circumstances, thoughts, and feelings around the guilt-provoking experience, especially the patient's perceptions and feelings at the time. Once the patient's actions are fully explicated, the therapist asks, "Recognizing all this, if you had it to do all over again, would you do the same thing?" Interestingly, when all the conditions are elucidated, patients typically answer that they would indeed do the same (formerly guilt-provoking) thing again. The therapist then suggests that since the patient would still act in the same way, it is time to move on, "from now":

> Ms. K. was plagued by intrusive guilt that she had withdrawn from her brother Mark when he was dying of lung cancer at home several years before. In the detailed review, Ms. K. realized that Mark had become extremely verbally abusive to her as he neared death, and that she had stayed away to avoid this. Discussion also included possible reasons for Mark's behavior—including envy of her life. Based on this review, Ms. K. decided that avoiding Mark had been a viable means of self-protection from attack and that she would have done things the same way now. With this perspective, she felt sad (regretful) about what had happened, but believed also that she had not simply abandoned Mark gratuitously. She went to Mark's grave, something she had repeatedly planned and avoided, and she made her peace with him by telling him of her newfound regret. The intrusive guilt resolved.

The more rare response, that no, the patient would do things differently now, is handled in a similar fashion. The therapist suggests that since we cannot go back in time and undo our mistakes, the issue is what can be done now. Problem-solving techniques (Goldfried & Davison, 1976) can help address this question.

A variation can be helpful when the patient fears change because he or she anticipates feeling unmanageably guilty if there is an undesirable consequence, especially to an intimate (e.g., if the mother's financial affairs deteriorate when the child stops bailing her out from avoidable difficulties). The therapist might address the likelihood of the feared consequence, but even if it is seen as quite improbable, it can be very compelling to patients. Although a standard cognitive therapy tactic would be to work to diminish the importance of the feared negative consequence, in my experience most patients find it very foreign and alienating to consider "decatastrophizing" damage to significant others. Instead, considering the reasons that they are stopping the guilt-preventing behavior often speaks more closely to their concerns. Based on these sobering considerations, affirmative self-statements can be developed that may give some help (e.g., "Even if X happens, I made my choice for good reasons"; "the alternative was to stay enmeshed in my family").

Conflict Resolution. Guilt is often tied to a sense of conflict between "inclination and duty," as Wright (1971, p. 14) put it. In such instances, recognition both of one's values and of the thoughts and feelings associated with one's desires may be helpful. Greenberg and Safran (1987, p. 218) described use of the Gestalt two-chair dialogue with guilt difficulties to help the patient integrate conflicting aspects of experience.

Changing Core Role Definitions

Explicit Redefinition. Explicit redefinition of a core role involves clarification and evaluation of the current role (i.e., the personal requirements for an important aspect of self-definition) and then implementing change efforts. Information from the assessment of implicit rules (see "Assessment Considerations") is a useful entry point for clarifying current role requirements. (For instance, "It seems that a lot of your guilt has to do with feeling that you're not being a good _____. Let's think about what you have to do to be a good _____.") Evaluation in relation to personal values involves questions like, "How does this work for you? How does it work for any other people involved in the situation?" (Parent–child issues—such as guilt over feeling angry or bored with one's children and guilt over feeling resentful of one's parents—lend themselves well to this approach.) Discussion can then help develop a more adaptive role definition that reduces or eliminates the perceived discrepancy of provocative behavior (e.g., "What's a good mother?" or, with a bow to Winnicott, 1971, "What's a 'good-enough' mother?"). Behavioral assignments to experiment with slightly different actions and observe the impact on self and others are also useful. Once conclusions are drawn, cognitive-behavioral techniques such as stress inoculation training (Meichenbaum, 1985) and behavior rehearsal (Goldfried & Davison, 1976) can be used to help implement new role definitions.

Self-Blame, Control, and Power. When patients show pervasive and persistent guilt, straightforward redefinition of the core role may need to be supplanted by a broader and less direct approach. Pervasive guilt can often be rendered intelligible by positing a tacit rule like, "I am to blame for anything bad that happens." Such a tacit rule is central, in that it involves fundamental experiences of the self and predicts responses to a wide range of situations (Safran *et al.*, 1986). Pervasive self-blame also implies that the individual could somehow prevent these outcomes from occurring and, thus, that he or she has a great deal of power and control over these events. In my experience, there is a strong investment in this belief system. Cognitive restructuring around whether the patient is factually responsible in specific instances seems to have little effect except to engender friction between therapist and patient.

Instead, addressing pervasive guilt in terms of self-blame, control, and power involves several elements: (1) establishing the theme, (2) social-learning analysis, (3) direct change efforts, and (4) exploration of investments. *Establishing the theme* traces the sense of self-blame in current experiences. The therapist discusses specific guilt-provoking incidents in light of an implicit sense of power and control:

> Mr. L. argued strenuously with an intensely bureaucratic personnel officer to get the paycheck issued for a new supervisee. When the officer refused to release it on a technicality, Mr. L. felt tremendously guilty about not having discharged his obligation to his supervisee. The therapist pointed out the implication that Mr. L. could have done more, although the locus of the refusal was the personnel officer.

In establishing the theme, an empathic and sympathetic stance is most helpful to reduce the chance the patient will feel invalidated or judged as having unreasonable feelings. For instance, "It's interesting. It's as if you feel you could make her act differently. What more are you envisioning that you could have done? Would that have been possible? How likely do you think it is that would have made a difference?"

The *social-learning analysis* involves exploring historical antecedents for guilt and self-blame. The therapist moves the focus from specific current incidents to the past, asking questions like, "Is that a familiar feeling? Can you remember other times, perhaps when you were younger, that you felt the same way? Can you see the person or hear the voice giving you this message?" Fossum and Mason (1986, p. 67) suggested asking, "How did you learn to be so . . . [guilty]?" Empathic and sympathetic responses are again helpful (e.g., "What a burden that must have been"). Moving back and forth between the current theme and historical experiences establishes the relevance of the social-learning analysis (e.g., "So when you feel guilty about X, it's as if you're jumping back to when you were 15 years old and you were blamed for . . ."). The name I give to making these links understandable to the patient is the "no-wonder" response, as in "No wonder you feel so guilty now, considering what you learned back then."

In exploring the social-learning history of self-blame, patients often remember explicit training that they were responsible for everything bad:

> When asked whether feeling to blame for everything was a familiar feeling, Ms. M. remembered that her mother had a miscarriage when Ms. M. was 10 years old. Her older brother told Ms. M. that it had happened because she had come home late from school that day. Ms. M. then recalled several other instances in which family members blamed her when she had no evident causal responsibility by ordinary standards and stated that although logically she did not believe in her culpability, it still felt like she was to blame. The therapist commented, "No wonder you blame yourself now for so many things, considering the messages you got then." Discussion then centered on the extreme causal attributions made in the family and on the idea that Ms. M. had not had resources to question them when she was a child.

The therapist should normalize the self-blame, however deviant it may appear. I discuss how from the child's point of view, the perception of a central personal role in causation makes perfect sense: Children view their elders as experts on reality (because they indeed are right about so many things), so that blaming messages are highly credible. Also, young children's normal egocentrism is consistent with generalized self-blame. I use the Piagetian example that the normal 4-year-old believes the sun follows him or her around—a belief that corresponds to perceptual reality.

Along with direct training in self-blame and the child's egocentrism, two additional sources of self-blame should be considered in the social-learning analysis, especially because the family of origin may have been dysfunctional (e.g., parental alcoholism, severe marital conflict). In such families, frightening quarrels and other out-of-control behavior are frequent. One source of self-blame can be that the child's efforts to prevent feared behaviors in the family sometimes were or seemed effective (intermittent or superstitious reinforcement). In addition, the child's efforts to prevent these frightening disruptions, which often feel like they threaten one's survival (Brown, 1988), may have been an alternative to intense passivity and depression. In summary, then, in the social-learning analysis, the therapist aims to indicate ways that current pervasive self-blame is an extension from earlier experiences, and thus to imply that it is understandable but unwarranted from the vantage point of today.

In a sense, then, *direct change efforts* are first pursued through the social-learning analysis, a detailed exploration of current and past themes to establish "the full meaning . . . [of the specific beliefs], in the context of the whole core cognitive constellation in which they are embedded" (Safran *et al.*, 1986, p. 518). Once this has been established, direct change efforts draw on standard cognitive and behavioral techniques as described earlier in the "Explicit Redefinition" section. Supportive self-statements to manage the stress of potential blame and to remind the patient of the social-learning history of the emotion can be especially pertinent.

Investments in this set of issues must often also be considered, for direct change efforts must frequently contend with the persistence of self-blaming perceptions, although changing them would seem to relieve guilt. A complete functional analysis, including anticipated consequences of change, allows one to consider covert reinforcers or investments in the ostensibly undesired guilt and self-blame. Brown's (1988) monograph on treatment of adult children of alcoholics sensitively discussed many sources of attachment to core beliefs about controllability that can support pervasive guilt. Although she only considered children of alcoholics, and perhaps for this reason emphasized denial, Brown's integration of cognitive and psychodynamic concepts seems more widely applicable. She tied the maintenance of core beliefs, however damaging, to the individual's compelling need to maintain attachment to parents, however poor they were at basic parenting functions. Brown's work also should alert clinicians to explore the family history of chemical dependency when they encounter pervasively guilty adults.

Brown's views are consistent with recent conceptualizations of self-schemas in interpersonal terms as tied to attachment to significant others (e.g., Safran, 1990). On this view, there are brakes on cognitive change when change threatens the individual with loss of such attachment. Considering investments in attachment suggests several additional sources for retaining a maladaptive sense of self-blame and power (Brown, 1988), including:

1. The sense that one is deeply bad can help maintain the belief that one's parents are good and thus maintain a sense of security.
2. Avoiding anticipated survivor guilt for improvement can maintain involvement with the family of origin.
3. Through feeling responsible, the individual does not have to experience threatening feelings of neediness that dysfunctional families can engender.

I believe that some individuals also tap into a rewarding sense of power and importance when they are pervasively self-blaming.

Successful challenges to such affect-laden core beliefs may therefore often depend on the development of new attachments, whether to significant others, an individual therapist, or a therapy group. For adult children of alcoholics, Brown advocated open-ended interactional group therapy with both insight-oriented and cognitive-behavioral elements. Some specific cognitive restructuring procedures may help cognitive-behavioral therapists who have more short-term orientations to address investments in self-blame, control, and power using these concepts. The primary entry points are exploration of social-learning history and of possible investments for the patient. After such discussion, developing self-statements that recognize and reframe self-blame and power can be helpful; a self-statement that many patients have found useful is, "It's kind of insulting, but I'm probably not to blame for everything," which recognizes investment in a light tone as well as providing a more constructive viewpoint. Brown suggested that the guilty self-blaming patient could view him or herself as a "recovering self-hater," thereby maintaining the primary attachment but offering a basis to change specific cognitions and behaviors (Brown, pp. 146–147). Another possibility is to reframe the symptom in terms of valid needs (Bandler & Grinder, 1979). The patient is asked to consider the question, "How can I meet my valid needs for being in charge in ways that are less destructive to me than feeling so guilty/blamed?" Standard problem-solving techniques (Goldfried & Davison, 1976) can be used to generate responses.

Changing Behavior

A third approach to dysfunctional guilt is to change the provocative behavior so that it is less role-discrepant or contradictory to one's central values. The assessment process may provide cues as to pertinent behavioral changes, which can be addressed using problem-solving techniques. For instance, "Let's think about ways that might fit better with your values than _____ and might also meet some of your other needs."

> Ms. N. was an agoraphobic who planned a large church wedding, one of her dreams but extremely stressful because of the feelings of being trapped under scrutiny that it evoked. Ms. N.'s sister Jane had bipolar disorder, and her behavior was not well controlled. She dearly wanted to be a bridesmaid. Ms. N. felt that having Jane as a bridesmaid would be much too stressful but felt intensely guilty, since "I am depriving Jane of something that would give her tremendous pleasure, and she will be deeply hurt." Using problem solving, Ms. N. came up with a compromise that substantially decreased her guilt. She shopped with Jane and bought her a nice dress for the wedding, and asked her to present the offertory—a time-limited participation that someone else could quickly retrieve if necessary.

Efforts at reparation and atonement would also fit under the rubric of changing behavior.

Treatment of Problem-Specific Guilt

Guilt over Assertive Refusal

Jakubowski and Lange (1978, pp. 58–64) provided a set of questions about guilt-related self-statements concerning assertive refusal situations that can help clarify whether guilt-provoking refusal violates personally valid moral standards and also aid in cognitive restructuring. Topics included the other party's needs (e.g., "What would really help this person?"), the patient's personal responsibility (e.g., "Am I the only one who can help?"), and alternative views of refusal (e.g., refusal may sometimes be genuine caring that fosters independence). To distinguish true help from maladaptive rescuing, Jakubowski and Lange suggested attending to the emotional, physical, and interpersonal effects of an actual or imagined decision to comply (e.g., pleased, resentful, tense). My research on guilt over assertive refusal (Klass, 1981) suggests an additional treatment consideration. It is often thought that criticism of the other party (e.g., "He is manipulative") reduces guilt. Among the women whom I studied, criticism of the other party was positively correlated with degree of guilt. While the finding was correlational, it suggests that cognitive responses that devalue others should be used with caution.

Guilt over Sexual Victimization

Victims of father–daughter incest suffer from high levels of intrusive guilt over childhood compliance with and concealment of the sexual abuse, over past enjoyment of the sexual experiences, and over the effects of disclosure on the family (Swanson & Biaggio, 1985). Swanson and Biaggio's literature review (1985) discussed treatment methods that I would construe as permission-giving: attributing incest to the specific disturbed family dynamics; pointing out that feeling guilty presumes adult concepts of sexuality and responsibility, while the child's sexual behavior essentially was a quest for affection in the context of severe emotional deprivation; group therapy for incest victims. Because abused daughters frequently report that their parents questioned the validity of all emotions that the daughters expressed, it is especially important to convey that the therapist finds understandable and legitimate all the patient's feelings, including guilt. Swanson and Biaggio also cautioned therapists about incest victims' frequent desire to confront their parents in order to resolve guilt, since the parents usually react with rejection, denial, and hostility. I suggest that some of the cathartic benefits of confrontation may be attained more safely through in-session imaginal exercises, such as the Gestalt empty-chair technique (Stevens, 1971).

With guilty victims of rape and battering, Frank and Stewart (1984) reported on their clinical experiences. They felt that thought-stopping to control intrusive guilty thoughts and images was needed before cognitive restructuring of guilt-related self-statements and assumptions could have impact upon guilt.

Guilt in Children of Alcoholics

Brown (1988) provided a valuable portrait of the psychological stresses confronting adult children of alcoholics who seek treatment and of sources in the early social-learning environment. She considered the difficulties faced by these individuals in the light of investments in controllability that maintain attachments to the parents, despite highly adverse experiences with them. Using an open-ended group therapy, Brown saw three steps: breaking denial; early recovery, with exploration of the conflict between threats of abandonment and the relief of acquiring new beliefs; and an ongoing recovery phase of deeper self-exploration and integration of a new identity. (See "Self-Blame, Control, and Power," which presented Brown's theory in more detail and discussed ways that cognitive-behavioral therapists can apply this viewpoint.) Brown's monograph provided a guide to her group treatment model with many vivid clinical vignettes.

Mother–Daughter Role Strain

Adult daughters frequently take responsibility for the care of elderly widowed mothers (Scharlach, 1987), often creating distress in the daughter due to conflicting demands and to guilt over not meeting all the mother's apparent needs. Scharlach's work on this problem is of special interest as a controlled study of a cognitive-behavioral intervention targeted to guilt-related symptoms. A two-session cognitive-behavioral workshop for care-giving daughters focused on supporting their own needs as legitimate and on establishing older persons' needs for control and choice rather than unwarranted dependency. Cognitive-behavioral techniques like challenging automatic thoughts and behavior rehearsal were also introduced. In comparison to a waiting-list control, the cognitive-behavioral intervention reduced daughters' sense of burden, and interestingly, the mothers' sense of loneliness was reduced more when their daughters received the cognitive-behavioral workshop than an education-support workshop that emphasized meeting the mothers' needs. Unfortunately, although the composite burden measure included ratings of guilt, effects on guilt were not separately reported.

Problem Areas in Need of Exploration

There has been little discussion pertinent to cognitive-behavioral treatment of guilt in the context of several disorders in which guilt is often noted. These include clinical depression, pathological grief, obsessive–compulsive disorder, and combat-related posttraumatic stress disorder.

For *depression,* Beck *et al.* (1979) described some specific techniques for guilt, which can be characterized as relatively explicit and directive. They included distinguishing thoughts from actions, a form of permission-giving; addressing an unrealistic sense of responsibility by pointing out that the patient is assuming he or she can control the uncontrollable and by reattributing responsibility to external sources; and presenting the idea that guilt over self-control lapses may increase rather than reduce self-defeating behavior.

Pathological grief has received cognitive-behavioral analyses (e.g., Brasted & Callahan, 1984), but there has not been extensive discussion of pathological guilt in cognitive-behavioral literature on this topic. (Miles & Demi, 1985, offered a typology of normal parental guilt reactions to the death of a child and suggested coping responses for these reactions.) In their research on guided mourning, Marks and his colleagues (Mawson, Marks, Ramm, & Stern, 1981; Sireling, Cohen, & Marks, 1988) collected data on a hostility–anger–guilt self-report measure, which was a composite of these phenomenologically different affects.

Among patients with *obsessive–compulsive disorder,* for whom excessive guilt has long been noted, Rachman and Hodgson (1980) suggested that high guilt is specific to one subset—patients whose checking compulsions express fear of already having done harm (e.g., retracing driving routes to see if they have killed someone)—and that guilt is the motive for checking in these cases. (Others have felt that checking compulsions to *prevent* harm to others and immoral behavior, along with checking and cleaning compulsions centered on fears of contamination, also stem from guilt. This disagreement would be, at least to some degree, susceptible to empirical test.) Rachman and Hodgson speculated that inappropriate guilt in obsessive–compulsives is due to high parental standards (as Wright, 1971, and Aronfreed, 1968, theorized for high guilt in general), coupled with intense parental criticism for failures to meet standards. This combination would heighten the fear of mistakes and doubt about whether they have been committed, classic obsessive–compulsive features. Rachman and Hodgson also thought that guilty obsessive–compulsives had been socialized to a disproportionate sense that they must protect other people and that harmful events are likely to occur. Regarding treatment, Rachman and Hodgson believed that treatment methods that directly addressed guilty obsessive–compulsives' definition and tolerance of unacceptable thoughts and impulses might impact on both guilt and checking compulsions. They did not, however, propose any specific techniques aimed at these guilt-related issues, although they thought that the behavioral treatment of exposure to feared thoughts might reduce patients' guilt.

There has been great social concern about *combat-related posttraumatic stress disorder* in Vietnam veterans, and cognitive-behavioral researchers have delineated a variety of psychological features of these patients (see Keane, Zimering, & Caddell's [1985] literature review). As far as I know, the first data on guilt in this population were reported in Keane, Fairbank, Caddell, and Zimering's (1989) controlled comparison of implosive therapy and a wait-list control group. Implosive therapy resulted in a decrease in therapist-rated guilt that showed a trend toward statistical significance. In describing a cognitive restructuring therapy for combat veterans, Keane, Fairbank, Caddell, Zimering, and Bender (1985, p. 287) reported their clinical impression that guilt is among the symptoms that are least responsive to this approach. They employed standard cognitive restructuring techniques to encourage reattribution of guilt-provoking experiences to the situational context of combat, with the intent of explaining, rather than excusing, the behavior. Keane, Fairbank, *et al.* (1985, p. 287) listed several self-statements that patients were coached to use (e.g., "I performed this behavior while in combat [and] . . . I would not do such a thing now"; "I hate what I have done but I must carry on with my life. The best I can do is to live now in such a way that I can benefit others and myself.")

Glover (1984) provided a pointed clinical discussion, from a psychodynamic perspective, of cognitive distortions in combat veterans with survivor guilt. He included an inappropriate sense of control (e.g., "I should have sat where my buddy did and been blown up instead of him") and the feeling that those who died were more worthy ("this form of thinking assumes that matters of life and death should be decided on the basis of merit," Glover, p. 394). For treatment, Glover recommended a thorough reexamination of guilt-provoking combat incidents in terms of the question of how much control the patient could have had over events. This technique would here be classed as changing guilt to regret (see "General Treatment of Guilt"). Other specific tactics that Glover recommended included therapist confrontation of cognitive distortions and helping the patient find some meaning to justify the fact of survival. Glover also made the clinical observation that depression and avoidance of intimacy are linked to survivor guilt. He suggested that when the clinician notes the former symptoms in a combat veteran, survivor guilt should be explored even if it has not been a presenting complaint.

For the related issue of guilt over transgressions committed during combat, Marin's (1981) alternative perspective has already been noted, with its emphasis on respect for the moral pain of guilty combat veterans and recognition of their struggle with legitimate moral values (see "Theories of Guilt"). An additional reflection is that military socialization and institutions induce considerations such as loyalty to buddies, duty to country, and definition of enemies as less than fully human (cf. Bandura, 1977, pp. 155–158), as well as straightforward reinforcement contingencies. Thereby, behavior that is ordinarily viewed as morally unacceptable (killing human beings) is redefined as justified and desirable. In a sense, then, military socialization has failed to have its full impact on veterans with combat-related guilt difficulties. Functional analysis may suggest that the veteran's guilt, however much in keeping with the magnitude of the original transgression, does not now serve a useful purpose. (It certainly cannot bring back the dead.) Developing appropriate forms of atonement thus may be an important treatment direction. Detailed case reports on treating veterans with survivor guilt and, particularly given the moral issues, those with transgression-related guilt may help us grapple with the implications of immediately working to reduce guilt (e.g., by imaginal exposure) as opposed to living with moral pain.

SHAME

Shame, a humiliating sense of exposure of central personal inadequacies, has received little attention in cognitive-behavioral circles.

Theories of Shame

Buss (1980) speculated that shame-prone persons have been "socialized to regard themselves as unworthy when certain kinds of wrongdoing are revealed" (p. 230). He implicated the combination of three parental socialization practices: (1) conditional love, which maintains dependency on external evaluation; (2) high standards that the child feels are attainable but that he or she frequently fails to meet; and (3) parental reactions to the child's failures with ridicule, disgust, and a strongly moralizing tone, as well as love withdrawal. Over time, this pattern of humiliation for failure becomes the child's own reaction to perceived personal failures. (Aronfreed, 1968, attributed shame to associations between generalized conditioned anxiety for transgressions, due to direct and vicarious punishment, and labeling that emphasized the visibility of the transgression to others.) Buss (1980) also suggested that any background circumstances that create the feeling one has a defect in a central aspect of oneself are conducive to shame. These sources would include (1) public self-consciousness, which expresses concern with how one looks to others; (2) the possession of stigmas, whether visible or secret, which other people would treat as shaming; and (3) low self-esteem, which increases the likelihood that the individual will view behaviors as reflecting central personal failings.

Interestingly, Buss's notion of stigma as a cause of shame has some parallel in Fossum and Mason's (1986) systemic theory of shame as the result of conceal-ment of shaming experiences within the family (e.g., incest, rape, and addic-tion). Fossum and Mason suggested that the shame-inducing family creates a sense of fundamental badness in the child through perfectionism and blame, so that the child acquires a sense that he or she cannot succeed at becoming accept-able. (As in Buss's [1980] theory, shame-inducing parents have rigidly high stan-dards and are harshly negative about children's failures to meet them. Unlike Buss, who believed that shame-inducing parents conveyed the attainability of success and thus kept the child involved in trying to please them, Fossum and Mason viewed the shame-induced child as fundamentally defeated.) Fossum and Mason emphasized the role of denial, including collusion in concealing a central family secret and implicit rules against intimate interactions. Fossum and Mason used the unfortunate term "inherited generational shame" for the con-cealment process, implying inevitability rather than active interactional pro-cesses. Collusion and the sense of fundamental badness result in "maintained shame," repetitive behaviors that induce the same painful feelings. Regrettably, Fossum and Mason reified this process as well: "Shame seeks itself in others in its magnetic field" (p. 47). The views of Brown (1988) and of Safran (1990), in which repetitive interpersonal cycles reflect attachments to beliefs about signifi-cant others, are more compatible with cognitive-behavioral thinking about such maladaptive patterning.

Treatment of Shame

Treatment of maladaptive shame would appear to require (1) decreasing the sense that the provocative behavior is a central failing, (2) decreasing the painful sense of exposure, or (3) increasing tolerance for personal failings. Permission-giving tactics (see "Reducing Perceived Role Discrepancies") are a major set of methods to diminish the sense that particular behaviors are personal failings. To reduce the painful experience of exposure, Beck et al. (1979, p. 179) thought that the therapist should suggest that the patient adopt a systematic antishame phi-losophy of admitting to shaming behavior. This practice could rob scrutiny by self or others of its power by putting it within personal control.

Increasing tolerance for personal failings can be addressed in several ways. The therapist can point out the intensity and global nature of negative self-evaluation, which Beck et al. (1979) viewed as overgeneralization from evalua-tion of behavior to evaluation of one's character, and work cognitively to alter these perceptions. Beck *et al.* (1979, pp. 178–179) also suggested developing the notion that shame is self-created, by tracing how the intensity of shame varies with the patient's mood. Another approach would be social-learning analysis (see the earlier section on "Self-Blame, Control, and Power"), informed by the theories of shame that I have described. Drawing on Buss's (1980) theory, the therapist can explore antecedent experiences in which significant others conveyed disgust and intolerance for the patient's failings. The therapist might also use Fossum and Mason's view of the importance of the family context in shame by exploring for stigmatizing family secrets, dysfunctional interactional styles, and impossible conditions for a sense of personal worthiness. Treatment of self-esteem difficulties may be particularly pertinent for shame-prone patients. An array of specific cognitive therapy tactics to enhance self-esteem is usefully summarized by Burns (1980, pp. 51–74). Rational-emotive therapy methods to develop an unconditional sense of self-worth are detailed by Walen, DiGiuseppe, & Wessler (1980, pp. 130–136).

EMBARRASSMENT

Embarrassment involves a sense of discomfort with presumed negative evaluation by others. Cognitive-behavioral therapists have considered maladaptive embarrassment somewhat more extensively than shame, though far less than guilt.

Theories of Embarrassment

Buss's (1980) social-learning view was that embarrassment arises when behavior is punished by ridicule and that this punishing consequence socializes children to inhibit several classes of behavior: improprieties that violate social norms, social incompetence, and breaches of privacy (both public displays of normatively private acts and revelation of deeply personal experiences). As being singled out becomes associated with ridicule for behavior in these classes, conspicuousness also becomes a stimulus for embarrassment. As a result of this aversive learning history, socialized individuals avoid behaviors that have previously provoked embarrassment and feel embarrassed if they do engage in them.

According to Buss, individual differences in embarrassability reflect proneness to engage in embarrassing behaviors in the classes listed above and also personality traits that involve a heightened sense of conspicuousness. Relevant behavioral tendencies included poor social skills (leading to more improprieties and hence more embarrassment through direct negative feedback from others or self-evaluation), an inexpressive personal style (which Buss thought led to unintentional leaks of embarrassing feelings), and blushing easily (since blushing is viewed as an impropriety). Buss thought that public self-consciousness was the most relevant background personality trait. It should be noted, though, that focus on oneself as a social object would not be a sufficient cause of embarrassibility, since it is possible to focus on expecting positive feedback from others. Buss suggested excessive modesty was an additional source of embarrassability, since very modest people may often feel that they are breaking social norms on bodily display or vanity; he further speculated that women may be more modest and hence more embarrassable.

In contrast, Edelmann (1987) proposed that any action can be embarrassing, if implicit cognitive appraisals make for negative self-evaluation. A personal investment in avoiding social disapproval as well as awareness of breaking a social norm must be parts of the appraisal, according to Edelmann. He argued that the individual is only embarrassed by a norm violation that others notice if he or she cares about the evaluation of the others. Edelmann's model also emphasized that the perception of norm violation is a personal appraisal that can have impact without being veridical. Edelmann proposed an information-processing model in which people continually appraise their behavior, others' reactions, their own subsequent reactions, and their own internal states, evaluating all these for conformity to external norms and internal personal standards. Perceived discrepancies elicit embarrassment, and subsequent reactions are subjected to the same appraisal process in a feedback process that can further increase or decrease embarrassment. Embarrassment thus involves heightened self-focus with overt physiological and nonverbal signs of embarrassment (e.g., gaze avoidance, increased body movement, speech disturbance) that, if attended to, can further increase embarrassment.

According to Edelmann (1987), individual difference variables that could heighten embarrassability include public self-consciousness, social anxiety, and neuroticism, with the latter two variables accounting for the negative expectancies expressed in embarrassment. Edelmann's (1987) research with the Embarrassability Scale (Modigliani, 1968) indeed found correlations between embarrassability and these personality variables. (In addition to his own theory of embarrassment, Edelmann's monograph includes extensive literature reviews on embarrassment, including theories, social psychology, physiological, nonverbal, and developmental factors, individual differences, and treatment.)

Treatment of Embarrassment

Intervention alternatives include self-statement modification, "shame"-attacking exercises (Walen et al., 1980), functioning despite embarrassment, planning, and attentional focus treatment. Treatment methods for social phobia, in which fear of embarrassment is a central issue, are also relevant and are reviewed by Heimberg (1989). While self-statement modification must, of course, be guided by the results of individualized assessment, two commonly pertinent areas for maladaptive embarrassment are perceptions of the probability and the importance of negative scrutiny by others. The probability of negative evaluations can be addressed by questions like, "How likely is it that others will think you're a jerk for asking for directions?" and "If someone asks you for directions, do you think he or she is a jerk?" It should be noted that at least some embarrassable people do indeed judge others by harsh standards and search for signs of embarrassment. It can be difficult to alter attributions of evaluation by others, for these are rarely susceptible to direct verification in the ordinary course of events. (The opportunity to provide such feedback is an advantage of group treatment for these problems.) Therefore, the central therapeutic emphasis often becomes the importance or meaning of negative social-evaluative consequences. Relevant areas of exploration include, "What is the worst that could happen? How bad is it? Do I want my sense of self to stand or fall with this person's view of me?" (Heimberg & Becker, 1984).

Rational-emotive *shame-attacking exercises* (Walen *et al.*, 1980) in present terms are most usefully construed as related to embarrassment, in that the patient is asked to violate trivial social norms on purpose and thus to risk social disapproval (e.g., warmly greeting a stranger and trying to talk with him or her as if already acquainted). Walen *et al.* (p. 226) list 11 such tasks. The stated therapeutic goal is to encourage cognitive and experiential alternatives to feeling personally devalued by negative interpersonal scrutiny. Such exercises can also be viewed as exposure-based treatment of fear of embarrassment and as paradoxical prescriptions that reduce the fearfulness and discomfort of embarrassment by putting the provocative behavior under voluntary control. The therapist should weigh the relative merits of instigating such unusual behaviors compared to more ordinary activities that the patient finds embarrassing and would value engaging in (e.g., striking up a conversation with an acquaintance). Cognitive preparation is likely to be important in either case.

The third approach, *functioning despite embarrassment*, may be particularly relevant when efforts to reduce embarrassment by cognitive means have been ineffective and the avoided activity is important to the patient. The task is framed as tolerating the negative feelings in the interests of one's goal and may be relabeled (e.g., as requiring courage). Self-control techniques are then used to overcome avoidance:

> Seven years after finishing college, Mr. O. discovered from his college transcript that he did not have a college degree, because the registrar had not been notified of the last course he had passed. Week after week, Mr. O. did not make the phone call to begin resolving the problem, due to painful embarrassment about being in this situation. Neither self-statement modification nor exploration of the advantages and disadvantages of embarrassment resulted in his making the call. The therapist then suggested considering ways to make the phone call despite embarrassment and relabeled phoning as a way Mr. O. could begin learning to take care of himself. Patient and therapist were then able to develop a self-control plan that included rewards for steps toward phoning. It also included an aversive contingency (instigated by the patient) of telling his plans to his wife, so that failure to act would lead to an alternative embarrassment.

Planning a strategy for times the patient expects to be embarrassed can also be helpful, as uncertainty about behavioral requirements heightens social anxiety if the individual has negative expectations about his or her ability to cope with requirements (Schlenker & Leary, 1982). Planning, along the lines of stress inoculation training (Meichenbaum, 1985), can include gathering information about the nature of the event, developing a script for one's actions (e.g., "Excuse me, I would like to know _____"), and preparing a set of overt and cognitive responses to use if one does encounter social disapproval. Self-reward contingencies can also be useful.

Attentional focus treatment was developed by Edelmann (1987) from his information-processing theory of embarrassment. The treatment emphasizes redirecting presumably excessive self-focus rather than restructuring specific cognitive content. The patient is urged to turn attention from self-evaluation to the social task at hand (including environmental stimuli, others' nonverbal behavior, and the possible impact of the patient's behavior on others' reactions). The treatment also includes anxiety management techniques, with coping self-statements, cognitive restructuring, and imaginal rehearsal.

CONCLUSIONS AND OPEN ISSUES

Themes in Treatment

As the reader concludes this survey of clinical theories and methods, the array and variety of interventions for guilt, shame, and embarrassment may raise questions about the choice of treatment. This is an open question in cognitive-behavioral therapy, not limited to the problem areas dealt with in this chapter. Beyond a judgment, based on thorough assessment, as to the controlling conditions for the target problem and continuing attention to treatment response, cognitive-behavioral writers have offered little specific guidance on choices among technical interventions. Noteworthy exceptions include Goldfried and Davison's (1976, pp. 18–36) discussion of issues in selecting target behaviors and Safran *et al.*'s (1986) work on assessment of core cognitive processes. The emerging literature on case formulation (e.g., Persons, 1989) is promising in this regard. Steps toward developing a unified cognitive-behavioral theory of guilt, shame, and embarrassment that would account for their similarities and differences are also needed.

The reader may have noted the considerable weight that I have given to verbal, as opposed to enactive, methods of intervention. The strong cognitive loading in guilt, shame, and embarrassment may make verbal methods and exploration of inner experience especially pertinent in treatment. It is also possible that clinicians who have focused on these difficulties, in which subjective experience is so salient, are more inclined to such verbal methods. The question arises as to how social-learning analysis in particular (see "Self-Blame, Control, and Power") differs from psychodynamic genetic interpretations that link the present to past experiences. (Storr, 1980, pp. 29–41, makes a very clear presentation of psychodynamic techniques of interpretation.) Clearly, the conceptual apparatus differs: Instead of transference, repetition compulsion, and other constructs related to unconscious motivation, cognitive-behavioral therapists draw on a vocabulary of cognitive and learning concepts such as schemata, covert reinforcement, and expectancies. I would venture that in cognitive-behavioral therapy, historical reconstruction is generally used to provide an awareness of controlling variables and is followed by direct change efforts, and that psychodynamic therapists more typically focus on developing a coherent narrative, relying for change on the implicit processes of working through. The array of methods that I have presented may also reflect recent trends in cognitive-behavioral therapy toward more exploration of inner experience, historical sources, and the therapist–patient relationship (cf. Safran *et al.*, 1986). As other cognitive-behavioral therapists report on their clinical work with guilt, shame, and embarrassment, these matters may become clearer.

The Place of Values

Because guilt, shame, and embarrassment imply comparison to standards or norms, values are inherent in these emotions and in their treatment. (Norms, which are implicit rules for appropriate behavior, express values, which are "socially shared ideas about what is good, right, and desirable"; Robertson, 1987, p. 64). It is widely recognized that therapists, like other members of their societies, bring their own values to bear as they consider other people, including their patients (cf. London, 1977). Issues arise around managing to keep one's values from interfering (see "The Therapist–Patient Relationship in Assessment and Treatment"), whether therapists are imposing their values on patients whose values differ, and the acceptability of doing so. Wachtel (1987, Chapter 10), for instance, has argued that contingent therapist response is not only inevitable but also frequently desirable. The cognitive-behavioral solution to issues about values in treatment direction has generally been a thorough functional analysis of the potential target problem. For guilt, shame, and embarrassment, assessment ought to consider explicitly the rules or values underlying the patient's emotional reaction. Further exploration of value issues and potential value conflicts that arise in cognitive-behavior therapy would be welcome.

Sex-Difference Issues

Within our society, sex differences in personality features, value structure, social roles, and stressors may have bearing on treatment of guilt, shame, and embarrassment. The case of guilt is illustrative (Klass, 1988a, 1988b). Recent personality research has suggested that women more than men strongly value maintaining a sense of interconnectedness with others (Stewart & Lykes, 1985). Gilligan's (1982) analysis of male and female moral decision-making processes proposed that men emphasize fairness, while women place more weight on responsibility for others. Sociologically, women bear greater responsibility for the care of family members throughout the life cycle (Scharlach, 1987). Guilt-provoking behaviors, the rules supporting guilt, and their susceptibility to change may thus differ between the sexes. An appropriate intervention for a patient of one sex might impose inappropriate values on a patient of the opposite sex.

In my research on sex differences in guilt using the Situational Guilt Scale (Klass, 1988b), although the overall self-reported guilt of men and women did not significantly differ, there were substantial sex differences in specific guilt-provoking actions. Responses of moderate-guilt men and women paralleled the normative themes suggested above: Men were guiltier about loss of emotional control and women, about harm to others. In the small subset of extremely guilty subjects, however, the pattern of sex differences diverged. High-guilt men were guiltier about failing to meet family obligations and about avoidance of stressful situations than high-guilt women. It may be important to consider sex-role identity as well as biological sex. Applications of cognitive-behavioral therapy to the treatment of guilt in women are presented in another paper (Klass, 1988a). Empirical analyses and clinical writing about sex differences in shame and embarrassment from a cognitive-behavioral perspective would be welcome.

Cognitive Processes in Guilt, Shame, and Embarrassment

In this chapter, I have portrayed guilt, shame, and embarrassment as cognitive-affective phenomena, in which discomfort is experienced as if there has been moral transgression, exposure of a central personal failing, or failure of a self-presentation effort. At the same time, it is evident that explicit cognitive appraisals are not required before an individual feels guilty, ashamed, or embarrassed. When patient and therapist identify maladaptive self-statements and underlying rules, they may be constructing a process that is more logical than what naturally occurs.

Some organizing principle is needed to account for the diversity in provocative behaviors and the fact that individuals can feel guilty, ashamed, or embarrassed about behaviors despite having had no direct training about their acceptability.[1] One explanation is stimulus generalization—that behaviors become provocative based on gradients of similarity to original learning experiences. An alternative is the schema construct—an organized cognitive structure, abstracted on the basis of past experience and capable of guiding current information processing (Fiske & Linville, 1980, p. 543). The conceptualization of schema operation proposes that when a schema is activated, it elicits an entire cognitive-affective reaction (e.g., proximity to harm to another person can evoke guilt and self-blame even in an accidental situation because in the past, harm and personal causality were associated). Schemata about the self have the greatest clinical relevance.

Safran (1990) proposed that the interpersonal self-schema, a set of tacit rules for self–other relationships abstracted from experiences with attachment figures, is most important, because it is most central to identity. In "Self-Blame, Control, and Power," I drew on Brown's (1988) and Safran's views about self-definition and attachment to speculate on the sources and treatment of pervasive guilt. For shame, experiences encoded as disgusting to self or significant others and therefore needing to be hidden may likewise reflect central conditions of attachment that are summarized in the interpersonal self-schema. For

---

[1]However one views the epistemological status of the superego construct in psychodynamic thinking, it does provide a unifying principle for the diversity in overt behaviors that provoke guilt and shame.

embarrassment, pertinent schemata may be more peripheral, including summaries of requirements for acceptable self-presentation and others' anticipated reactions to defects in self-presentation.

A related question is whether central schematic processes ought to be a direct focus of treatment for maladaptive guilt, shame, and embarrassment. I have presented some interventions that are aimed at central schemata (e.g., changing core role constructs, for guilt; increasing tolerance of central failings, for shame), and others that target more peripheral levels (e.g., changing behavior, for guilt; functioning despite embarrassment). Safran *et al.* (1986) pointed out that controlled outcome research comparing central to peripheral interventions will be needed to establish the merits of each strategy.

Areas in Need of Further Work

Clearly, empirical work is needed on the behavioral and physiological referents of guilt, shame, and embarrassment and also on the meanings of these terms to lay persons. Research on referents of the emotions might well be guided by Lang's three-systems approach (1968). With regard to the meanings of these emotional terms to lay persons, empirical evidence based on prototype methodologies has been sparse and inconsistent (Shaver, Schwartz, Kirson, & O'Connor, 1987; Wicker, Payne, & Martin, 1983). Research on the ways that nonpsychologists use the terms guilt, shame, and embarrassment may illuminate some of the definitional questions. It is possible that the provocative behaviors that others have viewed as required characteristics for guilt, shame, and embarrassment are prototypic instances, but not necessary for each emotional term. Prototype research might evaluate the relevance of the dimensions of moral weighting and concern with others' opinions that I proposed as characterizing the spectrum of guilt, shame, and embarrassment.

There are also important questions about the need for targeted treatment of guilt, shame, and embarrassment, as opposed to conceptualizing treatment at the level of more generic constructs like social anxiety and self-esteem. Certainly at the level of cognitive-behavioral clinical practice, it is useful to have available techniques that are closely tied to specific target problems, such as guilt, shame, and embarrassment. On the other hand, empirical data on treatment effects on these symptoms are lacking. Unanswered questions include whether and under what conditions maladaptive levels of these emotions change with generally successful treatment, and also the relations of pre- and posttreatment levels to relapse. The paucity of adequate measures of guilt, shame, and embarrassment probably accounts to some degree for the lack of such information. Additional general measures, especially for shame, are needed, and specific, narrow-band measures (e.g., for rape-related guilt) are needed. In the meantime, it should be of value for clinicians to write up cases in which guilt, shame, or embarrassment was a treatment target, including individualized assessment. It is thus my hope that this chapter will stimulate clinical writing and empirical research that increase our ability to help people with these difficulties.

ACKNOWLEDGMENTS. I would like to thank Dr. Janet E. Poppendieck and Dr. Zindel V. Segal for their generous help with preparation of this chapter.

REFERENCES

American Psychiatric Association. (1987). *Diagnostic and statistical manual of mental disorders* (3rd ed., rev.). Washington, DC: Author.

Aronfreed, J. (1968). *Conduct and conscience.* New York: Academic Press.

Bandler, R., & Grinder, J. (1979). *Frogs into princes: Neuro-linguistic programming.* Moab, UT: Real People Press.

Bandura, A. (1977). *Social learning theory.* Englewood Cliffs, NJ: Prentice-Hall.

Barlow, D. H. (1988). *Anxiety and its disorders.* New York: Guilford.

Beck, A. T., Rush, A. J., Shaw, B. T., & Emery, G. (1979). *Cognitive therapy of depression.* New York: Guilford.

Brasted, W. S., & Callahan, E. J. (1984). A behavioral analysis of the grief process. *Behavior Therapy, 15,* 529–543.

Brown, S. (1988). *Treating adult children of alcoholics: A developmental perspective.* New York: Wiley.

Burns, D. D. (1980). *Feeling good.* New York: Morrow.

Buss, A. (1980). *Self-consciousness and social anxiety.* San Francisco: Freeman.

Edelmann, R. (1987). *The psychology of embarrassment.* New York: Wiley.

Eisenberg, N., & Lennon, R. (1983). Sex differences in empathy and related capacities. *Psychological Bulletin, 94,* 100–131.

Ellis, A. (1962). *Reason and emotion in psychotherapy.* New York: Lyle Stuart.

Fairburn, C. G., & Cooper, P. J. (1984). The clinical features of bulimia nervosa. *British Journal of Psychiatry, 144,* 238–246.

Fiske, S. T., & Linville, P. W. (1980). What does the schema concept buy us? *Personality and Social Psychology Bulletin, 6,* 543–557.

Fossum, M. A., & Mason, M. J. (1986). *Facing shame.* New York: Norton.

Frank, E., & Stewart, B. D. (1984). Physical aggression: Treating the victims. In E. A. Blechman (Ed.), *Behavior modification with women* (pp. 245–272). New York: Guilford.

Freedman, J. L. (1970). Transgression, compliance, and guilt. In J. Macaulay & L. Berkowitz (Eds.), *Altruism and helping behavior* (pp. 155–162). New York: Academic Press.

Gilligan, C. (1982). *In another voice: Psychological theory and women's development.* Cambridge: Harvard University Press.

Glover, H. (1984). Survival guilt and the Vietnam veteran. *Journal of Nervous and Mental Disease, 172,* 393–397.

Goldfried, M. R., & Davison, G. C. (1976). *Clinical behavior therapy.* New York: Holt, Rinehart & Winston.

Greenberg, L. S., & Safran, J. D. (1987). *Emotion in psychotherapy.* New York: Guilford.

Heimberg, R. G. (1989). Cognitive and behavioral treatments for social phobia: A critical analysis. *Clinical Psychology Review, 9,* 107–128.

Heimberg, R. G., & Becker, R. E. (1984). *Cognitive-behavioral treatment of social phobia in a group setting.* Unpublished manuscript, State University of New York at Albany, Albany, NY.

Hoffman, M. L. (1976). Empathy, role-taking, guilt, and development of altruistic motives. In T. Lickona (Ed.), *Moral development and behavior: Theory, research, and social issues* (pp. 124–143). New York: Holt, Rinehart & Winston.

Hoffman, M. L. (1977). Sex differences in empathy and related behaviors. *Psychological Bulletin, 84,* 712–722.

Hoffman, M. L. (1983). Affective and cognitive processes in moral internalization. In E. T. Higgins, D. N. Ruble, & W. W. Hartup (Eds.), *Social cognition and social development* (pp. 236–274). New York: Cambridge University Press.

Jakubowski, P., & Lange, A. (1978). *The assertive option: Your rights and responsibilities.* Champaign, IL: Research Press.

Keane, T. M., Fairbank, J. A., Caddell, J. M., & Zimering, R. T. (1989). Implosive (flooding) therapy reduces symptoms of PTSD in Vietnam combat veterans. *Behavior Therapy, 20,* 245–260.

Keane, T. M., Fairbank, J. A., Caddell, J. M., Zimering, R. T., & Bender, M. E. (1985). A behavioral approach to assessing and treating posttraumatic stress disorder in Vietnam veterans. In C. R. Figley (Ed.), *Trauma and its wake* (pp. 257–294). New York: Guilford.

Keane, T. M., Zimering, R. T., & Caddell, J. M. (1985). A behavioral formulation of posttraumatic stress disorder in Vietnam veterans. *The Behavior Therapist, 8,* 9–12.

Kelly, G. A. (1955). *The psychology of personal constructs* (Vol. 1). New York: Norton.

Kelly, G. A. (1969). Sin and psychotherapy. In B. A. Maher (Ed.), *Clinical psychology and personality: The selected papers of George Kelly* (pp. 165–188). New York: Wiley.

Klass, E. T. (1978). Psychological consequences of immoral actions: The experimental evidence. *Psychological Bulletin, 85,* 756–771.

Klass, E. T. (1981). A cognitive analysis of guilt over assertion. *Cognitive Therapy and Research, 5,* 283–297.

Klass, E. T. (1983). *Guide to the use of a situational self-report measure of guilt.* Unpublished manuscript, Hunter College, City University of New York.

Klass, E. T. (1987). Situational approach to the assessment of guilt: Development and validation of a self-report measure. *Journal of Psychopathology and Behavioral Assessment, 9,* 35–48.

Klass, E. T. (1988a). Cognitive behavioral perspectives on women and guilt. *Journal of Rational-Emotive and Cognitive-Behavior Therapy, 6,* 23–32.

Klass, E. T. (1988b). *Sex differences in guilt: An empirical analysis.* Manuscript submitted for publication.

Kohlberg, L., & Kramer, R. (1969). Continuities and discontinuities in childhood and adult moral development. *Human Development, 12,* 93–120.

Lang, P. J. (1968). Fear reduction and fear behavior: Problems in treating a construct. In J. M. Shlien (Ed.), *Research in psychotherapy* (Vol. 3, pp. 90–102). Washington, DC: American Psychological Association.

Leitenberg, H., & Rosen, J. (1988). Cognitive-behavioral treatment of bulimia nervosa. In M. Hersen, R. Eisler, & P. M. Miller (Eds.), *Progress in behavior modification* (Vol. 23, pp. 11–35). Newbury Park, CA: Sage.

Lewis, H. B. (1986). Shame and the narcissistic personality. In D. L. Nathanson (Ed.), *The many faces of shame* (pp. 93–132). New York: Guilford.

London, P. (1977). *Behavior control* (2nd ed.). New York: New American Library.

LoPiccolo, J. (1978). Direct treatment of sexual dysfunction. In J. LoPiccolo & L. LoPiccolo (Eds.), *Handbook of sex therapy* (pp. 1–17). New York: Plenum.

Marin, P. (1981, November). Living with moral pain. *Psychology Today,* pp. 68–80.

Mawson, D., Marks, I. M., Ramm, L., & Stern, R. S. (1981). Guided mourning for morbid grief: A controlled study. *British Journal of Psychiatry, 138,* 185–193.

Meichenbaum, D. (1985). *Stress inoculation training.* New York: Pergamon Press.

Miles, M. S., & Demi, A. S. (1985). Guilt in bereaved parents. In T. A. Rando (Ed.), *Parental loss of a child* (pp. 97–118). Champaign, IL: Research Press.

Modligliani, A. (1968). Embarrassment and embarrassability. *Sociometry, 31,* 313–326.

Mowrer, O. H. (1966). *The new group therapy.* New York: Van Nostrand.

Persons, J. B. (1989). *Cognitive therapy in practice: A case formulation approach.* New York: Norton.

Rachman, S. J., & Hodgson, R. J. (1980). *Obessesions and compulsions.* Englewood Cliffs, NJ: Prentice-Hall.

Robertson, I. (1987). *Sociology* (3rd ed.). New York: Worth.

Safran, J. D. (1990). Towards a refinement of cognitive therapy in light of interpersonal theory: I. Practice. Clinical Psychology Review, 10, 107–121.

Safran, J. D., Vallis, T. M., Segal, Z. V., & Shaw, B. F. (1986). Assessment of core cognitive processes in cognitive therapy. *Cognitive Therapy and Research, 10,* 509–526.

Scharlach, A. E. (1987). Relieving feelings of strain among women with elderly mothers. *Psychology and Aging, 2,* 9–13.

Schlenker, B. R., & Leary, M. A. (1982). Social anxiety and self-presentation: A conceptualization and model. *Psychological Bulletin, 92,* 641–669.

Shaver, P., Schwartz, J., Kirson, D., & O'Connor, C. (1987). Emotion knowledge: Further exploration of a prototype approach. *Journal of Personality and Social Psychology, 52,* 1061–1086.

Sireling, L., Cohen, D., & Marks, I. (1988). Guided mourning for morbid grief: A controlled replication. *Behavior Therapy, 19,* 121–132.

Stevens, J. O. (1971). *Awareness: Exploring, experimenting, experiencing.* Moab, UT: Real People Press.

Stewart, A. J., & Lykes, M. B. (1985). Conceptualizing gender in personality theory and research. *Journal of Personality, 53,* 93–101.

Storr, A. (1980). *The art of psychotherapy.* New York: Methuen.

Swanson, L., & Biaggio, M. K. (1985). Therapeutic perspectives on father–daughter incest. *American Journal of Psychiatry, 142,* 667–674.

Wachtel, P. L. (1987). *Action and insight.* New York: Guilford.

Walen, S. R., DiGiuseppe, R., & Wessler, R. L. (1980). *A practitioner's guide to rational-emotive therapy.* New York: Oxford University Press.

Watson, D., & Friend, R. (1969). Measurement of social-evaluative anxiety. *Journal of Consulting and Clinical Psychology, 33,* 448–457.

Wicker, F. W., Payne, G. C., & Martin, R. D. (1983). Participant descriptions of guilt and shame. *Motivation and Emotion, 7,* 25–39.

Winnicott, D. W. (1971). *Playing and reality.* New York: Methuen.

Wright, D. (1971). *The psychology of moral behaviour.* Baltimore, MD: Penguin.

V

Evaluation Anxiety

13

Sport Performance Anxiety

Ronald E. Smith and Frank L. Smoll

The role of anxiety in sport has been a topic of great interest to coaches, athletes, and researchers for many years. The fact that emotional and motivational factors can cause one athlete to "peak" in the crucible of competition while another falters or "chokes" is evident to anyone who has watched or participated in sports. Coaches speak of "Wednesday All-Americans" who cannot perform up their capabilities on Saturday game days because of debilitating effects of anxiety. Conversely, coaches and athletes sometimes express the view that anxiety facilitates performance.

Anxiety affects other outcomes as well. Some children drop out of sports because they find athletic competition to be aversive and threatening rather than enjoyable and challenging. Trainers and sports medicine practitioners have observed that athletes who find the competitive situation to be anxiety provoking sometimes appear injury prone and/or seem to take longer to return to action following injury.

These and other observations suggest that the role of anxiety in sport has a range of practical implications that can potentially be addressed through a greater understanding of the antecedents, dynamics, and consequences of anxiety. Moreover, from a scientific perspective, sport would appear to offer a number of advantages as a setting for the study of anxiety. Here, large numbers of subjects are exposed to predictable, identifiable, and repetitive situations in which anxiety can be assessed and its consequences studied within a meaningful real-life context. Performance measures having unquestioned ecological validity are readily measurable within the athletic setting (Smith & Smoll, 1989). Moreover, depending upon the sport, athletes are required to perform behaviors that vary considerably along a number of task dimensions (e.g., simple vs. complex; speed vs. endurance; self-paced vs. reactive; cognitive vs. motoric), permitting researchers to assess the effects of anxiety (including its cognitive and somatic components) on various classes of behavior.

Given the range of practical and theoretical issues that can be addressed

Ronald E. Smith and Frank L. Smoll • Department of Psychology, University of Washington, Seattle, Washington 98195.

through the study of sport anxiety, it should not be surprising that it has attracted the attention of scientists for many years. In the past decade, however, a notable upsurge of scientific activity has occurred, due largely to the development of sport-specific measures of anxiety as well as increased interest among sport psychologists in developing anxiety reduction intervention programs for athletes (Apitzsch, 1983; Hackfort & Spielberger, 1989; Smith, 1989; Suinn, 1989).

Some of the earliest research on anxiety in sport focused on possible differences between athletes and nonathletes on measures of general trait anxiety. Researchers also assessed differences between elite athletes and less proficient ones. Ogilvie (1968) reviewed the sport personality literature and concluded that athletes, particularly superior athletes, have unique and specific personality profiles. According to Ogilvie, superior athletes are more emotionally stable, have lower levels of anxiety, and are more resistant to emotional stress. Other reviewers, however, (e.g., Cooper, 1969; Hardman, 1973; Johnson & Coffer, 1974; Martens, 1975) have concluded that no consistent differences in general trait anxiety exist among participants compared with nonparticipants or among athletes having different skill levels. For example, Hardman (1973) assessed anxiety among 42 different samples of athletes using Cattell's (1957) 16 PF. These samples included athletes from 16 different sports and several different countries, as well as athletes of superior and average skills. The data indicated that most of the athlete samples were well within the normal range of the trait when compared with Cattell's norms. It is important to note, however, that these studies assessed general anxiety, and not sport-specific anxiety.

More recent research has assessed the role of individual difference variables and situational factors as determinants of anxiety responses among athletes. A second important line of research has explored consequences of anxiety, including performance, physical well-being, and withdrawal from sport participation. Both of these areas of research are reviewed below.

Arousal, Stress, and Anxiety

Before discussing the measurement, antecedents, and consequences of sport performance anxiety, distinctions should be drawn between the related concepts of arousal, stress, and anxiety. These terms are often used interchangeably, resulting in no small measure of confusion within the literature.

Arousal is the most general of the three terms. Cannon (1929) used the term to refer to energy mobilization in response to situations that threatened the physical integrity of the organism. The concept of arousal has also occupied a prominent position in the theoretical formulations of Berlyne (1960), Duffy (1962), Hebb (1949), Malmo (1959), and others. If behavior is viewed as varying along two basic dimensions of direction and intensity, then arousal is the intensity dimension. Arousal, often used interchangeably with other intensity-related terms such as tension, drive, and activation, can vary on a continuum ranging from deep sleep to peak excitement.

The term *stress* is used in two different but related ways. First, it is used in relation to situations (termed *stressors*) which place significant demands on the organism. This situational definition of stress is frequently couched in terms of the balance between situational demands and the resources of the individual (e.g., Lazarus & Folkman, 1984). The second use of the term stress refers to the responses of individuals to stressors. Used in this sense, stress refers to a cognitive-affective response involving appraisal of threat and increased physiological arousal (Lazarus & Folkman, 1984; Spielberger, 1989). Though less general than arousal, the term stress is typically used to refer to a range of aversive emotional states, such as anxiety, depression, and anger.

Anxiety is one variety of stress response. It is an aversive emotional response and an avoidance motive characterized by worry and apprehension concerning the possibility of physical or psychological harm, together with increased physiological arousal resulting from the appraisal of threat. As a motivational state, anxiety is an avoidance motive which helps strengthen successful coping and/or avoidance responses through negative reinforcement.

The State–Trait Anxiety Distinction

The emotional reaction of anxiety varies in intensity and fluctuates over time. Physiological and psychological calmness and serenity indicate the absence of an anxiety response. Moderate levels of anxiety involve apprehension, nervousness, worry, and tension; very high levels of anxiety may involve intense feelings of fear, catastrophic thoughts, and high levels of physiological arousal. The momentary level of anxiety experienced by an individual is termed *state anxiety.*

Spielberger (1966) noted the important distinction between state anxiety and trait anxiety. *Trait anxiety* refers to relatively stable individual differences in anxiety proneness that are regarded as a personality disposition or trait. That is, people who are high in trait anxiety are more anxiety prone in that they perceive or appraise a wider range of situations as threatening than do individuals who are low in trait anxiety. High trait-anxious people are thus more likely to experience state anxiety, and their anxiety responses tend to be of greater intensity and duration.

It is now generally accepted that a comprehensive theory of anxiety must distinguish between anxiety as a transitory emotional state and individual differences in the relatively stable personality trait of anxiety. An adequate model of anxiety should also specify the nature of the cognitive processes that mediate the appraisal of threat as well as the consequences of such appraisals.

The Multidimensional Nature of Anxiety

As the above description of state anxiety would imply, the anxiety response consists of both cognitive and physiological components. Conceptualizations of anxiety have treated it as a multidimensional construct, distinguishing between its cognitive and physiological components (e.g., Borkovec, 1976; Davidson & Schwartz, 1976; Liebert & Morris, 1967; Sarason, 1984). Multidimensional conceptions of anxiety were stimulated in part by behavior therapy research in the 1960s and 1970s that indicated that anxiety involves three separate and largely independent cognitive, physiological, and behavioral response dimensions (Borkovec, 1976; Lang, 1971). Measurement of anxiety responses by means of self-report, physiological, and behavioral measures of anxiety in laboratory stress studies and in behavior therapy research often indicated that these three response systems were only loosely correlated with one another. Factor analytic studies of anxiety scales have likewise revealed the existence of statistically independent cognitive (e.g., worry) and somatic (e.g., physiological response) dimensions of anxiety (Morris, Davis, & Hutchings, 1981; Sarason, 1984). Cognitive anxiety is characterized by negative appraisals of situation and self, worry, and aversive mental imagery, whereas somatic anxiety is reflected in increased physiological arousal as typified by rapid heart rate, shortness of breath, and increased muscle tension.

One rationale for the distinction between cognitive and somatic anxiety is the likelihood that these dimensions may differentially affect behavior. For example, Morris *et al.* (1981) hypothesized that the differential nature and patterns of change in cognitive and somatic components of state anxiety would be expected to result in cognitive anxiety impairing task performance more frequently and more strongly than does somatic anxiety. They reasoned that somatic anxiety should primarily affect initial performance, when performers are feeling most nervous. On the other hand, cognitive anxiety should be a more powerful mediator of ongoing performance because expectations of failure may arise at any time during the performance. Likewise, it might be expected that performance on cognitive tasks would be particularly affected by cognitive anxiety. As we shall see, attempts have been made to test these hypotheses in recent studies of sport performance anxiety.

The General–Specific Anxiety Distinction

Since state anxiety is defined as a transitory emotional response, it is always measured within specific situations. Trait measures of anxiety, on the other hand, fall into two general categories. Some instruments measure anxiety as a global transituational trait, while others are designed to assess the tendency of individuals to experience anxiety within particular types of situations such as tests, social situations, or competitive sport situations. The study of situation-specific anxiety has been stimulated in part by interactional approaches to personality (e.g., Magnusson & Endler, 1977), in which behavior is assumed to be determined by the reciprocal interaction of personal traits and the characteristics of situations. If anxiety is a learned response to particular classes of situations, then we should expect that situation-specific anxiety measures would relate more strongly to behavior in the critical situations than would general transituational anxiety. An impressive array of research results supports this prediction. For example, test anxiety measures are more strongly related to test performance than are measures of general anxiety (see Sarason, Chapter 15, this volume). Moreover, situation-specific trait anxiety measures are better predictors of elevation in state anxiety for a particular class of stress situations than are generalized trait anxiety measures (Martens, 1977; Spielberger, 1972).

THE NATURE OF SPORT PERFORMANCE ANXIETY

As a trait construct, sport performance anxiety may be defined as a learned tendency to respond with cognitive and/or somatic state anxiety to competitive sport situations in which the adequacy of the athlete's performance can be evaluated. Although a number of specific sources of threat (including the possibility of physical harm) may reside in the sport situation, we believe that the most salient sources of threat are the possibilities of failure and of disapproval by significant others who are evaluating the athlete's performance in relation to some standard of excellence. Athletic performance anxiety is thus part of a family of performance-related fear-of-failure constructs that include test anxiety, speech anxiety, and the stage fright that actors, musicians, and dancers can experience within their evaluative performance situations (Steptoe & Fidler, 1987; Kendrick, Craig, Lawson, & Davidson, 1982). Like other forms of anxiety, sport performance anxiety has separate but related cognitive, affective, and behavioral components.

A conceptual model of athletic performance anxiety is presented in Figure 1. This model, derived from conceptions of emotionality and anxiety advanced by Arnold (1960), Ellis (1962a), Lazarus and Folkman (1984), Mandler and Sarason (1952), Smith (1986), and Spielberger (1966), includes both the trait–state distinction and the differentiation between situational, cognitive, physiological, and behavioral components of the process of anxiety.

The cognitive and somatic components of competitive state anxiety are shown within the appraisal and physiological response panels of the figure. The intensity and duration of the state anxiety response are assumed to be influenced by three major factors. The first of these factors is the nature of the competitive sport situation in which the athlete is involved. Obviously, such situations differ in the demands which they place upon the athlete, as well as the degree of threat that they pose to successful performance. Such factors as strength of opponent, importance of the contest, presence of significant others, and degree of social support received from coaches and teammates can affect the amount of threat that the situation is likely to pose for the individual.

Two classes of intrapersonal factors are also important determinants of the level of state anxiety experienced by the athlete. One of these is the performer's level of sport-specific cognitive and somatic trait anxiety. As noted above, this individual difference variable involves the individual's tendency to experience cognitive and somatic state anxiety reactions within competitive situations. The second intraindividual factor is the psychological defenses that the athlete may have developed to cope with anxiety-arousing competitive situations. As Spielberger (1966) has noted, defensive processes may be mobilized to avoid or reduce anxiety. These defensive processes operate at the level of appraisal and in some way modify or distort the perception or appraisal of the situation. To the

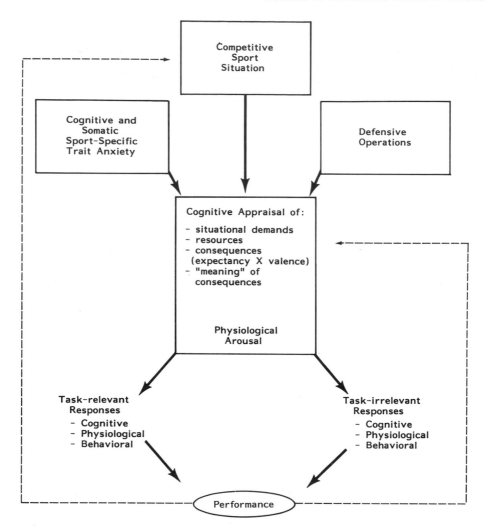

FIGURE 1. A conceptual model of athletic performance anxiety, indicating relationships between trait and state anxiety, as well as relevant situational, cognitive, physiological, and behavioral variables.

extent that a defensive operation is successful, the competitive sport situation would be seen as less threatening, with a resulting decrease in state anxiety. Thus, defensive processes may at times balance or mitigate the effects of the high level of sport-specific trait anxiety.

The objective situation, level of trait anxiety, and the individual's defenses are all assumed to influence the performer's appraisal processes. Four classes of appraisal are particularly important: appraisal of the situational demands; appraisal of the resources available to deal with them; appraisal of the nature and likelihood of potential consequences if the demands are not met (that is, the expectancies and valances relating to potential consequences); and the personal meaning that the consequences have for the individual. The meanings attached to the consequences derive from the person's believe system, and they often involve the individual's criteria for self-worth (Ellis, 1962b; Rogers, 1959). Thus, an athletic who defines the present situational demands as overwhelming, who appraises his or her resources and skills as insufficient to deal with the demands, who anticipates failure and/or disapproval as a result of the demands–resources imbalance, and who defines his or her self-worth in terms of success and/or the approval of others will clearly perceive this competitive situation as threatening or dangerous. Such appraisals are likely to generate high levels of physiological arousal, and this arousal, in turn, feeds back into the ongoing process of appraisal and reappraisal. High levels of arousal may convince the athlete that he or she is "falling apart" and help generate even more negative appraisals.

State anxiety may affect a variety of outcomes, including the athlete's enjoyment of the competitive situation; interactions with opponents, teammates, coaches, officials; injury proneness; and performance. Since the relationship between anxiety and performance has always been a central focus of sport anxiety research, we have included mechanisms assumed to influence performance. As Mandler and Sarason (1952) have noted, motivational and emotional states may generate two broad classes of task-related responses. Some of these responses facilitate task performance (task-relevant), whereas others are detrimental to performance (task-irrelevant responses). We suggest that the task-relevant and task-irrelevant responses may be cognitive, physiological, or behavioral in nature. Thus, cognitive responses such as concentration on the task and strategic planning may be facilitated by certain levels of state anxiety and would thereby contribute to performance. On the other hand, task-irrelevant cognitive responses such as worry and catastrophic thinking could readily interfere with task performance by disrupting attentional and problem-solving processes. Likewise, certain classes and intensities of physiological responding might facilitate task performance, whereas other types and intensities of physiological responding might interfere with task performance. Finally, behavioral responses such as persistence and smooth execution of motor responses would facilitate performance, while impulsive or inappropriate behaviors would interfere with it. The balance between task-relevant and task-irrelevant responses and the manner in which they are affected by the performer's anxiety level will thus affect the adequacy of performance. It should also be noted that ongoing appraisal of performance adequacy will influence the four basic appraisal elements shown in Figure 1.

This heuristic model of sport performance anxiety helps to provide a conceptual framework for the topics to follow. First, we discuss the measurement of sport performance anxiety from both a trait and a state perspective. Next, we describe what is known about situational and individual difference factors that influence competitive state anxiety. Finally, we review evidence concerning the manner in which anxiety affects performance and other athletic outcomes.

The Measurement of Anxiety in Sports

The development of adequate measurement techniques is critical to the study of any psychological construct. In research on sport anxiety, much progress has been made in the past decade as a result of the development of sport-specific state and trait anxiety measures. Because of the important distinction between state anxiety and trait anxiety, we describe both types of measures.

Trait Anxiety Measures

Until the late 1970s, no sport-specific trait anxiety measures existed. Consequently, investigators wishing to assess individual differences in trait anxiety employed general anxiety measures such as Taylor's (1953) Manifest Anxiety Scale, the anxiety factor from Cattell's (1957) 16 PF, and the Trait scale from Spielberger's State–Trait Anxiety Inventory (STAI; Spielberger, Gorsuch, & Lushene, 1970). Because general anxiety scales assess anxiety across a wide range of situations, these measures were minimally useful for assessing individual differences in sport-specific anxiety. For example, a high score on a measure of general trait anxiety does not guarantee that the person experiences high anxiety in the competitive sport situation, nor does a low score indicate that the person does not have a tendency to experience sport-specific anxiety. Thus, it is not surprising that general anxiety measures often bore little relationship to performance measures in sport (Martens, 1971).

The Sport Competition Anxiety Test

The need for a sport-specific trait anxiety measure stimulated the development of the Sport Competition Anxiety Test (SCAT; Martens, 1977). The SCAT is a 10-item scale with items specific to sport competition (see Table 1). Five additional spurious items were included in the scale in an attempt to disguise its purpose somewhat, and these items are not scored. The subject responds to each item according to how he or she *generally feels* in competitive sport situations on a 3-point Lickert-type scale labeled *hardly ever, sometimes,* and *often.* Parallel forms of the SCAT have been developed for adults and children. The SCAT has adequate test–retest reliability and good internal consistency. It correlates approximately .45 with general trait anxiety measures for both adults and children (see Martens, 1977).

TABLE 1. Sample Items from the Sport
Competition Anxiety Test (SCAT)

Before I compete I feel uneasy.
Before I compete I am calm. (reversed scoring)
I get nervous waiting to start the game.
When I compete I worry about making mistakes.

Note. From Martens, 1977. Items are answered on a
3-point scale labeled *hardly ever, sometimes,* and *often.*

The primary means of assessing construct validity involved comparing the SCAT with general trait anxiety measures in ability to predict state anxiety scores obtained prior to or within competitive sport situations. For example, in one study (Martens & Simon, 1976), members of 16 intercollegiate women's volleyball teams completed the SCAT and Spielberger's STAI–Trait measure. They later completed the STAI–State just prior to competition. The general trait anxiety measure correlated only .30 with precompetitive state anxiety, whereas the SCAT correlated .65 with this measure. This result parallels results of other studies in which situation-specific trait anxiety measures more successfully predicted state anxiety in the relevant situations than did general trait anxiety measures (Spielberger, 1972).

During the past decade, the SCAT has been a very important research tool within sport psychology. The vast majority of studies in which individual differences in competitive trait anxiety have been assessed in adults and children have utilized the SCAT. There is no question that the availability of this measure has stimulated research that has resulted in major advances in our knowledge of sport anxiety, its antecedents, and its consequences.

The Sport Anxiety Scale

The SCAT was designed as a unidimensional measure of sport-specific trait anxiety. Inspection of its 10 items indicates that 8 of them measure primarily somatic reactions; the other 2 items appear to tap worry. The demonstrated importance of differentiating between cognitive and somatic anxiety has stimulated the recent development of the Sport Anxiety Scale (SAS; Smith, Smoll, & Schutz, in press). Derived primarily through exploratory factor analysis, the SAS is a 22-item scale that consists of three subscales: Somatic Anxiety, Worry, and Concentration Disruption. Subscale scores can be summed to provide a total sport anxiety score. Both exploratory and confirmatory factor analyses show the differentiation between worry and concentration disruption as separate and essentially independent dimensions of cognitive anxiety. Sample items from each of the subscales are presented in Table 2.

Both the total scale and the individual subscales of the SAS have adequate internal consistency and test–retest reliability. The SAS correlates highly (.78) with the SCAT, and the Somatic Anxiety subscale correlates more highly with the SCAT than does either of the cognitive subscales. In an initial validity study, SAS scores were correlated with scores from an abbreviated version of the Profile of Mood States (POMS) that was completed as a state measure by college football players prior to an important game. The SAS correlated highly ($>.60$) with scores on the POMS Tension and Confusion subscales. Results from recently completed but as yet unpublished studies indicate that high scores on the Somatic Anxiety subscale are predictive of later athletic injuries, whereas scores on the cognitive scales are negatively related to athletic performance measures. The multidimensional nature of the SAS thus appears to contribute to its potential usefulness as a measure of individual differences in sport anxiety and in patterns of anxiety in athletes.

TABLE 2. Sample Items from the Sport Anxiety Scale

Somatic anxiety
  My body feels tense.
  I feel tense in my stomach.
  My heart pounds before competition.

Worry
  I'm concerned about choking under pressure.
  I'm concerned about performing poorly.
  I'm worried about reaching my goal.

Concentration disruption
  During competition, I find myself thinking about unrelated
    things.
  I have lapses in concentration during competition because of
    nervousness.
  I'm concerned I won't be able to concentrate.

Note. From Smith *et al.*, in press. Items are scored on a 4-point scale
ranging from *not at all* to *very much so.*

State Anxiety Measures

Although trait anxiety has been assessed primarily through self-report, state anxiety can be measured in a variety of ways. These include physiological measures, overt behavioral indications of anxiety, and self-report scales.

Psychophysiological Measures

The use of psychophysiological measures to assess arousal, stress, and anxiety has a long history in sport research (see Hatfield & Landers, 1987, for a review). A wide variety of physiological response systems have been through such measures as the electroencephalograph, galvanic skin response, cardiovascular measures, and electromyographic measurement of muscle tension. Biochemical measures of stress hormone levels have also been used to assess responses to potentially stressful athletic situations.

As in other areas of psychology, much frustration has resulted from the lack of consistent agreement among different physiological variables and questionnaire measures of arousal, stress, and anxiety (Hatfield & Landers, 1987). This state of affairs is not surprising, since humans exhibit marked individual differences in autonomic response patterns (Lacey, 1967). Because of autonomic response stereotypy, averaging one or a few physiological variables across groups of subjects may conceal individual arousal reactions. Use of multiple autonomic measures is clearly preferable for this reason.

A second consideration in the use of physiological measures to assess anxiety is the fact that arousal and even stress are not necessarily synonymous with anxiety. Thus, a high level of physiological arousal could result from a state of positive excitement resulting from anticipation of success, or from anger, rather than from a state of anxiety. The cognitive-affective model of anxiety presented in Figure 1 suggests that physiological arousal is appropriately considered a measure of anxiety only when the subject cognitively labels his or her arousal reaction as anxiety.

Self-Report Measures

Self-report measures have been the most frequently used indices of sport-specific state anxiety. Because state anxiety questionnaires require that the subject indicate his or her reactions at the present moment, the distinction between general and sport-specific reactions is not as crucial as it is in the case of trait measures. Thus, a variety of different state measures have been employed in sport research, including the Activation–Deactivation Check List (Thayer, 1967), the Affective Adjective Check List (Zuckerman, 1960), and Spielberger's STAI–State measure. The STAI–State has been the most frequently used state measure, having been employed in well over 100 studies in sport (Spielberger, 1989).

To provide researchers with a brief state anxiety measure that could be administered repeatedly in competitive situations, Martens, Burton, Rivkin, and Simon (1980) introduced the Competitive State Anxiety Inventory-1 (CSAI-1). The CSAI-1 consists of 10 items selected from Spielberger's state anxiety measure. The items chosen have high face validity in relation to competitive sport situations, and the CSAI-1 has been utilized in many recent sport psychology studies dealing with competitive state anxiety.

More recently, Martens and his associates have introduced a multidimensional state anxiety measure known as the CSAI-2 (Martens, Burton, Vealey, Bump, & Smith, in press). The 27-item scale is designed to measure cognitive state anxiety, somatic state anxiety, and a third variable termed self-confidence. Sample items are presented in Table 3. Inclusion of the self-confidence subscale in the CSAI-2 was based on factor analytic findings indicating that items of a

TABLE 3. Sample Items from the Competitive
State Anxiety-2 Inventory

Somatic anxiety
   I feel jittery.
   I feel my stomach sinking.
   My body feels tight.

Cognitive anxiety
   I'm concerned about this competition.
   I have self-doubts.
   I'm concerned about losing.

Self-confidence
   I feel self-confident.
   I'm confident of coming through under pressure.
   I'm confident about performing well.

Note. From Martens et al., in press. Items are scored on a 4-point scale ranging from not at all to very much so.

positive nature were independent of the remaining cognitive anxiety items refer-ring to negative reactions. Within the framework of the model we have present-ed, the self-confidence subscale could be viewed as reflecting an appraisal that resources are adequate to meet situational demands.

The CSAI-2 subscales have adequate internal consistency, and the items themselves are more relevant to competitive athletic situations than are the items on the STAI–State. The multidimensional nature of the scale constitutes a step forward in the assessment of state anxiety within sport situations. Initial studies to be reviewed in the section on anxiety and performance indicate that cognitive and somatic anxiety may be differentially related to performance in various sport settings. The current availability of both trait and state measures of cognitive and somatic sport anxiety may facilitate advances in our understand-ing of the antecedents, dynamics, and consequences of sport anxiety and its subcomponents.

DETERMINANTS OF SPORT PERFORMANCE ANXIETY

Athletes at all competitive levels must learn to cope with the demands and pressures of competition if they are to enjoy and succeed at sports. To gain a better understanding of the determinants of competitive anxiety, researchers have focused on stress in children's athletics. Approximately 20 million of the 45 million youngsters in the 6–18 year age range participate in nonschool sports (Martens, 1988). For many child athletes, sport is an important achievement arena where their ability is publicly tested, scrutinized, and evaluated. With social evaluation lying at the heart of the competition process, youth sport participation has the potential to provoke anxiety for some children in certain circumstances (Scanlan, 1986, 1988). Because of this, a substantial amount of research has been devoted to examining situational and intrapersonal factors associated with anxiety experienced by young athletes prior to, during, and following competitive events.

Most studies of anxiety experienced during youth sport competition have utilized psychophysiological measures of arousal. Most of the field studies in-vestigating pre- and postcompetition anxiety have employed variations of the following methodological paradigm: Individual difference factors (competitive trait anxiety, self-esteem) thought to be predictive of anxiety were assessed several weeks before a competitive event. On the day of competition, charac-teristic pregame thoughts and worries as well as youngsters' perceptions of adults were assessed a few hours before the contest. Ten to 20 minutes prior to the event, young athletes completed measures of personal and team perfor-mance expectancies and either the Spielberger State Anxiety Inventory for Chil-dren (Spielberger, 1973) or the children's version of the CSAI-1. Postevent mea-sures of state anxiety and assessments of the amount of fun experienced during the competition were made immediately after the contest. A smaller number of studies have employed psychophysiological measures to assess arousal during actual competition.

Precompetition Anxiety: Situational Factors

Some research has been conducted to determine whether certain types of sports are more anxiety inducing than others. Griffin (1972) administered the STAI–State to 682 female athletes within 1 hour prior to competition. The athletes were drawn from three age groups (12 to 13, 16 to 17, and 19 years and older) and from four individual sports and four team sports. Although the findings were not presented separately by age group, the results indicated that individual sports elicited higher precompetition state anxiety than team sports. Gymnasts had the highest anxiety scores, followed in rank order by participants in track and field, swimming, tennis, football, volleyball, basketball, and field hockey.

In another study, Simon and Martens (1979) administered the children's form of the CSAI-1 to 468 9- to 14-year-old boys 10 minutes before they competed in one of seven nonschool organized sports: baseball, basketball, football, ice hockey, gymnastics, swimming, and wrestling. Covariance analysis was used to control for between-athletic differences in basal state anxiety measured in a nonevaluative setting. Surprisingly, an overall comparison between contact and noncontact sports (wrestling, football, and hockey versus gymnastics, swimming, baseball, and basketball) revealed no significant differences in precompetition anxiety. However, the findings indicated that participants in individual sports had higher state anxiety prior to competition than athletes in team sports. Wrestling and gymnastics were the two most anxiety-inducing sports; they elicited significantly higher anxiety than football, hockey, and baseball, which were the least stressful activities. Thus, the results of Griffin (1972) and those of Simon and Martens (1979) are consistent in revealing that individual sports, which maximize the social evaluation potential of competition, generally elicit higher levels of precompetition anxiety than team sports.

In addition to the type of sport, the importance of the game or match is another situational factor that has been found to influence precompetition anxiety. Lowe and McGrath (1971) examined the effects of game criticality on the arousal level of 60 boys, 10 to 12 years of age, throughout an entire 18-game season of Little League Baseball. Game criticality was determined by a formula that took into account the ranking of the two teams within the league, the difference in their won–lost percentages, and the number of games remaining in the season. Two physiological measures, pulse rate and respiration rate, indicated that pregame arousal increased under conditions of increased game importance. More recently, support for a relationship between precompetition anxiety and criticality was indicated in a study of junior elite wrestlers, who rated "participating in championship meets" as a major source of stress (Gould, Horn, & Spreeman, 1983b). Similarly, Feltz and Albrecht (1986) found that participating in championship races was a major source of stress among junior elite runners.

The amount of time prior to competition is a third factor that affects precompetition anxiety. Gould, Horn, and Spreeman (1983a) asked junior elite wrestlers to retrospectively rate their typical level of anxiety at various times prior to a major competition (i.e., 1 week, 24 hours, i hour, and 2 minutes). Inspection of the means revealed a linear increase in anxiety across the precompetition time intervals, with anxiety increasing as the time of competition approached. Further research with 63 female high school volleyball players expanded these findings in two important ways (Gould, Petlichkoff, & Weinberg, 1984). First, actual state anxiety was measured on five different occasions (1 week, 48 hours, 2 hours, and 20 minutes) prior to a major tournament. Second, cognitive and somatic anxiety components and confidence were assessed separately by the CSAI-2. The findings revealed that cognitive anxiety and confidence remained very stable throughout the entire week and were higher than somatic anxiety. Somatic anxiety was fairly stable until it rose at the 2-hour mark, and then again at the 20-minute mark. Thus, only the somatic anxiety of young athletes increased as competition approached, a finding consistent with other sport psychology research (Martens et al., in press) as well as research on test anxiety (Morris & Engle, 1981; Morris & Fulmer, 1976; Smith & Morris, 1976).

In summary, situational determinants of precompetition anxiety include the type of sport, the criticality of the contest, and the temporal countdown to competition. Studies have generally shown that individual sports are more anxiety provoking than team sports, more important events are more stressful than less important events, and anxiety increases as the time of competition nears.

Precompetition Anxiety: Intrapersonal Factors

The amount of anxiety experienced in a particular sport setting varies considerably from one young athlete to another. Some children, for example, may feel very anxious before the start of a contest, while others feel relatively calm and relaxed. This has prompted researchers to identify intrapersonal factors that might account for the individual differences. One such factor is competitive trait anxiety. In several laboratory experiments and field studies, children's competitive trait anxiety was assessed by the SCAT a few weeks or months prior to a motor skill contest or an athletic event. The ability of this test to predict state anxiety responses to competition was then examined. The findings consistently indicated that prior to competition, high-competitive trait-anxious boys and girls experienced higher state anxiety than did low-competitive trait-anxious children (Gill & Martens, 1977; Martens & Gill, 1976; Scanlan & Lewthwaite, 1984; Scanlan & Passer, 1978, 1979).

Self-esteem is another personality factor that influences children's precompetition anxiety to some extent. In their studies of male and female youth soccer players, Scanlan and Passer (1978, 1979) found that self-esteem was a significant but weak predictor of pregame anxiety, accounting for only about 2% of the variance. In a field study conducted with 9- to 14-year-old wrestlers, self-esteem was moderately correlated with prematch anxiety ($r = -.39$), but was not a significant predictor (Scanlan & Lewthwaite, 1984).

Precompetition anxiety is also related to several intrapersonal factors that do not represent personality dispositions. Research with team (soccer) and individual (wrestling) sports has revealed an interesting pattern of results concerning the role of performance expectancies. Scanlan and Passer (1978, 1979) reported that boys and girls with lower expectancies for their team to be victorious experienced greater precompetition anxiety than children with higher team expectancies. With respect to individual performance expectancies, boys with lower expectancies to personally play well in a soccer game or to win a wrestling match experienced greater precompetition anxiety than boys with higher personal performance expectancies (Scanlan & Lewthwaite, 1984; Scanlan & Passer, 1978). This result was not found for female soccer players (Scanlan & Passer, 1979) and did not account for much of the anxiety variance for male soccer players. Overall, the results indicated that team expectancies were more important predictors of anxiety in team sports than personal performance expectancies. However, in individual sports, personal performance expectancies were strong predictors of precompetition anxiety.

Finally, Scanlan and Lewthwaite's (1984) study of male junior wrestlers revealed that certain prematch worries and perceptions of significant adults were associated with unidimensional precompetition anxiety as measured by the CSAI-1. Specifically, (1) boys who worried more frequently about failure experienced greater general state anxiety than boys who were less preoccupied with performing poorly and making mistakes, (2) boys who worried more frequently about the performance expectations and evaluations of their parents and coach tended to experience greater anxiety than boys who worried less frequently, and (3) boys who felt greater parental pressure to compete (i.e., having to wrestle in order to please one's parents) exhibited higher anxiety than boys who perceived less pressure from their parents to participate. The relationship between worries and CSAI-1 state anxiety found in this study may reflect the common variance shared by cognitive and somatic anxiety.

It might also be noted that children's precompetition state anxiety appears to be unrelated to several intrapersonal factors, namely, gender, age, and amount of sport experience. In comparing the results of their boys' and girls' soccer studies, Scanlan and Passer (1978, 1979) found that the state anxiety responses of the two sexes were remarkably similar before competition. Laboratory experiments also revealed that gender was unrelated to children's precompetition state anxiety (Gill & Martens, 1977; Martens & Gill, 1976). With respect to age and amount of sport experience, Gould et al. (1983a) asked junior elite wrestlers how anxious they usually became prior to competition. No significant differences were found in the ratings of younger (13- to 16-year-old) versus older (17- to 19-year-old) wrestlers, nor in the ratings of less experienced (1 to 5 years) versus more experienced (5 years or greater) wrestlers. Similarly, state anxiety measurements (CSAI-2) of female high school volleyball players taken at various times prior to competition revealed no differences in cognitive or somatic anxiety between experienced and inexperienced players (Gould et al., 1984).

In summary, a wide variety of intrapersonal factors are related to heightened precompetition state anxiety responses in young athletes. High-competitive trait-anxious athletes experience higher levels of precompetitive state anxiety than low trait-anxious participants. Similarly, low self-esteem children experience more competitive anxiety than do high self-esteem children. Finally, young athletes who experience high levels of state anxiety are characterized by low team and individual performance expectancies, they tend to worry more about failure, adult expectations and social evaluation, and they perceive more parental pressure to participate.

Anxiety during Competition

As we have seen, several situational factors are related to how much anxiety children experience prior to competing. Other investigations have examined how young athletes' anxiety during competition is affected by specific situational factors that accompany or occur within a particular contest. Lowe and McGrath's (1971) study of Little Leaguers also examined the effects of game and situation criticality on arousal during competition. As previously described, game criticality represented the importance of the game itself and was a function of the ranking of the two teams within the league, the difference in their won–lost percentages, and the remaining number of games in the season. Situation criticality reflected the importance of the immediate situation within the game and took into account the difference in score between the two teams, the inning of play, the number of outs, and the number and location of any baserunners. In addition to recording pregame pulse and respiration rates, the investigators took these physiological measures each time a player was in the dugout, waiting to go to the on-deck circle (i.e., the player who was two turns from coming to bat). As predicted, players showed greater arousal as the criticality of the game increased (e.g., when opposing teams were closer in ranking, as fewer games remained in the season) and as the criticality of the situation within the game increased (e.g., when players were on base, when the score was close). Overall, game criticality seemed to have a greater effect on players' arousal than did situation criticality, which led Lowe and McGrath to suggest that the importance of the total situation (i.e., the game) may be a greater determinant of arousal than specific events within the situation.

Another study examined arousal during competition as a function of the specific activity or role being performed within a sport. Hanson (1967) used telemetry to monitor the heart rates of 10 male Little League Baseball players. Recordings were taken when the player was at bat, standing on base after a hit, sitting in the dugout after making an out, standing in the field, and sitting at rest before and after the game. The most striking finding was the magnitude of response shown when players came to bat. When at bat, players' heart rates escalated dramatically to an average of 166 beats per minute (bpm), 56 bpm above their mean pregame resting rate of 110 bpm. In fact, no other game situation caused arousal increases that even closely approximated the levels experienced when batting. Substantial variation was found within and between players. The highest heart rate recorded while at bat was 204 bpm; the lowest was 145 bpm. Interestingly, after the game most players reported that they did not feel particularly nervous while batting. Based on players' physiological responses, Hanson concluded that the stress of being at bat was high, but short lived.

The studies by Hanson (1967) and Lowe and McGrath (1971) provided information about players' physiological reactions to various game conditions. Several laboratory experiments, however, have used self-report measures to assess children's anxiety during competition. For example, Martens and Gill (1976) and Gill and Martens (1977) had children compete at a motor skills task over a series of trials, with the won–lost outcome of each trial controlled by the experimenters. State anxiety was measured during midcompetition by Spielberger's (1973) State Anxiety Inventory for Children. The findings indicated that children who lost the early trials became more anxious than children who found themselves ahead.

A final factor affecting anxiety during competition merits attention, namely, competitive trait anxiety. Studies reviewed earlier indicated that prior to competition, high-competitive trait-anxious children experience greater state anxiety than low-competitive trait-anxious children. During competition, a similar but slightly weaker relationship has been obtained as ongoing success–failure outcomes begin to influence youngsters' anxiety (Gill & Martens, 1977; Martens & Gill, 1976).

In summary, the following situational factors affect anxiety during competition: the criticality of the contest, the importance of the situation within the contest, the specific task or activity in which the athlete is engaged, and whether the athlete is ahead of or behind the opposition. Furthermore, competitive trait anxiety is an important intrapersonal factor that helps predict midcompetition state anxiety.

Postcompetition Anxiety

Two major predictors of postcompetition anxiety have been identified. These are (1) the situational factor of victory versus defeat, and its various gradations, and (2) the individual difference variable involving the amount of fun children report having had during the event. The effects of success–failure outcomes on competitive anxiety were examined in Scanlan and Passer's (1978, 1979) youth soccer studies. In the first study 191 boys, 11 and 12 years of age, were administered Spielberger's (1973) State Anxiety Inventory for Children 30 minutes before and immediately after games. A preseason baseline measure also was taken as a control factor. The second study involved 176 10- to 12-year-old girls and employed the same procedure. The findings from the two studies were virtually identical, with losing players having substantially higher postgame anxiety than winning players. Game outcome accounted for 40% of the variance in boys' and 55% of the variance in girls' postgame anxiety. Furthermore, a direct comparison of players' pre- and postgame scores indicated that losers were more anxious after the game than before the game, whereas winners' anxiety decreased.

A third field study, conducted with 9- to 14-year-old male wrestlers, included an examination of whether won–lost findings generated in the team sport context generalized to the individual sport setting. Scanlan and Lewthwaite (1984) administered the children's form of the CSAI-1 to 76 junior wrestlers prior to and after two consecutive tournament rounds. Pretournament baseline anxiety was also recorded as a control factor. For both rounds losers experienced greater postgame state anxiety than winners.

In their study of male players, Scanlan and Passer (1978) also examined the relationship between game closeness and postcompetition anxiety. Based on the pattern of scoring and the final margin of victory or defeat, games were classified as being very close, close, and not close. The closeness of the game did not influence the postgame anxiety of winners, suggesting that a victory by an margin was sufficient to minimize anxiety. Game closeness, however, did affect losers' anxiety. Players who lost a very close game had higher postgame anxiety than players who lost either a moderately close game or a game that was not close. The latter two groups did not differ in postcompetition anxiety.

Because several games in Scanlan and Passer's studies happened to end in a tie, this allowed them to examine the effects of a tied outcome on players' anxiety. Data from three games in the girls' study indicated that players experienced a significant increase in pre- to postgame state anxiety after tie matches, and they had greater postcompetition anxiety than winners, but less than losers (Scanlan & Passer, 1978). The results from one tie game in the boys' study revealed that under some circumstances, a tie can be just as anxiety inducing as a loss (e.g., playing a bitter rival and relinquishing the lead within the final minute of play; Passer & Scanlan, 1980). Overall, the findings from both studies suggested that a tie is perceived as an aversive outcome, not a neutral one.

The amount of fun experienced while competing has been found to be a strong and consistent predictor of postcompetition anxiety for both genders across diverse sport contexts. Boys and girls who report having less fun during a game or match experience greater postcompetition anxiety than children who report having more fun (Scanlan & Passer, 1978, 1979; Scanlan & Lewthwaite, 1984). Moreover, and perhaps most importantly, the inverse relationship between fun and anxiety is independent of victory or defeat. In other words, it is not simply the case that winners have more fun than losers. This suggests that even among losing athletes, anxiety might be reduced by making the process of competition as enjoyable as possible.

In summary, several field studies have demonstrated that won–lost outcomes influence postcompetition anxiety in team and individual sports, and across both sexes. Furthermore, regardless of outcome, postgame anxiety is related to children's perceptions of how much fun they had.

Interactional Assessment of Anxiety Elicitors

It is now generally accepted that behavior is a joint function of what individuals bring with them to situations and the nature of the situation. This interactional perspective received major impetus from the research of Endler and Hunt (1966) on person-by-situation interactions in anxiety responses. Their S–R Inventory of Anxiousness contained 11 potentially anxiety-arousing situations and 14 modes of response (e.g., "feel anxious," "heart beats faster"). Each mode of response was paired with each of the 11 situations in a 14×11 matrix to generate 154 items, each of which was rated on a 5-point scale as to its occurrence. The responses of several large samples indicated that the majority of variance accounted for was explained by person $\times$ situation, person $\times$ response mode, and situations $\times$ response mode interactions.

Fisher and Zwart (1982) applied the S–R inventory methodology to the study of athletic anxiety among basketball players. Athletes rated the extent to which they experienced various types of anxiety responses in a variety of pregame, game, and postgame situations. It was assumed that the S–R data are a function of the specific demands they perceive in each situation and their cognitive and emotional makeup. A multidimensional scaling technique (INDSCAL) was applied to the matrix of responses in order to identify the anxiety dimensions underlying the athlete's ratings. Three factors were revealed by the analysis. The first and most important was ego threat resulting from inadequate performance. The other two factors related to outcome uncertainty and expectation of losing. This novel approach to the S–R data not only identified relevant situational elicitors of anxiety, but it also revealed the relative importance of each dimension for each athlete. Fisher and Zwart's approach appears to have great promise for exploring relationships among appraisals and reactions to anxiety-arousing situations in sport.

Consequences of Performance Anxiety

Anxiety and Performance

The manner in which emotional arousal affects performance is one of the classical issues in sport psychology. This question lies at the heart of every motivational theory that addresses sport performance, and it has received a great deal of theoretical and empirical attention over the years because of its practical implications.

One approach to assessing the stress–performance relationship involves asking athletes how they feel their performance typically is affected by anxiety. Pierce (1980) found that 31% of a sample of youth sport participants and 50% of sport dropouts reported that various worries prevented them playing up to their capabilities. On the other hand, 39% of a sample of elite wrestlers (Gould, Horn, & Spreeman, 1983a) and 50% of junior elite runners (Feltz & Albrecht, 1986) reported that anxiety and nervousness helped their performance. Thus, it appears that some athletes feel that anxiety usually hurts their performance, whereas others believe that they perform better when they are anxious. Much research and theorizing has been directed at resolving these seemingly contradictory reports.

Two theoretical frameworks have served as the major bases for predictions concerning the effects of arousal on performance. Hull–Spence drive theory (Spence & Spence, 1966) guided much of the early research on arousal and motor behavior. As we shall see, informal observation, intuition, and research results have increasingly favored an even older formulation, the Yerkes–Dodson Law (Yerkes & Dodson, 1908).

Drive Theory

Although the learning theory developed by Hull (1943) is a complex one having many theoretical constructs, the most important for our present purposes are reaction potential, drive, and habit strength. *Reaction potential* (sER) is the statistical probability that a particular response or set of responses will occur. *Drive* (D) was defined by Hull as a global, nonspecific energizer of behavior that resulted from presently salient motivational states within the organism. *Habit strength* (sHR), based on the frequency of past reinforcement of a response in the presence of particular environmental stimuli, was a third important factor. Within any situation, the organism's repertoire of learned and unlearned (reflexive) responses were assumed to be ranked hierarchically in terms of likelihood of occurrence. The key postulate of Hull's formulation was that reaction potential is a multiplicative function of drive and habit strength, or sER = f(sHR × D).

The appeal of drive theory was the fact that it generated specific and presumably testable predictions concerning the effects of individual differences and increases in drive based on knowledge of the individual's response hierarchy. That is, the multiplicative relationship predicts that in situations in which the correct or desired response is the dominant response in the hierarchy, increases in drive should result in enhanced performance. However, in situations where incorrect responses are high in the hierarchy (as in the early stages of learning a complex task), an increment in drive will result in poorer performance.

Drive theory was a dominant motivational theory in the 1950s, and many experiments were conducted to test the basic function posited by it. In research with humans, the Manifest Anxiety Scale (MAS; Taylor, 1953) was employed in many studies as an operational definition of chronic drive level. Perhaps the most impressive support for the theory occurred in paired-associates learning studies in which it was possible to infer on an *a priori* basis whether the correct response was dominant in the hierarchy by using lists of paired associates, such as "bacon–egg" (termed "noncompetitive"), or "competitive" lists in which the dominant response was incorrect as a result of previous learning and competed with the correct response (e.g., 2 × 4 =. . . .11). In several of these studies, high-MAS subjects performed significantly better than lows on noncompetitive lists, but more poorly on competitive lists, as the theory predicts (Spence & Spence, 1966).

Extrapolation of Hull–Spence principles to motor tasks would appear to be fairly straightforward. The key factor would be the extent to which the desired response is likely to be dominant in the subject's response hierarchy. Thus, Oxendine (1970) suggested that on relatively simple motor tasks involving strength or speed, increased arousal should facilitate performance in a linear fashion. Conversely, high levels of arousal would be expected to impair performance on tasks involving complex skills, fine motor control, steadiness, and high concentration. Deleterious effects would be especially evident early in the learning process, when many competing reaction tendencies were present.

Aside from general formulations like Oxendine's, drive theory has received few direct tests in the sport psychology literature, primarily because of the difficulties in specifying habit hierarchies. In one attempt to define habit strength, Hunt and Hillary (1973) used motor mazes with known floor and ceiling effects so that probability of a correct response could be specified. They found that arousal resulting from the presence of an evaluative audience facilitated performance on simple mazes but resulted in performance decrements on complex mazes. Using the same tasks with a variety of physical and psychological stressors, Landers, Brawley, and Hale (1978) found similarly supportive results. Despite these positive results, however, evidence supporting drive theory has been inconsistent in the motor behavior literature (see Martens, 1971, for a review). Although drive theory cannot be faulted in instances in which task characteristics were not carefully controlled or assessed, the difficulties in specifying habit hierarchies render it difficult to generate unequivocal tests of the theory. But perhaps the most important reason why tests of drive theory are no longer occurring in the sport or motor behavior literature is that the Hull–Spence formulation has quietly faded from the scene, supplanted by other models that emphasize more explicit cognitive, attentional, and motor control concepts.

The Yerkes–Dodson Law

The Yerkes–Dodson Law, originally advanced in 1908, has two main postulates:

1. There exists an optimal level of arousal for performance of any given task. Levels of arousal above and below this optimal level will be associated with relatively lower performance.
2. The more complex the task is, the lower will be the optimal level of arousal for its performance.

The first postulate yields the familiar "inverted-U" function between motivation and performance. The second indicates that task variables collectively subsumed under the rubric of "complexity" must be taken into account. While the latter is consistent with the important role of habit strength in the Hull–Spence model, the postulating of a curvilinear relationship rather than a linear one is not. (It is worth noting, however, that there may exist very simple and overlearned tasks, such as running or lifting, for which it would be difficult to have too high a level of arousal, in which case a linear relationship would also be predicted by the Yerkes–Dodson Law.)

One of the reasons for the intuitive appeal of the Yerkes–Dodson Law is that its first postulate conforms to the common observation that athletes can be "too flat" or, on the other hand, "too psyched up" to perform optimally. This is a common concern of both athletes and coaches. Moreover, as we shall see, there is considerable empirical support for a curvilinear relationship between anxiety and performance on motor tasks. Indeed, Yerkes and Dodson (1908) derived their law from the results of studies with mice in which both arousal (produced by oxygen deprivation) and task difficulty in negotiating underwater mazes were controlled experimentally.

Sport Anxiety Studies

Both the Hull–Spence and the Yerkes–Dodson formulations relate performance to the general concept of arousal under the assumption that arousal states resulting from various motivational and emotional states are functionally equivalent. This assumption has been challenged by models that differentiate among motivational states in terms of the extent to which they generate approach versus avoidance cognitions and response tendencies (e.g., Atkinson & Feather, 1966), or task-relevant versus task-irrelevant responses (Mandler & Sarason, 1952). Physiological arousal produced by engaging an approach motive like achievement motivation may be accompanied by entirely different cognitive and attentional responses than arousal produced by an avoidance motive like anxiety. Research on test anxiety (a fear-of-failure motive like sport anxiety) suggests that anxiety-generated cognitions tend to be self-oriented (rather than task oriented) and disruptive of problem-solving and attentional processes (see Sarason, Chapter 15, this volume). Our present concern is, therefore, with the effects of anxiety that are relevant to the sport environment, rather than with arousal in general.

Two research designs have been employed in research on the sport anxiety–performance relationship. The majority of studies have used between-subjects designs in which the performances of subjects differing in either trait or state anxiety have been compared. A smaller number of studies have utilized within-subjects designs in which both anxiety and performance are assessed under different conditions. It should be noted that a valid test of the inverted-U hypothesis requires that at least three points on the arousal continuum be assessed, regardless of the nature of the research design. Likewise, at least two levels of task complexity are required to assess anxiety × task complexity interactions.

Between-Subjects Designs. A classic series of studies involving self-report, projective test, and physiological indices of anxiety was performed with sport parachutists by Walter Fenz and his colleagues (Fenz, 1975; Fenz & Epstein, 1967; Fenz & Jones, 1972). Measures of respiration and heart rate were obtained periodically from the time the skydivers arrived at the airport until they were about to jump. Performance ratings were obtained from instructors. High levels of performance were associated with a pattern of increasing physiological arousal as the jump approached, but a lowering of arousal to moderate levels just before the jump. With experience, competent parachutists exhibited their "inverted-U" pattern of arousal increasingly earlier in the jump preparatory stage. Poor performers, on the other hand, continued to exhibit high levels of arousal. These findings suggest that on this task, high levels of anxiety at the point of performance negatively relate to performance, whereas moderate levels are associated with competent performance.

In another field study, Weinberg and Genuchi (1980) assessed the relationship between trait and state anxiety and the performance of collegiate golfers. Trait anxiety was assessed with the SCAT. The athletes completed the STAI–

State scale just prior to competition on three different days of a tournament. The golfers were divided into low, moderate, and high trait anxiety groups on the basis of their SCAT scores. Although the three groups of golfers were similar in ability, their performance differed sharply during the anxiety-arousing tournament rounds. The low trait-anxious golfers (who also had the lowest state scores) performed best, and the high-SCAT athletes (who had the highest state anxiety scores) most poorly. On the first day of competition, the average performance of the low-anxiety group was five strokes better than that of the high-SCAT group. On the last day of the tournament, the difference between the groups increased to nearly seven strokes. The moderate-SCAT group had intermediate scores. The investigators reasoned that since golf is a precision sport requiring fine muscle coordination and great concentration, the optimal level of arousal for its performance would be quite low, and their results are consistent with that expectation.

To test the inverted-U hypothesis, Martens and Landers (1970) subjected high, moderate, and low STAI–Trait-anxious junior high school boys to a motor tracking task under three levels of induced stress created by ego-involving conditions and threat of electric shock. A manipulation check indicated that the high-, moderate-, and low-stress conditions were successfully established. Martens and Landers found that the subjects in the moderate stress condition performed best, supporting the curvilinear hypothesis. They also found that moderate STAI–Trait subjects outperformed the high and low trait-anxious groups, which also is consistent with the inverted-U hypothesis. However, both high and low trait-anxious subjects performed best at the moderate situational stress level, suggesting that the experimental manipulation did not differentially affect the two groups. This finding is consistent with earlier findings suggesting that threat of shock does not produce differential state anxiety in high- and low-STAI–Trait subjects.

In a follow-up study in which negative evaluation and ego involvement were used to create three levels of situational stress, Weinberg and Ragan (1978) found an interaction between trait and state anxiety on a motor task. High trait-anxious subjects performed best under low-stress conditions, whereas low trait-anxious subjects performed best under high stress. State-anxiety measures indicated that the experimental manipulation had interacted with the subjects' trait anxiety to produce a moderate level of state anxiety. This study's results clearly support an optimal moderate level of anxiety interpretation.

Several investigators have assessed the relationship between performance anxiety and quality of performance in musicians (Leglar, 1979; Steptoe, 1983). In both studies, an inverted-U function was found, with moderate levels of musical performance anxiety being associated with superior performance.

Despite the findings described thus far, between-subjects designs have frequently yielded inconsistent and negative results. For example, Nideffer and York (1978) found that high physiological arousal assumed to reflect anxiety was associated with a decrement in performance in swimmers performing an overlearned speed swim, a result that is consistent with neither drive theory nor the inverted-U proposition. Both models predict a positive relationship between anxiety and performance on this "simple," "all-out-effort" task unless anxiety were at a virtual panic level (which was clearly not the case).

Sonstroem and Bernardo (1982) related pregame STAI–State scores obtained by 30 female college basketball players to their performance across three games of a tournament. They found no relationship between groups of subjects differing in state-anxiety scores. However, as we discuss below, an intrasubject analysis yielded far different results.

Development of the CSAI-2 has stimulated several studies which have assessed relationships between cognitive and somatic state anxiety and performance. McAuley (1985) found no relationship between subscale or total scores and gold performance over ten 18-hold tournament rounds. In a series of studies by Gould and his associates, significant relationships were found between CSAI-2 cognitive and somatic anxiety scores and wrestling performance in some matches, but not in others (Gould *et al.*, 1984). Inconsistent results like these have prompted investigators to consider intrasubject designs in studies assessing the notion of an optimal level of anxiety.

Within-Subjects Designs. In the between-subjects studies described above, optimal anxiety levels were assessed in a normative fashion (i.e., in terms of the anxiety distribution produced by all subjects). However, it is possible that the optimal level of arousal is itself an individual difference variable, and that optimal arousal may be specific to each subject.

One of the first studies to support this suggestion was reported by Klavora (1978). High school basketball players on 14 teams completed the STAI Trait and State measures. The state measures were completed just prior to participation in 8–14 games, permitting an analysis of anxiety–performance relationships across contests. Performance ratings by coaches served as the dependent variable. The intrasubject analyses indicated that both high and low trait-anxious athletes displayed inverted-U relationships between anxiety and performance. However, the truly notable result was that for low trait-anxious players, the optimal level of anxiety was on the low end of the continuum, whereas the optimal level was toward the high end of the state anxiety continuum for the high trait-anxious players. Klavora's results suggested the possibility that optimal performance may occur at a level of arousal that is similar to athletes' customary level of anxiety rather than at a normative level defined by the anxiety distribution for all subjects.

Sonstroem and Bernardo's (1982) data lend further support to this notion of an individualized optimal anxiety level. As noted above, Sonstroem and Bernardo found no relationship between absolute state anxiety levels and women's basketball performance. However, intrasubject analyses of state anxiety and performance scores across games disclosed that low-, moderate-, and high-anxiety athletes all displayed inverted-U functions, with the highest level of performance falling at the moderate (median) level as defined by their own scores. Thus, like Klavora's results, this pattern indicates that individuals may have their own personal optimal levels of arousal, a possibility that would have definite implications for performance enhancement strategies.

A recent study by Gould, Petlichkoff, Simons, and Vevera (1987) was the first to use the multidimensional CSAI-2 within an intrasubject design to assess the relationships between cognitive and somatic anxiety, self-confidence, and performance. The subjects were 39 police trainees who performed on five different occasions under conditions that were designed to vary in the amount of evaluation apprehension they elicited. The goal was to create at least the three levels of state anxiety needed to assess a possible curvilinear relationship between anxiety and performance. An advantage of the task was that it was constant from session to session and was constant for all subjects. Each subject's anxiety scores were converted to intrasubject standard scores to take into consideration individual differences in absolute state anxiety scores.

Contrary to expectations, no relationship was found between cognitive anxiety and performance. However, a significant curvilinear (inverted-U) relationship was found between somatic state anxiety and performance. This may be attributed to the fact that the shooting task requires fine motor control that could easily be interfered with by high somatic anxiety. On the other hand, little is required in the way of cognitive processing. An unexpected finding was that self-confidence exhibited a significant negative relationship with marksmanship.

A more recent study by Burton (1988) assessed the relationships between the CSAI-2 subscales and swimming performance in two samples of college and elite swimmers. The first sample completed the anxiety measure shortly before competing in three meets. This design fulfilled the minimal conditions required to assess curvilinearity. In the sample of 28 collegiate swimmers, CSAI-2 scores accounted for 18%, 25%, and 57% of the variance in performance at the three meets, respectively. Using the intrasubject analytic method introduced by Sonstroem and Bernardo (1982), Burton found that somatic anxiety was related to swimming performance in a curvilinear relationship, with the athletes' own moderate level of anxiety across the three meets being associated with their best performance. In contrast, cognitive anxiety was negatively related to performance, and self-confidence was positively related—both relationships being linear in nature. On the basis of regression analyses in which somatic anxiety, cognitive anxiety, and self-confidence scores were used as predictor variables for performance in a variety of different swimming events (e.g., breaststroke, freestyle), Burton concluded that cognitive anxiety bore a more consistent relationship to performance than did somatic anxiety, since ti generally accounted for far more variance in the regression equations.

A major objective of those investigators who have used the CSAI-2 to this point was to test theoretical propositions concerning the effects of somatic and cognitive anxiety on performance. They have explicitly assumed that the CSAI-2 taps independent dimensions of anxiety, since factor analyses using orthogonal rotations have revealed the existence of these independent factors. However, all of the investigators have used raw scores summed over the items that load on each factor, rather than factor scores. Data presented by Martens et al. (in press) indicate that, far from being statistically independent, subscale scores based on unit scores actually correlate substantially (.50 to .60) with one another. A clearer answer to theoretical questions concerning the correlates of somatic and cognitive anxiety would be forthcoming if factor scores were used instead of summed raw scores. The substantial variance shared by the three subscales of the CSAI-2 dictates that in a standard multiple regression analysis, the first variable that enters the regression equation is going to account for a major portion of the variance and may possibly mask the contribution of other variables. For example, in Burton's (1988) study, zero-order correlations of −.68 and −.61 were found between performance and cognitive anxiety and somatic anxiety, respectively, for one of the meets. When a regression analysis was performed, cognitive anxiety entered the equation first and accounted for 46% of the variance. The addition of somatic anxiety resulted in an increment of only 8% in variance accounted for, a result which could result in an inappropriate conclusion that cognitive anxiety was a far more potent predictor of performance than was somatic anxiety. (If, on the other hand, somatic anxiety were forced into the equation first, the opposite conclusion would result.) This, again, argues for the use of large samples and the derivation of statistically independent CSAI-2 factor scores in instances where the basic theoretical issue concerning the independent contributions of cognitive and somatic anxiety to performance is being addressed.

Task Characteristics. In the foregoing discussion, we have often speculated in a post hoc fashion about task characteristics. We have described tasks as simple or complex, as requiring motor rather than attentional precision, and so on. We also saw that the inability to measure task characteristics and relate them to habit hierarchies has, with the exception of a few laboratory tasks, impeded the testing of drive theory. It seems safe to conclude that at the present time, we can probably measure anxiety with greater precision than we can task characteristics. Clearly, progress in the latter area is needed if we are to advance our understanding of anxiety–performance relationships.

Landers and Boutcher (1986) have attempted to quantify task complexity and to specify optimal state anxiety levels for their performance. Drawing upon Billing's (1980) analysis of task complexity as involving decisional, perceptual, and motoric dimensions, Landers and Boutcher have developed scales for estimating these components on an *a priori* basis. For example, tasks differ in their decision requirements in terms of the number of decisions and alternatives in question, speed of decision required, and the sequence of the decisions. Perceptual demands are dictated by the number, duration, and intensity of stimuli present, the clarity of relevant and irrelevant stimuli, and so on. Motoric characteristics include the number and fineness of motor acts required, the amount of coordination needed, and the like. Using these scales to define task complexity, Landers and Boutcher have scaled athletic tasks along this multivariate complexity dimension and deduced a range of STAI–State and CSAI-1 scores that would likely be related to optimal performance. For example, very high scores would optimize performance on tasks like football blocking and sprinting, whereas low scores would facilitate performance on complex tasks like archery, golf, and field-goal kicking in football.

Utilizing this schema for defining task complexity, Ebbeck and Weiss (1988) attempted to assess the relationship between CSAI-1 scores and performance in a range of track-and-field events believed to differ in complexity. High school athletes competing in the javelin throw, the mile run, and the 400-m, 800-m, and 1600-m events completed the CSAI-1 prior to competing. Performance measures included postevent athlete and coach ratings as well as objective indices such as running times and javelin distance.

Relationships between the various performance measures were disappointingly low. Moreover, the track coaches who rated the events on the complexity scales gave all of the events similar complexity ratings. Finally, no evidence was found for an optimal level of state anxiety for any of the track-and-field events. Perhaps this is not surprising in light of previously discussed evidence for individualized as opposed to normative optimal anxiety levels. Individual differences in optimal arousal level would not show up in this kind of between-subjects design. Indeed, the assumption that one can specify optimal anxiety levels on an *a priori* basis may not be tenable if individualized optimal levels exist. The strongest test of the viability of the Landers and Boutcher task complexity scales may come from repeated-measures designs in which subjects perform tasks that differ on the various complexity dimensions. Finally, the fact that the first two dimensions (decisional and perceptual) would likely be most sensitive to the effects of cognitive anxiety, while the motoric dimension would seem to be most sensitive to variations in somatic anxiety invites the use of multidimensional trait and state scales such as the Sport Anxiety Scale and the CSAI-2 in future research.

Mechanisms Influencing Anxiety Effects on Performance

The fact that relationships have been found between anxiety and sport performance has prompted much speculation, theorizing, and research on the mechanisms that mediate the relationships. The inconsistency and sometimes conflicting nature of obtained results has stimulated attempts to identify mechanisms in the hope of reconciling the findings. Given the multidimensional nature of sport anxiety, it is not surprising that attention has focused on both cognitive and somatic mechanisms.

Information-Processing Effects. When performing an athletic behavior, the athlete must attend to, encode, process, and respond to both external and internal stimuli. Aspects of the anxiety response that affect information-processing capabilities could surely affect performance. Major advances in understanding the effects of anxiety in other evaluative situations have been made through the analysis of cognitive mechanisms (Sarason, Chapter 15, this volume; Wine, 1980).

A commonly reported consequence of emotional arousal is narrowing of attention. Research employing a dual-task paradigm has shown that increases in arousal can cause individuals to narrow their attentional focus to central cues while reducing their attention to peripheral cues (Landers, 1980). Recent sport psychology research has provided evidence for perceptual narrowing in rifle marksmen under conditions of increasing stress (Landers, Wang, & Courtet, 1985).

Perhaps the most widely cited explanation for the relationship between arousal and attentional deployment is Easterbrook's (1959) cue utilization hypothesis, as it would appear to account for the inverted-U function frequently found between anxiety and performance. Easterbrook suggests that a person operating under low arousal has a broad perceptual range. Therefore, through low selectivity or effort, task-irrelevant cues may be processed in an uncritical manner, which can result in low performance. As arousal increases to an optimal level, perceptual sensitivity and cue discrimination increase, and performance increases as a result of optimal attention to task-relevant cues. Further increases in arousal result in maladaptive perceptual narrowing in which task-relevant cues are no longer processed effectively, and performance deteriorates as a result. For example, one college football quarterback complained of a kind of "tunnel vision" under high arousal in which he could no longer pick out alternative pass receivers. He likened it to "looking through a toilet paper roll of toilet paper."

The cue utilization hypothesis is consistent with the inverted-U postulate of the Yerkes–Dodson Law. Easterbrook also suggested that the lower optimal level of arousal on complex as opposed to simple tasks could be accounted for in terms of task-related attentional demands. It seems reasonable to assume that the range of task-relevant cues is narrower for simple than for complex tasks. Thus, with more task-relevant cues to process as task complexity increases, the likelihood is higher that elevated arousal levels will lead to a performance decrement on a complex task as a result of failure to process and respond to task-relevant information.

Aside from its attentional disruption effects (as indicated on the Concentration Disruption subscale of the Sport Anxiety Scale), cognitive components of anxiety include worry and other self-oriented thinking that can directly interfere with thinking and decision making (Wine, 1980).

Somatic Mechanisms. The somatic component of the anxiety response also can affect motor output. Increased physiological arousal can include muscle tension that is capable of disrupting motor activity by affecting muscle and joint function (Beuter & Duda, 1985; Benter, Duda, & Widule, 1989). The more complex or precise the motoric demands of the athletic task, the more easily performance could be adversely affected by somatic anxiety responses.

Weinberg and Hunt (1976) studied the patterning of neuromuscular activity during task performance as a function of STAI–Trait anxiety and situational stress. Quality of movement was assessed by means of electromyograph (EMG) measures of anticipation, duration, perseveration, and amplitude of response in muscle groups involved in performance of a ball-throwing accuracy task. Following failure feedback designed to create stress, the performance of low-anxiety subjects improved, while that of high-STAI–Trait subjects deteriorated. Analysis of EMG results indicated that the high-anxious subjects used significantly more energy before, during, and after the throw than did low-anxious subjects. Moreover, they exhibited cocontraction rather than sequential contraction of the muscles involved in throwing, a highly inefficient muscular pattern. The low-anxious subjects, on the other hand, exhibited sequential muscle patterning and more efficient use of energy. So marked were the EMG differences that 95% of the subjects could be classified correctly as high or low anxious on the basis of their neuromuscular patterning in response to ego threat. It thus appears that by assessing the pattern of movements, researchers might gain increased understanding of the mechanisms underlying anxiety–performance relationships.

One additional point deserves consideration in the study of physiological mechanisms underlying performance. It is quite likely that different physiological systems influence performance on various tasks. Given the abundant evidence for the existence of autonomic response stereotypy (Lacey & Lacey, 1958), a critical factor influencing relationships between somatic anxiety and performance may be the extent to which the individual's physiological arousal pattern includes the system(s) that influence the particular task. For example, an athlete who reacts somatically with cardiovascular and electrodermal changes, but not with increased muscular tension, might not exhibit the neuromuscular patterning described above. In such an athlete, no relationship between somatic anxiety and performance would exist, even though the athlete might have a high score on a multidimensional sport anxiety measure because of responses to items involving the athlete's "hot" response systems.

Other Consequences of Athletic Anxiety

Some young athletes are fortunate in that they develop effective ways of coping with potential sources of stress and anxiety. Others, who are not so fortunate, are prone to suffer adverse psychological, behavioral, and health-related effects. Consideration is now given to these negative consequences of competitive anxiety.

Effects on Participation, Enjoyment, and Withdrawal from Sports

Youngsters are affected by competitive anxiety in many different ways. Because of anticipated stresses, some children actually avoid playing sports. In one study, Orlick and Botterill (1975) reported that 75% of a sample of 8- and 9-year-old sport nonparticipants indicated that they would like to compete, but were fearful of performing poorly or of failing to make a team. In a more recent study of 10- to 17-year-olds, Pierce (1980) found that 26% of agency-sponsored sport participants, 26% of sport dropouts, and 32% of nonparticipants reported that various worries bothered them so much that they might not play in the future.

In addition to influencing the decision about entering a sport program, competitive anxiety can detract from children's enjoyment of sports. Youngsters who play for relatively punitive or critical coaches, perceive more pressure and negative responses from their mothers, feel that their parents and coaches are less satisfied with their overall sport performance, and view themselves as having less skill express less enjoyment from their participation and like their sport less (Scanlan & Lewthwaite, 1986; Smith, Smoll, & Curtis, 1978; Wankel & Kreisel, 1985). Furthermore, young athletes who feel that winning is the most important aspect of sports (and who therefore may place themselves under added competitive anxiety) derive less enjoyment from their participation and are more apt to drop out (Orlick & Botterill, 1975; Roberts, 1986; Robinson & Carron, 1982).

Whether anxiety causes young athletes to withdraw from competition is another important issue. Pooley (1980) found that 33% of 10- to 15-year-old youth soccer dropouts attributed quitting to an overemphasis on competition and negative coaching behaviors (e.g., frequent criticism of players, pushing them too hard). Similarly, a study by Gould, Feltz, Horn, and Weiss (1982) of 10- to 18-year-old former swimmers revealed that over half of the youngsters rated "did not like the pressure" as either a very important (16%) or somewhat important (36%) reason for dropping out, and many rated "did not like the coach" as a very important (20%) or somewhat important (24%) factor. In a study of over 1,000 age-group swimmers, McPherson, Marteniuk, Tihanyi, and Clark (1980) found that too much pressure, conflict with coaches, and insufficient success were among the reasons swimmers reported for why their teammates dropped out of competition. Finally, in a recent study of 8- to 17-year-old wrestlers, a theoretically based comparison of dropouts' versus participants' won –lost records, performance expectancies, attributions, and sport values led Burton and Martens (1986) to conclude that youngsters appeared to drop out when their perceived ability was threatened by consistent failure. Existing evidence thus suggests that competitive stress contributes significantly to the dropout rate in youth sports.

Effects on Physical Well-Being: Illness and Injuries

A growing body of research literature is demonstrating positive, though modest, relationships between high levels of anxiety and the onset of a variety of medical and psychological dysfunction in children (Coddington, 1972; Dohrenwend & Dohrenwend, 1981; Rabkin & Struening, 1976; Rahe & Arthur, 1978). The unfortunate effects of severe competitive pressures are all too frequently seen in clinical reports of young athletes who develop anxiety-related headaches, stomachaches, and dermatological problems (Nash, 1987; Olerud, 1989). A condition known as reflex sympathetic dystrophy is a particularly alarming and extreme example of a physical malady that may be linked with athletic anxiety. This disorder involves an abnormal response of the sympathetic nervous system to an injury like a sprain. An entire arm or leg may swell up, turn blue, and become blotchy, while the muscles of that limb may atrophy and the bone may be reabsorbed. A sports medicine specialist, Lyle J. Micheli, reported treating reflex sympathetic dystrophy in 30 to 40 youngsters per year over a span of 4 or 5 years. He attributes the disorder to the stressful conditions of youth sports, stating that "very few children ever get reflex sympathetic dystrophy, but the ones who do are almost always involved in organized sports training and stressful competition, especially in individualized sports like gymnastics, dance, and figure skating" (Nash, 1987, p. 131).

In addition to the above, some data exist concerning the degree to which involvement in sports disrupts youngsters' eating and sleeping patterns. Skubic's (1956) survey of Little and Middle League Baseball players revealed that 11% of the respondents experienced diminished appetite after losing a game, and 60% reported occasional or frequent sleep disturbance the night before or after competition. A remarkably similar figure was obtained for a sample of junior elite wrestlers; 58% reported having "some" to "a lot" of difficulty sleeping the night before a match because of competitive anxiety (Gould *et al.*, 1983a).

The most definitive data on sleep disruption are provided by the Michigan Youth Sports Study (Universities Study Committee, 1978). This comprehensive survey included a statewide sample of 1,118 male and female youth sport participants. Of these children, 21% indicated that there were times when they did not receive enough sleep because of their involvement in sports. Of the athletes experiencing sleep loss, 46% rated worrying about performance as a contributing factor, and 25% indicated that being upset after losing was a cause. It should be noted, however, that other sources of sleep disruption were not directly related to competitive stress. Moreover, youngsters' sleep was disrupted somewhat less by sports involvement than by other achievement-oriented recreational activities (e.g., music, drama, clubs).

The widely recognized contribution of life stress to the development of physical illness and psychological distress has stimulated research on the possible role of anxiety in athletic injuries. Several studies have examined whether athletes who experience a high degree of "life stress" are at greater risk for athletic injury. May, Veach, Reed, and Griffey (1985) assessed life events, depression, and general well-being (health concerns, energy, life satisfaction, cheerfulness, tension, and emotional control) in 73 members of the U.S. Alpine Ski Team. These psychological factors were compared with subsequent surveys of general health, illness, and athletic performance. Higher scores on the life-change scales were clearly related to greater duration of ear, nose, and throat problems, headaches, musculoskeletal leg injuries, and sleep problems. On the other hand, positive well-being was associated with a shorter duration of ear, nose, and throat problems, headaches, digestive problems, sleep disturbances, and neurological conditions. Overall, the psychological scales predicted (at statistically significant levels) seven of the top ten health and injury problems of the alpine skiers.

Additional evidence derives from research on football injuries. Studies of college football players have shown injury rates of 68–73% in athletes who had recently experienced major life changes, compared with rates of 30–39% in athletes who had not experienced such events (Bramwell, Masuda, Wagner, & Holmes, 1975; Cryan & Alles, 1983). In another study of college football players, Passer and Seese (1983) obtained partial support for a relationship between injury and "object loss" (a subgroup of negative life events involving the actual or threatened loss of a close personal relationship). In the sole study of younger athletes, Coddington and Troxell (1980) found no relationship between overall life stress and injury rates among high school football players. However, athletes who suffered the actual loss of a parent were five times more likely to be injured than teammates who had experienced no object loss. It thus appears that life change, particularly negative events, may be a predisposing factor in youth sport injuries. This important issue warrants further empirical attention.

Future Directions in Sport Performance Anxiety Research

Considerable progress has been made during the past decade in understanding some of the antecedents and consequences of sport anxiety. This progress has been facilitated by the development of sport-specific measures of both trait and state anxiety. The availability of new multidimensional measures such as the SAS and the CSAI-2 will undoubtedly contribute to further advances in understanding the antecedents and consequences of both cognitive and somatic anxiety.

Antecedents of state anxiety have been the focus of many studies, but little is known about the developmental antecedents of sport-specific trait anxiety. Identification of the factors that contribute to the development of this trait (and, specifically, to its cognitive and somatic components) could have important implications for prevention. It seems likely that the pattern of causal factors will parallel that of other fear-of-failure motives, such as test anxiety. That is, we might anticipate a history of punishment or withdrawal of love by significant others (especially parents and coaches) in response to failure.

Given the negative consequences that anxiety can have for athletes, we can expect to see more systematic attempts to reduce or control it. The conceptual model in Figure 1 suggests a number of potential foci for research and intervention. At the situational level, for example, identification of factors that result in unnecessary anxiety (such as punitive approaches by coaches that can promote the development of fear of failure) can provide a focus for intervention. Thus, Smith et al. (1979) have developed an intervention program for youth coaches that is designed to help them to create a positive and enjoyable psychological environment for their athletes. Through didactic instruction, modeling and role playing, and the development of self-monitoring skills, coaches learn behavioral guidelines designed to increase positive control of player behaviors through reinforcement, encouragement, technical instruction, and team-building procedures. Experimental evidence indicates that the program promotes increased enjoyment of the sport experience, greater attraction toward coach and teammates, and increases in general self-esteem. However, the effects of this type of coach training on athletes' trait and state anxiety has not yet been assessed. A companion program has been developed to provide parents of young athletes with parallel guidelines for promoting the development of a positive desire to achieve rather than fear of failure (Smoll, 1984), but the effects of this program on parental behaviors and athletes' motives have not been evaluated experimentally. It seems likely that coming years will witness the development and evaluation of situational interventions designed to reduce anxiety. While some degree of anxiety is endemic to sport competition, there are unnecessary sources of anxiety that invite the attention of sport psychologists.

A major focus of contemporary sport psychology is in the application of psychological interventions designed to enhance performance in athletes. In addition to such procedures as mental rehearsal of skills and the application of goal-setting principles, stress management programs enjoy a wide range of application. Cognitive-behavioral interventions appear to be an effective approach to increasing self-control or performance anxiety in both athletes (e.g., Smith, 1989; Suinn, 1989) and in other performers, such as musicians (Kendrick et al., 1982; Steptoe & Fidler, 1987). Such interventions are typically directed at modifying cognitive appraisal processes through cognitive restructuring, self-instructional training, and other cognitive-change procedures. Coping-skills training for controlling somatic anxiety usually involves the learning of relaxation skills that can be applied prior to and within performance situations, as well as more general relaxation skills such as meditation. While training procedures in cognitive-behavioral anxiety control have been widely employed by sport psychologists for nearly a decade, there is a surprising dearth of controlled outcome research with athletes. Given the fact that the athletic situation is one in which anxiety and its consequences can readily be measured, it is likely that good experimental outcome studies will be forthcoming.

Clearly, an increasing number of psychologists are being attracted to sport as a naturalistic laboratory for the study of a wide range of psychological phenomena and as an ideal setting in which to develop and assess psychological interventions. It seems likely that because of its central role in sport competition, anxiety will continue to be a major focus of attention in the future. There are few naturalistic settings that are better suited to the study of anxiety.

ACKNOWLEDGMENT. Preparation of this chapter was facilitated by Grant 86-1066-86 from the William T. Grant Foundation.

REFERENCES

Apitzsch, E. (Ed.). (1983). *Anxiety in sport.* Magglingen, Switzerland: Guido Schilling, ETS.

Arnold, M. B. (1960). *Emotion and personality.* New York: Columbia University Press.

Atkinson, J. W., & Feather, N. T. (1966). *A theory of achievement motivation.* New York: Wiley.

Berlyne, D. E. (1960). *Conflict, arousal, and curiosity.* New York: McGraw-Hill.

Beuter, A., & Duda, J. L. (1985). Analysis of the arousal/motor performance relationship in children using movement kinematics. *Journal of Sport Psychology, 7,* 229–243.

Beuter, A., Duda, J. L., & Widule, C. J. (1989). The effect of arousal on joint kinematics and kinetics in children. *Research Quarterly for Exercise and Sport, 60,* 109–116.

Billing, J. (1980). An overview of task complexity. *Motor Skills: Theory into Practice, 4,* 18–23.

Borkovec, T. D. (1976). Physiological and cognitive processes in the regulation of anxiety. In G. Schwartz & D. Shapiro (Eds.), *Consciousness and self-regulation: Advances in research* (Vol. 1, pp. 261–312). New York: Plenum.

Bramwell, S. T., Masuda, M., Wagner, N. N., & Holmes, T. H. (1975). Psychosocial factors in athletic injuries: Development and application of the Social and Athletic Readjustment Rating Scale (SARRS). *Journal of Human Stress, 1,* 6–20.

Burton, D. (1988). Do anxious swimmers swim slower? Reexamining the elusive anxiety–performance relationship. *Journal of Sport and Exercise Psychology, 10,* 45–61.

Burton, D., & Martens, R. (1986). Pinned by their own goals: An exploratory investigation into why kids drop out of wrestling. *Journal of Sport Psychology, 8,* 183–195.

Cannon, W. B. (1929). The mechanism of emotional disturbance of bodily functions. *New England Journal of Medicine, 198,* 877–884.

Cattell, R. B. (1957). *The IPAT anxiety scale.* Champaign, IL: Institute for Personality and Ability Testing.

Coddington, R. D. (1972). The significance of life events as etiologic factors in the diseases of children: II. A study of a normal population. *Journal of Psychosomatic Research, 16,* 205–213.

Coddington, R. D., & Troxell, J. R. (1980). The effect of emotional factors on football injury rates: a pilot study. *Journal of Human Stress, 6,* 3–5.

Cooper, L. (1969). Athletics, activity, and personality. *Research Quarterly, 40,* 17–22.

Cryan, P. D., & Alles, W. F. (1983). The relationship between stress and college football injuries. *Journal of Sports Medicine, 23,* 52–58.

Davidson, R. J., & Schwartz, G. E. (1976). The psychobiology of relaxation and related states: A multi-process theory. In D. Mostofsky (Ed.), *Behavioral control and modification of physiological activity* (pp. 399–442). Englewood Cliffs, NJ: Prentice-Hall.

Dohrenwend, B. S., & Dohrenwend, B. P. (1981). Life stress and illness: formulation of the issues. In B. S. Dohrenwend & B. P. Dohrenwend (Eds.), *Stressful life events and their contexts* (pp. 1–27). New York: Prodist.

Duffy, E. (1962). *Activation and behavior.* New York: Wiley.

Easterbrook, J. A. (1959). The effect of emotion on cue utilization and the organization of behavior. *Psychological Review, 66,* 183–201.

Ebbeck, V., & Weiss, M. R. (1988). The arousal–performance relationship: Task characteristics and performance measures in track and field athletics. *The Sport Psychologist, 2,* 13–27.

Ellis, A. (1962a). *Reason and emotion in personality.* New York: Lyle Stuart.

Ellis, A. (1962b). *Reason and emotion in psychotherapy.* New York: Lyle.

Endler, N. S., & Hunt, J. M. (1966). Sources of behavioral variance as measured by the S–R Inventory of Anxiousness. *Psychological Bulletin, 65,* 338–346.

Feltz, D. L., & Albrecht, R. R. (1986). Psychological implications of competitive running. In M. R. Weiss & D. Gould (Eds.), *Sport for children and youths* (pp. 225–230). Champaign, IL: Human Kinetics.

Fenz, W. D. (1975). Strategies for coping with stress. In I. G. Sarason & C. D. Spielberger (Eds.), *Stress and anxiety* (Vol. 2, pp. 305–336). New York: Halsted.

Fenz, W. D. (1988). Learning to anticipate stressful events. *Journal of Sport and Exercise Psychology, 10,* 223–228.

Fenz, W. D., & Epstein, S. (1967). Changes in gradients of skin conductance, heart rate and respiration rate as a function of experience. *Psychosomatic Medicine, 29,* 33–51.

Fenz, W. D., & Jones, C. B. (1972). Individual differences in physiological arousal and performance in sport parachutists. *Psychosomatic Medicine, 34,* 1–8.

Fisher, A. C., & Zwart, E. F. (1982). Psychological analysis of athletes' anxiety responses. *Journal of Sport Psychology, 4,* 139–158.

Gill, D. L., & Martens, R. (1977). The role of task type and success–failure in group competition. *International Journal of Sport Psychology, 8,* 160–177.

Gould, D., Feltz, D., Horn, T., & Weiss, M. (1982). Reasons for discontinuing involvement in competitive youth swimming. *Journal of Sport Behavior, 5,* 155–165.

Gould, D., Horn, T., & Spreeman, J. (1983a). Competitive anxiety in junior elite wrestlers. *Journal of Sport Psychology, 5,* 58–71.

Gould, D., Horn, T., & Spreeman, J. (1983b). Sources of stress in junior elite wrestlers. *Journal of Sport Psychology, 5,* 159–171.

Gould, D., Petlichkoff, L., & Weinberg, R. S. (1984). Antecedents of, temporal changes in, and relationships between CSAI-2 subcomponents. *Journal of Sport Psychology, 6,* 289–304.

Gould, D., Petlichkoff, L., Simons, J., & Vivera, M. (1987). Relationship between Competitive State Anxiety Inventory-2 subscale scores and pistol shooting performance. *Journal of Sport Psychology, 9,* 33–42.

Griffin, M. R. (1972, Spring). An analysis of state and trait anxiety experienced in sports competition at different age levels. *Foil*, 58–64.

Hackfort, D., & Spielberger, C. D. (Eds.). (1989). *Anxiety in sports: An international perspective*. New York: Hemisphere.

Hanson, D. L. (1967). Cardiac response to participation in Little League baseball competition as determined by telemetry. *Research Quarterly, 38*, 384–388.

Hardman, K. (1973). A dual approach to the study of personality and performance in sport. In H. T. A. Whiting, K. Hardman, L. B. Hendry, & M. G. Jones (Eds.), *Personality and performance in physical education and sport* (pp. 136–152). London: Kimpton.

Hatfield, B. D., & Landers, D. M. (1987). Psychophysiology in exercise and sport research: An overview. *Exercise and Sport Sciences Reviews, 15*, 351–387.

Hebb, D. O. (1949). *The organization of behavior*. New York. Wiley.

Hull, C. L. (1943). *Principles of behavior*. New York: Appleton-Century-Crofts.

Hunt, P. J., & Hillary, J. M. (1973). Social facilitation in a coaction setting: An examination of the effects over learning trials. *Journal of Experimental Social Psychology, 9*, 563–571.

Johnson, W. R., & Cofer, C. N. (1974). Personality dynamics: Psychosocial implications. In W. R. Johnson & E. R. Buskirk (Eds.), *Science and medicine in exercise and sport* (pp. 71–92). New York: Harper & Row.

Kendrick, M. J., Craig, K. D., Lawson, D. M., & Davidson, P. O. (1982). Cognitive and behavioral therapy for musical-performance anxiety. *Journal of Consulting and Clinical Psychology, 50*, 353–362.

Klavora, P. (1978). An attempt to derive inverted-U curves based on the relationship between anxiety and athletic performance. In D. M. Landers & R. W. Christina (Eds.), *Psychology of motor behavior and sport—1977* (pp. 369–377). Champaign, IL: Human Kinetics.

Lacey, J. I. (1967). Somatic response patterning and stress: Some revisions of activation theory. In M. H. Appley & R. Trumbull (Eds.), *Psychological stress: Issues in research* (pp. 14–37). New York: Appleton-Century-Crofts.

Lacey, J. I., & Lacey, B. C. (1958). Verification and extension of the principle of autonomic response stereotypy. *American Journal of Psychology, 71*, 50–73.

Landers, D. M. (1980). The arousal–performance relationship revisited. *Research Quarterly for Exercise and Sport, 51*, 77–90.

Landers, D. M., & Boutcher, S. H. (1986). Arousal–performance relationships. In J. M. Williams (Ed.), *Applied sport psychology: Personal growth to peak performance* (pp. 163–184). Palo Alto, CA: Mayfield.

Landers, D. M., Brawley, L. R., & Hale, B. D. (1978). Habit strength differences in motor behavior. In D. M. Landers & R. W. Christina (Eds.), *Psychology of motor behavior and sport—1977* (pp. 420–433). Champaign, IL: Human Kinetics.

Landers, D. M., Wang, M. Q., & Courtet, P. (1985). Peripheral narrowing among experienced and inexperienced rifle shooters under low- and high-stress conditions. *Research Quarterly for Exercise and Sport, 56*, 57–70.

Lang, P. J. (1971). The application of psychophysiological methods to the study of psychotherapy and behavior modification. In A. E. Bergin & S. L. Garfield (Eds.), *Handbook of psychotherapy and behavior change* (pp. 75–125). New York: Wiley.

Lazarus, R. S., & Folkman, S. (1984). *Stress, appraisal, and coping*. New York: Springer.

Leglar, M. (1979). Measurement indicators of anxiety levels under various conditions of musical performance. *Dissertation Abstracts International, 34*, 5201A.

Liebert, R. M., & Morris, L. W. (1967). Cognitive and emotional components of test anxiety: A distinction and some initial data. *Psychological Reports, 20*, 975–978.

Lowe, R., & McGrath, J. E. (1971). *Stress, arousal, and performance: Some findings calling for a new theory* (Report No. AF 1161-67). Washington, DC: Air Force Office of Strategic Research.

Magnusson, D., & Endler, N. S. (Eds.). (1977). *Personality at the crossroads: Current issues in interactional psychology*. Hillsdale, NJ: Erlbaum.

Malmo, R. B. (1959). Activation: A neurophysiological dimension. *Psychological Review, 66*, 367–386.

Mandler, G., & Sarason, S. B. (1952). A study of anxiety and learning. *Journal of Abnormal and Social Psychology, 47*, 166–173.

Martens, R. (1971). Anxiety and motor behavior: A review. *Journal of Motor Behavior, 3,* 151–179.

Martens, R. (1975). *Social psychology and physical activity.* New York: Harper & Row.

Martens, R. (1977). *Sport Competition Anxiety Test.* Champaign, IL: Human Kinetics.

Martens, R. (1988). Youth sport in the USA. In F. L. Smoll, R. A. Magill, & M. J. Ash (Eds.), *Children in sport* (3rd ed., pp. 17–23). Champaign, IL: Human Kinetics.

Martens, R., & Gill, D. L. (1976). State anxiety among successful and unsuccessful competitors who differ in competitive trait anxiety. *Research Quarterly, 47,* 698–708.

Martens, R., & Landers, D. M. (1970). Motor performance under stress: A test of the inverted-U hypothesis. *Journal of Personality and Social Psychology, 16,* 29–37.

Martens, R., & Simon, J. A. (1976). Comparison of three predictors of state anxiety when competing. *Research Quarterly, 47,* 381–387.

Martens, R., Burton, D., Rivkin, F., & Simon, J. (1980). Reliability and validity of the Competitive State Anxiety Inventory (CSAI). In C. H. Nadeau, W. R. Halliwell, K. M. Newell, & G. C. Roberts (Eds.), *Psychology of motor behavior and sport—1979* (pp. 91–99). Champaign, IL: Human Kinetics.

Martens, R., Burton, D., Vealey, R. S., Bump, L. A., & Smith, D. E. (in press). The Competitive State Anxiety Inventory-2 (CSAI-2). In D. Burton & R. Vealey (Eds.), *Competitive anxiety.* Champaign, IL: Human Kinetics.

May, J. R., Veach, T. L., Reed, M. W., & Griffey, M. S. (1985). A psychological study of health, injury, and performance in athletes on the US Alpine Ski Team. *The Physician and Sportsmedicine, 13,* 111–115.

McAuley, E. (1985). State anxiety: Antecedent or result of sport performance? *Journal of Sport Behavior, 8,* 71–77.

McPherson, B., Marteniuk, R., Tihanyi, J., & Clark, W. (1980). The social system of age group swimmers: The perception of swimmers, parents and coaches. *Canadian Journal of Applied Sport Sciences, 4,* 142–145.

Morris, L. W., & Engle, W. G. (1981). Assessing various coping strategies and their effects on test performance and anxiety. *Journal of Clinical Psychology, 37,* 165–171.

Morris, L. W., & Fulmer, R. S. (1976). Test anxiety (worry and emotionality) changes during academic testing as a function of feedback and test importance. *Journal of Educational Psychology, 68,* 817–824.

Morris, L. W., Davis, D., & Hutchings, C. (1981). Cognitive and emotional components of anxiety: Literature review and revised worry–emotionality scale. *Journal of Educational Psychology, 73,* 541–555.

Nash, H. L. (1987). Elite child–athletes: How much does victory cost? *The Physician and Sportsmedicine, 15,* 128–133.

Nideffer, R. M., & York, T. J. (1978). The relationship between a measure of palmar sweat and swimming performance. *Journal of Applied Psychology, 61,* 376–378.

Ogilvie, B. C. (1968). Psychological consistencies within the personality of high level competitors. *Journal of the American Medical Association, 205,* 156–162.

Olerud, J. E. (1989). Acne in a young athlete. In N. J. Smith (Ed.), *Common problems in pediatric sports medicine* (pp. 219–221). Chicago: Year Book Medical Publishers.

Orlick, T. D., & Botterill, C. (1975). *Every kid can win.* Chicago: Nelson-Hall.

Oxendine, J. (1970). Emotional arousal and motor performance. *Quest, 13,* 23–30.

Passer, M. W., & Scanlan, T. K. (1980). The impact of game outcome on the postcompetition affect and performance evaluations of young athletes. In C. H. Nadeau, W. R. Halliwell, K. M. Newell, & G. C. Roberts (Eds.), *Psychology of motor behavior and sport—1979* (pp. 100–111). Champaign, IL: Human Kinetics.

Passer, M. W., & Seese, M. D. (1983). Life stress and athletic injury: Examination of positive versus negative events and three moderator variables. *Journal of Human Stress, 9,* 11–16.

Pierce, W. J. (1980). *Psychological perspectives of youth sport participants and nonparticipants.* Unpublished doctoral dissertation, Virginia Polytechnic Institute and State University, Blacksburg.

Pooley, J. C. (1980). Dropouts. *Coaching Review, 3,* 36–38.

Rabkin, J. G., & Struening, E. L. (1976). Life events, stress, and illness. *Science, 194,* 1013–1020.

Rahe, R. H., & Arthur, R. J. (1978). Life changes and illness studies: past history and future directions. *Journal of Human Stress, 4,* 3–15.

Roberts, G. C. (1986). The perception of stress: A potential source and its development. In M. R. Weiss & D. Gould (Eds.), *Sport for children and youths* (pp. 119–126). Champaign, IL: Human Kinetics.

Robinson, T. T., & Carron, A. V. (1982). Personal and situational factors associated with dropping out versus maintaining participation in competitive sport. *Journal of Sport Psychology, 4*, 364–378.

Rogers, C. R. (1959). A theory of therapy, personality and interpersonal relationships as developed in the client-centered framework. In S. Koch (Ed.), *Psychology: A study of a science* (Vol. 3, pp. 67–102). New York: McGraw-Hill.

Sarason, I. G. (1984). Stress, anxiety, and cognitive interference: Reactions to tests. *Journal of Personality and Social Psychology, 46*, 929–938.

Scanlan, T. K. (1986). Competitive stress in children. In M. R. Weiss & D. Gould (Eds.), *Sport for children and youths* (pp. 113–118). Champaign, IL: Human Kinetics.

Scanlan, T. K. (1988). Social evaluation and the competition process: A developmental perspective. In F. L. Smoll, R. A. Magill, & M. J. Ash (Eds.), *Children in sport* (3rd ed., pp. 135–148). Champaign, IL: Human Kinetics.

Scanlan, T. K., & Lewthwaite, R. (1984). Social psychological aspects of competition for male youth sport participants: I. Predictors of competitive stress. *Journal of Sport Psychology, 6*, 208–226.

Scanlan, T. K., & Lewthwaite, R. (1986). Social psychological aspects of competition for male youth sport participants: IV. Predictors of enjoyment. *Journal of Sport Psychology, 8*, 25–35.

Scanlan, T. K., & Passer, M. W. (1978). Factors related to competitive stress among male youth sports participants. *Medicine and Science in Sports, 10*, 103–108.

Scanlan, T. K., & Passer, M. W. (1979). Sources of competitive stress in young female athletes. *Journal of Sport Psychology, 1*, 151–159.

Simon, J. A., & Martens, R. (1979). Children's anxiety in sport and nonsport evaluative activities. *Journal of Sport Psychology, 1*, 160–169.

Skubic, E. (1956). Studies of little league and middle league baseball. *Research Quarterly, 27*, 97–110.

Smith, C. A., & Morris, L. W. (1976). Effects of stimulative and sedative music on two components of test anxiety. *Psychological Reports, 38*, 1187–1193.

Smith, R. E. (1986). A component analysis of athletic stress. In M. R. Weiss & D. Gould (Eds.), *Sport for children and youths* (pp. 107–111). Champaign, IL: Human Kinetics.

Smith, R. E. (1989). Athletic stress and burnout: Conceptual models and intervention strategies. In D. Hackfort & C. D. Spielberger (Eds.), *Anxiety in sports: An international perspective* (pp. 183–201). New York: Hemisphere.

Smith, R. E., & Smoll, F. L. (1989). Sport as a naturalistic laboratory for psychological theory development, research, and intervention. Manuscript submitted for publication.

Smith, R. E., Smoll, F. L., & Curtis, B. (1979). Coach effectiveness training: A cognitive-behavioral approach to enhancing relationship skills in youth sport coaches. *Journal of Sport Psychology, 1*, 59–75.

Smith, R. E., Smoll, F. L., & Schutz, R. W. (in press). *Reactions to competition: Measurement and correlates of sport-specific cognitive and somatic trait anxiety: The Sport Anxiety Scale. Anxiety Research.*

Smoll, F. L. (1984, December). Parent sport orientation: A workshop for athletes' parents. *Your Public Schools*, p. 11.

Sonstroem, R. J., & Bernardo, P. (1982). Intra-individual pregame state anxiety and basketball performance: A reexamination of the inverted-U curve. *Journal of Sport Psychology, 4*, 235–245.

Spence, J. T., & Spence, K. W. (1966). The motivational components of manifest anxiety: Drive and drive stimuli. In C. D. Spielberger (Ed.), *Anxiety and behavior* (pp. 291–326). New York: Academic Press.

Spielberger, C. D. (1966). Theory and research on anxiety. In C. D. Spielberger (Ed.), *Anxiety and behavior* (pp. 3–20). New York: Academic Press.

Spielberger, C. D. (1972). Anxiety as an emotional state. In C. D. Spielberger (Ed.), *Anxiety: Current trends in theory and research* (pp. 23–49). New York: Academic Press.

Spielberger, C. D. (1973). *Preliminary test manual for the State–Trait Anxiety Inventory for Children.* Palo Alto, CA: Consulting Psychologists.

Spielberger, C. D. (1989). Stress and anxiety in sports. In D. Hackfort & C. D. Spielberger (Eds.), *Anxiety in sports: An international perspective* (pp. 3–17). New York: Hemisphere.

Spielberger, C. D., Gorsuch, R. L., & Lushene, R. E. (1970). *Manual for the State–Trait Anxiety Inventory (STAI)*. Palo Alto, CA: Consulting Psychologists.

Steptoe, A. (1983). The relationship between tension and the quality of musical performance. *Journal of the International Society for the Study of Tension in Performance, 1,* 12–22.

Steptoe, A., & Fidler, H. (1987). Stage fright in orchestral musicians: A study of cognitive and behavioural strategies in performance anxiety. *British Journal of Psychology, 78,* 241–249.

Suinn, R. M. (1989). Behavioral intervention for stress management in sports. In D. Hackfort & C. D. Spielberger (Eds.), *Anxiety in sports: An international perspective* (pp. 203–214). New York: Hemisphere.

Taylor, J. (1953). A personality scale of manifest anxiety. *Journal of Abnormal and Social Psychology, 48,* 285–290.

Thayer, R. E. (1967). Measurement of activation through self-report. *Psychological Reports, 20,* 663–678.

Universities Study Committee. (1978). *Joint legislative study on youth sports programs: Phase II. Agency sponsored sports.* East Lansing, MI: Michigan Institute for the Study of Youth Sports.

Wankel, L. M., & Kreisel, P. S. J. (1985). Factors underlying enjoyment of youth sports: Sport and age group comparisons. *Journal of Sport Psychology, 7,* 51–64.

Weinberg, R. S., & Genuchi, M. (1980). Relationship between competitive trait anxiety, state anxiety, and golf performance: A field study. *Journal of Sport Psychology, 2,* 148–154.

Weinberg, R. S., & Hunt, V. V. (1976). The interrelationships between anxiety, motor performance, and electromyography. *Journal of Motor Behavior, 8,* 219–224.

Weinberg, R. S., & Ragan, J. (1978). Motor performance under three levels of stress and trait anxiety. *Journal of Motor Behavior, 10,* 169–176.

Wine, J. D. (1980). Cognitive-attentional theory of test anxiety. In I. G. Sarason (Ed.), *Test anxiety: Theory, research, and applications* (pp. 349–385). Hillsdale, NJ: Erlbaum.

Yerkes, R. M., & Dodson, J. D. (1908). The relationship of strength of stimulus to rapidity of habit formation. *Journal of Comparative Neurology and Psychology, 18,* 459–482.

Zuckerman, M. (1960). The development of an affect adjective check list for the measurement of anxiety. *Journal of Consulting Psychology, 24,* 457–462.

14

Speech Anxiety

WILLIAM J. FREMOUW AND JOSEPH L. BREITENSTEIN

INTRODUCTION

Speech anxiety is a popularly researched area, probably due to its prevalence, the availability of subjects (usually college students), and its similarity to common clinical presentations of anxiety (Turner, Beidel, & Larkin, 1986). Of adults, 25% report "much" fear when speaking before a group (Borkovec & O'Brien, 1976). Interestingly, the definition of speech anxiety is often ambiguous and frequently goes unstated, but it is most often defined by the particular dependent measures used (e.g., questionnaires; Watson & Friend, 1969). For this chapter, *speech anxiety* is defined as maladaptive cognitive and physiological reactions to environmental events that result in ineffective public speaking behaviors.

Other terms such as stage fright, communication apprehension, audience anxiety, or social anxiety are sometimes used to describe speech anxiety. *Stage fright* and *audience anxiety* are generally synonymous with speech anxiety and describe specific anxiety or fear when speaking to an audience. Communication apprehension and social anxiety, however, are broader forms of anxiety which occur in situations in addition to a public speaking format. *Communication apprehension* is often described as reticence or "unwillingness to communicate across many settings and audience sizes, not just public speaking." *Social anxiety* refers to social sensitivity or social inhibition in social contexts which may not even require oral communication (Daly, 1978).

Therefore, this chapter first reviews the currently used assessment procedures and major treatments for speech anxiety. The definition and measurement of effective treatments for anxiety are then addressed. Finally, recent research advances on the prediction of client–treatment interactions are discussed.

WILLIAM J. FREMOUW AND JOSEPH L. BREITENSTEIN • Department of Psychology, West Virginia University, Morgantown, West Virginia 26506-6040.

ASSESSMENT OF SPEECH ANXIETY

Assessment of speech anxiety consists of measurements of the three traditional domains of behavioral assessment: cognitive, physiological, and behavioral responses (Lang, 1969). Most of these assessment devices are paper-and-pencil measures. Some measures assess all three response modalities. For example, the Personal Report of Confidence as a Speaker (PRCS; Paul, 1966) is a 30-item (e.g., "I am in constant fear of forgetting my speech.") true–false self-report scale which measures cognitive, physiological, and behavioral responses experienced during the most recently delivered speech (see Figure 1). This is the most commonly used self-report measure of speech anxiety because the questions directly addresses a public speaking experience.

Other self-report measures are available which assess the broader constructs of communication apprehension and social anxiety. The Personal Report of Communication Apprehension (PRCA; McCroskey, 1970) is a 25-item measure which describes a reticence or avoidance of communication; while Watson And Friends's (1969) Social Anxiety and Distress Scale (SAD) is a 58-item scale which focuses on social anxiety and social sensitivity. These measures, although focusing on different aspects of social communication, correlate highly with each other and public speaking anxiety. Daly (1978) reported that the PRCS and PRCA correlated .88, the PRCS and SAD correlated .63, and the PRCA and SAD correlated .54. These broader measures of communication apprehension and social anxiety are often included in speech anxiety research as measures of generalization to other anxiety areas (e.g., Fremouw & Zitter, 1978).

Some instruments were designed to assess responses in one modality. For example, the Social Interaction Self-Statement Test (SISST; Glass, Merluzzi, Biever, & Larsen, 1982) is a 30-item questionnaire consisting of 15 positive cognitions (facilitative; e.g., "No worries, no fears, no anxiety") and 15 negative cognitions (inhibitory; e.g., "I hope I don't make a fool of myself") about performance in social situations. These statements are rated on a 5-point Likert scale where 1 is "*hardly ever* had the thought" and 5 is "*very often* had the thought" (Glass *et al.*, 1982). The SISST was adapted by Turner and Beidel (1985; see Figure 2) for speaking situations by changing the pronouns used in the questions from their singular to plural forms when necessary.

Physiological responses may be assessed with both paper-and-pencil questionnaires and more direct physiological measures. The Autonomic Perception Questionnaire (APQ; Mandler, Mandler, & Uviller, 1958) is one such paper-and-pencil measure. The APQ contains 21 items (e.g., "Did you experience accelerated heart beat?") which require subjects to rate on a 10-point scale such reactions experienced during a recently delivered speech. Many physiological indicators of anxiety, like heart rate, galvanic skin response (GSR), and systolic and diastolic blood pressure, are often directly measured before, during, and after speaking situations with standard psychophysiological measurement devices like electrocardiograms and syphgmomanometers. Paul (1966) first measured heart rate in speech-anxiety subjects by comparing beats per minute during the last 30 seconds of a 5–8 minute baseline with the first 30 seconds of the speech. Fremouw, Gross,

This instrument is composed of 30 items regarding your feelings of confidence as a speaker. After each question there is a "true" and a "false." Try to decide whether "true" or "false" most represents your feelings associated with your most recent speech, then put a circle around the "true" or "false." Remember that this information is completely confidential and will not be made known to your instructor. Work quickly and don't spend much time on any one question. We want your first impression on this questionnaire. Now go ahead, work quickly, and remember to answer every question.

1. I look forward to an opportunity to speak in public.   T   F

2. My hands tremble when I try to handle objects on the platform.   T   F

3. I am in constant fear of forgetting my speech.   T   F

4. Audiences seem friendly when I address them.   T   F

5. While preparing a speech I am in a constant state of anxiety.   T   F

6. At the conclusion of a speech I feel that I have had a pleasant experience.   T   F

7. I dislike to use my body and voice expressively.   T   F

8. My thoughts become confused and jumbled when I speak before an audience.   T   F

9. I have no fear of facing an audience.   T   F

10. Although I am nervous just before getting up I soon forget my fears and enjoy the experience.   T   F

11. I face the prospect of making a speech with complete confidence.   T   F

12. I feel that I am in complete possession of myself while speaking.   T   F

13. I prefer to have notes on the platform in case I forget my speech.   T   F

14. I like to observe the reactions of my audience to my speech.   T   F

15. Although I talk fluently with friends, I am at a loss for words on the platform.   T   F

16. I feel relaxed and comfortable while speaking.   T   F

17. Although I do not enjoy speaking in public I do not particularly dread it.   T   F

18. I always avoid speaking in public if possible.   T   F

19. The faces of my audience are blurred when I look at them.   T   F

20. I feel disgusted with myself after trying to address a group of people.   T   F

21. I enjoy preparing a talk.   T   F

22. My mind is clear when I face an audience.   T   F

23. I am fairly fluent.   T   F

24. I perspire and tremble just before getting up to speak.   T   F

25. My posture feels strained and unnatural.   T   F

26. I am fearful and tense all the while I am speaking before a group of people.   T   F

27. I find the prospect of speaking mildly pleasant.   T   F

28. It is difficult for me to calmly search my mind for the right words to express my thoughts.   T   F

29. I am terrified at the thought of speaking before a group of people.   T   F

30. I have a feeling of alertness in facing an audience.   T   F

FIGURE 1. Personal Report of Confidence as a Speaker (PRCS; Paul, 1966).

Directions:

It is obvious that people think a variety of things when they are involved in different social situations.

Below is a list of things when you may have thought to yourself at sometime before, during, or after this interaction. Read each item and decide how frequently you may have been thinking a similar thought before, during, and after the interaction. Using the following scale to indicate the nature of your thoughts:

Did you have the thought

1	2	3	4	5
Hardly ever	Rarely	Sometimes	Often	Very often

_____ 1. When I can't think of anything to say I can feel myself getting very anxious.

_____ 2. I can usually talk to guys pretty well.

_____ 3. I hope I don't make a fool of myself.

_____ 4. I'm beginning to feel more at ease.

_____ 5. I'm really afraid of what he'll think of me.

_____ 6. No worries, no fears, no anxieties.

_____ 7. I'm scared to death.

_____ 8. He probably won't be interested in me.

_____ 9. Maybe I can put him at ease by starting things going.

_____ 10. Instead of worrying I can figure out how best to get to know him.

_____ 11. I'm not too comfortable meeting guys, so things are bound to go wrong.

_____ 12. What the heck, the worst that can happen is that he won't go for me.

_____ 13. He may want to talk to me as much as I want to talk to him.

_____ 14. This will be a good opportunity.

_____ 15. If I blow this conversation, I'll really lose my confidence.

_____ 16. What I say will probably sound stupid.

_____ 17. What do I have to lose? It's worth a try.

_____ 18. This is an awkward situation but I can handle it.

_____ 19. Wow — I don't want to do this.

_____ 20. It would crush me if he didn't respond to me.

_____ 21. I've just got to make a good impression on him or I'll feel terrible.

_____ 22. You're such an inhibited idiot.

_____ 23. I'll probably bomb out anyway.

_____ 24. I can handle anything.

_____ 25. Even if things don't go well it's no catastrophe.

_____ 26. I feel awkward and dumb; he's bound to notice.

_____ 27. We probably have a lot in common.

_____ 28. Maybe we'll hit it off real well.

_____ 29. I wish I could leave and avoid the whole situation.

_____ 30. Ah. Throw caution to the wind.

FIGURE 2. Revised Social Interaction Self-Statement Test (SISST; Glass *et al.*, 1982).

Monroe, and Rapp (1982) similarly measured GSR in addition to heart rate. Such comparisons demonstrate the strongest physiological changes associated with speech tasks (Borkovec, Wall, & Stone, 1974). Recent research (e.g., Turner & Beidel, 1985) has utilized other dependent measures, like blood pressure, and variations of such temporal analyses.

Several measures have been designed for assessing the behavioral dimensions of anxiety. The most widely used measure is the Behavior Checklist for Performance Anxiety (Paul, 1966), which contains 20 behaviors (e.g., "voice quivers") derived from those collected by Clevenger and King (1961). Two to three raters complete the checklist in 30-second intervals while observing a 4-minute speech by the subject. An adapted version (Mulac & Sherman, 1974; see Figure 3) reduced the original 20 items to 14 items in order to increase interrater reliability. Subsequent research (Fremouw & Harmatz, 1975; Fremouw & Zitter, 1978) has demonstrated the reliability and validity of this abbreviated version.

In summary, in research projects speech anxiety is usually first identified by a self-report screening measure such as the Fear Survey Schedule (FSS-II; Geer, 1965). These measures have adequate normative data to derive inclusion criteria.

	1	2	3	4	Total
	1 2	3 4	5 6	7 8	

Name _____   Speech number _____

Date _____   Rater _____

1. Quivering, tense voice, giggles
2. Voice too soft
3. Voice monotone, lacks emphasis
4. Stammers, halting, stuttering
5. Vocalized pauses, ah's, you knows (2%)
6. Hunts for words, blocks (3 seconds$^+$)
7. Breathes easily
8. Eye contact avoided (50%$^+$)
9. Face tense, grimaces, twitches
10. "Deadpan" facial expression
11. Arms & hands rigid, tense, trembling
12. Arms & hands extraneous movements
13. Arms & hands immobile, lack gestures
14. Sways, paces, shuffles feet

Overall anxiety

1	3	5	7	9	11	13	15
None			Moderate				Extreme

FIGURE 3. Behavior Checklist for Performance Anxiety.

Individuals identified as anxious generally complete a 3- to 4-minute speech while being observed by raters who complete a behavior checklist and overall anxiety ratings. Physiological reactions like heart rate and GSR are monitored to obtain direct measures of autonomic reactivity. The speech-anxious person completes self-report measures of cognitive arousal, such as the SISST or the PRCS, after the speaking situation. This paradigm provides a multidimensional assessment of speech anxiety which can offer rich clinical data as well as permit comparisons with the current literature on these standard measures.

TREATMENTS FOR SPEECH ANXIETY

Anxiety disorders, including speech anxiety, have a variety of theoretical explanations. Theories of the etiology of speech anxiety can vary from an analytic, intrapsychic model to a cognitive-behavioral learning model. There is no specific theory for the cause of speech anxiety that is distinct from the general theoretical debates about the origins and maintenance factors for most anxieties.

Regardless of the unresolved etiological issues, beginning with Paul (1966), behavioral treatments have been demonstrated as the most effective for reduction of speech anxiety. This section briefly reviews the major treatments available and selected research supporting their effectiveness. For a more comprehensive review of this literature, see Last and Hersen (1988) or Heimberg, Dodge, and Becker (1987).

Systematic Desensitization

Systematic desensitization (Wolpe, 1958, 1969, 1973), involves the pairing of relaxed states with hierarchically arranged series of imagined or real events the client finds particularly stressful. Anxiety is reduced primarily through this counterconditioning, the prevention of avoidance responses, and the attainment of reinforcers through engaging in previously feared activities. Paul (1966) first demonstrated that systematic desensitization was effective in treating speech anxiety. In this classic study, systematic desensitization using an accelerated version of Jacobsen's (1938) progressive muscle relaxation was presented to subjects over five 1-hour sessions. Systematic desensitization was demonstrated as more effective than insight-oriented psychotherapy or three control conditions across cognitive, physiological, and behavioral measures of a public speaking task. An 18-month follow-up conducted by Paul (1968) demonstrated that these changes were maintained and that, contrary to psychodynamic theories, no symptom substitution occurred. Since then, others (e.g., Marshall, Preese, & Andrews, 1976) have replicated these results.

Relaxation Training

Relaxation techniques like transcendental meditation, designed to reduce the physiological aspects of anxiety, are thousands of years old. The first formal relaxation training program, progressive muscle relaxation (PMR), was developed by Jacobson in 1938. PMR consists of the successive tensing and relaxing of specific muscles in a lengthy sequence until all voluntary muscles in the body are relaxed. PMR assumes that muscle tension is related to anxiety, and that if muscle tension can be reduced, an associated decrease in anxiety will occur.

Current reformulations of PMR are numerous and diverse. Perhaps the most researched variation was developed by Bernstein and Borkovec (1973). Highly systematized, their approach consists of scripts presenting several PMR skills. Bernstein and Borkovec also pair cues (e.g., the word *calm*) with relaxed states achieved through PMR. This conditioning promotes the use of the cue to elicit relaxation when needed, and it theoretically facilitates generalization of training to stressful events in the environment. Other variants include teaching clients to use relaxation as a pragmatic self-control skill in order to monitor anxiety and replace it with relaxation, usually *in vivo* (Goldfried & Trier, 1974; Mikulas, 1976; Sherman & Plummer, 1973). Still another variant is autogenic training (Lindeman, 1973; Luthe, 1969), which utilizes self-suggestions, like "my right arm is heavy and relaxed," to promote relaxation. Cue-controlled relaxation (Lent, Russell, & Zamostny, 1981), and applied relaxation training (Osberg, 1981) are some of the variants of relaxation training that have been successfully implemented in reducing speech anxiety.

Flooding

Flooding acutely exposes a client, either imaginally or *in vivo*, to high levels of anxiety-producing stimuli while preventing avoidance responses (Malleson, 1959; Polin, 1959). By prohibiting avoidance behaviors, the patient is forced to experience the feared stimuli. While initially resulting in increased anxiety, with prolonged exposure, the anxiety response has been shown to extinguish (Rimm & Masters, 1979). While implosive therapy (Stampfl, 1961) is occasionally defined as being synonymous with flooding (cf. Kirsch, Wolpin, & Knutson, 1975), technically, implosive therapy exposes clients to psychodynamic themes thought to underlie the disorders, while flooding uses salient "real world" cues (Rimm & Masters, 1979). The research on such implosive procedures with speech anxiety is not comprehensive enough to be included in this review.

Early research with flooding (Calef & McLean, 1970; Grossberg, 1965; Hosford, 1969; Kirsch, Wolpin, & Knutson, 1975) established the effectiveness of *in vivo* and imaginal flooding procedures. Kirsch, Wolpin, and Knutson (1975) demonstrated that five brief (4–5 minute) weekly sessions of *in vivo* and imaginal flooding were significantly more effective in reducing speech anxiety than were treatments consisting of successive approximation and an attention placebo as measured by Paul's (1966) Behavior Checklist and Personal Report of Confidence as a Speaker (PRCS). More recent research has concentrated on refining flooding procedures. For example, Mannion and Levine (1984) examined various categories or "levels" of phobic stimuli in imaginal and *in vivo* flooding procedures. Results indicated that only stimuli directly relevant to the phobia were necessary and that *in vivo* procedures were generally more effective than imaginal procedures.

Rational-Emotive Therapy

A number of therapists have developed treatment regimens based on the role of cognitions in maintaining emotions and behavior (Beck, 1976; Ellis, 1962; Lazarus, 1972). The most prominent is rational-emotive therapy (RET), developed by Albert Ellis (1962). Rational-emotive therapy follows the A-B-C-D-E paradigm, where A (activating event) symbolizes an external event (e.g., giving a speech), B (belief) refers to the chains of self-statements that are responses to A (e.g., "I am terrible at giving speeches"), C (consequences) symbolizes the emotional and behavioral products of B (e.g., anxiety), D (dispute) refers to the defining and debating of those irrational beliefs that contribute to negative consequences (e.g., "I have no evidence that I am terrible"), and E (effects) refers to the products of the disputes—more functional emotions and behaviors. Basically, training consists of learning to modify problematic cognitions with appropriate behavioral and emotional changes following.

Trexler and Karst (1972) compared RET with relaxation training and a no-treatment control condition. Treatment consisted of four group sessions held several days apart. Results showed that RET was significantly more effective on an irrational beliefs scale (Jones, 1968) and Paul's (1966) PRCS. A questionnaire follow-up at 6 months revealed that these treatment effects were maintained.

Stress Inoculation Training

Stress inoculation training (SIT; Meichenbaum, 1969, 1972, 1985) differs from RET in that Meichenbaum's approach emphasizes ongoing self-control of overt behaviors. SIT attempts to inoculate clients by providing them with coping skills to use in successfully negotiating future problems. These problems are addressed in a systematic, usually hierarchical fashion, with the client applying cognitive self-control strategies to more difficult situations. While Meichenbaum's original research emphasized the role of adaptive cognitions (Meichenbaum, 1969, 1972), SIT has evolved to include other therapeutic techniques like relaxation training (Meichenbaum, 1985). SIT has proven effective in treating various disorders (Meichenbaum, 1985), including speech anxiety (Craddock, Cotler, & Jason, 1978; Fremouw & Zitter, 1978; Jaremko, 1978; Jaremko, Hadfield, & Walker, 1980).

Fremouw and Zitter (1978) compared SIT, public speaking skills training, an attention placebo, and a waiting-list condition among speech-anxious undergraduates reporting either high or low levels of social anxiety. The presence of speech anxiety was determined by a score in the upper quartile of the Personal Report of Communication Apprehension (PRCA; McCroskey, 1970) and above the median on the PRCS (Paul, 1966). High and low levels of social anxiety were determined by a median split of scores from the Social Anxiety Distress Scale (SAD; Watson & Friend, 1969). The treatment groups met for five 1-hour sessions, with the SIT group learning coping statements and relaxation and the skills group doing behavioral rehearsal of specific speaking skills, such as good posture, gesturing, and eye contact. Subjects were provided videotape feedback of practice speakers to help improve specific speaking behaviors (e.g., eye contact). Comparisons of pretreatment and posttreatment speeches showed that the treatment groups both improved significantly on two behavioral measures: the Behavioral Checklist and the duration of silence occurring during the speech. The treatment groups also improved on a subjective measure of social anxiety, the Anxiety Differential (Husek & Alexander, 1963). These improvements did not extend to the two measures of generalization, the PRCA and SAD, although there was some evidence supporting the efficacy of SIT for those indicating high levels of social anxiety.

Thus, research has demonstrated that speech anxiety can be significantly reduced by a variety of therapies, including systematic desensitization, relaxation training, flooding, RET, and SIT. Improvements in groups receiving one of these treatments have been maintained at up to 6-month follow-ups.

DEFINING EFFECTIVENESS OF TREATMENTS

The previously reviewed treatment literature for speech anxiety is based primarily upon statistical comparisons of improvements between various treatment groups. This between-group paradigm bases conclusions on statistically significant differences between groups without a careful examination of the clinical impact or significance of these changes. This is not unique to speech anxiety. There is a general limitation of much of the behavior therapy literature in that individual rates of improvement are often ignored when comparing treatments. Information about individual versus group effects is very important to help make decisions about which treatments are most likely to benefit a particular client.

The treatments in the speech anxiety area were generally compared to control groups (e.g., Karst & Trexler, 1970) and then later compared to other treatments and control groups (e.g., Meichenbaum, Gilmore, & Fedoravicius, 1971). Paul (1966) approached this problem by using statistical comparisons as well as an examination of individual rates of change. He calculated the standard error of the dependent measure and established a 95th percentile confidence interval. Data from each subject were then examined to determine whether the individual improved more than the standard error of the measure. This revealed that 100% of systematic desensitization subjects were greater than the standard error of the measure, as compared with 17% of the control group.

Glogower, Fremouw, and McCroskey (1978) were the next researchers in this area to examine treatment data in a similar manner. They calculated the percentage of subjects who "significantly improved" on behavioral and self-report measures of speech anxiety. Table 1 describes the results of this analysis when comparing components of a cognitive restructuring treatment. This analysis clearly demonstrated that the coping statement treatment was the major factor in subject improvement. Of the subjects in that group, 50% improved significantly on both measures, as compared to only 8 or 9% of subjects in the other two treatment components. Examination of the combination group re-

TABLE 1. Percentage of Subjects "Significantly Improved" on a Behavioral and a Self-Report Index

Treatment	N	FreqL[a] (%)	PRCA[b] (%)	Improved on both measures (%)
Waiting-list control	13	31	15	0
Extinction	12	17	67	8
Negative self-statements	11	36	54	9
Coping statements	12	67	83	50
Combination	12	67	100	67

Note. From Glogower et al. (1978).
[a]FreqL, frequency of long verbalizations.
[b]PRCA, Personal Report of Communication Apprehension (McCroskey, 1970).

vealed that all subjects improved on the self-report measure, and 67% improved on the behavioral measure. Overall, this approach demonstrates the usefulness of examining individual rates of improvements in treatment and measures to arrive at a clearer evaluation of the effectiveness of the treatment. The examination of group means can distort or hide the effect on individual subjects because of the impact of extreme scores on means.

A different approach to establishing the effectiveness of speech therapy treatments involves using normative group data from nonanxious subjects as well as data from high-anxious control groups. Meichenbaum et al. (1971) provided data from low speech-anxious subjects to establish norms and to permit comparisons with posttreatment levels of anxiety. At pretreatment, the high-anxious groups were significantly different from low-anxious groups on all but one dependent measure. At posttreatment, however, the speech-anxious subjects who completed cognitive therapy no longer differed from the low speech-anxious comparison group. The use of normative data for a speech-anxious population allows treatments to be evaluated in relationship to the amount of change required to eliminate speech anxiety.

While some researchers have begun to recognize the need to look beyond statistical differences between group means, few procedures have been developed or widely accepted to evaluate the importance of behavior change. Kazdin (1980) has suggested that behavior change can be determined through social comparisons and through subjective evaluation methods. In these methods, two dependent measures are generally assessed—the magnitude of the obtained improvement and the proportion of the subjects who improve.

A social comparison of normative criteria is used to evaluate each client's improvement in relation to his or her non-speech-anxious peers. These procedures differ from that used by Meichenbaum et al. (1971), because no statistical tests are used to compare subjects to the normative group. Instead, individual scores are compared to a normative group's performance to see if the individual falls in the range of a normal group. After treatment, the number and percentage of speech-anxious subjects who now score within the range of the nonanxious group is calculated. It is a simple, descriptive presentation of percentages. In using this approach, two importance issues must be considered. First, how to define membership in the normative sample range and, second, what level of improved performance defines clinical improvement.

The Gross and Fremouw (1982) study examined their outcome data with this approach. The subjects were selected on the basis of their responses to the item "speaking before a group" of the Fear Survey Schedule-II (Geer, 1965). If they scored at least 5 (*much fear*) on a 7-point scale, they were defined as high-anxious subjects. The normative group was defined by subjects who reported *very little* or *no anxiety* (1 or 2) on a 7-point scale for the same item. To evaluate the clinical significance of treatment, individual posttreatment scores for the formerly high-anxious subjects were compared with the low-anxious normative group. The treatment outcome was evaluated by using two different levels of clinical significance as summarized in Table 2. In one analysis, subjects were defined as clinically improved if their posttreatment scores were less or equal to the normative mean plus one standard deviation (84th percentile) of the low-anxious group. This criterion is suggested by Kendall and Wilcox (1980). In the second analysis, a more stringent criterion of less than or equal to the normative mean (50th percentile) is used. Table 2 demonstrates that changing the definition of clinical significance produces large differences in the percentage of subjects who could be classified as significantly improved. If the 84th percentile were used, 75 to 92% of treated subjects would be considered clinically improved. In contrast, if the 50th percentile were used, the improvement rates would range from 15 to 57%. Therefore, selection of the comparison levels could lead to different conclusions as to the effectiveness of a treatment.

In addition to examining posttreatment scores relative to normative groups, subjective ratings of improvement are important. As Kazdin (1980) suggests, subjective ratings by significant others best reflect how the client will be evaluated outside of the treatment setting. In addition, subjective ratings can help validate the behaviors that were targeted for change.

Fawcett and Miller (1975) obtained audience ratings of individual speakers

TABLE 2. Percentage of Subjects at Posttreatment
Meeting Two Criteria of Improvement

Variable	Percentage of subjects less than	
	50th percentile of low-anxious group	84th percentile of low-anxious group
PRCS[a]	25	75
SAD[b]	57	87
Behavior Checklist[c]	55	92
Overall anxiety rating	15	85

[a]Personal Report of Confidence as a Speaker (Paul, 1966).
[b]Social Anxiety and Distress Scale (Watson & Friend, 1969).
[c]Behavior Checklist for Performance Anxiety (Paul, 1966).

to demonstrate that changes in specific speaking behaviors improved global evaluations of a speaker's enthusiasm, sincerity, knowledge, and overall performance. This validated their selection of target behaviors by demonstrating the desired impact on the audience's perception of the speaker's abilities.

In this approach, the issue of determining the criteria for selection of the raters is important. Other members in a public speaking class, teachers, or strangers could all be appropriate audiences, depending on the goal of treatment and the type of public speaking being treated. Fawcett and Miller (1975) used an audience of people from the community in a real speech situation to provide these subjective evaluations of speaker effectiveness.

Overall, the treatment literature demonstrates many therapies that produce statistically reliable differences between groups. The above discussions suggest several additional ways to examine treatment outcome to better determine the magnitude of the treatment effects and the percentage of subjects who actually benefit from these specific treatments. Future research on speech anxiety should incorporate error measures, social comparisons, and clinical significance criteria to supplement the traditional between-group statistical comparisons.

PREDICTION OF TREATMENT OUTCOME

With the development of effective treatments and refined criteria for defining successful outcome, researchers (see Fremouw & Gross, 1983) have begun to address the concerns of Cronbach (1957), Kiesler (1966), and Paul (1969) to identify predictive idiographic variables regarding treatment efficacy. These idiographic variables are specific characteristics of clients, therapists, treatments, and situations. Paul (1969) has described this task quite succinctly in terms of an ultimate question: "What treatment, by whom, is more effective for this individual with that specific problem, under what specific circumstances, and how does it come about?" (p.44). Such predictors are obviously important, for if they can be established, then clients and treatments can be matched to provide the most effective intervention available.

Garfield's (1978) demographical analyses are an example of an early attempt to establish predictive idiographic variables with respect to psychotherapy in general. He reviewed a number of studies and arrived at some tentative and expected conclusions regarding broad client–treatment interactions; namely, clients who are less disturbed at the beginning of therapy will in general have higher levels of adjustment after therapy is complete. He also found that, in general, "YAVIS" (i.e., Young, Adult, Verbal, Intelligent, Single) clients reported the most success in therapy.

This section of the chapter discusses more specific strategies used to identify client–treatment interactions, including component analyses of treatments, comparing treatments within populations, comparing treatments between populations, establishing subtypes of anxiety, and cluster analyses.

Component Analyses of Treatments

One basic strategy to establish predictive idiographic differences is to analyze the components of a treatment in order to identify specific components needed by particular clients. For example, several such analyses have been performed examining what components of cognitive therapy (e.g., types of self-statements) are most important in RET and SIT when applied to speech-anxious subjects (Glogower et al., 1978; Meichenbaum, 1972; Thorpe, Amatu, Blakey, & Burns, 1976). Glogower et al. (1978) found that just the identification of irrational beliefs did not produce anxiety reduction. Instead, learning specific coping statements about speeches was necessary for improvement. This result differs from that of Thorpe et al. (1976), who concluded that "insight" about irrational beliefs was more helpful than learning coping statements.

Component analyses may also be more molar in scope. For example, Horan, Hackett, Buchanan, Stone, and Demchik-Stone (1977) have examined the various phases of SIT and have found that the skill acquisition phase plays the most important role in reducing speech anxiety. Skill acquisition is the actual rehearsal of a speech while using the new relaxation and coping strategies. However, component analyses suffer from the same limitations that many treatment outcome studies do; that is, they fail to establish definitive client–treatment interactions due to a lack of both standardized treatment components and careful assessment of individual differences prior to treatment.

Comparing Treatments within Populations

A preliminary method of analyzing client–treatment interactions is to compare different treatments among similar subjects and then perform post hoc analyses to identify subgroups of subjects who responded differently to the treatments. Goldfried and Trier (1974) compared applied relaxation training (a presentation of self-control rationale, progressive relaxation training, and in vivo training), PMR training, and an attention placebo among speech-anxious subjects scoring similarly on self-report and behavioral measures. Applied relaxation and PMR were demonstrated equally effective, and both were more effective than the attention placebo. Meichenbaum et al. (1971) compared groups receiving (1) insight (cognitive restructuring), (2) systematic desensitization, (3) a combination of the two, (4) an attention placebo, and (5) time spent on a treatment waiting list. The groups were assessed across two dependent measures—a timed behavioral checklist and the Personal Report of Confidence as a Speaker (PRCS; Paul, 1966). Both treatment groups were significantly more effective than the control groups in reducing speech anxiety. Interestingly, post hoc analyses indicated that insight was more effective for subjects who reported anxiety across a number of situations, as measured by the SAD, than for those experiencing anxiety primarily in public speaking situations.

Other comparisons involving speech anxiety include skills training versus flooding (Hayes & Marshall, 1984) and speech skills training versus coping skills training versus paradoxical treatment (Worthington, Tipton, Cromely, Richards, & Janke, 1984). None of these studies identified clearly superior treatments. As with studies investigating component analyses, it is difficult to address the issue of client–treatment match using studies that compare a variety of treatments. The determinations of client–treatment interactions depend upon better specificity of the treatments and homogeneity of the populations. Until these procedures are implemented, such approaches will not readily lend themselves to the establishment of client–treatment interactions.

Comparing Treatments between Populations

The post hoc analyses of scores on the Social Anxiety and Distress Scale (SAD; Watson & Friend, 1969) conducted by Meichenbaum *et al.* (1971) were very promising. As one of the first significant client–treatment interactions reported, it suggests that comparing interventions across *a priori* divisions of subjects could be useful. Casas (1975) established such differences by dividing subjects into high and low scores on self-report measures of imaginal abilities, irrational beliefs, physiological arousal, and speaker confidence. Self-report, behavioral, and physiological dependent measures were used to compare groups receiving self-control desensitization, rational restructuring, and time on a waiting list. Although no statistically significant differences were observed, some nonsignificant client–treatment interactions were mentioned. In general, subjects who primarily experienced anxiety cognitively (high on imaginal abilities and irrational beliefs, but low on confidence) benefited most from rational restructuring, while desensitization had the greatest effect upon those reporting primarily physiological arousal.

Fremouw and Zitter (1978) used median split scores on the SAD to divide speech-anxious subjects into those high in social anxiety and those low in social anxiety. Subjects were assigned to one of four conditions: (1) speaking skills training, (2) cognitive restructuring–relaxation training, (3) discussion placebo, or (4) waiting list. Both treatment groups improved significantly on one subjective and two behavioral measures of speech anxiety, but the improvement did not generalize to the social anxiety measure. Unlike the Meichenbaum *et al.* (1971) study, client–treatment interactions were not statistically significant. However, the trends indicated that speaking skills training was about equally effective for subjects scoring both high and low on social anxiety, while cognitive restructuring–relaxation training benefited those with high levels of social anxiety most.

Other *a priori* topics researched with speech-anxious subjects include introversion–extroversion (DiLoreto, 1971), assertiveness (Schwartz & Gottman, 1976), dysfunctional cognitions (Hammen, Jacobs, Mayol, & Cochran, 1980), and misattribution (Slivken & Buss, 1984). No clear client–treatment interactions were demonstrated in these studies. When subjects are accurately classified, *a priori* divisions of subjects are probably the best univariate predictors of client–treatment interactions. However, because anxiety is a multivariate phenomenon

(Borkovec, Weerts, & Bernstein, 1977), prediction of treatment outcome probably requires a more complex approach than just using a simple variable.

Establishing Subtypes of Anxiety

One approach to categorizing anxiety is based on examining several anxiety dimensions simultaneously. Turner & Beidel (1985) attempted to classify socially anxious subjects according to levels of physiological arousal and negative cognitions that they experienced while giving a speech. To be considered socially anxious, subjects had to score above the published cutoff score on each of three measures, the SAD, the Fear of Negative Evaluation Scale (Watson & Friend, 1969), and the State–Trait Anxiety Inventory (Spielberger, Gorusch, & Lushene, 1970). The Social Interaction Self-Statement Test (Glass *et al.*, 1982) served as the dependent measure of cognitions, and change in systolic blood pressure from baseline to a speech task served as the physiological dependent measure. The task consisted of a 10-minute baseline measurement period followed by the assignment of a speech topic, a 3-minute preparation period, and a 5-minute speaking period. Two subtypes of socially anxious subjects, containing more than 85% of the sample, were identified—high negative cognition–high physiological reactivity and high negative cognition–low physiological reactivity. While no interventions were proposed, the authors speculated that this categorization of subjects may prove helpful in developing an effective treatment plan. For example, cognitive restructuring and relaxation training should be differentially successful depending upon the particular responsivity of a subject.

Cluster Analysis

Cluster analysis (Johnson, 1967) examines *a priori* divisions based upon one or more determinants and describes the data as a continuum. The superiority of this strategy over *a priori* divisions by themselves lies in its ability to combine related variables (e.g., physiological arousal and irrational cognitions) along one dimension and its subsequent dismissal of division by median splits. Homogeneous groups may be established on the basis of existing conceptualizations of anxiety, like those reviewed previously (e.g., Borkovec, 1973; Davidson & Schwartz, 1976).

Fremouw *et al.* (1982) utilized the anxiety typologies of Borkovec (1973), Davidson and Schwartz (1976), and Lang (1977) to analyze client–treatment interactions. The dimensions of the Borkovec (1973) typology are high and low perceived and high and low actual physiological arousal. Davidson and Schwartz (1976) developed a four-factor typology of high and low cognitive and somatic activity. Lang's (1977) typology consists of high or low verbal (cognitive), motor (behavioral), and physiological responding. Assessment data were obtained from subjects across two situations—giving an extemporaneous speech and conversing with a student of the opposite sex. Dependent measures consisted of heart rate and skin conductance (physiological reactions), self-report of physiological responses (physiological perceptions), a cognitive measure of feelings (cognitive measure), a behavioral checklist (behavioral measure), and several other measures to assess the anxiety levels of the samples. Cluster analyses identified relatively homogeneous subtypes for both tasks and supported each of the four subtypes in the Borkovec (1973) and Davidson and Schwartz (1976) typologies (high or low physiological reaction and either high or low physiological perception or cognitive reaction). Little support was indicated for the Lang (1977) typology of verbal, motor, and physiological dimensions.

Gross and Fremouw (1982) extended the Fremouw et al. (1982) study by dichotomizing subjects into the Borkovec (1973) and Davidson and Schwartz (1976) typologies of anxiety and studying how members of various subtypes benefited from two interventions—progressive relaxation and cognitive restructuring. Physiological dependent measures included heart rate, skin conductance, and self-report. Behavior was measured using Paul's (1966) Behavior Checklist, an overall rating of anxiety, and an 11-item rating form assessing self-reported behavior (Trussell, 1978). Cognitive data were obtained using three self-report measures—the State Anxiety Scale (SAS; Spielberger et al., 1970), the SAD, and the PRCS. Cluster analyses generated all of the subtypes of the Davidson and Schwartz (1976) and Borkovec (1973) typologies. Results indicated that both treatment groups were more effective in giving a posttreatment speech than a waiting-list control group. However, only one significant subtype–treatment interaction was obtained. In subjects in which physiological reaction was low and either cognitive anxiety or physiological perception of anxiety was high, subjects did not appear to benefit from progressive relaxation. In contrast, subjects with high physiological reactivity benefited most from relaxation training.

Cluster analyses approaches appear to offer one of the best available strategies for identifying client–treatment interactions, because a number of specific variables can be combined in an *a priori* fashion to examine interactions with components of treatments.

In summary, a variety of effective treatments for speech anxiety are available, ranging from systematic desensitization (Paul, 1966) to SIT (Meichenbaum et al., 1971) to skills training (Fremouw & Zitter, 1978). Efforts to match an individual client with optimal treatment have not progressed beyond preliminary findings. In general, cognitive restructuring appears more promising for clients with generalized anxiety (Meichenbaum et al., 1971; Fremouw & Zitter, 1978) than other treatments such as skills training or progressive relaxation. Progressive relaxation training is only effective if the client has high physiological reactivity which can be reduced. Clients who only worry but do not react physiologically have little benefit from a physiologically oriented treatment (Gross & Fremouw, 1982). These tentative results need further refinement and replication before becoming widely accepted.

Future Directions

Although speech anxiety has been well studied, it is no longer a trendy area for research. Still, it offers a rich, clinical laboratory in which to examine anxiety in a readily available population. Speech anxiety is both clinically significant for individuals and is a window through which to further refine the assessment and treatment approaches for other anxiety problems.

At this point, further basic comparisons of well-established treatments no longer add to the literature. Efforts at component analyses and the examination of nonspecific factors in treatments appear more productive. The major challenge in this area is to identify predictors which would best permit matching of clients with individual treatments. Preliminary work is promising but requires much further examination. Further use of multivariate procedures such as cluster analyses may offer one direction for research. This approach relies on systematic studies of large groups of subjects screened with the same measures. In contrast, an extensive study of anxious subjects within a single-subject paradigm may also lead to the identification of some helpful predictors.

REFERENCES

Beck, A. (1976). *Cognitive therapy and emotional disorders*. New York: Plenum.

Bernstein, D. A., & Borkovec, T. D. (1973). *Progressive muscle relaxation: A manual for the helping professions*. Champaign, IL: Research Press.

Borkovec, T. D. (1973). The effects of instructional and physiological cues on analogue fear. *Behavior Therapy, 4*, 185–192.

Borkovec, T. D., & O'Brien, G. T. (1976). Methodological and target issues in analogue therapy outcome research. In M. Hersen, E. Eisler, & P. Miller (Eds.), *Progress in behavior modification* (Vol. 3). New York: Academic Press.

Borkovec, T. D., Wall, R. L., & Stone, N. M. (1974). False physiological feedback and the maintenance of speech anxiety. *Journal of Abnormal Psychology, 83*, 164–168.

Borkovec, T. D., Weerts, T. C., & Bernstein, D. A. (1977). Assessment of anxiety. In A. R. Ciminero, K. S. Calhoun, & H. E. Adams (Eds.), *Handbook of Behavioral Assessment*. New York: Wiley.

Calef, R. A., & McLean, G. D. (1970). A comparison of reciprocal inhibition and reactive inhibition theories in the treatment of speech anxiety. *Behavior Therapy, 1*, 51–58.

Casas, J. M. (1975). *A comparison of two mediational self-control techniques for the treatment of speech anxiety*. Unpublished doctoral dissertation, Stanford University.

Clevenger, T., Jr., & King, T. T. (1961). A factor analysis of the visible symptoms of stage fright. *Speech Monographs, 28*, 296–298.

Craddock, C., Cotler, S., & Jason, L. (1978). Primary prevention: Immunization of children for speech anxiety. *Cognitive Therapy and Research, 2*, 389–396.

Cronbach, L. J. (1957). The two disciplines of scientific psychology. *American Psychologist, 12*, 671–689.

Daly, J. (1978). The assessment of social-communicative anxiety via self-reports: A comparison of measures. *Communication Monographs, 45*, 204–218.

Davidson, R. J., & Schwartz, G. E. (1976). The psychobiology of relaxation and related state. In D. I. Mostofsky (Ed.), *Behavior control and modification of physiological activity* (pp. 280–306). New York: Prentice-Hall.

DiLoreto, A. O. (1971). *Comparative psychotherapy: An experimental analysis*. Chicago: Aldine-Atherton.

Ellis, A. (1962). *Reason and emotion in psychotherapy*. New York: Lyle Stuart.

Fawcett, S. B., & Miller, L. K. (1975). Training public speaking behavior: An experimental analysis of social validation. *Journal of Applied Behavioral Analysis, 8*, 125–135.

Fremouw, W. J., & Gross, R. (1983). Issues in cognitive-behavioral treatment of performance anxiety. In P. Kendall & J. Hollon (Eds.), *Advances in Cognitive-behavioral Research and Therapy* (Vol. 2, pp. 279–306). New York: Academic Press.

Fremouw, W. J., Gross, R. T., Monroe, J., & Rapp, S. (1982). Empirical subtypes of performance anxiety. *Behavioral Assessment, 4,* 179–193.

Fremouw, W. J., & Harmatz, M. G. (1975). A helper model for behavioral treatment of speech anxiety. *Journal of Consulting and Clinical Psychology, 43,* 653–660.

Fremouw, W. J., & Zitter, R. E. (1978). A comparison of skills training and cognitive restructuring for the treatment of speech anxiety. *Behavior Therapy, 9,* 248–259.

Garfield, S. L. (1978). Research on client variables in psychotherapy. In S. L. Garfield & A. E. Bergin (Eds.), *Handbook of psychotherapy and behavior change* (2nd ed., pp. 191–232). New York: Wiley.

Geer, J. H. (1965). The development of a scale to measure fear. *Behavior Research and Therapy, 3,* 45–53.

Glass, C. R., Merluzzi, T. V., Biever, J. L., Larsen, K. H. (1982). Cognitive assessment of social anxiety: Development and validation of a self-statement questionnaire. *Cognitive Therapy and Research, 6,* 37–55.

Glogower, F., Fremouw, W. J., & McCroskey, J. (1978). A component analysis of cognitive restructuring. *Cognitive Therapy and Research, 2,* 209–223.

Goldfried, M. R., & Trier, C. (1974). Effectiveness of relaxation as an active coping skill. *Journal of Abnormal Psychology, 83,* 348–355.

Gross, R. T., & Fremouw, W. J. (1982). Progressive relaxation and cognitive restructuring for empirical subtypes of performance anxiety. *Cognitive Therapy and Research, 6,* 429–436.

Grossberg, J. M. (1965). Successful behavior therapy in a case of speech phobia ("stage fright"). *Journal of Speech and Hearing Disorders, 30,* 285–288.

Hammen, C. L., Jacobs, M., Mayol, A., & Cochran, S. D. (1980). Dysfunctional cognitions and the effectiveness of skills and cognitive-behavioral assertion training. *Journal of Consulting and Clinical Psychology, 48,* 685–695.

Hayes, B. J., & Marshall, W. I. (1984). Generalization of treatment effects in training public speakers. *Behavior Research and Therapy, 22,* 519–533.

Heimberg, R. G., Dodge, C. S., & Becker, R. E. (1987). Social phobia. In L. Michelson & M. Ascher (Eds.), *Anxiety and stress disorders* (pp. 280–309). New York: Guilford Press.

Horan, J. J., Hackett, G., Buchanan, J. D., Stone, C. I., & Demchik-Stone, D. (1977). Coping with pain: A component analysis of stress inoculation. *Cognitive Therapy and Research, 1,* 211–221.

Hosford, R. E. (1969). Overcoming fear of speaking in a group. In J. D. Krumboltz & C. E. Thoreson (Eds.), *Behavioral counseling.* New York: Holt.

Husek, T. R., & Alexander, S. (1963). The effectiveness of the anxiety differential in examination stress situations. *Education and Psychological Measurement, 23,* 309–318.

Jacobson, E. (1938). *Progressive relaxation.* Chicago: University of Chicago Press.

Jaremko, M. E. (1978). A component analysis of stress inoculation: Review and prospectus. *Cognitive Research and Therapy, 3,* 35–48.

Jaremko, M. E., Hadfield, R., & Walker, W. (1980). Contribution of an educational phase to stress inoculation of speech anxiety. *Perceptual and Motor Skills, 50,* 495–501.

Johnson, S. C. (1967). Hierarchical clustering schemes. *Psychometrika, 32,* 241–254.

Jones, R. G. (1968). *A factored measure of Ellis's irrational belief systems.* Wichita: Test Systems.

Karst, T. O., & Trexler, L. D. (1970). Initial study using fixed-role and rational-emotive therapy in treating public speaking anxiety. *Journal of Consulting and Clinical Psychology, 34,* 360–366.

Kazdin, A. E. (1980). *Research and design in clinical psychology.* New York: Harper.

Kendall, P. C., & Wilcox, L. E. (1980). Cognitive-behavioral treatment for impulsivity: Concrete versus conceptual training in non-self-controlled problem children. *Journal of Consulting and Clinical Psychology, 48,* 80–91.

Kiesler, D. J. (1966). Some myths and psychotherapy research and the search for a paradigm. *Psychological Bulletin, 65,* 110–136.

Kirsch, I., Wolpin, M., & Knutson, J. L. (1975). A comparison of *in vivo* methods for rapid reduction of "stage fright" in the college classroom: A field experiment. *Behavior Therapy, 6,* 165–171.

Lang, P. J. (1977). Physiological assessment of anxiety and fear. In J. D. Cone & R. P. Hawkins (Eds.), *Behavioral assessment: New directions in clinical psychology* (pp. 177–195). New York: Brunner/Mazel.

Lang, P. J. (1969). The mechanics of desensitization and the laboratory study of human fear. In C. Franks (Ed.), *Assessment and status of the behavior therapies.* New York: McGraw-Hill.

Last, C. G., & Hersen, M. (Eds.). (1988). *Handbook of anxiety disorders*. New York: Pergamon Press.

Lazarus, R. (1972). A cognitively oriented psychologist takes a look at biofeedback. *American Psychologist, 30*, 553–560.

Lent, R. W., Russell, R. K., & Zamostny, K. P. (1981). Comparison of cue-controlled desensitization, rational restructuring, and a credible placebo in the treatment of speech anxiety. *Journal of Consulting and Clinical Psychology, 49*, 235–243.

Lindemann, H. (1973). *Relieve tension the autogenic way*. New York: Wyden.

Luthe, W. (1969). *Autogenic therapy*. New York: Grune & Stratton.

Malleson, N. (1959). Panic and phobia. *Lancet, 1*, 225–227.

Mandler, G., Mandler, J., & Uviller, E. (1958). Autonomic feedback: The perception of autonomic activity. *Journal of Abnormal and Social Psychology, 56*, 367–373.

Mannion, N. E., & Levine, B. A. (1984). Effects of stimulus representation and cue category level on exposure (flooding) therapy. *British Journal of Clinical Psychology, 23*, 1–7.

Marshall, W. L., Preese, L., & Andrews, W. R. (1976). A self-administered program for public speaking anxiety. *Behavior Research and Therapy, 14*, 33–39.

McCroskey, J. C. (1970). Measures of communication-bound anxiety. *Speech Monographs, 37*, 269–277.

Meichenbaum, D. (1969). The effects of instructions and reinforcement on thinking and language behaviors of schizophrenics. *Behavior Research and Therapy, 7*, 101–114.

Meichenbaum, D. (1972). Cognitive modification of test anxious college students. *Journal of Consulting and Clinical Psychology, 39*(3), 370–380.

Meichenbaum, D. (1977). *Cognitive-behavior modification: An integrative approach*. New York: Plenum.

Meichenbaum, D. (1985). *Stress inoculation training*. New York: Pergamon Press.

Meichenbaum, D. H., Gilmore, J. B., & Fedoravicius, A. (1971). Group insight versus group systematic desensitization in treating speech anxiety. *Journal of Consulting and Clinical Psychology, 36*, 410–421.

Mikulas, W. L. (1976). A televised self-control clinic. *Behavior Therapy, 7*, 564–566.

Mulac, A., & Sherman, A. R. (1974). Behavioral assessment of speech anxiety. *Quarterly Journal of Speech, 60*, 134–143. Englewood Cliffs, NJ: Prentice-Hall, Inc.

Osberg, J. W. (1981). The effectiveness of applied relaxation in the treatment of speech anxiety. *Behavior Therapy, 12*, 723–729.

Paul, G. L. (1966). *Insight versus desensitization in psychotherapy*. Stanford, CA: Stanford University Press.

Paul, G. (1988). Two year follow-up of systematic desensitization in therapy groups. *Journal of Abnormal Psychology, 73*, 119–130.

Paul, G. L. (1969). Behavior modification research: Design and tactics. In C. M. Franks (Ed.), *Behavior therapy: Appraisal and status*. New York: McGraw-Hill.

Polin, A. T. (1959). The effects of flooding and physical suppression as extinction techniques on an anxiety motivated avoidance locomotor response. *Journal of Psychology, 47*, 235–245.

Rimm, D. C., & Masters, J. C. (1979). *Behavior therapy*. New York: Academic Press.

Schwartz, R., & Gottman, J. (1976). Toward a task analysis of assertive behavior. *Journal of Consulting and Clinical Psychology, 44*, 910–920.

Sherman, A. R., & Plummer, I. L. (1973). Training in relaxation as a behavioral self-management skill: An exploratory investigation. *Behavior Therapy, 4*, 543–550.

Slivken, K. E., & Buss, A. H. (1984). Misattribution and speech anxiety. *Journal of Personality and Social Psychology, 47*, 396–402.

Spielberger, C. D., Gorsuch, R. L., & Lushene, R. E. (1970). *Manual for the state-trait anxiety inventory*. Palo Alto, CA: Consulting Psychologist Press.

Stampfl, T. G. (1961). Implosive therapy: A learning theory derived psychodynamic therapeutic technique. In K. Lebarba, & G. Dent (Eds.), *Critical issues in clinical psychology*. New York: Academic Press.

Thorpe, G., Amatu, H., Blakey, R., & Burns, L. (1976). Contribution of overt instructional rehearsal and "specific insight" to the effectiveness of self-instructional training: A preliminary study. *Behavior Therapy, 7*, 504–511.

Trexler, L., & Karst, T. O. (1972). Rational emotive therapy, placebo, and no treatment effects on public speaking anxiety. *Journal of Abnormal Psychology, 79*, 60–67.

Trussell, R. P. (1978). Use of graduated behavior rehearsal, feedback, and systematic desensitization for speech anxiety. *Journal of Counseling Psychology, 25,* 14–20.

Turner, S. M., & Beidel, D. C. (1985). Empirically derived subtypes of social anxiety. *Behavior Therapy, 16,* 384–392.

Turner, S. M., Beidel, D. C., & Larkin, K. T. (1986). Situational determinants of social anxiety in clinic and nonclinic samples: Physiological and cognitive correlates. *Journal of Consulting and Clinical Psychology, 54,* 523–527.

Watson, D., & Friend, R. (1969). Measurement of social-evaluative anxiety. *Journal of Consulting and Clinical Psychology, 33,* 448–457.

Wolpe, J. (1958). *Psychotherapy by reciprocal inhibition.* Stanford, CA: Stanford University Press.

Wolpe, J. (1969). *The practice of behavior therapy.* Oxford: Pergamon Press.

Wolpe, J. (1973). *The practice of behavior therapy* (2nd ed.). Oxford: Pergamon Press.

Worthington, E. L., Jr., Tipton, R. M., Cromely, J. S., Richards, T., & Janke, R. H. (1984). Speech and coping skills training and paradox as treatment for college students anxious about public speaking. *Perceptual and Motor Skills, 59,* 394.

15

Test Anxiety

IRWIN G. SARASON AND BARBARA R. SARASON

Test anxiety is a situation-specific personality trait generally regarded as having two psychological components: worry and emotional arousal. People vary with regard to the disposition to experience these components in academic settings. Test anxiety is an important personal and social problem for several reasons, not the least of which is the ubiquitousness of taking tests. It is a decidedly unpleasant experience, plays an important role in the personal phenomenology of many people, and influences performance and personal development. Indices of test anxiety reflect the personal salience of situations in which people perform tasks and their work is evaluated.

People come to evaluative situations with their distinctive sets of personal characteristics, including assumptions, concerns, and expectations. A useful starting point in analyzing anxiety begins with the objective properties of problematic situations and individuals' interpretations of them. Regardless of the objective situation, it is the personal interpretation or cognitive appraisal of the situation that leads to behavior. Someone who has failed a test, but isn't aware of it, will not become upset. Students who feel they have performed creditably on a test will relax and anticipate recognition for their achievements. Students who feel they have performed poorly will experience stress and see themselves as having a problem.

When stress is experienced, the individual feels on the spot: "What will I do now? It's up to me, I guess." There are several types of responses to stress. The most adaptive one is a task-oriented attitude that leads the individual to take specific steps toward successfully coping with the stress-arousing situation. Seeking a conference with the teacher and studying harder are two adaptive responses to failing a test. An example of a maladaptive response is denying its importance: "So what if I got a low grade? I can't have such bad luck next time. It was a dumb test." The anxious response to failure is to stew about the problem, engage in self-derogation, and anticipate future failure.

Whereas stress inheres in one's interpretation of a situation, anxiety is a response to perceived danger and inability to handle a challenge or unfinished

---

IRWIN G. SARASON AND BARBARA R. SARASON • Department of Psychology, University of Washington, Seattle, Washington 98195.

business in a satisfactory manner. Among the characteristics of anxiety are the following:

1. The situation is seen as difficult, challenging, and threatening.
2. The individual sees himself or herself as ineffective, or inadequate, in handling the task at hand.
3. The individual focuses on undesirable consequences of personal inadequacy.
4. Self-deprecatory preoccupations are strong and interfere or compete with task-relevant cognitive activity.
5. The individual expects and anticipates failure and loss of regard by others.

These characteristics can become linked to situations through experience. Anxiety might be associated with any or all of the following: anticipating a situation, experiencing it, and "recovering" from it. There are varied, often quite idiosyncratic, physiological concomitants of anxiety. Both the quantity of anxiety and the mix of situations in which it is experienced vary from person to person:

1. Anxiety can be experienced in well-defined situations, commonly seen as stressful, to which the individual feels unable to respond adequately.
2. It can be experienced in ambiguous situations where the individual must structure task requirements and personal expectations.
3. It might be linked to classes of situations defined in idiosyncratic ways (interpersonal relationships with certain groups of peers, family members, authority figures, members of the opposite sex; situations requiring verbal, mathematical, spatial, or motoric skills).

These concomitants are consistent with a view of anxiety as a state marked by heightened self-awareness and perceived helplessness. This helplessness can arise from inability to cope with a situational demand in a satisfactory manner, perceived inability to understand situational demands, or uncertainty about the consequences of inadequacy in coping. The self-preoccupations of the anxious person, even in apparently neutral or even pleasant situations, may be due to a history of experiences marked by a relative paucity of signals indicating that a safe haven from danger has been reached.

The reasons for the perception of danger are various, including the stimulus properties of situations and unrealistically high standards. Every teacher knows students who, although quite able and bright, are virtually terror stricken at exam time. In these cases, a student often expresses concern about the consequences of not performing at a satisfactory level and embarrassment at what is regarded as "failure."

Stress then is a call for action determined by the properties of situations and personal dispositions. The test-anxious person feels unable to respond to that call. Because of similarities between the responses of test-anxious and socially anxious individuals, it seems likely that some of the findings from the test-anxiety literature can be of value both in analyzing the effects of social anxiety and in understanding its meaning.

Single sentence definitions of anxiety often acknowledge its various aspects by referring to the individual's apprehension, experience of an unpleasant emotional state, and physiological reactivity. More important than acknowledging this variety of characteristics, however, is the possibility that they may not be very highly intercorrelated. If this is the case, thinking of anxiety as a unitary concept could be quite misleading. More research is needed on the components of anxiety and the correlations among them. At any given time, people can be characterized by their observable behavior (e.g., social withdrawal), their thoughts (e.g., worries), and their bodily reactions (e.g., heart rate). For a given individual, these components might or might not be correlated. Because we know little about the degree of synchrony or desynchrony that may exist among these anxiety components for particular aspects of life, this approach could be of considerable value in increasing the reliability of anxiety measurement and understanding the relationships among anxiety components. It could also be useful in selecting appropriate dependent measures, such as performance, sense of well-being, and the reactions of others to a target person as a social object. There is a great need to interrelate the behavioral, cognitive, and physiological components of anxiety and to consider their separate and interactive effects on a variety of behaviors. This chapter focuses attention mainly on the cognitive component because (1) it has been well studied and (2) it has been shown to be significantly related to intellective performance.

We review research and theory on test anxiety in four areas: test anxiety and performance; cognitive interference, worry, and self-preoccupation; the components of test anxiety; and intervention strategies. The concluding section of the chapter deals with points of intersection between research on test anxiety and social anxiety.

TEST ANXIETY AND PERFORMANCE

There are marked individual differences in reactions to evaluational situations, the range of the reactions extending from virtual immobilization in the face of potential criticism to exhilaration at the prospect of receiving accolades. From an information-processing point of view, it is important to identify the cognitive events that influence overt behavior and the personal meaning that an event has for the individual. The person who freezes on a final examination seems preoccupied with self-doubt and the consequences of failure, whereas the accolade seeker seems confident and approaches an examination as an opportunity for receiving recognition.

To study test anxiety, an index of the variable is needed. Over the years, several test-anxiety indices have been developed and shown to be useful. One of the first of these was the Test Anxiety Questionnaire, which consisted of a series of graphic rating scales (Mandler & S. B. Sarason, 1952). The 37 items of the true–false Test Anxiety Scale, which has been used in many field and laboratory investigations, are presented in Table 1 (Sarason, 1978). Spielberger has extended his analysis of general anxiety as a state and trait to test anxiety. The

Table 1. Test Anxiety Scale (TAS) Items

(T)   1. While taking an important exam, I find myself thinking of how much brighter the other students are than I am.
(T)   2. If I were to take an intelligence test, I would worry a great deal before taking it.
(F)   3. If I knew I was going to take an intelligence test, I would feel confident and relaxed, beforehand.
(T)   4. While taking an important examination, I perspire a great deal.
(T)   5. During course examinations, I find myself thinking of things unrelated to the actual course material.
(T)   6. I get to feeling very panicky when I have to take a surprise exam.
(T)   7. During tests, I find myself thinking of the consequences of failing.
(T)   8. After important tests, I am frequently so tense that my stomach gets upset.
(T)   9. I freeze up on things like intelligence tests and final exams.
(T) 10. Getting a good grade on one test doesn't seem to increase my confidence on the second.
(T) 11. I sometimes feel my heart beating very fast during important exams.
(T) 12. After taking a test, I always feel I could have done better than I actually did.
(T) 13. I usually get depressed after taking a test.
(T) 14. I have an uneasy, upset feeling before taking a final examination.
(F) 15. When taking a test, my emotional feelings do not interfere with my performance.
(T) 16. During a course examination, I frequently get so nervous that I forget facts I really know.
(T) 17. I seem to defeat myself while working on important tests.
(T) 18. The harder I work at taking a test or studying for one, the more confused I get.
(T) 19. As soon as an exam is over, I try to stop worrying about it, but I just can't.
(T) 20. During exams, I sometimes wonder if I'll ever get through college.
(T) 21. I would rather write a paper than take an examination for my grade in a course.
(T) 22. I wish examinations did not bother me so much.
(T) 23. I think I could do much better on tests if I could take them alone and not feel pressured by a time limit.
(T) 24. Thinking about the grade I may get in a course interferes with my studying and my performance on tests.
(T) 25. If examinations could be done away with, I think I would actually learn more.
(F) 26. On exams I take the attitude, "If I don't know it now, there's no point worrying about it."
(F) 27. I really don't see why some people get so upset about tests.
(T) 28. Thoughts of doing poorly interfere with my performance on tests.
(F) 29. I don't study any harder for final exams than for the rest of my course work.
(F) 30. Even when I'm well prepared for a test, I feel very anxious about it.
(T) 31. I don't enjoy eating before an important test.
(T) 32. Before an important examination, I find my hands or arms trembling.
(F) 33. I seldom feel the need for "cramming" before an exam.
(T) 34. The university should recognize that some students are more nervous than others about tests and that this affects their performance.
(T) 35. It seems to me that examination periods should not be made such tense situations.
(T) 36. I start feeling very uneasy just before getting a test paper back.
(T) 37. I dread courses where the professor has the habit of giving "pop" quizzes.

Note. Keyed answers are in parentheses.

outcome of this work is his Test Anxiety Inventory (Spielberger, 1980). The Reactions to Tests, a multidimensional measure of four components of test anxiety, has scales that include Tension, Worry, Test-Irrelevant Thinking, and Bodily Symptoms (Sarason, 1984). Most researchers regard test anxiety as debilitative and a source of interference with task performance (Sarason, 1958). Alpert and

Haber (1960) designed a Test Anxiety Questionnaire (the Achievement-Anxiety Test) to measure both debilitative and facilitative anxiety. They reported that the two scales of their questionnaire correlated $-.48$ with each other and that the debilitative scale correlated .64 with the Test Anxiety Questionnaire.

Academic Performance

Most of the available instruments have been used to determine correlations between test anxiety and various types of performance in both adults and children. Studies in academic settings, using a variety of indices, have found an inverse relationship between test anxiety and performance (e.g., grades, scores on aptitude tests) (Sarason, 1980). There is also considerable evidence that the performance of high Test Anxiety Scale (TAS) scorers on complex tasks is particularly affected by evaluational stressors (Sarason, 1975). The less complex, less demanding the task, the weaker the inverse relationship. Evaluative stressors are found in many naturally occurring academic situations. In laboratory studies, experimental manipulations often involve time pressure, failure reports, and achievement-orienting instructions that inform subjects that there will be some kind of evaluation of their performance.

An example of test-anxiety research that deals with traditional academic indices is Coes' (1987) study of performance on a college entrance examination. Using the Reactions to Tests (RTT), she found that, while the entrance examination provided a fairly accurate index of academic achievement for students with low test anxiety, there was a serious underestimation of intellectual potential among high test-anxious students. Coes concluded that high test-anxious individuals are penalized relatively more heavily than are low test-anxious individuals in evaluative situations like college entrance examinations. She found that the RTT's Tension, Worry, and Bodily Symptoms scales provided reliable indices of the degree of underestimation of college performance. Coes also found that women received higher scores on the RTT's scales than did men, a finding consistent with many other studies of test anxiety.

Illustrating applied studies of test anxiety outside school settings is one in which this individual difference variable was related to the performance of Marine Corps recruits (Robinson, Novaco, & Sarason, 1981). Using a shortened version of the TAS, recruits high in test anxiety performed more poorly than other recruits and were more likely to be separated from the service for various reasons (including health and uncooperativeness) than were recruits with low or midrange TAS scores. Another example of applied research is Haglund's (1987) investigation of the possibility that test anxiety might be related to performance on driving tests given to people applying for drivers' licenses. He found a negative relationship between test anxiety and performance on a driving test.

Laboratory Settings

An investigation by Sarason and Stoops (1978) illustrates the use of test anxiety in testing hypotheses about both performance and cognitive processes.

The investigation comprised a series of experiments concerning subjective judgments of the passage of time. After being given either achievement-orienting or neutral instructions, subjects waited for an undesignated period of time, after which they performed an intellective task. The achievement-orienting manipulation involved telling the subject that the task was a measure of intelligence. The dependent measures were subjects' estimates of the duration of the waiting and performance periods and their scores on the assigned task.

The experiments were aimed at providing information about the way in which individuals differing in anxiety fill time. It was predicted that, in the presence of achievement-orienting cues, time would pass more slowly for high than for middle and low TAS scorers. When these cues are not present, there should not be a significant gap in estimates of time duration among groups differing in test anxiety. Furthermore, it was felt that the effects of an achievement orientation should be as noticeable while the individual is waiting to perform as during performance itself.

The first two experiments supported the conclusion that not only is the performance of TAS subjects deleteriously affected by achievement-orienting instructions, but the subjects also tend to overestimate both the duration of the test period and the period during which they wait to have their ability evaluated. This appears analogous to the tendency to exaggerate time spent in the dentist's waiting room and office. Anticipating and going through unpleasant, frightening, or threatening experiences seem to take up a lot of time. If this interpretation is correct, the question arises: Do individuals differing in anxiety fill time periods in similar or dissimilar ways? The third experiment dealt with this questions.

In the experiment, college students worked on a digit-symbol task prior to a waiting period and then were asked to solve a series of difficult anagrams. The subjects then responded to a questionnaire dealing with their cognitive activity during the anagrams task. The experimental design encompassed two factors: (1) TAS scores and (2) achievement-orienting and neutral instructions. Each subject worked on the digit-symbol task for 4 minutes. This was followed by a 4-minute waiting period. At the end of the waiting period, subjects performed for 18 minutes on the anagrams. The experiment concluded with subjects responding to the Cognitive Interference Questionnaire, a self-report measure of what people think about while working on a task (Sarason, Sarason, Keefe, Hayes, & Shearin, 1986; see Figure 1). The experiment showed that under achievement-orienting conditions, high test-anxious subjects reported significantly more preoccupation with failure and their low ability while performing than did low test-anxious subjects. It appeared as though intrusive cognitions contributed to the relatively poor performance of high test-anxious individuals.

This type of evidence led Wine (1982) to an attentional interpretation of test anxiety, according to which people at high and low levels of test anxiety differ in the types of thoughts to which their attention is directed in the face of an evaluative stressor. Consistent with this interpretation are the results of Ganzer's (1968) experiment, which showed that while performing on an intellective task, subjects with high test anxiety make many more task-irrelevant comments than

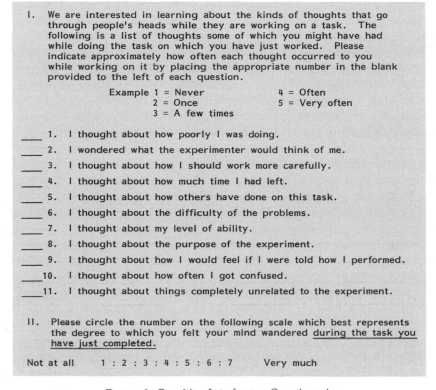

I. We are interested in learning about the kinds of thoughts that go through people's heads while they are working on a task. The following is a list of thoughts some of which you might have had while doing the task on which you have just worked. Please indicate approximately how often each thought occurred to you while working on it by placing the appropriate number in the blank provided to the left of each question.

Example	1 = Never	4 = Often
	2 = Once	5 = Very often
	3 = A few times	

____ 1. I thought about how poorly I was doing.

____ 2. I wondered what the experimenter would think of me.

____ 3. I thought about how I should work more carefully.

____ 4. I thought about how much time I had left.

____ 5. I thought about how others have done on this task.

____ 6. I thought about the difficulty of the problems.

____ 7. I thought about my level of ability.

____ 8. I thought about the purpose of the experiment.

____ 9. I thought about how I would feel if I were told how I performed.

____10. I thought about how often I got confused.

____11. I thought about things completely unrelated to the experiment.

II. Please circle the number on the following scale which best represents the degree to which you felt your mind wandered during the task you have just completed.

Not at all   1 : 2 : 3 : 4 : 5 : 6 : 7   Very much

FIGURE 1. Cognitive Interference Questionnaire.

do subjects with low test anxiety. A high percentage of these comments are self-deprecatory. Other researchers have found that people with high test anxiety are more likely than those with low test anxiety to blame themselves for their performance level (Doris & Sarason, 1955), feel less confident in making perceptual judgments (Meunier & Rule, 1967), and set lower levels of aspiration for themselves (Trapp & Kausler, 1958). These empirical findings have resulted in a variety of productive research issues, including that of anxiety's effects on cue utilization (Geen, 1976), its developmental antecedents (Dusek, 1980), and clinical and educational interventions that might influence its intensity and undesirable consequences (Denney, 1980; Meichenbaum, 1977).

Several studies have shown that individuals high in test anxiety differ from those who are low in test anxiety in the degree to which they exercise caution and conservatism in responding to tasks (Geen, 1987). When free to escape or actively avoid the testing situation, high test-anxious people tend to leave the situation if the opportunity to do so is available. When constraints against leaving are present, they often adopt a cautious and conservative mode of responding that takes the form of passive avoidance behavior.

That test anxiety plays a role in decisional and predecisional processes is illustrated by a study reported by Nichols-Hoppe and Beach (1987). Their study was stimulated in part by Geen's (1985) earlier examination of anxiety-induced cautiousness in the context of a signal detection task. Geen found that high-anxious subjects set a more stringent decision criterion for reporting detection of the signal; that is, they were more cautious about what constituted sufficient evidence that a signal had occurred. Nichols-Hoppe and Beach studied predecisional information seeking using a task requiring participants to decide among alternatives (e.g., apartments) on the basis of various dimensions of information about each (e.g., rent, size, noise level, etc.). Their subjects were allowed to examine whatever information they wanted to, in whatever order they wanted, before making the decision, and a record was kept of their search sequences. The researchers found that subjects who scored high on the TAS inspected more information in the course of predecisional searches, and that more of it was redundant, than did subjects who scored low in test anxiety. Nichols-Hoppe and Beach suggested that anxiety induces increased inspection of information prior to decision making, and that at least some of that increase consists of reinspection of previously observed information. Anxious decision makers are not only cautious but also have difficulty absorbing decision-relevant information, perhaps because of intrusive thoughts that are unrelated to the decision task. These results are consistent with other evidence concerning cognitive functioning and anxiety (Eysenck, MacLeod, & Matthews, 1987; Frey, Stahlberg, & Fries, 1986).

COGNITIVE INTERFERENCE, WORRY, AND SELF-PREOCCUPATION

Research on test anxiety has clearly established the detrimental effects of this personality characteristic on behavior in a variety of evaluative situations. A closer look at the mechanisms by which this decrease in performance level might come about suggests that interfering thoughts play a major role in the performance decrement. Thoughts that relate to worry about performance and to social comparison seem to be responsible for much of the performance decrement reported by high test-anxious people. Thoughts about off-task matters and a general wandering of attention from the task also contribute to performance deficits.

There is growing evidence of the significant role cognitive factors play in test anxiety. Covington, Omelich, and Schwarzer (1986) found that diminished ability perceptions and diminished perceptions of self-worth are key factors in the experience of anxiety and its effect on performance. Krohne and Hindel (1986) studied superior competitive table tennis players and found that top performers reported relatively few self-preoccupying thoughts while performing. Their findings suggest that while top performers generally are able to immerse themselves completely in the tasks that confront them, anxiety can cause a redirection of attentional focus from the task at hand to self and consequent failure.

Deffenbacher and his colleagues in a series of studies (e.g., Deffenbacher *et al.*, 1986) have investigated the belief systems of people differing in anxiety. They were interested in the possibility that particular classes of beliefs might be related to the types of intrusive thoughts experienced by individuals of varying anxiety levels. Overconcern for the negative consequences of personal behavior, perfectionism, the tendency to catastrophize, and beliefs about helplessness and personal isolation appear to be central beliefs significantly associated with the likelihood of experiencing anxiety. Highly anxious people become preoccupied with possible threat, their ruminations tend to persist, and they are most potent when situational threats are actually present. Hunsley (1987) found that test anxiety was related to the occurrence of frequent negative thoughts about personal abilities, the perceived difficulty of questions, and mood during exams.

In an analysis of the components of anxiety, Ingram and Kendall (1987) identified several critical cognitive features. One of these consists of schemata which relate to possible danger or harm to the individual. With regard to test anxiety this often means the perceived possibility of negative evaluation. The word "possibility" is important in relation to both general and specific anxieties, such as test anxiety. When not in an evaluational situation, or anticipating one, the highly test-anxious individual may not worry about possibilities of failure, embarrassment, and social rejection. But in evaluational situations these possibilities become active and salient. When this happens, the test-anxious individual becomes self-absorbed instead of being task-absorbed. Schwartz and Garamoni (1986) have estimated that cognitive functioning generally consists of a roughly 2 to 1 proportion of positive to negative thinking. Evaluational stressors heavily tip the balance for test-anxiety-prone individuals in the opposite direction.

The balance of positive to negative thoughts under evaluational circumstances is only part of what characterizes the cognitive life of the highly test-anxious person. Evaluational stress not only tips this balance but also influences other aspects of information processing. Naveh-Benjamin, McKeachie, and Lin (1987) have found that when compared with less-anxious students, highly test-anxious students have difficulties in organizing material to be learned. This suggests that one of the causes for the poor academic performance of highly test-anxious students is a deficit in organization of the material to be learned. A fully developed information-processing analysis of anxiety requires attention to pre-performance cognitions, as well as cognitions during performance and the individual differences associated with them.

Highly test-anxious individuals experience high levels of intrusive thinking. These interfering thoughts tend to center around worry and self-preoccupation. Although all people think about their personal capabilities in relation to the task at hand, anxious individuals seem to become overly preoccupied with these self-evaluative thoughts. Thoughts such as "I don't know what to do now" can be self-defeating if the person in fact has the wherewithal to handle the situation. One type of cognition that may be particularly relevant to anxiety in social situations consists of perceptions and thoughts about one's physical attributes. Many socially anxious people worry, often quite unrealistically, about what they see as unappealing or even revolting features of their appearance. These worries, of course, may or may not be based on reality. Anxious self-preoccupation may arouse emotions that interfere with the perception and appraisal of events and of the reactions of others. This is likely to produce errors and uncertainties in performance and interpersonal behavior. The anxious person may at the same time notice too much and too little and be prone to distort and misinterpret available cues.

Attributional Aspects of Test Anxiety

The study of anxiety requires analysis of both features of situations and the individual differences people bring to the situations. One pertinent source of individual differences is the attributional styles of people differing in test anxiety. The available evidence suggest that there usually is more to test anxiety than simply a history of failure experiences. Test-anxious people process their objective successes and failures in distinctive ways, and their anxiety is related importantly to how they, and significant others in their lives, view test-taking experiences.

An important aspect of attributional style is the way in which responsibility for outcome is assigned. Turk and Sarason (1983) studied the performance of subjects differing in test anxiety as a function of a prior success or failure experience and the subject's assignment of responsibility for the performance level achieved. Half of the subjects began the experiment by working on either insoluble or easy anagrams. For each difficulty level, the subjects were given either achievement-orienting or neutral instructions. All subjects were asked to check "passed" on their test if they solved three of the five anagrams and "failed" if they solved fewer than three problems. (All the subjects who worked on the easy anagrams "passed.") They then filled out a questionnaire that dealt with causal attributions. The questionnaire asked the subjects about the extent to which they interpreted their anagrams performance as being due to ability, effort, luck, and task difficulty. Attributions were made on a Likert-type scale of 7 points. In the next phase of the experiment all subjects worked on a series of moderately difficult anagrams.

Following the failure condition, the high test-anxious group performed at a lower level than did all other groups in the experiment. This is consistent with previous work on test anxiety. Following the success condition, the high test-anxious subjects were categorized on the basis of their causal attributions. Subjects who made internal attributions on the failure task (e.g., "I'm not good at solving problems") had relatively poor subsequent performance on the anagrams regardless of their anxiety score. Following the success condition, the best-performing group consisted of high test-anxious subjects who made internal attributions (e.g., "I'm an intelligent person"). This study illustrates the need to know more about the cognitive effects of success as well as failure experiences for subjects differing in test anxiety and in attributional style.

In a study that addressed this question of the interaction of test anxiety and attributional style, Goldberg (1983) correlated test anxiety, assessed using total scores on the Reactions to Tests, with the Attributional Styles Questionnaire, which yields scores for causal attribution regarding both good and bad (desirable and undesirable) events. She found that highly test-anxious subjects tend to attribute successful task performance to external factors (e.g., "It was an easy test"). She also found that test anxiety is positively correlated with scores on the Fear of Negative Evaluation Scale (Watson & Friend, 1969). Thus, highly anxious individuals worry about what other people think of them and attribute bad outcomes to "personal helplessness," while low test-anxious individuals tend to attribute their successes to personal competence and their failures to external factors. In other words, attributions to long-lasting pervasive causes rather than temporary situational factors are reversed for success and failure in the two groups.

Test anxiety can be interpreted as the tendency to view with alarm the consequences of inadequate performance in an evaluative situation. In a sense, the highly test-anxious person creates his or her own problem by processing too much information and making inappropriate attributions. The job of processing task-relevant information is complicated by maladaptive personalized feedback (e.g., "I'm dumb"; "What if I don't pass this exam?"). Conditions that evoke positive attributions might be particularly effective with highly test-anxious people because they counter the worrying and preoccupation that is characteristic of anxiety.

COMPONENTS OF TEST ANXIETY

Researchers who study general and specific types of anxiety, such as test anxiety, have wondered about the degree to which they are dealing with a unitary response or an amalgam of responses. One frequently mentioned distinction is the one between worry and emotionality (Deffenbacher, 1977, 1978; Kaplan, McCormick, & Twitchell, 1979; Liebert & Morris, 1967; Morris, Davis, & Hutchings, 1981). *Worry* refers to the cognitive side of anxiety (preoccupations, concerns); *emotionality* refers largely to a person's awareness of bodily arousal and tension. In their reviews of the literature on the worry–emotionality distinction, Deffenbacher (1980) and Tryon (1980) showed that while worry and emotionality are correlated, only worry is related to performance decrements in the presence of an evaluational stressor. Burchfield, Stein, and Hamilton (1985), after reviewing the literature, concluded that anxiety is primarily a cognitive event with physiological correlates.

Worry and emotionality, like anxiety, are concepts. They may or may not be unitary. A useful step would be to define more reliably the various types of reactions people have when placed in evaluational situations. Deffenbacher (1986) found that while performing on a test, high test-anxious subjects had higher pulse rates than those low in test anxiety. Pulse rate was unrelated to performance, while worry over evaluation was associated with poor performance.

There is a sizeable body of evidence consistent with the idea that proneness to self-preoccupation and, more specifically, worry over evaluation, is a powerful component of what is referred to as test anxiety. If, as several studies suggest, the most active ingredient of test anxiety is self-preoccupation, there are some important and practical implications for assessment. While both general and test anxiety are usually defined as complex states that include cognitive, emotional, behavioral, and bodily components, most anxiety measures reflect this inclusive definition by yielding only one global score. Wine (1982) has pointed out that it is not immediately obvious how to identify the active or most active ingredients in this complex and has suggested that test anxiety might fruitfully be reconceptualized primarily in terms of cognitive and attentional processes aroused in evaluational settings.

The Reactions to Tests (RTT) was created in order to assess separately several components of a person's reactions to test situations (Sarason, 1984). The RTT consists of four factor analytically derived scales:

1. Tension ("I feel distressed and uneasy before tests").
2. Worry ("During tests, I wonder how the other people are doing").
3. Test-Irrelevant Thought ("Irrelevant bits of information pop into my head during a test").
4. Bodily Reactions ("My heart beats faster when the test begins").

Table 2 presents of the items of the four scales. While the scales are positively intercorrelated, the correlations seem low enough to justify comparisons among them concerning their predictive value. In one study of performance on a digit-symbol task, the RTT was related to performance on a difficult digit-symbol task under evaluative conditions (Sarason, 1984). However, the Worry scale was more consistently related to performance and post-performance reports of cognitive interference than were the other scales. The Tension scale approached the Worry scale as a predictor of performance.

The RTT has been related to physiological measures obtained during a test-taking situation. Burchfield, Sarason, Sarason, and Beaton (1982) examined the relationship of the RTT to physiological indices gathered while college students worked on items of the type found on intelligence tests. Both the Tension and Worry scales were significantly correlated with skin conductance and finger-tip temperature changes during performance. There were no significant correlations with EMG changes. Interestingly, the Task-Irrelevant Thinking and Bodily Reactions scales were unrelated to all physiological change measures. More studies dealing with relationships among components of test anxiety, performance variables, and physiological measures are needed.

INTERVENTION STRATEGIES

With increasing evidence of the deleterious role test anxiety plays in performance, impetus has been given to ways of increasing test-taking coping skills. What can be done to strengthen the test-anxious person's ability to handle task-interfering tensions related to being evaluated? Experimental studies have used a wide variety of interventions to influence performance. Some of these manipulations may have opposite effects on people differing in test anxiety. For example, reassuring and neutral instructions at the outset of an experimental session

Table 2. The Four Factor Analytically Derived Reaction to Tests (RTT) Scales

Tension
1. I feel distressed and uneasy before tests.
2. I freeze up when I think about an upcoming test.
3. I feel jittery before tests.
4. While taking a test, I feel tense.
5. I find myself becoming anxious the day of a test.
6. I wish tests did not bother me so much.
7. I am anxious about tests.
8. I feel panicky during tests.
9. Before tests, I feel troubled about what is going to happen.
10. I have an uneasy feeling before an important test.

Worry
1. The thought, "What happens if I fail this test?" goes through my mind during tests.
2. During a difficult test, I worry whether I will pass it.
3. While taking a test, I find myself thinking how much brighter the other people are.
4. After a test, I say to myself, "It's over and I did as well as I could."
5. Before taking a test, I worry about failure.
6. While taking a test, I often think about how difficult it is.
7. Thoughts of doing poorly interfere with my concentration during tests.
8. During tests, I think about how poorly I am doing.
9. The harder I work at taking a test, the more confused I get.
10. During tests, I wonder how the other people are doing.

Test-irrelevant thinking
1. During tests, I find myself thinking of things unrelated to the material being tested.
2. Irrelevant bits of information pop into my head during a test.
3. My mind wanders during tests.
4. While taking a test, I often don't pay attention to the questions.
5. I think about current events during a test.
6. I have fantasies a few times during a test.
7. While taking tests, I sometimes think about being somewhere else.
8. During tests, I find I am distracted by thoughts of upcoming events.
9. I daydream during tests.
10. During tests, I think about recent past events.

Bodily reactions
1. I become aware of my body during tests (feeling itches, pain, sweat, nausea).
2. I feel the need to go to the toilet more often than usual during a test.
3. My heart beats faster when the test begins.
4. My stomach gets upset before tests.
5. I get a headache during an important test.
6. I get a headache before a test.
7. I sometimes feel dizzy after a test.
8. My hands often feel cold before and during a test.
9. My mouth feels dry during a test.
10. I sometimes find myself trembling before or during tests.

facilitate the performance of high test-anxious groups. Unfortunately, these same conditions may be detrimental for low test-anxious groups.

Observational opportunities and modeling can provide a person not only with demonstrations of overt responses but, if the model "thinks through" problems and tactics aloud, covert ones as well. Observing a model prepare for a test situation can shape and reshape one's views and expectancies concerning oneself and others. Whereas exposure to models who have failure experiences has a negative effect on the performance of high test-anxious subjects, exposure to models displaying adaptive behavior plays a discernible positive role in facilitating learning and performance. In one experiment, subjects differing in test anxiety were given the opportunity to observe a model who demonstrated effective ways of performing an anagrams task. Using a talk-out-loud technique, the model displayed several types of facilitative thoughts and cognitions. The major finding was that high test-anxious subjects benefited more from the opportunity to observe a cognitive model than did those low in test anxiety (Sarason, 1972, 1973). Cognitive modeling might have considerable potential in instructional programs as a means of demonstrating for students the differences between adaptive and maladaptive cognitions and the negative aspects of maladaptive attentional habits.

Another approach to facilitating the performance of highly test-anxious people is pertinent, easily understood pre-performance instructions that direct subjects' attention to the importance of task-relevant thinking. Sarason and Turk (1983) studied 180 undergraduate students differing in RTT Worry scores who performed on a difficult anagrams task in groups of 15 to 20. The subjects were told that performance on the anagrams task was a measure of the ability to do college-level work. After this communication, one-third of the subjects were given an attention-directing condition, one-third were given reassurance, and a control group received no additional communication.

The instructions for the anagrams task were contained in the test booklet. The attention-directing and reassuring communications were given by the experimenter after the subjects had read the task instructions, which included the achievement-orienting message. Subjects under the reassurance condition were told not to be overly concerned about their performance on the anagrams. The experimenter made such comments as "Don't worry" and "You will do just fine." Subjects under the attention-directing condition were told to absorb themselves as much as possible in the anagrams task and to avoid thinking about other things. The experimenter said, "concentrate all your attention on the problems," "think only about the anagrams," and "don't let yourself get distracted from the task." High-worry subjects under the control condition performed poorly compared to the other control subjects. High-worry subjects in the attention-directing and reassurance groups performed well. However, consistent with previous evidence, the study showed that reassuring instructions have a detrimental effect on people who are not worriers. Nonworry subjects in the reassurance group performed poorly, perhaps because nonworriers take the reassuring communication at face value; that is, they take the task lightly and lower their motivational level. The performance levels of all groups that received the attention-directing instructions were high. The attention-directing approach seems to have all of the advantages of reassurance for high-worry subjects, with none of the disadvantages for low-worry subjects.

After the anagrams task all the subjects responded to the Cognitive Interference Questionnaire (CIQ), which provided a measure of the number and type of interfering thoughts experienced in that particular situation. Cognitive interference at the end of the anagrams tasks was relatively low under the attention-direction condition for high- as well as low-worry subjects. Similar to previous findings concerning highly test-anxious subjects, the high-worry groups showed high cognitive interference under the control conditions.

The performance and CIQ scores were reanalyzed in terms of the other RTT scales, but none of these analyses revealed statistically significant results. The findings of this experiment support an attentional interpretation of anxiety and worry. They suggest that simply calling subjects' attention to the need for task-oriented behavior can have a salutary effect on their performance, with a reduction in intrusive thoughts.

Another approach to test-anxiety reduction is through social psychological processes and the relationship between the test taker and the tester. For example, Sarason (1981) employed a social support manipulation in an experiment with subjects who differed in test anxiety. Social support was provided by a group discussion focused on sharing concerns and solutions concerning students' problems of stress and anxiety in testing situations. Several confederates worked to heighten social association by suggesting a meeting after the experimental session. The group discussion was followed by an anagrams task which was presented as a separate, unrelated experiment run by another experimenter that was combined into the same session for the sake of efficiency.

The results showed that performance and self-preoccupation as measured by the CIQ were affected by this specially created opportunity for social association and acceptance by others. Performance on the anagrams task increased and self-preoccupation decreased as a function of the social support manipulation. However, this change was pronounced only in subjects who were high in test anxiety. The performance of those low in test anxiety was essentially unchanged by the support manipulation.

Modeling and pre-performance instructions are only two of the interventions aimed at reducing the deleterious effects of test anxiety on performance. There have been two general approaches to interventions pertinent to test anxiety, those that deal with aspects of the test situation and those intended to increase the individual's ability to perform in test-taking situations (Spielberger & Vagg, 1987). The modeling experiment described above and the experiment dealing with pre-performance instructions illustrate efforts to influence test anxiety through situational manipulations. In addition to these types of laboratory investigations, the number of investigations in actual classroom settings are increasing. For example, Helmke (1986) investigated academic performance across classrooms. He found that the more success-and-failure feedback to students is salient within the classroom, the stronger are the interfering effects of high test anxiety. He also found that orienting students by frequently giving them previews, heavily emphasizing review of learned material, and allotting sufficient time for answering questions reduce the debilitating effects of worry cognitions.

Further classroom research is needed to explore the interrelationship of achievement and achievement-oriented variables by comparing groups of classrooms differing in academic atmosphere and the relationship between teachers and students. There is a need also to compare the results of manipulations using individual students, as well as the classroom, as the unit of analysis.

Intervention research focused on the individual has been carried out in the form of treatments directed toward either or both the cognitive and the emotional dimensions of test anxiety (Allen, Elias, & Zlotow, 1980; Crowley, Crowley, & Clodfelter, 1986; Denney, 1980; Zeidner, Klingman, & Papko, 1988). Frequently used interventions include cognitive therapy, rational-emotive therapy, cognitive-behavioral treatments, systematic desensitization, relaxation training, and biofeedback training. Cognitively focused treatments seem to be effective in reducing test anxiety, and emotionality-focused treatments, such as biofeedback, are relative ineffective in reducing test anxiety unless these treatments include cognitive elements such as detailed instructions on how to use relaxation. The cognitively focused treatments have been found to generalize from individual treatment settings to school-related social-evaluative situations, such as giving a talk in class or talking with a teacher. Cognitive therapies directed toward the reduction of the worry component of test anxiety have been successful in reducing self-reported anxiety. While cognitive therapies have sometimes been successful in improving the academic performance of test-anxious students, the success has by no means been universal (Dendato & Diener, 1986).

Using test-anxious students as the unit of analysis requires attention not only to their cognitions and emotional reactions, but also to the poor academic skills which they often bring to academic situations. As several research studies have noted, highly test-anxious students have less effective study habits than do their low-anxious counterparts (Culler & Holahan, 1980). There is increasing evidence that inadequate study skills and ineffective test-taking strategies (measured independently of classroom performance) may have stronger negative effects on grades than test anxiety (Brown & Nelson, 1983). Dendato and Diener (1986) have found that while study skill training alone was not effective in reducing anxiety or improving test performance, and relaxation and cognitive training were effective in reducing anxiety but not in improving performance, the combination of these interventions was effective in both reducing anxiety and in improving performance. The superiority of Dendato and Diener's combined therapy condition suggests the value of having interventions sufficiently complex to deal with the major facets of the test-anxiety experience. The student who is unprepared or lacks effective test-taking skills may benefit little from attempts to reduce worry directly. Not only must self-evaluative statements and other off-task behavior be reduced, but effective on-task behavior must be substituted. Attempts to improve preparation and test-taking skills without treating anxiety, however, will also often prove to be an insufficient treatment for test-anxious students.

TEST ANXIETY AND SOCIAL ANXIETY

Anxiety is generally defined as having both cognitive (apprehension, dread, fear) and affective-emotional arousal (physiological responsiveness) components. The research we have reviewed reflects the roles these components play in test anxiety. Social anxiety, which encompasses dating anxiety, speech anxiety, stage fright, communication apprehension, audience anxiety, and social embarrassment, would appear to involve similar components. Just as a componential approach seems to hold promise of a better understanding of evaluational anxiety, the same approach may prove useful in the study of social anxiety and shyness. Although these two concepts are among the most widely used in analyses of social behavior, they refer to such a wide variety of phenomena that their referents are often difficult to identify. For example, social anxiety can be specific or general. Some people experience it prior to, during, or after their social interactions, whereas others experience it in particular situations. For some people, social anxiety and shyness are highly correlated, whereas for others there seems to be only a slight relationship. Although most shy people show anxiety and social inhibition in interpersonal situations, others may display timidity or introversion without apparent personal discomfort (Leary, 1983). Thus, two important problems present themselves: (1) How general or traitlike are the tendencies toward social anxiety and shyness? (2) What are the components of reactions to social situations and what is their interrelationship? A third question also needs an answer: (3) How do moderator variables (either within the individual or in the environment) influence social behavior and the experience of social anxiety and shyness?

Because the component analysis of test anxiety seems promising, we are using a similar approach to social behavior. The RTT described earlier consists of scales that assess tension or emotionality, worry, test-irrelevant thought, and bodily reactions. The RTT's items have been rewritten to refer to social rather than testing situations. An instrument called Reactions to Social Situations (RSS) has been administered to a large group of college students and factor analyzed. Essentially, the same four factors found for the RTT emerged in the factor analysis of the RSS (Sarason & Sarason, 1986). However, the RSS Tension and Worry factors were less pure than the comparable RTT factors.

When the RSS was correlated with three other individual difference indices, several significant relationships were found. One of these indices was the Social Competence Questionnaire (Com Q), a 10-item scale designed to tap the degree of comfort in social situations (Sarason, Sarason, Hacker, & Basham, 1985). Each Com-Q item is rated by the subject on a 4-point rating scale from *not at all like me* to *a great deal like me*. Table 3 presents the Com-Q's items. Whereas there were significant negative correlations between all four RSS scales and the Com Q for both sexes, those involving the RSS Tension scale were the highest ($rs = -.67$ and $-.63$ for males and females, respectively.) The comparable Worry scale correlations were $-.45$ and $-.49$. Thus, self-reported tension or emotionality and worry on the RSS is reflected in lower levels of self-described social competence.

The RSS scores were also correlated with the two scales of the Social Support Questionnaire (SSQ; Sarason, Levine, Basham, & Sarason, 1983). The SSQ has two scores: the Number score measures the number of persons that the individual perceives to be available if support were needed; the Satisfaction scores measures how satisfactory the available support is perceived to be. Just as

Table 3. Items Included in the Social Competence Questionnaire (COM Q)

1. Start a conversation with someone I don't know well, but would like to get to know better.
2. Be confident in my ability to make friends, even in a situation where I know few people.
3. Be able to mix well in a group.
4. Feel uncomfortable looking at other people directly.
5. Have trouble keeping a conversation going when I'm just getting to know someone.
6. Find it hard to let a person know that I want to become closer friends with him/her.
7. Enjoy social gatherings just to be with people.
8. Have problems getting other people to notice me.
9. Feel confident of my social behavior.
10. Seek out social encounters because I enjoy being with other people.

Note. Each item is marked on a 4-point scale ranging from *not at all like me* to *a great deal like me.*

was the case with the Com Q, the Tension scale correlated the most negatively of the four RSS scales with the SSQ Number score ($rs = -.35$ and $-.33$ for males and females, respectively).

The third individual difference measure with which the RSS was correlated was a specially constructed, slightly shortened version of the Thought Occurrence Questionnaire (TOQ) (Sarason, Sarason, Keefe, Hayes, & Shearin, 1986). The TOQ asks subjects to rate the frequency with which task-irrelevant thoughts generally occur while they work on various types of tasks. The 5-point rating scale extends from *never* to *very often*. Examples of TOQ items are, "I think about how poorly I am doing"; "I think about what someone will think of me"; "I think about how hard it is."

The correlation of the RSS score (summing over its 40 items) with the TOQ was .44 for males and .53 for females. Every item on the TOQ was correlated significantly and positively with the RSS's scores, reflecting the tendency to experience task-irrelevant thoughts in social situations. It may well be that task-irrelevant thinking plays as detrimental role in social behavior as it does in test-taking situations. In this shortened version of the TOQ, 22 of the 28 items correlated significantly with the RSS Tension scale, and 24 of the correlations with the RSS Worry scale were significant.

These findings using the RSS are only small first steps in specifying the relationships among dimensions of social behavior, personality and cognitive characteristics. They are presented here because it is possible that a multidimensional approach to social behavior will provide an empirically based vocabulary that reduces some of the semantic disagreements surrounding such terms as *shyness* and *social anxiety.*

A recent study by Schwarzer and Quast (1985) replicated the results presented above with German university students. In another study, C. Schwarzer (1986) provided replication evidence for both German and Turkish school children. These researchers suggested that when stressful events occur in either social or academic situations, people will shift their attention from task to self in the process of assessing their competence and likely outcomes. If competence and likely outcomes are perceived as being insufficient or inadequate, the situation will be appraised as threatening, and the individual will experience anxiety. There may also be a degree of resignation, the result of which would be that the individual does not invest enough effort and persistence in the task or in the social interaction, thus increasing the probability of ultimate failure (Carver, Peterson, Follansbee, & Scheier, 1983; Slapion & Carver, 1981).

In conclusion, our goal in this chapter has been to suggest the mechanisms by which test anxiety impacts performance and how this knowledge may lead to effective intervention strategies. We have argued that these same approaches can be useful in dealing with social anxiety. Finally, we have discussed a number of testing instruments that have proven useful in assessing the components of anxiety and in enhancing our understanding of the processes by which anxiety affects performance under stress.

REFERENCES

Allen, G. J., Elias, M. J., & Zlotlow, S. F. (1980). Behavioral interventions for alleviating test anxiety: A methodological overview of current therapeutic practices. In I. G. Sarason (Ed.), *Test anxiety: Theory, research, and applications* (pp. 155–186). Hillsdale, NJ: Lawrence Erlbaum.

Alpert, R., & Haber, R. N. (1960). Anxiety in academic achievement situations. *Journal of Abnormal and Social Psychology, 61,* 207–215.

Brown, S. D., & Nelson, T. L. (1983). Beyond the uniformity myth: A comparison of academically successful and unsuccessful test-anxious students. *Journal of Counseling Psychology, 30,* 367–374.

Burchfield, S. R., Sarason, I. G., Sarason, B. R., & Beaton, R. (1982). *Test anxiety and physiological responding.* Unpublished study.

Burchfield, S. R., Stein, L. J., & Hamilton, K. L. (1985). Test anxiety: A model for studying psychological and physiological interrelationships. In S. R. Burchfield (Ed.), *Stress: Psychological and physiological interactions* (pp. 35–66). New York: Hemisphere.

Carver, C. S., Peterson, L. M., Follansbee, D. J., & Scheier, M. F. (1983). Effects of self-directed attention on performance and persistence among persons high and low in test anxiety. *Cognitive Therapy and Research, 7,* 333–354.

Coes, M. (1987). *Test anxiety and the Brazilian College entrance examination.* Unpublished master's thesis, University of Illinois at Urbana-Champaign.

Covington, M. V., Omelich, C. L., & Schwarzer, R. (1986). Anxiety, aspirations, and self-concept in the achievement process: A longitudinal model with latent variables. *Motivation and Emotion, 10,* 71–88.

Crowley, C., Crowley, D., & Clodfelter, C. (1986). Effects of a self-coping cognitive treatment for test anxiety. *Journal of Counseling Psychology, 1,* 84–86.

Culler, R. E., & Holahan, C. J. (1980). Test anxiety and academic performance: The effects of study-related behavior. *Journal of Educational Psychology, 72,* 16–20.

Deffenbacher, J. L. (1977). Relationship of worry and emotionality to performance on the Miller Analogies Test. *Journal of Educational Psychology, 69,* 191–195.

Deffenbacher, J. L. (1978). Worry, emotionality and task-generated interference in test anxiety: An empirical test of attentional theory. *Journal of Educational Psychology, 70,* 248–254.

Deffenbacher, J. L. (1980). Worry and emotionality in test anxiety. In I. G. Sarason (Ed.), *Test anxiety: Theory, research, and applications* (pp. 111–128). Hillsdale, NJ: Erlbaum.

Deffenbacher, J. L. (1986). Cognitive and physiological components of test anxiety in real-life exams. *Cognitive Therapy and Research, 10,* 636–644.

Deffenbacher, J. L., Zwemer, W. A., Whisman, M. A., Hill, R. A., & Sloan, R. D. (1986). Irrational beliefs and anxiety. *Cognitive Therapy and Research, 10,* 281–292.

Dendato, K. M., & Diener, D. (1986). Effectiveness of cognitive/relaxational therapy and study-skills training in reducing self-reported anxiety and improving the academic performance of test-anxious students. *Journal of Counseling Psychiatry, 33,* 131–135.

Denney, D. R. (1980). Self-control approaches to the treatment of test anxiety. In I. G. Sarason (Ed.), *Test anxiety: Theory, research, and applications* (pp. 209–244). Hillsdale, NJ: Lawrence Erlbaum.

Doris, J., & Sarason, S. B. (1955). Test anxiety and blame assignment in a failure situation. *Journal of Abnormal and Social Psychology, 50,* 335–338.

Dusek, J. B. (1980). The development of test anxiety in children. In I. G. Sarason (Ed.), *Test anxiety: Theory, research, and applications* (pp. 81–110). Hillsdale, NJ: Lawrence Erlbaum.

Eysenck, M. W., MacLeod, C., & Mathews, A. (1987). Cognitive functioning and anxiety. *Psychological Research, 49,* 189–195.

Frey, D., Stahlberg, D., & Fries, A. (1986). Information seeking of high- and low-anxiety subjects after receiving positive and negative self-relevant feedback. *Journal of Personality, 54,* 695–703.

Ganzer, V. J. (1968). The effects of audience pressure and test anxiety on learning and retention in a serial learning situation. *Journal of Personality and Social Psychology, 8,* 194–199.

Geen, R. G. (1976). Test anxiety, observation, and range of cue utilization. *British Journal of Social and Clinical Psychology, 15,* 253–259.

Geen, R. G. (1985). Evaluation apprehension and response withholding in solution of anagrams. *Personality and Individual Differences, 6,* 293–298.

Geen, R. G. (1987). Test anxiety and behavioral avoidance. *Journal of Research in Personality, 21,* 481–488.

Goldberg, S. A. (1983). *Cognitive correlates of test anxiety: Examination of the relationship among test anxiety, fear of negative evaluation, social anxiety, and attributional style.* Unpublished Honors thesis, Brown University.

Haglund, M. (1987). *Driver licensing and test anxiety.* Unpublished manuscript, Uppsala, Sweden.

Helmke, A. (1986, July). *Classroom context mediates how anxiety affects academic achievement.* Paper presented at the 7th International Meeting of the Society for Test Anxiety Research in Jerusalem.

Hunsley, J. (1987). Internal dialogue during academic examinations. *Cognitive Therapy and Research, 11,* 653–664.

Ingram, R. E., & Kendall, P. C. (1987). The cognitive side of anxiety. *Cognitive Therapy and Research, 11,* 523–536.

Kaplan, R. M., McCormick, S. M., & Twitchell, M. (1979). Is it the cognitive or the behavioral component which makes cognitive-behavior modification effective in test anxiety? *Journal of Counseling Psychology, 26,* 371–377.

Krohne, H. W., & Hindel, C. (1986). *Trait anxiety, state anxiety, and coping behavior as predictors of athletic performance.* Paper presented at the International Conference on Stress and Emotion, Budapest, Hungary.

Leary, M. R. (1983). *Understanding social anxiety: Social, personality, and clinical perspectives.* Beverly Hills, CA: Sage.

Liebert, R. M., & Morris, L. W. (1967). Cognitive and emotional components of test anxiety: A distinction and some initial data. *Psychological Reports, 20,* 975–978.

Mandler, G., & Sarason, S. B. (1952). A study of anxiety and learning. *Journal of Abnormal and Social Psychology, 47,* 166–173.

Meichenbaum, D. (1977). *Cognitive-behavior modification: An integrative approach.* New York: Plenum.

Meunier, C., & Rule, B. G. (1967). Anxiety, confidence and conformity. *Journal of Personality, 35,* 498–504.

Morris, L. W., Davis, M. A., & Hutchings, C. H. (1981). Cognitive and emotional components of anxiety: Literature review and a revised Worry–Emotionality Scale. *Journal of Educational Psychology, 73,* 541–555.

Naveh-Benjamin, M., McKeachie, W. J., & Lin, Yi-Guang (1987). Two types of test-anxious students: Support for an information processing model. *Journal of Educational Psychology, 79,* 131–136.

Nichols-Hoppe, K. T., & Beach, L. R. (1987). *The effects of test anxiety and task variables on predecisional information search.* Unpublished manuscript. University of Washington, Seattle.

Robinson, G. L., Novaco, R. W., & Sarason, I. G. (1981). *Cognitive correlates of outcome and performance in Marine Corps recruit training* (Tech. Rep. AR-005). Seattle: University of Washington.

Sarason, B. R., Sarason, I. G., Hacker, T. A., & Basham, R. B. (1985). Concomitants of social support: Social skills, physical attractiveness, and gender. *Journal of Personality and Social Psychology, 49,* 469–480.

Sarason, I. G. (1958). The effects of anxiety, reassurance, and meaningfulness of material to be learned on verbal learning. *Journal of Experimental Psychology, 56,* 472–477.

Sarason, I. G. (1972). Test anxiety and the model who fails. *Journal of Personality and Social Psychology,* 22, 410–423.

Sarason, I. G. (1973). Test anxiety and cognitive modeling. *Journal of Personality and Social Psychology,* 28, 58–61.

Sarason, I. G. (1975). Test anxiety, attention, and the general problem of anxiety. In C. D. Spielberger & I. G. Sarason (Eds.), *Stress and anxiety* (Vol. 1, pp. 165–210). New York: Hemisphere/Halstead.

Sarason, I. G. (1978). *The Test Anxiety Scale: Concept and research.* In C. D. Spielberger & I. G. Sarason (Eds.), *Stress and anxiety* (Vol. 5). Washington, DC: Hemisphere.

Sarason, I. G. (Ed.). (1980). *Test anxiety: Theory, research, and applications.* Hillsdale, NJ: Lawrence Erlbaum.

Sarason, I. G. (1981). Test anxiety, stress, and social support. *Journal of Personality,* 49, 101–114.

Sarason, I. G. (1984). Stress, anxiety, and cognitive interference: Reactions to tests. *Journal of Personality and Social Psychology,* 46, 929–938.

Sarason, I. G., Levine, H. M., Basham, R. B., & Sarason, B. R. (1983). Assessing social support: The Social Support Questionnaire. *Journal of Personality and Social Psychology,* 44, 127–139.

Sarason, I. G., & Sarason, B. R. (1986). Anxiety and interfering thoughts: Their effect on social interaction. In W. H. Jones, J. M. Cheek, & S. R. Briggs (Eds.), *Shyness: Perspectives on research and treatment* (pp. 253–264). New York: Plenum.

Sarason, I. G., Sarason, B. R., Keefe, D. E., Hayes, B. E., & Shearin, E. N. (1986). Cognitive interference: Situational determinants and traitlike characteristics. *Journal of Personality and Social Psychology,* 51, 215–226.

Sarason, I. G., & Stoops, R. (1978). Test anxiety and the passage of time. *Journal of Consulting and Clinical Psychology,* 1, 102–109.

Sarason, I. G., & Turk, S. (1983). *Test anxiety and the directing of attention.* Unpublished study. University of Washington, Seattle.

Schwartz, R. M., & Garamoni, G. I. (1986). A structural model of positive and negative states of mind: Asymmetry and the internal dialogue. In P. C. Kendall (Ed.), *Advances in cognitive-behavioral research and therapy* (Vol. 5, pp. 2–63). New York: Academic Press.

Schwarzer, C. (Ed.). (1986). *Two studies of anxiety.* Unpublished report. University of Dusseldorf, West Germany.

Schwarzer, R., & Quast, H. (1985). Multidimensionality of the anxiety experience: Evidence for additional components. In H. M. van der Ploeg, R. Schwarzer, & C. D. Spielberger (Eds.), *Advances in test anxiety research* (Vol. 4, pp. 3–14). Lisse, The Netherlands: Swets & Zeitlinger.

Slapion, M. J., & Carver, C. S. (1981). Self-directed attention and facilitation of intellectual performance among persons high in test anxiety. *Cognitive Therapy and Research,* 5, 115–121.

Spielberger, C. D. (1980). *Test Anxiety Inventory. Preliminary professional manual.* Palo Alto, CA: Consulting Psychologists Press.

Spielberger, C. D., & Vagg, P. R. (1987). The treatment of test anxiety: A transactional process model. In R. Schwarzer, H. M. van der Ploeg, & C. D. Spielberger (Eds.), *Advances in test anxiety research* (Vol. 5, pp. 179–186). Lisse, The Netherlands: Swets & Zeilinger.

Trapp, E. P., & Kausler, D. H. (1958). Test anxiety level and goal-setting behavior. *Journal of Consulting Psychology,* 22, 31–34.

Tryon, G. S. (1980). The measurement and treatment of test anxiety. *Review of Educational Research, 50,* 343–372.

Turk, S., & Sarason, I. G. (1983). *Test anxiety, success-failure, and causal attribution.* Unpublished manuscript. University of Washington, Seattle.

Watson, D., & Friend, R. (1969). Measurement of social-evaluative anxiety. *Journal of Consulting and Clinical Psychology, 33,* 448–457.

Wine, J. D. (1982). Evaluation anxiety: A cognitive-attentional construct. In H. W. Krohne, & L. Laux (Eds.), *Achievement, stress, and anxiety* (pp. 207–219). Washington, DC: Hemisphere.

Zeidner, M., Klingman, A., & Papko, O. (1988). Enhancing students' test coping skills: Report of a psychological health education program. *Journal of Educational Psychology, 80,* 95–101.

16

Fear of Failure

The Psychodynamic, Need Achievement, Fear of Success, and Procrastination Models

ESTHER D. ROTHBLUM

> If at first you don't succeed, you're about average.
> —Fortune cookie proverb

In a society focused on achievement and success, the possibility of failure is often minimized or denied. Nevertheless, the very nature of a competitive society is that success can only be attained by a few. Although many individuals strive for success, others behave in ways that minimize the risk of failure, even at the cost of attaining success. The concept of fear of failure has been investigated from widely different perspectives, resulting in an enormous literature. This chapter focuses on four perspectives: (1) the psychodynamic conceptualization of fear of failure; (2) fear of failure as viewed by the need achievement literature; (3) fear of failure versus fear of success; and (4) fear of failure as an antecedent of academic procrastination. Each perspective has used different ways of assessing fear of failure and has conceptualized a specific model. Gender differences, and, when applicable, racial differences are reviewed, as is the research on fear of failure according to each model. Finally, each section provides implications for intervention.

PSYCHODYNAMIC VIEWS OF FEAR OF FAILURE

The psychodynamic literature has examined the concept of fear of failure from the perspective of inhibitions in intellectual pursuits and underachievement. This literature, which is quite limited in scope, has been labeled "the psychodynamics of flunking out" (Hendin, 1972). The focus is on understanding

ESTHER D. ROTHBLUM • Department of Psychology, University of Vermont, Burlington, Vermont 05405.

497

the motivations of individuals who fail or withdraw from academic pursuits despite sufficient ability, intelligence, or preparation to succeed. Fear of failure is consistently regarded as originating in early (preoedipal) relationships with parents.

Psychometric Scales and Assessment

Psychodynamic theorists describing fear of failure have not used psychometric scales to assess this concept. Hendin (1972) mentions use of projective tests as an "independent check on the data derived from the interviews" (p. 132), but this is the only mention of any systematic assessment in the literature, and the results of these tests are not reported. Nevertheless, the Thematic Apperception Test (TAT), which is based on psychodynamic principles, forms an important component of assessment in subsequent models of fear of failure which are discussed later on.

Research

In general, data on psychodynamic models of fear of failure have been obtained from case studies. Hellman (1954) describes the nonempirical nature of these observations when she states (p. 259): "the observations I shall be discussing here have not been collected systematically with the intention of doing research on the subject. They have been gained, as we usually gain material in psychoanalytic work, from cases which have come to us by chance, at intervals of several years." Hellman studied three children with intellectual inhibitions in great detail. She observed their mothers to present similar patterns: a close bond between them and their child, intense anxiety about losing this close relationship, and denial of this anxiety.

Using a similar case study approach, Hendin (1972) interviewed 15 male college students with academic difficulties yet with the intelligence to perform well in college. Students were seen twice a week over the course of several months in the context of short-term therapy. From these interviews, the author described an in-depth presentation of three cases which exemplify some of the themes of academic failure. These themes indicate that the students' failure often represented a means of coping with conflicting messages from parents about success and a way of maintaining ties with parents via conflict. "With fathers who often are afraid of their son's potency, and with mothers who constrict them, these students are the victims of families that have encouraged them to pursue goals they did not really want them to achieve" (Hendin, 1972, p. 131).

Thus, the psychodynamic theory of fear of failure has been developed from comprehensive observations and interviews with a small number of cases. The lack of controls (e.g., comparisons with individuals who are achieving well) and the small sample size should be kept in mind during the following review of the literature.

Model

Baker (1979) presents a theory of the development of fear of failure as the result of pathological family relations in which the child's failure comes to play an important function. According to Baker, the parents' role is to provide the child with empathic encouragement so as to minimize the child's frustrations and maximize self-esteem. Parents who cannot accept their child's shortcomings or who are highly critical will rear a child with little self-esteem and unrealistic personal standards. This child will have an unrealistic or *grandiose* sense of self. The combination of low self-esteem and high demands for performance results in failure or *narcissistic injury*. Poor self-esteem causes the child to search for external sources of evaluation. Any failure experienced by such a narcissistically vulnerable child will result in either rage or avoidance. Rather than engage in the repeated effort or trial and error necessary for academic achievement, the child begins to avoid studying and instead engages in activities with more pleasurable outcomes. By not studying, the grandiose self is kept intact: "if an exam is flunked, it is only due to lack of study, not due to the lack of ability; if, however, it is passed without study, it is doubly delicious, providing a good grade and 'confirming' magical powers of brilliance" (Baker, 1979, p. 422). Furthermore, the child avoids studying to prevent competition and thus direct comparison with the parent.

Gender Differences

Most psychodynamic theorists recognize the prevalence of fear of failure among women and focus on origins of this fear specifically from the perspective of female development. According to Kanefield (1985b), conflicts about achievement and fear of failure are prevalent in girls whose mothers are ambivalent about their daughter's independence. The mother in this case needs the presence of a daughter to maintain her sense of adequacy, and she may feel intensely threatened as her daughter matures and thus obviates the need for a protective caretaker. Rather than respond to her own maturity with pleasure, the girl associates mastery with anxiety, fear of abandonment, loss of love, or retaliation. Thus, females are prone to associate competitive or independent behaviors with loss of parental approval and interpersonal abandonment. "In this way, the desire to be loyal to the mother emerges as a major motivation for girls to postpone or undermine their accomplishments and individuation" (Kanefield, 1985b, p. 350).

Women's undermining of success as a solution to fears of retaliation by the mother has been termed *masochism* by psychodynamic theorists (Freud, 1957; Horney, 1967; Kanefield, 1985b). Yuen and Depper (1987) state: "Fear of failure may be a form of masochism, in that the constant sense of inadequacy which underlies fear of failure is, in one sense, a perpetuation of pain and suffering" (p. 31). The masochist pursues defeat rather than pleasure and is ". . . consumed by self-centered suffering" (Yuen & Depper, 1987, p. 31). Rather than accomplish success and thus symbolically risk surpassing their mothers, women devalue success or perceive themselves as worthless. The alternative involves triumphing over parents with terror about retaliation and loss of affiliation (Kanefield, 1985b). Kanefield states:

> In response to these social and psychological dilemmas, a woman takes the only recourse: she sabotages her accomplishments, devalues or disowns her achievements, or views herself as inadequate in spite of her activities to the contrary. Thus, she assuages her guilt for abandoning her mother, extricates herself from responsibility for her mother's rage, envy, or emptiness, excuses her mother's inappropriate dependency, and perpetuates the masquerade that she lacks what is essential for independent achievements. She remains loyal to her mother, but sacrifices her self-esteem. (pp. 358–359)

In contrast, boys are encouraged to enter into rivalry with their fathers in order to disidentify with their mothers. Consequently, Kanefield (1985b) argues that males do not have the fears of competition that females do.

Women's conflicts about achievement have also been interpreted as representing *penis envy* (Chessick, 1984; Kanefield, 1985b). Among current psychodynamic writers, the concept of penis envy does not connote women's actual wish for a penis but instead the desire for power, status, and independence awarded to men in our society. Given the devaluation of women in our culture and the restrictions and limitations placed on them, this results in women's denigration of their accomplishments, withdrawal from competition, work inhibitions, and feelings of fraudulence in their achievements (Kanefield, 1985b). It will also result in women's lowered self-esteem and in oversensitivity to the opinions of others rather than personal values (Chehrazi, 1984).

Finally, there has been discussion in the psychodynamic literature about women's achievement conflicts in light of women's relational ties. Notman, Zilbach, Baker-Miller, and Nadelson (1986) describe how women's self-esteem is tied to relations with others. Self-esteem is thus enhanced when women feel connected to others and receive feedback about such connectedness. In contrast, men's self-esteem is characteristically tied to feelings of personal accomplishment. Since our society regards achievement as an individual rather than a collective attribute, men are less likely to experience achievement-related conflicts than are women. Kanefield (1985a) has similarly described boys as wishing to achieve, motivated by their desire to separate from the mother. Girls, on the other hand, are fearful of achieving because of threats of isolation, and consequently they engage in self-defeating behaviors in order to maintain interpersonal relationships.

Intervention

There has been little focus in the psychodynamic literature on intervention specifically for fear of failure. Baker (1979) emphasizes the need to select an appropriate treatment goal for individuals who display fear of failure. Rather than focusing on improved academic performance or a successful career, the therapist should investigate developmental factors, particularly those related to the client's poor self-esteem. Because of the origins of poor self-esteem and lack of separation from parents in the preoedipal years, the prognosis for recovery is not considered good. Furthermore, the clients' difficult and ambivalent relationships with parents can result in poor transference during the therapeutic process, including rage, lack of interest in therapy, and increased failure in school or career. This in turn may result in the therapist feeling helpless, frustrated, and antagonistic toward the client (Baker, 1979).

Summary

The psychodynamic model of fear of failure has been based on intensive case observations rather than controlled research. Overly critical parental child-rearing practices result in an individual who has poor self-esteem, is sensitive to external sources of evaluation, and avoids activities with the potential of failure. Women with mothers who encouraged dependence and who feared maturity in their daughters will come to associate achievement with negative interpersonal consequences and possible retaliation by others. Interventions for fear of failure have a poor prognosis due to the long-standing nature of this phenomenon and the client's inability to form a good transference relationship.

FEAR OF FAILURE VERSUS NEED ACHIEVEMENT

During the 1950s and 1960s there was a tremendous proliferation of research on achievement motivation. In these postwar decades, the emphasis on genetic determinants of behavior decreased, and the focus on environmental influences of behavior escalated. Government programs were established to increase technical and academic skills, and individuals were sought out who had the motivation and ability to profit from these programs. Personal striving and competition with others were viewed as exemplary. Yet only a fraction of individuals can achieve success in a society that rewards individual rather than group achievement. Although the bulk of the research focused on the achievers, a few researchers began to examine those who chose to avoid the possibility of failure.

Models

The most widely cited theory of achievement motivation is that by McClelland, Atkinson, Clark, and Lowell (1953). They view achievement motivation as a stable trait, so that the high achiever is likely to strive for success in almost any situation that can be interpreted as achievement related, or as involving standards of excellence. Conversely, the low achiever tends to avoid achievement-related situations. This theory views achievement as a drive, with the individual motivated to reduce arousal and frustration through performance. The research to develop this theory was funded by the navy, and therefore subjects usually consisted of enlisted men. Thus, much of the achievement

motivation literature used male subjects and military tasks (such as rifle shooting). McClelland *et al.* are concerned with the societal implications of achievement rather than effects on individuals.

Atkinson and Feather (1966) regard achievement as the combination of two
motives: hope of success and fear of failure. Hope of success corresponds to
achievement motivation as conceptualized by McClelland *et al.* (1953). Fear of
failure is the motive to avoid a negative incentive and is operationally defined as
test anxiety. When fear of failure exceeds hope of success, the individual will
choose activities that are so easy or so difficult that they minimize anxiety about
failure. Atkinson and Feather view achievement as dependent on a variety of
factors in the individual, such as perceptions of task difficulty, attributions about
success and failure, and level of anxiety.

Both these theories view fear of failure and the motive to achieve as opposites. Thus, a great deal of the research literature that focuses on low achievers
is reviewed later, since these are viewed as individuals high on the motive to
avoid failure.

A third theory views achievement motivation and fear of failure as independent factors (Birney, Burdick, & Teevan, 1969). These researchers examined TAT
stories for evidence of avoidance of fearful situations. They found such stories to
contain central figures who were adjusting to some threat that had appeared by
itself (i.e., that was not the figure's fault) and that was blocking achievement.
When subjects underwent a failure task and were then given a TAT task, they
increased such threat imagery, which was termed *hostile press.* By including
external threats (e.g., court trials, attack, injury) in TAT stories designed to elicit
achievement themes, individuals were avoiding failure for the figures in their
stories by introducing insurmountable but legitimate barriers to success. Even
though individuals in these stories fail as the result of barriers, this constitutes
objective, rather than subjective or devaluative, failure (Teevan & Smith, 1975).
According to this model, individuals can score high on both need achievement
and fear of failure—they may have high achievement goals and yet indicate
barriers to such goals in their TAT imagery. Birney *et al.* also view fear of failure
as related to affiliative needs and as reflecting avoidance of either a lowered self-
estimate or a lowered evaluation by others.

Psychometric Scales and Assessment

TAT Imagery

McClelland *et al.* (1953) felt that the way to assess motivation was through
the use of fantasy. They modified the Thematic Apperception Test (TAT) for
experimental investigation by administering the TAT scenes in a group setting
and projecting them onto a screen. Subjects were asked to write stories about
each scene and had specific instructions intended to ensure a complete plot
(e.g., Who are the persons? What has led up to the situation? What is being
thought? What will happen?)

In order to arouse the achievement motive, McClelland *et al.* (1953) preceded the TAT with a 12-minute anagrams test. Subjects were told that they were taking a test which indicated level of intelligence, which had been used during the past war to assess officer candidates, and which demonstrated whether an individual had leadership capacity. The anagrams test also allowed the experimenter to manipulate success and failure by the use of artificial norms with which students could compare their scores. McClelland *et al.* used this procedure under relaxed (the importance of the test was de-emphasized), neutral (the test was not described as important nor unimportant), achievement-success (the test was described as important, and norms were low), achievement-failure (the test was described as important, and norms were high), and achievement-success-failure conditions (the test was described as important, the norms provided for an initial test were low so that subjects were led to believe they would succeed, and then norms provided for the actual battery were high so that subjects would receive low scores).

Scoring of the TAT which followed this anagrams test incorporated an elaborate and standardized procedure that included various types of achievement imagery, instrumental activity, obstacles or blocks to achievement, nurturance, and affective states (McClelland *et al.*, 1953). It became apparent that some subjects seemed to avoid achievement in their stories based on TAT scenes, or else they described characters in their stories who displayed negative emotional reactions in competitive situations. The authors referred to such responses as characterizing fear of failure.

Hostile Press Imagery

Birney *et al.* (1969) developed a scoring system specifically for TAT imagery which they felt demonstrated hostile press, the tendency to describe the central figure as adjusting to some external threat that was blocking achievement. They categorized three types of threats: (1) "legitimate demands," such as warnings or information that precluded achievement; (2) "exercise of judicial power," including arrest or reprimands from authority figures; and (3) "catastrophes," such as physical injury or impending death. In scoring hostile press, the experimenter looks for such evidence as reprimands for personal action, legal retaliation for actions, or hostile conditions that impede well-being. Furthermore, since Birney *et al.* presumed fear of failure to be associated with a need for affiliation, responses indicating deprivation of affiliative ties are also included in the hostile press scoring system.

Administration of the TAT is time consuming, and the scoring requires considerable training. There have also been criticisms of its test–retest reliability (e.g., Krumboltz & Farquhar, 1957). In her review entitled "To Dispel Fantasies about Fantasy-based Measures of Achievement Motivation," Entwisle (1972) critiqued the psychometric properties of TAT-based scoring systems of achievement motivation. She argued that test–retest reliability rarely exceeds .40 and thus that the predictive validity of these systems for school achievement and career success is limited. Females and individuals with high IQ scores and high socioeconomic status wrote more words per story, and such productivity predicts school grades more than scoring of achievement motivation (Entwisle, 1972). Nevertheless, the TAT is the predominant method of assessing need achievement and fear of failure in nearly all of the research that follows.

Goal-Setting and Risk-Taking Behavior

According to Atkinson (1957), individuals high in fear of failure will choose tasks that are either so easy that success is guaranteed or so difficult that no one could succeed at them. In contrast, the individual high on need achievement will choose tasks of moderate difficulty on which these is maximum challenge. Furthermore, whereas high achievers will increase goals as they master tasks, individuals high on fear of failure will remain with easy tasks despite success or with difficult ones despite failure. This concept, termed *goal-setting behavior* (Atkinson, Bastian, Earl, & Litwin, 1960), *risk-taking behavior* (Hancock & Teevan, 1964), or *level of aspiration* Birney et al., 1969), has been demonstrated repeatedly using such tasks as a ring-toss game (Atkinson & Feather, 1966), shuffleboard performance (Atkinson *et al.*, 1960), and placement of bets (Hancock & Teevan, 1964). Generally, individuals are asked to estimate their performance preceding each trial. Whereas high achievers tend to take moderate risks, individuals high in fear of failure behave in seemingly irrational ways by moving to harder odds after failure or easier odds after success. According to Hancock and Teevan (1964), this is so the individual high in fear of failure can reduce the amount of anxiety present due to continued success or failure. Because of the consistency with which this effect is demonstrated, goal-setting or risk-taking behaviors have been used to assess achievement and fear of failure (Birney *et al.*, 1969).

Mehrabian's Self-Report Scale of Achieving Tendency

In 1968, Mehrabian developed a self-report scale that measures the motive to achieve relative to the motive to avoid failure, based on Atkinson's (1957) model. The 38 items assess both positive feelings aroused by success and negative feelings aroused by failure. In order to incorporate research related to the achievement motive, items assessing the motive to achieve include independence in personal relationships, delay of gratification, future perspective, preference of moderate-risk situations, and preference for activity involving competition. Items assessing the motive to avoid failure include affiliation with others, immediate gratification, present perspective, preference for high- or low-risk situations, and preference for activity involving cooperation and chance (Mehrabian, 1968). The scale is scored by summing all items, with a high score indicating high motive to achieve and low motive to avoid failure. Thus, the motives to achieve and to avoid failure are viewed as direct opposites; it is not possible to be high on both. Mehrabian's scale has a test–retest reliability of approximately .75 and is not correlated with social desirability. The scale is negatively correlated with test anxiety. Because the scale correlates significantly with gender, separate male and female norms have been developed to account for females' lower achieving tendency (Mehrabian & Bank, 1978).

Other Self-Report Scales

Finally, some researchers have used the Debilitating Anxiety Scale of Alpert and Haber's (1960) Achievement Anxiety Test, which assesses anxiety in achievement-related situations, and the Achievement Scale of the Edwards Personal Preference Schedule (Edwards, 1959), which measures the number of times subjects chose achievement-related statements compared with other statements in a forced-choice format. Macdonald and Hyde (1980) factor analyzed both self-report and projective measures of need achievement, fear of failure, and fear of success. Their results indicated that a primary factor on which several self-report measures loaded accounted for about 10 percent of the variance and was termed "anxiety." Grade point average could be significantly predicted by scores on self-report measures of achievement, including the Debilitating Anxiety Scale (for both genders) and the Edwards Need Achievement Scale (for females).

Research

In comparison to the vast amount of research on need achievement, relatively little research has specifically investigated fear of failure. Much of the research on fear of failure was conducted by Richard Teevan, and is summarized by Birney *et al.* (1969). They describe a variety of studies designed to test the validity of the hostile press scoring system for fear of failure.

When male college students were asked to volunteer for a dart-throwing task that emphasized achievement, students high on hostile press were less likely to volunteer. On the other hand, when the same task was described in more affiliative terms (the task was important to the instructor), there was no difference in volunteer rates of students high and low on hostile press. When male high school students were asked to participate in a rifle-shooting task, students high on hostile press were more likely to set unrealistic levels of aspiration and to express displeasure with the task. Male high school students high on hostile press made more "irrational" (extremely risky) choices on a mathematical probability task. Birney *et al.* (1969) conclude that individuals high in hostile press are avoiding failure rather than approaching success.

What happens in situations (such as the school setting) in which individuals high on hostile press cannot avoid tasks measuring achievement? Birney *et al.* (1969) predict that one effective way to avoid failure is to succeed. In fact, research cited by the authors indicates that male elementary, high school, and college students high in hostile press do have higher grades than students low in hostile press. The authors conclude that students high on fear of failure use a number of strategies to avoid failure. If they have a choice about participation in achievement situations, they will choose not to participate. If they are forced into an achievement situation, they will do what they can not to fail, even if that also means not succeeding. If the only way not to fail is to succeed, they will work hard to succeed.

Individuals high on fear of failure are externally oriented in their definitions of success and failure. Birney *et al.* (1969) review research indicating that individuals high in hostile press are more influenced by the opinions of "expert" others, show greater conformity to peers, are more willing to give up recognition for achievement in exchange for a secure place in a group, cooperate rather than compete with others, and are more likely to join protest groups on college campuses. Whereas individuals high on need achievement compare themselves to an internal standard of excellence, individuals high on hostile press look to other people for evaluation (Birney et al., 1969). Nevertheless, comparison with others may be anxiety producing for the individual high on fear of failure. Based on this research, Birney et al. (1969) predict that high hostile press individuals would prefer comparisons with noncomparable groups, prefer imprecise rather than precise measures of performance, reject responsibility, and seek social support rather than perform alone.

In sum, Birney et al. (1969) state:

> As long as the self-estimate is kept vague, it remains unclear whether a performance confirms it or disconfirms it. We would therefore expect a person who is fearful of a self-estimate loss to avoid situations which promise to increase the precision of the self-estimate. It is true that one decreases the chances of success as well as failure, but a person who is particularly fearful of a loss in self-estimate may prefer to forego the opportunity of raising his self-estimate in order to ensure that there be no loss. (p. 211)

The concept that individuals will protect self-estimate even if this means failure has also been elaborated by Covington and Omelich (1979). Their research has indicated that students and teachers often have conflicting ideas about achievement. Teachers reward effort, yet students feel they lose face when they try and then fail. Thus, students may increase their positive self-image when risking failure by not studying—the very condition that teachers punish most severely. This is particularly important in the case of potential public shame (Brown & Weiner, 1984). Effort reduces guilt, but it also increases the possibility of feelings of incompetency in cases of failure. Covington and Omelich (1984) state (p. 159): "Although high effort may reduce the negative affect association with noncompliance to a work ethic, it also implies that the cause of failure is low ability, a realization that leads to shame and humiliation." Thus, students struggle to balance effort and competency without impeding self-worth.

Gender Differences

Most of the research on fear of failure used only male subjects. Furthermore, it is questionable whether dart-throwing and rifle-shooting tasks are relevant in arousing achievement motivation in females. Yet gender differences in achievement motivation were apparent from the results of the earliest studies (e.g., McClelland et al., 1953). Achievement imagery in females did not seem to be aroused by tasks stressing intelligence and leadership that aroused such imagery in males. On the other hand, females' scores under neutral conditions (when the task was described as unimportant) were as high as those of males under conditions of arousal. This gender difference was ignored rather than examined, with early studies selecting only male subjects from coeducational schools and colleges.

In 1973, Stein and Bailey reviewed the literature on achievement motivation in order to identify factors specific to women's pattern of achievement. First, they argue that leadership and intelligence are qualities that women are not socialized to value as much as men are. In fact, females place greater value on and have higher personal standards of performance for tasks that are labeled feminine or neutral rather than masculine (Stein, Pohly, & Mueller, 1971). Specifically, social skill and avoidance of social rejection are sources of achievement motivation for females (Stein & Bailey, 1973). For example, girls are more likely to seek contact during a failure situation than are boys (Zunich, 1964). Women competing against others report less confidence, lower goals, and less expectancies for success than women working alone (House, 1974). In contrast, there are no significant differences on these variables between men working alone and men competing against others. In sociological studies of coalition forming (Bond & Vinacke, 1961), males tend to use "exploitative" strategies (such as playing competitively), whereas females use "accommodative" strategies (such as displaying concern for the welfare of others). Females scoring high on the motive to avoid failure on Mehrabian's scale improved their performance when responsibility for the task was assigned to the group as opposed to themselves; males high on the motive to avoid failure did not show this pattern (Mehrabian, 1968). Hoffman (1972) has discussed the tendency for women to "sacrifice brilliance for rapport" (p.135) to reflect women's greater affiliative needs. Stein and Bailey disagree with the notion that women are more affiliation oriented and men more achievement oriented. They point out that social arousal leads to *achievement* imagery, not affiliative imagery, in women, and thus social performance is related to achievement striving, possibly because females have been reinforced for engaging in social activities more than males have.

Second, Stein and Bailey (1973) review gender differences in characteristics related to achievement that could account for women's achievement patterns. Females are more anxious about failing in academic situations than are males, and females score higher on measures of test anxiety. Furthermore, anxiety is negatively related to achievement and to learning. Although male and female college students have similar course grades, females expect to receive lower grades than do males (Battle, 1966; Erkut, 1983). Girls tend to be overly cautious when choosing tasks on which they expect to succeed, whereas boys tend to be risk takers, choosing tasks of undue difficulty (Veroff, 1969, in Stein & Bailey, 1973). Finally, women are rated as less competent even when performing in identical ways to men. When raters are asked to evaluate identical products that are attributed either to males or females, they rate the product more negatively when they are led to believe it is by a woman, whether the product is a professional article (Goldberg, 1968), a work of art (Pheterson, Kiesler & Goldberg, 1971), the credentials of potential faculty members (Fidell, 1970), or the ability of physicians (Feldman-Summers & Kiesler, 1974).

Third, Stein and Bailey (1973) review developmental differences in the socialization of achievement patterns of males and females. During the early school years, females achieve well in the academic arena. Even by first grade, however, boys prefer repeating previously failed tasks, whereas girls prefer repeating tasks on which they have been successful. Boys are also less dependent on peers and adults for assistance and approval than are girls, and girls are more likely to withdraw from a threatening situation (Crandall & Rabson, 1960). By adolescence, the value of academic pursuits decreases for females, career aspirations are less clear than are those of males, and parents and peers place a greater focus on the social accomplishment of females (Stein & Bailey, 1973). Females are more likely to assume responsibility for failure than are males at all grade levels, but this difference increases during adolescence (Crandall, Katkovsky & Crandall, 1965). Whereas male high school underachievers tend to have a history of underachievement from grade school on, female high school underachievers tend to have superior levels of achievement until junior high school, when achievement begins to decrease (Shaw & McCuen, 1960).

A fourth factor identified by Stein and Bailey (1973) to account for women's achievement patterns is that feminine sex-role stereotypes such as dependency, nonassertiveness, and nonaggressiveness are in conflict with achievement motivation as it is traditionally defined. How, then, do women cope with the dissonance of achievement? According to Stein and Bailey, women may do this in a variety of ways. They may view achievement as more appropriate for men than for women. Female underachieving students tend to produce more achievement imagery when presented with stimuli (pictures or stories) containing men than women, whereas the reverse is true for female students rated as achievers (Lesser, Krawitz, & Packard, 1963). A second strategy is to receive vicarious satisfaction through the achievements of husband or children. Women tend to value the accomplishments of their spouses more than their own accomplishments, particularly if they adhere to the traditional feminine role (Lipman-Blumen, 1972, in Stein & Bailey, 1973). Third, they may value achievement more than traditional female activities, which have lower status in our society. Thus, they may view achievement as compatible, rather than incompatible, with femininity. High school females who perform well in school define achievement as more gender appropriate than do females who perform more poorly in school (Lesser, Krawitz, & Packard, 1963). Fourth, they may choose a traditionally feminine career and achieve within that career. Fifth, they may conceal their accomplishments from others or reduce effort (this will be discussed more fully in the following section on fear of success). Finally, they may compensate for achievement by expanding equal effort to appear physically attractive and to engage in domestic activities. Clearly, achievement is less directly rewarding and more conflict laden for women than for men.

A number of studies have focused on gender differences in attributions following success and failure on achievement-related tasks. Women tend to be more external in their attributions for both success and failure (this contradicts the research cited earlier by Crandall et al., 1965, which found women to take responsibility for failure) by perceiving the causes for their performance to be due to task difficulty or luck (Bar-Tal & Frieze, 1977; Erkut, 1983; Feather, 1969). In contrast, men are more likely to cite internal attributions such as ability and effort for their performance. In this same study, women were also less confident about success and felt more inadequate during the task than were men. This tendency of women to externalize has been interpreted as reflecting women's powerlessness in a sexist society (Frieze, Whitley, Hanusa, & McHugh, 1982). Other research has found women to attribute success to luck and failure to poor ability (e.g., Nichols, 1975). This tendency for women to believe negative information but discount positive information has been termed the "self-derogatory" model and viewed as contributing to women's low self-esteem in achievement settings (Frieze *et al.*, 1982). In contrast, men have been found to attribute success to skill and failure to luck, which has been viewed as reflecting men's fear of failure (Levine, Reis, Sue, & Turner, 1976).

Women's attributions following success and failure are related to gender role, however. Women who were classified as feminine were unaffected by success but inhibited by failure (Welch & Huston, 1982). Androgynous women, on the other hand, were unaffected by failure but facilitated by success. Androgynous women also tended to attribute success to ability and failure to task difficulty, whereas feminine women did not differ in attributions for success and failure. The authors of this study speculate that the attributional patterns of androgynous women may help to increase their self-esteem. In a study relating sex roles to career achievement (Wong, Kettlewell, & Sproule, 1985), women's educational level, presence of masculinity, and absence of femininity all contributed as predictors of career achievement. In contrast, fear of failure was found not to be significantly related to sex roles classified as "traditional" (family oriented) or "nontraditional" (career oriented) (Steinberg, Teevan, & Greenfeld, 1983).

Racial Differences

A few studies have compared achievement motivation between blacks and whites. Early research on locus of control found that blacks were more externally oriented than were whites (Battle & Rotter, 1963; Lefcourt & Ladwig, 1965). Strickland (1971) states (p. 318): "This expectancy may well reflect the reinforcement history of members of minority or disadvantaged groups who often find that their behaviors have little to do with the subsequent events that happen to them."

Unfortunately, most of the research on race and achievement makes no specific mention of fear of failure. One exception is a study by Gurin and Epps (1975). These authors found that black men who exhibited fear of failure had lower course grades and performed more poorly on an anagrams task than did black men without fear of failure. However, no such relationships existed for black women with fear of failure (Gurin & Epps, 1975). Both black men and women with fear of failure had lower career aspirations than did those without fear of failure.

Childrearing Factors

A number of studies have investigated parent–child interaction factors that might contribute to the development of fear of failure. Birney *et al.* (1969) discuss the development of fear of failure as a consequence of parental reinforcement patterns. They argue that parents may either reward, punish, or remain neutral to their child for trying or not trying (effort) and for succeeding or failing (outcome), resulting in many patterns of reinforcement. The parent who remains neutral and thus ignores both effort and outcome will produce a child with low achievement motivation. The parent who rewards success and remains neutral to all other outcomes will presumably have a child high in hope for success and low in hostile press, who is eager to seek out achievement situations. Third, the parent who rewards success and punishes failure may have a child who learns to value success and hide failure. Finally, the parent who remains neutral to success and punishes failure would be expected to produce a child high in fear of failure. This child learns to avoid achievement situations when at all possible, since there is no reward for trying but instead a negative focus on failing.

Teevan and McGhee (1972) tested some of these hypotheses about parental reinforcement and resulting fear of failure. Mothers of male high school students were asked how they characteristically reward or punish their child. Mothers of male students who were high on hostile press were more likely to respond neutrally to satisfactory achievement situations, whereas mothers of students low on hostile press were more likely to respond positively to such successes. Mothers of students high on hostile press were also more likely to punish their sons for unsatisfactory achievement behavior than were mothers of students low on hostile press, but this difference was not significant. Thus, it seems that fear of failure may develop by maternal neutrality to success and some maternal punishment of failure, as predicted by Birney et al. (1969). Specifically, they argue that this parental reinforcement pattern creates low self-image in children and poor adjustment in an achievement-focused society.

Second, researchers have examined the role of parental expectations for independence in the development of fear of failure. Teevan and McGhee (1972) asked mothers of male high school students to list the ages at which they expected their son to accomplish various independence and achievement behaviors (e.g., tie his shoes right, stand up for his own rights around other children, earn his own spending money). Male students who were high in fear of failure had mothers with earlier expectations for their independence. However, other research (Winterbottom, 1958) has found early independence training by mothers to also be indicative of high achievement motivation among elementary school boys compared with boys low in achievement motivation. When research has compared boys and girls, mothers of girls cite later ages for their daughters to gain independence and begin achievement than do mothers of boys (Collard, 1964, in Hoffman, 1972).

A study by Hermans, ter Laak, and Maes (1972) compared Dutch elementary school boys and girls who were either high or low on achievement motivation and either high or low on fear of failure (as measured by the achievement motivation and debilitating anxiety subscales of a Dutch version of the Achievement Motivation Test for Children). Parent–child interactions at home were then observed as the child performed four difficult tasks to which the parents knew the solution. Parents of children with high debilitating anxiety showed fewer reactions when the child expressed insecurity, produced more negative tension releases (e.g., showing irritation) and fewer positive tension releases (e.g., expressing enthusiasm), and withheld more reinforcements after correct solutions. Children high in debilitating anxiety also expressed more negative and fewer positive tension releases than did children low in debilitating anxiety. Parents of children with high achievement motivation used more nonspecific help (e.g., hinting), less specific help (e.g., providing the solution), and more positive task-oriented reinforcements than did parents of children low in achievement motivation. Children high in achievement motivation tended to refuse help offered by parents. Parents of children who were high in achievement motivation and low in debilitating anxiety had the highest expectations of performance for their child. Teacher ratings in this study indicated that children high in debilitating anxiety were more socially dependent and that children high in achievement motivation were more goal oriented, had high personal responsibility, and high persistence. The authors conclude that children high in debilitating anxiety seem to receive less structure (both affectively and cognitively) from parents and more irrelevant information. Children high in achievement motivation and low in anxiety have parents who provide direction but also allow the child to perform independently. Finally, in a study of level of aspiration, children who tended to avoid failure in a goal-setting task had mothers high in protectiveness (Crowne, Conn, Marlowe, & Edwards, 1969).

Third, researchers have investigated parental warmth as a factor in children's achievement. Moderate, rather than high levels of warmth seem to be optimal for achievement (Stein & Bailey, 1973). Parents who are either highly nurturant or rejecting have children with low achievement behavior. However, warmth seems to have a greater effect in influencing boys' rather than girls' achievement (Crandall, 1963, in Stein & Bailey, 1973). There is little research on the relationship between warmth and fear of failure. Baumrind (1971) has postulated that moderate, rather than high, levels of warmth may assist the child in handling failure. In a study of parental warmth and children's attributions (Katkovsky, Crandall, & Good, 1967), girls whose fathers had been observed during home visits to be affectionate and nurturing were less likely to believe that they had caused their own failures on a self-report questionnaire of attributions.

Stein and Bailey (1973) have reviewed the literature examining parental modeling of achievement and parental acceptance of achievement in children. Not surprisingly, children high in achievement have mothers who reinforce achievement (Crandall, Preston, & Rabson, 1960) and who expect high performance (Kagan & Moss, 1962, in Stein & Bailey, 1973). High-achieving females tend to have working mothers (Nye & Hoffman, 1963, in Stein & Bailey, 1973). However, there has been little research examining the role of fathers in fostering achievement.

Finally, in the case of females, Stein and Bailey (1973) have described how the development of achievement motivation and the feminine sex role are incompatible. Girls are most likely to develop achievement motivation when mothers are employed, behave toward their daughter in a moderately warm manner, encourage independence, and encourage achievement behavior. In contrast, mothers who are very warm, permissive, and ignore achievement are more likely to have daughters who are conforming, dependent, and feminine (Stein & Bailey, 1973). Thus, traditional childrearing patterns for girls are in conflict with the development of achievement behavior. It is not surprising that achievement motivation is inversely related to femininity, as discussed earlier. Since models of achievement motivation may or may not consider fear of failure and need achievement to be polar opposites, this does not necessarily mean that fear of failure and femininity are positively related.

Intervention

Because of the origins of the achievement motivation literature in social psychology, there has been little treatment outcome research on changing fear of failure as defined by low achievement motivation or hostile press. One exception is a study by Montanelli and Hill (1969) that found achievement expectancies of elementary school children to increase following praise and decrease following criticism. Birney *et al.* (1969) also suggest that changes in patterns of reinforcement may reduce fear of failure, but they argue that at some point in a child's development (perhaps even by the beginning of school), fear of failure may be resistent to change or irreversibly entrenched in children's self-concepts. Additionally, much of the research on consequences of experimentally induced success and failure and of childrearing factors on fear of failure has implications for intervention to reduce fear of failure.

Summary

In the achievement motivation literature, fear of failure is defined either as low need for achievement, low hope for success, or hostile press imagery on the TAT. Individuals high in fear of failure choose extreme rather than moderate goals, are reluctant to participate in achievement situations, and will attempt to avoid failure even if this means not succeeding. Both women and blacks tend to attribute success and failure to luck rather than skill. Parental childrearing factors that are related to fear of failure include lack of reward for success and early expectations for independence. Females and individuals high in fear of failure place greater value on affiliative tasks. The nature of many achievement tasks is more relevant for males, whereas females score lower on need for achievement, particularly as they enter adolescence and if they are feminine in their sex roles.

FEAR OF SUCCESS

In 1964, a graduate student named Matina Horner was working on her dissertation at the University of Michigan. John Atkinson, her dissertation advisor, was described earlier as formulating a model of achievement motivation. Horner examined the relationships between need for achievement, need for affiliation, anagram performance, and level of aspiration (Tresemer, 1976a). Students enrolled in introductory psychology served as the subjects for this experiment, and they spent several hours completing stories to such headings as "Tom is looking into his microscope." After five such stories, subjects were given the heading "At the end of first-term finals, Anne finds herself at the top of her medical school class" (Tresemer, 1976a). Male subjects were asked to write about John at the top of his class and females, about Anne.

Horner found that this last story heading yielded strong gender differences, with 62.2% of females writing stories with a negative content to the medical school cue, compared with only 9.1% of males (Tresemer, 1976a). Her dissertation was completed in 1968, and the results were reported in *Psychology Today* under the title "Fail: Bright Women" (Horner, 1969). Soon, every major magazine and newspaper picked up the story, focusing on fear of success as an explanation for women's unequal occupational status in the United States (Tresemer, 1976a).

As early as 1916, Freud had used the term "wrecked by success" to describe his patients who appeared to become ill immediately after a wish had come true, such as a political appointment (in Cavenar & Werman, 1981). Psychodynamic writers (e.g., Fenichel) viewed fear of success to stem from guilt, fears of future failure, and conflicts around independence (Cavenar & Werman, 1981). What was significant about Horner's research, however, was that it represented the first achievement-related theory that dealt specifically with gender differences. As was described earlier, the early achievement motivation literature focused mostly on males, and results for females were not as replicable or clear-cut.

How is fear of success related to fear of failure? Tresemer (1976a) argues that to demonstrate fear of success, there must be a performance decrement in achievement-related activities in which success is a possible outcome. However, fear of success should not lead to performance decrements in activities in which only failure is a possible outcome. In contrast, fear of failure is demonstrated when people avoid situations in which there is possible failure but not situations in which there is possible success (Tresemer, 1976a). This differentiation in fact becomes very difficult to verify empirically, since most achievement-related activities have both success and failure as possible outcomes. Thus, the fear-of-success literature will be reviewed here, given its salience in the achievement literature and its overlap with fear of failure.

Model

According to Horner (1972), femininity has been viewed throughout history as incompatible with intellectual competence. Even today, as the educational system is designed to prepare males and females equally for future career success, females still perceive social and psychological barriers to stand in the way of this success. Specifically, women will be motivated to avoid success when they expect negative consequences (such as rejection by others or feelings of being unfeminine) as the result of succeeding. She argues that this is not the same as the motive to avoid failure, which consists of individuals expecting negative consequences from failing. Fear of success is more characteristic of high-achieving women; one cannot fear success if one is incapable of attaining it (Horner, 1972).

The motive to avoid success is most strongly aroused in competitive conditions. In Horner's original study, females high on fear of success decreased their performance in competitive group situations, whereas females low on fear of success and males increased performance in such situations (Horner, 1972). The most significant factor related to fear of success is the concern of negative reactions from peers (Horner, 1972).

Alternative explanations have been provided for Horner's theory of fear of success. Fear of success has been termed "fear of gender-inappropriate behavior" by Cherry and Deaux (1978), due to the nontraditional nature of medicine as a career for women in the 1960s. Similarly, fear of success has been conceptualized as reflecting cultural stereotypes about gender-appropriate occupations (Feather & Raphaelson, 1974; Monahan, Kuhn, & Shaver, 1974). Makovsky (1976) has argued that Horner's measure of fear of success is actually a measure of gender-role orientation, and that performance in situations that are incompatible with gender role will lead to role conflict. Finally, given women's relative lack of options in society compared to those of men, the personality approach taken by Horner has been termed "blaming the victim . . . of an oppressive social system" (Tresemer, 1977, p. 50).

The early conceptualization of the fear-of-success model viewed it as a personality trait or motive, sometimes referred to as the "motive to avoid success." Much of the research on fear of success, on the other hand, has viewed this concept as situationally determined behavior that is influenced by environmental cues. This trend has been paralleled by the journals in which fear-of-success articles have been published. Early studies were published in personality journals; by the mid-1970s the overwhelming majority of fear-of-success articles were published in the journal *Sex Roles* and stressed societal factors.

Psychometric Scales and Assessment

Although Horner originally gave subjects a variety of stories to complete, the majority of the research on fear of success has used only one: the heading "At the end of first-term finals, Anne (John) finds herself (himself) at the top of her (his) medical school class." Stories generated by subjects are scored for positive or negative content. Horner's original system of scoring focused on a number of specific indices that she regarded as indicative of concern with success, including

> (a) negative consequences because of the success, (b) anticipation of negative consequences because of the success, (c) negative affect because of the success, (d) instrumental activity away from present or future success, including leaving the field for more traditional female work such as nursing, school teaching, or social work, (e) any direct expression of conflict about success, (f) denial of effort in attaining the success (also cheating or any other attempt to deny responsibility or reject credit for the success), (g) denial of the situation described by the cue, or (h) bizarre, inappropriate, unrealistic, or nonadaptive responses to the situation described by the cue. (Lockheed, 1975, p. 44)

Furthermore, Horner found that the negative imagery tended to fall into one of three categories (Hyde, 1985, p. 205), consisting of:

1. Social rejection fears. For example, "Anne is an acne-faced bookworm. She runs to the bulletin board and finds she's at the top. As usual she smarts off. A chorus of groans is the rest of the class's reply . . ."
2. Worries about womanhood. For example, "Unfortunately Anne no longer feels so certain that she really wants to be a doctor. She is worried about herself and wonders if perhaps she isn't normal. . . . Anne decides not to continue with her medical work but to take courses that have a deeper personal meaning for her."
3. Denial of reality. For example, "Anne is a code name of a nonexistent person created by a group of medical students. They take turns writing exams for Anne."

There have been major criticisms of Horner's methodology (see Zuckerman & Wheeler, 1975, for a review). First, a published manual for scoring fear of success did not exist until 1977 (Horner & Fleming, in Macdonald & Hyde, 1980), resulting in multiple ways of scoring stories for fear-of-success content. In this revised scoring system by Horner, story cues are scored only for the presence or absence of fear of success, rather than the more specific scoring system that Horner used in her original study (Macdonald & Hyde, 1980). Second, stories were usually scored for the single cue of fear of success, so that the internal consistency of the measure could not be scored. Zuckerman and Wheeler (1975) present some evidence that studies which used multiple cues found fear-of-success imagery to fluctuate considerably across cues. Furthermore, fear-of-success rates fluctuate markedly between studies—ranging from 20 to 88% among females and from 9 to 76% among males (Zuckerman & Wheeler, 1975). Zuckerman and Wheeler (1975) speculate that this may be due to coding errors in labeling all negative themes (e.g., references to drug abuse, murder) as reflecting fear of success, when in fact Horner considered only negative themes resulting from success to constitute fear of success. Finally, the interrater reliability of scoring of fear of success via projective stories has been questioned. Robbins and Robbins (1973) found that female raters tended to score more content as related to fear of success in stories written by women than did male raters. Nevertheless, interrater reliability can be quite high. Lentz (1982) trained three male and three female raters for 10 hours and found that interrater reliability was .96 based on 26 practice protocols.

Although most of the fear-of-success literature uses Horner's original cues of "Anne/John" at the top of their medical school class, a considerable proportion of studies have modified these projective instructions to reflect other careers, to add more information about interpersonal factors, and so on, as will be described below. Interestingly, researchers have clung to the names "Anne" and "John" without exception. Additionally, a number of paper-and-pencil scales of fear of success have been developed in order to increase the objectivity of scoring.

Zuckerman and Allison's Fear of Success Scale consists of 27 items asking subjects to agree or disagree with items that describe the benefits of success, the costs of success, and subjects' attitudes toward success (Zuckerman & Allison, 1976). This scale has a low (.18) but significant correlation with Horner's original scale, and high fear-of-success scores predict poor anagram performance under competitive conditions and external attributions about success (Zuckerman & Allison, 1976).

Pappo's Fear of Success Scale consists of 83 items that measure academic fear of success, including self-doubt, preoccupation with competition, preoccupation with evaluation, rejection of competence, and self-sabotage (Gelbort & Winer, 1985). Although this scale is part of an unpublished doctoral dissertation completed in 1972, it has been used in several subsequent studies. Pappo's scale did not correlate significantly with Horner's original measure, but it was correlated with Alpert and Haber's Debilitating Anxiety Scale, which is used to measure fear of failure. Pappo deliberately avoided items related to gender roles, and consequently the scale does not yield different scores between males and females (Shaver, 1976).

Cohen's Fear of Success Scale, also based on an unpublished doctoral dissertation, views fear of success as broader than academic success (Shaver, 1976). This scale correlated highly with Pappo's scale and, like Pappo's scale, is uncorrelated with Horner's original measure. It predicted which subjects would perform poorly on a memory task after being told that they had qualified for the final stage of a memory contest. However, like Pappo's scale, it is difficult to know whether this scale measures fear of success or fear of failure.

Major's Revised Fear of Success Scale consists of two story cues: Horner's traditional cue about Anne and the cue "Mary has just received word that out of a class of 50, she alone passed the entrance exam and is being assigned the important position abroad" (Major, 1979). After each cue, subjects are asked to rate 30 items, half of which refer to positive consequences about the event and half to negative consequences. The two cues have been found to relate significantly to each other and to Horner's original measure (Major, 1979).

Spence's Objective Scoring System of Horner's story cues involves a 10-item questionnaire that follows presentation of the story cues (Spence, 1974). Items refer to attributions, external pressures against aspirations, career outcomes, noncareer outcomes, and cue denial.

Research

In contrast to the need for achievement literature, every study examining fear of success has used female subjects. Gender differences have been a part of the model from its inception. Much of the research was designed to test alternative explanations for Horner's concept of fear of success. Interestingly, because of the controversy regarding whether or not this term was valid, studies in which statistically significant results were not obtained have been published with some frequency as well as those in which significant results were found (Tresemer, 1976b).

When both male and female college students are given both the "Anne" and the "John" heading, males too are more likely to write stores with fear-of-success content for "Anne" (Feather & Raphaelson, 1974). Thus, the authors conclude that the instructions elicit cultural stereotypes rather than motives, since men are presumably not identifying with the female character.

When "Anne" and "John" are described as either at the top, in the top 5%, top 15%, top 25%, or top half of their medical school class, more positive imagery was projected onto "Anne" the lower her rank in class, whereas "John" was rated more negatively as he decreased in rank (Fogel & Paludi, 1984). Lentz (1982) suspected that the situation in which subjects complete the fear-of-success task can influence the outcome. She asked college women to complete the fear-of-success task, under instructions stating that the stories would be read by a panel of either males, females, or persons, who would evaluate subjects as either potential friends, coworkers, or acquaintances. Contrary to predictions, none of these instructions affected fear-of-success imagery. However, anagram performance was significantly affected by instructions about evaluators. Women who anticipated evaluation by males or by persons as potential friends performed significantly worse on the anagrams task than did women who anticipated evaluation by males as potential coworkers or acquaintances. Women who anticipated evaluation by women did not exhibit these effects (Lentz, 1982). Thus, it seems that the instructions aroused evaluation anxiety rather than fear of success.

Schnitlzer (1977) observed that women's fears described in their stories about "Anne" all focused on interpersonal factors, such as not being liked, not dating, not getting married, and not having children. In contrast, those men that exhibited fear of success to the "John" heading tended to write that John was becoming too one-sided or materialistic. She concludes that women are more likely than are men to experience a career as sacrificing friendship, marriage, or family. To assess this, Spence (1974) modified Horner's scenario to reflect a successful medical student who was either a single woman, married woman, or single male. Male and female undergraduates then answered objective questions about the story cues, using Spence's objective scoring system. Men were more likely than women to rate both the single man and single woman more negatively (Spence, 1974).

Lockheed (1975) postulated that women's fear of success is present only in situations in which women are considered deviant. Thus, medical school attendance is more normative, and thus less anxiety producing, for men than for women. She asked male and female college students to write stories to one of the two following headings:

1. "All Anne's classmates in medical school are men. After first-term finals, Anne finds herself at the top of her class."
2. "Half of Anne's classmates in medical school are women. After first-term finals, Anne finds herself at the top of her class" (p. 44).

When medical school attendance was described as more typical for women, men and women did not differ significantly in their story content about "Anne." However, when medical school attendance was described as more deviant for women, men were significantly more likely than were women to describe negative consequences for "Anne." Thus, women were more accepting of the successful woman in the heading, regardless of how deviant her role was, than were men.

In order to examine whether women who exhibited fear of success were more likely to aspire to traditionally female occupations than were women low on fear of success, Anderson (1978) asked college women to complete the fear-of-success task as well as answer questions about their career plans. Women low on fear of success were more likely to state that they wanted to make a major contribution to their field, that they had plans for nontraditional careers, and that they had mothers who were employed in nontraditional fields for women. Women low on fear of success were also more likely to have higher self-esteem, a more internal locus of control, and scores indicating more affection expressed to intimate others than were women high on fear of success (Anderson, 1978). Anderson concludes that women high on fear of success are more likely to have ambivalent feelings about career success, greater self-criticism, and greater need for affection.

Topol and Reznikoff (1979) compared female senior high school achievers and underachievers on fear of success, beliefs in women's roles, and educational and career goals. Female achievers had higher educational aspirations, less traditional career goals, and more commitment to their career goals than did underachievers. There was a tendency for achievers to exhibit lower fear of success and more feminist views of women's roles than did underachievers, but this did not reach significance.

Males and females at an adult religious conference center were asked to write stories for female headings that differed in deviance (engineering school versus nursing school) and role overload (happily married with children versus happily married without children) (Bremer & Wittig, 1980). Both men and women were more likely to write fear-of-success stories in response to deviant than to nondeviant situations, and to role overload rather than situations without role overload.

A number of researchers have been interested in correlating fear of success with gender role. For example, Major (1979) asked college women to complete the Bem Sex Role Inventory (Bem, 1974) and Major's Revised Fear of Success Scale. Androgynous women scored lower on fear of success than did feminine (sex-typed) women. Furthermore, masculine (sex-reversed) women scored higher on fear of success than did androgynous, feminine, or undifferentiated women. Major postulates that achieving women who are also feminine are more likely to experience positive consequences for success than are achieving women who reject feminine characteristics. Nevertheless, relatively few women are classified as sex-reversed on gender-role inventories. In line with this analysis, Makovsky (1976) found that high fear-of-success women perform best on anagrams tasks when competing against another woman and when the task is described as feminine.

Finally, a review by Tresemer (1976b) of over 100 fear-of-success studies yielded the following generalizations: (1) females tell a slightly greater proportion of fear-of-success stories than do males given a same-gender cue (i.e., "Anne" for women; "John" for men); (2) when males and females write stories to both male and female cues, there is no gender difference in fear of success; and (3) fear of success is not consistently related to academic ability or gender-role identification.

Racial Differences

With few exceptions, the subjects of the fear-of-success literature have been white college students. In two studies of fear of success comparing black and white college students (Puryear & Mednick, 1974; Weston & Mednick, 1970), black women showed less fear of success than did white women. Social class did not affect fear of success scores (Weston & Mednick, 1970).

Interestingly, women who endorsed more black militant attitudes were more likely to show fear of success (Puryear & Mednick, 1974). Fear of success and black militant attitudes were most strongly correlated among women who reported not being attached to a man. Puryear and Mednick speculate that women in this category may experience some of the same role conflicts first postulated by Horner. This corresponds with results by Caballero, Giles, and Shaver (1975), who found that women who hold liberal or radical political views and who favor the women's movement also score higher on fear of success than do women with more traditional beliefs.

Fear of Success among Children

There has been surprisingly little focus on fear of success and childrearing practices, given the large literature on childrearing and achievement motivation reviewed earlier. However, fear-of-success researchers have examined developmental factors in fear of success in an attempt to pinpoint at what age the phenomenon becomes salient.

Romer (1977) gave children in the fifth, seventh, eighth, ninth, and eleventh grades five story cues, with the heading "Anne (John) finds herself (himself) at the top of the (junior) high school class." Children were subsequently asked to perform an anagrams task in either a competitive or nonexplicitly competitive setting, either with one other individual or in a group. There was no overall gender difference in the frequency of fear-of-success content, although there was an effect for grade, with ninth graders of both genders most likely to write fear-of-success stories. Girls were more likely to write themes indicating loss of affiliation, followed by themes of denial. Boys were more likely to describe tragic events as the consequence of success, followed by themes related to loss of affiliation (Romer, 1977). Males with fear of success performed better in the competitive group condition than in the noncompetitive group condition; males with low fear of success showed the reverse pattern. The results for girls were not as clear-cut.

Hawkins and Pingree (1978) gave third-, sixth-, ninth-, and twelfth-grade students the original medical school scenario (reworded for simplicity) and then asked students to respond to semantic differential scales. "Anne" and "John" were rated as happier when they were successful than when they failed. When they failed, "John" was rated as much less nice than "Anne" was when she failed; when both succeeded, "Anne" was rated as slightly less nice than was "John" (Hawkins & Pingree, 1978). Monahan *et al.* (1974) similarly used Horner's original medical school scenario with 10- to 16-year-old boys and girls. Both boys and girls responded more negatively to the female cue, with boys responding significantly more negatively to "Anne" than did the girls.

Fear of success has been shown to increase from fourth to tenth grade but to decrease from tenth to twelfth grade (Kimball & Leahy, 1976), when children were asked to respond to the cue "After report cards, Anne (John) finds that she (he) is at the top of her (his) class." Gender differences in fear of success did not appear until high school, when females scored higher on fear of success than did males. Specifically, females enrolled in secretarial courses demonstrated low fear of success, and females in college preparatory classes showed high fear of success. The results were interpreted by the authors as demonstrating less conflict for high school girls involved in more gender-compatible tasks (Kimball & Leahy, 1976). Similarly, O'Leary and Hammack (1975) found high school girls with traditional career aspirations to demonstrate less fear of success.

Girls who had attended single-gender elementary and high schools were less likely to demonstrate fear of success than were girls from coeducational schools (Winchel, Fenner, & Shaver, 1974), even though these children came from similar religious backgrounds, neighborhoods, and social classes. The authors argue that coeducation ". . . increases the salience of cross-gender competition for academic and professional success" (p. 727).

Fear of Success versus Fear of Failure

Given the research described earlier that found evidence for women being more motivated by affiliative than by achievement needs, some researchers have speculated that women's needs for affiliation may motivate both their fear of success and fear of failure. For example, Jackaway and Teevan (1976) state: "If it is true that social approval is the achievement goal of many women, then fear of social rejection because of success (FOS) becomes tantamount to fear of failure" (p. 286). Consequently, there have been some attempts to compare fear of success with fear of failure. Furthermore, the scoring criteria for fear of success and for the hostile press scoring system of fear of failure show considerable overlap (Jackaway & Teevan, 1976). Both focus on negative consequences, reprimands for personal action, and relief for alleviation of the tension. Thus, the two are not independent concepts.

Jackaway and Teevan (1976) asked male and female high school students to write three stories, and included the prompt "John (Anne) is looking into his (her) microscope." Half the students were asked to compete with another student on a performance task and then to announce the "winner" publicly. Story content was then scored for both fear of success and hostile press imagery. Correlations between fear-of-success and fear-of-failure imagery ranged from .41

to .58, depending on condition and gender, and were highly significant. Thus, both males and females under neutral and competitive conditions demonstrated a relationship between the fear-of-success and fear-of-failure content of their stories.

Fear of success (using the Zuckerman and Allison Fear of Success Scale) and fear of failure (using the Alpert and Haber Debilitating Anxiety Scale) among male and female engineering undergraduates were correlated with the Bem Sex Role Inventory (Mulig, Haggerty, Carballosa, Cinnicak, & Madden, 1985). Fear of success and fear of failure were significantly correlated among females ($r = .62$) and among males ($r = .45$). Regression analyses indicated that fear of failure was best predicted from subjects' gender (females). However, fear of success was best predicted from subjects gender *role*, with masculine and neutral (androgynous and undifferentiated) subjects higher on fear of success (Mulig et al., 1985). These results are similar to those of Kimball and Leahy (1976) and of O'Leary and Hammack (1975) described earlier, that found females involved in gender-incompatible tasks and courses to exhibit higher fear of success than those involved in more traditionally feminine tasks.

In one of the most comprehensive studies comparing fear of success with fear of failure, Macdonald and Hyde (1980) factor analyzed male and female college students' responses to four measures of fear of success (Horner's original scoring system of fear of success, Horner and Fleming's revised system of fear of success, Cohen's Fear of Success Scale, and Zuckerman and Allison's Fear of Success Scale); three measures of fear of failure (Birney et al.'s hostile press scoring system, an alternative TAT scoring system, and Alpert and Haber's Debilitating Anxiety Scale); and three measures of need achievement (McClelland's TAT measure, the Achievement Scale of Jackson's Personality Research Form, and the Achievement Scale of the Edwards Personal Preference Schedule). Additionally, they included the Marlowe–Crowne Social-Desirability Scale, the Taylor Manifest Anxiety Scale, and three statements: "I am motivated to avoid success," "I am motivated to avoid failure," and "I have a need for achievement."

Results of the factor analysis indicated similar patterns for males and females. Specifically, Factor 1, labeled Anxiety, consisted of the Taylor Manifest Anxiety Scale, Alpert and Haber's Debilitating Anxiety Scale, and Cohen's Fear of Success measure. Factor 2 consisted of the three individual statements, and was thus hard to label. Factor 3 was labeled Fear of Success, and consisted of Zuckerman and Allison's Fear of Success Scale and Horner's original scoring system. Females scored higher than did males on every fear-of-success measure. Fear of failure did not appear as a distinct construct in the factor analysis (Macdonald & Hyde, 1980).

Gelbort and Winer (1985) correlated a number of fear-of-success and fear-of-failure scales, including Horner's fear-of-success scoring system, Pappo's Fear of Success Scale, Zuckerman and Allison's Fear of Success Scale, the Alpert and Haber Debilitating Anxiety Scale, and Birney et al.'s hostile press scoring system. The hostile press measure of fear of failure was significantly correlated with Horner's scoring system of fear of success (thus, it could be argued that it was the projective nature of these measures that was similar, rather than content) but negatively correlated with the Zuckerman and Allison Fear of Success Scale. The Debilitating Anxiety Scale was positively correlated with the Zuckerman and Allison Fear of Success Scale and Pappo's Fear of Success Scale.

In sum, it is unclear whether fear of success and fear of failure are separate concepts. Tresemer has stated that the "motive to avoid success may not be a motive and may have little to do with avoiding success" (in Zuckerman & Wheeler, p. 932).

Has Fear of Success Decreased since 1965?

Given the onset of the second wave of feminism in the late 1960s and the increasing numbers of women entering medical school, has fear-of-success motivation decreased over the years when the scenario of "Anne" is presented? Some studies have not found a decrease in fear of success over the years. In 1971 Hoffman (1974) carried out Horner's study under the same conditions at the same university. The percentage of fear of success among women was identical in 1965 and 1971—about 65%. Among men, fear of success rose from 9% in 1965 to 77% in 1971—a tremendous increase. Consequently, there were no gender differences in fear of success in 1971. Yet there were gender differences in content of fear-of-success stories: women indicated that "Anne" suffered a loss of affiliation, whereas men tended to question the value of achievement.

In a similar vein, Alper (1974) replicated Horner's study on Wellesley College women in the academic year 1970–1971. About 89% told avoidance stories about "Anne," and 50% told avoidance stories about "John." When Dartmouth College males were given the same story cues, 62.5% told avoidance stories about "Anne," a statistically significant difference (Alper, 1974).

On the other hand, Tresemer's (1976b) review of the fear-of-success literature indicated that both men and women decreased in fear-of-success content when the results of more recent studies are compared with earlier ones. Tresemer compared these results with national statistics on the percentages of women entering medical school. For women rating "Anne" over the years, fear of success began to decrease markedly in 1969 and continued to decrease rapidly until 1975, when Tresemer's review was written. The proportion of women entering medical school increased slightly in 1969 and continued to increase until 1975, although not at the same marked rate as that of the decrease in fear-of-success scores among women. Thus, other social changes presumably contributed to this change in women's attitudes.

Whether or not fear of success is decreasing, it continues to receive its share of coverage in psychology and women's studies textbooks. The term "fear of success" has become part of the general vocabulary but is also beginning to lose its specificity. For example, Sherman (1983) described high school girls who took advanced math courses as reflecting less "fear of success." Thus, the term as used here is synonymous with positive attitudes toward math. When researchers examine fear of success these days, they need to realize that "Anne" and "John" have become familiar to college students. One student wrote the following story in response to the traditional medical school cue: "Anne is being congratulated by the male and female members of her class. The males are somewhat chagrined, as is Anne. However, Anne has read *Psychology Today* and knows that studies such as this indicate that this is an expected reaction" (Tresemer, 1977, p. 104).

Finally, Shaver (1976) speculates that what is fearful about success is not that different from what is fearful about failure: people who deviate from normative scores ". . . may pay a high price in strained interpersonal relations" (p. 317). He argues that had Horner used the cue "Anne is by all accounts the most beautiful coed at the University of Michigan," she would have found similar themes of negative interpersonal consequences and denial, yet she would hardly have termed her results "fear of beauty." The very term *success* is defined as one that involves ". . . obtaining desirable outcomes as a result of an action or performance. Thus, a distinction should be made between quality of performance and the consequences of the performance" (Jellison, Jackson-White, Bruder, & Martyna, 1975, p. 382). Success and failure are synonymous when a positive outcome also implies rejection and negative consequences in the future.

The peak period of research on fear of success occurred in the early 1970s, corresponding with the beginning of the focus on gender differences in the psychological literature. A decade later, fear-of-success research has all but ceased, and Horner's original conception of the term is no longer used.

Intervention

There has been no focus on interventions for fear of success. Although Horner originally conceptualized fear of success as a personality trait, the emphasis quickly changed to environmental explanations, particularly those focusing on gender roles. Currently, the term fear of success is not used much either in research or intervention. Presumably, if a client described her academic or work-related difficulties as stemming from a fear of success, the therapist would reinterpret these as reflecting women's roles in society and would inquire about the negative consequences of success.

Summary

Horner viewed fear of success as the consequence of women's roles in society, in which women are rejected or considered unfeminine when they succeed. In fact, fear of success and fear of failure are difficult to separate empirically, since most situations have both success and failure as possible outcomes. Furthermore, some of the fear-of-success scales overlap with scales on fear of failure. Research on fear of success indicates that women are more likely to tell negative stories about other women who are described as at the top of their medical school class, but that both males and females write more negative stories about successful females than successful males. Specifically, female children and adults fear interpersonal loss as the consequence of academic or professional success. There is some evidence that fear of success among women decreased in the decade following Horner's original study, and the concept is rarely used in current research.

FEAR OF FAILURE AS AN ANTECEDENT OF PROCRASTINATION

In the early 1970s, as record numbers of U.S. students attended college, behavior therapists became interested in improving the performance of individuals who were failing academically. The initial focus was on students who were on academic probation or failed to complete coursework. Procrastination, poor study habits, and lack of goal setting were found to be prevalent among these students (Green, 1982). This resulted in an enormous literature that provided study skills training and time management strategies (Bristol & Sloane, 1974; Greiner & Karoly, 1976; Mawhinney, Bostow, Laws, Blumenfeld, & Hopkins, 1971; McReynolds & Church, 1973; Richards, 1975; Richards, McReynolds, Holt, & Sexton, 1976; Ziesat, Rosenthal, & White, 1978). Interventions focused on improving the "time–work relationship" (Semb, Glick, & Spencer, 1979) by such methods as stimulus control, self-reward, and self-punishment (Ziesat *et al.*, 1978), increasing time spent studying (Mawhinney *et al.*, 1971), planning skills (Greiner & Karoly, 1976), and study skills advice (Richards, 1975).

It soon became apparent that academic procrastination was not limited to students performing poorly in college or to those deficient in study skills. A survey of 500 students at five colleges (Hill, Hill, Chabot, & Barrall, 1978) found that only 12% of students reported that they seldom procrastinated. Of the remaining students, 38% reported procrastinating occasionally, 23% about half the time, 17% frequently, and 10% stated that they usually procrastinated. Faculty estimates of student procrastination in this survey were even higher. Only 1% of faculty stated that students seldom procrastinated, 30% occasionally, 27% about half the time, 35% frequently, and 7% felt that students usually procrastinated. Furthermore, faculty rated themselves as occasional procrastinators: 18% reported that they seldom procrastinated, 51% occasionally, 13% about half the time, 15% frequently, and 3% usually (Hill *et al.*, 1978). Despite these data indicating that procrastinators included some high-performing students and faculty members, the intervention for procrastination continued to focus on study skills improvement.

In 1983, Burka and Yuen published their clinical observations of the reasons for procrastination, based on treatment groups of nonstudent populations. They found a number of cognitive and affective factors to precede procrastination, including evaluation anxiety, difficulty in making decisions, rebellion against control, lack of assertion, and perfectionism. In the first empirical study of cognitive-affective antecedents of academic procrastination, Solomon and Rothblum (1984) asked students and faculty for reasons for academic procrastination and found 13 possible antecedents of procrastination: evaluation anxiety, perfectionism, difficulty making decisions, dependency and help seeking, aversiveness of the task and low frustration tolerance, low self-esteem, laziness, lack of assertion, fear of success, poor time management, rebellion against control, risk taking, and peer influence. These reasons for procrastination were subsequently incorporated into a scale, described below.

A factor analysis of college students' reasons for procrastination yielded two major factors. The first, termed Fear of Failure, consisted of five items reflecting evaluation anxiety (anxiety about meeting the expectations of others), perfectionism (concern about meeting one's own standards), and low self-esteem, and it accounted for 49.4% of the variance. The second factor, termed Task Aversiveness, consisted of items reflecting aversiveness of the task and laziness, and it accounted for 18% of the variance. Factors 3 through 7 tapped dependency, risk taking, lack of assertion, rebellion against control, and difficulty making decisions, respectively. Interestingly, given the large intervention literature, time management was not found to be an independent factor for reasons for procrastination. Nor was fear of success, despite the large literature on this topic in the 1970s. Given that fear of failure accounted for half the variance of reasons for academic procrastination, research on fear-of-failure-related procrastination has continued and will be described below.

Psychometric Scales and Assessment

The Procrastination Assessment Scale—Students (PASS) was developed to measure the frequency and cognitive-behavioral antecedents of academic procrastination (Solomon & Rothblum, 1984). The first part assesses the frequency of procrastination in six academic areas: (1) writing a term paper, (2) studying for exams, (3) keeping up with weekly reading assignments, (4) performing administrative tasks, (5) attending meetings, and (6) performing academic tasks in general. Subjects are asked to indicate on 5-point Likert scales the extent to which they procrastinate on each task and the extent to which procrastination on each task is a problem for them.

The second part of the PASS describes a procrastination scenario (delay in writing a term paper) and then lists 26 possible reasons for procrastination on the task (two statements for each of the 13 reasons listed above). Subjects rate each statement on a 5-point Likert scale according to how much it reflects why they procrastinated the last time they delayed writing a term paper. For example, the two items reflecting evaluation anxiety are "You were concerned the professor wouldn't like your work" and "You were worried you might get a bad grade." The two items related to perfectionism are "You were concerned you wouldn't meet your own expectations" and "You set very high standards for yourself and you worried that you wouldn't be able to meet those standards" (Solomon & Rothblum, 1988). Males and females do not differ in frequency of academic procrastination on the PASS.

The PASS has also been modified to reflect the British-based university system of Australia (APASS; Beswick, Rothblum, & Mann, 1988) and for use in assessing procrastination among employees (PASE, Rothblum, 1986). Finally, Jeffers (1986) developed a scale of social procrastination (SPASS).

Self-reported frequency of procrastination on the PASS correlates significantly with delay in completing self-paced quizzes (Solomon & Rothblum, 1984;

Rothblum, Solomon, & Murakami, 1986), delay in submitting course assignments (Beswick *et al.*, 1988), delay in participation in psychology experiments (Solomon & Rothblum, 1984), and lower course grades (Beswick *et al.*, 1988; Rothblum *et al.*, 1986). Frequency of procrastination on the PASS also correlates positively with self-report measures of irrational cognitions, depression, and anxiety, and negatively with self-esteem and study habits (Solomon & Rothblum, 1984).

Research

Fear of failure has been found to account for most of the variance in factor analyses of reasons why students procrastinate, both in the United States (Solomon & Rothblum, 1984) and Australia (Beswick *et al.*, 1988). Although males and females are equally likely to report procrastination, females are significantly more likely to endorse the Fear-of-Failure factor than are males. The five items that make up the Fear-of-Failure factor are endorsed by about 6–14% of students as extremely reflective of why they procrastinated. Thus, a small but very homogeneous group of female students seem to experience fear of failure. In contrast, males are more likely to endorse items reflecting risk taking and rebellion against deadlines.

Fear of failure as a reason for academic procrastination was found to correlate positively with anxiety, depression, and irrational cognitions, and negatively with self-esteem and organized study habits (Solomon & Rothblum, 1984). In contrast, the second factor, Task Aversiveness, was endorsed by more students, was more heterogeneous (accounted for a lower percentage of the variance) and did not correlate significantly with anxiety. There also were no significant gender differences in the endorsement of Task Aversiveness as a reason for procrastination.

In order to examine more specifically how anxiety-related factors are related to procrastination, high and low procrastinators were assessed weekly as an academic deadline approached (Rothblum *et al.*, 1986). Women were more likely than were men to report test anxiety and low self-control (consisting of delay of gratification, perceived self-efficacy, and perceived control over emotional reactions). High procrastinators were more likely than were low procrastinators to report test anxiety and low self-control. High procrastinators were also more likely to attribute success on a task to external and temporary factors, whereas low procrastinators attributed success more to internal and stable factors. High and low procrastinators did not differ on attributions of failure, and there were no gender differences on attributions. Female high procrastinators were more likely to report state anxiety and anxiety-related physical symptoms across time periods than were female low procrastinators. Finally, fear of failure was viewed as an obstacle to effective study by all groups, and it decreased in salience as the deadline approached (Rothblum *et al.*, 1986). Thus, the results of this study indicate that procrastination is associated with high and stable levels of anxiety across time, especially for women.

Is fear of failure as a reason for procrastination related to fear of failure as defined by the need achievement literature? Dalton, Rothblum, and Solomon (1984) asked subjects to complete the Fear-of-Failure factor of the PASS and Mehrabian's self-report scale of achieving tendency (a low score indicates greater motive to avoid failure). There was a small ($r = -.24$) but significant negative correlation between the two measures, indicating some overlap between the two conceptualizations of fear of failure.

Given the importance placed on evaluation from others in the Fear-of-Failure factor, Jeffers (1986) developed a version of the PASS that focused on social rather than academic procrastination (SPASS). The first component of the SPASS focused on procrastination in eight social situations (e.g., communicating with roommates, meeting new people). The second component provides two scenarios: contacting a roommate or family member about conflict, and contacting a boyfriend/girlfriend/lover about conflict, and asks subjects to think of the last time they were involved in these situations. Both scenarios were found to be high-frequency areas of social procrastination in a pilot study, and each scenario is followed by 15 statements reflecting reasons for procrastination in these scenarios. Separate factor analyses of each scenario indicated that Fear of Rejection (including items reflecting fear of not being liked, not wanting to be hurt, feeling judged or advised, and not wanting to deal with the consequences) accounted for approximately 30% of the variance of the first scenario (conflict with roommate/family member), followed by a factor termed Lack of Responsibility that accounted for 7% of the variance. For the second scenario (conflict with lover), Fear of Rejection again accounted for about 30% of the variance, followed by a factor termed Fear of Causing Pain or Anger. This second factor, which accounted for 10% of the variance, was endorsed significantly more by women than by men (Jeffers, 1986).

Childrearing Factors

There has been no research using the PASS with children. However, McKenna, Solomon and Rothblum (1986) speculated that fear of failure, consisting of high evaluation anxiety and perfectionism, is likely to result from childrearing patterns. Specifically, they hypothesized that children with overly critical parents who demand high standards might learn to avoid important tasks rather than risk disapproval. They asked college students to complete the PASS and measures of parental affection and control. Subjects high on fear of failure were less likely to report their fathers to have been accepting, to demonstrate caring, and to allow cognitive independence, while they were growing up. When males and females were compared separately, it was females high on fear of failure who experienced these childrearing styles from fathers while they were growing up; these relationships were not significant for males high on fear of failure. Additionally, females high on fear of failure showed a small but significant tendency to report paternal overprotectiveness while they were growing up (McKenna et al., 1986). There were no significant relationships between fear of failure and maternal childrearing styles.

Model

Solomon and Rothblum (1983) have developed an avoidance model of pro-crastination, depicted in Figure 1. According to this model, high fear-of-failure procrastinators will experience some worry and anxiety as the deadline for a task approaches. A way to reduce this anxiety is to avoid the task by procrastination, resulting in relief from anxiety and thus reinforcement of the avoidance behav-ior. Thus, fear-of-failure procrastinators may be similar to individuals with pho-bias. There is some evidence that high procrastinators, especially those also high on fear of failure, are unconcerned with performance until anxiety and worry reach peak levels (Solomon, Murakami, Greenberger, & Rothblum, 1983).

Additionally, the research on attributions (Rothblum et al., 1986) indicates that high procrastinators attribute success to more external and fleeting circum-stances than do low procrastinators. In this way, high procrastinators do not take credit for their own performance and may not feel as competent. Group discussions with high and low procrastinators (Solomon et al., 1983) indicated that high procrastinators begin work on academic tasks immediately preceding the deadline, in part so as not to test their true ability. If they then succeed on the task, they can attribute performance to luck; if they fail, to lack of effort. In this manner, they are protecting their self-esteem, and avoiding a true test of their competence. Because performance is thus attributed to unstable circumstances (i.e., luck or effort), feelings of competence are unlikely to generalize to subse-quent tasks. The procrastinator thus approaches each new academic task with slight aversion, resulting in additional avoidance.

The avoidance model of fear-of-failure-based procrastination has similarities to three areas of cognitive-behavioral research. The first, termed *self-handicapping*

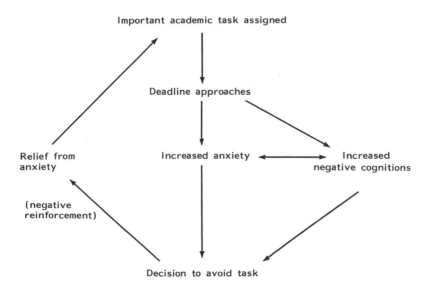

FIGURE 1. Solomon and Rothblum's avoidance model of procrastination.

(Berglas & Jones, 1978), argues that individuals may enhance the difficulty of tasks in order to externalize failure and thus "save face." Self-handicapping strategies may include choosing performance-inhibiting drugs (Berglas & Jones, 1978; Kolditz & Arkin, 1982), drinking alcohol (Jones & Berglas, 1978; Tucker, Vuchinich, & Sobell, 1981), reporting shyness (Snyder, Smith, Augelli, & Ingram, 1985), or reporting physical illness (Smith, Snyder, & Perkins, 1983), as decrements to performance. In this way, individuals can avoid a true test of their ability, given that their maladaptive behavior serves as an "excuse" for poor performance.

The second area, termed *defensive pessimism* (Norem & Cantor, 1986b), focuses on the strategies used by people to cope with situations that present the possibility of failure and risks to self-esteem. According to Norem and Cantor (1986a), individuals can cope with anticipatory anxiety by setting low expectations and can cope with actual failure by restructuring their cognitions of the situation.

Finally, Clance (1985) has coined the term *imposter phenomenon* to describe individuals who feel like fakes or frauds despite successful careers. Clance argues that such individuals do not take credit for their success, believing that it was due to a mistake or to kindness on the part of others. Because individuals experiencing the imposter phenomenon do not view themselves as competent, they will worry unduly about new tasks, procrastinate, engage in frenzied work immediately before the deadline, and then attribute success to chance. In this way, they will perpetuate the cycle of anxiety and self-doubt and avoid new tasks or responsibility.

Intervention

The procrastination model of fear of failure originated from intervention studies using study skills and time management strategies. Given cognitive and affective components of procrastination, and especially the salience of fear of failure as a reason for procrastination, what are the implications for intervention?

A few researchers have incorporated cognitive strategies into the intervention of procrastination and study skills training. Jason and Burrows (1983) provided "transition training" for students about to graduate from high school. High school seniors who were provided with relaxation, cognitive restructuring, and problem solving demonstrated greater self-efficacy and rational beliefs than did students not given this training. Wilson and Linville (1985) found that attributional retraining increased the academic performance of college freshmen. Freshmen who were told in class that low grades in the freshmen year are temporary had significant increases in grade point average during the following semester, compared with freshmen who were not told this information (Wilson & Linville, 1985). Borkovec's research on treating worry has found stimulus control (i.e., telling worriers when and for how long to worry) decreased the daily frequency of worry for these individuals (Borkovec, Wilkinson, Folensbee, & Lerman, 1983). Finally, collective, rather than individual, performance on difficult tasks decreases anxiety, a phenomenon known as "social facilitation" (Jackson & Williams, 1985).

Solomon and Rothblum's avoidance model of fear-of-failure-based procrastination implies that the treatment of procrastination may need to use similar techniques as that for phobias. If individuals are motivated to avoid performance because this avoidance is reinforcing, then they may not comply with programs that require them to gradually increase anxiety. Thus, flooding may be an effective intervention for fear-of-failure-based procrastination. Research on flooding as a treatment method for fear-of-failure-based procrastination is currently in preparation (Loew, Solomon, Rothblum, & Kaloupek, 1988).

Summary

A small but homogeneous group of female college students endorsed fear of failure as the primary reason why they procrastinated. Fear of failure as an antecedent of academic procrastination remains at high levels across time and is related to a number of anxiety-related measures. Solomon and Rothblum have conceptualized an avoidance model of fear of failure that is similar to the anxiety-relief model of phobias.

CONCLUSION AND FUTURE DIRECTIONS

The four perspectives on fear of failure differ in their theoretical conceptualization and assessment of the term fear of failure. Nevertheless, the research on fear of failure yields some consistent themes. First, women generally report more fear of failure, and behave in ways that express more fear of failure, than do men. What is fearful about failure seems to be the expected interpersonal consequences (such as fear of rejection) rather than the specific academic performance. Individuals with fear of failure are motivated to avoid situations that run the risk of poor performance, even at the expense of less success. When presented with a choice to receive feedback about their performance, individuals with fear of failure would rather not know how they are doing. Yet those individuals high on fear of failure are often performing adequately, even successfully. The cycle of avoidance and external justification for success is associated with poor self-esteem and increased self-doubt.

Furthermore, the importance of achievement for women seems to decrease in adolescence. The research on fear of success indicates that our educational system is more relevant for the career goals of men than of women. Finally, parental childrearing practices interact with gender to influence children's self-perceptions of competence and achievement.

Most of the literature on fear of failure has focused on college students, and there have been a few studies on children. Little is known about the achievement patterns of older adults, particularly as they become secure in their careers and face retirement. Theories of gender differences in adult development (e.g., Gilligan, 1982; Levinson, 1978) indicate that men and women face different changes in attitudes, values, and work satisfaction as they mature. There is some evidence to indicate that for women achievement motivation declines during the childrearing period and then increases when children mature (Baruch, 1967). Kaufman and Richardson (1982) have argued that such "vicarious achievement" through children and spouses among homemakers should be investigated more thoroughly.

There is little information on fear of failure among minority groups and members of lower socioeconomic groups. Presumably, achievement and success as they are traditionally defined may have little relevance for oppressed groups. More emphasis needs to be placed on redefining achievement as it relates to the priorities of groups other than white, middle-class, young people.

There is little question that fear of failure as defined by images of barriers to success and by test anxiety should be ameliorated. The term itself connotes an aversive affective state and poor academic performance. However, much of the research reviewed above suggests that, in many ways, individuals who score high on fear of failure are cooperative rather than competitive and socially rather than personally oriented. Thus, individuals low on achievement motivation possess important affiliative skills. Perhaps a more important question is whether high striving for success is a desirable goal for clinicians to prioritize for their clients.

Because of the focus on males in early achievement motivation research, the models of achievement single-mindedly emphasize academic achievement to the exclusion of all other areas, such as athletic, domestic, social, and community performance. Hoffman (1972) has argued that a mentally healthy society needs to emphasize greater flexibility, and that the more diffuse achievement patterns of women should serve as a model for a fuller life. Developing affiliative and social skills is preferable to encouraging competitive striving for goals that can be won by, at most, a few individuals.

The peak period of achievement-related research took place during the postwar decades, when emphasis on career and academic success was primary. The social change of the late 1960s, affirmative action for women and minorities, and women's increased participation in the labor force may (or may not) have affected achievement patterns. It remains to be seen whether changes in childrearing, the work setting, and family constellations will change the nature of achievement and fear of failure in future years.

REFERENCES

Alper, T. G. (1974). Achievement motivation in college women. *American Psychologist, 29*, 194–203.
Alpert, R., & Haber, R. N. (1960). Anxiety in academic achievement situations. *Journal of Abnormal and Social Psychology, 61*, 207–215.
Anderson, R. (1978). Motive to avoid success: A profile. *Sex Roles, 4*, 239–248.
Atkinson, J. W. (1957). Motivational determinants of risk-taking behavior. *Psychological Bulletin, 64*, 359–372.
Atkinson, J. W., Bastian, J. R., Earl, R. W., & Litwin, G. H. (1960). The achievement motive, goal setting, and probability preferences. *Journal of Abnormal and Social Psychology, 60*, 27–36.

Atkinson, J. W., & Feather, N. T. (1966). *A theory of achievement motivation.* New York: John Wiley & Sons.

Atkinson, J. W., & Litwin, G. H. (1960). Achievement motive and test anxiety conceived as motive to approach success and motive to avoid failure. *Journal of Abnormal and Social Psychology, 1,* 52–63.

Baker, H. S. (1979). The conquering hero quits: Narcissistic factors in underachievement and failure. *American Journal of Psychotherapy, 33,* 418–427.

Bar-Tal, D., & Frieze, I. H. (1977). Achievement motivation for males and females as a determinant of attributions for success and failure. *Sex Roles, 3,* 301–313.

Baruch, R. (1967). The achievement motive in women: Implications for career development. *Journal of Personality and Social Psychology, 6,* 32–37.

Battle, E. S. (1966). Motivational determinants of academic competence. *Journal of Personality and Social Psychology, 4,* 634–642.

Battle, E. S., & Potter, J. B. (1963). Children's feelings of personal control as related to social class and ethnic group. *Journal of Personality, 31,* 482–490.

Baumrind, D. (1971). Current patterns of parental authority. *Developmental Psychology, 4,* (1, Pt. 2).

Bem, S. L. (1974). The measurement of psychological androgyny. *Journal of Consulting and Clinical Psychology, 42,* 155–162.

Berglas, S., & Jones, E. E. (1978). Drug choice as a self-handicapping strategy in response to noncontingent success. *Journal of Personality and Social Psychology, 36,* 405–417.

Beswick, G., Rothblum, E. D., & Mann, L. (1988). Psychological antecedents of student procrastination. *Australian Psychologist, 23,* 207–217.

Birney, R. C., Burdick, H., & Teevan, R. C. (1969). *Fear of Failure.* New York: Van Nostrand-Reinhold.

Bond, J. R., & Vinacke, W. E. (1961). Coalitions in mixed-sex triads. *Sociometry, 24,* 61–75.

Borkovec, T. D., Wilkinson, L., Folensbee, R., & Lerman, C. (1983). Stimulus control applications to the treatment of worry. *Behaviour Research and Therapy, 21,* 247–252.

Bremer, T. H., & Wittig, M. A. (1980). Fear of success: A personality trait or a response to occupational deviance and role overload. *Sex Roles, 6,* 27–46.

Bristol, M. M., & Sloane, H. N. (1974). Effects of contingency contracting on study rate and test performance. *Journal of Applied Behavior Analysis, 7,* 271–285.

Brown, J., & Weiner, B. (1984). Affective consequences of ability versus effort ascriptions: Controversies, resolutions, and quandaries. *Journal of Educational Psychology, 76,* 146–158.

Burka, J. B., & Yuen, L. M. (1983). *Procrastination: Why you do it. What to do about it.* Reading, MA: Addison-Wesley.

Caballero, C. M., Giles, P., & Shaver, P. (1975). Sex-role traditionalism and fear of success. *Sex Roles, 1,* 319–326.

Cavenar, J. O., & Werman, D. S. (1981). Origins of the fear of success. *American Journal of Psychiatry, 138,* 95–98.

Chehrazi, S. (1984). Female psychology: A review. *Journal of the American Psychoanalytic Association, 34,* 141–162.

Cherry, F., & Deaux, K. (1978). Fear of success versus fear of gender-inappropriate behavior. *Sex Roles, 4,* 97–101.

Chessick, R. D. (1984). Was Freud wrong about feminine psychology? *The American Journal of Psychoanalysis, 44,* 355–367.

Clance, P. R. (1985). *The imposter phenomenon: When success makes you feel like a fake.* New York: Bantam Books.

Covington, M. V., & Omelich, C. L. (1979). Effort: The double-edged sword in school achievement. *Journal of Educational Psychology, 71,* 169–182.

Covington, M. V., & Omelich, C. L. (1984). Controversies or consistencies? A reply to Brown and Weiner. *Journal of Educational Psychology, 76,* 159–168.

Crandall, V. C., Katkovsky, W., & Crandall, V. J. (1965). Children's beliefs in their own control of reinforcements in intellectual–academic achievement situations. *Child Development, 36,* 91–109.

Crandall, V. J., Preston, A., & Rabson, M. (1960). Maternal reactions and the development of independence and achievement behavior in young children. *Child Development, 31,* 243–251.

Crandall, V. J., & Rabson, A. (1960). Children's repetition choices in an intellectual achievement situation following success and failure. *The Journal of Genetic Psychology, 97,* 161–168.

Crowne, D. P., Conn, L. K., Marlowe, D., & Edwards, C. N. (1969). Some developmental antecedents of level of aspiration. *Journal of Personality, 37,* 73–92.

Dalton, E., Rothblum, E. D., & Solomon, L. J. (1984). *Fear of failure, test anxiety, and task importance as
predictors of academic procrastination.* Unpublished manuscript. Department of Psychology, University of Vermont, Burlington.

Edwards, A. L. (1959). *Edwards Personal Preference Profile.* New York: Psychological Corporation.

Entwisle, D. R. (1972). To dispel fantasies about fantasy-based measures of achievement motivation.
Psychological Bulletin, 6, 377–391.

Erkut, S. (1983). Exploring sex differences in expectancy, attribution, and academic achievement. *Sex
Roles, 9,* 217–231.

Feather, N. T. (1969). Attribution of responsibility and valence of success and failure in relation to
initial confidence and task performance. *Journal of Personality and Social Psychology, 13,* 129–144.

Feather, N. T., & Raphaelson, A. W. (1974). Fear of success in Australian and American student
groups: Motive or sex role stereotype. *Journal of Personality, 42,* 190–201.

Feldman-Summers, S., & Kiesler, S. B. (1974). Those who are Number Two try harder: The effect of
sex on attributions of causality. *Journal of Personality and Social Psychology, 30,* 846–855.

Fidell, L. S. (1970). Empirical verification of sex discrimination in hiring practices in psychology.
American Psychologist, 25, 1094–1097.

Fogel, R., & Paludi, M. A. (1984). Fear of success and failure, or norms for achievement? *Sex Roles, 10,*
431–434.

Freud, S. (1957). Some characters met with in psychoanalytic work: II. Those wrecked by success. In
J. Strachey (Ed. and Trans.), *The Standard edition of the complete works of Sigmund Freud* (Vol. 14, pp.
316–331). London: Hogarth Press.

Frieze, I. H., Whitley, B. E., Hanusa, B. H., & McHugh, M. C. (1982). Assessing the theoretical
models for sex differences in causal attributions for success and failure. *Sex Roles, 8,* 333–343.

Gelbort, K. R., & Winer, J. L. (1985). Fear of success and fear of failure: A multitrait–multimethod
validation study. *Journal of Personality and Social Psychology, 48,* 1009–1014.

Gilligan, C. (1982). *In a different voice: Psychological theory and women's development.* Cambridge, MA:
Harvard University Press.

Goldberg, P. A. (1968, April). Are women prejudiced against women? *Trans-Action,* 28–30.

Green, L. (1982). Minority students' self-control of procrastination. *Journal of Counseling Psychology,
29,* 636–644.

Greiner, J. M., & Karoly, P. (1976). Effects of self-control training on study activity and academic
performance: An analysis of self-monitoring, self-reward, and systematic-planning components. *Journal of Counseling Psychology, 23,* 495–502.

Gurin, P., & Epps, E. (1975). *Black consciousness, identity, and achievement.* New York: Wiley.

Hancock, J. G., & Teevan, R. C. (1964). Fear of failure and risk-taking behavior. *Journal of Personality,
32,* 200–209.

Hawkins, R. P., & Pingree, S. (1978). A developmental exploration of the fear of success phenomenon as cultural stereotype. *Sex Roles, 4,* 539–547.

Hellman, I. (1954). Some observations on mothers of children with intellectual inhibitions. *Psychoanalytic Study of the Child, 9,* 259–273.

Hendin, H. (1972). The psychodynamics of flunking out. *Journal of Nervous and Mental Disease, 155,*
131–143.

Hermans, H. J. M., ter Laak, J. J. F., & Maes, P. C. J. M. (1972). Achievement motivation and fear of
failure in family and school. *Developmental Psychology, 6,* 520–528.

Hill, M. B., Hill, D. A., Chabot, A. E., & Barrall, J. F. (1978). A survey of college faculty and student
procrastination. *College Student Journal, 12,* 256–262.

Hoffman, L. W. (1972). Early childhood experiences and women's achievement motives. *Journal of
Social Issues, 28,* 129–155.

Hoffman, L. W. (1974). Fear of success in males and females: 1965 and 1971. *Journal of Consulting and
Clinical Psychology, 42,* 353–358.

Horner, M. S. (November, 1969). Fail: Bright women. *Psychology Today,* pp. 36–38, 62.

Horner, M. S. (1972). Toward an understanding of achievement-related conflicts in women. *Journal of
Social Issues, 28,* 157–175.

Horney, K. (1967). The problem of female masochism. In H. Kelman (Ed.) *Feminine psychology* (pp. 214–233). New York: W. W. Norton.

House, W. C. (1974). Actual and perceived differences in male and female expectancies and minimal goal levels as a function of competition. *Journal of Personality, 42,* 493–509.

Hyde, J. S. (1985). *Half the human experience: The psychology of women.* Lexington, MA: D. C. Heath.

Jackaway, R., & Teevan, R. (1976). Fear of failure and fear of success: Two dimensions of the same motive. *Sex Roles, 2,* 283–293.

Jackson, J. M., & Williams, K. D. (1985). Social loafing on difficult tasks: Working collectively can improve performance. *Journal of Personality and Social Psychology, 49,* 937–942.

Jason, L. A., & Burrows, B. (1983). Transition training for high school seniors. *Cognitive Therapy and Research, 7,* 79–92.

Jeffers, P. (1986). *Prevalence of and reasons for social procrastination.* Unpublished honors thesis, Department of Psychology, University of Vermont, Burlington.

Jellison, J. M., Jackson-White, R., Bruder, R. A., & Martyna, W. (1975). Achievement behavior: A situational interpretation. *Sex Roles, 1,* 369–384.

Jones, E. E., & Berglas, S. (1978). Control of attributions about the self through self-handicapping strategies: The appeal of alcohol and the role of underachievement. *Personality and Social Psychology Bulletin, 4,* 200–206.

Kanefield, L. (1985a). Psychoanalytic constructions of female development and women's conflicts about achievement—Part I. *Journal of the American Academy of Psychoanalysis, 13,* 229–246.

Kanefield, L. (1985b). Psychoanalytic constructions of female development and women's conflicts about achievement—Part II. *Journal of the American Academy of Psychoanalysis, 13,* 347–366.

Katkovsky, W., Crandall, V. C., & Good, V. (1967). Parental antecedents of children's beliefs in internal–external control of reinforcements in intellectual achievement situations. *Child Development, 38,* 765–776.

Kaufman, D. R., & Richardson, B. L. (1982). *Achievement and women: Challenging the assumptions.* New York: The Free Press.

Kimball, B., & Leahy, R. L. (1976). Fear of success in males and females: Effects of developmental level and sex-linked course of study. *Sex Roles, 2,* 273–281.

Kolditz, T. A., & Arkin, R. M. (1982). An impression management interpretation of the self-handicapping strategy. *Journal of Personality and Social Psychology, 43,* 492–502.

Krumboltz, J. D., & Farquhar, W. W. (1957). Reliability and validity of the n achievement test. *Journal of Consulting Psychology, 21,* 226–228.

Lefcourt, H., & Ladwig, G. (1965). The American Negro: A problem in expectancies. *Journal of Personality and Social Psychology, 1,* 377–380.

Lentz, M. E. (1982). Fear of success as a situational phenomenon. *Sex Roles, 6,* 987–997.

Lesser, G. S., Krawitz, R. N., & Packard, R. (1963). Experimental arousal of achievement motivation in adolescent girls. *Journal of Abnormal and Social Psychology, 66,* 59–66.

Levine, R., Reis, H. T., Sue, E., & Turner, G. (1976). Fear of failure in males: A more salient factor than fear of success in females? *Sex Roles, 2,* 389–398.

Levinson, D. J. (1978). *The season's of a man's life.* New York: Ballantine.

Lockheed, M. E. (1975). Female motive to avoid success: A psychological barrier or a response to deviancy? *Sex Roles, 1,* 41–50.

Loew, D. E., Solomon, L. J., Rothblum, E. D., & Kaloupek, D. (1988). *Modification of fear of failure-based academic procrastination: A comparison of flooding and study skills training.* Unpublished manuscript. Department of Psychology, University of Vermont, Burlington.

Macdonald, N. E., & Hyde, J. S. (1980). Fear of success, need achievement, and fear of failure: A factor analytic study. *Sex Roles, 6,* 695–711.

Major, B. (1979). Sex-role orientation and fear of success: Clarifying an unclear relationship. *Sex Roles, 5,* 63–70.

Makovsky, V. P. (1976). Sex-role compatibility of task and of competitor, and fear of success as variables affecting women's performance. *Sex Roles, 2,* 237–248.

Mawhinney, V. T., Bostow, D. E., Laws, D. R., Blumenfeld, G. J., & Hopkins, B. L. (1971). A comparison of students studying behavior produced daily, weekly, and three-week testing schedules. *Journal of Applied Behavior Analysis, 4,* 257–264.

McClelland, D. C., Atkinson, J. W., Clark, R. A., & Lowell, E. L. (1953). *The achievement motive.* New York: Appleton-Century-Crofts.

McKenna, C., Solomon, L. J., & Rothblum, E. D. (1986). *Academic procrastination and childrearing factors.* Unpublished manuscript, Department of Psychology, University of Vermont, Burlington.

McReynolds, W. T., & Church, A. (1973). Self-control, study skills development and counseling approaches to the improvement of study behavior. *Behaviour Research and Therapy, 11,* 233–235.

Mehrabian, A. (1968). Male and female scales of the tendency to achieve. *Educational and Psychological Measurement, 28,* 493–502.

Mehrabian, A., & Bank, L. (1978). A questionnaire measure of individual differences in achieving tendency. *Educational and Psychological Measurement, 38,* 475–478.

Monahan, L., Kuhn, M., & Shaver, P. (1974). Intrapsychic versus cultural explanations of the "fear of success" motive. *Journal of Personality and Social Psychology, 29,* 60–64.

Montanelli, D. S., & Hill, K. T. (1969). Children's achievement expectations and performance as a function of two consecutive reinforcement experiences, sex of subject, and sex of experimenter. *Journal of Personality and Social Psychology, 13,* 115–128.

Mulig, J. C., Haggerty, M. E., Carballosa, A. B., Cinnicak, W. J., & Madden, J. M. (1985). Relationships among fear of success, fear of failure, and androgyny. *Psychology of Women Quarterly, 9,* 284–287.

Nichols, J. G. (1975). Causal attributions and other achievement-related cognitions: Effects of task outcome, attainment value, and sex. *Journal of Personality and Social Psychology, 31,* 379–389.

Norem, J. K., & Cantor, N. (1986a). Anticipatory and post hoc cushioning strategies: Optimism and defensive pessimism in "risky" situations. *Cognitive Therapy and Research, 10,* 347–362.

Norem, J. K., & Cantor, N. (1986b). Defensive pessimism: Harnessing anxiety as motivation. *Journal of Personality and Social Psychology, 51,* 1208–1217.

Notman, M. T., Zilbach, J. J., Baker-Miller, J., & Nadelson, C. C. (1986). Themes in psychoanalytic understanding of women: some reconsiderations of autonomy and affiliation. *Journal of the American Academy of Psychoanalysis, 14,* 241–253.

O'Leary, V. E., & Hammack, B. (1975). Sex-role orientation and achievement context as determinants of the motive to avoid success. *Sex Roles, 1,* 225–234.

Pheterson, G. I., Kiesler, S. B., & Goldberg, P. A. (1971). Evaluation of the performance of women as a function of their sex, achievement, and personal history. *Journal of Personality and Social Psychology, 19,* 114–118.

Puryear, G. R., & Mednick, M. S. (1974). Black militancy, affective attachment, and the fear of success in black college women. *Journal of Consulting and Clinical Psychology, 42,* 263–266.

Richards, C. S. (1975). Behavior modification of studying through study skills advice and self-control procedures. *Journal of Counseling Psychology, 22,* 431–436.

Richards, C. S., McReynolds, W. T., Holt, S., & Sexton, T. (1976). Effects of information feedback and self-administered consequences on self-monitoring study behavior. *Journal of Counseling Psychology, 23,* 316–321.

Robbins, L., & Robbins, E. (1973). Comment on "Toward an understanding of achievement-related conflicts in women." *Journal of Social Issues, 29,* 133–137.

Romer, N. (1977). Sex-related differences in the development of the motive to avoid success, sex role identity, and performance in competitive and noncompetitive conditions. *Psychology of Women Quarterly, 1,* 260–272.

Rothblum, E. D. (May, 1986). *Women and procrastination.* Invited workshop. University of Connecticut Health Sciences Center, Farmington.

Rothblum, E. D., Solomon, L. J., & Murakami, J. (1986). Affective, cognitive, and behavioral differences between high and low procrastinators. *Journal of Counseling Psychology, 33,* 387–394.

Schnitzler, P. K. (1977). The motive to avoid success: Exploring the nature of the fear. *Psychology of Women Quarterly, 1,* 273–282.

Semb, G., Glick, D. M., & Spencer, R. E. (1979). Student withdrawals and delayed work patterns in self-paced psychology courses. *Teaching of Psychology, 6,* 23–25.

Shaver, P. (1976). Questions concerning fear of success and its conceptual relatives. *Sex Roles, 2,* 305–320.

Shaw, M. C., & McCuen, J. R. (1960). The onset of academic underachievement in bright children. *Journal of Educational Psychology, 51,* 103–108.

Sherman, J. (1983). Girls talk about mathematics and their future: A partial replication. *Psychology of Women Quarterly, 7,* 338–342.

Smith, T. W., Snyder, C. R., & Perkins, S. C. (1983). The self-serving function of hypochondriacal complaints: Physical symptoms as self-handicapping strategies. *Journal of Personality and Social Psychology, 44,* 795–805.

Snyder, C. R., Smith, T. W., Augelli, R. W., & Ingram, R. E. (1985). On the self-serving function of social anxiety: Shyness as a self-handicapping strategy. *Journal of Personality and Social Psychology, 48,* 970–980.

Solomon, L. J., Murakami, J., Greenberger, C., & Rothblum, E. D. (1983). *Differences between high and low procrastinators as a deadline approaches: A qualitative study.* Unpublished manuscript. Department of Psychology, University of Vermont, Burlington.

Solomon, L. J., & Rothblum, E. D. (1983). An avoidance model of academic procrastination. Unpublished figure.

Solomon, L. J., & Rothblum, E. D. (1984). Academic procrastination: frequency and cognitive-behavioral correlates. *Journal of Counseling Psychology, 31,* 503–509.

Solomon, L. J., & Rothblum, E. D. (1988). Procrastination Assessment Scale—Students (PASS). In M. Hersen & A. S. Bellack (Eds.), *Dictionary of behavioral assessment techniques* (pp. 358–360). New York: Pergammon Press.

Spence, J. T. (1974). The thematic apperception test and attitudes toward achievement in women: A new look at the motive to avoid success and a new method of measurement. *Journal of Consulting and Clinical Psychology, 42,* 427–437.

Stein, A. H., & Bailey, M. M. (1973). The socialization of achievement orientation in females. *Psychological Bulletin, 80,* 345–366.

Stein, A. H., Pohly, S. R., & Mueller, E. (1971). The influence of masculine, feminine, and neutral tasks on children's achievement behavior, expectancies of success, and attainment values. *Child Development, 42,* 195–207.

Steinberg, C. L., Teevan, R. C., & Greenfeld, N. (1983). Sex-role orientation and fear of failure in women. *Psychological Reports, 52,* 987–k992.

Strickland, B. R. (1971). Aspiration responses among Negro and white adolescents. *Journal of Personality and Social Psychology, 3,* 315–320.

Teevan, R. C., & McGhee, P. E. (1972). Childhood development and fear of failure motivation. *Journal of Personality and Social Psychology, 3,* 345–348.

Teevan, R. C., & Smith, B. D. (1975). Relationships of fear-of-failure and need achievement motivation to a confirming-interval measure of aspiration levels. *Psychological Reports, 36,* 967–976.

Topol, P., & Reznikoff, M. (1979). Achievers and underachievers: A comparative study of fear of success, education and career goals, and conception of woman's role among high school senior girls. *Sex Roles, 5,* 85–92.

Tresemer, D. (1976a). Editorial: Current trends in research on "fear of success." *Sex Roles, 2,* 211–216.

Tresemer, D. (1976b). The cumulative record of research on "fear of success." *Sex Roles, 2,* 217–236.

Tresemer, D. (1977). *Fear of success.* New York: Plenum.

Tucker, J. A., Vuchinich, R. E., & Sobell, M. B. (1981). Alcohol consumption as a self-handicapping strategy. *Journal of Abnormal Psychology, 90,* 220–230.

Welch, R. L., & Huston, A. C. (1982). Effects of induced success/failure and attributions on the problem-solving behavior of psychologically androgynous and feminine women. *Journal of Personality, 50,* 81–97.

Weston, P. J., & Mednick, M. T. (1970). Race, social class and the motive to avoid success in women. *Journal of Cross-Cultural Psychology, 1,* 284–291.

Wilson, T. D., & Linville, P. W. (1985). Improving the performance of college freshmen with attributional techniques. *Journal of Personality and Social Psychology, 49,* 287–293.

Winchel, R., Fenner, D., & Shaver, P. (1974). Impact of coeducation on "fear of success" imagery expressed by male and female high school students. *Journal of Educational Psychology, 66,* 726–730.

Winterbottom, M. (1958). The relation of need for achievement in learning experiences in independence and mastery. In J. W. Atkinson (Ed.), *Motives in fantasy, action and society* (pp. 453–478). New York: Van Nostrand.

Wong, P. T. P., Kettlewell, G., & Sproule, C. F. (1985). On the importance of being masculine: Sex role, attribution, and women's career achievement. *Sex Roles, 12,* 757–769.

Yuen, L. M., & Depper, D. S. (1987). Fear of failure in women. *Women and Therapy, 6,* 21–39.

Ziesat, H. A., Rosenthal, T. L., & White, G. M. (1978). Behavioral self-control in treating procrastination of studying. *Psychological Reports, 42,* 59–69.

Zuckerman, M., & Allison, S. N. (1976). An objective measure of fear of success: Construction and validation. *Journal of Personality Assessment, 40,* 422–430.

Zuckerman, M., & Wheeler, L. (1975). To dispel fantasies about the fantasy-based measure of fear of success. *Psychological Bulletin, 82,* 932–946.

Zunich, M. (1964). Children's reactions to failure. *The Journal of Genetic Psychology, 104,* 19–24.

Index

Academic ability/performance
  shyness and, 59, 67
  social anxiety and, 492–493
  test anxiety and, 479, 483, 492–493
  interventions, 489–490
Achievement Anxiety Test, 505
Achievement motivation
  fear of failure and, 501–512
    childrearing factors, 509–512
    interventions, 512
    models, 501–502
    psychometric scales and assessment, 502–505
    research, 505–506
    sex factors, 506–509
    parental factors, 510–512
  sex factors, 506–509, 511, 530–531
Addiction, social phobia and, 14
Adjustment disorder with withdrawal, 162
Adolescence, social phobia during, 279
Affiliative response, toward strangers, 89, 102
Aggression
  peer factors, 166, 168
  school phobia and, 180
Agonic mentality, 17–18, 20, 34
  case example, 40–41
  hedonic mode versus, 37
  social anxiety and, 23
  therapeutic implications, 39
Agonistic behavior, ritual, 16–17
  yielding routine, 17, 18
Agoraphobia
  anxiety disorder comparison, 271, 272
  onset age, 279
  prevalence, 278
  psychophyisological measures, 298
  school phobia and, 181
  social phobia and, 14, 280–281
  socioeconomic factors, 280
  somatic symptoms, 282
  stranger anxiety and, 22
Alcohol abuse, 283–284
Alcoholics, adult children of, 398, 400–401
Alprazolam, as social phobia therapy, 299
Androgyny, fear of success and, 518

Animals. *See also* Primates, nonhuman
  antipredator system, 16, 17
  courtship, 17, 18
  separation distress, 88
Anorexia nervosa, 277
Antipredator system, 16, 17
Anxiety Disorders Interview Schedule, 289
Anxiolytic drugs, social phobics' use of, 284
Apology, 36
Appetite loss, sport performance anxiety-related, 447
Appraisal-coping model, of social anxiety, 22–36
  appraisal system, 28–33
  coping system, 33–36
  description, 23–24
  function, 25
  social environment component, 27–28
  structure, 24–25
  theory integration, 25–27
Arousal
  affective-emotional, 490–491
  cognitive, 490–491
  definition, 418
  emotional, 252
  physiological, 24
    attention and, 443–444
    behavioral inhibition and, 140–141
    dating anxiety and, 221
    shyness and, 49
    social anxiety and, 30–31
    social interaction and, 298
    social phobia and, 285, 286
    somatic anxiety and, 420
    sport performance anxiety and, 423, 426–427, 428, 429, 432
    stranger anxiety/reactions and, 22
  sexual
    affect and, 372–375
    anxiety and, 358
    anxiety induction studies, 361–363
    attentional factors, 367–377
    attentional focus, 369–371
    attentional resource allocation and, 367–369, 371–372

Arousal (*cont.*)
  sexual (*cont.*)
    autonomic component, 364–366, 372–377, 379, 380–381
    inhibition, 359
    subjective estimates, 372–374
    voluntary control, 366–367
Assertiveness
  assessment, 170
  as self-presentation standard, 37
  of socially anxious individuals, 34
Assertiveness training, 39, 311
  for children, 172
Atenolol, as social phobia therapy, 300, 301
Athletic performance anxiety. *See* Sport performance anxiety
Attachment system, 19, 89
Attachment theory, of stranger anxiety/-reactions, 107–108
Attentional factors
  in arousal, 443–444
  in schizophrenia, 338
  in sexual arousal, 367–372
Attentional focus treatment, for embarrassment, 408
Attention-deficit hyperactivity disorder, 162
Attributional style
  achievement and, 508–509
  in dating anxiety, 224
  in shyness, 70
  in procrastination, 528–529
  in test anxiety, 484–485
Audience anxiety, 55, 455
Authority, fear of, 281
Autonomic factors, in sexual arousal, 364–366, 372–377, 379, 380–381
Autonomic Perception Questionnaire, 456
Autonomic response stereotypy, 445
Avoidance behavior
  assessment, 297
  shyness and, 56
  social phobia and, 281, 284
Avoidant disorder of childhood or adolescence, 162
Avoidant personality disorder
  defensive self-representation and, 32
  definition, 315
  diagnostic criteria, 57, 271, 273, 274
  embarrassment and, 386
  shame and, 386
  social phobia and, 22, 273–274, 279
  stranger anxiety/reactions and, 22

Behavioral activation system, 153, 154
Behavioral Approach/Avoidance Test, 297

Behavioral Assertiveness Test, 329–330
Behavioral Checklist, 463
Behavioral factors, in social anxiety, 3–4
Behavioral inhibition system, 153–154
Behavioral measures
  of social phobia, 294–297
  of stranger reactions, 97–99
Behavioral observation
  of dating phobia, 227–228
  of school phobia, 193–195
  of social withdrawal, 167–169
Behavior Checklist and Personal Report of Confidence as a Speaker, 461
Behavior Checklist for Performance Anxiety, 459, 465
Beliefs, irrational
  in schizophrenia, 346
  in shyness, 69
  in social phobia, 285
Belief systems, anxiety and, 482–483
Bem Sex Role Inventory, 518
Benzodiazepines, as social phobia therapy, 299
Beta-blockers, as social phobia therapy, 299–300, 301, 316
Biofeedback training, as test anxiety intervention, 490
Biological factors, in social phobia, 286
Birth order
  separation reactions and, 122–123
  stranger reactions and, 106–107
Blood-injury phobia, 286
Blood pressure
  as social phobia indicator, 277, 282
  as speech anxiety indicator, 456, 459, 469
Blushing
  embarrassment and, 55, 405
  genetic factors, 286
  onset age, 278
  shyness and, 49
  social anxiety and, 36
  social phobia and, 277, 282, 286
Body dysmorphic disorder, 277
Breeding behavior, 16–17
Bulimia, shame and, 388–389

Cardiovascular measures. *See also* Electrocardiogram; Heart rate; Pulse rate
  as sport performance anxiety indicators, 426, 445
Career development, shyness and, 67
Care-giving, as guilt cause, 401
Child abuse, 86
Child Behavior Checklist, 169, 175
Childrearing factors. *See also* Parental factors
  in fear of failure, 509–512

Children
  achievement motivation, 509–512
  of alcoholics, 398–399, 400–401
  assertiveness training, 172
  behavioral inhibition
    assessment, 145–147
    biological models, 150–151
    distress and, 145–146
    heart rate in, 143, 144, 147
    model, 153–155
    peer factors, 142–143, 151
    psychopathology and, 155–156
    respiratory rate in, 144
  clinical fears, 179–180
  death of, 401
  egocentrism, 397
  fear of success, 519–520
  loneliness, 256–257
  phobias, psychoanalytic theory of, 186
  procrastination, 527
  shyness, 61, 62, 63–64, 65
    fearful, 147, 148–149
    self-conscious, 147–149
    social anxiety and, 147–150
  socially withdrawn, 155–156, 161–178
    assessment, 163–170
    definition, 161
    DSM-III diagnostic criteria, 161–162
    interventions, 170–174, 175, 176
  sport performance anxiety
    consequences, 435–436, 445–448
    determinants, 428–434
Children's Action Tendency Scale, 170
Children's Behavior Questionnaire, 146, 149
Children's Manifest Anxiety Scale, 183, 192
Coaching, as social withdrawal intervention,
    171–173
Cognitive anxiety
  characteristics, 420
  sport performance anxiety and, 430, 441–442
Cognitive-behavioral theory, of guilt, 390–393
Cognitive-behavioral therapy
  for embarrassment, 408–409
  for guilt, 408–409
  for shame, 408–409
  for sport performance anxiety, 449
  for test anxiety, 490
Cognitive factors/processes
  assessment, 335–337
  in embarrassment, 410–411
  in guilt, 410, 411
  in sexual responsivity, 366–375
  in shame, 410, 411
  in shyness, 70–72
  in social anxiety, 4, 91–93

Cognitive factors/processes (cont.)
  in social phobia, 285, 293–294
  in stranger anxiety/reactions, 91–93
Cognitive-information processing model, of
    schizophrenia, 334–341
Cognitive interference, test anxiety and, 480,
    481, 482–485, 488–489
Cognitive Interference Questionnaire, 480, 481,
    488–489
Cognitive restructuring
  for dating anxiety, 233–234
  for guilt, 398
  for posttraumatic stress disorder, 402
  for procrastination, 529
  for speech anxiety, 470
Cognitive self-schemata, 24
Cognitive-Somatic Anxiety Questionnaire, 289,
    290–291
Cognitive therapy, 39, 40. See also Cognitive-
    behavioral therapy
  for schizophrenia, 347
  for social anxiety, 310–311
  for social phobia, 311–313
  for test anxiety, 490
Cohen's Fear of Success Scale, 516, 521
Colorado Childhood Temperament Inventory,
    152
Communication apprehension, 56, 455
Competition, sex factors, 507
Competitive State Anxiety Inventory–1, 427,
    428, 429, 431, 434, 442, 443
Competitive State Anxiety Inventory–2, 427–
    428, 431, 440, 441–442
Concern for Appropriateness Scale, 37
Conditioning. See also Counterconditioning;
    Extinction
  operant, as school phobia intervention, 188,
    189, 202–204, 206
  in social phobia etiology, 284–285
  vicarious, school phobia and, 199–202, 206
Conflict behavior, 107
Conflict model, of shyness, 53–54
Conflict resolution, as guilt intervention, 395
Contingency management, of school phobia,
    204
Conversational behavior
  of children, 172–173
  in dating anxiety, 222, 228
  in loneliness, 257–258
  in schizophrenia, 337–338
  in shyness, 261
  in social anxiety, 34–35, 37–39
Cooperation, hedonic social structure and, 20
Coping skills, 33–36. See also Appraisal-coping
    system

Coping skills (*cont.*)
  as speech anxiety intervention, 467–468
Core role, guilt and, 395–399
Counterconditioning, 195–196
Courtship, 17, 18
Creativity, shyness and, 68
Cues, social
  dating behavior and, 224
  schizophrenic's perception of, 336
  social anxiety and, 29, 285
Cultural factors
  in shyness, 64
  in stranger reactions, 106

Date rape, 223
Dating anxiety, 217–246
  assessment, 227–228
  behavioral factors, 221–223, 227–228
  cognitive models, 223–225
  definition, 218–220
  disruptive effects, 217–218
  future research, 240–241
  interventions
    case example, 234–239
    desensitization, 221, 229, 230, 233, 240
    practice dating, 229, 230, 234, 240
    social skills training, 229–231, 232, 233, 240
  nature of, 220–227
    conditioned anxiety and, 221
    physiological factors, 221
  physical attractiveness and, 225–226, 227, 228
  self-presentational model, 226–227
  shyness and, 219
  social anxiety and, 219
  social phobia and, 219–220
  social skills deficits, 221–223, 226
Dating behavior, 40. *See also* Courtship
Day care, 86, 91, 123
Debilitating Anxiety Scale, 505, 521, 522
Decatastrophizing, 395
Decision-making
  moral, 409
  test anxiety and, 481–482
Defense mechanisms, 15–18
  coping system and, 33–36
  interaction with safety system, 20–21
  social anxiety and, 23
  sport performance anxiety and, 421–422
  subsystems, 16–18
    antipredator, 16
    group living, 17–18
    territorial breeding, 16–17
Defense Mechanisms Inventory, 70

Denial, shame and, 404
Departure protest, 119–120
Depression
  dating anxiety and, 218
  guilt and, 401
  loneliness and, 252
  ritual agonistic behavior and, 17
  school phobia and, 180
  sex factors, 71
  shyness and, 57
  social phobia and, 57, 283, 315
  survivor guilt and, 403
Depressive disorders, social phobia and, 14
Desensitization, systematic
  for dating anxiety, 221, 229, 230, 233, 240
  for school phobia, 196, 196–197, 198, 206
  for sexual dysfunction, 357
  for social phobia, 300, 303, 304, 305
  for speech anxiety, 460
  for test anxiety, 490
Developmental changes/factors
  in fear of failure, 499–501
  in separation reactions, 85–86, 91–93, 120–122, 127–128, 129–130
  in shyness, 61–65
  in social anxiety, 91–93
  in stranger anxiety/reactions, 85–86, 101–103, 127–128, 129–130
Diagnostic and Statistical Manual-III (DSM-III), diagnostic criteria
  avoidant personality disorder, 271, 273, 274
  childhood withdrawal and isolation, 161–162
  panic disorder, 273
  school phobia, 183
  social phobia, 270–271, 274–275, 282
Diazepam, as social phobia therapy, 299
Disaffiliative behavior, 260–261
Discrepancy theory, of social anxiety, 92, 93
Disengagement, 33
Divorced individuals, dating anxiety, 220
Dominance schemata, 29–30, 32
Dominant personality, appraisal-coping responses, 27
Down syndrome, 129
Drive theory, 435, 436–437
Driving test, 479
Dysmorphophobia, 277–278
Dystrophy, reflex sympathetic, 446–447

Eating disorders, embarrassment and, 386
Edwards Personal Preference Schedule Achievement Scale, 505
Egocentrism, 397
Electroencephalogram (EEG)
  as stranger reactions indicator, 99

Electroencephalogram (EEG) (*cont.*)
  as sport performance anxiety indicator, 426
Electromyograph, as sport performance anxiety
    indicator, 426, 444–445
Embarrassability Scale, 390, 406
Embarrassment
  adaptive role for, 385
  assessment, 388–390
  cognitive processes in, 410–411
  conversation and, 38
  definition, 386–388
  interventions, 406–408, 411
  self-presentation failure and, 32
  shyness and, 55, 71
  smiling and, 35
  theories of, 405–406
  values and, 409
Emotionality, definition, 485
Emotionality, Activity, Sociability and Im-
    pulsivity Scale, 152
Empty chair technique, 400
Environment, social
  appraisal-coping system and, 27–28
  positive reinforcement in, 20
Erectile dysfunction. *See* Sexual dysfunction
Escape, reverted, 17–18, 26, 33, 35, 38, 39
Etiquette, 20
Evaluation anxiety. *See also* Test anxiety
  definition, 12–13
  onset age, 22
  shyness and, 29
Evolutionary factors
  in separation anxiety, 88–90
  in social anxiety, 14–22
    defense/safety systems interaction,
        20–21
    defense system, 15–18
    in infancy, 88–90
    safety system, 18–20
Excuses, 36
Expectancy
  behavior-outcome, 24
  in dating anxiety, 226–227
  efficacy, 33
  efficacy-outcome, 24
  in infancy, 91, 105, 108
  outcome, 33
  self-efficacy, 226–227
  in shyness, 68–69
  in sport performance anxiety, 430–431
  stimulus-outcome, 24, 28–30
Exploratory system, 89
Exposure
  guided, 39
  in vivo, 302, 307–311

Extinction, as school phobia intervention, 195,
    196, 198–199
Eysenck Personality Inventory, 218

Failure
  attribution of, 263, 484, 485
  cognitive effects, 484
  fear of. *See* Fear of failure
  handicap-related, 35
  responsibility for, 33
  test anxiety and, 484
Family Environment Scale, 152
Family size, stranger reactions and, 106–107
Father–daughter relationship, incestuous, 400
Father–infant relationship, in separation reac-
    tion, 124
Fear
  definition, 140
  negative affect and, 141
  response systems, 364
  shyness and, 149
  of strangers. *See* Stranger anxiety/reactions
Fear face, 35
Fear of failure, 497–537. *See also* Achievement
    motivation
  childrearing factors, 509–512
  fear of success versus, 520–522
  interventions, 500–501, 512
  need achievement versus, 501–512
  parental factors, 509–512
  as procrastination antecedent, 524–530
  psychodynamic views of, 497–501
  school phobia and, 183
  sex factors, 499–500, 513
  sport performance anxiety and, 421, 423, 448
Fear of Negative Evaluation Scale
  of dating anxiety, 230
  of embarrassment, 390
  of schizophrenia, 343
  of social phobia, 289, 292–293
  of speech anxiety, 469
  of test anxiety, 485
Fear Questionnaire, 289, 290
Fear Survey Schedule, 57, 289–290, 459
Fear Survey Schedule for Children, 192
Fear Survey Schedule II, 465
Fear-wariness system, 89
Feedback. *See also* Biofeedback
  as schizophrenia intervention, 330–331
Female development, fear of failure and, 499–
    500
Femininity
  achievement and, 508, 512
  fear of success and, 513–514, 518
Fight-flight-freeze-faint system, 16, 31

Flooding
    as social phobia intervention, 199, 205, 300,
        302, 303
    as speech anxiety intervention, 461
Freud, Sigmund, 513
Friendship skills, 39–40

Galvanic skin response
    as behavioral inhibition indicator, 146–147
    as speech anxiety indicator, 456, 459, 460
    as sport performance anxiety indicator, 426
    as speech anxiety indicator, 456, 459
Gaze avoidance, 35
Genetic factors
    in anxiety disorders, 286
    in shyness, 64–65, 151–153
    in social anxiety, 11
    in stranger reactions, 105
Gestalt empty-chair technique, 400
Gestalt two-chair dialogue, 395
Goal-setting behavior, 504
Grandiosity, 499
Grief, pathological, 401
Grinning, 35
Group living system, 17–18
Group therapy
    for guilt, 398
    for social phobia, 313–315
Guilt
    adaptive function, 385
    assessment, 388–390
    cognitive processes in, 410, 411
    definition, 386–388
    interventions, 393–403
        behavior changes, 399
        core-role definition changes, 395–399
        perceived role discrepancy changes, 394–
            395
        problem-specific guilt, 399–403
        targeted, 411
    military combat-related, 392, 402–403
    personal construct theory, 392–393
    positive functions, 385, 391
    posttraumatic stress disorder-related, 386
    as psychological problem, 385–386
    as regret, 394–395
    social learning and, 396–399
    survivor, 402–403
    theories of, 390–393
    values and, 409

Habit strength, 436
Handicap, as failure cause, 35, 528–529
Headache, sport performance anxiety-related,
    446

Health, loneliness and, 247
Heart rate
    as behavioral inhibition indicator, 143, 144,
        147
    as dating anxiety indicator, 221, 227
    as social phobia indicator, 282, 297–298
    as speech anxiety indicator, 456, 459, 460
    as sport performance anxiety indicator, 432,
        438
    as stranger reactions indicator, 99
Hedonic mode, 19–20, 21, 35
    therapeutic implications, 39
Helplessness
    anxiety and, 476, 483, 485
    shyness and, 69
    as threat response, 26
Heterosexual anxiety. See Dating anxiety
Heterosocial skills training, 40
Homosexuals, dating anxiety, 220
Hormonal factors, in shyness, 67
Hostility, as submissiveness response, 22

Imagery
    emotive, 197–198
    hostile press, 503–504, 505–506, 520–512
Implosive therapy, 199, 461
Impotence, dating anxiety and, 218
Incest, 400
Individual therapy, for social phobia, 313–315
Industrialized society, stranger anxiety/-
    reactions in, 106
Infancy
    behavioral inhibition, 142–145, 146
    separation reactions, 85–86, 91–93, 118–127
        conceptual issues, 118–120
        developmental changes, 120–122
        evolutionary approaches, 88–90
        influences on, 122–127
        methodological issues, 120
        psychoanalytic approaches, 87–88, 93
        socialization and, 90–91
    shyness, 61, 63, 95
        parental factors, 152–153
    stranger anxiety/reactions, 85–86, 95–118
        birth order and, 106–107
        cultural factors, 106
        developmental changes in, 101–103
        family size and, 106–107
        infant's characteristics and, 104–109
        influences on, 103–118
        measurement, 97–99
        mother–infant relationship and, 107–108
        onset age, 103
        research methodology, 100–101
        research setting, 99–100

Infancy (*cont.*)
  stranger anxiety/reactions (*cont.*)
    situation's characteristics, 113–116
    stranger's characteristics, 109–113
    temperament and, 104–105
    in twins, 105
    types of reactions, 95–97
Infant Behavior Questionnaire, 146
Inferiority, fear of, 30
Information processing
  in embarrassment, 406
  in separation anxiety, 129
  in sport performance anxiety, 443–444
  in stranger anxiety/reactions, 129
Inhibition
  behavioral
    assessment, 145–147
    biological models, 150–151
    definition, 140
    distress and, 145–146
    heart rate in, 143, 144, 147
    in infancy, 142–145, 146
    model, 153–155
    peer factors, 142–143, 151
    psychopathology and, 155–156
    respiratory rate in, 144
  reciprocal, 357
    anxiety induction studies, 361–363
    definition, 359–360
Injury, athletic, 447–448
Integrity therapy, 392
Intermediate Level Social Skills Assessment
    Checklist, 297
Interpersonal Behavior Role-Play Test,
    329
Interpersonal dysfunction
  etiology, 326–327
  in loneliness, 252–254, 255–257, 262, 263
  in schizophrenia, 325–355
    cognitive-information processing model,
      334–341
    dysfunctional thoughts and, 345–347
    interventions, 330–334
    social anxiety and, 341–345
    topographic model, 327–334
  in social anxiety, 37–39
Interview, behavioral/clinical
  for embarrassment, 389
  for guilt, 389
  for school phobia, 190–191
  for shame, 389
  for social phobia, 288–289
Introversion, shyness and, 53–54
Introvert personality, appraisal-coping re-
    sponses, 27

Jackson's Personality Research Form
  Achievement Scale, 521

Learning
  guilt and, 390–391, 396–399, 408
  mood and, 23
  vicarious, 284–285
Lehrer–Woolfolk Symptom Questionnaire, 289,
    291
Loneliness, 247–266
  assertiveness and, 34
  definition, 248, 251
  depression and, 252
  emotional, 250
  emotional arousal and, 252
  failure attribution and, 263
  incidence, 247
  interpersonal environment and, 261–262
  interpersonal relationships and, 252–254
  measurement, 248–251
  psychological concomitants, 251–252
  relational stress and, 254
  self-esteem and, 251–252
  shyness and, 57, 259, 260
  social, 250
  social anxiety and, 247–266
  state, 250, 251, 260
  trait, 250–251
  UCLA Loneliness Scale, 248–251
Loneliness Questionnaire, 170
Louisville Fear Survey for Children, 192–193,
    198

Major's Revised Fear of Success Scale, 516
Manifest Anxiety Scale, 424, 436
Marital factors
  in loneliness, 253, 254
  in social phobia, 280–281
Marlowe–Crowne Social-Desirability Scale, 521
Masculinity
  dating anxiety and, 218
  fear of success and, 518
Masochism, 499–500
Mehrabian's Self-Report Scale of Achieving
    Tendency, 504
Memory
  recall, 87
  selective, 21
  situational appraisal and, 94
Metacognition
  definition, 51
  in shyness, 50–53, 54, 68
Meta-self-consciousness, 51–53, 71
Military combat, guilt related to, 392,
    402–403

Minnesota Multiphasic Personality Inventory, 291
 Social Introversion Scale, 53
Modeling
 as schizophrenia intervention, 331
 as school phobia intervention, 199–202
 as social withdrawal intervention, 170, 173
 as test anxiety intervention, 487–488
Modesty
 excessive, 406
 shyness and, 47–48, 65
Monoamine oxidase inhibitors, as social phobia therapy, 299, 301
Mother–child relationship
 school phobia and, 186
 shyness and, 64
Mother–daughter relationship, guilt in, 401
Mother–infant relationship. See also Separation anxiety
 attachment, 19, 89
 stranger reactions and, 107–108, 115–116, 117
Motor skills, assessment, 329–330

Need achievement, fear of failure versus, 501–512

Object loss, 447–448
Obsessive–compulsive disorder, 278
 guilt related to, 386, 401–402
Operant conditioning. See Conditioning, operant
Oppositional defiant disorder, 162
Overanxious disorder, 162

Paired comparison method, of peer evaluation, 165–166
Panic
 social phobia and, 32, 272–273, 283
 stranger anxiety-related, 22
Pappo's Fear of Success Scale, 516, 521, 522
Paranoia, phylogenetic basis, 21
Parental factors
 in fear of failure, 509–512
 in guilt, 390–391, 402
 in procrastination, 527
 in school phobia, 187, 194–195
 in separation reactions, 124, 126
 in shame, 403–404
 in shyness, 152–153
 in social anxiety, 287
 in social phobia, 185, 286–287
Peer evaluation, 163–170
 peer assessment, 166
 sociometric assessment, 163–166

Peer factors
 in aggression, 166, 168
 in behavioral inhibition, 142–143, 151
 in childhood disorders, 162
 in shyness, 64
 in school phobia, 183, 187, 188
 in social withdrawal
  behavioral observation, 167–169
  evaluation, 163–170
  intervention strategies, 170–173
  significant issues regarding, 173–176
Peer nomination, 164–165
Peer socialization, 171
Perceived Competence Scale for Children, 170
Performance anxiety
 sexual. See Sexual anxiety
 sports-related. See Sport performance anxiety
 test-related. See Test anxiety
Permission-giving, 394
Personal construct theory, of guilt, 392–393
Personality disorders, social phobia and, 14
Personal Report of Communication Apprehension, 456, 462, 463
Personal Report of Confidence as a Speaker, 456, 457, 460, 465, 467, 470
Pessimism, defensive, 529
Phenelzine, as social phobia therapy, 299, 300, 301
Phobia(s)
 of children, 180. See also School phobia
  psychoanalytic theory of, 186
 flooding therapy, 461
 social. See Social phobia
Phobic disorders
 anxiety disorder comparison, 271–272
 lifetime prevalence, 278
 onset age, 279
Physical appearance/attractiveness. See also Dysmorphophobia
 dating anxiety and, 225–226, 241
  assessment, 228
 shyness and, 59, 65–66
 social skills and, 225–226
 test anxiety and, 483–484
Physiological factors. See also Electroencephalogram; Electromyograph; Galvanic skin response; Heart rate; Pulse rate; Respiratory rate
 in shyness, 49
 as social phobia indicators, 275, 277, 286, 297–298
 as sport performance anxiety indicators, 426–427, 429, 432–433
 as stranger anxiety/reaction indicators, 99
Posttraumatic stress disorder, 386, 402–403

Practice dating, 229, 230, 234, 240
Predators, defense system responses, 16
Primates, nonhuman
    hedonic mode of, 19–20
    parental attachment system of, 19
    submissive behavior of, 18
Procrastination, fear of failure-related, 524–530
    intervention, 529–530
    model, 528–529
    psychometric scales and assessment, 525–526
Procrastination Assessment Scale—Students, 525–526, 527
Profile of Mood States, 425
Profile of Nonverbal Sensitivity, 336
Progressive muscle relaxation, 460–461, 467, 470
Psoriasis patients, 278
Psychiatric illness, maternal, 184
Psychoanalytic theory
    of childhood phobias, 180
    of separation anxiety, 87–88
    of stranger anxiety/reactions, 87–88
Psychobiological theory, of social anxiety, 13–22, 36–41
    antipredator system, 16
    attachment system, 19
    defense/safety systems interaction, 20–21
    defense system, 15–16
    group living system, 17–18
    hedonic system, 19–20
    individual safety system, 19
    safety system, 18
    territorial breeding system, 16–17
Psychodynamic theory
    of fear of failure, 497–501
    of fear of success, 513
Psychopharmacological therapy. See also names of specific drugs
    for social phobia, 298–300, 301
Psychotherapy
    for guilt, 392
    for school phobia, 198, 207
Public speaking phobia, 31, 281
Pulse rate
    as sport performance anxiety indicator, 429
    as test anxiety indicator, 485
Pupil Evaluation Inventory, 166

Racial factors
    in achievement motivation, 509
    in fear of failure, 509
    in fear of success, 519
Rape, date-related, 223
Rape victim, guilt of, 394

Rational Behavior Inventory, 293–294, 312, 313
Rational-emotive therapy, 39
    for embarrassment, 407
    for social anxiety, 309–310
    for speech anxiety, 462, 462, 467
    for test anxiety, 490
Reaction potential, 436
Reactions to Tests, 478, 479, 486, 487, 488, 489, 491–492
Reassurance signals, 20
Refusal, assertive, 399–400
Regret, guilt as, 394–395
Rehearsal, behavioral
    as guilt intervention, 401
    as schizophrenia intervention, 330
    as social withdrawal intervention, 172
Reinforcement. See also Conditioning
    in fear of failure, 510
    safety system and, 19
    as schizophrenia intervention, 330–331
    in separation anxiety, 90
    in social environment, 20
    as social phobia intervention, 302
    as social withdrawal intervention, 170–171, 172
Relaxation training
    as procrastination intervention, 529
    progressive muscle, 460–461, 467, 470
    as school phobia intervention, 198
    as social phobia intervention, 312
    as speech anxiety intervention, 460–461, 467, 468, 469, 470
    as sport performance anxiety intervention, 449
    as test anxiety intervention, 490
Resource holding potential, 16, 25, 29
Respiratory rate
    as behavioral inhibition indicator, 144
    as sport performance anxiety indicator, 429, 438
Retirement, 67
Retrieval, mood and, 23
Revised Children's Manifest Anxiety Scale, 175
Revised Fear Survey Schedule for Children, 183
Risk-taking, 257, 504
Role-playing
    as dating anxiety assessment method, 227–228
    limitations of, 295

Safety system, 18–21, 28
    interaction with defense system, 21–22
    subsystems
        attachment, 19

Safety system (*cont.*)
  subsystems (*cont.*)
    hedonic, 19–20
    individual, 19
Same-sex interactions. *See also* Sexual anxiety
  dating anxiety and, 218
Schizo-form disorders, 22
Schizoid personality disorder, 22, 57, 315
Schizophrenia, 325–355
  interpersonal dysfunction in, 325–355
    cognitive-information processing model,
      334–341
    dysfunctional thoughts and, 345–347
    interventions, 330–334
    social anxiety and, 341–345
    topographic model, 327–334
  negative syndrome, 325–326
  subtypes, 348–349, 350
School phobia, 179–214, 278
  assessment, 189–195
    behavioral interview, 190–191
    behavioral observation, 193–195
    rating instruments, 191–193
  characterological, 184, 185
  concurrent disorders, 183
  description of, 180–182
  diagnostic issues, 182–186
  etiology, 186–189
  incidence, 182
  interventions, 195–208, 209
    behavioral, 207–208
    classical conditioning, 195–199, 202–204,
      206
    integrative treatment, 204–208
    operant conditioning, 202–204
    vicarious conditioning, 199–202
  maternal psychiatric illness and, 184
  neurotic, 184–185, 205
  onset age, 181
  parental factors in, 187, 194–195
  separation anxiety and, 182–184
  sex factors in, 181
  subtypes, 185
  as symptom, 195
  truancy versus, 181, 184
Self-awareness, 32–33, 476
Self-consciousness
  embarrassment and, 405–406
  meta-, 51–53, 71
  shyness and, 49, 67–71
  social anxiety and, 4, 21, 32–33
Self-disclosure, loneliness and, 258
Self-efficacy, shyness and, 68–69
Self-esteem
  dating anxiety and, 218, 224

Self-esteem (*cont.*)
  fear of failure and, 501
  loneliness and, 34, 251–252
  parental factors, 20
  shame and, 405
  shyness and, 58–67
  sport performance anxiety and, 430, 431
  of women, 500
Self-handicapping, 35, 528–529
Self-help groups, as guilt intervention, 394
Self-identity, social anxiety and, 25, 26
Self-instructional training, as social anxiety intervention, 309–310
Self-perception
  dating anxiety and, 224–225
  loneliness and, 255
Self-preoccupation
  shyness and, 69–70
  social anxiety and, 281–282
  test anxiety and, 482–486
Self-presentation, 28
  acquisitive, 34
  avoidant personality disorder and, 32
  coping response, 33
  neutral, 34
  protective, 34–35, 37
  shyness and, 69–70
  social anxiety and, 29
  standards, 37, 38
Self-regard. *See* Self-esteem
Self-report measures
  of achievement motivation, 504–505
  of embarrassment, 389–390
  of guilt, 389–390
  of shame, 389–390
  of social phobia, 289–293
  of sport performance anxiety, 427–428
Self-statements
  modification, 406
  in schizophrenia, 346–347
Separation anxiety
  in children, 183–184
    school phobia and, 182–184, 187
  in infancy, 118–127
    cognitive-developmental perspectives, 91–
      93
    conceptual issues, 118–120
    developmental changes in, 120–122
    evolutionary approaches, 88–90
    future research, 127–130
    influences on, 122–127
    methodological issues, 120
    psychoanalytic theory of, 87–88
    socialization and, 90–91
  in nonhuman primates, 150–151

Separation distress, 119–120
Separation-individuation, 87–88
Sex factors
  in achievement motivation, 506–509, 511,
      530–531
  in competition, 507
  in depression, 71
  in embarrassment, 406
  in fear of failure, 499–500, 506–509
  in fear of success, 513–519, 520–521
      among children, 519–520
  in guilt, 409–410
  in procrastination, 526
  in school phobia, 181
  in separation reactions, 122
  in shyness, 60–61, 70–71
  in social phobia, 280
  in stranger reactions, 108, 109
  in test anxiety, 479
Sex role
  achievement motivation and, 511–512
  stereotypes, 508
      fear of success and, 514
Sexual anxiety. See also Arousal, sexual; Sexual
      dysfunction
  anxiety induction studies, 361–364
  components, 360–361
  conceptualizations, 359–360
  definition, 364, 364
  reciprocal inhibition and, 357, 359–363
Sexual dysfunction. See also Arousal, sexual
  affect and, 374–375
  attentional factors, 367–369, 370–372, 373–
      374, 376–377
  etiology, 360
  interventions, 357–358
  social phobia and, 379
  test anxiety and, 379–380
  working model, 377–379
Sexual experience, dating anxiety correlation,
      218
Sexual Opinion Survey, 375
Sexual victimization, guilt related to, 400
Shame
  adaptive role for, 385
  assessment, 388–390
  cognitive processes in, 410, 411
  definition, 386–388
  interventions, 404–405, 411
  self-representation failure and, 32
  shyness and, 55
  social anxiety and, 13, 36
  theories of, 403–404
  values and, 409
Shame-attacking exercises, 407

Shaping, 302
Shyness
  assessment, 146
  audience anxiety and, 55
  cognitive factors, 70–71
  conversational behavior and, 261
  dating anxiety versus, 219
  definition, 47, 48, 140
  developmental aspects, 61–65
  diagnostic criteria, 56–57
  disaffiliative behavior and, 260–261
  embarrassment and, 55
  fearful, 147, 148–149
  fear of social evaluation, 29
  genetic factors, 64–65, 151–153
  hormonal factors, 67
  incidence, 13, 47, 56, 60
  in infants, 61, 63, 95, 152–153
  loneliness and, 259
  misinterpretation, 261
  negative affect and, 141
  normal, 47
  parental factors, 152–153
  positive aspects, 47–48
  self-concept and, 67–71
  self-conscious, 147–149
  self-esteem and, 58–67
  self-handicapping and, 35
  sex factors, 60–61, 70–71
  shame and, 55
  social anxiety and, 147–150, 491
  as three-component syndrome, 48–58
Shyness disorder and introverted disorder of
      childhood, 162
Shyness Scale, 55–56, 59, 66
Siblings, stranger reactions and, 106–107
Simulated Social Interaction Test, 329–330, 336,
      343
Situational Guilt Scale, 390, 409–410
Situation Questionnaire, 230, 231
16 PF, 152, 424
Sleeping disorders, sport performance anxiety-
      related, 447
Smiling, in embarrassment, 35, 36
Social anxiety
  appraisal-coping model, 22–36
      appraisal system, 28–33
      coping system, 33–36
      description, 23–24
      function, 25
      social environment component, 27–28
      structure, 24–25
      theory integration, 25–27
  assessment, 456–460
      in schizophrenia, 342–343

Social anxiety (*cont.*)
  behavioral factors, 3–4
  cognitive factors, 4
  consequences, 4–5
  dating anxiety versus, 219
  definition, 1, 11, 13, 140, 455
  genetic factors, 11
  negative affect and, 141
  parental factors, 185, 286–287
  phenomenology, 3–4
  psychobiological aspects, 13–22, 39–41
    antipredator system, 16
    attachment system, 19
    defense/safety systems interaction, 20–21
    defense system, 15–16
    group living system, 17–18
    hedonic system, 19–20
    individual safety system, 19
    safety system, 18
    territorial breeding system, 16–17
  schizophrenia and, 341–345
  self-concept and, 21
  self-preoccupation and, 281–282
  shyness and, 147–150
  situational factors, 2–3
  subtypes, 469
  types, 1–3
  world view in, 21
Social Anxiety and Distress Scale, 456, 462–
    463, 465, 467, 468, 469, 470
Social Anxiety Inventory, 342
Social Anxiety Scale, 55
Social Avoidance and Distress Scale
  dating anxiety applications, 219, 230, 232
  schizophrenia applications, 343
  social phobia applications, 289, 292–293
Social behavior, loneliness and, 257–259
Social Competence Questionnaire, 491, 492
Social contact, loneliness and, 253–254, 261–
    262
Social-evaluation anxiety, incidence, 2
Social facilitation, 530
Social Interaction Rating Scale, 169
Social Interaction Self-Statement Test
  dating anxiety applications, 228
  Revised, 458
  schizophrenia applications, 346–347
  social phobia applications, 289, 294
  speech anxiety applications, 456, 460, 469
Social isolation, of children. *See* Social with-
    drawal, in children
Socialization. *See also* Parental factors
  achievement patterns and, 507–508
  embarrassment and, 405
  military, 403

Socialization (*cont.*)
  peer-related, 171
  separation anxiety and, 90–91
  shame and, 403–404
  social anxiety and, 90–91
  social environment internalization in, 28
Social learning, embarrassment and, 405–406
Social learning analysis, 396–397
  as embarrassment intervention, 408
  as guilt intervention, 396–399, 408
  as shame intervention, 405, 408
Social phobia, 269–324
  anxiety disorder comparison, 271–274
  assessment, 287–298
    behavioral measures, 294–297
    cognitive measures, 293–294
    psychophysiological measures, 297–298
    self-report measures, 289–293
  avoidant personality disorder versus, 273–
    274
  characteristics, 278–284
    behavioral factors, 281
    cognitive factors, 281–282
    concomitant fears, 283
    duration, 280
    marital status, 280–281
    psychophysiological reactions, 282
    restrictions related to, 282–283
    sex differences, 280
    situations feared, 281
    socioeconomic factors, 280
    somatic symptoms, 282
    substance abuse, 283–284
  cognitive-behavioral therapy, 39
  cognitive-inhibition model, 302
  conditioned-anxiety model, 302
  dating anxiety and, 219–220
  definition, 270–271
  diagnostic criteria, 57, 274–275
  dysmorphophobia and, 277–278
  epidemiology, 278
  etiology, 284–287, 315
    biological factors, 286
    cognitive factors, 285
    conditioning, 284–285
    parental attitudes, 286–287
    skills-deficit hypothesis, 285
    vicarious learning, 284–285
  generalized, 12, 270
  interventions, 298–315
    psychological, 300, 302–315, 316
    psychopharmacological, 298–300, 301, 313–
      314
  models, 11
  onset age, 273, 278–279

Social phobia (*cont.*)
  panic disorder and, 32, 272–273
  primary, 272
  as psychiatric disorder, 2
  secondary, 272
  sexual dysfunction and, 379
  social skills deficits, 275, 281, 285, 302
  specific, 12, 270
  subtypes, 274–278
Social Phobia and Anxiety Inventory, 289, 293
Social Reaction Inventory, 342–343
Social Referencing, 90, 115–116
Social Reticence Scale, 55
Social skills
  global ratings, 296
  of infants, 105, 108
    mother–infant relationship, 91
  physical attractiveness and, 225–226
Social skills deficits
  in dating anxiety, 221–223, 226
  in embarrassment, 405
  in loneliness, 257–259
  in schizophrenia, 328–329
  in school phobia, 188
  in shyness, 49
  in social anxiety, 3–4, 36
  in social phobia, 275, 281, 285, 302
  in social withdrawal, 162, 163
Social skills training, 39–40
  as dating anxiety intervention, 229–231, 232, 233, 240
  as schizophrenia intervention, 330–334, 341, 343–344, 345, 349–350
  as social withdrawal intervention, 170, 171–173
  as social phobia intervention, 304, 305, 306, 307, 312–313
Social status, of children, 162
Social support, as test anxiety intervention, 489
Social Support Questionnaire, 491–492
Social withdrawal, in children, 155–156, 161–178
  assessment methods, 163–170
    behavioral observation, 167–169
    informants, 169–170
    peer evaluation, 163–170
  DSM-III diagnostic criteria, 161–162
  definition, 161
  interventions, 170–173
    age-specific, 174
  anxiety and, 174–175
  future developments, 175–176
  individualized, 175–176
  social skills training, 170, 171–173
  target behaviors, 173–174
  unidimensional approach, 170–171

Socioeconomic factors, in social phobia, 280
Sociometric assessment, of peers, 163–166
Somatic anxiety
  characteristics, 420
  sport performance anxiety and, 430, 441–442, 445
Speech anxiety, 455–474
  definition, 455
  etiology, 460
  interventions, 460–470, 471
    effectiveness, 463–466
    flooding, 461
    rational-emotive therapy, 462
    relaxation training, 460–461
    stress inoculation training, 462–463
    systematic desensitization, 460
  intervention outcome prediction, 466–470
Speilberger State-Trait Anxiety Inventory, 291, 425–426
Speilberger State-Anxiety Inventory for Children, 428, 433
Spence's Objective Scoring System, 516
Sport Anxiety Scale, 425–426
Sport Competition Anxiety Test, 424–425, 438–439
Sport performance anxiety, 417–454
  appraisal processes, 422–423
  arousal and, 423, 426–427
    performance effects, 435–444
  assessment, 424–425
  cognitive anxiety and, 430, 441–442
  conceptual model, 421, 422, 448
  consequences, 435–448
    drive theory and, 435, 436–437, 438
    illness and injuries, 446–448
    sports avoidance, 445
    sports enjoyment, 445–446
    sports withdrawal, 446
    task characteristics and, 442–443
    Yerkes–Dodson law and, 437, 438, 444
  defense processes, 421–422
  definition, 421
  determinants, 428–435
    intrapersonal factors, 421, 430–432
    situational factors, 429–430
  fear of failure and, 421, 423, 448
  future research, 448–449
  interventions, 448–449
  intraindividual factors, 421–422
  somatic anxiety and, 430, 441–442, 445
  state anxiety and, 421–422, 423, 423, 431–432, 434
    measurement, 420, 426–428, 433
    precompetition, 429, 430
  stress and, 429

Sport performance anxiety (*cont.*)
    task-irrelevant response, 423, 438
    task-relevant response, 423, 438
    trait anxiety and, 422–423, 431, 433, 448
        measurement, 420–421, 424–426
Spouse, loss of, 261–262
S–R Inventory of Anxiousness, 434–435
Stage fright, 421, 455
Stanford Shyness Survey, 55–56
State anxiety
    definition, 419
    measurement, 420, 426–428, 433
    sport performance anxiety and, 421–422,
        423, 431–432, 434
    precompetition, 429, 430
State Anxiety Inventory, 231
State Anxiety Scale, 470
State-Trait Anxiety Inventory
    dating anxiety applications, 230
    speech anxiety applications, 469
    sport performance anxiety applications, 424,
        425, 427, 428, 438–439, 440, 442, 444
State-Trait Anxiety Inventory for Children, 183
State-Trait Anxiety Scale for Children, 192
Stereotype
    autonomic response, 445
    sex-role, 508, 514
Stigma, as shame cause, 404
Stranger anxiety/reactions, 17, 19
    adaptive value of, 47
    in children, 153–154
    in infancy, 85–118
        birth order and, 106–107
        cognitive-developmental perspectives, 91–
            93
        cultural factors, 106
        developmental changes, 101–103
        evolutionary approaches, 88–90
        family size and, 106–107
        future research, 127–130
        genetic factors, 105
        infant's characteristics and, 104–109
        influences on, 103–118
        measurement, 97–99
        mother–infant relationship and, 107–108
        onset age, 103, 106
        psychoanalytic viewpoints, 87–88
        research methodology, 100–101
        research setting, 99–100
        sex factors, 108, 109
        situational context, 113–116
        socialization approaches, 90–91
        stranger's characteristics and, 109–113
        temperament and, 104–105
        theoretical perspectives, 86–94

Stranger anxiety/reactions (*cont.*)
    in infancy (*cont.*)
        in twins, 105
        types of reactions, 95–97
    onset age, 22, 103, 106
    phylogenetic basis, 21–22
    loneliness and, 255–256
Stress
    definition, 418–419
    loneliness and, 254
    relational, 254
    responses, 475
    school phobia and, 188–189
    sport performance anxiety and, 429
    sport-related injury and, 447–448
    test anxiety and, 475, 476
Stress inoculation training, as speech anxiety
    intervention, 462–463, 467
Stress management, as schizophrenia interven-
    tion, 345, 347
Submission
    arousal and, 31
    hostility response to, 22
    social anxiety and, 34
    as threat response, 17–18, 26
Subordinate personality, appraisal-coping re-
    sponses, 27
Substance abuse, loneliness and, 247
Success
    fear of, 512–524
        among children, 519–520
        fear of failure versus, 520–522
        interventions, 523, 523
        model, 513–514
        psychometric scales and assessment, 514–
            516
        research, 516–519
        sex factors, 513–514, 514–519, 522–524
    hope of, 502
    psychodynamic theory of, 513
Suicide
    loneliness and, 247
    school phobia and, 180
Superordinate dominance schema, 23–24
Sweating, social phobia-related, 277

Temperament
    behavioral inhibition and, 141
    biologically-based model, 153
    definition, 139
    individual differences, 141
    shyness and, 147–150
Territorial breeding system, 16–17
Test anxiety, 475–495
    attributional aspects, 484–485

Test anxiety (*cont.*)
  cognitive interference and, 482–485
  components, 485–486
  decision-making and, 481–482
  definition, 475
  interventions, 486–490
  measurement, 420
  performance and, 477–482
  self-preoccupation and, 482–485
  sex factors, 479
  social anxiety and, 490–493
  stress and, 475, 476
  worry and, 482–485
Test Anxiety Inventory, 478
Test Anxiety Questionnaire, 477, 479
Test Anxiety Scale, 477–479, 480, 479
Thematic Apperception Test, 498, 502–504, 521
Therapeutic relationship, 316
  in embarrassment assessment and treatment,
    389
  in guilt assessment and treatment, 389
  in shame assessment and treatment, 389
  values in, 409
Topographic model, of schizophrenia, 327–334
Trait anxiety
  definition, 419
  general, 420–421
  measurement, 420–421, 424–426
  situation-specific, 420–421
  sport performance anxiety and, 422–423,
    431, 433, 448
Trauma. *See also* Posttraumatic stress disorder
  as school phobia cause, 187

Trembling, social phobia-related, 277
Tribal society, stranger reactions in, 106
Twins
  anxiety of, 286
  stranger reactions of, 105

UCLA Loneliness Scale, 262
Unemployment, 67

Vietnam War veterans
  guilt, 392, 402–403
  posttraumatic stress disorder, 402–403

Walker Problem Behavior Identification Check-
    list, 169
Wariness. *See also* Stranger anxiety/reactions
  of infants, 95, 96, 101–102
Willoughby Personality Schedule, 289, 291
Worry
  definition, 485
  interventions, 529
  shyness and, 49
  sport performance anxiety and, 431, 435
  test anxiety and, 482–485, 485, 486, 488–489

Yerkes–Dodson law, 437, 438, 444
Yielding routine, of ritual agonistic behavior,
    17, 18

Zuckerman and Allison's Fear of Success Scale,
    515–516, 521, 522